DATE DUE

DEMCO 38-296

DEATH IN THE
VICTORIAN FAMILY

DEATH IN THE VICTORIAN FAMILY

PAT JALLAND

OXFORD UNIVERSITY PRESS

1996

ss, Walton Street, Oxford OX2 6DP

ford New York

kland Bangkok Bombay

Town Dar es Salaam Delhi

ng Kong Istanbul Karachi
Kuala Lumpur Madras Madrid Melbourne
Mexico City Nairobi Paris Singapore
Taipei Tokyo Toronto
and associated companies in
Berlin Ibadan

Oxford is a trade mark of Oxford University Press

Published in the United States
by Oxford University Press Inc., New York

British Library Cataloguing in Publication Data
Data available

Library of Congress Cataloging in Publication Data
Jalland, Patricia.
Death in the Victorian family / Pat Jalland.
p.   cm.
Includes bibliographical references and index.
1. Funeral rites and ceremonies—Great Britain—History—19th
century.   2. Funeral rites and ceremonies—Great Britain—
History—20th century.   3. Death—Social aspects—Great Britain.
4. Bereavement—Great Britain.   5. Great Britain—Social life
and customs—19th century.   6. Great Britain—Social life and
customs—20th century.   I. Title.
GT3243.A2J35   1996   306.9´0941´09034—dc20   96-2389
ISBN 0-19-820188-5

1 3 5 7 9 10 8 6 4 2

Typeset by Best-set Typesetter Ltd., Hong Kong
Printed in Great Britain
on acid-free paper by
Biddles Ltd
Guildford & Kings Lynn

For my father
George Hoffman Case

and in loving memory of my mother
Esther Case

ACKNOWLEDGEMENTS

The Australian Research Council awarded me a two-year ARC Large Grant to fund research assistance for this project in the United Kingdom. A Visiting Fellowship in the History Program, Research School of Social Sciences (RSSS), Australian National University, provided the perfect base for writing many chapters of this book in 1991–2. The early stages of research were facilitated by a semester's study leave from Murdoch University in 1989.

Special thanks are due to Dee Cook for her outstanding work as my graduate research assistant. Dee's patience, exceptional efficiency, and careful attention to detail in transcribing difficult holograph material in archival collections were exemplary.

I am deeply indebted to good friends and colleagues who read and commented on my entire draft with great generosity and wisdom: Peter Clarke, John Hooper, Ken Inglis, Oliver MacDonagh, and Barry Smith. John again gave unfailing personal and professional support, encouragement, and advice throughout this project, including invaluable practical assistance as proofreader and index compiler. Marion Stell, Geoff Bolton, and Deryck Schreuder contributed thoughtful comments on individual chapters; and Marion also provided additional research assistance.

Warm thanks go to my helpful and skilful friends in the History Program, RSSS, at the Australian National University, who shared between them the production of the typescript: Janice Aldridge, Anthea Bundock, Bev Gallina, Helen Macnab, and Marie Penhaligon. The final corrections were efficiently and cheerfully completed by Anne McBride and Robyn Pease in the History Program at Murdoch University. I am grateful to the staff of the many libraries and archives who facilitated the research for this book; and to the staff at Oxford University Press, who embody the qualities of a world-class University Press, especially Tony Morris, Anna Illingworth, Mick Belson, and Laurien Berkeley.

Permissions

Permissions for quotations from manuscript collections have been kindly granted by Sir John Acland and Lt.-Col. Sir Guy Acland (Acland Papers); the Earl of Balfour (Balfour Papers); the Bodleian Library (Acland, Bickersteth, Bryce, Carrington, Harcourt, Horsley, Phillipps–Robinson, Lovelace–Byron, Hughenden, Thorold Rogers, Selborne, Somerville Papers); the British Library (Balfour, Carnarvon,

Gladstone, Layard, Holland House Papers, Wentworth Bequest); Lord Carnarvon (Carnarvon Papers); Mr J. N. Llewellen Palmer (Carrington Papers); the University of Birmingham (Chamberlain Archive); the Master, Fellows, and Scholars of Churchill College in the University of Cambridge (Chandos Papers); the British Library of Political and Economic Science (Courtney Collection); the Syndics of Cambridge University Library (Charles Darwin Papers); Mr David Lethbridge (Galton Papers); Sir William Gladstone (W. E. Gladstone, Glynne–Gladstone, and Mary Drew Papers); Surrey Record Office and the depositor (Goulburn Papers); the Trustees of the National Library of Scotland (Haldane and Minto Papers); the Hon. Mrs E. A. Gascoigne (Harcourt Papers); the Trustees of the Royal Botanic Gardens, Kew (Hooker Papers); Miss Rosamund Strode (Horsley Family Papers); the Earl of Lytton (Lovelace Byron Papers); the Public Record Office (Ramsay MacDonald Papers); the University of Liverpool Library (Rathbone Papers); Dr M. A. T. Rogers (Thorold Rogers Papers); the Earl of Selborne (Selborne Papers); Dr Sarah Pearson and the Librarian, University College London (Sharpe Papers); Somerville College, Oxford (Mary Somerville Papers); the Board of Trustees of the Chevening Estate (Stanhope Papers); Mrs Mary Colville (Tait Papers); Mr Charles Talbot (Talbot Papers); the Trustees of the Trevelyan Family Papers in the Robinson Library, University of Newcastle upon Tyne, and Mr George Trevelyan, c/o Messrs Longman, Publishers (Trevelyan Papers); the Principal and Chapter of Pusey House, Oxford (Mrs Humphry Ward Papers).

SCM Press Ltd. kindly granted copyright permission for extracts from Owen Chadwick, *The Victorian Church, pt. 1: 1829–1859*, 1992. I offer my apologies to any copyright owners I have been unable to locate.

CONTENTS

List of Plates   xi

Introduction   1

PART I. DEATH AND DYING

1. The Evangelical Ideal of the 'Good Death'   17
2. The Revival and Decline of the Good Christian Death   39
3. Bad Deaths, Sudden Deaths, and Suicides   59
4. Death and the Victorian Doctors   77
5. Nurses, Consultants, and Terminal Prognoses   98
6. 'That Little Company of Angels': The Tragedies of Children's
   Deaths   119
7. Death in Old Age   143
8. In Search of the Good Death: Death in the Gladstone and
   Lyttelton Families 1835–1915   161

PART II. GRIEF AND MOURNING

Introduction to Part II   193
9. Funeral Reform and the Cremation Debate   194
10. The Funeral Week   210
11. Widows: Gendered Experiences of Widowhood   230
12. Widowers: Gendered Experiences of Widowhood   251
13. Christian Consolations and Heavenly Reunions   265
14. The Consolations of Memory   284
15. Rituals of Sorrow: Mourning-Dress and Condolence Letters   300
16. Chronic and Abnormal Grief: Queen Victoria, Lady Frederick
    Cavendish, and Emma Haden   318
17. 'A Solitude beyond the Reach of God or Man': Victorian
    Agnostics and Death   339
18. Epilogue. After the Victorians: Social Memory, Spiritualism,
    and the Great War   358

Notes   382
Location of Manuscript Collections   443
Index   447

LIST OF PLATES

Between pp. 244 and 245

Plate 1   Emma Haden in Mourning Dress *c.*1858
           [MS. Eng. b 2008, item 5, The Horsley Papers, The Bodleian Library,
           Oxford]

Plate 2   *Fading Away* by Henry Peach Robinson, 1858
           [Royal Photographic Society]

Plate 3   Death in old age
           [*Sunday at Home*, 1873, courtesy of the Mary Evans Picture Library]

Plate 4   Henry Rogers, who committed suicide at seventeen in 1876
           [The Papers of the Family of J. E. Thorold Rogers, The Bodleian
           Library, Oxford]

Plate 5   Henry Rogers' grave in Oxford
           [The Papers of the Family of J. E. Thorold Rogers, The Bodleian
           Library, Oxford]

Plate 6   Mary Ann Rogers in her bath chair *c.*1870
           [The Papers of the Family of J. E. Thorold Rogers, The Bodleian
           Library, Oxford]

Plate 7   Cast of three-year-old Harry Horsley made by his father after
           Harry's death
           [MS. Eng. b 2264, item 5, The Horsley Papers, The Bodleian Library,
           Oxford]

Plate 8   Lord Frederick Cavendish after his assassination in 1882
           [The Trustees of the Trevelyan Family Papers in the Robinson Library,
           University of Newcastle upon Tyne]

Plate 9   Lord Frederick Cavendish lying in state at Chatsworth, 1882
           [*Illustrated London News*; courtesy of the Mary Evans Picture Library]

Plate 10   The Gladstone Family at Hawarden, 1894
           [From Mary Drew, *Catherine Gladstone*, London, 1919]

Plate 11   The room in Hawarden Castle in which W. E. Gladstone died
           [Courtesy of the Mary Evans Picture Library]

Plate 12   The twelve children of the fourth Lord Lyttelton by his first
           marriage
           [The Royal Archives © Her Majesty The Queen]

Plate 13   Mary, Lady Lyttelton
           [From Mary Drew, *Catherine Gladstone*, London, 1919]

Plate 14   Margaret Gladstone (née King)
           [Ramsay MacDonald Papers, Public Record Office 30/69/929]

xi

Plate 15   The death certificate of Lord Lyttelton
             [The design of the death certificate is Crown copyright and is reproduced
             with the permission of the Controller of HMSO]
Plate 16   The Duke of Wellington's triumphal funeral car, 1852
             [Courtesy of the Mary Evans Picture Library]
Plate 17   An exhibition of perishable coffins at Stafford House, 1875
             [Courtesy of the Mary Evans Picture Library]
Plate 18   New mourning gowns, 1887
             [*Girl's Own Paper*; courtesy of the Mary Evans Picture Library]
Plate 19   The London General Mourning Warehouse, Regent Street
             [*Art Journal*, 1849; courtesy of the Mary Evans Picture Library]
Plate 20   *The Father's Grave*: an engraving by W. Egleton after a painting
             by John Callcott Horsley
             [Courtesy of the Mary Evans Picture Library]

INTRODUCTION

D EATH IS AN INEVITABLE EXPERIENCE FOR US ALL, BUT THE MANNER OF dying varies greatly, as do individual and family responses to death and their mourning rituals. As a leading French historian Michel Vovelle has observed about death, 'in the human adventure it stands as an ideal and essential constant. It is a constant which is quite relative, moreover, since people's relationships with death have changed, as have the ways in which it strikes them . . . Pierre Chaunu was right when he said that every society gauges and assesses itself in some way by its system of death.'[1] The study of death and bereavement in the past helps us to understand the present, especially in the context of the modern tendency to avoid the subject of death and to minimize the public expression of grief. Scholars in the social sciences and humanities have recognized the need to study death and grief in contemporary society, but historians of modern Britain have been relatively slow to contribute to this important field. David Cannadine noted in 1981 that 'we still know quite extraordinarily little about attitudes towards death in the nineteenth century. At all levels of society . . . much more research needs to be done.'[2] This remains largely true today.

My book aims to expand our knowledge of the experiences of dying and death, grief and mourning among the middle and upper classes in nineteenth- and early twentieth-century Britain. It is concerned with the attitudes, beliefs, and behaviour of the educated and literate part of the population, in the hope that other scholars will examine working-class families. My research supports Ruth Richardson's argument about 'the existence of distinct class-bound death cultures in Victorian Britain'.[3] The material and cultural gulf between rich and poor affected most aspects of life, including death. There were enormous differences between the upper and lower classes in attitudes and customs relating to death and in the management of the dying. We should beware of assuming that the behaviour and beliefs about death of the middle and upper classes automatically filtered down to the working classes.

My exploration of the world of Victorian and Edwardian experience began with *Women, Marriage and Politics 1860–1914*, first published in 1986.

My commitment to experiential history is based on the view that the people of the past must first speak to us in their own words, if we can retrieve them, and that their most significant texts are often those in which their innermost lives are revealed. Death is one of the most important facts in human life, and experiences of dying and responses to death take us to the heart of human history. In studying the history of human experiences of death and grief, we approach the meaning of human life. However, that meaning is embedded in a world of private experience which has to be reconstructed from family manuscript collections, and contextualized within the profound cultural transformations of the nineteenth and early twentieth centuries.

My focus is on death within the family because the family was the primary Victorian and Edwardian social institution in which the meaning of individual deaths was constructed and transmitted across the generations. Leonore Davidoff observes that 'throughout the nineteenth century, the family was central to the economic, religious, social and emotional life of the middle class'.[4] The Victorian family has often been idealized, as in John Ruskin's influential definition of the family in *Sesame and Lilies* as 'a sacred place, a vestal temple' and 'the place of Peace'.[5] In 1936 G. M. Young depicted the family as 'a vital article of the common Victorian faith . . . as a Divine appointment for the comfort and education of mankind'.[6] Twenty years later Walter Houghton conceived the Victorian family as a shelter for moral and spiritual values threatened by the stress of modern life.[7]

The Evangelical movement played a vital role in this Victorian idealization of the family, because Evangelicalism was the religion of the home as well as the heart, enabling family and faith to reinforce each other. The family was conceived as a divine institution favoured by God, which was continued in heaven (irrespective of biblical injunctions against marriage in the afterlife). Evangelicalism exercised a strong and widespread influence on the nineteenth-century upper- and middle-class family, establishing the representative pattern and values of family life, even for many who were not avowedly Evangelical. It was responsible for many characteristic features of the Victorian family, including family prayers, reading aloud around the fireside, religious instruction of the children, and the moral earnestness of the more pious homes.

The major motors of change affecting attitudes to death between 1830 and 1920 were the transformations in religious beliefs and the demographic pattern, both reinforced by the trauma of the Great War. The Evangelical revival had a profound impact on the way the Victorian family approached death, as Chapter 1 will demonstrate. Evangelicalism revitalized the traditional Christian ideal of the 'good death', which required piety and fortitude in the face of suffering. In the Victorian Evangelical version, this good Christian death took place in the home surrounded by a loving and support- ive family, whose affection expressed itself afterwards in sorrow for its dead. Death was ideally a family event interpreted in terms of a shared Christianity, with the assurance of family reunion in heaven. When the fervour and piety of Evangelicalism began to wane in the last quarter of the nineteenth century, traditional assurances about death and immortality declined with it.

The Victorian family has sometimes been depicted as claustrophobic and oppressive, because it has been assumed that a surfeit of earnest piety must have been gloomy and repressive. The testimony of Victorians such as Edmund Gosse and Samuel Butler has reinforced this perception. But Evan- gelical families were often cheerful families—William Wilberforce's family certainly benefited from his view that parents should 'labour to render religion as congenial as possible'.[8] Noel Annan described the educated upper- middle-class Evangelical family of Leslie Stephen as leading 'happy, gentle lives', joining in the comfortable routine of family prayers twice daily and treating Jesus 'as if another member of the family were living under the same roof'.[9]

Religion played a vital and pervasive role in the lives of the majority of Victorian middle- and upper-class families, for whom church attendance was not usually just a matter of convention. Intensive analysis of the manuscript collections of fifty-five families leaves me singularly impressed by the depth of piety and spiritual commitment of the majority, at least up to the 1880s. Contemporary testimonies to the strength of Victorian religion in the family abound. Elizabeth Haldane commented on her childhood in the 1860s: 'Religion permeated our lives, and the sense of sin and its consequences seemed to dog our footsteps,' noting that home life had a stronger influence than the church in this process. She added, 'We were brought up to remem- ber that death was an essential part of life, and must be faced without fear.'[10] Frances Balfour wrote of the impact of the Church of Scotland on family life in the 1880s:

I want to describe a state of things where religion was not talked about, it was lived. 'By their fruits you shall know them', the church was the centre of the life that abides, its precepts were followed, the Christian Year, and Sunday was kept, and a happy peace rested on the homes that remembered the blessings which attend Faith and Order.[11]

Leading historians have confirmed this view of the central role of religion in Victorian life. Owen Chadwick opened his classic history of the Victorian Church with the statement: 'Victorian England was religious . . . Public law and private morals, mental philosophy and social convention—the life of the nation was rooted in age-long conviction of the Christian truth.' Comparing the cabinets of 1837 and 1901 Chadwick concluded that the leadership of the nation was no less Christian at the end of Victoria's reign than at the start.[12] More recently Jose Harris has largely shared Chadwick's conclusion: 'Religion or reaction against it permeated the lives, language, institutions and moral imaginations of large numbers of people living in Britain in the late nineteenth and early twentieth centuries.'[13]

The role of the upper- and middle-class family at the deathbed also assumed greater significance in the nineteenth century because of the increase in affection within the family, documented in Lawrence Stone's classic work *The Family, Sex and Marriage in England 1500–1800*. Stone argued that marriage in 1500 was primarily an economic and reproductive relationship involving little emotional commitment, but by 1800 'there developed much warmer affective relations between husband and wife and between parents and children'.[14] The increase in affection within the family in nineteenth-century Britain was a response to both the Evangelical and the Romantic movements. Evangelicalism has been called 'the religion of the heart' and emotionalism was an integral part, expressed in sorrow as well as joy. On Mrs Henry Thornton's death in 1815 William Wilberforce understood that even good Christians were sorrowful on the deaths of their loved ones, despite their confidence in heavenly family reunions. Wilberforce commented that '"Jesus wept", and He will allow His people to weep also' to express their natural human sorrow.[15] Early and mid-nineteenth-century Evangelicals, men as well as women, expressed the intensity of their grief in weeping together without shame. This emotional upsurge was reinforced by the literature, particularly the poetry, of the Romantic movement, which largely coincided with the Evangelical revival, and which also demanded social expression of feelings.

Death evoked the most intense emotions in family life, and Evangelicalism and Romanticism encouraged early and mid-Victorians to give full scope to their expression. They were able to talk and write freely of their sorrow as well as their joy and their love, with a simple sincerity. They were not shy about expressing the depth of their suffering in tears and in words, with varying degrees of restraint depending on family circumstances.[16] Where some modern readers see sentimental piety and excessive emotionalism at Victorian family deathbeds, in Victorian eyes they were simply communicating their sorrow, love, and faith as honestly as they knew how. There was an acceptable range of expressive behaviour, which could include public displays of extreme grief. For example, in 1848 Sarah Courtauld described the reaction of an unidentified father on the death of an only child: '*he* has been almost frantic—sometimes rolling on his bed and tearing his hair'.[17] On his wife's death in 1857 George Lyttelton completely abandoned himself to his grief: 'weeps openly—talks of his feelings—and seems *sure* we are all feeling alike and will help him'. The day after his wife's death George sat sobbing with his mother and for days afterwards wanted to 'weep and muse and pine'. Even as late as 1875 A. J. Balfour avoided the funeral of his beloved May Lyttelton, preferring instead to weep under a tree in Hagley Park, her home.[18] But the age of open emotional expression was already passing in the 1870s and 1880s with the decline of Evangelicalism and Romanticism, accelerated for men by the ethos of the public schools with their cult of manliness and masculine reserve.[19]

However, this world of the Evangelical Victorian family was increasingly transformed by the demographic reality of a declining mortality rate which, in combination with other factors, changed the frequency and the experience of death in late Victorian and Edwardian society. A new demographic pattern was established from about 1870 which had a significant impact on the history of death, especially from the late 1890s. Before 1870 mortality had remained high, with a shorter life expectancy and a particularly high death-rate for infants and children—a demographic picture which still exists in the Third World. The death-rate for infants scarcely changed between 1850 and 1900, and the deaths of babies still numbered one-quarter of all deaths by the end of the century. The Victorian preoccupation with death was under-standable—an honest realism given relatively high mortality rates.

There was a noticeable decline in the death-rate in England and Wales from 21.8 per 1,000 per year in 1868 to 18.1 in 1888, after which the fall was more rapid, moving down to 14.8 in 1908 and 11.7 in 1928.[20] This decline in mortality has been continuous since the late nineteenth century and has affected different age cohorts in stages. Children between 1 and 15 were the first to enjoy the benefits from the 1870s, followed by young adults and the middle-aged a decade later. However, an improvement in mortality for infants, children in their first year, and those over 55 was delayed until the twentieth century.[21] The fall in mortality was caused by a combination of factors, including an improved standard of living, better nutrition, public-health reforms, and the natural reduction of deaths from infectious diseases. In the 1870s the birth-rate began to fall at the same time as the death-rate, initiating a half-century of steadily falling fertility when the number of children born to married couples fell.

The gradual move from infancy to old age as the most probable time of death is a crucial development dating initially from the late Victorian period. Life expectancy at birth in England and Wales improved from around 40 years in about 1850 to 52 for males and 55 for females by 1911–12, and up to 66 and 72 for 1950–2. Again, the impact was far more marked after the turn of the century.[22] Obviously society's concern with death was likely to decline once mortality rates fell and life expectancy rose, allowing death to be perceived as a natural and timely event concluding a long life.

The importance of Victorian medicine as a force for change in the history of death and dying was less significant than that of religion or demography because Victorian doctors still had very limited power to cure. In the early and mid-Victorian periods the good Christian assumed that death was divinely ordained and submission to the will of God was all-important. But growing uncertainty about the Christian faith in the late Victorian period coincided with a revised view of disease, as death was increasingly attributed to specific diseases rather than divine intervention. The medical practitioner was seen as playing a more significant role during a terminal illness in reducing pain and physical discomfort, even if he could not cure the disease. More effort was made to relieve pain and suffering by judicious use of opiates and alcohol, and careful attention was paid to the 'economy of the death chamber'. Victorian physicians such as Henry Halford and William Munk anticipated the work of modern experts on the care of the dying, emphasizing effective palliative management, the value of family care in the home, and good communication between patient, family, and doctor. As Munk observed, when death was expected 'we dismiss all thought of cure, or of the prolongation of life', to concentrate rather on alleviating pain and giving moral support and practical advice to the family.[23] This was an important contribution, but it concerned care rather than cure. Only the advent of modern 'miracle' drugs in the 1930s resulted in cures for a wide range of diseases, and the possibility of prolonging life and challenging death.

The First World War initiated further change in attitudes to death, and also reinforced and accelerated the effects of the major demographic, religious, and medical changes already in progress since 1870. It can be argued that there were two major turning-points in the history of death between 1830 and 1920. The first was the gradual process of change generated by the combination of demography, religious decline, and medical advance in the decades after 1870, while the second was the trauma of the Great War. The enormous loss of human life and the subsequent mass grief transformed the experiences of death and mourning for survivors and bereaved families. Deaths in the Great War were far removed from the peaceful, gradual deaths at home among the family which provided the model of the early and mid-Victorian good Christian deaths. War deaths were sudden, violent, premature, ugly deaths of young healthy adults, with bodies often smashed and unidentifiable, and burial at home impossible. Such deaths were rare in the nineteenth century, but they could promote abnormal and long-term grief when they did occur. The Great War not only shattered Victorian customs of deathbed farewells, burial, and mourning ritual; it also happened when these Christian ideals and rituals about death were already in decline.

Since David Cannadine expressed concern in 1981 about the 'puddles of ignorance' surrounding the history of death, grief, and mourning in modern Britain, some excellent work has been produced, including his own valuable essay on the impact of the Great War.[24] Recent studies have tended to concentrate on specialized areas, such as Ruth Richardson's fascinating 1987 analysis of the impact of the Anatomy Act, which is very revealing about working-class attitudes and rituals relating to the dead.[25] Michael Wheeler's 1990 book *Death and the Future Life in Victorian Literature and Theology* is an excellent study of 'the theological questions associated with death, judgment, heaven, and hell in the nineteenth century' and their treatment by creative writers such as Tennyson, Dickens, and John Henry Newman.[26] Wheeler's book helps to clarify and contextualize the complex theological questions associated with death in nineteenth-century Britain, as did the earlier work by Geoffrey Rowell *Hell and the Victorians*.[27] The increasing interest in death as a significant subject for historical analysis across the centuries has also been demonstrated by the useful collection of scholarly essays edited by Ralph Houlbrooke in 1989.[28] Literary critics, such as John Reed and Elisabeth Jay, have also provided valuable work on which historians can draw.[29] But we are still some way from a more comprehensive social history of death, grief, and mourning in Victorian and Edwardian Britain.

By contrast, French historians have been developing a 'new history of death' for France from the 1970s and earlier, acting as pioneers in the history of death, as in so many other areas of social history.[30] As Michel Vovelle observed in 1990, 'The history of death occupies a far from minor place in the new history of mentalities . . . The history of death retains a specific and exemplary value within this complex system.'[31] The originality and creativity of the contribution to this field by historians of France is illustrated by the work of Michel Vovelle, Pierre Chaunu, Philippe Ariès, John McManners, and Thomas A. Kselman.[32]

However, much of the historiography of death for France is limited in its application to the nineteenth-century British experience, firstly because it provides an interpretation of a predominantly Catholic rather than Protestant culture; secondly, because it has mostly not been translated; and, thirdly, much of it relates to earlier centuries. Philippe Ariès has been the only French historian to have a major impact on British research through his pioneering work *The Hour of our Death*, which was translated into English and widely distributed in paperback from 1981. Ariès provided a fairly simple yet ambitious model of five stages of death in many countries over the centuries. His model has been especially influential at a more popular level and has been widely used by non-historians seeking a historical framework, including psychologists, sociologists, and literary critics.[33] Ariès's model has also been used by historians of earlier centuries.[34]

Ariès presented a stereotypical view of death in nineteenth-century Britain as 'the beautiful death', whereby Romanticism transformed death from the fearful to the beautiful, to be almost eagerly awaited as Victorians glorified the act of dying and the deathbed scene. His sources for Victorian Britain were limited and eccentric, largely based on the writings of the Brontë family, which was decimated by tuberculosis. The value of Ariès's work for Britain is further restricted by his emphasis on the paradigmatic experience of Catholic France and his failure to evaluate the impact of the Protestant Reformation. Rather, if death in nineteenth-century Britain is to be characterized in terms of a single model or an ideal, then it should be the Evangelical 'good death' and not Ariès's 'beautiful death'. Death itself and the process of dying were rarely greeted with joy or conceptualized as subjects of beauty, except in romantic fiction or didactic literature. If we look to the historical world of family experience, then the 'good' Christian death had the most importance as a model for most Christians.

David Cannadine has underlined the need to understand 'the world of private experience' of death, while noting the immense obstacles to doing so. Research in this field has been limited by the assumption that 'the world of private experience' is impossible to enter.[35] But rich experiential source material certainly does exist, though the research process involved in exploring numerous family manuscript collections is indeed laborious. My book focuses on the experiences of large networks of families in the British middle and upper classes, ranging from the professional middle classes to the aristocracy, drawing on their private diaries, extensive correspondence, wills, and memorials of death. The archival evidence is complemented by a wide range of secondary and primary published sources, including Victorian biographies, memoirs, and periodicals, Evangelical tracts, theological treatises, medical journals, and texts.

Fifty-five family manuscript collections have been examined for a period of almost a century (1830 to 1920), enabling comparative analysis of the dynamics of change over time. My sources have been drawn as broadly as time and resources permitted, from dozens of family archives rather than a small sample. The families in this study span a broad spectrum of middle- and upper-class society, including politicians, scientists, clergymen, diplomats, landowners, doctors, and intellectuals. There is no reason to suppose that these families were unrepresentative of the professional middle class and the upper-middle and upper classes as a whole.

The fifty-five families were selected from a far larger number of Victorian and Edwardian families by a process of elimination. The starting-point was the fifty families of politicians studied in my earlier book, *Women, Marriage and Politics*. Some of these family collections had to be excluded because they were less rewarding as sources for death than they had proved to be for women's history. Many families of scientists, churchmen, and diplomats were added, with the invaluable assistance of the *Guides to Sources for British History* compiled by the Royal Commission on Historical Manuscripts.[36] Those selected were chosen because they had preserved valuable material for the study of death, grief, and mourning. The majority of the fifty-five family collections were of Anglican families—not surprisingly, given the identification of the Church of England with the upper and upper-middle classes in England. Selected families also encompassed Presbyterian, Unitarian, Quaker, and Roman Catholic religious affiliations, while six more families included unbelievers (the families of Ada Lovelace, Charles Darwin, Joseph Hooker, T. H. Huxley, W. S. Blunt, and the Trevelyans). Many manuscript collections had to be eliminated because families had kept only material which related fairly narrowly to the categories of politics, diplomacy, science, or the Church. Some family archives contained little or nothing of relevance to this book, though evidence survived in some cases to demonstrate that rich material had once existed. The final fifty-five collections which yielded valuable material on the history of death, grief, and mourning included twenty massive collections which spanned two or three generations.

The family correspondence included a vast number of condolence letters, as well as the more regular correspondence between family members and friends throughout a terminal illness and the months of mourning. Such letters were sometimes the Victorian equivalent of today's telephone conversations and were not written with publication in mind. Many of these correspondents tried to convey their feelings of grief through letters, often expressed with an intensity, directness, and precision which would be rare today. Many hoped, like Caroline Fox in 1840, to convey 'exactly things as they are or *that I believe them to be*, free from all colouring and prejudice'.[37] Not all correspondents succeeded, of course, nor were they always aware of their own biases. The intensity of their efforts to convey their feelings accurately is captured in a letter of 1843 from Eleanor Fazakerley to her sister, both recently bereaved mothers: 'I am glad always to write to you just as I feel when my pen is in my hand . . . Although one's feelings have been just what one describes when writing, they so soon vary, and one's weak faith so soon fails, that unintentionally, one's letters often convey a false idea of one's habitual state to a correspondent.'[38] However, when such letters were written frequently, often daily, and were supported by other correspondence and evidence such as diaries or memorials, a wide range of emotions could be conveyed very graphically.

Diaries were particularly important as a source for this book, especially those death memorials which were kept in the form of a diary. Nineteenth-century Evangelicals revived the Puritan habit of keeping diaries to testify before God to their worthy spiritual life, and to aid self-scrutiny and self-improvement. John Wesley, Henry Venn, and William Wilberforce, for example, took Jeremy Taylor's advice to record 'a daily examination of our actions . . . that we may see our evil and amend it'.[39] The model set by the founding fathers of Evangelicalism was followed by many Victorians, including W. E. Gladstone, Archbishop A. C. Tait and his wife Catharine, and countless others, who often extended the habit into a detailed accounting for family deaths as well as lives. Such private memorials are far more reliable than edited and published accounts as sources for deathbed scenes, attitudes, and experiences. As Paul Fussell pointed out, 'The further personal written materials move from the form of the daily diary, the closer they approach the figurative and the fictional.'[40]

Diarized deathbed memorials flourished with the Evangelical movement, and provide the most intimate accounts of deathbed scenes in many families up to the 1860s and 1870s when Evangelical fervour began to decline. While these memorials were chiefly intended as spiritual accounting to God, they also served as personal therapy for the writer and as a written record to preserve the memory of the loved one for the immediate family. They usually recorded daily, even hourly, events in the sick-room, including the symptoms, medical treatment, visitors, and conversations. Details of religious significance were also included, such as references to passages from the Bible and the prayer-book which were read aloud, visits from clergymen, the administration of holy communion, and edifying statements testifying to the spiritual preparation of the dying person. The medical and spiritual accounts were often uneasily juxtaposed, even within the same paragraph, as the diarist moved between a prosaic clinical narrative and a symbolic spiritual discourse.

The majority of these Victorian deathbed memorials have almost certainly been destroyed, but enough have survived to act as a crucial source for this project. Twentieth-century responses to these characteristic Victorian documents are revealing of the gulf between the two centuries in relation to

death and to religion. In 1956 E. M. Forster, in his biography of Marianne
Thornton, described her sixty-page memorial written when she was only 18
on the deaths of both her Evangelical parents in 1815. Forster was impatient
with her pietism and the 'superabundance' of information in this 'Pronouncement', which he regarded as 'far removed from us in spirit'. In his
view Marianne should merely have stated that Henry Thornton died at the
age of 50 of tuberculosis:

Why cannot his daughter leave it there—keeping the rest in her heart? . . . On goes
her sad narrative, gently, relentlessly, as if the spirit of the age, which adored death
beds, was speaking through her lips. Nothing is insincere, nothing strained or in bad
taste, but on it goes, on . . . The twentieth-century observer has to remind himself
that inside all this cocoonery of words there was love, there was pain. It was the
technique of the age and of a section of the middle class.

Forster observed that when bereaved people in the twentieth century reduce
or eliminate mourning, they lessen the pain, 'and with pain they cut down
love'.[41] Despite Forster's impatience and repugnance in response to Marianne
Thornton's 'Pronouncement', he believed that it signified values and emotions such as love, religious faith, and 'loyalty of soul', which have been in
decline in the twentieth century. Such 'protracted obsequies' were common
in the Thornton family between 1815 and 1857, and in other families, such as
the Gladstones and Lytteltons, they continued into the 1870s. They provide
an insight into the world of private experience of dying and death which has
no parallel today.

This book is structured thematically—the first half examines Victorian and
Edwardian experiences of dying and death, and the second half considers
grief and mourning. Part I analyses the changing nature of the Christian ideal
of the 'good death' and the massive effect of the Evangelical movement in
reviving that ideal, with its emphasis on the art of dying well. Yet even in the
early Victorian period, few actual deathbed experiences imitated the Evangelical ideal of the good death, which demanded an unusual mixture of
prolonged but painless illness, fortunate family circumstances, and virtuous
life. Detailed accounts in diaries, letters, and death memorials illustrate the
gulf between the family reality and the idealized deathbed scenes in biography, Evangelical tracts, and literary fiction. In real life ugly or sudden deaths
were not reserved for sinners and unbelievers, as so often represented in
novels and Evangelical literature. There were many Victorian ways of death,
according to major variables such as age, disease, size and nature of the
family, religious beliefs, wealth, and class. Chapters on the deaths of children
and old people examine the different family responses and behaviour accord-

ing to the stage of the life-cycle at which death occurred and the nature of the disease which caused it.

Part II examines the ways in which Victorian middle- and upper-class families came to terms with grief, and assesses the function and value of funerals, cremations, mourning customs, and rituals. The evidence indicates that most nineteenth-century mourning rituals helped to meet the psychological needs of the bereaved; they structured the grieving process within a coherent framework which reduced the terrifying aspects of death and also rallied the support of family and friends. The four primary forms of consolation were religious belief, time, private and social memory, and the sympathy of friends and relatives; but most Victorian Protestants relied above all on their expectation of happy family reunions in heaven. Chapters 13 and 14 analyse the consolations of Christian faith and private memory, exploring the transformation in ideas and beliefs relating to heaven, hell, and immortality between 1830 and 1920. Unbelievers seem to have coped with death less effectively, and the first-generation agnostic could be overwhelmed by 'the utter grimness of death unbrightened by faith'.[42] Later generations of unbelievers were more resourceful in constructing alternative strategies to make their losses more bearable, such as spiritualism and the creation of new forms of civic ceremonies and rituals of public memory.

Several important gendered differences in the experiences of death, grief, and mourning are explored in the book. Some differences were biological, in that women lived longer and some diseases were gender-specific, such as puerperal fever and certain forms of cancer. But other gendered differences—notably those relating to nursing and widowhood—were powerfully affected by the cultural conditioning which emphasized the separation of the spheres and the 'natural' female roles as good wives and mothers. Nurses were almost always female since Victorians considered that devoted care of sick and dying loved ones was a normal part of women's nurturing role within the family. Wives, mothers, and daughters undertook the demanding work of terminal care at home, though wealthier families often sought assistance from trained female nurses from the 1870s. Paradoxically, women were likely to be more familiar than men with the physical realities of dying bodies, despite ideal notions of the delicacy and refinement of Victorian ladies.

Gender also made a significant difference to the experience of widowhood, as we will see in Chapters 11 and 12. The very large surplus of widowed women in Victorian society increased with age, since widows lived longer than widowers. Widows often had a more difficult life than widowers because the consolations of paid employment and remarriage were generally reserved for men. The financial problems and social isolation of widows were often greater too, as the death of a husband could mean the loss of income, home, and social status as wife. Victorian women were also less likely than men to express anger in response to the death of a spouse or a child, perhaps because religious and social training taught women the virtues of submission to the will of God, as to that of husbands and fathers.

PART I

DEATH AND DYING

THE EVANGELICAL IDEAL OF THE 'GOOD DEATH'

Early Catholic and Protestant Ideals of the 'Good Death'

For most human beings the theory of death precedes the practice. Cultural models of the nature and meaning of death are transmitted from the old generation to the new. The dominant ideal of death shapes the approach and to some extent the experience of the dying and their descendants. These representations of death guide the living and construct the meaning of death at the heart of a culture.

Pious Christians have been most anxious to achieve a 'good death'. In late medieval and early modern England a vast body of devotional literature known as the *ars moriendi*, the art of dying, taught people how to die well, since dying was seen as a test of both courage and virtue, and a good death might go some way to compensate for a less worthy life. The state of the individual's soul at the moment of death was deemed of vital importance, since there was an immediate divine judgement on each individual at death, making constant preparation essential. Advice on the art of dying was initially written by and intended primarily for clergymen, but such literature continued to be popular after the Reformation among lay people.

The Catholic ideal of the good death is clearly defined in the *ars moriendi* and in modern scholarly works such as John McManners's *Death and the Enlightenment*. Catholics believed that the small minority of saints would go directly to heaven and the unrepentant sinners straight to hell, while the majority who were to be saved went to purgatory 'to be cleansed by tribulation'. In seventeenth-century France, a massive resurgence in devotional literature by members of religious orders advised people how to prepare for death. They were admonished to live every moment of their lives as if death might come at any time, with a regular routine of prayer and meditation accompanying 'sacrificial living'.[1]

McManners explains that noble and bourgeois deathbeds in seventeenth- and eighteenth-century France were ideally seen as occasions for public ceremony, though the custom of dying in public was in decline by the late eighteenth century. The Catholic model of the good death included solemn farewells and pious advice to spouse, children, and servants, the resolution of worldly affairs, and the public reading of the will. The ceremonies of the Catholic Church, presided over by the priest, started with confession and absolution, followed by the administration of the viaticum, the last Eucharist, and extreme unction. The procession carrying the viaticum into the dying person's house was a public ceremony, when all neighbours and friends could follow the sacrament into the death chamber to offer their prayers and support.[2]

The Protestant model of the good death, as it developed in Britain, was based on this Catholic tradition, but certain distinctive Protestant features were introduced by the Reformation, as Ralph Houlbrooke has shown. After the Reformation the clergyman's role at the deathbed became far less significant and the Catholic last rites were simplified or disappeared entirely, though practice varied greatly between sects. The spiritual and emotional role of the family and neighbours became more important, as their prayers replaced the priest's last rites. The abolition of purgatory and prayers of intercession for the dead left Protestants with the stark alternative destinations of heaven or hell, which enhanced their fear of judgement and eternal punishment.[3]

The Christian ideal of the good death remained vitally important after the Reformation. The devotional tradition of the *ars moriendi*, begun in the late Middle Ages, lasted over 250 years and still flourished in seventeenth-century Protestant England as well as Catholic France. The most famous Anglican contribution to the genre was Bishop Jeremy Taylor's *The Rule and Exercises of Holy Dying*, first published in 1651, and reprinted many times in the following centuries.[4] The English novelist George Eliot identified Taylor's *Holy Dying* as a standard reference book in Victorian homes, which her character Adam Bede read for moral improvement.[5] *Holy Dying* continued to influence nineteenth-century Anglicans, especially those of the High Church, though Evangelicals were also affected.

Jeremy Taylor, Anglican Bishop of Down, opened his treatise with an attack on Catholic deathbed practices, including deathbed conversions, prayers for the dead, and even the last sacraments.[6] However, he retained the Catholic emphasis on preparation for a holy death by strict piety throughout life, with daily prayer and examination of all actions through devotional exercises: 'He that would die well must always look for death, every day knocking at the gates of the grave.' Taylor, like the Evangelicals later, emphasized the example of 'Holy Jesus upon the Cross', and the value of suffering as a punishment for sins: 'Sickness . . . is that agony in which men are tried for a crown.' In the High Church tradition, Taylor advocated an important role for the minister of religion at the deathbed: 'the Spiritual man is appointed to restore us, and to pray for us', inspiring the sick man's confession of his sins.[7]

Other seventeenth- and eighteenth-century devotional literature in the *ars moriendi* tradition was also popular among Victorian Protestants and contributed to the nineteenth-century ideal of the good death, though none had the impact of Taylor's work. Christopher Sutton's *Disce Mori: Learn to Die*, first published in 1626, appeared again in 1839, exhorting 'every Christian man to enter into a serious remembrance of his end'.[8] Standard Victorian devotional reading also included Charles Drelincourt's *The Christian Defence against the Fears of Death*, written by a French Protestant in the seventeenth century, and published in numerous editions in many languages. Drelincourt urged Christians to overcome the fear of death by frequent meditation on the subject, and by expecting it every moment, as well as 'by Repentance and an holy Life'.[9] More research is needed on death and dying in the eighteenth century, but it does seem that the fervour of the *ars moriendi* tradition was in decline in the age of Enlightenment, to be rekindled by the Evangelical revival.

The Influence of the Evangelical Movement on the Protestant 'Good Death'

In the late eighteenth and the first half of the nineteenth centuries the Protestant ideal of the good death was powerfully revitalized by the Evangelical movement, which restored the seventeenth-century emphasis on spiritual piety. Evangelicalism drew heavily on the *ars moriendi* for inspiration and ideals of death and dying, as Michael Wheeler observes: 'Conventions associated with the *ars moriendi*, familiar to the educated English reader from Jeremy Taylor's *Holy Dying* (1651), were deeply rooted in the corporate memory of the faithful.'[10]

Evangelicalism had great influence on large portions of the population during the nineteenth century, not just those who belonged to its churches, as G. M. Young observed: 'Evangelicalism had imposed on society, even on classes which were indifferent to its religious basis and unaffected by its economic appeal, its code of Sabbath observance, responsibility, and philanthropy; of discipline in the home, regularity in affairs.' The Evangelical impulses of seriousness, piety, discipline, and duty 'showed at their best in the upper ranks of society', and became the basis for Victorian morality and Victorian values.[11] Evangelicalism was a vital force in the development of Methodism, and it transformed the Church of England, as well as influencing such dissenting sects as the Congregationalists, the Baptists, the Presbyterians, and even the Quakers. Evangelicalism touched all denominations and all sections of the Church of England, including even the High Church. David Bebbington has recently charted the history of Evangelicalism, acknowledging its debt to the rationalism of the Enlightenment as well as to the emotionalism of the Romantic movement. He also recognizes its inheritance from the High Church tradition, noting especially the impact of Taylor's *Holy Dying* on John Wesley, who adopted Taylor's suggestions for a rule of life.[12]

The central teaching of the Bible for early Evangelicals was the doctrine of atonement, which argued that Christ died as a substitute for sinful human beings, and faith in the sacrifice on the Cross was essential to salvation. Evangelicalism also emphasized the doctrine of assurance of faith, usually acquired at conversion rather than baptism. This assurance contributed largely to the dynamism of the Evangelical movement, for assurance meant forgiveness of sins and ensured a cheerful, enthusiastic piety. The doctrine of assurance led directly to the emphasis on preaching the gospel to win converts, with the stress on the Bible (as inspired by God, rather than by Church tradition or authority) as the source of spiritual truth. The message of the Bible was disseminated through preaching and prayer rather than through sacraments administered by priests.[13]

Evangelicalism changed over time, and the emphasis on atonement and conversion declined from the 1880s, when biblical criticism made it difficult even for most Evangelicals to adopt a literal interpretation of the Bible.[14] Evangelicalism probably reached the peak of its social and spiritual influence in Britain in the 1850s and 1860s. Its greatest impact within the Anglican Church came in the 1850s, when Evangelicals accounted for over a third of the clergy, including even the Archbishop of Canterbury J. B. Sumner. Its influence began to contract and that of the High Church to increase from about 1865. Even so, Bebbington sees the activism and influence of the Evangelicals as sufficiently strong to justify the title 'the Evangelical century' for the entire period from 1815 to 1914.[15]

The Evangelical movement affected most aspects of Victorian life, not least the approach to death. Yet while historians are agreed about its crucial role in defining Victorian morality and religious seriousness, and in transforming behaviour and even politics and family life, most fail to mention its equally central role in relation to death and dying. Geoffrey Best is an exception: 'Death had no terrors for the Evangelical . . . The Evangelical's confidence in the face of death was unusually comforting and homely; it lay at the heart of Evangelical religion.'[16]

The Evangelical revival had enormous influence on deathbed behaviour and on the ideal of the good Christian death in the first half of the nineteenth century and up to the 1870s. It continued to affect many Christians thereafter, though to a diminishing degree. Thousands of didactic deathbed scenes in nineteenth-century Evangelical tracts and journals attested to the zeal to save souls by showing people how to die. Death was a primary concern of Evangelical theology, since the doctrines of sin, assurance, and atonement emphasized Christ's sacrifice on the Cross to save people from their sins. For those who professed to be saved through conversion, the manner of their dying could provide the final proof of salvation. For devout Evangelicals who feared that they had missed the experience of conversion, the hour of death was the last opportunity. Early and mid-Victorian Evangelicals thought earnestly about sin, judgement, and the possibility of everlasting torment, and they viewed suffering and death as the punishment for sin.

At the heart of these Evangelical death scenes was the traditional belief that most people were doomed at death to eternal physical punishment in hell, and that the individual judgement took place at the time of death. Among more liberal Christians, belief in a literal interpretation of hell was diminishing in the nineteenth century; but Evangelicals, like Tractarians and Roman Catholics, continued to preach and produce popular literature on the perpetual punishment awaiting the damned, thus maintaining the traditional significance of the hour of death. Evangelicals used the term 'triumphant death' to describe the victory, through Christ's atonement, over both death and the devil, whose temptations were supposed to be especially potent at deathbeds.

The Evangelical model of the good Christian death was widely disseminated through Evangelical journals and tracts, which were intended primarily to provide spiritual edification and example—to save souls by showing people how to live and die well. These were usually designed to demonstrate the earnest piety, upright character, and resigned death of dying 'saints'. The *Evangelical Magazine*, which was published from 1793 to 1892, usually included a memoir of the life and death of a recently deceased Evangelical Christian at the start of each monthly issue. Clergymen were the subject of eight of the ten memoirs in 1837 because they were presumed to set the most pious examples; only one memoir was of a woman. Each memoir was about five pages long, including up to one page on the deathbed scene, out of a total journal length of about fifty pages. The opening memoir in the January 1837 issue for the late Mrs Ann Lloyd explained its purpose and justified the inclusion of a woman:

The lives *and deaths* of the faithful disciples of Christ, in successive ages furnish a constantly accumulating testimony, often more affecting than the most elaborate arguments, in favour of Christian principles. The memorials of pious women are equally instructive with those of pious men, as they reveal the silent influence of the religion of the Gospel in forming the character, and sustaining the mind under circumstances, often of difficulty and trial.[17]

Such memoirs were evidently considered of less interest to readers in the late Victorian period, for in 1890 they were replaced by a briefer 'In Memoriam' section, which appeared in only two of the ten issues.

The *Christian Guardian and Church of England Magazine* was published from 1807 to 1849. As in the *Evangelical Magazine*, each monthly issue opened with a memoir of about six pages, but most of the *Christian Guardian*'s memoirs extolled the virtues of long-dead bishops, clergymen, and saints, especially in the seventeenth century, seeming to presume that the more recently deceased provided less edifying examples. The memoirs in both journals usually described the Christian endeavours of devout clergymen and their attempts to triumph over the sufferings of the deathbed by testifying to their faith in their final hours. These memoirs will be used in the last section of this chapter to illustrate various features of the Evangelical model of the good death.

Where clerical memoirs in Evangelical journals were characterized by deep piety and high moral seriousness, those published in popular Evangelical tracts were often more notable for sentimentality and dramatic emphasis on the raptures of death triumphant. One Evangelical tract will suffice to illustrate the character of this popular Victorian genre. An account of Sophia Leakey's death from tuberculosis in 1858 was first published anonymously in 1860 by her sister Caroline in the Evangelical journal *Sunday at Home*, under the title 'Holy Living, Happy Dying'. Over twenty years later, another sister, Emily Leakey, reproduced the story in a memoir of Caroline's life and death called *Clear Shining Light*. Caroline Leakey's account told how Sophia was tempted by the devil during the last few days of her life. After suffering great pain with no complaint, Sophia had a serious convulsion four days before her death in 1858, while her sister prayed earnestly that heavenly strength might sustain her through the trial. Early next morning Caroline was amazed to find that Sophia had lost the habitual lines of suffering: 'Her face was as it had been the face of an angel . . . surprise and rapture were in that upturned face.' The dying woman exclaimed, 'Yes, it is heaven. It is Jesus come to fetch me. Oh, it is lovely, glorious! It is mag-ni-fi-cent.' But then the devil tempted her, and a look of 'unutterable horror' transformed her face, until she declaimed with triumph, 'Get-thee-behind-me-Satan.' The victory was complete as Sophia 'triumphed through the blood of the Lamb'.[18]

Such deathbed scenes in journals and tracts were highly selective and much depended on presentation and editing. As Geoffrey Best reminds us:

In these descriptions of death-bed scenes there was of course much art; art certainly in the narrator, fashioning the incident to fit the model he had in mind; art perhaps also in the subjects of the stories, who knew well enough the model to which they were meant to approximate and who presumably took pains not to disappoint their loved ones by failing to produce it.[19]

Evidence survives to demonstrate that Evangelical deathbed scenes intended for publication could indeed be reconstructed to fit the required model. Emily Leakey's memoir, *Clear Shining Light*, provides a revealing commentary on the manner in which Evangelical deathbed scenes found their way to the press, and the didactic purpose behind publication. Revd J. Rashdall wrote to Caroline Leakey soon after her sister Sophia's death in 1858, encouraging her to relate this 'lovely instance of the Christian's victory over death':

You cannot have a better subject for a tract. Mind that whilst you keep back names and places you make it quite clear that it may be depended on as an authentic history, not merely a story founded on facts. The value of it will be, that it all happened so, and that *we* may look for the same loving visitation when our hour of transition comes.

However, while Sophia's resistance to the devil's temptation was a major element of the published death scene, it was not mentioned in family correspondence about her death. Indeed, Sophia's own brief account suggests that she had energy and inclination for nothing 'but to sleep or cough'. Even the vision of the 'clear shining light' in Emily Leakey's account of Caroline's death in 1880 had little basis in the historical record.[20]

A number of Victorian Christians commented that deathbed scenes in their own experience were quite different from the triumphal accounts published for popular edification. Even William Wilberforce, founding father of Evangelicalism, noted on his daughter's death in 1821 that 'there was none of that exultation and holy joy which are sometimes manifested by dying Christians.' Yet he needed no dramatic signs of grace, for he was already confident that Barbara 'is gone to a better world', a happy place with God.[21] Some years later Henry Acland also revealed his conviction that 'raptures were not necessary to a happy Christian death'.[22] The most outspoken criticism of stage-managed and heavily edited deathbed scenes was made in a sermon preached in 1852 by Revd F. W. Robertson of Brighton, a liberal Anglican critical of Evangelicalism.

It is the easiest thing to represent the dying Christian as a man who always sinks into the grave full of hope, full of triumph, in the certain hope of a blessed resurrection. Brethren, we must paint things in the sober colours of truth; not as they might be supposed to be, but as they are. Often that is only a picture. Either very few death-beds are Christian ones, or else triumph is a very different thing from what the word generally implies . . . Rapture is a rare thing, except in books and scenes.[23]

In Robertson's view, the true Christian death was signified by a calm fearless-ness rather than ecstatic 'parade'.

Not all Evangelicals wanted for themselves the idealized deathbed scene in tracts and journals. Revd William Carus recorded that Revd Charles Simeon, the Cambridge evangelist, had always wished for privacy at his death, and asked Carus to 'keep everyone away from him' at the end. Three weeks before his death in 1836, Simeon was distressed that Carus permitted a 'crowd' of six (Carus, the physician, the curate, and Simeon's three servants) to gather round his bed for a short time. Next morning Simeon told Carus that he was hurt at the previous night's 'scene': 'a death-bed scene I abhor from my inmost soul'.[24] The deathbed account published in the *Evangelical Magazine* made no reference to Simeon's insistence on a solitary deathbed, while the statement that 'his last hours were peaceful' actually meant that he was unconscious for the last two days.[25]

Deathbed scenes in Victorian fiction were also heavily influenced by the Evangelical movement and further helped to disseminate the Evangelical model to a large reading public. As Walter Houghton observed, the purpose of death scenes in Victorian novels was partly religious: 'They are intended to help the reader sustain his faith by dissolving religious doubt in a solution of warm sentiment.'[26] Dickens and Thackeray were the most famous creators of fictional deathbed scenes, notably represented by the deaths of Little Nell in *The Old Curiosity Shop* and Colonel Newcome in *The Newcomes*. Many other novelists imitated their treatment of such scenes because of their immense popular success, though not Anthony Trollope, who was more restrained. Deathbed scenes in novels were usually melodramatic occasions of moral judgement and emotional farewell, the worthy heroes dying with dignity and the sinners in agony. These stereotypical scenes often included proof of spiritual salvation, with minor miracles, haloes of light, and edifying last words. Death scenes in Victorian fiction tended to be more melodramatic and sentimental than those in Evangelical tracts, but it was often a matter of degree. However, the fictional scenes made no claims to historical accuracy; they were deliberate devices for emotionally engaging the reader in an age when sentimental stories were very popular.[27]

In practice, the Evangelical model of the good death was moderated for many Anglicans by the Oxford or Tractarian movement of the 1830s and 1840s, which reinforced the essential practical piety of Evangelicalism while restraining its excesses. Through a series of widely read 'Tracts for the Times', John Henry Newman, Edward Pusey, and John Keble initiated debate on such issues as the authority of the visible Church, the sacraments, and church tradition. Many Tractarians were initially drawn from the ranks of the radical Evangelicals, whose views in the 1820s were remarkably similar to those of the Oxford movement in the following decade.[28]

These links between the Evangelical and Tractarian revivals help to explain why the fundamentals of their deathbed practice were so similar. As David Newsome argues, 'The tightest knot which bound the Evangelicals and the Tractarians together . . . in these early years was the common pursuit of holiness.'[29] This 'pursuit of holiness' was at the core of their attitudes to death and dying, and both movements identified strongly with the precepts of Jeremy Taylor's *Exercises of Holy Dying*. They agreed about the emphasis on moral earnestness, self-discipline, self-scrutiny, and the call for a life of prayer, contemplation, and sanctity. Evangelicals such as Charles Simeon, Hannah More, and William Wilberforce shared Newman's goal of 'passionate and sustained earnestness after a high moral rule, seriously realised in conduct'.[30] The Tractarians contributed in a small way to the tradition of didactic deathbed literature with John Warton's *Death-Bed Scenes*, published in three volumes in 1827.[31] This illustrated the major theoretical difference between the two deathbed traditions, notably the High Church stress on the attendance of the clergy to administer the last communion, as against the Evangelical emphasis on the visible signs of grace. But such variations were more apparent in theory than family practice, given the common link of the 'pursuit of holiness' through piety in life and at death.

Features of the Evangelical Model of the Good Death: Evangelical Theory and Victorian Family Practice

The major features of the Evangelical model of the good Christian death will be demonstrated by comparing published prescriptive Evangelical tracts and journals with middle- and upper-class family practice and experience. Private family correspondence, diaries, and deathbed memorials were often heavily influenced by the Evangelical movement, but they were not usually deliberately edited and stage-managed; they were mostly written very close to the time of the death, and under the stress of intense emotion. The detailed

accounts of deathbed scenes were usually written for the writer or the immediate family only, primarily as part of the Evangelical process of accounting
to God for their lives and deaths. They were sometimes disarmingly frank
about moral weakness, unpleasant physical symptoms, or unworthy deathbed
behaviour. The published Evangelical deathbed accounts in tracts, journals,
and biographies were intended, by contrast, primarily for popular moral
instruction, with the undesirable features edited out.

The Victorian Evangelical version of the good death included several
features which can be traced back to the early modern period. Death ideally
should take place at home, with the dying person making explicit farewells to
each family member. There should be time, and physical and mental capacity, for the completion of temporal and spiritual business, whether the latter
signified final Communion or informal family devotions. The dying person
should be conscious and lucid until the end, resigned to God's will, able to
beg forgiveness for past sins and to prove his or her worthiness for salvation.
Pain and suffering should be borne with fortitude, and even welcomed as a
final test of fitness for heaven and willingness to pay for past sins.

All Victorian Christians were agreed on certain desirable features of deathbed behaviour, especially those which asserted the human need for family
support. The vital importance of family solidarity and sympathy in coping
with death and participating in its rituals tended to be taken for granted in
middle- and upper-class families. It rarely required stating in writing, especially because family members were usually together at times of death. Mary
Ann Wildman urged her brother A. C. Tait to return home for their father's
death in 1832: 'In an affliction like this we want the society of those who feel
as we do . . . Such sorrow makes us cling the more firmly to each other.'[32]
Many Victorians commented that no amount of preparation for death could
remove the pain of the final parting from the family. But as Caroline Parker
observed in 1853 on the death of her sister-in-law Catharine Sharpe it eased
that pain immensely 'that so many of those she loved were near her' in her
final days.[33] On the death of her brother Herbert in 1877, Angelina Acland
prayed that all her brothers and sisters might continue to keep the family
chain unbroken at deathbeds and afterwards.[34]

The custom of dying in public at the centre of a crowded deathbed scene
had been abandoned by the nineteenth century. The attendants at middle- or
upper-class Victorian deathbeds were usually far fewer than the 'crowd' at the
deathbed in early modern England or eighteenth-century France. Victorian
deathbed scenes were private affairs which were usually limited to a relatively
small number of members of the immediate family, together with a nurse or
a servant, and occasionally a doctor. Formal portraits of public deathbed

scenes of royalty give a false impression of a customary crowd of onlookers, in addition to family participants, because royal births and deaths required statesmen as witnesses. William Walton's lithograph of the last moments of Prince Albert in 1862 shows twenty-one onlookers, including at least thirteen politicians and public servants. The deaths of famous statesmen, such as that of Gladstone in 1898, also give an inaccurate impression because they were regarded as public events for the nation, with visiting politicians occasionally swelling the size of an already large family.

Victorian deathbed attendants usually increased in number for a few hours only for the final farewells, the sacraments, and sometimes for the last vigil; otherwise attendants were restricted to one or two people, for fear of exciting the patient. There were considerable variations in the number and composition of the attendants at the last vigil, according to personal preference, family size and status, the age of the dying person, and the nature of the disease. At the death of John Keble's niece by marriage 'Kenie' Keble in 1858, her husband and her mother were the only attendants in the final hours.[35] Gib Acland was nursed for twenty months by his stepmother and other relatives before his death in 1874. Five family members took turns in sitting with him in the final hours, and they all knelt round the bed to read the commendatory prayer at the end.[36] On the death of Sarah Acland, a mother of seven, in 1878, her husband and two of the children were present, in addition to the nurse and doctor.[37] The Dowager Countess of Carnarvon died in 1876 attended by a sister and four children and presumably also a nurse, the doctor having left earlier in the day.[38]

Modern psychologists such as John Hinton have written of the frequent emotional disengagement of relatives in today's society from the person known to be dying. By contrast, Evangelicalism encouraged the expression of love, sorrow, and faith at the nineteenth-century deathbed.[39] There are countless examples of Victorian families' recognition of the need of dying relatives for affection and companionship, particularly in the final days, when holding the hand or stroking the hair could be more meaningful than words. When May Lyttelton lay dying of typhus in 1875 she was comforted by her aunt Catherine Gladstone 'lying by her, petting and stroking and soothing her'.[40] In 1876 the dying dowager Countess of Carnarvon held her son's hand constantly in the final hours, telling him how much pleasure his presence gave her.[41] In 1879 Lord Carrington held his dying sister 'Minim' in his arms till the last.[42] Agnes Anson soothed old Lady Acland in 1892, recognizing her need for touch as well as companionship: 'I have had so much love-making with her.'[43] Even in the Potter family, which was uncertain about how to cope with Lawrencina Potter's death in 1882, Beatrice 'lay by her side and petted her' during one of her long watches.[44] Relatives kept their vigils by the dying, often alone or with a nurse, holding the hand of the dying person, and reciting poetry or psalms or other extracts from the Bible.

However, the defining features of the Evangelical model of the good death were inevitably those which related most closely to its primary religious concerns. Thus Evangelicals and Tractarians shared Jeremy Taylor's conviction that spiritual readiness was crucial. So devout Christians preferred a long illness because it allowed time for devotional preparation by the sufferer and the family. As Lord Grosvenor wrote to Revd William Harcourt on the death of his daughter in 1839, 'Your affliction may have been, and I hope was, alleviated by the preparation of a long illness and the anticipation of a fatal result.'[45] Conversely, Jane Goulburn lamented the sudden death of a villager in the 1850s, fearing death must have found him ill prepared for such an 'awful' change. She took the opportunity to warn her daughter Jane that she should learn from such a melancholy event: 'I hope my darling that you do not forget to think on the necessity of being prepared for death at any age, and that you pray to God to sanctify you, and make you meet for the inheritance of the saints in light.'[46]

Preparation for death was usually most advanced in the elderly and the pious, but many sick people discussed their feelings about death with sympathetic relatives. For instance, when Evelyn Lady Carnarvon was told by her doctor in 1875 that she was dying of puerperal fever, she talked about her spiritual readiness for death with her husband, keeping 'perfectly quiet and calm and resigned'.[47] When Margaret Kelvin was approaching death in 1869 she chose to reveal her troubled spiritual journey to her beloved niece Margaret King, ending with a calm acceptance:

[Margaret Kelvin] spoke calmly and freely of the doctor's opinion and her own approaching death, and of that feeling of [the] loneliness of the other world which she cannot get over; of the sad days they [she and Uncle William Kelvin] have had in the very dark valley itself, it seemed. But now she is calmer, more willing, and wants to interest herself in us all, in her sister's baby, and all my preparations [for marriage]. She said she had wanted to tell me all about it herself that I might see as she sees, and enter into her feelings . . . Though we were both crying, there *was* no shadow on the happiness.[48]

This example bears some resemblance to the stages of response to approaching death identified by modern psychologists, moving (in varying order) through denial, bargaining, anger, depression, and acceptance.[49] But this late twentieth-century model has only limited application to Victorian Christians, whose religious beliefs interpreted earthly life as transient, urged them to prepare for a better life after death, and taught resignation to the will of

God. Moreover, death was too frequent and familiar in the nineteenth century to be easily denied, while Christianity's message of hope in the resurrection of Christ reduced the anger.

The Evangelical model of the good death encouraged the rapid settlement of worldly affairs to minimize distractions from spiritual preparation. In 1856 Henry Goulburn recognized that his 'departure' was not far removed, and returned home 'to set his papers in order', allowing him to depart in peace.[50] Lewis Dawnay acknowledged his impending death after the failure of an exploratory operation in 1910, as his wife reported: 'The following morning he gave me so many messages and directions to follow. He dictated a few letters, said goodbye to our servants, thanking them so gratefully, and spoke of my future and what he wished me to do.' Dawnay said farewell to his two sons, explained where he wished to be buried, and arranged the details of the funeral service. As his wife said, 'He really had "set his house in order" . . . Nothing was left undone and he was so fully prepared and glad to go.'[51]

The Evangelical model placed great weight on the didactic value of death-bed scenes, to enable witnesses to learn from the triumphant examples of the final hours of departing saints. Henry Venn's classic devotional text *The Complete Duty of Man*, first published in 1763 and reissued many times up to 1841, put a strong case for children to witness deathbeds:

And if an opportunity could be found of bringing your son or daughter to the bed-side of a departing saint, it will infinitely exceed the force of all instruction, to let them see with their own eyes, and hear with their own ears, the faithful servant of God speaking good of his name . . . proclaiming the peace of his own mind under the pains of an approaching dissolution.[52]

Parents should seize opportunities offered by the deaths of friends, neighbours, or servants to teach their children early that death was the start of endless sorrow for wicked unbelievers, but the 'door to endless joys, and the perfection of glory' for those who loved God.[53]

William Wilberforce, like many of his Evangelical colleagues in the early nineteenth century, frequently referred in his correspondence to the exemplary value of good deathbed scenes. He tried to comfort Lady Waldegrave on the death of her daughter in 1805 with the reminder that death sometimes produced 'everlasting benefit and joy'; 'There is scarcely any providential dispensation which is so often rendered the instrument of producing a happy effect on the hearts of men as the death of friends. I have known several who ascribe to it their own conversion.'[54] Even the sad consumptive death in 1815 of the recently widowed Mrs Henry Thornton, leaving nine orphaned children, demonstrated for Wilberforce the victory of Christianity over death: 'It is a scene which must be witnessed to produce its full effect upon the heart . . . [demonstrating] a happiness felt in the moments of the deepest outward dejection and sorrow . . . Triumphs . . . of the believer's faith.'[55] Some Evangelicals, notably Hannah More, carried this sentimental piety over the deaths of the faithful to extremes, as Robin Furneaux observed: 'She positively wallowed in the delicious agonies of the death-bed. "I know of nothing so interesting", she wrote, "as the closing scenes of a champion of righteousness." In 1792 she visited the death-bed of Bishop Horne, "a more delightful or edifying death-bed cannot well be imagined".'[56] Evangelical zealots such as Hannah More followed the deaths of sinners and unbelievers equally avidly, to testify to their well-earned suffering or their belated repentance. Following her daughter's death in 1821, William Wilberforce's wife, Barbara, kept a commonplace book in which she noted deathbed scenes, especially the unpleasant deaths of sinners.[57]

There is abundant evidence that both High Church and Evangelical Anglicans recognized the didactic value of the deathbed scene. Two weeks after the consumptive death of her son Harry in 1843, Jane Goulburn included a prayer in her diary, indicating her awareness of Venn's advice: 'Preserve a lively recollection of the awful scenes which they have witnessed to abide in the heart of my three remaining children and quicken them with thy heavenly spirit so that they may all be made meet for the inheritance of thy saints.'[58] When Dorothea Palmer was dying of consumption in 1852 she told her sisters to 'make all the use of me that ever you can' in teaching the local children at the school and the church about God.[59]

Victorian Christians were eager to learn the details of family deathbed scenes, to be reassured that the death was a good one and their loved one truly saved, rather than to wallow in the suffering as Hannah More appeared to do. Thus Richard Cavendish thanked Edward Goulburn 'with all my heart' for his detailed letter describing the death of his brother Harry in 1843.[60] Elizabeth Herbert wrote to W. E. Gladstone in 1857 on the death of Mary Lyttelton: 'I am so grateful to you for making time to give me all those details which I longed but scarcely hoped for.'[61] Similarly, Revd W. V. Harcourt wrote to his youngest sister, Georgiana Malcolm, in 1853 on their brother's death: 'I feel very thankful to you for the detail into which you have gone in your affecting account of Henry's last moments upon earth.' Harcourt was particularly grateful to learn of the restoration of his brother's consciousness and reason and 'the calmness and prayerfulness of his end'.[62]

The most important difference between Evangelical and Tractarian deathbeds related to the role of the clergyman and the significance attached to the sacraments. For Evangelical Anglicans and Nonconformists the clergyman's administration of the last rites was less important than a sincere faith in God, supported by the prayers and Bible-reading of the family faithful. The Evangelicals emphasized the scriptures rather than the authority of the Church as the source of spiritual truth. The Evangelical Christian achieved salvation theoretically through faith alone, so that the word of the gospel expressed through prayer and Bible-reading had more significance than the priestly administration of the sacraments. Illustrations abound of families repeating hymns, verses of the Bible, and suitable prayers to their dying relatives at regular intervals. In few Victorian Evangelical families did the clergyman's visit have the same impact as that of the doctor, especially towards the end of the century.

Samuel Beckett, a provincial surgeon who wrote a memoir on his sister's death in the early 1850s, perceptively described the restricted role of the clergyman at the Evangelical deathbed. The Beckett family's 'valued pastor' called daily during his sister's illness, but did not visit the sick-room on every occasion, recognizing the importance of rest for the sufferer, as well as the limitations of his own offices:

What can a faithful pastor do in sickness more than he has . . . done in health? Had he preached himself, instead of Christ, as the sinner's hope—a reliance on sacraments, instead of a dependence upon His merits—a legal routine instead of a lively faith, his presence would now have been of the utmost importance . . . Simple evangelical truth however, habitually proclaimed, relieves both the minister and the afflicted member of his flock from such a vague and dreadful responsibility.[63]

Beckett described his family's devotional routines during his sister's long illness. At regular intervals the 'pious parents' offered short prayers, often at their daughter's request, or read appropriate passages from the Bible, especially from the books of Isaiah and Revelation. The parents were assisted by the daily visits of their 'beloved pastor' and even by their unusually devout nurse, 'who embraced every opportunity of reading Scripture and engaging in prayer'. The pastor became convinced that the sufferer 'was trusting alone in Christ, as the "sinner's only hope"'.[64] The Evangelical family had largely taken over the responsibility for spiritual preparation for the dying from the clergyman, accelerating a very slow process which started with the Reformation.

At the other end of the Christian spectrum, it was vitally important for dying Catholics, by contrast, that there be a final confession and that the viaticum be administered by a priest. Francis and Alice Blunt, brother and sister of Wilfrid Scawen Blunt, the poet, were Catholics who died of tuberculosis in 1872. Francis took the last sacrament a week before his death in April 1872, and was several times visited by a priest. Three months later, when Alice was dying, she received the last sacrament from an old family friend, Canon Wenham, on 13 July, after a particularly bad night, and felt 'very cheerful' afterwards. On the day of her death, over two weeks later, she asked for their local priest, Father Wenneslaus, who prayed with her and gave her the last blessing.[65]

Most High and many Broad Church Anglicans also believed that it was important to receive the last Communion from a clergyman on their death-bed. The timing of the final sacrament was often problematical since, ideally, it should take place after all concerned had accepted that death was inevitable but while the sufferer still retained clear mental faculties. Catharine Tait, a devout Anglican and wife of A. C. Tait, the Archbishop of Canterbury, died in 1878 at the age of 59. She had planned to receive her final Communion on Advent Sunday, but became distressed about her deteriorating condition the day before, as Archbishop Tait recorded: 'We were now in great alarm of some sudden termination, or of unconsciousness coming on, and it would have left a sad memory if she had departed without that solemn rite through which her soul had always rejoiced to hold communion with her saviour.'[66] The family physician, Dr Carpenter, at first seemed 'averse for fear of disturb-ing her', but later that day allowed the Archbishop to administer Holy Communion to his wife, their two daughters, and the doctor. Catharine joined in as far as her impeded speech would allow, 'her mental faculties entire'. Her daughters then sang several favourite hymns, including 'Jesu Lover of my soul', followed by her husband repeating biblical texts and short prayers, until the doctor said she needed some rest. Later that day Catharine lapsed into a coma and the Archbishop said the commendatory prayer shortly before she died.[67]

Catharine Tait's death raises two further points of interest. It was not uncommon for the clergyman who administered the final sacrament in large upper- and upper-middle-class families to be a member of the family. Archibald Tait was only unusual in his eminence as Archbishop of Canter-bury. The Gladstone and Lyttelton families, for example, at various death-beds, called upon the services of W. E. Gladstone's son Revd Stephen Gladstone, his brother-in-law Revd Henry Glynne, his nephew Arthur Lyttelton, or his nephew by marriage Edward Talbot. Secondly, Dr Carpen-ter was not the only doctor to advise against the last Communion on medical grounds. When Lord Beaconsfield, the Conservative statesman, was dying in 1881, his physician 'peremptorily forbade the suggestion [of final Commun-ion] being made, on the ground that the patient would realise at once that his case was hopeless and would turn his face to the wall and die'.[68] Though medical advice against the final sacrament was proffered more often in the later Victorian period, it was not unusual in earlier decades, as with Sir John Gladstone in 1851.

Another major difference between Evangelical and High Church death-beds, at least in theory, related to the rapturous triumphalism of the Evangelical model, including uplifting last words and joyful signs of grace. The last words of the dying had special significance for Evangelicals, who believed that conduct in the final hours was a vital test of fitness for salvation. Departing saints, and even the less worthy, were supposed to be supremely aware of their proximity to divine judgement and to the afterlife at the hour of their death, and therefore capable of uttering words of heavenly wisdom. At the very least, it was hoped they would make a statement testifying to their humble, penitent, and hopeful state of mind. The *ars moriendi* and many uplifting Evangelical tracts of the nineteenth century provided advice on appropriate final words. The anonymous author of *Death-Bed Thoughts* in 1838 produced nearly 100 pages of purple prose, written 'in daily expectation of her final summons' and given to the press at the wish of her friends.[69] As late as 1893 a tract entitled *Final Triumph* provided readers with suitable examples from the elevated last words of saints, martyrs, and assorted famous people. Sir Henry Havelock was reported as saying in 1857 that he died unafraid, 'happy and contented', asking for his eldest son to 'see how a Christian can die'. *The Art of Dying* in 1894 used poets and writers as exemplars for the popular reader.[70] The published last words in Evangelical tracts ranged from the sublime to the mundane, such as Caroline Leakey's '*Farewell*, dear drawing-room, you have long been devoted to God.'[71]

Evangelical journals and tracts provide abundant evidence of dying people testifying to their personal state of repentance and submission in their final days. The *Evangelical Magazine* recorded in 1837 the dying words of the Revd John Humphreys at the age of 79. He told his family he had no fear of death, was resigned to God's will, and believed 'God will be more glorified in my salvation than in my destruction.'[72] According to the *Evangelical Magazine*, as a consequence of his good life and death 'his happy spirit rose to enjoy the light and glory of an everlasting day'. The *Christian Guardian and Church of England Magazine* recorded in 1827 the final days of the Revd Samuel Knight, apparently based on his family's memorial. Several weeks before his death, despite great suffering, Revd Knight called his family to hear his dying testimony to his faith: 'You will be desirous to learn what is the state of my mind, and with what feelings I contemplate the near approach of death. All my trust is in the promises of the Gospel . . . I know no refuge but the cross of Christ.' At the hour of his death, the 'departing saint' spoke a few words which expressed his communication with the world above: 'All is ready . . . They are waiting . . . I see Jesus.' The suspense ended as his family knelt to commend his soul to the hands of God.[73]

But some departing saints suffered too much at the end to sustain any coherent testimony to their spiritual state. In such cases Evangelicals sometimes conducted a catechetical exchange to establish the sufferer's spiritual condition, illustrated in the account of Revd John Witherington Peers's death in the *Christian Guardian and Church of England Magazine* in 1837. His zealous family sought to ascertain his spiritual state, despite his excruciating pain, mental degeneration, respiratory problems, and deafness. A family member asked, 'Are you comfortable in the prospect of eternity?', to which Revd Peers managed a remarkable reply in the circumstances: 'I desire to rest entirely upon him, though I want the manifestation of his presence . . . All my trust is in Jesus Christ.' Despite extreme distress at the very end he managed to say, 'I am saved only by Christ . . . Nothing but Christ crucified.'[74]

A number of Evangelical tracts and privately published memorial pamphlets also demonstrated this use of a litany of questions about the state of the dying person's soul. A woman described only as 'Mrs W———', aged 84, was deprived of sight and reason by a stroke in 1862. As her death approached, her husband, 'a veteran Christian soldier', searched eagerly for signs of her salvation. He took advantage of a brief restoration of her mental faculties, which he considered a miracle, to subject her to a series of questions seeking evidence of repentance. She struggled to answer before she 'soared on angel wings to her everlasting home above'.[75]

Private accounts of deathbed scenes which were unedited and unpublished suggest, by contrast, that few dying Victorians actually succeeded in producing the required testimonies to their readiness for heaven. Revd Dr Thomas Somerville, a 90-year old Scottish Presbyterian, was one of the few to meet these high expectations outside the pages of the Evangelical journals and tracts. According to his son's private account, a day or two before his death in 1830 Revd Somerville assembled his family and delivered his last sermon: 'Even pain leads me to bless God, I look upon it as one of the proofs of a glorious Resurrection . . . The pains of death I firmly believe are to be succeeded by joys that cannot be conceived . . . Jesus Christ was sent to save us by the atonement.'[76]

Such edifying dying statements were rare outside the published didactic deathbed literature, and usually came from the most devout families. For example, William Roundell, an Anglican, described his wife's ideal death in the early 1850s in a letter to his son-in-law:

The Manner of her Death was what she had always prayed for, her Illness was short, and not attended with Pain, and her Intellects were perfect. From the first she was sensible her Time was come, and she desired not to continue, but said I am ready to go or stay as seems best to the Allmighty. I am in Charity with all human Beings, and I commend myself to the Mercy of God, trusting to the Merits and Intercession of Jesus Christ for the forgiveness of all my Sins. And having so said, she expired without a groan, or single struggle.[77]

Like Revd Somerville's final statement, this reads like a prepared speech, possibly embellished for the benefit of the clerical son-in-law. It was certainly an unusual testimony in the private family records, though a number of dying people managed to recite brief familiar biblical texts or short passages from memorized prayers until shortly before the end. Such were Harry Goulburn's last words as he lay dying of consumption in 1843: 'Don't grieve for me . . . Blessed, blessed is he whom the Lord chasteneth.'[78]

But most accounts of deathbed scenes recorded bland or banal last words during the final vigil or, more often, none at all. Many final words inevitably referred to requests concerning physical needs and comfort, such as Sir John Gladstone's 'Bring me my porridge' in 1851—not in fact his very last words, but remembered as such.[79] Many terminal illnesses concluded with days of delirium or unconsciousness, which prevented meaningful communication. On learning that Jane Goulburn died after a stroke in 1857, Louisa Cane regretted that 'the state of unconsciousness is trying to witness and one longs for parting words'.[80] Similarly, Louisa Clemens was disappointed at her family's 'detail of particulars' of the death of her mother, Ruth Courtauld, at the age of 92 in 1854: 'You gave me none of her last words: not one word, or *action* of her last two months of decline indicative of the last mental exercises.'[81]

John Tait, aged 80, was delirious during his final illness in 1877 and '*raving so continually*' that he was unable to follow any prayers. His brother James Tait honestly admitted to the third brother, Archbishop A. C. Tait, that 'We find the less we talk to him the better, as he takes up some idea, often disagreeable and goes on for hours.'[82] Adelaide Drummond found her last visit to her father, Lord John Russell, in 1878 very distressing: 'I stood at the foot of his bed. The sight was unutterably pathetic. He began to speak very rapidly and rather loudly, but his articulation was so much affected by his illness that I could not understand what he said, and I knew that he could not hear the poor answers I tried to make to his earnest speech.'[83]

Occasionally the family was able to take advantage of 'pre-mortem clarity', a lucid interval immediately before death.[84] After several hours of unconsciousness in 1911, Lady Carrington's mother 'rallied in the most wonderful way and saw us all one after another and seemed more like herself than she had been for some time'.[85] But even clarity of mind did not ensure the production of suitable final words which could be recorded. Lady Harcourt was relieved that her husband, Sir William, was able to attend his brother's deathbed in 1891, though there is no record of what was said: 'Thank God that you went . . . It will be a life long satisfaction to you—I had been terribly afraid that you would *not* have been able to have that precious interview. There is nothing like those words that come from a conscious mind and heart when death is near. I have known it but I believe that it is very rare.'[86] It was rare indeed, even when people understood the significance of such final words and knew from Evangelical literature, and from previous experience, what was expected of them.

Two Victorian doctors who attended numerous deaths made some revealing observations about last words. In 1863 the eminent physician William S. Savory, FRS, delivered a lecture entitled 'Death: Its Signification' to the Royal Institute of Great Britain. He pointed out that the brain usually fails first in the dying process, and that: 'We hear and read of persons retaining a clear and vigorous intellect up to the moment of departure; but in truth, such ideas and statements rest upon very shallow evidence. A few reasonable sentences uttered at intervals, or the repeated expression of some prevailing idea, can hardly go for so much.'[87] In the early 1850s Dr Samuel Beckett, a devout Christian, contended that serious mistakes were made in expecting 'manifestations of gracious feeling', which were not always physically possible. During many painful deaths dying people were unable to communicate, while fevers paralysed the powers of verbal expression. Dr Beckett concluded that many 'candidates for immortal felicity' were denied a good Christian death because of the nature of their disease:

In many such cases, it is only in half-broken accents, or by the significant movement of the head or of the hand, that we can arrive at the assurance of the Divine presence and support; and the oppression of pain and disease may be so fierce, that even our inquiries seem to become almost an impertinence. Perhaps it may be truly affirmed that comprehensive and earnest views of life, death, and futurity, do not usually originate with such circumstances; apathy on the one hand, or nervous depression and irritability on the other, being far more usual. In fact, serious illness often becomes a touchstone of character; revealing weakness, instability, and impatience, where firmness and grandeur of demeanour might have been expected.[88]

Some features of the Evangelical model of the good death were primarily literary myths which were rarely, if ever, realized in the historical evidence. In tracts and novels, Evangelicals looked for 'signs' of salvation, or even for deathbed miracles, and found them in abundance, as in the famous death of Little Nell in Dickens's *Old Curiosity Shop*. Novelists and authors of Evangelical tracts often satisfied their readers by manufacturing proof of the salvation of departing heroes and heroines, depicting the rapture on their faces as they caught their first glimpse of the wonders of Heaven. Sometimes they were represented as hearing heavenly music, or seeing a bright triumphal light or a vision of a loved one waiting to welcome them.

The rare references in Victorian family papers to such phenomena usually seem contrived and unconvincing. The account by Emily Harcourt of the death of her sister Selina Lady Morshead from bowel cancer in 1884 attempted to depict an inspirational death despite dreadful physical suffering:

I want you to know how the state Selina was in *mentally*, helps me on as far as the wonderful spirituality went—all her thoughts up in Heaven with my Father—his name always in her mouth . . . and the last time I was with her consciously, she took my arm and with hers pointing direct up said *most urgently* twice, 'Emmie, Jesus Christ'.

It was clear to Emily Harcourt that Selina had 'left us long ago for Heaven'.[89] But if this extract is read in the context of the rest of the family correspondence, its effect is undermined by the evidence that Emily herself was so exhausted by prolonged nursing and grief that she was rambling and confused when she wrote it.

Although most members of these families failed to see signs of salvation in the form of beatific visions or clear shining lights, they sometimes compensated in their descriptions of the countenance of the deceased. The process of dying was rarely described as beautiful, but beauty was sometimes attributed to corpses, particularly their facial expression in the 'smile of death', though rarely so ecstatically as in Dickens's description of the dead Little Nell. If these families almost never saw rapture on the face of the sufferer before death, they partly made up for it with their tributes to the faces they saw after death. The smile of death was thought by some to suggest that the soul had sighted the glory of heaven—it was interpreted as a sign of salvation. Victorian scientists understood that the facial muscles sometimes contracted after death, but some people preferred an ethereal explanation.[90] It was comforting to find physical signs which might confirm the heavenly destination of the departed.

The historical evidence also suggests the more mundane explanation that the bereaved family often experienced a sense of relief on seeing their relative's face free from the suffering of disease. On the death of her eldest sister in 1813, Hannah More thought it 'pleasant to see death without its terrors. We visit the cold remains twenty times a day.'[91] Caroline Fox commented in 1840 on the death of her brother the third Lord Holland that she kissed the 'beautiful forehead' and saw 'the angelick countenance as serene as in life with no trace of suffering'.[92] Lady Anne Blunt described the face of her brother-in-law Francis Blunt immediately after his death from tuberculosis in 1872: 'His face was beautiful like the face of a saint as I imagine it to be . . . Death is horrible but at the first moment there is something beautiful in it too.'[93] The wife of Charles Vaughan, Dean of Llandaff, described his appearance at his death in 1897, at the end of a long, excruciating illness: 'He *looks* beautiful . . . with an expression of such heavenly peace and love on his countenance that it would seem as if already he belongs to the Celestial City.'[94] But responses to the sight of the corpse varied greatly, and Marianne Thornton's experience on her father's death in 1814 was not uncommon either. At the moment of death, those who had seen him in pain were comforted by the expression of 'ever deepening repose'. Half an hour later they were taken to see the body after it had been laid out: 'but we only took one glance—it was all so sadly altered' and 'looked like death indeed'. Her mother exclaimed that she could not bear it and they did not enter the room again.[95]

This chapter has explored the Evangelical model of the good Christian death and the gulf between the literary ideal and the family reality. The Evangelical model published in journals, tracts, and fiction could not possibly represent the infinite variety of deathbed experiences, with their immense range of diseases, religious beliefs, and family circumstances. Indeed, the didactic aspirations of the Evangelical ideal limited its capacity to represent the multifarious reality of death. In practice, the good Evangelical death required a rare combination of good luck, convenient illness, and pious character, and was achieved more often in Evangelical tracts than in family life.

2

THE REVIVAL AND DECLINE OF THE GOOD CHRISTIAN DEATH

The Ideal of the Good Christian Death to 1870

Many Victorian deaths illustrated one or more of the characteristic features of the Evangelical ideal, though even the most pious men and women usually attained, at best, only a modest approximation to the ideal. These families had enough direct experience of death to know that the practical reality was usually very different from the ideal stereotypes of the didactic Evangelical tracts. Most written records of deathbeds were usually private, spontaneous outpourings of grief, which paid little attention to literary presentation. This chapter begins with four case-studies of death which most closely approximated the Evangelical ideal, selected from the few such documented examples which have survived. Changing perceptions of the good death from the 1870s will then be explored, demonstrating the impact of the decline in Evangelical fervour and piety.

It is no accident that all four initial case-studies are from the early and mid-Victorian periods, or that all come from devout Christian families—three Anglican and one Presbyterian. All were influenced by the spiritual revivals of the early nineteenth century—the Oxford and Evangelical movements—which both encouraged zealous spiritual preparation for death and emphasized the vital significance of the final hours. Their faith gave these dying Christians courage, patience, and submission to their fate, thereby reducing emotional stress and fear of death. Modern psychiatrists who work with dying patients have observed that those who had a strong religious faith and attended church frequently had the greatest freedom from anxiety about dying.[1] It is not surprising, either, that these four deaths are of young adults, aged between 23 and 31, because the untimely death of an 'adult child' was a particularly painful loss for parents, then as now.[2] Victorian parents sometimes idealized the deaths of grown-up children because children over 10 were expected to live out their natural life-span and parents' emotional investment in them was great.

It is also significant that three out of the four cases died of tuberculosis. It seems paradoxical that a disease which was a product of poverty, overcrowd-ing, and unsanitary conditions should have been idealized, especially as consumptives usually fitted the romantic stereotype by virtue only of their youth. As Barry Smith demonstrates in *The Retreat of Tuberculosis*, most consumptives were poor, enfeebled people suffering from a chronic, debilitat-ing, and painful disease which could be neither cured nor prevented: 'as a fundamental destructive social force it was rivalled among illnesses only by the venereal diseases and insanity'. Tuberculosis killed more people than smallpox and cholera combined, though from 1850 it did so at a gradually declining rate. Between 1840 and 1960 'the death-rates attributed to infec-tious diseases fell steadily from about 11 per 1,000 to about 2.5 per 1,000; tuberculosis accounted for nearly half this diminution'.[3] Though Robert Koch identified the bacillus in 1882, doctors had no cure for tuberculosis until streptomycin was isolated in 1943, and Victorian treatment was empirical and inadequate.

Most Victorians familiar with the disease, especially poor working-class families, did not idealize death from consumption. The *Christian Remembrancer* noted in 1842, 'The subject is, to half the families of England, too fraught with painful reality to be thus introduced . . . amid dreamy sentiment.'[4] The *Lancet* in 1882 denounced the romantic view of consump-tive death, 'which seems to us as false as can well be'.[5] Charlotte Brontë's letters described the stark physical reality of the death of her consumptive sister Emily in 1848: 'She is *very* ill. A more hollow, wasted, pallid aspect, I have not beheld. The deep tight cough continues; the breathing after the least exertion is a rapid pant; and these symptoms are accompanied by pains in the chest and side . . . moments so dark as these I have never known.'[6] Another testimony to the bleak reality of consumption, even among the wealthy, came from Charty Ribblesdale, whose family had a history of tuberculosis, and who died of the disease herself in 1911 after years of nursing and isolation. Despite Charty's horror of consumption, she nursed her dying sister Pauline at Davos, the Swiss Alpine consumptive resort, in 1886: 'This is a sad, dreary little place, and I feel as if I were living in a graveyard . . . I always think of the Dance of Death! There is such a fearful satire about it! The people are deadly dull as well as deadly ill. I feel a sort of sense of suffocation when they come to tea here.'[7]

Yet death from consumption was romanticized by early and mid-Victorian poets, artists, and novelists, including D. G. Rossetti, W. Holman Hunt, and John Millais. Such portrayals as H. P. Robinson's *Fading Away* of 1858, Burne-Jones's *Fair Rosamund* of 1863, and the opera *La Traviata* depicted consumptives as young, beautiful, innocent, and frequently female. As Barry

Smith acutely observes: 'Tuberculosis had, in the tragic mode, replaced the semi-comic gout of the eighteenth century. It seems that writers and painters draw on one disease and its connotations at a time. Other prevalent chronic, life-threatening illnesses, heart disease, diabetes, cancer, never became aesthetic or emotional devices . . .'.[8] Hearing of the death of a young female friend from consumption, Edgar Allan Poe responded: 'I would wish all I love to perish of that disease. How glorious! To depart in the heyday of the young life, the heart full of passion, the imagination all fire.'[9] Despite the Brontë sisters' intimate knowledge of the actual horror of consumption, Philippe Ariès was able to draw on their fictional representation of the disease to illustrate the alleged Victorian cultural tendency to romanticize death.[10]

Consumption was also idealized by many clergymen and even the occasional Evangelical doctor as a blessing in disguise which allowed time and mental clarity for spiritual reflection and improvement. A sermon by Daniel C. Eddy, DD, in 1885 argued that 'of all diseases [consumption] is best calculated to bring out the better traits of human character and develop the graces of the Christian life'.[11] While this was not an unusual perspective in a clergyman, it was more surprising in a young provincial surgeon such as Dr Samuel Beckett. In the early 1850s Beckett wrote a memorial on the death of his sister, in which he used his experience of several hundred deathbeds to demonstrate that the nature of the dying process varied greatly according to the disease. He considered slow consumption an infinitely better way for the Christian to die than the various fevers, insanity, or sudden accident. In Beckett's view it was delightful 'to witness the calm, heavenly, and truly edifying bearing and conversation of a pious young person slowly wearing away under pulmonary consumption', sometimes described as 'the death of the chosen' because of its gradual approach and its non-interference with the mental faculties.[12]

Beckett's memorial helps to explain the paradoxical idealization of death from tuberculosis by Victorian Christians, who still saw death as a trial of Christian fortitude. A devout man or woman who had led an upright Christian life and achieved spiritual preparedness could triumph over death from certain unpleasant diseases. The committed Christian could purify his or her soul through suffering, provided the disease allowed time and a clear mind for spiritual preparation. Conversely, certain types of disease made a good death very difficult, if not impossible, to achieve, even where the sufferer and his family were devout Christians. These included most infectious diseases and the many illnesses loosely described as fever, including typhus, scarlet fever, and puerperal fever, as well as mental illness and particularly painful forms of cancer.

Harry Goulburn's last illness in 1843 illustrates the process of spiritual purification which a slow death from consumption was supposed to permit. His case is unusual because the dying man himself described his final year in his daily diary, which reveals a devout Anglican's self-conscious spiritual preparation for death. Harry Goulburn was an outstanding young lawyer of 30, son of Henry Goulburn, Chancellor of the Exchequer in Peel's cabinet. Harry's diary reveals his daily struggle to reach a state of submission to God's will as he gradually became an invalid confined to the family home in Hastings. In the early months of 1843 he regretted his miserable inactivity and listlessness, caused by growing weakness and discomfort. On 7 March he lamented, 'Woe is me that the flesh should have such power to weigh down and oppress the spirit.' On 12 March he was able to accept 'Thy will be done:—but rather with a listless acquiescence than a thankful and faithful submission.' He feared he was not benefiting sufficiently from God's 'chastening' and from the months of warning.[13]

On 19 April 1843, two weeks after his thirtieth birthday, Harry Goulburn paid a last visit to London to resign from the Bar: 'God grant that I may indeed find it one step of weaning away from this world, one lesson of preparation to depart.' After that his condition deteriorated rapidly, though he continued to regret his 'shrinking from pain and suffering'. By 8 May his physical problems hindered concentration on prayer and spiritual devotions because his weakness increased and his cough was more painful. Recognizing that his death was near, Harry prayed for support to endure suffering and death as a Christian should. His recurrent use of the term 'chastening' demonstrated his belief that his ordeal was God's punishment for his sins. He asked for strength to find joy and peace through his ordeal and for forgiveness for his 'innumerable transgressions'.[14]

Harry Goulburn's spiritual anguish abated from the time he acknowledged his approaching death on 8 May, accepting with resignation that his physical torment was intended 'to wean away my soul from the earth'. He occasionally admitted to fear, though never to anger, and felt increasingly contented as he submitted to God's will. On 20 May Harry looked back on his life and asked forgiveness for his sins: 'Teach me to know Jesus Christ and him crucified.' The entries for the remaining eighteen days of his life were few. Harry was frustrated by his inability to think, read, or pray: 'O Lord suffer not my faith to fail' was one of his last appeals.[15] There was no detailed record of his final days, but his mother's diary for 7 June, the day of his death, noted a 'day of agony'. Subsequent references to 'awful scenes' suggest that this was a particularly distressing death, though she described the last three hours as quiet.[16] Yet Harry Goulburn's parents and friends were convinced of his perfect faith and more than usually certain that his triumph over suffering and his spiritual preparedness assured him of a place in heaven.

The consumptive deaths of Dorothea Palmer and Elvira Horsley, both in 1852, were described by their families in correspondence and diaries. They also demonstrate their assurance that the prolonged trial of suffering transformed a disagreeable physical death into a good Christian death by purifying the patient's faith. Dorothea Palmer and Elvira Horsley were High Church Anglicans whose intense piety made their deaths remarkably like the Evangelical ideal in fundamental respects, reinforcing the earlier point about 'the common pursuit of holiness' in the two religious revivals.

Dorothea Palmer, sister of the first Earl of Selborne, died of consumption in 1852 at the age of about 23. She came from a particularly devout High Anglican family; besides her father, Revd William Jocelyn Palmer, four of her eleven siblings went into the Church, including Emily, who became a nun, and William, who converted to Rome in 1855. The story of her death was chiefly told through her family's correspondence with her brother William, already in exile in Greece as he renounced Protestantism and moved towards the Catholic Church. Hers was such a perfect example of a good Christian death that it could have been published without alteration as a didactic tract. The physical suffering was given little prominence in her family's accounts, and Dorothea displayed none of Harry Goulburn's early reluctance to submit to fate.

Dorothea Palmer's death was a story of absolute resignation to God's will and a strong but simple faith. Six months before her death Dorothea warned her brother William that she did not expect to recover and now did not wish to do so. She assured her father she was 'quite happy', prayed that God's will be done, and asked for forgiveness for her sins: 'I do not shrink either from death or illness: on the contrary, the first would be joy,' and illness would be a blessing. Her brother Revd George Horsley Palmer hoped to follow Dorothea's example when his turn came to die: 'I cannot wish or desire more blessedness—her faith—her meekness—her brightness and resignation indeed deprives death of every sting.'[17]

The family accounts all emphasize the importance of Dorothea's death at home, surrounded by her family: 'Of human comforts, it was a great pleasure to her to be *at home* at the last with all her sisters, her father and her mother.'[18] Dorothea talked quite freely with her sisters about death, drawing comfort from John Keble's consolation poetry, *The Christian Year*, which helped to express her own feelings; several times she quoted the verse for All Saints' Day, 'Waiting their summons to the sky, | Content to live, but not afraid to die.' Dorothea self-consciously viewed her own death as exemplary, telling her sisters to use it in teaching the local Mixbury children about God.[19] Though she could speak little in her final week, her family was uplifted by 'heavenly incidents' uttered in sleep and delirium: 'such thoughts as one can well believe are sent as anticipations of Heaven to those whom God is about to take to Himself'. Her broken words were written down to be cherished by her family.[20]

The family's only regret in the last days of Dorothea's life was that Revd William Palmer discouraged his daughter from taking Holy Communion on her final Sunday, believing that she was too weak and misjudging the proximity of death. Unfortunately that was the last opportunity, as Dorothea was unconscious for most of her remaining three days, except for a brief lucid interval on the Monday which allowed her to say affectionate farewells. She died at last on Wednesday, 27 January 1852 'in the presence and among the prayers of them all', as her father knelt saying the Lord's Prayer. Her brother Roundell, later Lord Selborne, arrived too late to see Dorothea alive, but found his family behaving 'as Christians ought to be under such a dispensation—not as sorrowing without hope'. On his journey home to Mixbury, Roundell had read Revd Richard Baxter's *Saints' Everlasting Rest*, a popular treatise of 1650 'on the blessed state of the saints' in heaven, as an appropriate preparation for seeing his sister for the last time. He viewed her 'dear remains' soon after arrival, though he knew 'she is in Heaven, already enjoying the happiness of the Saints'.[21] The sisters and brothers were convinced that Dorothea was an exalted example of Christian life and death. Mary urged them to pray that 'none may fall short of this!', while Emma asked God to 'make me fit enough at last to die'.[22]

Later that same year John Callcott Horsley, a popular painter of portraits and domestic scenes, described in detail in his diary the death of his first wife, Elvira. She died from consumption at the age of 31 on 1 December 1852, leaving three sons, aged 2, 3, and 5, all of whom were to follow her to the grave within a few years. Elvira's condition had been stable for some time, but began to deteriorate from March 1852.[23] From May she was again spitting blood, and by June it was heartbreaking to see her wasted state, 'but God's will be done'.[24] On the night of 30 July husband and wife spoke freely for the first time of the probability of Elvira's early death. John described their discussion as one of 'bitter grief', during which Elvira remained calm, working hard to console her husband. Elvira observed that their talk might be premature, but it was a comfort that they could speak about death and face it together. John confessed to his inadequacies in their married life, but she reassured him that he had nothing to regret since she had been very happy. Elvira insisted that she wished him to marry again, as did a number of other

Victorian wives on their deathbeds. John assured her that the children would be his primary obligation, and they spoke of their efforts to prepare their eldest child, Edward, for his mother's impending death. Elvira had warned Edward that she was soon going to 'a happy place in Heaven' where he could join her if he learned to love God. Husband and wife concluded their discussion with a long and warm embrace, with 'many fervent kisses'.[25]

Throughout her long illness, Elvira's spiritual preparation included frequent prayer and requests to John to read prayers and Bible extracts aloud. During the emotional discussion of 30 July she asked him to read a portion of Revelation aloud, and later she repeated the Lord's Prayer and parts of the Litany after him. On many occasions Elvira talked of 'feeling more and more the presence of Jesus'. Any earlier fear of death disappeared from the time she knew that she was likely to die soon. However, she still dreaded what she termed 'the last gasps of death', though John encouraged her to believe that God would allow her to die in her sleep—wishful thinking which was to be far from the truth. He noted that her suffering was at times intense, for the 'bitterness of death' was already upon her.[26]

In the final weeks Elvira Horsley was calm and resigned in the face of suffering which was often acute. Towards the end, when told that her brother-in-law Dr Seth Thompson could do nothing more to relieve her pain, she said, 'I feel I am in the arms of Jesus. He will bear me in safety, oh my trust is in Him.' She assured John that they would meet again in the 'many mansions' in heaven, where they would be eternally happy. On 26 November, after Elvira had taken her dose of morphine, husband and wife received Holy Communion from their rector, Archdeacon Sinclair, one of the few signs that this was a High Church death. Two days later Elvira asked John if she should continue to beg daily forgiveness for all her past sins; he reassured her that she should only remember the current sins of each day, for he was certain she had performed a long mental penance for all past sins.[27]

Elvira's final two days of life were harrowing, but this did not undermine her family's belief in her 'good death', which was based on her spiritual rather than her physical state. She was suffering too much for any formal family farewells, though a few close friends and relatives had previously called to say goodbye individually. She saw 5-year-old Edward for a few minutes on 26 November for the last time, but was too exhausted to see the two younger children as intended. On 1 December John was woken by the nurse with the news that Elvira had endured a dreadful night and death was near. She was breathing with immense difficulty, with a terrible rattling sound, and her suffering was agonizing to witness, though John understood that the convulsions were probably less distressing for her than they appeared to be. The only two witnesses of Elvira's death were her husband and the nurse. Ten minutes before Elvira died, John begged his mother, Elizabeth Horsley, not to join them in the death chamber: 'she could do no good and it would only be unnecessarily distressing'.[28]

Elvira Horsley's death was far removed from the idealized image of the large family around the deathbed saying their farewells at the end. Afterwards John took the three children and his mother to see Elvira's body, but the scene was 'evidently incomprehensible' to the silent children, 'and who would wish it otherwise!' Their response decided the father not to take them in to see their mother again, and to disregard their usual family custom of taking casts or drawings of the corpse.[29] Elvira's death would probably have been depicted as a bad death a century later, because of the depth of suffering and the nature of the disease. In 1852 her family saw it as a good Christian death because her soul was fully prepared and her faith gave her strength and resignation to triumph over suffering. Above all, they were convinced that Elvira's 'glorified Spirit' was in the presence of Christ in the Kingdom of God.[30]

The importance of the particular construction of the good death is more obvious in the death of Margaret Gladstone from puerperal fever in 1870 than in the three consumptive deaths examined so far. Victorian Christians most feared death from any kind of rapid infectious disease, which allowed neither the time nor the mental clarity to make final peace with God. Fever of all kinds also struck terror into the families of the afflicted because there was no cure, and it usually prevented meaningful communication between the family and the sufferer. Dr Samuel Beckett commented in the early 1850s, 'The whole class of fevers . . . so completely prostrate the powers of life, as to paralyze, almost at the onset, alike the powers of emotion, will and expression.'[31]

Margaret Gladstone died of puerperal fever on 16 August 1870, at the age of 26, four weeks after the birth of her only child. Her father, Revd David King, was a Scottish Presbyterian minister who had raised his family in strict, earnest piety. Margaret was a deeply religious young woman who read sermons at night and did voluntary work as a Bible-class teacher. In 1869 she married Dr John H. Gladstone, a widowed scientist with four young children.

Puerperal fever was the disease dreaded by all pregnant women. Maternal mortality was high in the Victorian period, and remained so even after the introduction of antisepsis in the 1880s. William Farr calculated that in the thirty years from 1847 to 1876, on average five mothers died for every 1,000 children born alive. Puerperal fever caused between 33 and 38 per cent of maternal deaths in England and Wales from 1847 to 1874, though this was likely in reality to have been closer to the 50 per cent recorded for the last quarter of the century.[32] A cure was not available until the widespread use of antibiotics in the 1940s.

Women had great difficulty in coming to terms with the deaths of mothers in childbirth. When Theresa Cripps nearly died in childbirth in 1882, her sister Kate Potter wrote: 'I always think that the death of a young Mother is one that it is difficult to think right, however submissively one may believe in a divine providence.'[33] Margaret Gladstone was well aware that childbirth could be dangerous and discussed the possibility of her death with her husband early in the pregnancy. Her view of death reflected her deep Christian beliefs: 'I felt as if I could leave even this intense and overflowing happiness on earth to be with Jesus.'[34] She added: 'It is well that we can talk of these things freely', finding some relief in honest discussion with her husband, as had Elvira Horsley. Twelve days after the baby's delivery, in August 1870, Margaret was 'taken dangerously ill', starting with a 'terrible seizure'. The details of her two-week illness were carefully recorded in a sixteen-page journal kept by her pious mother, Elizabeth King, who attended her throughout.[35]

Margaret Gladstone was unfortunate to contract puerperal fever during the period of medical confusion about its cause and treatment, and she was well aware of the doctors' inability to cure. The family doctor, Dr Philip, soon called in two consultant physicians, Dr Morris and Dr Hewitt, who avoided naming the dreaded disease, which would have been seen as a death sentence. The doctors treated the more obvious symptoms and gave 'no decided opinion' during the first week, though later they mentioned kidney disease. The medical conspiracy of silence may have left Mrs King with some hope in the first week, but the doctors' belief in the terminal nature of the case was signalled by the prescribed treatment of opium, champagne, and brandy and soda every three hours. The doctors knew they had no cure and could only ease the dying woman's pain. On the day of Margaret's death, when it was abundantly clear to all concerned that death was near, the three doctors stood round the bed as she told them 'to learn what they could from her case'.[36]

Elizabeth King's Evangelical account of her daughter's death was written only for herself and possibly her immediate family, not for the edification of a wider public. She evidently jotted down in pencil every word Margaret uttered in her last two days, transferring these in full to her journal immediately after the death, and adding a few consolatory texts from Margaret's own journal. The account of the last twenty-four hours makes it seem to last much longer.

Elizabeth King composed this journal in the full knowledge that her daughter was dying, searching for spiritual hope in the midst of medical hopelessness. She and her daughter found more Christian consolation than might have been expected at a death from puerperal fever, reflecting the family's intense devotional habits and deep faith. The night before her death, Margaret asked her husband, John, to read aloud a favourite passage from Tennyson's great poem *In Memoriam*, 'Her eyes are homes of silent prayer', describing Mary's response to the resurrection of Lazarus. This was an appropriate choice for a Presbyterian family in 1870, as was Keble's *Christian Year* twenty years earlier for the High Church Palmer family. While Margaret's mind was wandering, she recited fragments of biblical texts and favourite hymns, such as 'There is a happy land'.[37] Early next morning the two nurses were busy elsewhere, leaving Mrs King alone with her daughter: 'She looked upward for some minutes with a calm fixed far off look. Then a smile overspread her countenance and she uttered the word "Angels" and after a little she said clearly and loudly "I am *so* glad to go" while her face was all radiant. After breakfast John said to her "I think, my love, God is going to take you to Himself." '[38] Later Margaret talked of the prospect of meeting relatives and friends gone before, while her mother recalled that she had often told her sister Agnes, 'we should meet above'. The mother found a vital source of consolation in her daughter's assurance of salvation and her references to their future family reunion in heaven.

About noon on her final day, Margaret asked to see her four young stepdaughters, and took the hand of each child in turn with a kiss to say farewell. When the servants briefly joined the children in the sick-room, making 'a great company', Margaret shook their hands, asking them to look after her baby. Mother and husband began to despair on the Monday afternoon, particularly when the three doctors insisted on 'torturing the poor patient suffering lamb' with a 'lamp bath', an obviously unwelcome and unexplained device.

Margaret Gladstone spoke little throughout her illness and never complained. Alongside the more uplifting last words, her mother noted the sad confession, 'Some die so bravely—I die so stupidly', a typically authentic touch in this account. Towards the end Margaret admitted that she was 'so frightened', to which her mother responded, 'Safe in God's hands'. It was anguish to her mother to hear Margaret say, 'but I must suffer now', then 'nothing else disturbed the perfect peace of that solemn time'. Her very last words were about 'classes', referring to her Sunday School teaching. Her mother repeated part of the twenty-third Psalm, holding her daughter's hands. At the very end her husband stood by her pillow while her mother lay beside her on the bed, until Margaret motioned her mother to leave, 'and crossed her hands on her breast and so passed very gently away'. Mrs King added a personal note: 'I do not fear death as I did since I have seen thee die.'[39]

This account of Margaret King's death may seem morbid, sentimental, or contrived to the late twentieth-century reader, but it was perfectly in keeping with the devout tone of Margaret's daily journal, informed by a living faith. The consolatory religious discourse of much of her mother's account of her death drew on the language of well-loved hymns and familiar Bible passages which the family usually read and sang on a daily basis. John Gladstone comforted his father-in-law, Revd David King, two weeks later, in the same language, reminding him that he had 'a daughter somewhere in the "many mansions" above, awaiting your summons and mine to the Heavenly Father's home'.[40] Again, the primary consolation lay in the prospect of a family reunion in heaven.

This was indeed a good Christian death despite the medical odds against it. Death from puerperal fever was always unpleasant, but in this case the physical ordeal was aggravated by the doctors' confused diagnosis and interventionist treatment at the end. That Margaret Gladstone's death could be considered in any sense 'a good death' owed little to the doctors or the disease, and everything to the devout Evangelical faith of the dying woman, her mother and husband. Mrs King's journal account of her daughter's dreadful death recorded a triumph of faith over disease, whereby the physical ordeal and the medical incapacity contrasted markedly with the spiritual hope and faith. There was little artifice in the simple account, merely a minimal description of the physical suffering, and a more complete record of the devotional consolations.

These four examples of the good Christian death are derived from families strongly affected by the spiritual revivals of the first half of the nineteenth century—the Oxford and Evangelical movements. These families kept copious records of their family deaths which were represented in terms of the Evangelical ideal. However, it must be acknowledged that many good Christian deaths obviously went unrecorded or were described in terms which do not appear to fit the Evangelical model. Three related Unitarian families, the Sharpes, Reids, and Kenricks, provide an interesting case in point, for their death scenes—when described at all—were economical, factual, and surprisingly unemotional. The Unitarians were the Protestant denomination least affected by the enthusiasm and fervour of Evangelicalism, but they still reflected its piety. Samuel Sharpe, an Egyptologist and a translator of the Bible, was even more restrained than most of his family on this subject. He described his wife's death in his journal on 3 June 1851: 'My dear wife Sarah breathed her last. The three eldest children were with me in constant attendance at the time. She had been ill for five days. They had been helpful nurses. I bid them bear their grief without crying, for they had done their duty. God's will be done.'[41] The many deaths of young people from tuberculosis in the Sharpe, Reid, and Kenrick families, including four of Samuel Sharpe's six children and at least two of Mary Reid's nine children, are mentioned briefly and apparently dispassionately. On Kenrick Reid's death in 1852, the family records reveal minimal information on his symptoms and medical care, and nothing at all about his spiritual or emotional state or that of his family.[42] We merely learn from her family's correspondence that Kenrick's mother, Mary Reid, did not 'show much outwardly', as was her custom.[43]

But the lack of detailed information on deaths in the Sharpe, Reid, and Kenrick families should not mislead us. There is enough to show that their ideal of the good death was the same as that of the Goulburns, Horsleys, and Palmers. It is clear from their brief references that the feelings of love and grief were intense, despite the detached and prosaic presentation. It seems to have been less important to these three Unitarian families to construct detailed memorials of deathbed scenes, though apparently this was not always the case. A few hints suggest that individual family members occasionally wrote longer accounts which have not survived, because they were seen as highly personal and confidential. Anne Rowley thanked her friend Lucy Sharpe in 1853 for the account of Catharine Sharpe's last hours, which provided assurance that her 'noble mind triumphed over the suffering body'.[44]

The family correspondence reveals relatively little about Letty Reid's death from consumption at the age of 17 in 1844, but enough to suggest that it was a good Christian death. Her married sister, Lucy Sharpe, thought Letty's state of mind 'most truly Christian and Heavenly' at their last meeting, so they should bow in 'humble submission to our Heavenly Father's will'. Lucy was sure that Letty's 'pure spirit . . . is fit to return to Him who gave it'.[45] Letty's brother, Dr James Reid, a medical practitioner, agreed that Letty's death was the work of God's 'merciful hand, and our religion teaches us to bear it with grateful resignation'. They should thank God for the time given them to prepare for the calamity—a characteristic reference to the advantages of consumption.[46] The only mention of Letty's deathbed was brief and indirect; her parents saw no need to record the deathbed particulars, even for the family, preferring to treasure their memories of her final day in their hearts.[47]

Like early Victorian Evangelicals, these three Unitarian families believed in the just dispensation of God and the purification derived from suffering, accepting that 'it is good to have been afflicted' on the death of Daniel Sharpe, who fell off his horse in 1856. Mary Reid's response to the death of her sister-in-law in 1853 was not to question 'why pain and suffering are prolonged . . . since we cannot understand we must submit ourselves in patience to the ways of the Lord'.[48] In 1874 Revd John Kenrick, a Unitarian minister from York, admitted that the death of his brother Revd George Kenrick was 'one of those mysterious events which try our faith', though they might reasonably believe there was some beneficent purpose in such painful events.[49]

Changing Perceptions of the Good Death 1870–1914

For early and mid-Victorian Christians, death and suffering were acts of divine providence which Christians must accept with submission. Christians, such as John Kenrick and William Wilberforce, when faced with the unedifying death of a committed Christian, took refuge in the view that humans could not understand the 'mysterious' providence of the Almighty. They preferred to believe that suffering and death served several useful purposes. The ordeal could provide punishment for past sins, while also purifying, testing, and strengthening the Christian faith of sufferer and attendants. Indeed a good death could display the power of true Christianity with its assurance of ultimate victory over death in the knowledge that the contrite Christian was 'gone to glory'. But their emphasis was usually on the spiritual struggle and ultimate triumph rather than the physical ordeal.

This emphasis changed as the Evangelical model of the good death declined in influence in the late Victorian period, when the enthusiasm of the Evangelical movement was past its peak. Family accounts of deathbed scenes from the 1870s and 1880s lacked the intense piety and spiritual fervour of earlier decades. This change is captured by the response of young Agnes Acland, a sincere Christian of the 1880s, on first reading the prayers and deathbed memorials written by her grandmother Lady Mordaunt nearly sixty years earlier on the death of her husband. Agnes Acland wrote to her fiancé, Fred Anson, in 1884, in considerable awe:

Imagine her writing an account of [the death of] her husband, and with it a sort of exhortation to herself of the *most* practical kind ten days after his death. She had such a high standard as makes me feel how far below such self discipline I fall . . . She seemed so *always* to be serving God. It ought to do one a lot of good to read such things, and brace one up and I suppose one ought to aim at that very high standard of self government.[50]

By the 1880s most families ceased writing and keeping such lengthy memorials on the deaths of their loved ones. Even in the devout Acland family such a practice was already seen by Agnes in 1884 as awesome and unusual.

The decline in Evangelical piety and passion in the late Victorian period was paralleled by an increase in anxiety about the physical suffering of dying. For early and mid-Victorian Christians there must often have been some conflict between the desire to display courage in the face of suffering and the human wish to die with as little pain as possible. However, though devout Christians were usually grateful for freedom from pain, they tried to regard it as a secondary consideration. For example, Henry J. Coleridge described the death of his brother Fred in 1843 as a most severe blow inflicted by God, because Fred's mind was clouded through two weeks of fever, though he suffered no pain.[51] The Coleridge family did not consider Fred's painless death a primary benefit, but merely a secondary compensation for the lack of mental clarity.

In the late Victorian period the balance swung slowly away from primary concern with the state of the soul in the final days, towards a greater emphasis on a death free from physical suffering. At one level it was simply a matter of dying people and their families expressing more anxiety about the degree of pain and less about the state of the departing soul. Lady Caroline Kerison was thankful in 1875 that Lord Stanhope's death was 'so calm and easy'.[52] A year later, on his mother's death, Edward Harcourt was grateful 'that there is no suffering, and that the end is as peaceful as sleep'.[53] Katharine Childers used almost identical words on the death of Lady Minto in 1882: 'how thankful I am that the end was so peaceful and free from suffering'.[54] There was also an increasing preference by those not directly involved to avoid information about the more unsavoury aspects of deaths. Where early and mid-Victorian Evangelicals earnestly requested such 'particulars' as evidence of Christian triumph over suffering, many Edwardians preferred reassurance that all was peaceful and painless. In 1908 Constance Connolly attempted to console Margaret MacDonald on the death of her brother, but made a remark unimaginable fifty years earlier: 'I trust the manner in which he met his death was not accompanied by any harrowing incidents.'[55] The Edwardian fear of dying uncomfortably was a world removed from that of the early Victorians.

On the many occasions when the process of dying was mentally or physically harrowing, many late Victorians and Edwardians seem to have coped less well than their parents and grandparents. From the 1880s there were more accounts of deathbed scenes which described dreadful physical or mental suffering with little or no reference to spiritual and devotional consolation, and none at all to the state of the soul in the final hours. Mark Pattison, an Oxford scholar and clergyman, died in 1884 from stomach cancer, after excruciating pain and 'uncontrollable rage'. This manner of death imposed intense strain on his wife, Frances, who was nursing him, and she prayed, 'Let not my last days be like his! The moral misery is awful.'[56] In 1886 Arthur and Clement Rogers visited their uncle Francis the day before his death: 'His mind had completely gone, and he could not recognise us. He was lying in bed and crying like a child.'[57] No family prayers around the bed mitigated this pathetic end, though the family was Anglican. The spiritual resources of late Victorian and Edwardian attendants were often less robust than they might have been a generation or two earlier, when they were more convinced that suffering was divinely ordained and had its own devotional value.

From 1900 the change extended beyond the expression of gratitude for freedom from pain to thankfulness in cases of sudden death that the dying person was unaware of impending death. In 1900 Sarah Bailey was grateful that her mother died peacefully and without pain, after her illness developed into blood-poisoning. She was unconscious throughout this critical period, and 'never knew how ill she was, I am thankful to say'.[58] In 1902 Alethea Grenfell confided to Lord Aldenham that death from pneumonia was the death her husband would have chosen and she thanked God for his mercies: 'He [Henry] was unconscious from the moment the Pneumonia seized him and 36 hours after his end was peace.' Early Victorian Christians would have been less welcoming of a sudden death from pneumonia.[59]

It was only a short step from this position to a deliberate family decision to withhold from the sufferer the knowledge that he or she was dying. In March 1901 Dorothy Ward, daughter of Mrs Humphry Ward, had tea with 'dear Aunt Fanny Lucy', knowing that her aunt had terminal cancer: 'I all the time *knew* she was fatally ill, and knew she did not know, and this knowledge almost choked me at times.' Dorothy felt it was terrible to keep 'cheerful and bright' in the dying woman's presence, but her family considered it best.[60] In April 1917 Lady Gainford told her daughter that 'poor Charlie Hunter is dying of cancer—it cannot be long now'. The doctors had known for seven months that nothing could be done to save him, but 'he did not know and his family thought he should not be told'.[61] That denial of knowledge was the converse of the good Victorian death. Occasionally the knowledge was shared between the dying person and just one relative or friend. In 1902 Lady Knutsford was the only person aside from Alice Dugdale who knew that Alice was dying. She was 'bound over not to tell', but suffered from the heavy burden: 'Alice, poor soul, chose *utter solitude*—and knew she was dying ever since October last. Her one dread was that her friends should know and pity her.'[62] It is hard to tell who gained from their conspiracy of silence.

In the late Victorian and Edwardian periods there were signs of a growing uneasiness about dying, combined with greater emotional inhibition and a loss of the familiarity and assurance about death characteristic of the early Victorians. Anne Lady Cowper died in 1880, having insisted that the family continue with Christmas and New Year festivities as usual, with the 'half dread of emotion that she had'. The grief of her daughter Dolly Herbert a year later was heavily touched by regret: 'I often wish now that we had broken down the reserve and talked freely about it all . . . Of course now that it is all gone, one does not remember the impossibility it then was.'[63] Such remarks became more frequent after the turn of the century. Lady Paget was in deep mourning in 1900 on the death of her daughter-in-law, but she was unable to postpone her house-party because her son Victor informed her that he did not want his wife's death spoken about at all. Betty Balfour considered this behaviour 'horribly constrained: to consciously avoid a painful subject must be such a dreadful strain on the nerves. I don't think I could stand it.'[64]

Another revealing indication of a transformation of attitudes and expectations was Geoffrey Howard's response to the extremely painful death of his father, Lord Carlisle, in 1911. Geoffrey told Molly Trevelyan that 'no one ought to be called on to see a man die', that it was 'shocking'.[65] Geoffrey and Molly were almost certainly both agnostics by this time, though they had been brought up as Unitarians, like Lord Carlisle. The very assumption here that death was 'shocking', and witnessing a death something to be avoided, would have been shocking earlier, though it is common enough in the twentieth century.

This chapter closes with two case-studies of the responses to death and dying in two late Victorian families whose religious beliefs were far from secure. These responses are not presented as archetypal, unlike the case-studies of the good Evangelical death earlier in the century, because increasingly there was no one accepted model. Uncertainty, uneasiness, fear, and avoidance were new features which did not dominate between 1870 and 1914 but were becoming more common, at the same time as the historian's archival sources on family deaths diminish.

Richard Potter, a substantial businessman and entrepreneur, was a Unitarian with a tendency to sample different churches which offered a variety of preachers. His wife, Lawrencina, had a stronger Christian commitment, while their nine daughters (including Beatrice Webb) later ranged between devout Anglican and agnostic beliefs.[66] The death of Lawrencina Potter in 1882 illustrates how a family with a rather tenuous Christian commitment might no longer know how to behave or to communicate at the mother's deathbed, especially if her death was unexpected and the doctors' signals ambiguous.

After two weeks of serious illness, Lawrencina Potter died on 13 April 1882 of 'Brights disease of kidneys and double pleuro pneumonia' according to the death certificate. The two doctors had considerable difficulty in isolating the cause of the illness, which was variously attributed to pleurisy, a 'rheumatic affection', and distended bowels. As Lawrencina's daughter Kate Courtney reported in her diary on 6 April 1882: 'She [Lawrencina] thought herself the whole trouble was in her bowels which had not acted and unfortunately the two doctors were led into devoting their attention to this and somewhat neglected symptoms of pleurisy . . . We had no conception yet that Mother was in any danger and the doctors gave us none of the directions we ought to have had about the nursing.'[67] The doctors gave no warnings and made no attempt to prepare the family or the dying woman. Beatrice did not like the trained nurse they hired, describing her as a 'roughish woman', and one of the sisters always attended their mother. It took Mrs Potter about two weeks to die, though no precise dates were given in her daughters' diaries. Lawrencina was semi-conscious in the last two days, muttering incoherently, clutching nervously at the bedclothes, and was quietened by morphine.[68]

There was little or no spiritual or material preparation for Lawrencina Potter's death. Her only practical preparation took place a few days before-hand when she told Beatrice that she thought she was mortally ill; she begged her daughter to write down instructions about division of her jewellery, and trusted that all the daughters would look after their father and their two youngest sisters. Beatrice was 'very much affected, but was too anxious not to appear so, and too certain that her fear was a delusion, to encourage her to tell me more—perhaps now I regret it'.[69] This was the only approach to discussion of the mother's impending death with any of the daughters, as Kate explained at length:

Whether she ever realized that she was dying while she was fully conscious we could not tell as when she became worse she gave no directions and left no messages or goodbyes even for Rosie [her youngest daughter] but appeared to concentrate her remaining energy in struggling against the disease and she specifically asked that none of her absent daughters should be sent for. We also never spoke to her of her danger, fearing to take away the last chance of life, so what she thought or felt during those sad last days we shall now never know . . . Would any speech about her death have been a comfort to her or not? I do not know for her but for myself I think that when my end comes, if I am conscious, I should like those nearest and dearest to me to break the silence and wish me God speed on my journey.[70]

Both daughters, more explicitly Kate, here expressed a yearning for a traditional Christian death with farewells and blessings and some discussion of the significance of dying. But to this late Victorian Unitarian family such an ending seemed impossible for a combination of reasons, including lack of personal experience of the good death, uncertainty about their own faith, and personal inhibitions. Beatrice and Kate only accepted they were 'in the presence of coming death' two days before the end. By then all the sisters had been summoned home, but they still thought it better not to excite the patient.[71]

The deathbed scene itself was in keeping with the rest. Mary Playne, another sister, woke them all at 4 a.m. on 13 April, saying 'You must come now', in a tone which Kate Courtney would never forget. They all assembled in their mother's boudoir, where they spent 'a miserable hour waiting for death'. Kate noted that 'we sat and stood mostly looking at each other silently', while their father and Maggie Harkness, another sister, stayed with Lawrencina in the bedroom next door, their father holding her hand 'and giving way to no grief that could disturb her'. The sisters went in one by one to kiss her, 'but she took no notice', and they did not stay as she appeared troubled when there were many people around her. Finally 'her spirit passed away without struggle and without pain' at 11.45 a.m., in the company of her husband and Maggie Harkness, who spent the last six hours at her side 'and felt the awefulness of death tragically'. The only religious reference in the two sisters' accounts is a mention of their father praying in his wife's room for a few minutes after she was dead, but then he 'came down and tried hard to be cheerful'.[72]

Lawrencina Potter's death was the antithesis of the traditional good Christian death and it is difficult to imagine it taking place in a Christian family fifty years earlier. If the doctors did recognize at an earlier stage that death was likely they gave no hint to the family, who were uncertain how to conduct themselves in the absence of such direction. Beatrice discouraged her mother's one attempt to communicate her fear of approaching death, preferring not to believe the end was near. Kate might have been more receptive, though she shared the general family anxiety that it would upset their mother to talk about death. There were no farewells or touching last words and little attempt by the dying woman to set her house in order. Both Beatrice and Kate were left with deep regrets. Looking back four months later, Beatrice wrote in her diary: 'Her death was so sad—so inexpressibly sad in its isolation. Is all death like that—can we not in that supreme moment, bind the past with the future, and through our influence forge one link in the chain of human develop-ment—and our last mental act be one of prayer and blessing? And who knows that Mother did not bless us with her last breath.'[73] Beatrice experi-enced a spiritual crisis as a result of her mother's death, which confirmed her feeling that she needed a satisfying spiritual alternative to Christianity, which agnosticism could not provide.

The death of the eighth Duke of Argyll at Inverary on 24 April 1900 was even further removed from the Christian model of the good death, and provided several pointers to the future. The Duke had been a staunch Christian and a prominent politician with a first-class mind who had retained a lively and active interest in politics and natural science into old age. At the age of 77 he suffered from an extreme form of senile dementia, which involved delirium and the delusion that he was actually experiencing his father's imprisonment in France during the French Revolution. The Duke knew he was dying and implored his family to rescue him from prison before his death. It was a gruesome death, as described in detail by his daughter Frances Balfour, a writer and suffragist, in her letters to her brother-in-law A. J. Balfour.

This was a twentieth-century rather than a nineteenth-century death in several respects. Frances Balfour's account scarcely mentioned religious belief except to note that her father's mental suffering made her aware that 'death comes not more lightly to those who have nothing to fear'—that her father's Christian belief provided no assurance of an easy passage. Her account was entirely dominated by the sayings and doings of the doctors, to an extent unusual in the early Victorian period. The doctors' theories were as varied as their prognoses, though they must have been sure, at least, that they had no cure. They attributed the delirium to 'gout' in the brain, but confessed that many 'unique' symptoms puzzled them.[74]

Frances Balfour's letters emphasized her extreme horror and fear of death, reflecting her inexperience on her first encounter with death. This would have been unusual for early or mid-Victorians who had reached her age of 42, but would be more common today. Frances's dread of death was accentuated by two aspects of the medical management of her father's death. First, the doctors several times warned the family to prepare for immediate death, only to talk later of possible recovery. As Frances reported to Arthur Balfour on 10 April, two weeks before her father's death:

On Thursday we were all told he was just sinking, body cold, and other signs of dissolution. As I waited in the next room, the nurse asked me some questions about things she would need after death, in fact no gruesome or horrible experience was omitted. My horror of death is such, that these summonses [to the deathbed] always give me deadly faintness, and I have a great struggle with myself.

But on each occasion until the very last Frances was reassured on seeing her father, as he seemed not to be dying.[75]

Secondly, the Duke's death became even more of an ordeal for the family because the doctors worked so hard to prolong his life—another link with death in modern society. Since they were treating a duke, they felt that they had to be seen to be doing everything in their power to prolong life. They even argued that the Duke fought harder for life because of his aristocratic blood: 'the high breeding makes life almost incapable of leaving the body'. But 'high breeding' also ensured that highly paid doctors expended more time in seeking to prolong life by greater intervention than Victorian doctors usually contemplated. After the episode of near-death reported on the Thursday, the doctors gave oxygen and injected strychnine, and by evening the Duke was eating a large meal. Earlier in the week Frances had acknowledged reluctantly, 'I suppose it is right to keep him alive, but he will live as long as he takes the nourishment freely, and inhales the quantity of oxygen he does.' Later she admitted that she shrank from his recovery: 'It seems to me senile decay has set in, and who could wish life.' The doctors certainly put all their efforts into keeping him alive, Dr Brunton only taking five hours' sleep in fifty-four.[76] Frances Balfour's accounts did not include the ultimate deathbed scene—another departure from Victorian precedent. There was no artifice in her descriptions, for she had no particular ideal of a good death, merely a horror of death in general, and she lacked the spiritual resources to construct a model.

While these case-studies document the two extremes of the early and mid-Victorian model of the good Christian death and the departure from that model after 1870, this is not to suggest that every family can be categorized in one or other extreme. Most deaths were somewhere in between, and family experience was infinitely varied. What is more, an agnostic family in 1910 might easily have defined a bad death in terms which would have signified a good death to a Christian family in 1840. This question of definition underlines the extent to which the model of the good death was transformed between the early Victorian period and 1914.

❧ 3 ☙

BAD DEATHS, SUDDEN DEATHS, AND SUICIDES

Bad Deaths

Sudden deaths could be bad deaths for Christians because they allowed no time for spiritual preparation and contrition for past sins. Suicides were terrible deaths for all concerned, and the most appalling fate for committed Christians. Early and mid-Victorian Christians were primarily concerned about bad deaths in the spiritual sense of concern for the unrepentant or unprepared sinner doomed to the eternal punishment of hell-fire. By the end of the nineteenth century the perception of the bad death had changed, with the decline in both Evangelical fervour and the fear of hell; less emphasis was placed on the soul unprepared to meet its maker, and more on the suffering of the body.

Records of bad deaths are inevitably in shorter supply than those of good deaths. Where good Christian deaths might be recorded and idealized by family members, the bad deaths of unbelievers were rarely documented. Victorians recognized that most deaths would fail to emulate the stereotypical ideal for many reasons, including lack of faith, family circumstances, and painful diseases. They were also aware that ugly deaths were not reserved for sinners and unbelievers, as so often in fiction and Evangelical tracts.

The concept of the bad death was intimately linked to traditional Christian fear of judgement at the moment of death on the sins of life resulting in eternal punishment in hell. Protestants excluded themselves at the Reformation from the Catholic hope of purgatory, where repentant sinners could be cleansed by tribulation, aided by the prayers of the living. Protestant theology presented stark, absolute alternatives. God's judgement at death determined whether souls ascended to heaven or joined the majority of sinners to burn in hell for all eternity. This doctrine provided preachers and theologians with abundant material for lurid sermons and frightening treatises on the precise nature of the horrors of eternal torment and the urgent need for repentance long before death. This terror of hell as a judgement on the sinner was largely responsible for fears of death in earlier centuries.

In the nineteenth century some Evangelical and Roman Catholic preachers continued to frighten their congregations with literal descriptions of the flames of hell. One of the very few representations of hell which survives in family archives was the product of the vivid imagination of a lapsed Catholic and poet, Wilfrid Scawen Blunt:

There is the feeling of Infinity, of the Eternity of suffering, of the absolute prostration of the soul to a formless terror which encompasses it. The pain of the body which in itself seems beyond endurance, is overpowered, and almost hidden under the colossal anguish of the mind. There is neither recollection there, nor hope, nothing but an absolute unchanging and unchangeable Present, which crushes out the rest.[1]

Elizabeth Lady Holland protested in 1797 at the power of the Church to promote such horror of dying:

The worst part of the Christian dispensation is the terror it inculcates upon a deathbed. The wisest dread it; no person who is strictly brought up in the principles of Christianity can ever thoroughly shake off the fear of dying.[2]

Such criticisms of the Christian concept of hell increased in the nineteenth century, and the comments of an agnostic doctor in 1875 were typical. Dr Keith MacDonald believed that the dissemination of the dogma of eternal punishment created incalculable misery for those who were dying and their surviving families.[3] This fear of perpetual punishment stimulated the spiritual devotions of many earnest Christians in the first half of the century, often reinforced by the experience of didactic deathbed scenes. Elizabeth Palmer, a committed Christian, expressed this well on the death of her aunt in 1841:

Could any one feel he had *steadily* pursued the path leading to eternal life, there would be little cause, I apprehend, to fear death. It is the proneness to evil, with its long train of (at least) sins of omission, added to a doubt of the genuineness of repentance, that makes *me* at times shrink, disturbing the calm which I for the most part feel.[4]

Unbelievers had much more to fear, especially if theirs were sins of commission.

From about 1700 onwards, some intellectuals and more liberal Christians found increasing difficulty in accepting the literal interpretation that a just God could order an eternity of torment for the majority of people. Between 1830 and 1880 this debate about hell gathered strength, and more people came to doubt that they were wicked enough to deserve perpetual pain and damnation.[5] Indeed some critics argued that the doctrine of eternal punishment was immoral and unjust, since most people were neither total saints nor utter sinners, and God was not a retributive tyrant. Accordingly, the doctrine of hell was sanitized and minimized in various ways. Some Victorians, such as Edward Pusey, depicted hell in metaphorical terms, as separation from

God; others developed the 'intermediate state' as the Protestant version of the Catholic purgatory, between the moment of death and the Last Judgement, when souls were either 'sleeping in Jesus' or more actively engaged in spiritual progress; others argued that everybody was ultimately saved. By 1898, as W. E. Gladstone observed, the doctrine of hell had been 'relegated to the far-off corners of the Christian mind . . . there to sleep in deep shadows as a thing needless in our enlightened and progressive age'.[6] Many of the families encountered in this book were intelligent liberal Christians who increasingly dismissed the fear of hell from their thoughts.

An Archetypal Bad Death: The Case of Ada Lovelace

The agonizing death in November 1852 of Ada Lady Lovelace, daughter of Lord Byron, would be considered a bad death by most standards, irrespective of creed. As a free thinker who was uncertain of the existence of an afterlife and whose unorthodox life was scarcely unblemished by Christian standards, Ada had some reason to fear the prospect of hell in 1852. She was cut down in the prime of life at 37 from cancer, variously diagnosed as cervical and uterine, with her potential as a mathematician perhaps not fully developed. Her suffering was excruciating and protracted, while her family was bitterly divided around her deathbed. Moreover, she was a free thinker in an age when unbelief was still remarkable among her class, while her disease allowed her ample time to ponder her uncertain fate beyond the grave. The sources for Ada's death are unusually rich; they include Ada's daily letters to her mother up to three months before her death, her husband's journal for August 1852, and her mother's journal for the last few months of her life. Ada's own letters provide a rare example of a self-conscious, if unsuccessful, attempt to manage and observe one's own death.

For more than a year Ada Lovelace dreaded 'that horrible *struggle*, which I fear is in the Byron blood. I don't think we die easy.' She hoped for 'a *spasm* to kill me *at once*', rather than an awful, lingering death.[7] She confessed to her mother in February 1852: 'What most disturbed me, at the time when I certainly apprehended a fatal termination, was the idea of the *length* of illness and suffering there would be. Dying by inches in a horrid way, is a dreadful fate, and did appall me when it seemed impending.'[8] By April the pain was terrible, despite the opiates, as her friend, Mary Somerville, observed later: 'I never heard of anyone who suffered such protracted intolerable agony.'[9] Having concealed the truth for many months, Dr Charles Locock finally confirmed that Ada was dying in late July 1852. Ada responded calmly that she feared the pain 'more than anything', though she was willing to consider her mother's view of pain as a moral challenge. She was quite clear about the meaning of death, however; she saw it as 'escape both from bodily and mental suffering'. Its worst aspects were that it must be done alone and it was so slow.[10]

The pain of the cancer was terrible enough, but Ada's spiritual dilemma added another awful dimension to her ordeal. Throughout her life her formidable mother, Lady Byron, sought to control Ada's religious and moral beliefs, and at her death aimed to achieve a deathbed repentance. Indeed Lady Byron brought a self-righteous missionary zeal to her daughter's deathbed, inspired by her own peculiarly 'eclectic mixture of unfocused Christianity, mesmerism, and spiritualism',[11] as she revealed on 14 July: 'I have found my daughter on the brink of the grave. My one object will be to make myself the medicine of Christian influence, elevating and cheering . . . I must strive for the spirit of "O Death where is thy Sting?"'[12] Lady Byron was not in the least deterred by her daughter's expressed contempt for deathbed repentances. While conceding that '*life*-repentances' were better, Lady Byron insisted that 'the truth was often seen more clearly towards the close'.[13]

Ada Lovelace was normally a highly intelligent and logical free thinker, but she was vulnerable to her mother's bullying, especially when exhausted, racked with pain, and drugged with opium. According to her biographer, Dorothy Stein, Ada was a manic-depressive who suffered at least two nervous breakdowns and tended to experience a 'religious mania' in her manic phases.[14] From an early stage of her illness her ideas about a future life were dominated by doubt: 'I really don't *exactly* know what I *do* or do *not* believe. How *can* one? These are not matters upon which we can get at *certainties*.'[15] But Ada Lovelace heeded her mother's warnings to contemplate her spiritual fate. In February 1852, in the early stages of her illness, she yearned at times for faith: 'I would indeed part with all *present* happiness for anything like *hope* and *faith*, anything like certainty of some ulterior and benevolent destiny for living things.'[16] She tried to retain 'a *faint* gleam of hope' about the objects of existence, for it was appalling to believe that there was no purpose at all except to 'die like a dog'.[17]

Ada's letters to her mother ceased in August 1852, to be succeeded by the versions of her death prepared for their own particular purposes by her husband and her mother. These two accounts demonstrate the manufacture of self-interested literary representations of the deathbed, as well as the fear of both writers that Ada would not die a Christian death. Lord Lovelace and Lady Byron had in earlier years co-operated in an attempt to control Ada's life, but their alliance had recently collapsed, leaving them bitter enemies.

During August, when Ada's agony was at its height and Lord Lovelace expected her to die within a few weeks, he kept a journal which idealized her response to her illness and his own devotion. His journal recorded Ada's calmness, fortitude, and resignation in the face of unremitting pain: 'it was so angelic, the character of her beauty so pure, and disengaged from bodily elements that she was quite fit to pass away from among us into a higher sphere'. On 21 August Lord Lovelace reported his wife's last wishes to be buried by the side of her father, Lord Byron, and to see her two sons. She felt all was 'fast ending in this life', and was anxious to be allowed a day or two in full possession of her faculties, for preparation and farewells.[18] This version could have been almost any Victorian Christian deathbed scene in a contented family.

But Lord Lovelace's idealized journal account of his wife's death stopped suddenly at the end of August, nearly three months before her death. At that point the gulf between his literary representation of a good death and the awful actuality may have become intolerable. On 29 August Ada was having convulsions day and night, with little consciousness and the loss of her sight. On 1 September there were scenes of great agony and three days later she seemed to be dying. There were additional reasons for the husband to cease his idealized record of his wife's death. During August the indomitable Lady Byron was slowly gaining control of her daughter's sick-room, limiting visitors to those whom she approved and excluding Ada's devoted maid and her friend Charles Babbage, the scientist, among others. By 22 August Lady Byron had moved into the Lovelace household and emerged successful in her bitter feud with Lord Lovelace for control of Ada's affairs and her death. On 1 September she destroyed his sentimental image of his innocent tormented wife by pressing Ada to confess to her husband her adultery with John Crosse, a scientific friend and neighbour. Lady Byron knew full well how painful this would be to both parties and took some pleasure in Lovelace's subsequent coolness and bitterness towards his dying wife.

Lady Byron's representation of her daughter's death was quite different in motivation, tone, and content from that of her son-in-law. She sent a series of self-congratulatory letters in the form of a journal to Miss Emily Fitzhugh, an adoring friend, intending to retrieve them later as a record of her 'faultless reputation as a mother', and of her campaign to secure a deathbed repentance. The journal was also a triumphant record of success in her battle with her son-in-law, even claiming at one point that 'I cannot imitate him in firing across a Death-bed.'[19] Lady Byron noted, one by one, her victories against Lord Lovelace, including her own appointment as guardian of Ada's younger child on 16 August.

In late August and early September 1852 Lady Byron, by her own account, appears to have been successful in converting her increasingly passive daughter to a belief in God and an afterlife, or at least to not opposing her mother's beliefs. Where Lord Lovelace stopped at misrepresenting the record, Lady Byron was ruthlessly determined to alter the events themselves. By the end of August Ada Lovelace was in a supremely vulnerable state. Her rare periods of clear consciousness were haunted by fears of being buried alive, and by guilt about her adultery, which her mother had so deliberately intensified. On 30 August Lady Byron noted, with an astonishing degree of clinical detachment, 'stupor and faintness—scarcely any consciousness . . . loss of sight, vacant eyes—idiotic gestures'.[20] When Ada whispered next day that she still hoped to live, her mother quashed the faint wish for life: 'You are dying—you may not have another day—use it well.'[21]

The climax of Lady Byron's representation of Ada's death was her daughter's act of contrition on 31 August. During a lucid interval Ada admitted her terror of the everlasting torment of hell; she confessed that she was 'guilty towards God, and should have "a million of years" of the horrible pains she had suffered in this disease. It was in vain to talk to her generally of God's mercy in Christ—she could not *hope*—and her terror and distress were great.' Ada then begged forgiveness from God for her sins against both her mother and her husband.[22] Next day Lady Byron reported that brain fever was feared, for 'the eyes have a Maniacal expression', and only she could control her daughter's 'distracted feelings'. Early in the morning of 4 September Ada Lovelace again appeared to be dying and gave Lady Byron instructions 'to have her opened if it could be of use'—a most unusual deathbed request in England in 1852.[23]

As Ada became weaker and more emaciated, so her mother's pressure for repentance increased. From 7 September Ada's memory of the previous six months was obliterated and she entered a more passive state, so 'there is no anxious watching medically'.[24] Lady Byron composed an account of 'Thoughts of Ada' at the end of August and in the first week of September. These were allegedly dictated by Ada, though her mother protested too much that 'the thoughts were spontaneous and not suggested by any conversation of mine'. Ada confessed, for instance, that her 'greatest errors were commenced "innocently"', but could have been avoided by stricter adherence to biblical principles. According to Lady Byron, her daughter was seeking strength to die in meditation and prayer, in studying 'the character of our Saviour' and listening to her mother read aloud from the Gospels.[25] These claims ring false, not least because Ada hated such reading aloud.

Ada Lovelace's last hours in November 1852 brought little comfort: 'For some hours the last agonies—Once she was supposed gone—Not an interval of rest or comfort—Faintings and fierce pains alternating . . . In the next room [Lovelace,] whose feelings are far from in harmony with mine.' To be sure her daughter was dead, Lady Byron 'tried the breath and the eyes with a candle'.[26] Ada lacked the support and consolation of a loving, united family around her deathbed. Not only were her husband and mother bitter rivals, but her two sons responded to her death with the indifference that she had shown to them in life. In 1845 she had described her children as 'irksome *duties*' who gave her no pleasure.[27] At the age of 13, her eldest son, Byron, had been sent away to join the Navy, which he hated, while Ralph had lived with Lady Byron from the age of 9. Lady Byron reported on 11 August that Ada 'can't bear to see her children except one in the day', because they were so distressed at her condition.[28] Ralph had scarlet fever during much of Ada's final illness, and Byron was 'unhappily indifferent about his Mother'.[29] Annabella, who was later to marry Wilfrid Scawen Blunt, was the only child who spent much time wiping her mother's fevered brow.

Lady Byron was not the only person anxious about the state of Ada Lovelace's soul. Ada's friend Agnes Greig, daughter-in-law of Mary Somerville, the scientist, visited the dying woman frequently in her final year to offer practical and spiritual ministrations. Mary Somerville, a devout Anglican like Agnes, wrote to her daughter-in-law in June 1852: 'Had you ever any conversation with her upon religious topics, or was her mind *capable* of such subjects at the time you were with her . . . I trust her sufferings have led her to think of a future state and that she is more disposed for serious things than she used to be.' Mary Somerville judged Ada's medical case to be hopeless, and evidently considered Ada's spiritual outlook almost as bleak as that of her body. She found the subject of Ada's impending death so difficult that she lacked the courage to write to her friend Lady Byron.[30] Years later Mary Somerville criticized Lady Byron's will for her insufficient gratitude for Agnes's efforts 'in recalling [Ada] while on her death bed to a sense of Christianity and to the study of her bible'.[31] It was generally difficult to construct a convincing good death without the essential ingredients of a Christian life and committed faith.

Sudden Deaths

A modern psychiatrist, Beverley Raphael, has noted the potential shock and trauma of sudden death, especially if the circumstances are violent or unpleasant:

When death occurs with little or no warning, and especially if it occurs in the younger years, then an extra parameter is added. There has been no opportunity for anticipation, for preparation beforehand. The death brings an extra effect of shock over and above the normal . . . It is not surprising that sudden, unexpected, and untimely deaths are associated with greater problems for the bereaved than are anticipated deaths.[32]

Sudden deaths are more likely than other deaths to leave the bereaved feeling guilty and angry, full of regrets, as well as shocked and sad. In 1967 John Hinton reported a survey which suggested that approximately one death in ten was unexpected, though comparable statistics for the nineteenth century are not available.[33]

Many sudden deaths in the nineteenth century were doubtless similar in many respects to those today. Agnes Greig described in 1865 the shock of her husband's sudden death from a heart attack at the age of 60, despite his apparently good health. While dressing, Woronzow Greig complained of a bad attack of heartburn, which prompted Agnes to consult the family medicine book and call the doctor. Woronzow lay down on the bed and breathed several times with 'such agony that I was alarmed'. The doctor arrived to say Woronzow was already dead, but Agnes would not believe him, insisting her husband was asleep after the pain. The kind servants surrounded the bed, weeping and saying prayers, until they finally carried Agnes away while they laid out her husband's body. As Agnes confessed to her sister-in-law later that day: 'I am perfectly stunned. It has been awfully sudden . . . I try to be calm—but I hardly can . . . I thank God that he suffered for only a few moments—neither of us thought of Death, there was not a moment for a farewell word.'[34]

Sudden deaths in public and on social occasions were dreadful for all concerned. In 1878 Lucy Cavendish recorded in her diary a 'terrible and piteous' death at a London dinner-party, to which she had invited the Duke and Duchess of Argyll, despite concern about the Duchess's 'precarious state' following a stroke. At the dinner the Duchess's words were indistinct, she was unable to eat or drink, 'and we then saw too plainly that another stroke was upon her'. They laid her on a mattress in the study, where she slipped into unconsciousness 'after a short time of very terrible distress, when she seemed struggling in vain to speak and make signs'. Lucy and Catherine Gladstone cut off her clothes, and applied mustard blisters to her feet. Within a few hours as many as five doctors and two nurses had been called to the scene. 'Things were tried, and for an hour or two the bleeding on the brain was checked and there was a little rally of the pulse.' The Duchess's children were all summoned, but five of them were out of London, though other relatives added to the 'sad bewilderment and confusion'. The Duchess of Argyll died at 3.30 a.m., unconscious and free from pain. The Gladstones, Cavendishes, and Campbells who attended the death must all have been acutely aware of the stark contrast between this pathetic death and family deathbeds in kinder circumstances. Lucy Cavendish commented sadly, 'A terrible sorrow it was to the poor Duke not to have one look, one word, of farewell; but, if she had been roused, it would have been to piteous distress.'[35]

Early and mid-Victorian Christians most feared sudden death because it allowed no opportunity for spiritual preparation and repentance, depriving them of the potential consolations of a Christian deathbed. Jeremy Taylor reminded Christians in 1651 of the perils of sudden death: 'sin is sometimes by natural causality, very often by the anger of God and the Divine judgment, a cause of sudden and untimely death'.[36] Victorian theologians differed over how far sudden death was a sign of God's retribution on the unrepentant sinner, while agreeing that this traditional view encouraged holy living.[37]

Sudden death was even more traumatic if it involved a young person and if it took place while the family was separated. Nineteen-year-old Henry Palmer set sail in the *Elizabeth* in late November 1834, but his ship was never heard of again. The family was kept in suspense for many months, as rumours and false information sustained their hopes. In February 1835 they read in the newspapers that the *Elizabeth* had sunk in the St Lawrence River—a report which was later found to be a mistake. The devout High Anglican family was intensely concerned about the state of Henry's soul at the time of his death. Henry's brother Roundell Palmer, later Lord Selborne, an earnest student at Oxford at the time, responded with guilt for his own contribution to Henry's youthful sins: 'what I feel so heavily is my own responsibility for too many of the faults for which he is now called to account before the tribunal of God'. The sudden death of so young a brother reminded Roundell Palmer forcibly of his own mortality and the need for constant spiritual preparation, as he confessed to his father: 'The solemn warning of his death forces upon me the consideration of the state of my own mind. I fear much that if I had been called so suddenly away your trust in my salvation might not have been equally well grounded.'[38]

Revd William Palmer responded to his son's letter in February 1835 with an emphasis on the doctrine of atonement: 'as the Son of God died, in whom our brother believed, and for whose sake he sought forgiveness of his offences, his offences have been forgiven and he is in peace'. But even the devout clergyman found submission to God's will more difficult when it became clear that the February reports were false, and the following months prolonged the agony of uncertainty. By July 1835 Palmer had finally accepted that Henry had gone down with his ship, so they must resign themselves to God's will in their calamity. But his letter to Roundell revealed more of the deep impact of the family tragedy, as he admitted that 'your poor Mother feels this state of things most keenly—she is still in a manner unable to persuade herself of the truth'.[39] It was very hard to come to terms with Henry's death without seeing his body, with no confirmation of his death and no burial ceremony. Psychiatrists agree that mourners may find it more difficult to come to terms with their grief and to accept death's finality when they have not seen the body, and that their grief may be abnormally prolonged.[40]

Dr A. B. Granville's son Charles died in England in the late 1830s from accidental drowning caused by a sudden heart seizure while taking the waters for his health. The rest of the family was in Germany. Granville had resisted his son's entreaties to accompany the family with the argument that Charles needed to recuperate from a recent illness. Consequently 'no relative was at hand to attend the dead', and the body had to be buried temporarily, awaiting its removal to the catacombs in Kensal Green on the family's return. Granville was still racked by guilt and regret as long as three decades later: 'The heart is bleeding still, after thirty-five years, as if the wound had been only fresh inflicted'; had he taken his beloved son to Germany, Charles might still be alive. Granville recalled this as 'the most painful period of my life' and 'an irreparable and fatal loss which has embittered my days'.[41]

George Colville, who was in the Navy, was drowned when his ship sank in 1861 near the West Indies. His sister-in-law Caroline Colville believed 'this heavy affliction' fell most severely on her husband, Henry, who was deeply attached to his brother: 'It is indeed a sad sad grief, and the shock at first was almost stupifying, we could not realize the truth, it seemed almost impossible that one so loved and admired could in such a moment be taken away with all belonging to him—and no one left to say *how* and *when* the fearful tragedy happened.' Like the Palmers twenty-five years earlier, the Colvilles were obliged to accept that it was 'the Lord's Will'.[42] This was the fate of many families of men serving in the armed forces and in distant outposts of the Empire in the nineteenth century, culminating in the mass tragedy of the First World War.

In 1877 Herbert Acland, son of Dr Henry Acland (later Regius Professor of Medicine at Oxford), died of typhoid in Ceylon, where he had arrived only a few months earlier to become a tea-planter. The family did not learn of his illness until two weeks after his death and never saw his body, though they were given details of his final hours and his burial place in a Colombo cemetery. Herbert's mother, Sarah Acland, was devastated by her beloved son's death, even though she had six remaining sons and a daughter. The depth of her grief was so great that her daughter noted, 'from this blow Mother never rallied'.[43] Sarah was in shock for several weeks, and without her son's body to bid farewell and bury, she found it impossible to accept the reality of his death and to mourn. A few weeks after Herbert's death Sarah told her son Willie that his father was making arrangements for the cross for Herbie's grave: 'Can it be that he really lies there, so many thousand miles away? . . . It was such a terrible shock as well as sorrow.'[44] Sarah Acland reread her son's letters from Ceylon and found some solace in the love of her remaining children: 'But one wound aches and bleeds, though the rest of the body is whole.' She experienced a battle with her faith, regretting that she was not more fully resigned to God's will: 'Should not a Christian Mother rejoice when one of [her] loved ones is beyond the reach of pain or sorrow or temptation? If her faith were perfect she surely would. May mine be strengthened; let this be the prayer of all who love me.'[45] Sarah Acland struggled on for the sake of her husband and family, suffering from an insidious, quiet grief, and rarely complaining. She spoke at length of her 'great grief' to Elizabeth Marriott, confessing that it had been 'like tearing my very heart out' to allow Herbie to go to Ceylon in the first place. Her words of grief were all 'so *intense*' and yet so quiet, as if she always felt herself under an obligation to suppress her sorrow. Soon afterwards Sarah's health collapsed, and she died of a 'broken heart' in October 1878, according to Sophia Marriott's account, though the exact cause of her death was not specified.[46]

Later in the century people were inclined to observe that sudden death was often easier for the departed, especially if they were elderly. This represented a pronounced shift in perspective from the anxiety for the state of the unprepared and unshriven soul expressed by Jeremy Taylor and the Palmer family. In 1891 Lady Southwark considered her father's death from heart failure while sleeping ideal from his perspective since he was well prepared 'to face eternity', though the loss to his family was 'crushing'.[47] W. H. Smith's friend and political colleague Lord Iddesleigh died suddenly in his house in 1887, which was a great shock to his family and friends. Yet Smith believed it was not an unhappy death for Lord Iddesleigh, who had shown only a few minutes earlier, by manner and conversation, that he was at peace with all men.[48] Louisa Lady Antrim told her mother in 1892 that the family was broken-hearted at the sudden death of the Dowager Lady Antrim, her mother-in-law. They were not even able to kiss the old lady to say farewell: 'it was so sudden at the end—merciful for her but terrible for them'.[49]

Suicide

If sudden deaths were traumatic for the families, suicide was the negation of the good death which could test them beyond endurance. Suicide was traditionally regarded as a form of murder, seen as a felony in criminal law and as an offence against God. Michael MacDonald and Terence Murphy have shown how hostility to suicide and the enforcement of savage punishments fluctuated in the centuries before 1800.[50] In the Middle Ages, suicide was condemned by the Church and the common law, but juries were reluctant to punish surviving families, generally returning verdicts of *non compos mentis*— innocent of self-murder because of a disturbed mind. The Reformation fuelled religious hostility to suicide, ensuring that the law was enforced far more rigorously in early modern England.[51] After 1700 an increasing aversion developed towards savage penalties, which included forfeiture of all property and goods, denial of Christian burial, and harsh rites of desecration of the corpse.[52] Coroners' juries in the eighteenth century, influenced by Enlightenment ideas, objected to the penalties and increasingly applied the *non compos mentis* verdict.

Parliament abolished the religious penalties for suicide in 1823 by repealing the custom of profane burial, while the forfeiture of property was repealed in 1870. Repeal simply recognized that the law had rarely been applied for decades, since coroners' juries presumed that the majority of suicides were insane. But suicide continued to be regarded with fear and aversion, as the converse of the good death. Most Christians in the nineteenth century still considered suicide a sin against God, and wished to deter potential suicides. As MacDonald and Murphy argue: 'Even if Victorians were unwilling to resume the punishments that their ancestors had inflicted on suicides and their families, they still believed that self-killing was bad. The families of suicides shrank from the stigma such a death attached to them; they tried as hard as ever to conceal suicides whenever they could.'[53] Parliament did not repeal the common-law felony of self-murder until 1961.

There was considerable opposition to the repeal of the penalties for suicide in the nineteenth century, especially from conservatives in the Anglican Church. Indeed, from the 1850s, when the Church was challenged by biblical criticism, scientific progress, and religious doubt, its conservatives became more outspoken on the subject of suicide. As Olive Anderson has shown, a considerable debate developed from 1850 regarding the trend towards greater leniency in treatment of suicides.[54] Many conservatives, both doctors and churchmen, were concerned that coroners' juries and medical witnesses generally interpreted the law mercifully for the sake of the survivors, returning verdicts of 'temporary insanity' instead of *felo de se*.[55] From the 1880s there was a growing belief that the incidence of suicide was increasing and that a stricter interpretation of the law might act as a deterrent. The *Lancet* argued in 1884 that 'scarcely one in a hundred of the so-called cases of "temporary insanity" are correctly so described'.[56]

In the last three decades of the century doctors, theologians, and philosophers debated whether suicide could best be explained in traditional moral terms as a sin against God, or by broader socio-economic forces, or by mental depression. The conservative moralists were still influential. Wynn Westcott, deputy coroner for Central Middlesex, argued in 1885 that 'the cultivation of a religious conviction of the sanctity of life and the sin of a self-inflicted death is a more certain hindrance to suicide' than most others.[57] The *Lancet* took the view in 1884 that genuine 'temporary insanity' was not a common cause of self-murder; in the great majority of cases 'it is not their psychical, but their moral condition which is at fault. They want to flee from the trials and troubles of life.'[58] Revd H. H. Henson in 1897 regarded the perceived increase in the number of suicides in recent decades as an indication of the decline of Christian influence.[59] Even in 1900 Revd J. Gurnhill in *The Morals of Suicide* still deplored suicide with horror as 'this deadly sin'.[60]

Yet in later Victorian Britain a secular view of suicide gained support, explaining suicide either as the result of mental illness or as a rational choice based on socio-economic circumstances. These perspectives had been developed since the Enlightenment, but had been less influential while the Evangelical movement was powerful. They were reinforced in the later decades of the century by the scientific challenges to religious orthodoxy and the increasing secularization of social thought. Writers placed greater emphasis on socio-economic factors in suicide, while recognizing the importance of genuine mental disorders as causes of a minority of suicides. Émile Durkheim's classic *Suicide: A Study in Sociology*, first published in 1897, was the most influential of the books developing the argument that suicide was a social problem rather than a moral crime.[61]

These archives reveal evidence of the personal reactions of family members to three suicides which all coincidentally took place in 1876 in devout Anglican families. These families still perceived suicide primarily as a moral crime, which helps to explain why their trauma may have been greater than for those who adopted Durkheim's view. Professor James Thorold Rogers's family in Oxford had to face the suicide by hanging of their eldest son, Henry, and the Palmer family the shooting by his own hand of their relative Currer Roundell. The Lyttelton and Gladstone families had to deal with the suicide of the head of the Lyttelton family, the father of twelve children and a respected public figure—as we shall see in a later chapter. Lord Lyttelton's suicide was the result of a clear instance of recurrent acute melancholia, so that the family's 'terrible anguish' was to some extent alleviated by their belief that their father was not accountable for his actions and that his faith in God continued strong until the end. Even so, they made some effort to conceal the manner of his death. Enrico Morselli observed in 1881 that the infamy attached to suicide for centuries impelled families to hide or falsify the true cause and particulars of death.[62]

The family of Professor James Thorold Rogers, the historian, could not console itself with the possibility that Henry had suffered from long-term depression, and the father had to take public refuge in the subterfuge that the death in September 1876 was an accident. The suicide of a beloved eldest son, aged only 17, must have been one of the worst forms of parental torture. Henry's younger brother Bertram, aged 15, later described the tragedy at the inquest and in an account for the family history entitled 'Black Sheep and Tragedies'. Henry and Bertram were spending the school holidays at home in Oxford, while their father was in Germany and their mother was in bed for a day or two with a bad toothache. The two boys had practised cricket and played card-games in the drawing-room before retiring to bed at their usual time. When Henry did not appear for breakfast next morning Bertram went to his room to call him, and found him 'suspended by a strap from the hook on the door, quite dead'. The 15-year-old boy cut the strap and laid his brother's body on the floor. Henry had not been to bed and the body was quite cold, so he must have died the previous evening. After making the 'dreadful discovery' Bertram rushed to his mother's room and summoned his father and sister home from Germany.[63]

The inquest was held in the dining-room, where Bertram testified that Henry had given no indication that he 'meditated self-destruction' and had no cause to do so. Their doctor said the death was caused by mental derangement due to overwork, no doubt hoping for a verdict of 'temporary insanity', but Bertram privately thought that was nonsense. The housekeeper testified that Henry seemed 'very happy', with no particular problems. The verdict of suicide was damning: 'That deceased hanged himself . . . and [that] there was no evidence laid before the jury to show the state of his mind at the time'.[64] The implication was that Henry was sane and therefore responsible for his actions. Fifty years later Bertram remained unable to explain his brother's suicide, though 'the horror of it is still fresh in my mind'. He felt sure Henry was happy at home, he was captain of Westminster School, and appeared to have good prospects at Oxford. Some light was cast on his school performance by a letter of May 1876 from a master at Westminster School to Mrs Rogers; he regretted that Henry had not recently been successful in his work and attributed this to his apparently poor health, already discussed with his mother, especially his low level of energy.[65] Henry may have been suffering from mononucleosis, with incipient severe depression.

Even at the time of Henry's death Bertram was aware that his father 'feared to face the real fact and tried to persuade himself that it was else than a deliberate act'.[66] It helped James Thorold Rogers to try to believe this fiction. Neither parent ever again spoke of the tragedy to Bertram, presumably because he continued to insist it was suicide, and they preferred to believe otherwise. Whatever their own grief, the parents left this 15-year-old boy to carry an extraordinarily heavy burden of grief and guilt with no parental support. The bereaved parents were unable to respond to the boy's grief because of their own sorrow and shame. Possibly also the mother was hostile to Bertram because he survived, while her favourite, the eldest son, did not. Nine days after Henry's death, Professor James Thorold Rogers distributed a most unusual black-edged, printed 'open letter' to friends and colleagues concerning the circumstances of his son's death. Ostensibly this two-page document was an expression of gratitude for the many letters of condolence, but the father's protests that he would not deceive himself or 'argue falsely on behalf of my dead son' are not convincing in the light of Bertram's evidence. James Thorold Rogers contended that Henry's death was caused by a school-boy experiment while performing 'dangerous gymnastic practices' in his room. The father affirmed that to argue that such a diligent and contented boy deliberately took his own life 'would be to insult humanity, to outrage reason, to dishonour the providence of God, to reduce human life to chaos or chance'.[67] A copy of this extraordinary open letter was bizarrely pasted into the family album of photographs, press cuttings, and records of achievements,[68] a sad family claim for posterity.

James Thorold Rogers also went to much trouble over his son's grave. The family archives include a 'faculty', or licence, from the ecclesiastical authorities for the construction of a brick family vault in perpetuity on the south side of Saint Sepulchre's Burial Ground in Oxford,[69] where Henry's parents were eventually to join their son. The remainder of the family appear to have been buried elsewhere. The significance of these special burial procedures relates back to the ancient customs which denied Christian burial to suicides, whose bodies were interred in a pit at a crossroads, with a wooden stake hammered through them. Though rites of desecration were abolished by the Act of 1823, private night-time burial between 9 and 12 p.m. continued, and clergymen could decline to perform the customary rites over the bodies of suicides or could amend them. Between 1852 and 1880 legislation permitted suicides to be buried with religious rites if co-operative clergymen could be found, but no clause compelled ministers to perform the burial service.[70] Popular opinion continued to oppose the burial of suicides in consecrated ground. Suicides judged *non compos mentis* were often buried in the shaded north side of churchyards, along with unbaptized infants and executed criminals. Burial practices varied, and some suicides, including Henry Rogers, were placed in family vaults or other more agreeable locations, at the request of privileged families.[71]

Ann Rogers's obsessive visits to her son's grave over many years may reflect her lingering concern about the state of his soul, as she endeavoured to beautify and sanctify his last resting-place. Her diary shows that she did not delude herself about the cause of her son's death, whatever consolation such vain hopes brought to her husband. Ann had four other sons and one daughter, but she could not assuage her grief for Henry. She recorded in her diary on 11 September 1876, the day of his death: 'God have mercy upon us for what happened today. My son my son.' Ann Rogers always visited Henry's 'dear grave' at least once a week, and frequently twice or more often, to plant flowers or bulbs, lay a wreath, or clean the marble cross. Tending his grave was an essential ritual which brought her some sense of closeness to her dead son. Numerous diary entries simply recorded 'very low. Always thinking about my poor darling'; and at Christmas, 'Oh so miserable, longing for my poor Boy.'[72] Of the first anniversary of Henry's death she wrote, 'Oh terrible anniversary so miserable thinking about my poor Darling. This awful mystery. God help me.' On New Year's Eve 1877 she wrote: 'A year of great mental agony to me. My precious Boy always present in my thoughts and his terrible death a source of unceasing suffering. God help us.'[73]

Bertram Rogers observed that his mother never recovered from Henry's suicide, and remained in mourning for the rest of her life: 'I think his image was always before her.'[74] Ann Rogers was unable to resolve her grief. On the third anniversary of the death she observed, 'all the past seems vivid as ever . . . how vexed is the recollection of that day 3 years'. In 1882 she wrote on 11 September: 'The terrible day. My sweet darling Boy I can hardly bear it even now.' She was still visiting the grave at least weekly and discussing her loss with her two sons Arthur and Clem, though never with Bertram. At least she was able to note an improvement in her health on New Year's Eve 1882, despite continued depression, and 'my darling Boy not forgotten but more gone into the past'.[75] Ann Rogers was 51 at the time of Henry's death and mourned him for twenty-three years until her own death in 1899 when she joined Henry in the vault.

Chronic grief will be examined more fully in the second half of this book, but we may notice here that it was closely associated with suicide on two out of the three occasions recorded in these archives. Obsessive long-term grief seems to have been rare in Victorian Britain, but it afflicted Ann Rogers, the mother of a suicide, and Lucy Cavendish, the daughter of a suicide. Both these women were devout Christians who could not avoid seeing suicide as a sin against God, and for them there was no resolution of their grief. In Ann Rogers's case the trauma was magnified because it involved a son who was still a dependent adolescent. As psychiatrist Beverley Raphael notes, 'Violent and accidental deaths are all the more shocking, abnormal and difficult to assimilate when they involve children.'[76]

We gain further insight into family responses to suicide from the Palmer family correspondence about the suicide of a cousin, Currer Roundell, also in 1876. Currer had been encouraged to buy a plantation in Wilmington, North Carolina, where he was found shot in his bedroom. Lord Selborne learned of the circumstances of his cousin's death from W. L. de Rosset, a shipping merchant of Wilmington, who was certain it was suicide because of 'the downward course of the ball' and the position of the body. A careful examination of Currer Roundell's effects revealed nothing to explain the cause of the 'terrible act'.[77] Lord Selborne concurred with the suicide verdict: 'When the time of night, and the state of the body as to clothing, are borne in mind, the theory of accident seems to me to be so entirely against reason, that the mere suggestion and discussion of it could only add unnecessarily to the inevitable pain, which must at all events be endured.'[78]

Lord Selborne and his two brothers, Revd George Horsley Palmer and Revd Edwin Palmer, Chaplain of Balliol College, were executors for Currer Roundell's estate, and all three were committed Anglicans. Their correspondence emphasized their view that Roundell died while of unsound mind. Lord Selborne's immediate response to the news of the death was that Currer Roundell '*died by his own hand*, doubtless . . . under mental aberration'. Selborne was aware that Roundell was mentally unstable when he left for America, having delusions about his own genius and wealth.[79] De Rosset, the Wilmington agent, was anxious to explain to the family the circumstances of Currer Roundell's burial, since he knew they were 'Church of England people'. Knowing the family would want an Anglican minister, the only episcopal minister in Wilmington presided over the burial service. Unfortunately he was 'a very particular man and strict constructionist', who could not conscientiously use the full burial service for a suicide, reading instead selections from it. De Rosset could not blame the minister, but hoped the family shared his preference for a selective burial service by an Anglican minister over a full service by a Dissenter.[80]

The three Palmer brothers were justifiably anxious about communicating the news to Currer Roundell's widowed mother, Laura Roundell, and his two young sisters. His mother instantly responded by blaming herself: 'poor woman, she naturally takes the turn of self-accusation'. She requested as much secrecy as possible: 'nothing should be said, beyond what may be absolutely necessary,—and especially nothing as to the circumstances'. Laura informed all friends, and even her solicitor, only that Currer died suddenly in America.[81] The three Palmer brothers became intimately involved in the affairs of the bereaved mother and daughters, sorting out their incomes and finding places for them to live. Within two months of Currer Roundell's suicide, Revd George Horsley Palmer feared that Laura Roundell's mind could 'give way at any moment'. Lord Selborne thought that the case was one of 'aggravated hysteria, rather than of mental derangement', occasioned by grief and shock at her son's suicide. The Palmer brothers, as executors, resolved to consult Laura Roundell's brother Mr Cornish on the advisability of mental treatment or care for his sister. The two girls were also 'to a certain extent demoralized by the most grievous trial that could ever befall two young girls'. The Palmer brothers agreed that the three poor women would be a lifelong cause for anxiety, but they would continue to do their best to assist.[82] There the archival evidence ends.

The particular problems created by a suicide in a Victorian Christian family are demonstrated vividly by the cases of Henry Rogers and Currer Roundell. They reveal the 'legacy of suicide' which still prevails; '. . . of uncertainty, of guilt, of blame, and hostility', as Beverley Raphael has expressed it.[83] Suicides were, of course, the most extreme cases. But the other instances of bad deaths explored in this chapter—violent, sudden, or ungodly—were abnormal deaths which were feared throughout the Victorian and Edwardian periods. Such deaths were in a minority among these families up to 1914, and their numbers seem even smaller today because few families chose to record them for posterity. The Great War was to be such an awful catastrophe in part because abnormal, sudden, and violent deaths became the norm, where previously they had been largely unrecorded and regarded as outside the realm of good Christian deaths.

✣ 4 ✣

DEATH AND THE VICTORIAN DOCTORS

THERAPEUTIC MEDICINE HAD A VERY LIMITED POWER TO CURE DISEASE before the advent of the sulphonamide drugs in the 1930s, but Victorian doctors compensated with a remarkably good record of terminal care, comfort, and palliative management. The work of Victorian physicians such as William Munk on the care of the dying anticipated that of such modern experts as John Hinton and Elisabeth Kübler-Ross. This chapter examines this Victorian contribution to improved terminal care and considers the doctors' response to ethical questions about prolonging life and hastening death. The next chapter will assess more specifically the role of nurses and consultants in the care of the dying and explore the extent to which doctors told the truth to terminal patients.

Between 1830 and 1920 the emphasis moved gradually away from spiritual concerns at a deathbed towards a greater anxiety to minimize physical suffering. In part this transition reflected a general decline in religious belief and the reduced vigour of Evangelicalism. It also signified a gradual change in attitudes to death and disease, with an increasing tendency to perceive death as being caused by particular diseases rather than divinely ordained. If death was God's will, then there was still a very definite limit to the doctor's power, but if the natural effects of disease were to blame, then the doctor might be expected to contribute rather more. If he could do little to cure disease before the 1930s, at least he could provide invaluable assistance in reducing the pain, discomfort, and fear associated with dying. But it was not a simple case of medicine replacing religion at the deathbed. The most important developments in therapeutic medicine and in hospitalization for the dying did not take place until after 1920, when the decline of Christian faith was already well advanced. In practice, religion and medicine often co-operated in the Victorian period, when Christian doctors shared with the families they treated many of the same aspirations for the 'good death'. By the time doctors had more substantial powers to cure disease fewer doctors or patients were Christians.

The Limits of Victorian Medicine and the Doctor's Role

As Roy Porter and Barry Smith have shown, the medicine of the Victorian general practitioner was not much more advanced than that of his predecessor two centuries earlier, because he had few effective medications. Up to the late nineteenth century, 'advances in basic medical science could not be translated into therapeutic weapons, not least because the causes of disease and the nature of the body's morbid responses remained deeply obscure and much contested'. Before the advent of antibiotics from the 1930s medicine could do little to deal with infectious diseases such as cholera and typhus. The decline in the death-rate from the 1870s owed far more to public-health reforms, better living-standards, and improved diet than to medical innovation.[1] The major nineteenth-century advances related to surgery, notably anaesthesia and antisepsis, and to the late Victorian diagnostic developments initiated by the discovery of the germ theory of disease.

Doctors and patients alike were well aware of the limits to the healing powers of Victorian medicine. Dr C. J. B. Williams, FRS, in his 1862 Lumleian Lecture to the Royal College of Physicians, reminded his colleagues of the uncertainty of their art, with its continuing failures caused by the intractability of certain diseases, and the ultimate inevitability of death. In the case of cholera, for example, 'as soon as it is disease it is death'.[2] Dr Charles Elam of Harley Street was even more gloomy in his commentary in the *Lancet* on the Registrar-General's report on deaths in London in 1868. Medicine appeared to be failing in its primary function of healing, given the increase in mortality rates in London for younger people, and the failure to reduce deaths from fever and epidemics.[3] Lord Holland in 1844 was not the only patient to question the claims and competency of 'those egregious humbugs the doctors': 'The longer one lives the less one can place faith in the [doctors] I think—theirs at best is a science of guess work—how often their guesses are wrong and how seldom will they ever reveal their real guesses even as they are.'[4]

Victorian doctors usually gave better care to patients suffering from diseases which could be identified and which developed slowly. Physicians were often at their worst with illnesses with a fast onset, especially fevers, for their treatment was necessarily empirical and they could not be sure whether the disease was terminal. Then they often had to rely on experience or instinct, while adopting a confident manner designed to encourage faith in their remedies. Victorian families learned from bitter experience that medicine was not an exact science. Lucy Sharpe expressed no surprise at the contradictory diagnoses of the two doctors who puzzled over her sister Letty's symptoms of consumption in 1843. Lucy still harboured faint hopes that the more optimistic doctor might yet prove to be correct: 'God grant the doctor may be mistaken. I cannot but have hopes he may be if he formed so positive an opinion so few days after Dr Watson had said there was no existing disease.'[5] As we have seen, Margaret Gladstone's death from puerperal fever in 1870 was made more traumatic because she and her mother were well aware that the doctors did not understand the nature of the disease and had no cure for it. Such cases can be multiplied, especially in the first half of the century.

Here is a paradox. Victorian doctors themselves admitted the limitations of their scientific knowledge and their inability to cure many conditions. Yet they were held in high regard by the middle and upper classes, who often developed an intimate relationship with their doctors, akin to that with loyal family retainers. Edward Shorter helps to explain this paradox with his suggestion that the doctor's concern for the patient's personal life and general well-being varied inversely with his ability to cure: 'Because therapeutic horizons were so limited, these modern physicians needed everything they had going for them, and that meant relying therapeutically upon the psychological dimension of the doctor–patient relationship.' Shorter contrasts the friendly and supportive Victorian family doctor with his 'post-modern' successor after the Second World War, who had immense therapeutic power, but less interest in the patient's general health and personal history.[6] Thus progress in palliative care and effective management of the terminal stage of disease could readily coexist in the nineteenth century with a continuing failure to make significant improvements in therapeutic medicine.

The large measure of co-operation between wealthy Victorian families and their doctors was encouraged by the substantial rise in doctors' professional and scientific status during the nineteenth century. Despite their weaknesses in therapy, advances in pathological anatomy, surgery, and microbiology began to develop the image of doctors as scientists by the end of the century.[7] It remained more common, however, for general practitioners to be of lesser social standing than their wealthy patients, and therefore more deferential, though the social gap was reduced in this period. Doctors were naturally eager to please such patients, to enhance their own reputation and the rise of their practice. But the families felt free to obtain additional medical opinions or change their doctors if they did not like their doctor's advice or his manner.

By the time a death occurred in a family, a firm relationship of long standing had usually been established with the local practitioner as well as one or more consultants. *Cassell's Household Guide* advised in 1869 that 'amongst

great families the doctor is treated like the clergyman', invited to the funeral
and supplied with mourning-scarf, -band, and -gloves.[8] The medical attendants of the deceased were frequently provided with a carriage in the funeral
procession, which was often stipulated in the will, as was the case at the
funerals of Lord Canterbury, Earl Spencer, and the Marquis of Westminster
in 1845.[9]

At times of death in the family gratitude to the doctors far outweighed any
criticism. Even when his wife and daughter were dying in 1839, John Horsley
Palmer had every confidence in the professional skill of Dr Peter Latham,
besides admiring 'the feeling and generous character of our excellent friend'.[10]
Thirteen years later, when Palmer's niece Dorothea Palmer was dying of
tuberculosis, she expressed her thanks to that same family doctor: 'Dr
Latham's care, kindness and attention deserve all our gratitude. Dr Watson
was just the same, only the one is an old friend and the other a new one . . . I
quite love Dr Latham—he was like a father.'[11] Dorothea's father, Revd
William Palmer, left £100 in his will to Dr Peter Latham in gratitude for his
kind attention to all the family, especially Dorothea.[12]

In the 1840s George Cornish informed John Keble that two eminent
physicians had declared the case of 'poor Louisa' hopeless. Nevertheless,
Cornish concluded with a comment which was reiterated by many Victorian
family members in their dealings with death and the doctors: 'There is the
satisfaction of feeling that all has been done which human skill can do.'[13] In
1838 Mary Somerville responded with similar fatalism to the sad news of the
approaching death of a child in her husband's family; but she also found
some consolation in the knowledge that 'they have the best medical aid so
there is at least the melancholy satisfaction [of] knowing that all has been
done'—almost the same words as those used by George Cornish.[14] On her
sister-in-law's death of a tumour in 1844, Mary Somerville was thankful that
all conceivable remedies had been tried: 'you at least have the consolation to
know that no earthly means have been wanting for the medical profession
stands as high in Scotland as in any part of the world'.[15]

The doctor's vital role as friend of the family and source of invaluable
moral support, rather than medical cure, was also exhibited in the account of
the death of Lady Morshead, sister to Sir William Harcourt. She died a
particularly painful death in 1883 which appears, from the symptoms and
treatment, to have been caused by cancer of the bowel. The confidence of her
husband, Sir Warwick Morshead, in one particular doctor was evident from
his comment that he had specially asked the physician, Priestly, to come, 'as
we wish to be quite sure of the treatment, as I don't wish any one but him to
make any examination'. He was relieved at the outcome, since Priestly was

satisfied with her progress: 'I don't know what I should have done without him in my anxiety.' The patient also testified to her faith in 'our dear doctor', but in her case this was the family doctor rather than Priestly: 'What Dr Macleod has been and is to me—twice he has saved my life during this illness.'[16] Neither Macleod nor Priestly was able to save Lady Morshead, but their constant attendance and cautious advice helped sustain patient and husband through long, painful months.

Improved Medical Care of the Dying: Munk's 'Euthanasia'

Upper- and middle-class Victorian families placed great reliance on their doctors while relatives were dying, despite their recognition of medicine's therapeutic weakness. To understand why this was so, beyond the obvious psychological value of reassurance, it is necessary to examine the record of nineteenth- and early twentieth-century doctors on the care of the dying. Increasingly they emphasized a more supportive and caring management of the dying, combined with improved palliative care. The role of the medical profession at the final stage of disease increased, but it was a benign influence. This is seen in the frequent use of the term 'euthanasia' by nineteenth-century doctors, in the classical Greek sense of a peaceful, easy, and painless death, to express their aim and role with dying patients. The doctor's role was still necessarily limited in the nineteenth century, for he could not yet cure many diseases and he lacked the technological means to prolong life. But he could help to make the terminal stage easier, without any sense of failure attached to the admission that death was inevitable.

The Lumleian Lecture delivered by Dr C. J. B. Williams to the Royal College of Physicians in 1862 illustrated the importance attached by Victorian doctors to the care of the dying. While conceding the curative limitations of the art of medicine, he also testified to its successes, including improved terminal care: 'I speak of the Prolongation and Utilization of Life, and the Alleviation of Suffering. These may seem very subordinate at first, but often they are far from being so in the estimation of the patient.' Many physicians received more gratitude, in his experience, from relieving pain and making death more comfortable and dignified than from effecting a cure.[17] Williams believed his colleagues were often at their best in ministering to the dying.

Victorian doctors did their best to allay the fear of death, especially the widespread notions that the terminal stage involved great suffering and that the moment of death was one of agony. The Christian ideal of the good death tended to exacerbate such fears in some, by its stress on the virtue of fortitude in the face of suffering at the deathbed. By allaying these anxieties, doctors were implicitly reducing the moral significance attached by Christianity to the hour of death itself. Sir Benjamin Brodie in 1854 indicated that the act of dying was seldom a painful process, except in cases such as death from tetanus or hydrophobia. Usually 'both mental and bodily suffering terminate long before the scene is finally closed', by which time fear of death had long abated.[18] William S. Savory, FRS addressed this issue further in 1863 in his well-known collection of lectures *On Life and Death*. The most acute mental distress occurred when people first realized they were about to die, but the fear of death usually declined when death drew near. Savory emphasized the gradual nature of the dissolution of the body and 'the gradual severance of the ties between the conscious man and the world around him by the decay of the senses'.[19]

The landmark in the Victorian history of the medical care of the dying was the publication in 1887 of Dr William Munk's influential textbook *Euthanasia: or Medical Treatment in Aid of an Easy Death*. Munk drew on his own experience, combined with that of doctors such as Halford, Brodie, Hufeland, and Savory, to provide a comprehensive text on the best management of the dying. Munk was the Victorian equivalent of modern experts like Kübler-Ross, Cicely Saunders, and John Hinton, and it is remarkable how much of their work he anticipated. The book provides a guide to the care of the dying endorsed by the highest medical authorities of the period. The *Lancet*, in an editorial and a review of *Euthanasia*, described Munk as 'one of our rare medical scholars', and 'a thoughtful and experienced physician' whose excellent advice was entirely supported.[20]

William Munk was among those who defined 'euthanasia' in the classical sense of 'a calm and easy death'. He noted that medical texts and treatises had little to say on the management of the dying or on the treatment required to relieve their suffering, while the subject was not specifically addressed in medical schools, leaving young physicians to learn for themselves. He promised the systematic treatment of a special study to correct this situation.[21]

Munk began by addressing popular fears, augmented by fictional representations and Evangelical literature, that 'mortal agony', or the 'death struggle', was inseparable from the process of dying. Drawing on the work of Savory and Brodie, he reassured readers that the urgent symptoms of disease usually subsided when the process of dying commenced and that extreme pain was unusual in the terminal phase. Munk explained the remarkable variety in the manner of death, according to whether its source was the heart, the lungs, or the brain. Popular belief that the act of dying involved severe bodily suffering was partly caused by confusing the terminal stage of dying with those 'urgent symptoms of disease that precede'. Common fears were also fuelled by 'theoretical views of the nature of the event itself'—the closest he came to admitting that the medical perspective might conflict with the traditional Christian ideal of death as a trial of faith against suffering.[22]

Munk devoted a large part of his book to advice on the alleviation of pain and distress. He emphasized that when death was approaching 'we dismiss all thought of cure, or of the prolongation of life', to concentrate instead on the relief of pain and discomfort. Much suffering associated with the deathbed was not necessarily related to the act of dying, and could be reduced. Restlessness was often due to the weight of bedclothes, which could be lightened; gasping and difficulty in breathing could be improved by admitting fresh, cool air to overheated rooms, and by change of posture. Indeed the doctor should take pains to regulate 'the economy of the bedchamber'—the temperature, ventilation, and degree of quiet required by the patient. Munk criticized the custom of excluding daylight from death chambers, since most dying people complained of failing sight and sought more light in their gloomy rooms. Attendants should not whisper or talk in undertones in the presence of the dying: 'What has to be said, and the less that is the better, should be in a clear, distinct, ordinary tone.' Munk also advised that the deathbed was no place for exclamations of grief or for 'officious interference or obtrusive curiosity'. Those entitled to be present should be limited to the immediate family, a nurse and doctor, and a minister of religion, who should refrain from crowding around the bed and eliminate 'all noise and bustle' when death was imminent.[23]

Munk believed that opium was invaluable in relieving pain, a subject I will discuss in the next section. He also considered that distilled or fermented alcohol had a special value in the treatment of the dying, since it passed readily into the blood, stimulated the failing heart, promoted circulation, and aided the digestive process. Alcohol should be administered in small quantities repeated at frequent intervals. Sherry and port were the most useful since champagne's effects were evanescent, but brandy was often better than wine, particularly if the stomach was upset. The correct administration of food was also vital, since mistakes in diet were responsible for much of the discomfort connected with dying, especially giving too much food when the stomach had already lost its digestive powers. The wishes of the dying patient were the most accurate indicator of the food and stimulants needed.[24]

Some physicians provided families with written regulations for the daily routine of their terminal patients, which demonstrate that Munk's advice on diet and alcohol reflected general medical practice. Dr W. D. Freeborn gave the Acland family instructions for the care of Sarah Acland, dying in 1878 of 'chronic bronchial catarrh' (according to the death certificate). The daily timetable started at 7 a.m. with two ounces of milk and two drams of brandy. Wine accompanied all meals, and was prescribed at regular intervals, ending with milk and brandy at 2 a.m. An enema was to be administered every other day, and a 'hypodermic injection of morphia when required to relieve pain'.[25]

The authority of Dr Munk's text was in part founded on his ready admission that he drew widely on the practice and teaching of the previous generation of doctors, especially Sir Henry Halford and Professor James Simpson. Munk's respect for Halford was evident in his biography of this distinguished physician of the early nineteenth century—President of the Royal College of Physicians for twenty-four years and consultant to many eminent English families, including royalty. Halford was recognized by the *Lancet*, as well as by Munk, as 'a master in all that concerned the management of the dying'.[26] Munk saw Halford as 'essentially a practical bedside physician' with a broad and accurate knowledge of available drugs and treatment and a supreme ability to inspire hope and confidence. Halford concentrated on alleviating pain, ensuring rest and sleep, maintaining the appetite for as long as possible, and providing 'such aid as medicines could supply'. So effective was he that one lady declared she preferred to die under Halford's care than recover under any other doctor. Munk claimed that Halford 'by his sympathy, his gentleness of manner and the hope he inspired, often did for his patient more than any drugs could effect'.[27]

The essential continuity between Munk's text of 1887 and the experience of earlier Victorian physicians in the care of the dying is also illustrated by the work of Professor James Young Simpson. W. E. Gladstone's lengthy account of the death of his 87-year-old father, Sir John Gladstone, in 1851 illustrates the potential for conflict between progressive medical advice and early Victorian family application of the Evangelical ideal. Simpson was brought to Fasque, the Gladstone family home in Scotland, 'by special engine' from Edinburgh, after the family and the three local doctors agreed on the need for expert advice on Sir John's deteriorating condition. When Simpson objected that the sick-room was too hot and stuffy, William Gladstone explained that many hands were required to move his father; 'this and instinctive feeling without particular guidance had caused the room to be somewhat crowded and close until Dr Simpson required that a better arrangement should be made'. Simpson later stipulated that there should be no more than four attendants in the death chamber at a time, since oxygen was as vital as food in the fight for life. Consequently, the family moved from their father's bedroom to the hall outside, making it habitable with chairs and a curtain to separate it from the staircase, 'and it continued to be our principal living room until the final close'.[28]

William Gladstone felt confident after Simpson's departure that both 'food and atmosphere were pretty successfully regulated', attributing his father's temporary improvement to the 'admirable nourishment' prescribed by Simpson, who recommended egg-whites as the food requiring least digestion. In the next twenty-four hours Sir John consumed the whites of thirteen eggs, a little brandy, and beef tea and toast. However, as the hour of Sir John's death approached, Simpson's rules for the economy of the death chamber were increasingly disregarded. Servants and chief tenants came to make their farewells, as the family sat or lay about the bedroom and the hall. William noted, in an understatement, that 'the bustle and efforts about [Sir John] must have tended to excite', while the 'strong fumigation' and coughing of some attendants greatly annoyed him.[29] But 1851 was still an early point in the educational process for families, and later Victorian deathbed records do suggest that the advice of Munk and other experts was more effectively implemented towards the end of the century.

Munk's *Euthanasia* remained the authoritative text on medical care of the dying for the next thirty years, when other medical experts, such as Oswald Browne in 1894 and Robert Saundby in 1902, added little to Munk's work. Browne's pamphlet for nurses *On the Care of the Dying* followed Munk closely, and reaffirmed the importance of such care: 'I can only express my own deep conviction that amongst the many privileges which fall to us who wait upon the sick, there is none touches or approaches this (the care of dying persons), nor is there any part of our work that more amply repays most careful study.'[30]

Munk and his colleagues were seeking to divest the process of dying of its worst terrors, even if this meant challenging the Christian belief that death was a test of fortitude in the face of suffering. It must be emphasized, however, that many Victorian doctors were committed Christians who sought to harness the more constructive features of their religion, such as faith, hope, and belief in an afterlife. Sir Benjamin Brodie was convinced in 1854 that 'a pure and simple religious faith' would contribute most 'to disarm death of its terrors'.[31] Professor Charles Williams believed in 1884 that, even with the most skilful medical resources at the deathbed, 'an absolute reliance on the overruling Providence of God is the only true source of confidence and peace'.[32] Munk himself became a Catholic at the age of 26 in 1842, and was described by the *Lancet* as a doctor whose medical experience was tempered by Christian philosophy.[33] Munk shared Halford's trust in the consoling effects of faith in a future life, when all hope of life in the present had vanished: 'A firm belief in the mercy of God, and in the promises of salvation will do more than anything in aid of an easy, calm, and collected death.'

Moreover, Munk argued from his personal experience with dying people that believers were more likely to die a calm and comfortable death than unbelievers (though we might wonder about the size of his sample of atheists): 'In the aggressive *dis*believer, as in the mere passive agnostic, doubt and anxiety as to his future is all but sure to obtrude itself on his last conscious moments, disturb them, and render such an euthanasia as we contemplate, impossible.'[34] Munk agreed with Halford's view that the patient should be informed of his terminal condition in time for 'a contemplation of his more important spiritual concerns', and the expression of contrition for his sins.[35]

But if religious belief was regarded by most Victorian doctors as supportive, it also came to be seen as subordinate to medical imperatives by the early twentieth century. A pamphlet entitled *Medicine and Religion*, edited in 1910 by Dr Charles Buttar, revealed the influence of secularism on late Victorian and Edwardian doctors. Buttar believed doctors and clergymen could work hand in hand, but they should never encroach on each other's territory. Another contributor was concerned lest energy required to fight disease be wasted on a melancholy, passive piety, obsessed with remorse and repentance.[36]

Palliative Care: Medical Theory and Practice

One of the most important aspects of Victorian doctors' care of the dying was the relief of pain and the use of opiates. Opium was widely used in the nineteenth century to relieve pain, while aspirin was not introduced until 1899. Patent remedies based on opium included Dover's Powder, Godfrey's Cordial, and laudanum or tincture of opium, which was a combination of opium, alcohol, and distilled water. From the 1860s a more effective hypodermic injection of morphine, the alkaloid isolated from opium, was used for incurable and painful diseases like cancer, causing some concern a decade later about the dangers of addiction. Heroin was first produced in 1874, but not used in medical practice in Victorian Britain. Berridge and Edwards show that legal and public attitudes to the widespread and open use of opium changed in the second half of the century because of fears of working-class dissipation, so that severe restrictions were introduced in 1868 and 1908 to discourage such general use and easy access.[37]

Roy Porter argues that the eighteenth century was an 'anaesthetized age, precisely because of the startling surge in the use of powerful narcotics, drawing above all upon alcohol and opium', approved by doctors and stimulated by a free market in drug sales. Leading physicians in the 1760s, such as Erasmus Darwin, used opiates widely 'as medical magic' to 'smooth the path to death'. Porter finds it difficult to be sure whether 'the pharmaceutical fix was intended to calm, stimulate, or to kill' in the eighteenth century, when 'people increasingly died insensible, stupefied with drugs, often medically prescribed', no longer prepared at every instant to meet their Maker.[38]

The Victorian evidence demonstrates a more disciplined use of opium in treating terminal pain, combined with a recognition of its value. Increasing regulation of opium developed in the later nineteenth century, as well as more precise management of doses, especially with the use of hypodermic injections of morphine. Devout Victorian Christians deprecated an extensive use of opium because it undermined the traditional 'good death' of fortitude in the face of suffering. But if dying people did not take opiates to alleviate the pain of diseases such as cancer, no other effective pain-killers were available, and their minds were likely to focus on their pain rather than the state of their souls.

The work of two later twentieth-century psychiatrists familiar with the use of opiates in modern British hospices is helpful in assessing their value in treating the dying. Dr Colin Murray Parkes argues, on the basis of his own experience as consultant psychiatrist at St Christopher's Hospice in Sydenham, that morphine can relieve most pain if properly administered. He considers it best introduced in treatment of painful diseases at an early stage, as soon as aspirin and other analgesics cease to work. Morphine remains in the blood for three to four hours, but it must be administered at regular intervals to sustain freedom from pain. If it shortens the life of a dying patient a little, this is less important than its ability to improve the quality of life in the terminal phase.[39]

John Hinton, Professor of Psychiatry at the Middlesex Hospital Medical School and an expert on the care of the dying, also argues that in a good hospice, 'with proper care and avoiding unnecessary parsimony over drugs, it was always possible to control pain in terminal cancer'.[40] Various studies have shown that about one person in eight suffers pain in the terminal illness, whereas hospice care substantially improves this figure. Hinton agrees with Parkes that regular and adequate doses of opiates are unequalled in controlling pain, while they also have a marked psychological action in easing fear and promoting calm. He also maintains that increased tolerance of large doses of morphine should not prevent its use for dying patients with chronic, severe pain.[41]

All nineteenth-century medical authorities on the care of the dying paid tribute to the supreme role of opiates in the control of pain. In the 1830s Professor C. W. Hufeland, the influential Prussian physician, declared that opium could not only remove the pangs of death but also impart 'courage

and energy for dying': 'Who would be a physician without opium in attendance on cancer or dropsy of the chest? How many sick has it not saved from
despair? For one of the great properties of opium is, that it soothes not only
corporeal pains and complaints, but affords also to the mind a peculiar
energy, elevation, and tranquillity.'[42] But Hufeland was not advocating massive overdoses, and was most concerned that 'dangerous remedies' should
never pass into the hands of the patient, especially in such quantities as might
endanger life.[43]

William Munk in *Euthanasia* in 1887 entirely agreed with Hufeland and
Sir Henry Holland that opium was invaluable in the care of the dying:
'Opium is here worth all the rest of the materia medica.' Munk emphasized
that opium should not be administered timidly or inadequately, but the
correct dosage should be measured by the relief afforded: 'If judiciously and
freely administered it is equal to *most* of the emergencies in the way of pain,
that we are likely to meet with in the dying', whereas doses that were too
small would be ineffective. He believed that opium's most important function was the relief of the feeling of 'sinking', that dreadful distress around the
stomach and heart, thus allowing the sufferer to die more easily and with
some composure, though not more quickly.

Munk insisted that the intended effects of the administration of opium to
the dying must be clearly defined; it should be used either as an anodyne to
relieve pain, or as a cordial to allay 'sinking and anguish about the stomach
and heart', but it should not be given primarily as a mere hypnotic to induce
sleep, though it might encourage sleep indirectly through pain relief. In
Munk's experience it was rare for the administration of opium to the dying
to cause confusion of the senses or the mind, and this would seldom occur if
its use were restricted to the relief of pain or severe sinking. Where such
confusion did occur, it was probably caused by either an 'idiosyncrasy' on the
patient's part or the inadequacy of the dose. Munk was careful to warn of the
contra-indications to the use of opium where it might actually hasten death,
for example where the air passages were obstructed, or the heart seriously
weakened, 'and where the conditions, directly or indirectly induced by opiates, especially that of sleep, may be just enough to turn the balance against
it'. Victorian doctors strongly advised against the indiscriminate opium abuse
and overdosing apparently so common a century earlier.[44]

Later medical authorities, such as Oswald Browne writing in 1894 and
Robert Saundby in 1902, followed Munk closely regarding the use of opium,
as also did the *Lancet*, which argued in 1888 that it was a neglect of medical
duty 'to withhold the inestimable boon afforded by opium in full doses' in
the last days of life.[45] As Saundby noted in his 1902 treatise on *Medical Ethics*,

opium could be given in large doses in hopelessly incurable and painful diseases, because 'the risk of the drug habit sinks into insignificance in the presence of approaching death'.[46]

Thus the nineteenth-century medical authorities were remarkably close to modern experts in their view of the use of opiates for the dying. They agreed that addiction was not a concern when a painful disease was terminal, and that the beneficial effects, if properly administered, vastly outweighed the rare detrimental influences. They also believed that opiates allowed the sufferer to die with some dignity, relatively free from pain and the distressing effects of sinking, and agreed that their aim was not to promote premature death or insensible stupefaction.

There are strong indications that Victorian physicians generally practised what they preached in relation to opiates. One of the most agonizingly painful deaths, already described in the previous chapter, was that of Ada Lady Lovelace from cancer in 1852. The detailed evidence of her case illuminates medical practice in the decade before hypodermic injections of morphine made pain relief both more effective and more precisely controlled. A number of Dr Locock's drug prescriptions for Lady Lovelace have survived. One directed: 'Take 10 drops of the Laudanum every 4 hours till I see you', while another stipulated 'no more Battly till the bowels have been relieved', unless the pain drove her to it.[47] (Battley's Sedative Solution was opium mixed with calcium hydrate, alcohol, sherry, and water.) On 6 January 1852, almost a year before her death, Ada told her mother, Lady Byron, that the pain was indescribable but the opiates were helping her to cope stoically: 'You think me philosophical about it; but I should *not* be so, if I did not get occasional intervals [free of pain]. *This* however, is only by means of narcotics, which *fortunately* produce no bad effects on me.'[48]

By spring 1852 laudanum could no longer control the pain and Ada was desperate enough to try anything her doctors would allow, orthodox or otherwise. Sir Gardner Wilkinson informed her of the benefits of cannabis in March 1852, but she did not take it constantly because it seemed to '*put me to sleep* rather strongly, and to be very quieting'. She recognized that it was not a drug to trifle with for the effects were 'very *definite*'.[49] This letter implies that laudanum had a less soporific effect, leaving her with more control. By April the pain was 'very hard to bear' after so many months: 'I believe we have tried *everything*, both local and general, to meet this evil. When very severe, *Chloroform* is the best and most effectual, but unfortunately only transient in its power.'[50] Chloroform was still a novelty in 1852 and, while effective in dealing with the temporary pain of operations and childbirth, it was hardly appropriate for long-term cancer pain. Ada Lovelace's mother, Lady Byron, was a forceful advocate of mesmerism (or hypnotism) as a therapeutic technique, but Ada found it less effective than opium for her '*Real* pains', just as her three sceptical doctors had warned in advance.

From mid-July 1852 the pain was constant and by 24 July Ada was at last informed that her disease was terminal and 'the *best* we can hope for is *only* continued pain'.[51] By 10 August she suffered 'the *severest* possible pain—which has quite appalled everyone'. Dr West now insisted on a rigorous regimen of pain management, calculating the maximum daily opium dose and its timing far more carefully, moderating the pain, though 'with the utmost difficulty'.[52] Lady Byron was able to report that Ada was much more composed on 17 August, owing to the suspension of the pain by opiates.[53] On many nights, however, despite the opium, Ada was 'dead sleepy and absolutely *torn* awake by agony'.[54] Detailed evidence ceased towards the end of August, but Ada's tormented suffering continued until 27 November, prolonged far beyond the expectations of the doctors, who clearly did not even contemplate an overdose of opium to end the torture. It would seem that Ada's doctors struggled to give appropriate doses of opiates to control almost continuous agonizing pain, though with increasingly limited success in the final months. In view of the detailed evidence of extreme pain for months, and insomnia and mental clarity despite the opiates, it is clear that Ada Lovelace was not deliberately rendered insensible by excessive doses of opiates.

Opium was regarded as highly beneficial in managing a number of terminal diseases in addition to cancer, 'from its power of sustaining the nervous and vascular systems', as well as helping difficulty in breathing. Several family references testify to its use in the final stages of consumption. When Mary Walcot was dying of tuberculosis in 1857, 'she managed to get thro' the night with taking Ether, Morphine, Brandy and Port Wine', which helped her to cope with extreme weakness, breathing difficulties, and pain.[55] The combination of ether, brandy, and port wine was commonly used as a stimulant for the weak heart and to promote the circulation, while brandy was additionally favoured for its aid to the digestive process. Ether was usually mixed with opium or laudanum as a powerful anti-spasmodic to treat difficulty in breathing.[56]

During Francis Blunt's prolonged consumptive illness in 1871–2 he was obliged 'to be constantly taking morphine. If he leaves it off even for a single day he falls away again.' The morphine was usually administered by his brother Wilfrid, the poet, but when he was away in March 1872 the local doctor found a man to follow Wilfrid's instructions: 'F wants his morphia at 7 in the morning, at 12, at $\frac{1}{2}$ past 5 and again before he goes to bed. It does not do to give much at a time and directly the effect wears off he is frantick for another dose.'[57] The only suggestion that Francis's mind was wandering a little as a result of the morphine came on the day of his death, but even in the hours before his death this confusion was only 'a little'.[58] Wilfrid's note on the required dosage suggests they were giving the minimum consistent with pain alleviation at intervals determined by the period of the drug's efficacy— perhaps a little less than Munk would have advised.

Family evidence suggests that the fear of addiction, so powerful in the later twentieth century, was already influencing medical behaviour as early as the 1890s. By then, morphine was not usually employed until a terminal illness was actually diagnosed, even if the patient was previously suffering pain from an unknown cause. Emily Giberne was suffering very severe pain which she could scarcely tolerate in 1896, but was only given morphine to ease the pain the night before she died. On the day of her death she said how nice it was to be free of pain, before sinking into a heavy sleep.[59] In 1898 after many months of fearful pain, which the doctors clearly believed the patient exaggerated, a cancerous swelling was finally diagnosed on W. E. Gladstone's palate. His daughter Helen commented, 'Now the doctors can feel it right to do all they can to ease the pain.'[60] In 1911 Geoffrey Howard thought his father's death 'shocking, fighting with great pain for some time until the doctor at last gave him opium, but only when he realised it was a hopeless case'.[61]

Prolonging Life and Hastening Death

Later twentieth-century doctors have a major ethical problem in deciding when to stop active treatments for dying patients. They have to determine how far they have a responsibility to prolong life, even poor-quality life dominated by unpleasant medication or technology. A minority of patients fear death so much that they prefer any misery and are willing to try any medical treatment which might just keep them alive. Parkes, Hinton, and others have argued that it is hard to justify such meddlesome medicine and that doctors have a responsibility to suspend treatment at a certain point.[62] The problem is exacerbated by technological advances, which enable mechanical aids to maintain an increasing number of vital functions during the terminal phase of a fatal disease. Hinton believes that there is little justification for using such aids, 'if they can only maintain a truncated semblance of life, as in a permanently unconscious being'.[63]

Victorian doctors were not faced with the same degree of difficulty in addressing this ethical question, for they lacked the later technological means to prolong life. Sir Henry Halford, in the early decades of the century,

recognized that 'disease runs a definite course, which cannot be advanta-
geously altered'.[64] Henry Holland in 1839 considered 'more mischief to be
done by needless protraction of the use of medicines' than by their premature
abandonment.[65] William Munk in 1887 argued 'the fewer the drugs and the
less of medicine' the better in treatment of the dying. He quoted Dr Ferriar's
injunction: 'The physician will not torment his patient with unavailing
attempts to stimulate the dissolving system.'[66] Dr Robert W. Mackenna,
writing as late as 1917, entirely agreed. Though it was the doctor's duty to
fight death, a wise physician would know when to cease the administration of
powerful stimulants like digitalis and strychnine.[67]

The family evidence suggests that doctors usually followed their own
advice on this question. For example, in 1876 the three doctors and the family
decided against medical intervention when the dowager Countess of
Carnarvon was dying of jaundice, as her son recorded in his diary: 'This
morning a serious question considered but decided in the negative as to
proposing an operation for plugging the nose. But it would involve pain, the
use of chloroform, in itself dangerous to her, and the gain would be so
problematical that we decided against it.' Lord Carnarvon felt that his mother
was dying so gently and mercifully, with so little suffering, that it would be
cruel to torment her needlessly. He had refused to allow such meddlesome
medicine when his first wife was dying, and he was equally opposed in his
mother's case.[68]

Victorian patients and their families generally preferred that the terminal
phase should not be prolonged by stimulants, once it was identified as
terminal. Many Christians who obviously knew that they were dying believed
that it was the will of God and had prepared themselves for death. Sir Charles
Mordaunt, who was dying of 'asthma' in 1823, suffered spasmodic pain and
prolonged attacks of fever. In the final days he was 'averse to medicine and
remedies' and only allowed his wife to apply a blister to his chest after much
persuasion. On the day of his death he commented that a visit by Dr
Johnstone would do no good. When his wife proposed some of Johnstone's
remedies, such as 'cataplasms' and embrocation for the feet, Sir Charles
objected gently and she apologized for 'teizing' him with such remedies.[69]
Sometimes the family felt stimulants were administered for too long, as did
Lord Lyttelton in the case of his wife's death from heart disease in 1857.
Similarly, in 1865, when Charlotte Keble was dying of dropsy and a weak
heart, John Keble feared that all the brandy and turtle soup they gave his wife
by day and night only served to enable her weakened system to live longer.[70]

The question of mercy killing was not debated with any great urgency in
the nineteenth century because doctors did not then possess mechanical aids,

such as cardiac stimulators and mechanical respirators, to prolong a limited form of life in a terminally ill patient. The issue of when to cease the application of such life-prolonging treatment did not arise, avoiding one of the most difficult aspects of the modern euthanasia debate. Until the late nineteenth century, as we have seen, Victorian doctors used the term 'euthanasia' to mean 'a calm and easy death', and the timing of its change of meaning is significant. It did not lose its original meaning until almost the turn of the twentieth century when doctors began to use it in the modern sense of mercy killing.[71] C. W. Hufeland used the term in the older, classical sense, stating that it was the doctor's most 'sacred duty' to effect 'the euthanasia', when he was unable to prevent termination.[72] Hufeland was totally opposed to any suggestion of hastening death. He admitted that when a patient occasionally prayed for death to end his incurable suffering, the doctor might consider whether it was permissible 'to rid the miserable sufferer of his burden a little earlier'. But he argued that such reasoning was false, 'and a mode of action based upon such principles would be a crime', for the aim of medicine was 'to preserve and, if possible, to prolong life'.[73]

Occasional essays by non-medical men advocated that doctors should be allowed to administer sufficiently strong doses of drugs to end cases of incurable and painful illness. Lionel Tollemache made such a case in the *Fortnightly Review* in 1873, claiming that doctors already gave strong narcotics to alleviate the final agony of the last stages of cancer, sometimes incidentally shortening the ordeal.[74] The *Lancet* in 1887 condemned such proposals by laymen, who usually called on the medical profession to confer the *coup de grâce* to hopeless cases, but who failed to appreciate the moral and legal obstacles in the path of such a course, which would be open to abuse by the unscrupulous. Doctors wisely declined such a responsibility because it was their primary duty to save life, sometimes even restoring it when all seemed to be lost. The *Lancet* proposed, however, that 'if the physician or surgeon may not shorten life methodically even under the most pressing circumstances, he may shorten pain and make the inevitable death easy and tranquil'. The *Lancet* warmly recommended Munk's *Euthanasia* as a guide to doctors on how far they could ethically aid an easy death, 'to the extent of alleviating acute sufferings, and, without hastening death, of making the approach to death peaceable. To this extent medical art may go; no further.'[75]

From the turn of the century the debate took a more modern turn, with a new and more familiar definition of euthanasia. In 1902 Dr Robert Saundby of Edinburgh discussed the subject in *Medical Ethics: A Guide to Professional Conduct*. He defined euthanasia quite clearly in its modern sense, rather than that used by Munk and others in the nineteenth century: 'By euthanasia, I understand the doctrine that it is permissible for a medical practitioner to give a patient suffering from a mortal disease a poisonous dose of opium or other narcotic drug in order to terminate his sufferings.' But the modern definition should not change the medical response. Euthanasia was contrary to the fundamental rule that doctors must 'hold human life sacred' and take no action which would deliberately destroy it. However, Saundby conceded that a distinction might be drawn between a dose of opium deliberately intended to cause death and a dose primarily to relieve pain, even though the latter might indirectly hasten death. In 1906 Dr S. Russel Wells addressed the Medico-Legal Society on the question of whether mercy killing was ever justifiable, concluding that it was not, since the dangers of abuse were too great. Errors of diagnosis and prognosis were possible, relatives might seek the death for personal gain, and it would create fear of the doctor as a purveyor of death rather than life.[76]

Two books written in the second decade of the twentieth century foreshadowed the modern euthanasia debate, assuming technological progress and the increasing medical ability to prolong life. Maurice Maeterlinck, a Belgian philosopher and poet, argued in 1911 that doctors contributed to the popular fear of death by their efforts to prolong life, instead of allowing people to die easily: 'As science progresses, it prolongs the agony which is the most dreadful moment and the sharpest peak of human pain and horror, for the witnesses, at least . . . All the doctors consider it their first duty to protract as long as possible even the most excruciating convulsions of the most hopeless agony.' This is a familiar charge today and one more justified in the 1990s than in 1916. Maeterlinck argued that people most dreaded 'the awful struggle at the end', while admitting that by then the sensibility of the dying person was often muted.[77]

Dr Robert Mackenna in 1916 devoted a chapter of his volume *The Adventure of Death* to a rather weak response to Maeterlinck's charges. He argued that the act of death was usually free from pain, and that pain-killing drugs such as opium relieved much of the suffering. He was aware that laymen and philosophers like Maeterlinck often argued that doctors should administer lethal doses of morphine to hopeless cases which were attended by great suffering. But such laymen did not have the final responsibility for the action, and it was easy to argue in the abstract for medical science to kill all incurables as acts of mercy. Mackenna insisted that medicine was the art of healing, 'not of dealing death', especially as human judgement was fallible and some sick people recovered. The physician's duty was to relieve the more intolerable pain by careful use of analgesics, and to make the last stage of life more comfortable, but not to become the 'arbiter of another's right to live'.

Mackenna further contended that arguments like Maeterlinck's were often primarily selfish: 'It is not the suffering of the patient, which applied medical skill is probably alleviating, but our own intolerance of personal distress which makes us shrink from the death-bed of a friend.'[78] This exchange again reflected fundamental changes in attitude and expectations since the early Victorian period.

It is scarcely surprising that most of the families examined in this book shared the ethical view of the doctors about mercy killing, since most of them were Christians, and any temptations to hasten death would have been stifled or remained secret. Only two such references survive, and these were fleeting temptations not acted upon. The first was the response of Lord Lovelace to his wife's agonizing suffering from cancer in 1852. Ada Lovelace, as a free thinker, told her husband, mother, and doctor in August 1852 that 'she was prepared to die and did not wish for life, as there were now no objects she could fulfil by living'. At this stage she still had three more months of appalling pain and suffering to endure, and she discussed this with her husband: 'She thinks the struggle may go on for months and prays that the termination may be near at hand. Alas when I witness the agony I am almost tempted to ask Is this necessary. Can not her slight and delicate organizations be spared this excess of aggravation?'[79] Even had Lord Lovelace considered acting on this temptation, he was given no opportunity, since, as we have seen, the final months of agony were presided over by Ada's formidable mother, who believed pain and suffering served a moral and spiritual purpose. As Ada's modern biographer noted, 'Surprising as it seems, so far from bringing her final relief with an overdose of narcotic, her attendants employed every possible precaution to extend her life.'[80]

The only extant discussion in these archives of mercy killing as a practical possibility in a Christian family came in 1886 at the final stage of a harrowing death from 'softening of the Brain'. Frank Rogers was just conscious, but 'childish and maudlin', and did not recognize his two nephews the day before his death:

[Uncle Frank] cried like a little child. It was a painful sight. Aunt Sabina discussed whether she should 'pull the pillow from under his head' by which [she] meant hasten his end by suffocation, after the manner of Othello or otherwise. She said she had heard that sometimes when people died the blood rushed to their faces and they were a horrible sight. However she [did] not murder him and the next day, when we called, he was dead and his face was of course the usual colour.[81]

The work of Dr Munk and other Victorian pioneers of medical care of the dying was largely forgotten in the half-century or so after 1920 and had to be reinvented by later twentieth-century writers who knew nothing of their predecessors. Twentieth-century progress in medical science has helped to transform attitudes to death, not only for doctors but also for other members of the community. The 1930s marked a significant turning-point in the relationship between medicine and death, with the advent of the sulpha drugs which could cure a wide range of disorders and vastly reduce mortality from bacterial diseases. Once doctors came to believe that they could cure most diseases, the death of a patient represented failure, rather than a landmark in life to be thoughtfully prepared for. The doctor is no longer perceived as the comforter of the dying, but as the medical professional who exercises scientific skills to avoid death, and who often prefers to evade the topic with patients. The fact that in Western societies modern death increasingly takes place in hospital has contributed to this transformation in outlook; death is now often removed from family life to a sterile institution concerned with routine and technical efficiency, inevitably depersonalizing the process of dying.

In 1965 the *Lancet* regretted that care of the dying was not a subject much discussed in the training of doctors—the very point made by the same medical journal in 1888—as if Munk had never lived. Medical students in the 1960s saw patients die in hospitals and were taught the basics of drugs and procedures, but were unlikely to know the earlier case histories or to appreciate the sufferers' emotional or spiritual needs. The *Lancet* in 1965 reiterated the Victorian belief that 'medicine has a duty to relieve suffering equal to that of preserving life'. It recommended that 'terminal illness was more likely to be managed successfully in well-organized, secure homes', with family support and familiar surroundings, rather than the intense loneliness of busy hospital wards catering for survivors: 'Advances in medical science and technology now make it possible to delay death and keep people "alive" long after what used to be the final crisis. Doctors strive to preserve life and relieve suffering, but the two may be incompatible. In mortal illness there comes a time when death alone will give relief and life-saving procedures can only prolong the act of dying.'[82]

In 1971 Russell Noyes, Jr., an American psychiatrist working in an Iowa state hospital, appealed for an increase in the doctor's knowledge of the dying process and its treatment, and much of his American evidence has relevance for modern Britain. He argued that 'the outlook for the dying person of today appears to be bleak despite the advancements of modern science'. According to Noyes there is no modern 'ideal to be striven for in dying', and the sufferer often faces pain, isolation, and indignity very much alone and unprepared, with few guide-lines and little comfort. Noyes argued that it was the physician's duty to continue the personal care of his patient throughout the terminal stage: 'He should strive to assist his patient in achieving a death which is fitting and appropriate according to the patient's character. The physician also must help to restore, maintain, or enhance his patient's faith in a universal order.'[83]

Modern medicine is still a substantial way from achieving Noyes's goal in the medical management of dying, but there has been some progress, generated in part by the AIDS epidemic. More hospices have been established on the lines of St Christopher's Hospice, Sydenham, to care for cancer patients in the terminal phase, which include the patient's family in the caring process; and some large hospitals and hospices now have a palliative-care team, including specialist nurses, psychologists, and social workers, to make home visits to facilitate domiciliary care of the dying. The work of doctors and psychiatrists concerned with terminal care, such as John Hinton, Elisabeth Kübler-Ross, and Cicely Saunders, has generated a rich literature analysing the subject from medical, sociological, and psychological perspectives. A 1991 text by an American medical sociologist, F. W. Hafferty, aims to educate doctors about death and the care of the dying, just as William Munk tried to do a century earlier.[84]

❧ 5 ❧

NURSES, CONSULTANTS, AND TERMINAL PROGNOSES

Women's Role as Nurses

Victorian medical experts on the care of the dying placed great emphasis on the all-important role of the family—especially its female members—in nursing the dying. Dr Oswald Browne expressed the doctors' view that the special secret of nursing the dying was 'the most constant close unwearying waiting upon them', combined with 'untiring thoughtfulness' about them.[1] Women in the family were expected to provide the major part of the loving care and the 'unwearying waiting' upon the dying. All sick people in these families were nursed at home, with rare exceptions at the end of the period when surgery was involved. Doctors observed that middle- and upper-class families were well situated to give excellent care to the dying, provided they received frequent reassurance and advice from their local doctors and consultant physicians. An editorial in the *Lancet* in 1861 argued that rich and poor alike had similar, simple needs when they were dying, but that these were best provided by the families of the comfortable classes:

Of medicines and drugs [the dying] need comparatively little, and the amount of food required is but small. What are needed are comforts. A little tender nursing other than by a pauper nurse, a cushioned chair to sit occasionally by the bedside . . . a small quantity of varied and delicate food, a draught of some refreshing or effervescent drink, all tendered with a little sympathy and kind forbearance . . . By such things as these it is that the kind and affectionate relatives of the sick of the better classes strive, and not unsuccessfully, as we all know, to mitigate the pains and penalties which attend the latter days of fading humanity.[2]

The care of the terminally ill depended above all on the quality of nursing care. Whether nurses were relatives, domestic servants, or trained or untrained nurses from outside the home, they were almost always female. Victorian social thought emphasized the 'natural' separation of the spheres along gender lines, with a rigid division of labour whereby males were supposedly fitted for the public sphere and females for the domestic realm. Nursing duties were regarded as women's work, just as much as domestic service, as Charlotte Maddon indicated in an essay entitled 'Nursing as a

Profession for Ladies' published in 1871: 'Where does the character of the "helpmeet" come out so strikingly as in the sick-room, where the quick eye, the soft hand, the light step, and the ready ear second the wisdom of the physician.'[3]

Nursing the sick and dying was a primary function of Victorian wives and mothers. Mary Ann Rogers, mother of Professor James Thorold Rogers, was frequently called on to nurse her brood of sixteen children through the decades, since she lived to 89 and eleven children predeceased her. At the age of 74 in 1856–7 Mary Ann Rogers and her daughter Louisa nursed her eldest son, George Vining Rogers, an alcoholic apothecary, for nine months. 'George's long illness has almost worn me and Louisa out, indeed I sometimes think it will be too much for her . . . [George was] obliged to be fed like a child and watched day and night, you cannot conceive the trouble and heavy expense he is to me.'[4] Mary Ann concluded that at her advanced age 'it is a sore grievous trial'. Nearly a decade later, at the age of 82 in 1865, she nursed her daughter Elizabeth, who was gravely ill with jaundice, but also demanding and selfish. Two months before her death, Elizabeth paid tribute to her mother's nursing skills: 'My dear mother is a splendid nurse. I only wish you could see how she plans and arranges for an invalid, old as she is she has lost none of the vigour of her mind, dear soul.'[5]

Many testimonies have survived to the tireless dedication of numerous wives and mothers at the deathbeds of their loved ones. In 1839 Canon W. V. Harcourt confessed that his wife's strength of mind and body had been severely tried by 'long and constant watching for three years, the last in extreme and ever-increasing anxiety' over the sick-bed of his young daughter Louisa, who died in 1839.[6] In 1852 Sir Henry Layard remarked on the wonderful devotion and patience of Lady Charlotte Guest in nursing her dying husband during his final year. Her attention to Sir John Guest was 'unremitting and nothing can exceed her watchfulness and devotion'. She endured the 'greatest trials' with exemplary good will, and 'is much harassed but bears up wonderfully'.[7] On the death of her husband in 1858 Elizabeth Horsley was grateful that her physical strength had allowed her to continue nursing him to the end. She knew that wives often reproached themselves when they had been persuaded to resign the care of their husbands to paid nurses.[8]

Nursing the sick and dying was also regarded as a natural role for daughters, especially spinster daughters, who regularly cared for elderly parents until they died. One spinster often remained at home in each generation of the larger Victorian families, suggesting that this may have been partly due to parental pressure, conscious or otherwise. W. E. Gladstone's unmarried sister

Helen was the chief family nurse when her mother died in 1835 and her father in 1851. Caroline and Louisa Cane were devoted spinster daughters who nursed both parents through degenerative illnesses. The void was immense when their father's death followed their mother's in the 1850s. As Louisa sadly observed, 'The loss or rather blank may be more felt when the greatest object in your life was the fostering and tending that loved one.'[9] In the Harcourt family, Sir William Harcourt's spinster sister Emily was the woman expected to nurse the sick and dying, including her father in 1871, her mother in 1876, and her sister Selina Morshead in 1883. Her brother's response in 1880, after she had nursed a dying relative, Colonel Francis Vernon, shows how far her work was taken for granted, referring to her 'labour of love and care which I know is that most congenial to your nature'. Sir William assured Emily that she had the 'consolation of feeling that you made his closing days more easy to him as you did to others before'.[10]

It is clear, however, that the wives, mothers, and daughters who nursed the dying in upper- and middle-class families often drew on the help of their female domestic servants, especially in the early and mid-Victorian decades. Brian Abel-Smith points out that 'historically the antecedents of the nursing profession were domestic servants. Indeed at the beginning of the nineteenth century, nursing amounted to little more than a specialized form of char-ring.'[11] Loyal family retainers often played a major role in nursing the elderly, and in caring for younger families struck by infectious diseases. When Eleanor Fazakerley's family was afflicted with typhoid in 1843, outside help from her sister was forbidden for fear of infection. Eleanor paid warm tribute, however, to the kindness of her two servants in sharing the nursing of her dying daughter: 'Charlotte and Bowles feel like relatives towards the dear child, and Charlotte's services no money could purchase or repay.'[12] When the five little daughters of A. C. Tait died of scarlet fever in 1852, his wife, Catharine, was only just recovering from her confinement, and all the practical nursing was shared between the family's housekeeper and the governess.

Domestic servants performed many of the heavier and more unpleasant tasks, sharing the vigils by the sick-beds, and laying out the body in the absence of a nurse. In 1865 the octogenarian Mary Ann Rogers received help in nursing her daughter Elizabeth from a servant named Sarah, who was 'almost worn out with fatigue'. A month later, however, Sarah was rewarded for her trouble by Elizabeth's widowed husband, Robert Parker, who gave her 'a pound and a suit of mourning, she deserved it, she did all in her power for poor dear Titty [Elizabeth]'.[13] These domestic servants attending the dying were usually female, though Sir John Gladstone insisted that his male retainers attend him in 1851, as well as his daughter. Three male servants were mentioned by name, including Sir John's clerk and his coachman, who were zealous about all 'external and manual offices' and shared the night watches.[14]

Family doctors also carried out many duties during terminal illnesses which would be regarded as part of the nurses' function today, further explaining why these doctors were so much in demand. The general practitioner frequently spent a substantial part of the final days with a wealthy dying patient, often staying the night to administer opiates or purgatives where necessary, though usually assisted by a female family member. The three local doctors who attended Sir John Gladstone's last illness in 1851 were described by his son as 'most kind and unwearied' in their attentions, with one of the three always present by day and night. They applied mustard plasters, fussed endlessly about the state of the old man's bowels, and advised when the time had come for the final farewells and the clergyman's last offices.[15] No doubt the doctors were well paid, but their presence and their care reassured the family that everything possible was being done.

Two general practitioners played a vital role in the last three months of Ada Lady Lovelace's prolonged illness in 1852. Ada described Drs West and Barwell as 'most attentive and excellent', quite willing to take turns at the night vigils, and to supervise her regime of food and opiates.[16] Late in August 1852 Barwell was obliged to take to his own bed, 'being quite exhausted with the severe labour of watching, mixing food and stimulants and the constant stooping down' to Ada's mattress on the floor.[17] Lady Byron, Ada's mother, also noted Dr Barwell's diligence, though with more than a hint of condescension: 'I have been obliged to provide another Medical Watcher, as Barwell was *seriously* affected by his extraordinary fatigues—he has been by far the most valuable and efficient . . . but he has less command over his feelings than I have, in looking at the victim.'[18] Barwell returned to Ada's side after his recovery, to be rewarded for his sympathetic attendance by a personal bequest of £200 on Ada's death, with the explanation that 'he has been very kind and good to me'.[19] Drs West and Barwell were not unusual in their diligence, and while they were well paid for their labours, they performed nursing duties far beyond the expectations of twentieth-century doctors.

Many family letters attest to the nursing services of local general practitioners, especially in the early and mid-Victorian years, before the nursing reforms of the 1870s. In 1844, during the last illness of Caroline Fox, niece to Charles James Fox, her nephew reported that Dr George had been most attentive, sleeping in the house for two nights: 'he really seems quite touched and attached'.[20] Frederick Goulburn in 1856 was immensely grateful to Drs

Martin and Watson for their 'constant and unremitting attendance' during his father's final illness; Frederick had not even dared to offer Dr Watson a fee for his extra morning visits, for fear of offending him.[21] Even late in the century, when professional nurses were available, wealthy families still sometimes employed their devoted general practitioner to nurse the dying patient. On the twentieth day of his wife's fatal typhoid fever in 1890, Herbert Luckock observed that the family's regular doctor was living in the house day and night, while a Cambridge doctor had also spent three or four nights there.[22]

These family papers contain few references to the employment of trained or untrained nurses from outside the household before the 1870s. In 1844 Mary Reid employed a nurse named Mrs Winks to help with the terminal care of her consumptive daughter Letty, which had become too great a burden for her mother. Letty was pleased with her new nurse, who was cheerful and 'knows exactly what to do', owing to previous experience with consumptive patients.[23] In 1866 Sarah Acland reassured her son that his grandfather William Cotton had an excellent nurse, 'such a tall person, who can lift him very comfortably'.[24] The occasional reference to these early nurses could be favourable, but more were critical. Few families employed nurses before the 1870s because they had a poor reputation, aptly characterized by Mrs Gamp in Charles Dickens's *Martin Chuzzlewit*. Elizabeth Horsley in 1854 wished that her daughter-in-law had a more efficient nurse during her last illness: 'Ann means well but she is very stupid,' causing a good deal of annoyance.[25] In 1862 Lady Clarendon consoled her sister-in-law Lady Lewis on the imminent death of her little grandson Julian Harcourt, and shared her anxiety about the role of an alcoholic nurse: 'I wish Ferguson [the doctor] had not mentioned his apprehensions about the spirit drinking nurse for it can only be a conjecture and it will make them both think that the calamity might have been averted if they had dismissed the woman sooner.'[26] The Tait family had the same problem in 1877, during the last illness of the elderly John Tait in Edinburgh. The male nurse, Scott, was considered very attentive, 'but he requires not to be let out alone [because of] his sad longing for *drink*'.[27] This unsavoury perception of early and mid-Victorian nurses was reinforced by Charlotte Maddon's statement in 1871 in a journal article on nursing: 'Many a wife and mother has continued night and day to watch by the sick-bed, who would gladly have taken proper rest had she been able to trust the nurse.'[28]

Looking back from the lofty heights of the progress made in nursing by 1887, Dr William Munk condemned 'the class of old, ignorant and prejudiced nurses' who could do so much harm at the sick-bed. By contrast, 'In the intelligent trained nurses of the present day, we have the best security against such barbarity,' reinforced by female family attendants.[29] Only twenty years earlier, Florence Nightingale had described nurses as generally 'too old, too weak, too drunken, too dirty, too stolid, or too bad to do anything else'.[30] As a reformer Miss Nightingale overstated her case, but from the 1870s the standard of nursing care did improve immeasurably, with the introduction of nursing training for educated gentlewomen, initiated by the Nightingale training school in 1860, and spreading throughout the voluntary hospitals by 1900. By 1901 there were over 69,000 nurses in England and Wales, mostly female, and over half of these worked in patients' homes.[31]

Abel-Smith has shown that the wealthy classes, who preferred to look after their sick at home, began to recognize the value of employing skilled nurses from the 1870s. Hospitals were still regarded as institutions for the poorer classes, where cross-infection and death were likely companions. From the 1870s the prosperous classes increasingly employed trained nurses, who welcomed work in private households because the pay was higher and the work less exacting than in the hospitals. A nurse working in private homes could expect to earn two guineas per week with meals included, or £30 to £50 a year on a salaried basis, while the domestic servants could be called upon to assist with heavier labour. Outside London the demand for qualified nurses outstripped the supply, though in the metropolis the wealthy could employ the best domiciliary nurses from the voluntary hospitals or the more reputable nurse-supply agencies.[32]

The positive response to nursing reforms was reflected in the rapid increase in the employment of trained nurses for dying patients from the 1870s. Two 'regular sick-nurses' were engaged to care for Margaret Gladstone, dying of puerperal fever in 1870, and the sick woman thanked the nurses several times for their kindness. A nurse was employed for Alice Blunt when she was dying of tuberculosis in 1872, and for Mark Pattison, dying of stomach cancer in 1884, though the women in these families shared the load with the professional nurses.[33] In a few cases the family did not find the nurse congenial or trustworthy and continued to do most of the nursing themselves, as during the last illness of Lawrencina Potter in 1882.[34] Few of these employed nurses were recognized in family letters or diaries as human beings with full names; they were treated like occasional staff, with a status somewhere between that of governesses and domestic servants.

Despite the welcome assistance of trained nurses from the 1870s, female members of middle- and upper-class families like the Aclands continued to carry a large share of the burden of nursing the dying, often at considerable cost to their own health. After the death of Sir Thomas Acland, tenth baronet, at Killerton in Devon in 1871, his daughter Agnes Mills and her sister-in-law Mary Acland were both ill for some time as a result of their 'long watching'.[35] While Lieutenant Gilbert Acland was dying slowly over twenty months up to March 1874, he was nursed by his stepmother, Mary Lady Acland, and his sister Agnes, still living at home before her marriage. Sarah Acland commented that 'poor Aunt Mary is getting much worn' after such prolonged strain.[36] Angie Acland, a 38-year-old spinster, described the family's nursing arrangements at her mother's death in Oxford in 1878. One of the 'three Miss Greens' came as nurse at night, remaining until the doctor called in the morning, when Angie shared the daytime nursing with Minnie Buckland, the 'nice' Devonshire housemaid. Angie's father, Dr Henry Acland, a successful physician, considered that his daughter was 'acting nobly', and evidently saw no need for a professional daytime nurse. She was subsequently expected to devote the next twenty-two years of her life to her widowed father's health and comfort, including nursing him through his final illness.[37]

Further down the social scale it was also expected that the women in the family would supplement the trained nurses, when the family could afford them. When Margaret MacDonald was dying in 1911, a friend, Edith Bell, wrote to offer her own services as 'an exceptionally experienced nurse', when the trained nurse was off duty, but she supposed Margaret's half-sister would be 'supplementing the professional nurses'.[38] Ellen Webster, another friend of the Ramsay MacDonald family, 'managed wonderfully' in nursing her husband alone until about two months before his death, when she was obliged to employ a trained nurse, for she was near collapse through want of sleep; by then her husband was unconscious most of the time, and she was 'content to have the Nurse relieve me'.[39] In cases where the family could not afford trained nurses at all, as when Mary Middleton was dying of cancer in 1911, female relatives and friends took up all the responsibilities of nursing. Mary's sister Agnes looked after her 'with quiet devotion', even when herself unwell, until she was called north by pressing duties, when a close friend, Alice Todd, replaced her in the final weeks of suffering.[40]

This pattern of care of the dying, based in the home and with the family assuming a significant role in the nursing, is increasingly seen today as a model to be copied. Many of those involved in modern hospice work believe most people still prefer to die in their homes, and encourage hospice terminal care in the home rather than in-patient hospice units. But even today a disproportionate burden of home care of the dying still falls to wives and daughters, who may also have to resolve the competing demands of paid employment and other family commitments.

Consultants and their Advice

Wealthy families frequently requested consultations with additional physicians. Irvine Loudon has shown that general practitioners have been regarded as subordinate to the élite consultants and specialists since 1850, but before that time the medical hierarchy was more fluid and confused, particularly outside London.[41] Since there was no medical cure for most serious illnesses, and treatment was largely empirical, individual doctors often varied widely in their advice. If the ministrations of the local doctor failed to improve the patient's situation, the family might then turn to one or more fashionable consultants who were favoured at the time by the wealthy families they knew. The number of such specialists consulted could be quite large when a family was confronted with the likely death of a loved one and wanted to be sure they had explored all possible avenues. Indeed doctors joked among themselves about the farcical situations which could arise through over-use of consultations. Dr F. Parkes Weber recalled the common joke that 'the more doctors there are in consultation on a case the less likely the patient is to recover'. In similar vein, Sir William Lawrence claimed that he had not known patients to recover when more than seven doctors had been consulted.[42]

Nineteenth-century medical authorities discussed the value and the limitations of consultations. Professor C. W. Hufeland offered detailed advice in 1846, prefacing his remarks with a general comment on the problematical nature of consultations. If doctors agreed, then a consultation seemed of no value, while diverse opinions caused confusion in treatment. He conceded that consultations could be useful when a disease was complex, leaving the doctor uncertain about his treatment, or when the patient lost confidence in the doctor. But Hufeland insisted that several conditions must apply to render a consultation useful. No more than two, or at most three, experienced physicians should be consulted, who should not be enemies, nor 'obstinate partisans of different sects'. He was concerned that physicians often seemed chiefly anxious to demonstrate their own importance, and to discredit the treatment of the ordinary medical attendant. Accordingly he advised that the patient should never be allowed to witness the consultation—only be informed of its result afterwards. Hufeland believed it was cruel to the patient to indicate that earlier treatment had been wrong, but if consultants and attendant doctors could not agree on diagnosis and treatment, an appeal to the patient's verdict was necessary.[43]

Further light on the work of the consultant physician is provided by the 1884 memoir of Dr Charles J. B. Williams, Professor of Medicine at University College London in the 1840s. In 1847–8 Williams received only £420 as Professor of Medicine, compared with £2,749 from his rapidly growing private practice, which largely comprised consultations. Most of his cases were new, seen for the first time and often for that one time only. Like most consultants Dr Williams believed the early Victorian fee of one guinea was insufficient remuneration for the time and skill bestowed on a new case.[44] According to the *Lancet*, many consultants were charging three times this amount by 1858, compared with the meagre 5s. to 10s. 6d. received by the general practitioner.[45]

An anonymous patient recalled his physicians from a rather different perspective in 1891. He remembered the attentions of consultant specialists as 'most expensive and elaborate', especially when called from London to the provinces at a fee of a guinea a mile. The patient suspected that most consultations were unnecessary, for they often took place when it was too late to be of use, yet 'it is a satisfaction for friends to know that everything has been tried'. The patient concluded ironically that medical men had no sympathy with the contemporary educational doctrine of payment by results.[46]

Family records suggest that the anonymous patient was correct in his claim that most consultations were too late, but they still provided immense reassurance. In 1843 Miss Catharine Sharpe had considerable faith in Dr Bright's opinion on the brain injury of her brother Sutton, but she still insisted on the necessity of outside advice from Dr Chambers. She wished to ensure that no family members could blame any future deterioration in Sutton's condition on Dr Bright's current medical treatment. It was also important 'to let Sutton hear from Dr Chambers a confirmation of the plan Dr Bright has pursued . . . At any rate two being of the same opinion will have more weight with him than one.'[47]

Relatives were often comforted by the frequent attendance of several consultants, even though they seemed able to do little, as at the death of the third Earl of Carnarvon in 1849, after a series of strokes. His wife was prepared to pay a substantial sum for at least two consultants to travel fairly frequently from London or Oxford to Richmond, sometimes staying overnight. In February 1849 Lady Carnarvon consulted a new physician in search of an opinion other than that of Dr Bunny, their old family doctor, as she told her eldest son:

We are just come from Mr Jolly, and I cannot help having much hope that he has discovered a new cause for dear Pappy's Illness . . . You must take care when you see Bunny not to allude to anyone else having been consulted privately. At all events, whether there be anything or not in it, it has done [Pappy] good, cheered him, roused him, given him something of a different kind to think about.[48]

Two months later, Lady Carnarvon had evidently lost faith in Jolly's new approach and was again writing to Dr Meryon, her London physician, describing her uneasiness about her husband's condition, 'begging him to come if he thought it necessary'.[49] When Dr Acland of Oxford visited another patient in Richmond, only two days after Dr Meryon's visit, she took advantage of the situation to obtain still further advice—eliciting Dr Acland's cautious verdict that her husband was no worse.[50] Lady Carnarvon was under prolonged strain in nursing her husband for so many months, and evidently gained comfort from such consultations, though her family understood that medical knowledge had its limits, and believed that death was in the hands of God.

W. E. Gladstone's account of his father's death in December 1851 shows that Lady Carnarvon's need for the reassurance of medical experts was not an isolated experience. Sir John had reached the advanced age of 87, but he was a formidable baronet and head of the clan, as well as being an exceptionally wealthy man. Therefore no expense was spared in satisfying family, retainers, and friends that the best medical advice had been taken, even with little or no hope. In such cases the local practitioners were usually only too happy to obtain second and third and even fourth opinions of the experts, especially if they were baffled or simply wanted to cover themselves against any charge of liability if the patient died. Often the local doctor initiated the suggestion to seek expert advice. In Sir John Gladstone's case, the three local Fasque doctors expressed their fears of imminent death, prompting the family to discuss with them the advisability of sending for a consultant physician— either Professor Miller or Professor James Simpson from Edinburgh. The local doctors 'quite approved of sending to Edinburgh for the best aid'. Sir John Gladstone's daughter Helen, his chief nurse, selected Simpson as the family's first choice of consultant, but the family was clear about Simpson's role: it was agreed between William Gladstone, Dr Guthrie, one of the local doctors, and Mr Irvine, the family's clergyman, that Professor Simpson's visit was a 'propriety more than anything else'.[51]

Professor James Simpson arrived at Fasque at 11 p.m. on 1st December 1851 and stayed for ten hours throughout the night, taking just three hours' rest. After a careful examination, Simpson concluded that Sir John was suffering from 'old man's fever', a diagnosis which reduced the consultant's scruples about departure, since medical science could do little, whereas family support was crucial. When Sir John had a stroke on 4 December, Helen asked the local doctors if they should send for Simpson again, but Dr Guthrie saw no medical reason for this, though it might give 'moral satisfaction'. Under these circumstances the three sons agreed that it was not proper to divert Simpson again from his normal practice.[52]

In most cases consultant physicians seem to have reached agreement about the nature of the case by the time they passed their verdict on to the family. Since they were so often called in at an advanced stage of the disease, this often meant no more than an agreement that death was likely, with some advice on nursing care. But in a minority of cases, consultants disagreed with each other, or with the local doctor, about either diagnosis or treatment. As Hufeland's book noted, in such cases the patient or his family had to decide between the conflicting opinions. Poor Archibald Tait, Dean of Carlisle, faced such a dilemma in 1856, when he was suffering the ordeal of watching five little daughters die of scarlet fever within three weeks. Four had already died when May became the subject of medical debate, as Dean Tait noted in his detailed account: 'There was a disagreement of opinion amongst the doctors. I shall never forget being called in to decide between them.' Dr Barnes thought May's brain was affected, while Mr Page and Dr Goodfellow attributed the continued delirium to the accumulated weakness of the disease. The immediate question at issue was whether to apply leeches or use stimulants to keep up the patient's strength. The father considered it 'a sad trial' to be called to reach a verdict which might determine his daughter's fate, and his decision against the leeches did not save May's life. None the less, despite this traumatic experience, Dean Tait was full of praise for the consultants and the local medical attendants, commenting that 'nothing could exceed the attention of all the Doctors', with tributes to their care and kindness.[53]

Telling the Truth to Dying Patients

Roy Porter has cited Thomas Sheridan to argue that, in the later eighteenth century, 'people were no longer allowed their own deaths; for, in the name of sympathy and avoiding distress, their families and doctors were allowing them to slip away oblivious to their fate'. Porter recognizes that this degree of evasion and outright concealment of danger may not have been characteristic, but he notes that such practice continued in the early nineteenth century with the career of Sir Henry Halford: 'With patients he recognized to be dying, it was Halford's policy long to withhold the truth, and instead to give prevarications or cheerful prognostications.'[54]

But the family evidence suggests that Victorian medical practice differed substantially from that described for the Georgian period when doctors were more likely to be influenced by the rationalism of the Enlightenment. If Sir Henry Halford's practice is examined more closely, the truth about mortal illness was divulged in the most considerate way. Halford presented his view of the physician's duty towards a dying patient in his 1831 lecture to the College of Physicians. He saw the doctor's first duty as extending the patient's life by 'all practicable means'. But 'at the same time I think it indispensable to let his friends know the danger of his case the instant I discover it', to allow the patient time to repent and set his or her spiritual affairs in order.[55] Halford argued that it was better for the family to warn the patient of the danger, under the guidance of the doctor, because relatives did not entirely destroy hope, whereas there was no appeal against a physician's sentence of death (except perhaps to another physician). But, if the family was not available, Halford always advised the patient that death was approaching, believing that no human being should meet his Judge unprepared. Halford concluded that no inflexible rule could be established, for every such case must be considered on its merits.[56] Dr William Munk, in his 1895 biography, emphasized that Halford was keenly aware of the influence of the mind on the body, especially the power of hope in aiding nature's recuperative powers. Halford's sanguine temperament encouraged him to take the most favourable view he honestly could of a patient's condition.[57]

Professor C. W. Hufeland of the University of Berlin was the only prominent medical authority published in Victorian Britain to support full concealment of a patient's terminal condition. In 1836 Hufeland published *On the Relations of the Physician to the Sick*, which was reprinted in many editions and was translated into several languages, including English in 1846.[58] Hufeland provided an extreme statement of the argument that the physician should never reveal to a patient that the illness was incurable:

The Physician, therefore, must be careful to preserve hope and courage in the patient's mind, represent his case in a favourable light, conceal all danger from him . . . Least of all should he betray uncertainty or irresolution, even though there be cause for doubt . . . To announce death is to give death, which is never the business of him who is employed to save life.[59]

However, Hufeland's work, while evidently well known in Britain, appears not to have influenced British medical opinion on this sensitive issue. In a preface the editor of the English edition of Hufeland's book took pains to dissociate himself from Hufeland's extreme views on this vexed question. Even the sanguine Sir Henry Halford, while sharing Hufeland's belief in the power of hope, stopped short of the Prussian doctor's conclusion.

Most Victorian authorities on medicine and medical ethics advocated telling the truth to dying patients, but there were considerable differences as to timing and manner. An editorial in the *Lancet* in 1869 on 'the ethics of prognosis' came close to Halford's view on the ethical question, while admitting the differences which existed among medical men. Some physicians were hopeful, even when they feared patients must eventually succumb, whilst others were gloomy at the slightest deterioration, and both approaches enjoyed a degree of success. The *Lancet* advocated a favourable prognosis, as far as this could be given consistently with the facts, since the primary duty of the physician was to bring comfort and to prolong life. Placing the best construction on unfavourable symptoms might extend a life because doctors could be wrong about the gravity and significance of symptoms. But where a hopeful diagnosis was inapplicable, then a plain statement of the truth, however unpalatable, was the doctor's clear duty. In all cases where death was the inevitable outcome, it was immoral as well as unkind for a doctor to be otherwise than candid.[60]

Dr William Munk, a devout Catholic as well as being the most influential Victorian writer on the care of the dying, emphasized the importance of informing the patient of impending death, earlier rather than later. He advised against postponing this warning until dissolution had already commenced, for it was important to allow time for the dying person to recover from the initial shock and regain a natural serenity: 'if the communication be made tenderly and with prudence, nothing but good is likely to result from it'. Munk shared Halford's view that this warning was best imparted by the family 'under the suggestions of the physician', but if this was impossible, then the doctor should prepare the patient 'to meet his Creator and Judge'.[61]

Most other nineteenth-century medical writers agreed with Munk and Halford rather than Hufeland. Sir Henry Holland in 1855 believed that the risks supposed to follow from telling a dying person the truth were usually overstated: 'Suspicion of a painful truth often disturbs more than the truth plainly stated.'[62] Professor Charles J. B. Williams recognized that the ignorance or fear of some patients made it occasionally expedient to 'minimise or mitigate' a serious announcement of dangers to their health; 'But to conceal them altogether, and still more to flatter false hope by denying their existence, is as unwise and unfeeling, as it is immoral.'[63] The prominent obstetrician and surgeon Dr Matthews Duncan argued in 1886 that adults had the right to know the condition of their own bodies and their likely prospects, and doctors had no right to mystify or deceive their patients.[64] Dr Robert Saundby's treatise on medical ethics, first published in 1902, insisted that in all cases of serious illness the patient's family should be told the truth first. Where a patient insisted on knowing the truth he should be informed, 'saying no more than is expedient', which was not usually difficult because few patients pressed such questions. This was a painful duty for the doctor, but unavoidable.[65]

Family evidence shows that medical practice on this issue broadly followed the guide-lines of Halford, Munk, and the *Lancet*. But there were variations in timing and manner, according to the religious beliefs and the temperament of the doctor, his relationship with the patient, and his assessment of the patient's ability to come to terms with the medical diagnosis. Halford, Munk, Charles Williams, Alfred Carpenter, and Sir Benjamin Brodie, to name but a few, were all influenced by their Christian belief in the need for spiritual preparation and in the consolations of a life after death. Two other relevant variables were the state of medical knowledge of the disease concerned, and the doctor's ability to make an accurate diagnosis. Despite such variations, the majority of cases demonstrated the physician's candour in informing the patient that his or her condition was dangerous, with some tendency towards increased reticence in the early twentieth century.

Where the doctors understood the nature of the disease and the signifi-cance of the symptoms, they were usually honest and direct. Two cases from the early 1850s show that even the same physician, Dr Charles Locock, could vary his prognostic behaviour according to the nature and speed of the disease and the age of the patient. As the Gladstone family physician, Locock was open and explicit in his advice to W. E. Gladstone about his 4-year-old daughter's illness from tubercular meningitis in 1850. As soon as Locock began to think Jessy was suffering from inflammation of the brain, he informed Gladstone accordingly. Locock was able to identify the dreaded disease with certainty and knew its fatal impact would be swift. Two days before Jessy's death, Locock 'explained the peculiar malignancy of the disease, its insidious character and fluctuating form and symptoms', warning that the crisis could be prolonged for up to three weeks. The next day Locock 'did not conceal from us that humanly speaking all was at an end'.[66]

Dr Locock treated the case of Ada Lady Lovelace very differently, because the disease was prolonged over eighteen months and he was initially uncer-tain of his diagnosis. Ada died a slow and excruciatingly painful death in November 1852, as we have seen. Dr Charles Locock evidently thought that a terminal prognosis should be revealed slowly in a prolonged illness, but that broad hints at earlier stages might prepare the patient, though the final bad news should be given honestly and bluntly. In June 1851 Dr Locock con-firmed in a letter to Lord Lovelace, Ada's husband, that there was 'a very deep and extensive ulceration on the neck and mouth of the womb'; surprisingly, Locock pronounced this condition 'perfectly curable' with proper care and rest over a prolonged period.[67] Sir James Clark and Dr Robert Lee, who were consulted at the same time, were more pessimistic, suspecting uterine cancer.[68] This difference of opinion indicates that Locock's reputation for optimistic diagnoses was justified. Dr West, Ada's general practitioner, later defended Locock: 'There seemed for some months to be reason for hoping that the disease might not be cancerous, and clinging to that hope various measures both local and constitutional were employed by Dr Locock with temporary benefit.'[69]

As Ada's anxiety and pain increased, she experimented with different treatments and sought more varied medical advice, orthodox and unorthodox. By November 1851 'the constant *locomotion*' of visiting so many doctors was causing exhaustion as well as confusion. But she concluded that Locock's treatment of her 'miserably disagreeable case . . . must be right', since Sir James Clark, Dr Cape, Mr Henderson, and Dr Robert Lee all confirmed it.[70] Two months later, Ada Lovelace was far more uneasy about Locock's optimistic diagnosis, as she confessed to her mother, especially as his comments to her family were more cautious: 'It seems such a formidable complaint, and Dr L's tone both to you and to others was *not* that of confidence.'[71] Ada learned from her mother and husband that Dr Locock feared that her 'uterus is *destroyed* as to all vital functions' and her case might become ultimately incurable. But Ada's desire to call in Dr Protheroe Smith for a further opinion met with an arrogant and emotional veto from Dr Locock, prompted perhaps by frustration at his own failure, combined with irritation at the array of consultants questioning his judgement:

I wish to have no consultations—they will only hamper me, and I will have none of them, unless at my own proposition, feeling at a loss or in a difficulty. No one who has not watched the case as I have done can possibly judge fairly, and if I am to be bothered with strange people coming in, I decline having any further charge of you . . . and I have no particular confidence in Dr Protheroe Smith.[72]

By July 1852 Ada Lovelace came to a complete understanding of the full horror of her situation, though she learned the truth by degrees and partly at second hand through her family. Two doctors examined her and afterwards made Lord Lovelace '*fully aware* of the grave nature of the case', so that he was unable to elicit any words of hope or encouragement. This impressed Lovelace so powerfully that he asked his wife to 'leave nothing *unsettled*'.[73] Some days later Dr Locock at last told his patient the truth: 'Dr Locock does *not conceal* his *now* less favorable view of my case. He always promised me to be open and truthful to me, and I believe he is. He now no longer speaks with any *confidence*. He simply hopes.' Locock conceded that the best to be hoped for was '*only* continued pain', but assured Ada that 'you will take a long time in killing'.[74] Dr West informed her in August that her disease was making 'great progress', and her life might last a few months but not a year.[75] She survived another three months, with the 'intolerable anguish' intermittently controlled by careful administration of opiates.

This case shows the doctors in a poor light in the earlier stages of the disease, when the diagnosis was still in doubt. Locock's temperament encouraged hope, since there was no cure and he knew that the illness would be prolonged and agonizing. Only when Ada was in continual, excruciating pain was Locock prepared to remove all hope from his patient, allowing her time to prepare to die. As in other instances, once all the doctors were agreed that the case was terminal and had so informed the patient, their care of the sufferer improved substantially.

Other early and mid-Victorian evidence also suggests that medical candour was the norm, though the timing varied, and sometimes the initiative was left to the patient. In 1864 Jane May Gladstone, suffering from diphtheria, asked the family physician, Mr Phillips, if he thought she was dying, and he replied that he 'greatly feared it was really so'.[76] A year later, the doctors were gentle in telling John Keble that his wife, Charlotte, was dying, but their diplomacy did not conceal the truth. At first they merely said they did not expect a cure, but the family might hope for some improvement. Later they ceased to say even that, but expressed surprise that 'the worst symptoms do not come on so fast as [they] expected'.[77] When Francis Blunt was dying of consumption in 1871, the doctors were always frank about their grave opinion of the case in talking to his brother and sister-in-law; four months before his death, as in Ada Lovelace's case, they warned the patient himself how serious his illness was.[78]

There are many examples of doctors continuing to tell the truth to the dying patient in the late Victorian and Edwardian periods. In April 1878 Dr Andrew Clark confirmed the family's fear that Samuel Sharpe's daughter Mary would be the fourth of his children to die from consumption. Yet the patient and her family were relieved by this announcement, as Mary's aunt Lucy Sharpe explained: 'She [Mary] is better however today; and wonderfully bright and cheerful,—relieved I feel sure in her mind, that her family know what she has long felt sure of—and they too are cheered by her cheerfulness and so will help each other thro' another nursing if that must be.'[79] In 1885 Adelaide Anson wrote of her father's impending death, 'Yesterday Dr Huxley took quite another tone—very kind and sympathetic, but telling us we must expect increased pain, and not giving us any hope of any cure, or restored power of walking.'[80] The fourth Earl of Carnarvon died in 1890 at the age of 59, suffering from cancer of the liver, attended by E. B. Turner, FRCS. Early in the course of the illness, Carnarvon asked Turner to tell him the nature of the disease and the likely outcome, saying that he trusted Turner to explain the exact condition in plain words which he could understand. When the doctor obliged, Lord Carnarvon displayed courage and perfect faith under a sentence of death which he thoroughly understood.[81] When Louisa Duchess of Atholl was dying of galloping consumption in 1902, at least one doctor spoke his mind plainly; Dr Anderson told her that if she wanted to settle her affairs she should do it immediately or she might soon get worse and lose control of her mind.[82]

But there were many occasions when Victorian doctors could not be certain of the prognosis or its timing, however great their desire for honesty. In many chronic illnesses, even today, it is difficult to assess at all accurately the period of remaining life. This was even more problematical a century ago, when doctors were more often uncertain of the diagnosis and understandably reluctant to commit themselves to the likely timing of death. Three examples will demonstrate how Victorian doctors reacted in such circumstances, especially when there was considerable pressure on them for an honest verdict— at the deaths of Henry Goulburn in 1856, Revd Cyril Wood in 1870, and Revd Crauford Tait in 1878. All three families were committed Christians who believed that the final verdict depended rather more on the will of God than on the doctors.

In 1855 Frederick Goulburn was particularly anxious to discover the doctors' honest prognosis on the lung disease of his father, Henry Goulburn, MP. If his father was really dying, then it was imperative to recall home to England his elder brother, Edward Goulburn, for a final farewell. By the end of December 1855 Dr Watson, the London consultant, and the two local doctors considered the case 'very precarious' and the outcome 'eminently uncertain'.[83] Frederick explained his dilemma to his brother, Edward:

The fear is, that should it be God's will that he should get worse—which not being able to see into the future we none of us can say—and which all the doctors cannot decide for me further than I have explained . . . His amount of strength being so small there might not be time to get you back. I can but act by the joint opinions of the 3 doctors and even they can but little relieve me from the anxious responsibility of my position. . . . We can only trust in God.[84]

Frederick kept a detailed diary of the final weeks of his father's illness, partly, at least, to justify his conduct in his brother's eyes, particularly stressing all the occasions on which the two or three doctors entirely agreed. Frederick eventually telegraphed for his brother on 7 January 1856, five days before their father died. Only on 9 January was Dr Martin able to tell Frederick that his father had 'no hope of ultimate recovery', and Edward did not receive the message in time to return home for his father's death on 12 January 1856.[85]

The doctors attending the final illness of Revd Cyril Wood in 1869–70 had an equally strong reason for telling patient and family the truth about the patient's condition, but again the illness did not permit an exact prognosis about the timing of death. In this case there were strong humanitarian reasons for sympathetic doctors to prevaricate. Wood was dying very slowly of heart disease, aggravated by overwork and repeated attacks of gout, lung congestion, and rheumatism.[86] The problem became more complex because he believed he should resign from his living if he could be certain that he was dying, thereby relinquishing the family home and income. His wife, Eleanor Wood, was most reluctant for her husband to resign the living unless they were absolutely certain that he would not recover.[87]

In this delicate situation the doctors were well aware how much depended on their medical prognosis. Given the nature of the disease they did not know how long Wood was likely to live, but the family circumstances encouraged them to be sanguine. In November 1869 Eleanor Wood reported to her brother Roundell Palmer that both Dr Blake and Mr Rowse held firm to their original diagnosis of 'organic' heart disease.[88] Eleanor Wood's sister Emma Palmer saw little to give them hope in Dr Blake's comments over the past week: 'He makes no absolute verdict, but he has seen enough former practice not to dare to say there is no organic mischief in any doubtful case . . . I know Dr Blake does not *expect* him to be downstairs again though he is very cautious in predicting anything.'[89]

Three months before Revd Cyril Wood finally died in May 1870, Dr Henry Acland assumed a role which transcended the purely medical in advising the family as to their most appropriate course of action. Dr Blake and Mr Rowse had led the family to believe it was almost impossible for Wood to recover, and that immediate resignation of the living was necessary. Dr Acland reassessed the family's total situation. He told them he considered the case to be dangerous and 'unusually complicated', but he did not despair of recovery, and was more hopeful of the outcome than the other doctors. Dr Acland did not recommend Wood to resign the living at that point, but rather to apply to the Bishop for leave of absence for a year. Eleanor Wood was grateful for the kindly doctor's sanguine and humane interpretation of the case. She could see that Dr Acland did not expect her husband to be again equal to the responsibilities of his demanding parish; but if the larger living was not surrendered now, it would remain possible to exchange it for a smaller one if his health later improved. Mrs Wood concluded her account of Dr Acland's advice to her brother: 'altogether his visit has been a very great comfort to me and I feel most thankful for it'.[90] Dr Acland clearly interpreted his role in the broadest sense, offering advice which allowed the family, in good conscience, to retain the income from the living for a few months longer.

The case of Revd Crauford Tait, who died in May 1878, also demonstrated the pressures which could operate on a well-meaning Christian physician, inclining him towards optimism in a doubtful case. Years earlier Archibald Tait, Archbishop of Canterbury, and his wife, Catharine, had suffered the terrible loss of five young daughters, which increased their emotional invest-ment in their only son, Crauford, aged 29. Knowing of the Tait family tragedy, the doctors were more than usually reluctant to deliver a fatal prognosis in Crauford Tait's difficult case of 'insidious deterioration of the blood', which they feared was incurable. For the sake of the parents, the family doctor, Alfred Carpenter, refused to abandon hope, reminding the family that medical science was finding treatment for diseases once consid-ered incurable. As in the case of Revd Cyril Wood, the doctors advised against Crauford resigning his new parish, possibly fearing that this would destroy all hope.[91] A month before Crauford died, Dr Alfred Carpenter wrote to Catharine Tait, explaining his fears and justifying his sanguine attitude:

I do not like to let you remain any longer in ignorance of the great anxiety I feel on Crauford's account ever since he visited Sir James Paget. I have had my suspicions as to the nature of the disease and although I have refused to look at it in the same light that others do it is because I have the[?] hope that his case may prove an exception to the rule. . . . The disease under which he is suffering has been generally fatal sooner or later. I have steadily refused to look at it in that light but I cannot find the history of a case which has been cured. . . . I write this first trusting that we may together ask for guidance from one above as to the best course to be followed. I dread the effect of such a knowledge upon the Archbishop. . . . I shall still consider that he is to get well again in spite of all I read and all I am told about it. He has youth, he has a good heart and a resigned spirit. Surely we shall have a favourable answer to our prayers.

Pray forgive me for having kept my own suspicions and my fears from you so long. It is so necessary for his possible recovery for all about him to be cheerful that I have thought it best not to communicate them to you earlier than I have done.[92]

This letter was evidently written from the heart by a doctor deeply commit-ted to the welfare of the Tait family, and desperately hoping for a miracle from God. Dr Carpenter was a Christian doctor who believed that Provi-dence played a major role in sickness, especially in incurable cases beyond the doctor's skills.

There are few examples of doctors deliberately withholding the truth to the end, when they knew death was inevitable. Even in these cases it is sometimes possible to understand why the doctors chose to evade giving a direct prognosis of death. The case of the third Earl of Carnarvon reveals that a doctor might refrain from giving an explicit death sentence if he sensed that the family badly needed reassurance and a little hope in a chronic terminal case. After Carnarvon's death in 1849, Dr Meryon, the chief consultant, wrote a polished letter of sympathy to the widow, offering 'heartfelt condolence on the melancholy loss', conceding only at this late stage that 'the fatal issue was inevitable'. He believed Lady Carnarvon must have been 'more or less prepared' for the loss, 'notwithstanding the many flattering presages which I hope and trust never formed more to be the comfort of despair than the foundation of any expectation of recovery'.[93] This letter demonstrated that Dr Meryon provided the rhetoric of hope, which could be justified later as the 'comfort of despair', refraining from the direct statement that death was inevitable. The tone and vocabulary of the letter suggested the smooth character of his bedside manner, combining a warm personality with elegant language. Yet, in the absence of greater scientific knowledge, such equivocal words of reassurance could raise family morale substantially, and were occasionally judged necessary to sustain relatives' strength for nursing. Meryon was one of the tiny minority of doctors who followed Hufeland's advice against giving a fatal prognosis. Clearly Lady Carnarvon was an unusual Victorian who did not wish to be told of her husband's inevitable and early death, and Dr Meryon read her wishes correctly.

The grim news of approaching death was concealed more often from the patient than the family, especially from the 1880s. The patient was obviously more likely to die in ignorance if he or she died suddenly from a rapid-onset fever, where the outcome was uncertain and the mental state confused. Such silence could be as much the decision of the family as the doctor. Leo and Katherine Maxse did not tell their father in 1900 that he was dying of typhoid, because they genuinely continued to hope for his recovery:

He was conscious nearly to the end—and always gave a welcome . . . He had no idea of dying—and we hoped till the last hour . . . The one thing the Doctors urged was that we were to be cheerful—and give him no idea of mental anxiety . . . The oxygen was kept going all the time . . . He repeatedly said he had no pain—volunteered it— you can hardly imagine the devotion of the nurses and Doctors . . . The end was absolutely peaceful—it looked just like falling asleep.[94]

This was indeed a twentieth-century perception of a good death, where the emphasis was placed on the medical need for rest and freedom from stress, in the faint hope of recovery, rather than on the spiritual need to prepare for death. It was important to the sufferer and his family to appear normal and cheerful, and to give no hint that death was conceivable. The sufferer stressed his freedom from pain, perhaps the truth or perhaps to spare his family, and his death was easy, 'like falling asleep'. This is the kind of death with which many twentieth-century medical practitioners seem more at ease, uncluttered by emotional confessions and farewells, and by scenes of intense religious significance. But there is a hint in this scene of a mutual conspiracy of silence to spare the feelings of the other, for it is hard to believe that none of them mentally prepared for the worst. This scene was far removed from Evangelical deathbeds of a half-century earlier, lacking the religious consolations that supported the previous generations.

☙ 6 ❧

'THAT LITTLE COMPANY OF ANGELS'
THE TRAGEDIES OF CHILDREN'S DEATHS

L IKE US, MOST VICTORIANS BELIEVED THAT THE DEATH OF A CHILD WAS
the most distressing and incapacitating of all. What consolation could
any parent find on the death of a beloved child—then or now? How could
parents possibly come to terms with such a loss? On hearing of the death of
a friend's baby from scarlet fever in 1893, Lady Desborough knew that no
words of consolation could soothe the desolate mother: 'I think there must be
no heartache like that of losing a child—for lovers love, childrens love,
husbands love, are none of them so deep and high as mothers love—*it* is the
highest shape love wears on earth . . . Poor Mary, what can we do—what can
*any*thing *ever* do, to make it well for her?'[1] Victorians felt that it was far harder
to lose a child than an elderly parent; the parent's death could more often be
prepared for, coming at the end of a natural progression in life, whereas the
child's death meant the loss of all hope at the start. Mary Fairfax contemplated the death of an elderly man in 1830, thinking back over her own grief
at the loss of several children:

At the great age to which he had attained death can hardly be considered an affliction
to the survivors. It is when the order of nature is reversed, and the parent witnesses
the death of the child over whom he has watched with an unremitting anxiety in
infancy, who had been entwined around the heart with every succeeding year, and to
whose life he looked with the fullest hope and confidence, resting on the blessing of
such existence, it is then that affliction is really felt.[2]

Even a devout Christian mother from one of the most prominent Evangelical Anglican families, the Bickersteths, found it infinitely harder to accept
the sudden death of her baby son in 1854 than the previous losses of her father
and sister. Elizabeth Birks confessed to her sister:

I did not know the parting would be such a pang—a peep into a gulf I had not
looked down before. It is something very different from our former losses; something
all my own; part of my daily life. But, darling—, I had been praying to be taught to
hate sin more; ought I to murmur when God answers my prayer by showing it to me
in its hateful fruit, death? for oh! death in itself is very, very evil. Our treasure seemed
to suffer fearfully yesterday . . . When the bitterness comes it seems almost too

weariful . . . I almost dread losing the sound of God's voice. I never expected it to be a life-embittering trial; but it was a sharp wrench.

But by the time of her baby's funeral her bitterness and anger had receded and Elizabeth was more reconciled, thinking more positively that it was a blessing to have enjoyed her baby for even a short time. She found the funeral 'not so bitter as I thought', though she felt 'enervated and unstrung' as a result of God's 'chastening hand resting on us'. Like other Christian parents, Elizabeth was unable to understand why God should cause the death of an innocent baby, except to punish the parents. Three months later, just as she seemed more able to accept the 'absolute necessity of each suffering' in 'the whole economy of God's providence', another wave of grief reminded her that this was her beloved baby: 'I dare not at times trust myself with what brings back to me my *baby*. My child in heaven I can think of, but not the *baby* I have lost; it makes me long too much to have such a fountain of joy again.'[3]

Victorians had to face the terrible tragedies of the loss of their children far more often than we do today. The deaths of babies and children were a common fact of life which afflicted all classes, though to varying degrees. The statistics for infant mortality record a particularly grim story of a consistently high death-rate throughout the nineteenth century, despite improvements in public health, diet, and sanitation. The death-rate in England and Wales per 1,000 live births for infants under 1 year varied remarkably little up to 1900, standing at 154 in 1840, 148 in 1860, 153 in 1880, and 154 in 1900. The turning-point in this appalling child mortality rate was not reached until the Edwardian period. A slow decline began between 1902 and 1906, and then accelerated, falling from 132 in 1906, to 105 in 1910, and down to 100 from 1916, to reach less than 16 in 1983.[4]

This 'massacre of the innocents', in Anthony Wohl's chilling phrase, totalled over 100,000 infants a year dying before their first birthday—one-quarter of all deaths.[5] Deaths in the first year of life were chiefly attributed to diarrhoea, pneumonia, bronchitis, and convulsions, while measles and whooping-cough became more lethal in the second year. Scarlet fever had its most fatal impact between the years of 2 and 5.[6] The major reason for the decline in the infant and child mortality rate in the Edwardian period was the dramatic reduction in deaths from infectious diseases, which mainly affected the young.

The incidence of infant and child mortality was naturally considerably lower among the middle and upper classes. William Farr's statistics documented class differentials in the mortality rates for children under 5 years of age between 1851 and 1861. The mortality of peers' children under 5 was

2.069 per cent, and 3.027 for children of the clergy, compared with over 10 per cent for all children in such industrial cities as Sheffield, Coventry, Leeds, Manchester, and Liverpool.[7] R. C. Ansell's analysis of infant mortality rates for the professional and upper classes in 1874 showed that 8 per cent died during their first year, which compared with over 14 per cent for the population of England and Wales as a whole between 1840 and 1900.[8] The middle and upper classes benefited from better diet, sanitation, and living-conditions, but even they experienced the deaths of an unacceptably high proportion of their children.

Lawrence Stone argues that parents in earlier centuries limited their emotional investment in young children because of high infant mortality: 'The omnipresence of death coloured affective relations at all levels of society, by reducing the amount of emotional capital available for prudent investment in any single individual, especially in such ephemeral creatures as infants.'[9] This view has influenced academics in other disciplines, such as the psychiatrist Colin Murray Parkes, who notes that parents in earlier centuries expected to lose several young children and 'accepted their losses more readily than we do today'.[10] But Linda Pollock firmly rejects Stone's assumption that a strong correlation exists between high child mortality rates and reduced parental affection, arguing instead that relations between parents and children have changed remarkably little through the centuries. She finds no significant increase in levels of affection between parents and children in England and America between 1500 and 1900; most parents in all centuries were anxious and distressed at the illness and deaths of their children.[11]

The nineteenth-century family archives investigated for this book fully support Pollock's conclusions. There is no evidence that parents in the early Victorian period invested less affection in their children and felt less distress at their deaths than Edwardian parents, despite lower expectations of their survival. For example, Margot Tennant described her mother's desolation in the 1850s: 'She had suffered too much over the deaths of her first three children (who died before I was born) to care for society . . . Sorrow had sapped her vitality.'[12] Victorian parents did not feel that several remaining children would compensate for the loss of any one, however alarming the child mortality statistics. In 1842 Lord Holland observed that the loss of a friend's child had broken her spirit, despite the birth of a new baby: 'the newcomer does not seem at all to make up to her'.[13] Mary Lyttelton was able to share in her sister's sense of loss after a miscarriage in 1851, even though she already had nine children: 'even I with so many should feel it very much'.[14] Lawrencina Potter already had eight girls when her 2-year-old son died in 1864, yet 'the greatest sorrow of her life was the death of this little boy'.[15] A similar response can be found in larger families after the turn of the century. A friend wrote to console Margaret MacDonald on the death of her son David in 1911: 'If one had twenty children one could never in the least take the place of another—there would always be twenty yearnings and twenty gaps in one's heart.'[16]

The death of a child was the supreme test of Christian faith. The Churches recognized this, producing a mass of consolation literature to explain the meaning of such deaths in Christian terms and to show mourners how their faith could console them, with titles such as *Our Children's Rest* and *To a Christian Parent, on the Death of an Infant*.[17] This devotional literature was more extensive in relation to child deaths because they constituted one-quarter of all deaths, and were so difficult to rationalize in Christian or any other terms. The problem was accentuated by the theological assumption that the doctrine of original sin applied to babies and children as well as adults.

Religious tracts insisted that the death of a child was a 'providential dispensation', a trial intended as a spiritual challenge which could purify the parents' souls: 'Are you really willing that this affliction should prove really beneficial? Are you willing to be improved by it?' Grieving parents were informed that this trial should teach them the lesson of submission to God's will, but were warned that this would not be easy. Some of them would find it 'hard to bear up against this heavy trial' and might even harbour rebellious thoughts against God in their grief.[18] Authors of consolation literature refrained from addressing the problem that such a terrible trial could be interpreted as God's punishment, though that was how many sorrowing parents perceived it.

Such arguments were used by many mourners in their attempts to find meaning on the deaths of their children. Canon William Vernon Harcourt believed that the death of his 13-year-old daughter Louisa in 1839 was 'the most moving of all calls to God', transforming his family's suffering into 'the greatest of God's blessings'.[19] Thomas Acland informed his sister in 1851 of his little daughter's death from scarlet fever: 'God be praised for All his Mercies which are great indeed—I feel this to be a serious call to us and beg your prayers that it may be blessed to us.'[20] W. H. Smith assured himself that God must have a higher purpose in the otherwise pointless death of his baby son in 1866, for the baby's death was God's will in his 'infinite wisdom'. Smith's mother-in-law, Charlotte Danvers, reinforced this message: 'God's ways are wrought in mystery, but . . . we shall see all things have been for our good, difficult as they are to bear here.'[21]

The consolation literature offered a further rationalization to bereaved parents with the argument that a benevolent God had removed their children early from an unhappy world of pain, sin, temptation, and doubt. In the words of the poet Caroline Roberts in 'The Two Little Graves', these children were now 'Free from care and pain and sorrow, | Oh, rejoice! They are at rest.'[22] The 1852 tract mentioned above, addressed to 'a Christian Parent' provided a prose equivalent: 'Why should you lament that your little ones are crowned with glory before the sword was drawn, or the conflict begun? . . . O remember your little one is not lost, but only taken from the evil to come.'[23] These sentiments were repeated hundreds of times by grieving parents and their families, trying to find some justification for their loss. W. H. Smith used the familiar biblical phrase on his baby son's death in 1866: 'and so he is taken from the sorrow to come'. This consolation affirmed that dead children were spared the suffering of a sinful world and were permitted to retain the relative innocence of childhood.[24]

The argument which offered the most positive consolation to Christian parents was that early death was God's act of mercy 'to those whom his grace hath prepared for heaven'. *To a Christian Parent* reassured parents of the Bible's revelation that 'your dear child is now a glorious, happy spirit . . . in heaven'.[25] The 1861 SPCK tract *Early Death* encouraged grieving parents to think of a lost daughter as a 'bright angel permitted to watch over your path' and cited John Keble's popular poem 'Bereavement':

> What if hence forth by Heaven's decree
> She leave thee not alone,
> But in her turn prove guide to thee
> In ways to Angels known?[26]

The anonymous author of *Our Children's Rest; or Comfort for Bereaved Mothers*, published in 1863, found the greatest consolation on her own loss of three children in the knowledge that '*my beloved ones were safe*! SAFE WITH JESUS! and that there would be a blessed and glorious reunion in a brighter and happier world'. The belief in family reunions with the lost children in heaven gave meaning to otherwise futile premature deaths. This tract emphasized that Christ's resurrection had 'taken from death *its sting*, from the grave *its victory*': 'There shall be blessed reunions in that holy MEETING-PLACE; there shall be joyful recognitions, living, loving, singing, praising, serving and worshipping God FOREVER. Each and *every member* of many dear families will be there, all safely gathered.'[27]

Many bereaved parents, like W. H. Smith in 1866, found the greatest source of consolation and justification in this belief that 'we have one of our own in heaven, ready to welcome us when we are there'.[28] Lord Grosvenor's young daughter died of typhus in 1839, but he trusted in God, and hope was therefore mingled with sorrow. He was comforted by the certainty that 'her innocent spirit winged its way to Heaven to join the company of the pure in heart . . . In the full possession of a happiness such as they could not have enjoyed on earth'.[29] In 1864 Lord Skelmersdale found spiritual solace on the death of his young child: 'It is a very comforting thought that our little bright one is now most certainly one among the many that surround the throne of our Saviour.'[30] But not all Christians found a belief in immortal life adequately consoling in the case of babies, as Lady Selborne confessed in 1914:

I never think the doctrine of the immortality of the soul is the same comfort with regard to a baby that it is with regard to older people—at least from a mother's standpoint—because it is the body that she loves at that age . . . She does not know what the soul is like yet, so she can only love that vaguely—but the other instinct is so strong that she suffers cruelly if she loses her baby.[31]

This chapter will closely analyse the impact on two families of scarlet fever, an infectious disease which was particularly destructive in the early and mid-Victorian periods. Two of the most revealing accounts of nineteenth-century child deaths were recorded in the 1850s, in the devout Anglican families of the Horsleys and the Taits, each devastated by the deaths of five children from scarlet fever. Jose Harris has recently observed that grief at the all-too-frequent loss of babies and young children in the nineteenth century was 'a phenomenon that still awaits imaginative historical reconstruction'.[32] These case-studies will attempt a reconstruction of two families' experiences of the deaths of five children and their own agony of grief.

Barry Smith has shown that the mortality rate of scarlet fever doubled between 1840 and 1870, after which its virulence diminished, until it practically disappeared in the 1920s. Infants under 12 months suffered the highest mortality rate, but the incidence of scarlet fever was greatest among children aged between 4 and 8. It was caused by streptococcal infection of the throat or middle ear and spread by droplet infection or contaminated milk or food. Symptoms of scarlet fever included a red rash, fever, headache, nausea, skin irritation, and ulcerated throat, but there was no effective medical treatment. The poor were undoubtedly more seriously afflicted by this childhood disease than the wealthy, but this tended to be disguised by the recurrent outbreaks of local epidemics, often due to infected milk supplies.[33]

The isolation of child victims in cases of infectious diseases made the idealized Evangelical deathbed scene impossible. John Callcott Horsley, already a widower, lost four sons and a daughter to scarlet fever in the 1850s and 1860s. His three sons by his first wife, Elvira, showed the first symptoms on 26 February 1854; Frank recovered by 7 March but Edward, the eldest, aged 7, was 'most alarmingly ill'. He died on 11 March, followed a week later by 3-

year-old Harry. John Horsley described the first two tragedies in letters to his fiancée, Rose Haden, daughter of Charles Haden, a surgeon; he was not allowed to see Rose, who had not been exposed to scarlet fever. On 7 March Edward's illness was diagnosed when the scarlet fever rash appeared, and his head was shaved to prevent infection. Next day John Horsley reported that Edward's 'cries and moans are at times most piteous and heart-rending'. He was forbidden to enter Edward's room in case he then spread the disease to the two younger boys: 'I could only be a most painful spectator of his sufferings, therefore it is as well.' He was relieved they had found a kind and efficient nurse, since 'that dear child can have none but a *hired* female hand about him'.[34] During the next few days John Horsley found it agonizing to hear from the nurse that his son was sinking rapidly, yet not be allowed to see him. Servants frequently played a major caring role in such household epidemics, when fear of infection prevented female family members from looking after their sick children.

John Horsley became resigned to Edward's death in the last three days. 'God is our all, and if it is His wish that my dearest child should die, I shall dwell but upon the thought that he is removed from the evil of this world, and joined to his dear mother in her everlasting rest!' On 11 March 1854 John informed Rose Haden: 'Our darling boy is now we trust with his dearest mother in the mansions of Heaven . . . I watched his last breath and closed his dear eyes.'[35] But it required prayer and contemplation by the grave of the boy's mother on 9 March to reach this state of submission to God's will. John Horsley interpreted his child's illness as a punishment from God, intended as a warning to mend his own ways and prepare for his own death. After visiting his first wife's grave he wrote to his fiancée:

I am enabled I believe to view this trial in its right light, and trust whatever may be the issue to be able to say from my heart God's will be done . . . I believe firmly that this affliction was needed, and most deserved—I was getting into a reckless careless state (comparitively speaking) thinking much too deeply on my work and worldly plans, and far too little of God, and being cold and listless in my services to Him. I am sure, dearest love, there is no better discipline, than to keep the uncertainty of this life ever in view, to think and meditate constantly and habitually on 'the hour of death', to familiarise it as far as possible to one's mind, and to endeavour in all ways to prepare oneself for it.[36]

John Horsley continued to contemplate death and its meaning as preparations progressed for his son's funeral. On seeing Edward's body for the last time on 12 March, John wrote to Rose: 'Oh! What a terrible awakening of the soul such a calamity as this is. With what intensity of shame do I view my sins of omission and commission, since I last knelt by the form of death!'[37]

Perhaps he was thinking about his first wife's death and his forthcoming marriage less than two years later.

The day after Edward's funeral the night nursery in which he died was cleaned and whitewashed before 3-year-old Harry was transferred there. Harry was still in a critical state, but his father only saw him when 'Mrs Pollard exhibited him to me at the window, looking of course very ill.'[38] As John Horsley began to fear the worst, his strong faith continued to provide sorely needed comfort. If Harry was to die also, John would 'bow meekly to God's will' and think only of his son's happiness in his next life. During the final twenty-four hours the quarantine was abandoned as John insisted on being with his dying son. A few hours before the end John Horsley could not entirely suppress his bitterness, though the hope of a heavenly family reunion remained his primary consolation:

Such a pang of bitterness came over me when I thought I should never see that merry little form run to meet me again! But in an *instant* came the consoling reflection, that if I only endeavour to live a life of faith and obedience to God's will on earth, that, and other most dear forms illumined by God's radiance, will welcome me (let me say *us all*) in the Courts of Heaven![39]

On 18 March John announced to Rose that 'Our darling is an angel in Heaven! His pure little soul parted from his sweet form about ½ past 3 oclock . . . Heaven is indeed the home of such innocents.'[40] He resolved to move from 'the Mall' in Kensington, 'that once happy home so utterly, so awfully changed! What two short weeks had done no words can express!' He found the week of Harry's funeral passed 'much like a dream', with the dismal repetition of all the burial tasks performed so recently for Edward.[41]

John Horsley's faith enabled him to bear the sudden deaths of his two small sons with commendable fortitude. He was told not to see his fiancée for at least a week after Harry's death, so he went alone to Brighton to recuperate and to ensure he was not infectious. He had plenty of time there to think about death and its implications. His supreme 'source of consolation in the loss of these dear children, is that *certainty* of their salvation', which he never questioned. This conviction of his children's innocence and purity contributed to his belief that their deaths were a punishment from God for his own sins. He was vividly reminded of his 'angels in Heaven' when he saw a father walking with a little boy, but concluded that he would not summon Edward and Harry back to earth even if he had that power: 'I believe most firmly with our good Archdeacon Sinclair that all the pure enjoyments of this world will be ours (intensified immeasurably) in the "New Heaven and *new earth* wherein dwelleth righteousness".' He believed it was important not to speak of his sons as 'dead', but to remember the words of Christ, 'He that believeth in me shall never die,' for death was merely the transition from one state of existence to another.[42]

After the deaths of Edward and Harry in 1854 John Horsley agreed with Rose that 5-year-old Frank, his third son by Elvira, and now his only surviving child, should become their chief care. Frank was bewildered by the deaths of his two brothers in 1854, and his father was worried by Frank's 'awestruck' expression as they regarded each other through the quarantine window. Frank was too young to understand why his father did not go in to see him and felt a mystery surrounding the whole proceeding. John Horsley was anxious that Frank should be cheered up in every possible way, that his memories of his brothers should be happy and his thoughts not directed towards them too often.[43] Indeed, after the first month, Frank seemed to remember very little about his two brothers.[44] This is an illustration that Victorian children may not have been unduly obsessed with death, even in devout families which had been struck by tragedy on many occasions.

John Horsley lost three more children to scarlet fever, but the detailed record disappeared with his second marriage, as daily letters to Rose were no longer needed. Frank died of scarlet fever in February 1857, aged 7. The two infant sons by Rose were sent away from the infected home, and the parents were again obliged to look at their children through a window. Nine years later, the younger of these, Hugh, also died of scarlet fever at the age of 10. John attempted to console Rose on her birthday soon afterwards by enumerating their sources of consolation, notably their memory of Hugh and the prospect of their family's reunion in heaven:

We may be infinitely happy in the thought that our great affliction has brought us nearer to each other than we were before—still *more* happy in the hope that the memory of our dear child will *ever* be an incentive to us so to live our lives here, that when our hour comes we may look forward with earnest faithful trust to re-joining him and other most dear ones gone before. I have a little memorial of the day for you, a locket in which you can place dearest Hugh's hair.[45]

Less than three years later, scarlet fever struck the Horsley family again. This time it was 10-year-old Emma, the fourth of Rose's seven children. As one friend wrote to Rose, 'After your experience even a slight case of this most cruel disease would be a torture while it lasted.'[46] Rose and John Horsley survived into the next century, with three remaining sons and two daughters.

A particularly virulent form of scarlet fever ravaged Carlisle in March and April 1856, killing five of Dean Tait's seven children. 'Five little weeks did the work of more than fifty years,' Archibald Tait succinctly noted. Chattie, aged $5\frac{1}{2}$, was taken ill on 6 March and died the next day, soon after the dreaded diagnosis of probable scarlet fever. She was buried on 10 March, followed by

Susie, aged $1\frac{1}{2}$, a day later. Frances, aged 4, died on 20 March, after a longer illness of five days. The greatest blows of all to the devoted parents were the last two deaths, of the two eldest daughters, Cattie, aged 10, and May, aged 9, on 25 March and 8 April. Only the new baby daughter and a 7-year-old son were left.

Archibald Campbell Tait became headmaster of Rugby School in 1842, Dean of Carlisle in 1850, Bishop of London in 1856, and Archbishop of Canterbury in 1869. While at Rugby he married Catharine Spooner, daughter of the Archdeacon of Coventry, a sympathetic woman of strong character and deep piety, raised in the teaching of the Evangelical movement. Tait was a liberal Broad Church Anglican who was rather more sympathetic to the Evangelical Low Church than the High Church. He had acquired Evangelical sympathies from his upbringing in an impoverished Scottish gentry family which had been Presbyterian for two generations. As his biographer, Peter Marsh, suggests, he was 'not at all a Romantic. He scorned emotive, mystical thinking'; his personal religion was a combination of Presbyterian piety, devotion to duty, and common sense.[47] Tait was well acquainted with death before the Carlisle tragedy—his mother died when he was 2, and as an adolescent he was shattered by the death of his brother.

Both husband and wife wrote very detailed accounts of their family catastrophe soon afterwards. Archibald Tait commenced his record on 14 March 1856, following the deaths of his first two daughters, but abandoned it after only five pages when the third child was taken ill on 15 March. He did not have the heart to continue the narrative until 8 May, a month after the final funeral. The father's journal account was 128 pages long, with numerous additional notes giving further details. It seems to have been written for his eyes alone, as part of the private daily diary in which he normally accounted to God, in Evangelical manner, for his life.[48]

His wife's account was similar in substance, detail, and length (139 pages) but different in purpose—exemplary and consolatory, as well as therapeutic. A few days after the fifth child died, Catharine Tait wrote to her dear friend Mrs Wordsworth, 'You shall know all the particulars of those most sweet deaths. It will touch you very deeply to hear about them, yet I know you will like it. They were Christian lives and Christian deaths.' She commenced her memorial account of her children's deaths shortly afterwards, intending it for her family and a few close friends. Catharine wrote to one such friend over a year later, promising that she should read the memoir of 'that little company of angels . . . as they left us one by one for their home in heaven'. After her death, a note was found in her dispatch-box, dated nearly twenty years later, in 1874, addressed to her remaining children. This note suggested that they might like to publish her account of 'that time of trial': 'As the suffering is one which must recur over and over again while the world lasts, it may speak a word of help and comfort to those upon whom a similar burden is laid.'[49] Family and friends pressed the Archbishop for publication, to which he agreed, and it was printed without alteration. The language of both parents' accounts alternated between a descriptive narrative of physical and emotional suffering, in prosaic terms, and a discourse of spiritual consolation drawn from hymns and Scripture.

The nature of scarlet fever and its regime made the tragedy more dreadful for the Taits, as for John Horsley. The doctors had no cure and no palliatives of any value. Moreover, the quarantine precautions to avoid further infection inevitably separated the family when they most needed to be together. Once Chattie was diagnosed as having scarlet fever, the other children were placed in rooms at the far end of the deanery, and forbidden to cross to Chattie's side of the house. The family met briefly only in the connecting public rooms after the parents had changed their dress and washed their hands following entry to Chattie's room. As Dean Tait noted, these basic precautions against infection 'added to the gloom'. But even this limited family communication ceased entirely after Susie was taken ill, when the other four children were removed to the house of their neighbour, Mr Gipp, opposite the deanery, accompanied by Miss Godding, the governess, who had first 'purified herself'. As Catharine noted: 'How greatly did this necessary separation increase to us the agony! I longed for communication with those darlings, I longed to strengthen and cheer them.' Instead they had to make do with looking at each other through the windows of Mr Gipp's house. The parents' pain was increased because the elder children understood the implications of the quarantine.[50] When Cattie in turn became ill, Mr Gipp's house became the new quarantine centre, and the two remaining children were moved to yet another house. After Cattie's death, Dean Tait discussed with Dr Goodfellow the condition of the rooms and the drains, ordering lime washing of all rooms touched by the disease, in a vain effort to save May.[51] Each daughter had her long hair cut off and burned once the disease was diagnosed, an action which came to symbolize approaching death. Each daughter in turn was buried in haste in a zinc coffin, closed almost immediately. Once again two family servants, the housekeeper and the governess, played a major role in caring for the dying children, owing to quarantine precautions and Catharine's recent confinement.

In these appalling circumstances idealized deathbed scenes were impossible, if they were ever feasible with young children, even with less virulent illnesses. Two of the five Tait deaths will be examined here in more detail—

that of Susie, who was the second to die, and the eldest daughter, Cattie, who died more slowly. The first three victims were the youngest, who died fairly quickly, including $1\frac{1}{2}$-year-old Susie, who was taken ill three days after Chattie's death. Susie was nursed by Mrs Peach, the housekeeper, while Catharine Tait looked after the new baby, as she was still recovering from childbirth only a month earlier. While Susie lay critically ill, the mother watched Chattie's funeral from the window, as the doctor had pronounced her still too frail to attend. All that the parents could do was keep their watch by Susie's bed and pray together, but in vain. After having a fit Susie became unconscious and all hope was surrendered, though the doctor 'tried every-thing' to revive the stiff body with the twitching limbs. The mother felt so ill that she was obliged to lie down in her own room, whence her husband recalled her to the deathbed. The parents did not attempt to conceal or idealize the traumatic reality of their child's suffering in their written memo-rials: 'It was a sight full of agony; the conflict with death was long. Between six and seven more hours we kept our sad watch, expecting every moment that all would be over.' After Susie's death, the parents retired to the drawing-room while Mrs Peach laid her body out, to be buried next day in the same grave as Chattie.[52] Susie was far too young and the illness too swift to permit any kind of romanticized death scene.

The fourth death, that of 10-year-old Cattie, the eldest, on 25 March, was the most agonizing for the parents, though it approached most closely to the ideal of the good Evangelical death. Both parents described the 'deepest darkness' of that dreadful Easter, when they kept watch by the deathbed of their 'sweet saintly girl', the little mother of the family and the father's favourite daughter. They suffered an 'agony of our spirits' on 20 March as they knelt by the body of 4-year-old Frances, who died on the day Cattie was taken ill. The mother dared not stay too long with Frances's body, as she needed 'calmness of spirit to enable me to take my watch beside my first-born'. The parents prayed for their eldest daughter to be spared, but Catharine confessed to the doctor that it was hard to start work by another sick-bed, with no hope. As she cut off her daughter's lovely long hair, an acceptance of the dreaded diagnosis, she felt 'as if by this act I was giving up my child'. Catharine interrupted her watch by Cattie's sick-bed to attend Frances's funeral on 21 March, for she could not bear to wait in agony at home while a third daughter was buried. They tried to keep the news of Frances's death from Cattie, fearing the shock would worsen her condition, so the bell did not toll and carriages were not allowed to come to the door. The family stole out of the deanery with the little coffin, which they placed in the hearse outside the gate. By a sad irony Frances's funeral was followed by the churching ceremony which gave thanks for the mother's safe delivery and the birth of the new baby.[53]

The parents returned home from the third funeral 'in sad anguish of heart', unable to contemplate the possibility of losing Cattie as well as the three younger girls. Miss Godding, the governess, undertook the practical nursing while the fever increased, but Catharine sat with her daughter almost constantly while Dean Tait carried out his clerical duties. The parents maintained their prayers for Cattie's recovery, for while three of their family were now beyond human help, God might still restore to them their eldest daughter as part of Easter's message of hope. In a sense they were close to bargaining with God for Cattie's life, as Catharine recognized, but Easter Sunday brought only the grim news that 9-year-old May was also ill. Their mother saw these two eldest daughters as deeply religious children who seemed 'ever to have walked straight to heaven'. The parents were constantly with Cattie, 'only leaving her to find some vent for our suffering, and to pray with a very agony of prayer' for her recovery.[54]

Two additional physicians were called in on Easter Monday, including Dr Goodfellow from London, but their reports were bleak. The doctors indeed played no more than a supportive role in the background, with the Almighty as the primary force determining life and death, and the parents, especially the mother, expecting little of medicine in cases of scarlet fever. For a while Catharine Tait felt utterly weak and hopeless, as if she could not live without Cattie, but 'God was with us to strengthen us even in that darkness . . . At length God heard my cry for help, and gave me calmness and a little strength.' Both parents prayed with Cattie together and separately: 'it was by those prayers her soul had been trained for heaven'. Cattie was unable to speak but followed the familiar prayers and hymns with her lips. The parents spoke to her of joining her three sisters, for by now she understood that Frances was also dead. 'She pointed upwards with her finger as if to show us where we should all meet.' At this point her father burst into tears, so the dying child beckoned him to her and wiped away the tears with her hand 'and tried in every way to comfort him'. These significant details were recorded in different words but similar meaning in the separate accounts of both parents. They were aware their eldest daughter was ready to die and were grateful for this long period of clarity in the middle of her last day. They felt she saw the angels waiting to convey her to 'that place in the many mansions of our Father's house' to join her three sisters. Catharine believed that God had sent 'this blessed hour of triumph over death to comfort us'.[55] The parents' accounts demonstrate that Cattie had learned how to conduct her own deathbed scene in appropriate Evangelical manner, in so far as her illness allowed.

But the interval of calm ended, as Cattie's suffering again increased so that she often seemed unconscious, though still tossing about. 'How we passed through the next few hours I really do not know, so intense was the agony,' as her mother confessed. 'They are hours which burn into one's soul.' Again the realism of the descriptive narrative of the child's suffering is painful to the reader. The doctors made one last effort at relieving the swelling in Cattie's throat by applying two leeches—the same two leeches which had been attached to the first victim, Chattie, with the same result. The father 'hoped much from these leeches', but in vain. By ten in the evening the pulse told the doctors that all hope was gone, though they felt too sorry for the parents to tell them immediately. On hearing Cattie was dying, all the servants came into her room 'and with loud and bitter crying all knelt down around her bed', while her father prayed aloud. Despite the 'exceeding bitterness' of that hour, the father, who had hoped until the end, at last had to say 'Thy will be done' before them all, as he read the Prayer of Commendation. The house-hold did not stay long, but left the dying girl with her parents, and Mrs Peach and Miss Godding. The parents knelt down again to pray beside Cattie, but the protracted agony became too much for the mother, whose strength gave way in the early hours. Catharine could bear the long death-watch no longer, so Miss Godding took her to lie down on her bed in the deanery.[56]

Dean Tait watched his child die at last at 4 a.m. on Easter Tuesday, and then went to tell his wife, noting in his diary only 'the unspeakable agony of that announcement'. He thought of rushing into the Abbey grounds and shrieking aloud in his grief, but instead lay down on the floor of Mr Gipp's dining-room, underneath the room where Mrs Peach and a maid dressed Cattie's body. The father noted sadly in his journal: 'The Sunshine was gone for ever from our earthly life. Oh may God grant us a happy meeting in a better world.' Later on Easter Tuesday, the parents saw Cattie one last time, but found the corpse most unlike their 'bright girl', as they read Keble's consolation poetry by her side. Cattie's funeral followed next day, but the father had only 'a vague recollection of this fourth repetition of the melancholy scene'—a reminder that the parents endured this ordeal not once but five times. After Holy Communion all their hopes and thoughts were directed towards May, who was already delirious with fever.[57]

The accounts of the Tait parents reveal some insights into children's perceptions of death and dying, even though they are filtered through adult descriptions. Children's attitudes towards death are obviously more difficult to document than those of adults. We should not expect Victorian children to respond to death in the same way that children do today, since their attitudes were inevitably conditioned to a large extent by those of their parents and other adults. Children's responses also varied according to their age, although here the differences are almost impossible to document from these family archives. The deaths of children were regarded as a fact of life by the Tait children. When one child was infected by scarlet fever, they knew it was likely that she might die and several others could follow. Their understanding of death came from family discussions combined with familiarity with Bible stories and the themes of countless hymns, which were read and considered daily in the family. The story of Christ's crucifixion and resurrection, like the story of Lazarus, was well known to all but the youngest.

Catharine Tait's description of their life in a clerical family before their tragedy shows just how far every day was a day of prayer and spiritual dedication. Each morning, shortly before 8 a.m., Crauford, Chattie, and Frances, the middle children in age, came to their mother to learn a psalm and a verse of a hymn, which they followed by saying their prayers. Meanwhile Cattie and May, the eldest, stayed in their own room to say their prayers together, and to learn a complete hymn and a psalm, which they subsequently repeated to Catharine. The family had prayers together every morning at nine, after which their father questioned them on their Bible-reading and explained difficult passages to them. They read aloud numerous books together, including Shakespeare, *Pilgrim's Progress*, and even the *Infant Pilgrim's Progress*. After the youngest children had gone to bed, the older children sang hymns and chanted psalms until their own bedtime. This routine was carried out in a spirit of sheer happiness and spontaneous enjoyment which illustrated that Evangelical piety need not be gloomy.[58]

James Walvin has emphasized the didactic purpose of the plethora of Victorian children's literature on the subject of death, in secular tales as well as religious texts: 'The spectre of death was constantly used to frighten the young reader or listener into good behaviour, "to edify by recording pious deaths".' These stories taught children that life on earth was often wicked and sinful, that death was omnipresent and able to wipe out entire families, and they must always be prepared for it.[59] The Tait family records suggest that where such literature was more constructively used by loving parents, it could also reduce children's fears by its emphasis on death as the entry to a happier life in heaven. Moreover, it could teach them to cope with the likelihood of death among their own siblings, relatives, or friends.

Hymn and Bible passages on the subject of death were frequently recited, sung, and discussed before scarlet fever struck. On the Sunday before her death, Chattie requested that the family sing a favourite hymn of hers: 'Oh! that will be joyful, when we meet to part no more!' The family then studied religious pictures, including one of St Stephen, which led to a discussion of martyrdom and the conclusion that even little children might be called upon to die for Christ. When Chattie died on 6 March 1856, their father told the four elder children that 'Jesus had come for her and taken her away.' Their mother was struck by the 'simple loving faith' of the three older children and their desire to comfort their parents. Cattie, the eldest, was the most dis-tressed at the news of her little sister's death, and her mother was anxious in case the 'presence of death should impress her over-sensitive mind too much'. Soon after, about 9 March, 10-year-old Cattie asked if all the children could sing together a hymn she thought appropriate on the subject of death:

> Here we suffer grief and pain,
> Here we meet to part again,
> In heaven we part no more . . .
> All who love the Lord below,
> When they die to heav'n will go,
> And sing with saints above.[60]

After Chattie's death the elder children understood the implications of the quarantine precautions and knew it was quite possible more of them would die. When 7-year-old Crauford was told that Susie was also ill with scarlet fever, he asked: 'Will Susan die? for you know scarlet fever is quite like a plague and carries off whole families.' Their mother tried to cheer them by saying that was not often the case, and soon afterwards they were all playing in the garden—another illustration that Victorian children often responded to death in a positive, matter of fact manner, even in its midst. Both parents commented several times that none of their children seemed to be afraid of death for themselves. When it was May's turn to be the victim of the disease, she knew at the age of 9 what to expect and insisted that Crauford be kept away from her. May asked for a favourite hymn called 'Victory in Death' to be read aloud. It was entirely unknown to her mother, but the child gave directions that it was to be found in the book of sacred poetry given to one of their maids the previous Christmas. Once the book was found May located the hymn immediately and had it read to her several times:

> Away, then dying saint, away,
> Fly to the mansions of the blest,
> Thy God no more requires thy stay,
> He calls thee to eternal rest.

As her father remarked, 'Her dear mind had plainly been much fixed on the thought of death.' He considered May remarkably devoid of any fear of death, while continually aware of its nearness. She told her parents they should not be sorry if she died, for they knew she would be happy in her new life. Her father observed that May preserved this 'calm view of death' to the end. Her mother recalled that even in health May found for herself hymns about death and chose them for the children to sing: 'From her earliest babyhood, death had seemed to my May a great and blessed reality, the way by which she was to attain her real life.'[61]

At the heart of the Tait family's attitude to death was their simple belief that it signified a transition to a happier world with God, where they would eventually be reunited. Their parents' firm convictions about the afterlife were well known to the children, and often illustrated in familiar hymns and Bible passages. When 5-year-old Chattie was dying, she told her parents, 'I must go away.' Her mother reminded her that she would be going to 'that much brighter home above, to that portion of those heavenly mansions ready for us: and not long to be separated from those sweet playmates of your earthly home'. The Tait family used this language of religion in daily conversation—it was not a formal discourse reserved for holy days and times of death, rather it was familiar and comforting to them at all times.[62]

After Chattie's death Catharine soothed herself and her remaining children with the conviction that her daughter's 'bright spirit . . . had flown to a region far more suited for it than this world of sin and sorrow'. Catharine contemplated 'the blessedness of having our sweet little one in heaven'. As the parents prayed besides Chattie's coffin, they gained strength from the prospect of a heavenly reunion: 'We know that we shall have her again, though not in this world.' After the second death, Catharine comforted herself that her two daughters were keeping each other company in heaven, and watching over the family left behind. When May was dying, Catharine found her daughter reading the twenty-fifth chapter of St Matthew's Gospel, 'about the Last Day'. The mother was consoled by the knowledge that the Last Day 'would bring no terror to my child'.[63] Dean Tait's references to the afterlife in his account of his children's deaths were fewer, but they also were couched in the language of the Bible and the hymnal. On Chattie's death he commented: 'She was to be but the first of that bright band of sisters all of whom were to spread their wings and fly away from us to the mansions where Christ keeps the blessed souls waiting for the resurrection.'[64]

For both parents a struggle was required to reach the point of complete submission to God's will, but it took place at quite different stages of their ordeal. The clergyman's account of his children's deaths was more prosaic and less emotional than his wife's, and did not mention any struggle to come to terms with the tragedy as it was happening. In almost every case, he continued to hope for each child's life until the bitter end, while Catharine accepted the inevitable much earlier. Archibald Tait's shock at each death was greater, and his struggle for resignation was postponed until after the children were dead. His wife, by contrast, endured a battle with her faith while her children were actually dying one by one, and for her the process of acceptance was swifter. Perhaps this was possible because she had more time for contemplation and prayer than her husband, and perhaps it also reflected a temperamental difference. But supporting evidence suggests there was also an important gender difference at work here.

Catharine Tait's struggle for submission was recounted in detail in her lengthy memorial. As an Evangelical, Catharine had been trained from childhood in the virtue of submission to God's will; and as a woman she had learned the additional virtues of patience, obedience, and humility. These virtues were tested to the full in the course of this ordeal. During Chattie's illness, their first death, the parents 'kept a watch of agony, but strove to have no will but His who had lent us this little lamb'. The mother, her spirits calm but full of anguish, knelt down by the dying child to seek strength, through faith and prayer, to surrender Chattie to God. As she watched Chattie's funeral procession from her room Catharine 'strove to realise the gain for my beloved lamb', and prayed for strength for the ordeal still to come. When she was informed that Susie also had scarlet fever, she instantly responded 'We are in God's hands.' Catharine was able to accept little Susie's death in the same spirit of submission to God's will, even though the quarantine by now entirely separated her from the remaining children.[65]

But with two children already dead, it became far more difficult for Catharine to accept that God might require still more deaths. She suffered a greater struggle to attain a state of submission at the prospect of 4-year-old Frances's death:

I knelt down beside her; her life was in the balance, but Who was directing it? Should I take the choice upon myself, and crave at any cost the life of this sweet child now so very precious to us? . . . If her Home in Heaven was ready, should I wish to keep her here? No! I knelt and asked Him who could see all that was before her and us, to do as He saw fit with this our blessed child, and I knew that He would strengthen us.[66]

Once the critical stage of Frances's illness was reached, Catharine was soon aware from the rapid, short breathing that the end was near. Dean Tait was not prepared for the onset of death, and sent for the doctor in a desperate bid to prolong hope in the face of the inevitable. Catharine walked about Frances's room in agony as her daughter lay dying, but noted afterwards that 'My will was subdued enough to feel that at our Father's call we could give up this one also.' But Catharine dreaded the thought that the ordeal so far was mere preparation for further losses, and she was not ready to surrender any more than three children. Eventually she calmed herself and was able to kneel down to pray beside her dying daughter. She comforted herself that Frances suffered little pain, she had no fear of dying, and would soon be safe in 'His Home above, safe with the sweet companions of her nursery.'[67]

Frances's death left the parents in greater anguish for the remaining children. Now the process of intercession with God commenced in earnest. The parents had three children in heaven and a new baby to start the nursery again, but the three eldest were their dearest companions of many years. They prayed earnestly that God would now spare the rest of the family. Terror assailed Catharine as she dreaded the possible loss of her entire family. The news of Cattie's illness fulfilled her worst forebodings. Catharine prayed beside Frances's body for calmness and strength and for Cattie's survival. The mother's fear increased, but the father continued to insist that Easter meant hope. Their agony grew with the onset of May's illness, but gradually prayer brought some calmness and strength. The knowledge that Cattie in the end wanted to join her sisters in death helped her mother to accept God's will: 'Our Father's hand had given it, He only could strengthen us to drink it.' But on this occasion the anguish of the deathbed watch was too great for the mother, who had to leave.[68]

The parents prayed that God would spare May, and they retained some hope during the long illness of over two weeks: 'almost everything seemed at stake for us in that bed of suffering'. During the fortnight of watching and of prayer, Catharine Tait arrived at a state of total submission to God's will: 'The greatness of eternity in comparison to time came fully over me. I could even rejoice in the certainty of that blessedness into which my darlings had entered, and calmly could I leave in the hands of my Saviour the future of this sweet sufferer.' When May died her mother 'turned my anguish into prayer,—prayer that God would comfort us in our extreme desolation and strengthen us to bear and suffer all His will'.[69]

The father's journal account of his five children's deaths contained no similar discussion of his own state of mind at the time. During each illness Dean Tait retained hope for longer than his wife, and his shock was correspondingly greater. When Cattie was dying and Dr Graham told the parents that 'the sooner it was over the better for all', this still came as a great shock to the father, who had continued to hope for a miracle: 'in spite of hopelessness I was buoyed up by hope'. His journal revealed no suggestion of a struggle to submit to God's will while the children were dying. Dean Tait's deepest agony was postponed until the subsequent months of grieving, whereas his wife experienced considerable preparatory grief before they died.

The surviving family left Carlisle on 10 April 1856, immediately after May's funeral, and never slept in the deanery again. The parents spent the next five months with their son and baby girl in a borrowed house in Ullswater in the Lake District, where they read, walked, and prayed together, soothed a little by the lovely countryside.

Dean Tait's grief and his struggle to accept God's will were more delayed, more prolonged, and more problematic than in his wife's case—complicated by his greater knowledge of Christian theology, and his deeper sense of sin and divine retribution. For nine weeks Tait lacked the heart to continue his journal, but he resumed it on 8 May 1856, a month after May's death. His opening sentences confessed that 'our hearts are well nigh broken'. His was a soul in torment as he struggled to accept the death of five children as God's merciful will. Like John Horsley, but unlike his own wife, he felt certain the severity of the trial was a divine punishment for his own sin: 'Oh Lord I feel the dreadful want in my case which has perhaps necessitated this chastisement.' He prayed for a 'truly spiritual mind' which dwelt less frequently upon earthly prospects, and he recognized that his wife was coping with this ordeal in a greater spirit of submission: 'Give me more of that genuine piety with which thou has blessed her. Oh Lord I fear that my sin necessitating this judgement as the [cure] for my worldly mindedness has involved her in this deep grief.'[70] At times Dean Tait felt additional guilt because he seemed to mourn more intensely for Cattie, the eldest daughter, 'as a husband almost would mourn for a wife', and had to accept that he loved her the most. On many days the parents 'wept together for our darlings' as they contemplated a future on earth without them. The pain of the loss often seemed unbearable, especially on anniversaries of the children's birthdays, when they began the day by reading together the baptismal service and ended with the burial service.[71]

Dean Tait slowly found consolation in the same two beliefs which had sustained his wife during their daughters' illnesses. He continually reminded himself that his daughters had received blessings from death and he should not weep for them. By mid-May, 'I feel now more calm conviction and am able better to realize the great gain it has been to those dear children to be rescued out of this sinful and suffering world.' They were in a land where earthly love was purified and perfected.[72] He never doubted that they had all gone to join Christ, 'whom each loved according to the capacity of her years'. He was especially soothed by a chapter on the intermediate state in an unnamed volume of consolation literature, which reassured him that his daughters were in paradise with Christ, a far better condition than earth.[73]

But the overarching consolation for Archibald Tait, as for his wife, was the prospect of a future reunion with their beloved daughters. Almost every journal entry returned from the agony of loss and separation to focus on the hope of meeting again. He continually thanked God 'for the bright hopes of a happy reunion, when we shall meet to part no more'.[74] On 20 July Dean Tait experienced renewed agony on visiting his daughters' graves in Carlisle: 'but comfort real comfort flows from the unhesitating conviction that they are with Christ—and that we shall meet in heaven'.[75] Occasionally the future Archbishop was afflicted by guilt that his spiritual priorities were unsound in that he over-valued the prospect of a heavenly reunion with his daughters: 'Sometimes I almost think that I idolise them too much now when they are gone. It is the thought of meeting the Lord Jesus Christ that ought to be the most sustaining when we look forward to death'.[76]

A similar gendered difference was evident in the response of Edward White Benson and his wife, Mary, to the death of their eldest son, Martin, in 1878. Martin died at the age of 17 from tubercular meningitis, and his father wrote a thirty-four-page diary account of his death a week later. Like Dean Tait, Bishop Benson was used to working through his problems in writing, and it helped him to document in detail this most severe test of his faith. He recorded that 'My dearest wife understood it all more quickly—better—more sweetly than I. At once she knew she had never cared for anything but his happiness.' Mary Benson's response was similar to Catharine Tait's. The day after her son's death Mary wrote to Beth Cooper, the family nurse, 'He is in perfect peace, in wonderful joy, far happier than we could ever have made him . . . free from fear, free from pain, from anxiety for evermore.' The Bishop, however, was shattered by the blow, and never able to understand fully why God had allowed his promising and beloved son to die so young. In his diary account he wrote that Martin's death seemed 'inconceivable': 'It has changed all my views of God's work as it is to be done both in this world and the next, to be compelled to believe that God's plan for him really *has* run on sweetly, and rightly for him and for all—and yet—he is dead.' At the age of 60, when he had succeeded A. C. Tait as Archbishop of Canterbury, Edward Benson still saw Martin's death as the 'inexplicable grief' of his life, as he confessed in his diary: 'To see into that will be worth dying.'[77] It would be speculative to generalize too far from the experience of two fathers who became Archbishops of Canterbury. But if churchmen of their calibre had greater difficulty than their wives in accepting their children's deaths as the will of God, it seems likely that men of weaker faith might also have submitted to God's purpose with reluctance.

Tait's elevation to the bishopric of London later in 1856 spared the family the ordeal of returning to the Carlisle deanery. Many shared the view of Tait's son-in-law Randall Davidson that the Taits 'carried consciously upon them the consecration-mark of the holy sorrow they had known'.[78] In 1869 Tait was enthroned as Archbishop of Canterbury, by which time they had two more daughters. For both parents the Carlisle tragedy was a lifelong sorrow. In 1878, twenty-two years later, they had to confront the death of a child once more, this time their only son, Crauford. Following the premature deaths of five young daughters, the parents' emotional investment in the one son over the next two decades was immense. Crauford died at the age of 29, shortly after his engagement and his appointment to a London parish, with a promising clerical career and marriage before him. He died of a bladder infection involving months of fever, pain, and chronic weakness. Crauford prepared himself for death by frequent prayer, and by careful reading of Jeremy Taylor's *Exercises of Holy Dying*. The medical attendants 'hoped against hope' until almost the very end, adopting the optimistic perspective on the value of hope. Crauford was 'living in faith and prayer, and God sustained him', until a haemorrhage ended his life. Crauford asked his father for the truth about his medical condition and received it with the utmost calmness, and 'set himself to use the hour', saying he was 'ready to leave all in God's hands'. After Holy Communion, Catharine offered up their daily family prayer that they should all eventually meet those five beloved sisters who died at Carlisle.[79] Many entries in the Archbishop's journal referred to his grief on the death of his only son: 'Our sad loss has greatly shattered my nerves. I can scarcely speak in public without tears.'[80]

But Catharine Tait, who had resigned herself to the deaths of her five little daughters twenty-two years earlier, seems to have found the death of this beloved son literally unbearable. She died suddenly of an unspecified illness only six months after Crauford, at the age of 59, following a bilious attack.[81] Canon William Benham suggested that she virtually died of grief: 'The cup was again held to her lips, bitter as ever, and she drank it in unshaken faith and trust; but Nature was exhausted now, and she immediately drooped and died.' Benham concluded that Crauford's death was 'too much for her, and she joined him in the Paradise of God'.[82] The gold-edged memorial card printed for distribution to family and friends on Catharine Tait's death included a poem, possibly written by the Archbishop, which dwelt on her need to join her son in paradise:

> O might of mother-love! O mother's heart
> That, knowing safe, beyond Time's changeful shore,
> Her child in Paradise for evermore,

Yet could not here enduring live apart.
. . . Now, both are blest in Thee, no more to part.[83]

These two deaths devastated Archbishop Tait, whose journal revealed the depths of his grief at the loss of his wife and only son within a year. The memorial poem for his wife acknowledged this impact: 'And he, again bereaved—in weakened form | And sorely smitten left.'[84] On the anniversary of Crauford's death he wrote in his journal: 'As time wears on I feel more and more desolate . . . How have I hungered for the sweet society of mother and of son. I shall go to them, but they will not return to me.' The Archbishop found it even harder to accept the premature death of his adult son than the death of his beloved wife:

It was a crushing blow indeed to see the young minister of Christ cut off with all the fair hopes of a long and blessed ministry dashed; but God could not have taken him except that he were wanted for some other work. Beloved Catharine—even she was ripe and had done her work—his was but beginning . . . Surely there is much work to be done in my own soul, and these two awful trials may by God's blessing do it.[85]

In the four years remaining before his own death, Archbishop Tait's response to his family's deaths was seen as an example to others. He was venerated as a man set apart by his profound experience of suffering. F. Max Muller wrote to the Archbishop soon after Crauford's death, 'to show you in how many ways your sufferings, your patience and your strength have been a help and a blessing to others'. Muller had lost his eldest daughter three years earlier, and his life had been shattered ever since. He often asked: 'Why all this irregularity? Why do the young leave before the old?' But when he could find no answer and no help, he looked to the Archbishop's example and felt ashamed.[86]

The 1879 publication of the memorial volume on the deaths of Archbishop Tait's children and his wife was one of the most widely read Victorian books of consolation literature, and letters of thanks poured in from bereaved parents who found it helpful. One simple letter to the Archbishop from Sarah Jones of Liverpool, who had lost four children to scarlet fever, asked for a copy of the book, which many sympathetic friends had recommended to her, 'to afford my stricken heart some consolation'. Sarah enclosed a press cutting of the recent death notice of her four children, aged between 1 and 6 years, all within four days.[87] A Congregational minister from Bristol, W. H. Jellie, wrote to Tait that he and his wife were heartbroken on the sudden death of their 4-year-old daughter. A friend suggested that they read Catharine Tait's account of the loss of her daughters. They felt they were reading about their own painful experience, 'so truly does the record of the sudden and heartrending loss of your little "Chatty" express the anguish of heart, the struggles of faith, and the sense of desolation through which we have just passed'. Their faith was strengthened as they read Catharine Tait's record of loving resignation to God's will. They believed it must be soothing to the Archbishop to know that 'in this way your sainted wife is fulfilling so precious a "ministry of consolation" still on earth'.[88]

Another letter of gratitude, from Robert Spence of North Shields, also testified to the grief of countless families who had lost children and to the value of such consolation literature as Catharine Tait's memorial. Spence had lost eight out of nine children, before his wife had also died just over a year earlier. Only one little girl lived to 13 years, and her 'deathbed was to us much as those of your two oldest girls had been to you'. Yet their Christian faith meant that 'all this sorrow is full of tenderness and sweetness and love and thankfulness for all that life was, and for all that the memory of it is now'. Spence could feel for the Archbishop, having experienced the same depth of sorrow. He also understood what it must have cost to give such a 'sacred record' to the wider world beyond their family, 'but your heart must have told you all the good it will have done, all it must ever do and how its intense patient tenderness will help to bear up many a sinking sorrowing heart'.[89]

Such public memorials of the deaths of children depended for their impact on two variables. They spoke to an age when most people had either experienced the loss of a child in their own family or knew personally of such losses in other families. They carried the greatest value as a source of consolation to Christians, since their primary message was that of faith. The experience of the Horsleys and the Taits demonstrates vividly that they survived their terrible ordeal to a great extent with the help of their faith, reinforced by the warm sympathy of family and friends. Their strong religious beliefs and everyday practice of Christianity gave them an exceptionally powerful structure for coping with death, and a language of consolation. The decline of religious faith in our own age has combined with demographic change and advances in medical science to transform our world of experience of the deaths of children, creating a gap which can only be bridged by history, or by the reality of lives in the Third World today.

⁊ 7 ⊱

DEATH IN OLD AGE

I N THE LATE TWENTIETH CENTURY DEATH IS WIDELY REGARDED IN WESTERN societies as almost the monopoly of the aged. People no longer expect to die in childhood and the majority live to old age, but it was not always so. The close association of death with old age is a major historical change dating from the late Victorian period. Life expectancy at birth in England and Wales began to rise from about 40 years in 1850 to about 52 for males and 55 for females by 1911–12. The death-rate began to decline slowly from 22 per 1,000 in the 1870s to 13 per 1,000 by 1910. This fall did not affect those over 45 until after 1900, and was more marked for women than for men. The age distribution of the population was transformed by the remarkable increase in life expectancy, whereby the percentage of the population over 65 rose from 4.7 per cent in 1861 to 5 per cent by 1901 and 13.2 per cent by 1971.[1] Michael Anderson estimates that in 1826 1 person in 15 in England and Wales was aged 60 or over, increasing steadily to 1 in 13 by 1911, and rising faster to 1 in 8 by 1931 and nearly 1 in 6 by 1951. He sees this as 'the most striking change in proportional terms' which occurred in the age structure of the population. The proportion of very old people over 75 was fairly stable in the nineteenth century and did not rise rapidly until after 1911.[2]

The major causes of the decline in mortality were the improved standard of living and diet, the reduction in deaths from infectious diseases as their intensity fell, and the impact of public-health reforms on sanitation, sewerage, and slums. Between 1851–60 and 1891–1900 the fall in mortality from tuberculosis in England and Wales was 47.2 per cent, from typhus and typhoid 22.9 per cent, and from scarlet fever 20.3 per cent.[3] While infectious diseases were a major cause of death among old people in nineteenth-century Britain, the dominant cause today is physical deterioration, including strokes, coronary attacks, and cancer.[4]

Observers began to comment on these demographic trends in the last two decades of the century. The *Lancet*, for example, noted in 1881 that life expectancy for the population of London had risen by a whole year within the previous decade; men over 60 were now more robust both physically and mentally, for human health had been substantially improved and death deferred. The *Spectator* thought the chief gain was made between the ages of 60 and 70, 'that a man of sixty-five was visibly younger than he would have been at the same age forty years ago'.[5] At the same time it was recognized that the increase in life expectancy carried with it new problems, such as the higher incidence of cancer, which was more common in 1893 than a century earlier, because it was a 'disease of degeneracy', as Sir James Paget acknowledged.[6]

The calculations of Edwin Chadwick, Charles Ansell, and Dr William Guy demonstrated that 'the richer classes' in general had higher life expectancies than the less fortunate classes in the nineteenth century. Chadwick's famous 1843 *Report on the Sanitary Condition of the Labouring Population of Great Britain* estimated that the average age at death for gentry and professional families in London, including their children, was 44, compared with 25 for tradesmen and clerks, and 22 for labouring families.[7] He subsequently calculated that by 1888 the mean age at death of men and women of the comfortable classes in Brighton had risen to 63, whereas that of the 'not well to do' was still only 28.8.[8] The upper and middle classes had lived longer than the working classes for many decades,[9] because their superior economic status permitted better diet, housing, and standard of living, and they did not have to fear old age and death in the workhouse. The chief problems for older members of the upper-middle and upper classes were deteriorating mental and physical health, a declining sense of usefulness, decreasing mobility, loneliness, and increased dependency on family, friends, or servants.

For the older men in our Victorian families, compulsory retirement had not yet encouraged a distinction between worthwhile occupation and useless old age. Social attitudes towards the role and status of older men in middle and upper class families were still generally very supportive, especially while they continued their professional occupations. Politicians and professional men, such as lawyers and clergymen, who often continued their careers until death or ill health intervened, were valued by their family and the community, rather than seen as burdens to be carried. Some prominent politicians, such as Lord Palmerston, died in office, prompting Lord Cowper to remark, 'His death is a terrible loss, but he himself could not have done better; for he is, as it were, in the Zenith of his glory, and had not begun to go downhill. He died with his own Parliament, and proved that old and weak and sick, he alone could manage it.'[10] Disraeli died at the age of 77, less than two years after his defeat in the 1880 general election. Gladstone would have preferred to share Palmerston's fate, but was instead persuaded by his colleagues to retire reluctantly in 1894 at the ripe old age of 85, despite his family's valiant efforts to conceal his failing eyesight and hearing, and increasing physical exhaustion. In 1908 Sir Henry Campbell-Bannerman, at the age of 72, refused to allow his last illness to force his retirement, and died in office at 10 Downing Street.[11] The status and sense of usefulness of the older woman was usually much lower, especially after widowhood, as will be seen later.

Some characteristic features of old age have changed little with time. Many elderly Victorians described their experience of a process which modern psychologists, such as Beverley Raphael, define as 'disengagement': 'a process in which many of the relationships between an older person and members of his social group are relinquished and others attenuated so that there is a mutual withdrawal'. Loneliness and isolation are common problems of the elderly today, together with a sadness about reduced social contacts and the deaths of friends and loved ones.[12] This enforced disengagement is vividly illustrated by a number of letters from elderly Victorians to younger members of their families. Henry R. Reynolds wrote from Hull in 1846 to his granddaughter:

I think we are both too old for going out—I particularly: I used to like it—and I still like my friends: but I feel so conscious of decayed powers, that I prefer sitting in silence, with those I love about me, though I scarcely speak to them, to the effort of Society. I am anxious for information, but almost abhor disputation and discussion.[13]

In 1843 Caroline Fox, at the age of 76, told her nephew that she had nothing to report, since she went out little and saw few people, and her memory was so treacherous that it retained only a little of what she did hear, and that incorrectly.[14] By the age of 80 in 1859, even the indefatigable scientist Mary Somerville ceased venturing out in the evenings, preferring to play patience, work crochet, or read the newspapers.[15]

An important aspect of this disengagement was the loss of valued friends, relatives, and former colleagues, as the older person survived many peers, and even some members of the younger generation. In 1840, shortly before his death, Lord Holland wrote sadly to his son: 'Another of my best [closest?] and sincerest friends dropped off—! One prays for long life but what is it but outliving what one values most in it, those one esteems and loves.'[16] Similar sentiments were expressed at the end of the period, as elderly writers were constantly reminded of their own mortality. In 1911 Lady Stepney found it 'simply ghastly and heartbreaking' to keep the anniversaries of all her friends and relatives; as she grew older, her year became 'just a row of 365 tombstones'. But it was impossible to forget them because 'some deaths are burnt in'.[17] After the death of Edward VII in 1910, Kate Courtney regretted that 'Death and impending death seems to be all round us at the present time and I doubt if I live myself whether I shall be much out of mourning for years. It is inevitable as we get older . . . There comes a continuous procession of the departing friends.'[18] Sir Aloitius Watt revealed something of his frustration at advancing age to Elizabeth Haldane in 1909: 'He is almost 80, I fancy, and feels old age. Not that he is not well, but he has lost some friends and after a very full life feels that people don't ask him to do things that he wants to do. The futility of the life that he and his friends have been having seems to weigh upon him. It was rather tragic.'[19]

But there were fewer Victorian references to the futility and frustrations of old age than might be expected, even today. Elderly people in our Victorian families wrote almost as much about the compensations of old age as about its miseries. For some, the disengagement from social life offered time and peace for spiritual contemplation, as Mary Haldane discovered by 1903, when she was about 80:

The detachment that arises from inability to take part in the activities of life certainly throws one more directly on God, and gives us an insight into the things of Eternity which balances all loss. Our life is in Him after all, whether we die or live, it is the same. I felt almost rebellious when I first realized being, as it were, laid on the shelf, but my children have been an unspeakable comfort to me and I endeavour as far as I am able to lift my thoughts away from my self to them.[20]

Edith Lyttelton also believed that growing old brought a new perspective on this life, as the prospect of an afterlife came closer. She admitted in 1911 that growing old seemed at times 'such an indignity' with its reminders of decay, but more often she felt that old age should not necessarily mean increasing sadness: 'It changes the direction of your thoughts and aims of course . . . daily aware of the great destiny in which we are caught . . . this life helps to fashion us in the next life . . . and it makes us understand that the attitude to the trivial as well as to the great things of life is vitally important.'[21]

Moreover, for most elderly people disengagement from their former social circle did not usually apply equally to their family, and the need for family contact remained vitally important. As we will see later, most widows sought consolation in their family, their children, and grandchildren. Caroline Fox at the age of 76 in 1843 prayed 'to retain to the very last her affection for her nephews and nieces when all else fades'.[22] More than half a century later, Anna Merivale appreciated the vital function of family in old age: 'For my own old age I am well provided with affectionate helpers—nieces abound all round me, and the nephews, though not so many, are not slack in their attentions . . . [Antony] and Janet are most kindly anxious that I should keep the old home, with more or less of the family about me.'[23]

The problems and compensations of old age for Victorian women are illustrated by the experience of the indomitable Mary Ann Rogers, widowed mother of sixteen children, including Professor James E. Thorold Rogers. She died at the advanced age of 89 in 1873, having married at 16 or 17 and lost her husband in 1846. She represents the 'very large surplus of widowed women' in old age in Victorian society, dependent on male family members for support.[24] Women generally married younger than men, died at a later age, and remarried less frequently. Mary Ann had a tough life, with eleven of her children dying before her, including two the worse for drink, one a vagrant, and one a sea-captain murdered by pirates. Her youngest child, Edmund, born when she was 44, died of brain fever at the age of 22, and she herself nursed several of her dying children over the years. In 1851, at the age of 68, she apologized that she was 'an old Woman and am become garralous'; but her services were still indispensable in giving 'constant attention' to her invalid spinster daughter Louisa. She considered it 'a great mercy that I have been spared so long and that my health on the whole is pretty good at my time of life I have little reason to complain few persons can do more than I can'.[25]

At the age of 80 in 1864 Mary Ann Rogers wrote to her son James E. Thorold Rogers on the birth of her grandson, an occasion which elicited reflections on old age and mortality. She regretted that few of her children remained, Louisa having also died earlier that year, and 'there is no *youth* in the family *now*'. She looked upon her last surviving daughter, Elizabeth, 'with fear and trembling there is disseas none of my daughters were stronge I have but one *now*'. She concluded: 'I find it very dull at times I am getting quite an old woman and cannot get out in the cold weather but I should not complain I can read and work which many cant at my age I wish you had a good living near me then I could see the dear children often I often think of the little dears.'[26]

A few days later Mary Ann wrote to her fifteenth child, Richard Norris Gandy, that 'poor Louisa's death has aged me much'. She could no longer walk far, but did not complain as she had much to be thankful for: 'kind children, kind friends, and attentive servant, I hope she wont think of marrying'.[27] At the age of 82, in 1865, it was a strain to help in nursing her surviving daughter, Elizabeth, during her last illness: 'it is a great trial for me, I find the infirmities of age, I cannot bear things as I did, little things put me out now'.[28] Two years later she decided to acquire a dog as 'something to love', provided the dog tax was reduced to 5s. a year; she needed company and missed her daughter Elizabeth very much.[29] On her eighty-fourth birthday Mary Ann divided a £10 note between her surviving sons, 'as a little remembrance of the event when I may be gone hence and no more seen', since she could not anticipate many more birthdays.[30] By 1870 few people came to see her, she was sometimes bedridden, and found the cold weather 'a great trial' which confined many people over 70 in her village to their beds.[31] At 89 she found it very dull being so much alone, with few friends left in the village and so many friends and children dead. But she had no interest in new faces.[32] Despite the miseries of extreme old age, Mary Ann Rogers complained little and was sustained by her Christian faith. A poem about old age in her handwriting, entitled 'Hymn for eighty and three months' began:

> With years oppressed, with sorrows worn
> Dejected, harrassed, sick, forlorn,
> To thee, O God! I pray.[33]

The grief experienced by family and friends on the death of the very old was usually less intense and prolonged than for young people, because the loss was anticipated and prepared for. The inevitability of death in old age was accepted and it was easier to come to terms with the death of a person who had lived out the allotted span of years. On the death of his sister-in-law in the prime of life in 1867, Roundell Palmer observed that grief varied in nature and intensity according to the stage in the life-cycle reached by the deceased:

My dearest Mother was taken away after the long preparation of a gradual decay of years, and at a ripe age: we were all prepared for it, and, while we could not but feel deeply the separation, we were not tempted to repine. It is not the same thing, when one appears likely to be taken, whom we had thought in the prime of life, and by whose strength we had hoped to see others supported, and ourselves helped and encouraged, for many years to come.[34]

In 1879 Archbishop Tait compared his own responses to the recent deaths of his 80 year-old brother James and his 29-year-old son Crauford. At 80, the death of a frail old man was 'only what we expect', and though it caused sadness, it was impossible to wish his life of weakness prolonged, whereas Crauford's death was a 'crushing blow', because his mature life was just starting.[35]

The family's grief was likely to be especially muted if the death of the elderly relative involved extensive pain or suffering, and prolonged anticipatory sorrow. Frances Lupton recorded the death of her aged aunt Mrs Martineau in 1891, 'which though a matter of tender concern, can bring no *grief* even to her nearest family, who will rejoice that she is released (at 90 years) from a condition which might, if prolonged, have led to much suffering'.[36] Charlotte Portal responded in like manner to the death of her brother

Lord Minto that same year: 'I never wished for a long old age for him even during this illness—I felt almost as great a fear of recovery to a life of invalidism as of death.'[37]

Old people themselves sometimes appeared to find bereavement easier to endure with advancing years. Maud Lady Selborne commented on Edward Cavendish's death in 1891: 'I don't expect it will affect the Duke as much as you fear—as very old people do not feel so keenly about death—knowing that they themselves have but a short time to live.'[38] Marion Bryce remarked on the death of 86-year-old Aunt Lizzie in 1901 that she trusted the aunt's aged sister would be helped by 'the merciful deadening of these blows which comes with age', particularly since the parting must be brief.[39]

The reduced impact of grief among elderly people may have been partly due to the decline of their own fear of death, especially as they approached and came to terms with the prospective end of their lives. This altered perspective has been noted by modern psychologists, as well as Victorian doctors such as Sir Benjamin Brodie and Sir William Savory.[40] As Brodie pointed out in 1854, people who reached extreme old age were often anxious to die, even when they were not suffering from any particular disease. In his view, God removed the dread of death when it was intended that people should die,[41] and most old people died resigned to their fate, having undergone a period of emotional and physical accommodation to the imminence of death. This was partly a matter of having the time to prepare, and also, for Christians, a question of resignation to God's will. As Ann Reynolds of Lancaster wrote to her granddaughter in 1841, 'This Life is very transitory— we are taken off in a moment—but "God's Will be done" as we say daily in our prayers. He alone knows what is best for us.'[42] Mary Lady Affleck, mother of Lady Holland, died in 1835 at the age of 88. Her grandchildren recognized that she was 'quite ready and resigned to her fate' and 'often prays fervently for Death', though still capable of 'wonderful rallies'.[43]

Mary Somerville, the scientist, died in 1872 at the age of 92. She had been grateful that her intellect was unimpaired, even into extreme old age, and that her two unmarried daughters 'support my tottering steps, and, by incessant care and help, make the infirmities of age so light to me that I am perfectly happy'. She was prepared for death, and the expectation brought 'neither pain nor regret'. She viewed the prospect of death as 'a solemn voyage, but it does not disturb my tranquillity'. As she wrote to Frances Power Cobbe shortly before her death, she 'never had a doubt of the immortal life'.[44]

These points are also well illustrated by the death in 1842 of Elizabeth Fox, widow of Charles James Fox, the statesman, at the age of 92. In April 1842 Caroline Fox reported on the condition of her aunt-by-marriage: 'Very comfortless accounts, nothing immediately to destroy life, but everything to render its continuance unenjoyable to herself—and painful to those around her witnessing as they do the daily decay of the mind.' Two months later Caroline Fox found her old aunt in 'dismal decay', suffering little or no pain but growing thinner and weaker; the doctor said she had no disease other than old age and 'lives upon suctions like an infant'. The patient spoke little, except to thank her loving attendants for their goodness, and did not seem to want them to speak.[45]

Caroline Fox wasted no energy describing a deathbed scene so far removed from any ideal, Christian or otherwise. Instead she promised to spare her family 'all painful and useless details', commenting only that death would be a blessing to the sufferer and her attendants, ending the 'hopeless but lingering suffering'. She applauded the unwearied vigilance of Mrs Fox's faithful attendants, Miss Marston, her companion and friend, and Mrs Tucker, her servant, who did all they could to alleviate her suffering, night and day. However 'strange and uncomfortable' it might seem, these attendants welcomed death when it came at last on 12 July 1842:

It would be impossible to regret her release from a state of hopeless suffering when all of life and its enjoyments were gone—and she was alive only to breathe and to suffer—the mind and the senses too she had outlived and it was torture to those affectionately devotedly attached to her, to behold sufferings beyond their power to alleviate so that dear Miss Marston says they almost uttered a cry of thankfulness when they saw the struggle was over.[46]

This death had long been anticipated and the preparation was complete, but it left Caroline Fox with a feeling of 'restless nervous irritation'. The death of her aged relative probably made Caroline, herself aged 75, acutely aware of her own mortality, prompting anticipatory mourning for her own death. Elizabeth Fox's death broke the last link of the chain of family life connecting Caroline to the eighteenth century, 'and brings before my eyes all my past life with all its chequered scenes of joy and sorrow'.[47] Such reminiscing about the past, reviewing memories over many decades, was a common feature of the grief response in the very old. Caroline knew her own death could not be long delayed—in fact she survived only three more years, when she died after a series of strokes.

For most Victorians and Edwardians, death in old age had the advantage that it allowed them to prepare for death, in both spiritual and temporal senses. A strong Christian faith was a significant comfort for many old people and their families, particularly because death in old age did not usually arouse the spiritual doubts, questioning, and anger sometimes evoked by deaths of children and young adults. A self-conscious preparation for death by the dying person, as well as the family, was more common in old age than youth, precisely because death was anticipated and regarded as inevitable.

The importance of such preparation and faith are well illustrated by the deaths in the 1890s of Lady Acland and Elizabeth King. The final illness and death of Mary Lady Acland in May 1892 was recounted in letters from her granddaughter Agnes Anson to her husband. Agnes reported her first long talk with her grandmother about the prospect of death in 1887, over five years before Lady Acland's death: 'She says she does not wish to die. I was *very* glad to open the door for such like conversation with her.' Lady Acland wanted to live until after the birth of Agnes's baby, because she feared that the sorrow of her death would otherwise hurt the new mother. The old lady conceded that she was less concerned about death than previously, because her husband was 'so much happier and employs himself more without her'.[48] On another occasion during this earlier illness, Lady Acland 'hunted up some old books', including her own daily journals and her mother's memorial of her father's death; the two women read them aloud together, Agnes sharing her grandmother's review of her past life, in anticipation of her death.[49]

Over five years later, Agnes Anson went to the Acland family home, Killerton in Exeter, for her grandmother's death. Lady Acland and her family had five years' preparation for her death, as well as considerable experience with dying people. Agnes took turns with her sister and other family members in sitting through the night vigils with Lady Acland, who hoped she would go 'at the beautiful daylight' of dawn. The Acland family understood the value of physical touch and reassurance when nursing those they loved who were dying. On the day of Lady Acland's death, Agnes wrote: 'I am sorry to say I did not kiss her when I went to bed—but I have had so much love-making with her that I have much to look back on.' Lady Acland and her family found their religious faith a comfort. The old lady was too weak to speak very much and wanted Agnes to read passages from the Bible, as well as prayers and her favourite hymns. She died at dawn on 14 May, just before Agnes's next watch, but 'I got to her before she died and said two texts.' The family was prepared and resigned to this death, certain that Lady Acland would be united with God and 'thanking God for her rest'.[50]

The death in 1896 of Elizabeth King, grandmother of Ramsay MacDonald's future wife, Margaret Gladstone, had many similar characteristics. Mrs King, now in her seventies, was loved and well cared for by her two spinster daughters Elizabeth and Agnes, as well as by her granddaughter Margaret Gladstone. This family was also deeply religious; Mrs King's husband had been a Scottish Presbyterian minister and she had raised her five

children within a strict regime of earnest piety. In 1894 one daughter, Elizabeth, wrote a revealing letter about their mother's preparation for death to
her sister Agnes: 'It is strange how often [Mother] has lately referred to the
subject of death. We have had some very quiet solemn talks about it, which
I hope have been reassuring and comforting to her. She had been saying how
terribly she dreaded the great change—the passing from this familiar world
into the utterly unknown.'[51] Elizabeth made no attempt to postpone the
discussion, but reminded her mother 'how peacefully she had lain on the
borderland' during her serious illness a decade earlier, when she felt no
terror but saw 'the other side as near and as natural as this'. Mrs King looked
pleased at the memory. This letter provides a good illustration of Victorian
religious and psychological preparation for death, supported by a strong faith
and a loving family. Relatives did not usually press the probability of impending death when the dying person seemed unwilling to accept it, but generally
responded honestly when such questions were raised.

Over a year later, Margaret Gladstone was at her grandmother's bedside as
she lay dying. Old Mrs King was very weak, with pain sometimes so bad that
it was 'almost difficult for her to feel the "God of Comfort" near her'. But
throughout the long, weary wait, her religious faith reassured her there was a
purpose to the suffering, although at times her tired mind obviously dwelt on
the prospect of judgement: 'My grandmother had a rather bad night: she was
rather distressed this morning—, said she had been so wicked she deserved
it all—So Aunt E. [Elizabeth] read her the prodigal son and she liked it. I
couldn't think why Aunt E. chose that last night—it seems not suitable to a
good old lady—but I suppose it really is to all of us.'[52] Margaret Gladstone
was convinced, however, that 'through it all she knows that God is behind the
clouds, and is sending her these trials in love'. Mrs King's spiritual expectations were focused on seeing her Lord in the next life, with just the
one expressed hope of reunion with the daughter who died at Margaret
Gladstone's birth in 1870.[53] Despite the strain of waiting for the end, 'there
is no gloom: it is bright and peaceful', for Mrs King and her family were fully
prepared for her death in July 1896.[54]

There were other deaths in old age where the religious faith was strong and
the family was well prepared and wholly supportive, but the nature of the
disease made the death more distressing and the spiritual consolation more
elusive. Lady Salisbury, wife of the Conservative Prime Minister, died of
'peritoneal dropsy' in 1899, at the age of 72, following a prolonged, painful,
and miserable illness which allowed patient and family three years of preparation, at the cost of great suffering. Mary Drew, a family friend, described
the patient's condition in 1897:

She has been tapped 4 or 5 times. Each time it has been a great success, and made them hopeful, and the Doctors do not say she cannot recover. . . . She is a good deal changed, face and hands wasted and her deafness has increased. Lord Salisbury sits by her petting her and stroking her hand and she is tremendously keen about politics and all that is going on, and she encourages him not to be depressed by her illness.[55]

Lady Salisbury was comforted by the tender care of a devoted family, but the disease was oppressive, as her lungs were emptied of fluid weekly and the pressure of liquid caused considerable pain.[56] Frances Balfour reported early in 1899 that Lady Salisbury was weaker, her mind usually wandering and deluded, but when she could think clearly she was very depressed by her condition: 'What wonder, they are tapping her *weekly* and taking 17 pints of fluid away.' Yet Frances could see some reason for thankfulness in Lord Salisbury's sensitivity and care of his wife, 'his complete absorption in her . . . I think this long drawn parting is a merciful weaning for him, and I believe [she] will be more to him, than had she died 3 years ago when the illness first set in.' He was certainly facing up to the grim truth and was 'really very low'.[57]

After Lady Salisbury's death in 1899, her eldest son, James, said there had been constant anxiety for months, so the end was 'not exactly a shock'. Lord Salisbury and their three sons were present when she died, though James Cecil explained their reluctance to record the scene in detail:

I have only [just] realised how terribly my father has felt that long strain of anxiety. He has almost a sense of restfulness now though very, very sad. The patience, submission, matter-of-course reality of his faith are wonderful to watch. . . . I know that his greatest anxiety is that our lives should not be darkened. . . . He speaks of my mother quite naturally as if she were still alive or had been dead a long time,—but of her death itself hardly a word. . . . Once I said to him that I thought the past anxiety had been worse for him to bear than now,—he assented, made a religious allusion to explain his resignation. . . . The death was quite peaceful,—she had been quite unconscious for some days,—practically so for some weeks.[58]

Alice Cecil, James's wife, felt the loss of 'the sort of Centre to everything and a figure which seemed as if Death could never touch'.[59] The Cecil family was well prepared for this death and consoled by their strong religious faith. It also helped that the loving husband was still alive to comfort and care for his sick wife, and in sufficiently good health to cope with the loss of his spouse.

Mental deterioration was the harshest aspect of some deaths for families to endure, illustrated by Beatrice Potter's sensitive response to her father's mental degeneration after a series of strokes. All but one of her sisters were married, leaving a reluctant Beatrice to preside over Richard Potter's household in his declining years. In 1883 she sadly noted her father's continuing grief for his wife, who had died a year earlier, and his frustration at his diminishing capacity to work at the age of 66:

Father really anxious for work. Still suffers silent agony and lonely grief for mother . . . this sorrow is permanent though intermittent. There is a deep sadness in decaying power, more terrible to me than death itself. And all who have passed the prime of life, who have lived those few golden years for work, must exhibit this decline in the power for *persistent* work.[60]

By 1889 Beatrice Potter could no longer maintain this philosophical approach to her father's 'slow decay', and began to anticipate his death as a blessed release: 'He lies in his bed in a state of complete apathy. His life can no longer be a pleasure to him or to those around him: it would be merciful if he should be taken.' The breaking of the central family tie would be sad, but she longed for the 'complete holiday' only possible on his death. Beatrice found her father's companionship 'inexpressibly depressing in its soullessness', only lightened by rare glimpses of calm reason and warm feeling. She wondered if her family was justified in assuming 'that he is a creature, whose effectual life is gone', and 'ignoring all responsible thought or action in him'. Perhaps they were all degrading some 'immortal principle' in him by assuming that he was morally dead, and that love and duty required them only to make him physically comfortable.[61] Four years after the most serious stroke Beatrice felt depressed and guilty: 'Father lying like a log in his bed—a child . . .—an animal . . . The consciousness of his presence falls like a black pall overhanging all things and deadening all thought and feeling. One longs for release and yet sickens at the thought of this weary desire for the death of one's Father.'[62] Moreover, her socialist philosophy was affronted by the thought that ten servants in the household were 'living on the fat of the land in order to minister to the supposed comfort of one poor imbecile old man'.[63]

Richard Potter died at last on New Year's Day 1892 at the age of 75. Beatrice and her sister Kate Courtney watched him through his last night as he lay in a heavy stupor. He was granted 'beautiful rest from the weary struggling life of a day ago', while Beatrice was finally free to move on to a life of socialist service and marriage with Sidney Webb.[64] Kate's sadness was also mixed with relief: 'We have been so long prepared and the last stages of Father's illness have left him so little alive that it seems hardly a shock— indeed a relief. The one happy thing to look back upon during the long illness is his freedom from care about himself.'[65] Beatrice Potter was an exceptional woman with outstanding intellectual capacity, but there is no reason to suppose that her emotional response to her father's slow mental decline was unusual, except in her ability to express her feelings so fluently.

A long illness accompanied by senile dementia could be agonizing for the family, since it prevented spiritual preparation for death, it often altered the sufferer's personality, and it made a good Christian death impossible. Watching a father die so slowly was a dreadful experience for a daughter, as Beatrice Potter found, but it could be a greater trauma for a spouse or partner whose life had been entirely entwined with that of the dying person for decades. The experience of the King sisters reveals the agony of death and separation for loving and mutually dependent spinster sisters. It also illustrates the extreme stress which could occur when one elderly partner had to bear the total burden of the other's care, without the professional nursing assistance and the ten servants available to Beatrice Potter.

On 26 May 1914 Elizabeth King died at the age of 64, of 'senile decay and heart failure', according to her death certificate. Elizabeth and Agnes King were fairly typical spinster sisters who escaped the usual obscurity of unmarried women only because their niece Margaret Gladstone happened to marry the Labour leader, Ramsay MacDonald. After a repressive Presbyterian upbringing they nursed their father through a mental breakdown in the 1870s and cared for both elderly parents for nearly two decades until their deaths. The King sisters accepted their domestic caring role with religious acquiescence, reinforced by their love for each other, and supported by a very small private income. Their relationship was in some respects like that of an elderly married couple, but with greater equality of roles and probably greater mutual dependence.

Agnes King was overwhelmed by intense grief at Elizabeth's suffering and by the strain of nursing her beloved elder sister through an agonizing final illness from 1911 to 1914. Her sorrow was exacerbated by the earlier loss of her beloved niece Margaret MacDonald in 1911. Agnes compared her own mental collapse with that of her father forty years earlier and, like him, she suffered a severe religious crisis. The mutual affection and dependence between the sisters were revealed in their correspondence during two brief separations in 1911 and 1912, intended to allow Agnes to recuperate. In April 1911 Agnes wrote to Elizabeth: 'I am going to try and leave it all with God . . . The doctor thinks that before long I shall have regained the calm which used to help you, and that with feeding and rest my heart will get all right and that there will be no further risk of its breaking down. Dear, dear love.'[66] One of the rare responses was a pathetic note from Elizabeth asking Agnes to refrain from writing such beautiful letters: 'Things with me are far too ghastly for that. Once more my dearest love to my darling.'[67]

Agnes King's 'Prayers during the long struggle' are a moving record of her mental breakdown and deep despair, as she failed to cope with Elizabeth's illness and impending death. Watching her sister's decline and remembering their father's mental breakdown, she had well-founded fears for her own sanity. Agnes was also most concerned about her own increasing dependence on her remaining family, especially her brother. She wrote in September 1911:

Oh God, I know my mind is going. I cannot stem the tide of sleeplessness and sorrow. Keep me safe, keep me safe, I beseech thee, that I may not live long to be a burden to those I love so dearly. I have tried to see my way but I have failed all round. This is an agony far, far worse than death, yet I know I must cling to life, however useless and broken it is.[68]

A life of deep Presbyterian devotion seemed of little avail in this crisis. Agnes feared that her sister's soul was doomed by her senility, and she nurtured thoughts of rebellion against God as well as suicidal yearnings: 'My brain is confused and tired with the long strain and the loss of sleep, guide it for me, Oh God, and help me to keep down rebellious and wrong thoughts.'[69] Agnes failed to rise above it all, to cope with the 'agony that sweeps over me from my strained nerves', filling her with 'wild dismay'.[70]

The final surviving *cri de cœur* was written in February 1912, more than two years before Elizabeth's death. Agnes confessed that even the love which had always been the mainspring of her life, love of God, her sister, and her family, seemed to be evaporating. People advised her to divert her thoughts elsewhere, but she considered this impossible, since her sister had filled her thoughts for more than fifty years: 'I never cared for anything she did not share.' She longed for death and increasingly her troubled mind dwelt on the prospect of recapturing her lost love again in heaven: 'Keep all this passionate love safe, Oh God, and give it me back, if not in this world, in Thy great heaven.' But in the meantime, she prayed to be kept 'safe from evil' and 'to do least harm and give least trouble and pain to those I love'.[71] This ordeal continued for two more years, but Agnes no longer found it possible to commit her prayers to paper. Her grief at Elizabeth's prolonged senile decay was like that of a wife about to become a widow, though a widow's social status and support network would probably have been greater, and her isolation less overwhelming.

Mental degeneration in old age was traumatic enough for all concerned when the families were supportive and caring, but it could be dreadful when they were not. Sir John Dashwood King, fourth baronet, died in 1849 aged about 83, afflicted with advanced senility. Four of his seven children predeceased him, while the remaining three had been alienated to varying degrees by his irascibility and difficult temperament. His eldest son, George Henry Dashwood, MP, had such severe differences with his father that they scarcely ever met in Sir John's final years, while his daughter Mary Berkeley had her own problems with her husband's mistress and his gambling debts.

The family physician, Dr Edmund Lambert, seemed to be the only genuinely concerned person who visited Sir John Dashwood at Halton in Berkhamsted at all frequently in 1848, the year before his death. Dr Lambert corresponded at regular intervals with George Dashwood, warning him of his father's precarious health and hazardous financial affairs. Early in January 1848 Dr Lambert advised George Dashwood that his father's mental decay rendered him totally incompetent to manage his business affairs: 'There can be no doubt that you are the proper person to protect him.' Dr Lambert recommended the transfer of Sir John's property and business matters to George's management and control.[72]

But the best efforts of the kindly family doctor could not persuade the eldest son to shoulder his filial responsibilities, and the situation rapidly deteriorated. Late in 1848 Dr Lambert reported that George Dashwood was urgently needed at Halton to look after his father and supervise the necessary financial changes. Moreover, Sir John was now in the hands of an unscrupulous attorney, who was acting without any controls and whose interests conflicted with those of the family. Two months later the doctor reported that the lawyers were 'getting pretty pickings out of Sir John', whose 'dotage is daily becoming more obvious', and who was now utterly incompetent to manage even his ordinary affairs.[73] In early March 1849 the exasperated doctor sent a strongly worded letter urging George Dashwood to attend to his father at Halton. Once more he exhorted the eldest son to take immediate action to protect his father's property and person:

[Sir John] is now arrived at a time of life when he only requires kindness and attention which undoubtedly he ought to experience in the bosom of his own family. And it is my opinion that the establishment at Halton is attended with a vast and useless expenditure under the superintendence of subordinate people and that by breaking it up Sir John would not be deprived of a single comfort. I am also of opinion that if you could agree in visiting the establishment, your own influence and the respectability of the family would be greatly increased.[74]

In the absence of a supportive family, Dr Lambert took a liberal interpretation of his role as family doctor, in the belief that the general welfare of his senile patient required him to act as personal and financial adviser. But the extended role of the family practitioner was in this case thankless and futile.

Possibly the good doctor had also been sending warning letters to George Dashwood's sister Mary Berkeley, for she belatedly began to visit her father and recognize the family responsibilities in May 1849, after an absence of eight months. She was horrified on arrival to find the house filled with sheriff's officers, and to learn that everything was to be sold. Mary found her father in bed, crying in his despair, as he greeted her with the words, 'I am as miserable as a man can well be!' She appealed for her brother's help in their father's declining years instead of abandoning him to the servants: 'Believe me George, that old man is pining away his days, *neglected* and *alone*, and if anything should happen to him, it is an awful thing to think *no one* has stept forward to alleviate and soothe his latter days.' Somebody must regulate their father's way of living, since it was clear Sir John had been 'shamefully cheated' by his lawyer for the last two years. Mary did not believe her brother had any conception of the depredation at Halton, with all the contents up for sale and the servants dismissed. She requested her brother to arrange a decent house for their father, who was in abject misery, having taken to his bed to 'shut out the evils by sleep'. In her view their father ought to have one of his family constantly with him, though her own family responsibilities prevented her from taking on this role: 'Of all the misfortunes I have endured this last of seeing my poor old father sinking (at his time of life) in poverty and misery is the greatest of *all,* it haunts me by night as well as by day.'[75]

But neither doctor nor sister could prevail on the eldest son. As Mary Berkeley reported on 11 June 1849, the old man was moved first to the inn at Berkhamsted, and then confined to a tiny room in 'small lodgings' in London, which he shared with his footman. Mary begged her brother, as head of the family, to place their father in a more 'wholesome' house immediately, because he was deteriorating rapidly. Six weeks later Sir John was still living in the same small room with his footman, who apparently let his master lie in bed to save trouble. Mary believed her father was entirely at the servant's mercy, and she and her brother should visit more often to check the situation.[76] George Dashwood finally visited his father in July 1849, in time to pronounce his legs paralysed and recovery impossible. Sir John Dashwood King died in October 1849, a 'happy release' as a relative confessed, and his eldest son at least attended the funeral.[77]

Many of these Victorian deaths in old age are described by adult children, who felt a special grief at the loss of a parent. Dolly Herbert spoke for other adult daughters when she lamented the death in 1880 of her mother, Anne dowager Countess Cowper: 'One delights in feeling how her love and life are part of one's very bone and marrow, and will surround one's thoughts and life as much as they have ever done, with perhaps increased love, as I am full of reproaches, at the greater love and tenderness one could have returned to her.'[78] Like Lady Salisbury, Lady Cowper had been the pivot of the family, 'the ground and the walls of one's life'. Margot Asquith captured the essence of a daughter's loss, remarking that 'the death of one's mother is the end of one's youth', in response to a letter of condolence on her mother's death in 1895.[79] Joseph Hooker, the scientist, felt 'as if *orphaned*' on his mother's death in 1872, even though he was already 55; she had never divided her affections and 'my prosperity was her chief joy'.[80] Violet Cecil commented in 1909: 'nothing on earth can ever in any way approach the loss of parents and children—when our Fathers and Mothers go, the world gets suddenly cold and our backs feel all bare as if the great shelter of life was gone'. She missed her own father hourly and would go to her grave missing him.[81]

For most adult children, the natural and inevitable deaths of parents in old age were accepted as a source of sorrow, but not a cause of longer-term psychological problems. However, in a minority of cases difficulties seem to have resulted from particularly intense and dependent relationships. Lady Abercromby's response to her mother's death in 1898 suggested an unhealthy devotion, if not dependence. She was stunned by her mother's death and likened her illness to a bad dream: 'How shall I live without her to share my thoughts with?' Even fourteen years later: 'This house and place are full of thoughts of my Mother. Everything that she has touched is as if her hand had just rested on it—It seems but yesterday that she was here.' Such references occurred in many letters to her friends, suggesting an unusually strong bond between mother and daughter.[82]

An extreme response to a parent's death is well illustrated by the plight of an unmarried daughter on the death of a father she had lived with and cared for over many years. As the only daughter, Sarah Angelina Acland became housekeeper and social secretary to her father, Sir Henry Wentworth Acland, Regius Professor of Medicine at Oxford, following the death of her mother in 1878 and her brothers' marriages. Angie promised her dying mother to 'do all in my power' for her father, but their relationship was formal over the next twenty-two years, characterized by adoration and subservience on her part. Her purpose in life was demolished at a stroke on his death in 1900, when she was 60, even though he had not made her happy: 'I shall never be the same again. I feel an old woman now that my only object in life is gone—and cannot imagine what I shall do—if I still have to live on. All my interest in life has so entirely gone during the long nursing of Father.' Her brother, with his home and family, could not possibly realize the impact of the loss of 'Father and home and position in a moment'.[83] In the following months Angie felt ill, desperately lonely, and uprooted by the necessary move away from the old family home. Her increasing involvement in philanthropy in subsequent years did not entirely fill the void left by her father's death.

It is well known that bereavement can affect physical health, and among elderly people who have lost a spouse it can occasionally contribute to death from heart disease. Studies by British psychologists have found that the death-rate rises in the first year of bereavement, heart disease being the most frequent cause of death. In 1963 Michael Young reported increased mortality rates among 4,486 widowers over the age of 54 during the first six months of bereavement, reaching a level 40 per cent higher than the expected rate for married men of the same age.[84] Psychiatrist Beverley Raphael explains this phenomenon:

The older the person is when the spouse dies, the less the future he or she perceives. There are fewer years left, and thus so much less motivation to suffer the pain of the mourning process and relinquish the spouse . . . The widow(er) holds on for the few years left, living on together with the lost person, maybe cherishing this image while awaiting reunion in some form of afterlife . . . Clinical observations suggest that some of the bereaved elderly just give up and die.[85]

There are numerous Victorian and Edwardian examples of elderly widows and widowers dying within a few months or years of their departed spouse. In 1858 May Gladstone's mother died, to be followed three years later by her grief-stricken husband, terminally ill with heart disease for the last eighteen months.[86] Evelyn Lady Stanhope died of a chill in 1873, leaving a 'broken-hearted' husband who followed her to the churchyard precisely two years later. Just before his death, his daughter-in-law warned her husband, the heir to the earldom, 'Your father is not getting on at all . . . There is a total absence of vital power or rebound. . . . It is his weak heart that is the serious thing and therefore you must not shock him.'[87] Emma Ribblesdale mentioned in her diary for 1886 that her mother's old aunts Jemima and Kate Mure died within a week of each other.[88] Anna Merivale commented in 1902 on her sister's death soon after the loss of her husband: 'Dear Rose was of course never the same after the trial of John's long illness and death.'[89] In May 1905 Kate Courtney noted in her diary that Lady Hobhouse had quickly followed her husband: 'I think she would have chosen to do so as soon as she had looked over his papers and letters and left things in order.'[90]

Historians have observed that old people rarely speak for themselves in the historical record because of the effects of poverty and disability.[91] Victorian family archives at least allow the voices of some old people from the privileged classes to be heard. From today's perspective, these accounts of deaths of the elderly in the nineteenth century seem far more familiar than those of the deaths of children, because we are primarily accustomed to death in old age. Death at the end of a long life calls forth a more gentle and muted response, lacking the emotional trauma of the premature deathbeds of the young and middle-aged.

ᵉ⅏ 8 ⅏ᵉ

IN SEARCH OF THE GOOD DEATH
DEATH IN THE GLADSTONE AND LYTTELTON FAMILIES
1835–1915

T HIS CHAPTER EXPLORES THE APPLICATION OF EVANGELICAL IDEALS OF
the good death over eighty years in two large and closely related Anglican families: the Gladstones and the Lytteltons. Analysis of the experiences of
these two families over eight decades reveals the effects of change over time,
and the differential impact of deaths at different stages of the life-cycle, and
from different sorts of diseases. The Gladstone and Lyttelton families are
broadly representative of many middle- and upper-class families who were
devout Anglicans. They spanned the professional spectrum, including politicians, clergymen, public servants, diplomats, landowners, and industrialists,
as well as William Ewart Gladstone himself, four times Prime Minister.
Excellent source material has survived about their experiences of death, grief,
and mourning over three generations from the 1830s to 1900, with some
additional evidence for the Edwardian period, whereas the evidence in most
families tends to be more fragmented.

A study of death in the Gladstone and Lyttelton families also facilitates a
closer analysis of the influence of Evangelicalism on deathbed expectations,
attitudes, and behaviour. In the early and mid-Victorian periods the impact
of Evangelicalism on these two families was profound, even though W. E.
Gladstone and his family gradually joined the Lytteltons in the High Church
fold. This case-study demonstrates the extent to which the influence of the
Evangelical movement transcended those groups who can be identified as
Evangelicals. It also shows how far an Evangelical childhood and upbringing
could still affect behaviour and expectations at times of crisis, particularly at
death, despite changes in doctrinal beliefs. Further, it suggests that the
devotional piety displayed by Evangelicals and Tractarians at the deathbed
was very similar, despite doctrinal differences.

W. E. Gladstone's father, John Gladstone, was a successful merchant who
had moved from a Unitarian viewpoint to that of the Evangelical wing of the
Anglican Church, even founding two Anglican churches in Liverpool in 1815.
His second wife, Anne, was an intensely pious Evangelical, as well as a

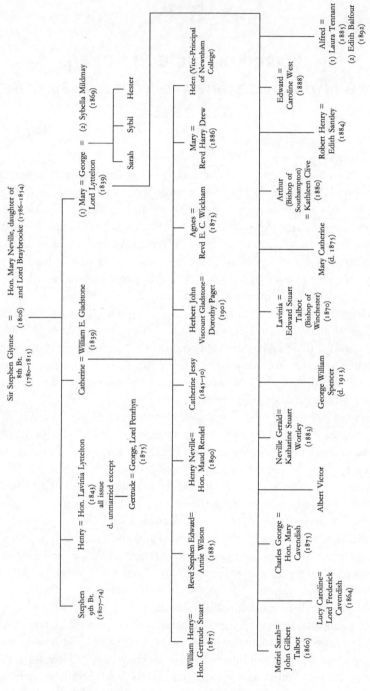

FIG. I. The Gladstone and Lyttelton families.

Source: Mary Drew, *Catherine Gladstone* (1919), 293.

neurotic invalid obsessed with sin and suffering. Anne set the strict religious tone of the young Gladstone family, teaching them the fervent language and behaviour of Evangelicals, with daily Bible-reading and a continuous self-scrutiny reflected in their daily diaries and their detailed accounts of deathbed scenes. Anne Gladstone's intensely personal struggle for salvation through faith was transmitted to all her children, but most of all to the precocious William.[1]

The Lytteltons and Gladstones became intimately connected in 1839, shortly after the start of Queen Victoria's reign, when the two beautiful and lively Glynne sisters, Mary and Catherine, married Lord Lyttelton and William Gladstone at a joint wedding. George Lyttelton could match Gladstone in scholarship and surpass him in rank, but he fell considerably short in professional accomplishment, physical appearance, and temperament. Like his wife, Mary, George was an unquestioning and committed Christian, and like his brother-in-law, he was influenced by High Church teaching at university, later reinforced by the Glynnes and by Gladstone. The Tractarianism of the Lytteltons was always tempered by Mary's simple faith and by the tolerant Low Church influence of George's brother William, Rector of Hagley, the family living. The Gladstones had four boys and four girls, while the Lytteltons had eight boys and four girls, who grew up together and drew their friends from the ranks of siblings and cousins. The lives of these two families were pervaded by a deep sense of cheerful but highly committed Christianity, very different from the stern and narrow practice of William's childhood. Family Bible-reading and prayers took place daily, and church attendance was frequent, even daily when possible, but it was all enjoyed rather than endured.

William Gladstone's personal journey from Evangelical to Tractarian in the 1820s and 1830s is well known, but as Colin Matthew emphasizes, he retained some Evangelical characteristics despite the High Church nature of his devotional habits. William's marriage to Catherine Glynne in 1839 was seen by both partners as a deep religious commitment, though it was also an alliance between the rising middle-class politician and the sister of a baronet with impressive aristocratic connections. Catherine brought emotional and spiritual balance to the Gladstone household, for she was a very different woman from her mother-in-law.[2] Lord Lyttelton later described his wife's faith as 'simple and entire' though she was disinclined to dwell on details. This applied equally to both Glynne sisters, who practised an uncomplicated but deeply committed religion, which they discussed rarely but took very much for granted. Georgina Battiscombe described Catherine as 'a soul turned instinctively towards God' and both sisters derived great pleasure from the practice of their faith.[3]

The private records of death kept by these two families illuminate the nature and significance of such memorials for many Victorian Christian families. George Lyttelton and William Gladstone each composed detailed, intimate accounts of family deaths on a daily and even hourly basis, in diary form, placing their emphasis on the physical and medical detail, as well as the spiritual state of the sufferer. William Gladstone compiled memorials of the deaths of his mother in 1835, his daughter Jessy in 1850, his father in 1851, and his son in 1891, while George Lyttelton constructed an astonishingly long record of his first wife's death in 1857. These memorials are complemented by the voluminous correspondence of many family members and by the private diaries of William Gladstone, his daughter Mary, and his niece Lucy Lyttelton.

The younger generation of Gladstones and Lytteltons continued their fathers' custom of keeping detailed records of family deaths. These accounts were valued as consolation, memorial, and therapy, and were often copied out lovingly by relatives and friends to support them through subsequent bereavements. Above all, these memorials were Evangelical in purpose. Just as family members kept diaries to account to God for the way they spent their lives, these memorials accounted for their deaths, and were intended to have a beneficent effect on the preparation for death of those who read them. Sometimes they were bequeathed in women's informal wills, and subsequent deaths added to the record. The long account of Lady Lyttelton's death in 1857 was partially copied in 1871 by her daughter May, who was only 7 when her mother died, with May's additional note, 'For the future reading (among others) of those, so dear to her, Who were yet too young to feel their loss'.[4] At her death in 1875 May bequeathed her own unfinished copy of this 'Hagley Record' to her friend and cousin Mary Gladstone, who added her own account of May's death. Ten years later Mary Gladstone confided to Lord Rosebery, a close family friend, that her own copy of the Hagley Record was 'rather specially precious' because it originally belonged to May Lyttelton. She was prepared to allow Lord Rosebery to see the family memorial because she knew he would be 'tender and reverent' about it, understanding how sacred it was to the family.[5]

In 1888, while she was searching for a letter at her father's request, Mary (by then Mary Drew) accidentally came across his account of the life and death of her sister Jessy in 1850. Mary wrote a note to her mother asking permission to copy this memorial: 'I want to know whether I may copy [it] into my Record? I shall much value a copy, and besides that I think there ought to be more than one copy in the world, in case any accident happened to the original . . . it is a *perfect* thing, and should be classed with the [Hagley] Record for sacredness and beauty and pathos.'[6] Mary did copy the moving account of her father's spiritual and emotional crisis on Jessy's death from meningitis in 1850, marked 'most private'. It was probably intended at first for Gladstone's eyes alone—certainly not for anybody outside his immediate family—as personal therapy and spiritual accounting to God and posterity. Mary copied out the sad text during a religious retreat, for it held deep spiritual significance for her: 'the record of a child, the mainspring of whose brief life was Love, the record of a father, the mainspring of whose resignation and faith was Love, and finally a record which is in itself an undying witness of the Love of God'.[7] At the time Mary Drew asked to copy Jessy's memorial, she was a busy, mature, well-balanced woman of 41. In time her Hagley Record accumulated to include, *inter alia*, her brother William's death in 1891 and her father's death in 1898, but with those two the Record ended.

In Search of the Good Death 1835–1875

The first four deaths to be analysed here are those of W. E. Gladstone's mother in 1835, his daughter in 1850, his father in 1851, and George Lyttelton's first wife in 1857. The account of Mary Lyttelton's death is the best example of the Victorian Evangelical ideal of the good death in all these family archives, while that of Anne Gladstone in 1835 demonstrates the self-conscious desire of Evangelicals to transform a difficult death into an inspiring spiritual occasion.

By 1835 William Gladstone had moved to a High Church position, but when it came to facing death the Evangelical foundations of his faith were still the most powerful. Memories of his Evangelical childhood must have been revived when, at the age of 26, he witnessed his mother's death. William was familiar with most treatises on the good death, including Jeremy Taylor's *Exercises of Holy Dying*, and was apprehensive lest his pious mother should not attain one. The day after Anne's death, he composed a lengthy memorial in the Evangelical form entitled 'Recollections of the Last Hours of my Mother', which became the model for the later family accounts of death. This memorial is remarkably prosaic, devoting obsessive attention to the practical details of the illness, and very different from published Evangelical effusions like *Clear Shining Light*. It was also pompous and self-conscious, characteristics not shared by the later family memorials.

The second Mrs Gladstone was delicate and self-effacing, 'asking only to set the religious tone of the household at a somewhat fanatical level of intellectually undemanding piety', as Richard Shannon observes. She bore six children, two girls and four boys, and her life of invalidism enabled her to evade the responsibilities posed by her husband's considerable achievements in business and politics.[8] She became a permanent invalid in 1827, two years before the death of her consumptive daughter, Anne. At the age of 63 in September 1835, Anne Gladstone deteriorated rapidly during a three-week illness diagnosed as erysipelas, and characterized by fever, pain, and general prostration. The patient rallied on 20 September, after a second medical opinion and an alarm about impending death, and the symptoms of erysipelas declined. The doctors turned their attention instead to the new symptom of 'alarming' constipation, which they treated with spirits of turpentine. When the pain increased next day the doctors administered an opiate to reduce Mrs Gladstone's suffering. Instead of welcoming the pain relief, Gladstone seemed concerned that his mother's mind was 'thus removed a step further from us' and was less able to concentrate on preparing her soul for death. The family was reassured by the presence of the two doctors, even though they seemed uncertain what to do for the best, their advice occasionally conflicted, and their treatment was sometimes painful. No doubt any kind of medical advice was better than none, especially as there was no professional nurse at this early date and the family needed reassurance as they shared the nursing.[9]

If the medical side of Mrs Gladstone's decline was unsatisfactory, the spiritual dimension failed utterly to fulfil her son's expectations of the good Christian death. Anne's death was probably typical of deaths from fever, but Gladstone left no doubt that he would have preferred the death scene to develop differently. Dr Hunter summoned the family from bed at 5 a.m. on Sunday 20 September 1835, with the premature warning that death was likely within a few hours:

We all . . . gathered round her bedside, unaware that we were likely rather to injure her by causing a bewildered astonishment as to the occasion of our presence. Whey was given her and a little wine. Tom asked her if she had any wish or sentiment to express. She answered in the negative: but presently asked for me [William Gladstone], and when I went up to her said, 'You all give me the idea that this is my last hour, but I have no such notion . . . [She] evinced a great weakness and difficulty in speaking though she recognized us all perfectly . . . It appeared soon that she was better informed than we were as to the strength of her constitution.[10]

The only remotely edifying statement was Mrs Gladstone's remark that 'all was right' between her husband and herself. She said she knew she was about to die and was 'weary to be off', and refused the offer of her son John to read prayers, protesting she was unequal to it. William was obliged to accept his mother's inability to respond to his earnest entreaties:

There was an evident incapacity, both in the organs of speech to act for any length of time, and in mind to deal with any complex combination of ideas . . . I once or twice attempted to say more on the subject of her sufferings, well knowing that the poorest attempt to remind her of her consolation would be a delight to her spirit, if her strength was sufficient to enable her to comprehend it . . . The vigour was gone which would have enabled her to evince more instructively in what way it was that Death was to her disarmed of its terrors, and that she was ready, without a moment's trepidation or reluctance, to go forth and meet the bridegroom.[11]

Several significant points emerge from William Gladstone's sanctimonious memorial. The convergence of the family around the bedside signified to all that death was near, and this could shock the unprepared patient. No mention was made of Holy Communion, despite William's Tractarian views, presumably because his mother was such a staunch Evangelical. William and his brother Tom, at least, had hoped for a final speech from the dying woman, to demonstrate that she did not fear death because she was well prepared. William's use of the term 'instructively' in this context underlines his frustration at his mother's inability to provide an exemplary Evangelical death scene.

In the next two days, the brothers and sisters shared the watches, taking it in turns to sit by their mother's side, while she suffered considerable pain from repeated applications of turpentine. Anne told William, in an unusual period of consciousness, 'My dear, this is become an awful case: I am in the depths of despair.' Frequent 'mutterings of prayer' were interspersed with bouts of pain. When Mrs Gladstone reached her second and final deathbed scene, she was unconscious, and far beyond the reach of spiritual exhortation from her son. On 23 September the family was again called into her room, but the 'descent into the dark valley' lasted for eight hours, with the family and Dr Guthrie watching at her side throughout, except to retire in couples to dine. Gladstone described the deep purple flush on his mother's face, the fatal rattling in the throat, the flesh sunk upon the features, and the occasional strong convulsive movements. However dreadful it looked and sounded, especially as 'the fearful rattle grew louder and louder', the family knew she was quite unconscious. Gladstone made no attempt to represent his mother's death as less ugly than it was, though he would dearly have liked it to be so.[12]

A few hours later the family took it in turns to visit the 'Chamber of Death' and kiss the 'claycold' face—again no attempt to idealize the reality. William wrote his lengthy account of his mother's death that night, and arrangements were made about mourning next day. On 25 September William noted in his diary: 'Most beautifully did my Father speak to me before dinner of the visitation, its wise and kind intent, and its softening effects: with the full recognition of the truth that such things are *necessary* for our peace.'[13] He had been unable to express such pious consoling thoughts in the account written two days before. At this early stage in his life he was familiar with the Evangelical ideal of the good death, but completely unprepared for an actual death which failed to conform. In his distress he made no attempt to misrepresent his mother's death and needed his father's help in appreciating any positive sources of consolation.

If the death of Gladstone's mother warned him that some deaths did not conform to the Evangelical model, the dreadful death of his eldest child, Jessy, must have shattered any remaining illusions. On 9 April 1850 4-year-old Jessy died from tubercular meningitis. Gladstone kept two accounts, one in his daily diary, the other a more detailed memorial of his daughter's illness marked 'most private', started two days before her death. He justified the writing of the memorial on the grounds that Jessy was 'great in Love', so 'the record of her may do us good, when we peruse it in a world where love is sorely nipped and blighted, not by sorrow, which waters and feeds it, but by the sharp and bursting blasts of Sin'. This record was far more emotional than Gladstone's stark account of his mother's death, since his feelings were far more deeply engaged.[14] He and Catherine were almost overcome by the horror of this death of a young child, which caused even Gladstone to question his faith.

Gladstone's memorial of Jessy's death began with an account of her young life and character which was less idealized than many, and proceeded to describe her illness. The disease developed so slowly that the parents noticed little until it was too late, when they could only assume that it was God's 'especial pleasure to remove her'. Jessy's health was broken from February 1850, marked by emaciation, slow circulation, and problems of the liver and digestive organs. By 29 March her condition looked very serious, with a complete loss of appetite and energy, followed by great pain and fever, despite her mother's 'affectionate and unwearied' nursing. On 1 April the parents sent for Dr Charles Locock, who initially reassured them, until the pain intensified next day, causing Jessy to toss and scream in the arms of one or other parent. Up to that time Dr Locock had not appeared greatly concerned, attributing the illness to a problem of the stomach or the intestines. But he now became thoroughly alarmed and admitted the symptoms indicated 'tubercular inflammation of the membranes of the brain, a most insidious form of disease', though still not a hopeless case.[15]

At that critical juncture Gladstone's diary switched abruptly from the prosaic recital of medical details to the consolatory language of Christianity, expressing his spiritual struggle to accept God's will: 'And now O Father can we readily yield her up to Thee? O how much better will she be cared for than in this sad and evil world. His will be done.'[16] But his statement of resignation was not convincing. The diary account concentrated on the medical symptoms and treatment, whereas the 'most private' memorial revealed Gladstone's emotional crisis. The doctor treated Jessy with blisters and Dover's Powder, a popular patent medicine based on opium,[17] which seemed to help initially. During the last few days the doctor concerned himself unduly with Jessy's constipation, giving repeated applications of calomel, leading Gladstone to report the daily state of her bowels in his diary. The greater the helplessness of the Victorian doctor, the more likely he was to become obsessed with purgatives. By 6 April Jessy was experiencing convulsions, and Catherine was near exhaustion. Next day Dr Locock explained 'the peculiar malignancy of the disease' and its fluctuating symptoms, warning that the crisis might be prolonged for up to three weeks.[18]

On 8 April Catherine sensed that her daughter was losing the 'deadly struggle' and the case was almost hopeless. The convulsions grew stronger, sickness developed, and her face was 'an awful hue'. Dr Locock finally admitted that the end was inevitable and suggested they should pray that 'the passage of the departing spirit should be quickened'. The doctor tried to comfort them by saying that Jessy could not feel pain in such a deep stupor, despite her 'piteous cries' as convulsions racked her entire body. Gladstone struggled hard to accept the agonizing death of his near innocent child as consistent with a loving God. As he watched the 'beloved child in her death battle, powerless to aid her', it was not easy to acquiesce in the verdict of divine providence. 'Our hearts again very sick yet I trust neither of us are so blindly selfish as to murmur at the Lord's being about to raise one of our children to Himself.' At the last the parents prayed for their daughter's 'speedy release . . . since it seems now to be plainly His will that her little life should not blossom here'. The little girl's body was racked with shattering convulsions for the last six hours, ending in a death agony of one prolonged convulsion for thirty minutes.[19]

This awful experience forced Gladstone to question the love of a God who could make a young child suffer for the sin of the human race, given the common early Victorian belief that the doctrine of original sin applied to children as well as adults:

It was, I must own, a heavy trial to flesh and blood to witness her death-struggle; to see that little creature, who had never sinned, paying the forfeit of our race; to see her little frame torn with throes . . . and to be powerless to give her aid; to feel as we moistened her lips, that it was a mockery. Though our reason told us that not being conscious, her soul did not let her suffer really, yet this sight was sad and terrible to flesh and blood.[20]

That morning Gladstone read family prayers with some difficulty, as he sought to convince himself that Jessy's suffering and death served some divine purpose, and had not been in vain:

What a witness was before us of the intensity of sin, and the wide range of its effects, when she was so torn by their powers, tho through God's grace, not tainted by their pollution: what a lesson of penitence and humility, and of the heavenly life in Christ which only saves us!

Gladstone struggled to come to terms with the idea that little Jessy preceded her parents into eternity; they should now revere her as a soul taken 'to immortality without the stain of wilful sin, and in the robe of purity, with which she rose from her baptism'.[21]

The parents endeavoured to explain Jessy's death to their three older children, who were taken to kiss the corpse 'with affectionate concern', though only Willy, the eldest, entirely understood. For two days the parents were consoled by having Jessy's body close to them, surrounded by flowers in the boudoir, acknowledging that it was the physical closeness which comforted, 'for of her spirit we know not'. On 12 April 1850 Gladstone undertook the pilgrimage to accompany 'the dear remains' on the long train journey from London to the Gladstone family home of Fasque in Scotland. He closed the carriage blind to exclude interruptions to his 'thoughts of her who seems incessantly to beckon me and say "Come Pappy come:" and of the land whither she is gone'. But practical problems intruded on his mournful contemplation, since three changes of carriage and five payments were required, despite his prior precautions. Gladstone was comforted by the outpouring of sympathy from family and friends at Fasque, and by sharing the funeral office and Holy Communion in the family chapel. When the last sacrament was celebrated Gladstone was struck by the solemn expression which seemed to cross Jessy's face, interpreting it to mean that she had seen her God and was now in eternal peace with him for ever. Gladstone's faith was severely tested by Jessy's death, but he had attained some measure of peace when she was finally placed in the family vault.[22]

Jessy's death was a dreadful experience for both parents, and perhaps especially for Gladstone. Christian consolation was inadequate, for the child's age and virtual innocence made it impossible for them to accept the traditional concept of the hour of death as a supreme trial, while the child had no 'wilful' sins to atone for. Last words and farewells were out of the question when the dying child was so young and in such terrible pain. The only possible comfort seemed to rest in the thought that Jessy had moved to a better place while she was still quite pure, while Gladstone could not yet find consolation even in the idea of being reunited in heaven.

One of the most remarkable of these family memorials was Gladstone's thirty-three-page account of the death of his father, Sir John Gladstone, at the age of 87 in 1851. In his final three years Sir John's strong constitution gradually collapsed, as his sight, hearing, and memory slowly failed, leaving him dependent and mildly senile. He settled his business and estate affairs reluctantly, loath to abandon the material matters which dominated his life in order to compose his mind for death. He became very demanding, insisting that both a son and a daughter be in regular attendance, but he had the time to compose outstanding quarrels and divide his estate between his children. Despite an exceptionally strong constitution, Sir John died of 'old man's fever' according to Professor James Simpson, suffering intermittent fever, repeated sickness, weakened mental capacity, and the inevitable consti- pation. Three days before the end he had a stroke and was unconscious for much of the remaining time.[23]

Gladstone's long memorial on his father's death reflected an ambivalent relationship 'in which, though both had prospered, neither had found much more than a business intimacy', as Colin Matthew has suggested. Matthew is probably correct, also, in sensing 'a craving for affection, or at least for recognition, by William at the deathbed'.[24] Though Gladstone's personal devotional observances were Tractarian by 1851, this memorial strongly re- flected the Evangelicalism of his youth. The first third of the document dealt with Sir John's spiritual state of mind, but thereafter it turned into a medical diary, recording the most trivial details of the old man's physical deteriora- tion and treatment, his son even borrowing the doctor's notes to ensure accuracy.[25] Gladstone probably provided such a meticulous clinical account for several reasons. In the absence of a professional nurse, the family was sharing the nursing and was all the more aware of its demands. Moreover, since the physical and mental degeneration made the good Christian death impossible, Gladstone felt impelled to justify and explain this at inordinate length. He may also have been using the mass of clinical detail to distance himself from the unwelcome dearth of spiritual assurance, as well as his own ambivalent feelings. William's memorial was oddly detached in tone and style, even at times a shade theatrical; it was apparently written for a larger family audience, in a style utterly unlike that of his account of Jessy's death, even including occasional interjections and instructions addressed to the reader.

The first few pages of William's memorial convey its Evangelical tone and purpose and document his father's spiritual preparedness during the final three months when it was his turn to be his father's companion at Fasque. William took his responsibility as spiritual adviser exceptionally seriously, recognizing that the roles of father and son were reversed. He read aloud from the Psalms and the prayer-book every morning and evening while Sir John listened with real effort, taking genuine delight in the prayers, and occasionally interrupting with a question or a correction.[26] As a Tractarian, William Gladstone was deeply concerned that his father should receive the Holy Communion before he died, according to his expressed wish. On 1 December, when the doctor warned that death was near, William asked whether his father wished for the last sacrament, but Sir John replied that he was 'not able—it is impossible'. William had promised Dr Guthrie not to press the issue if his father seemed reluctant, because the mental effort might strain the brain: 'So I trust that by his own spontaneous intention he communicated and received from Christ that heavenly manna so needful for support in the dark passage of Death.' William, undoubtedly disappointed, read instead the prayer for the sick, but for him that lacked the consolation and spiritual grace of the Holy Communion.[27]

By 3 December William's three brothers had arrived and the old man asked if he was dying. Early next morning Sir John called out in a loud and clear voice, 'Get me some porridge'; this was hailed at the time as a sign of improvement, but shortly afterwards he had a severe stroke and these were to be his last clear words. In the afternoon the doctor warned William that the time had come to read the Commendatory Prayer; once again the doctor prompted the family to make the necessary spiritual preparation for death. After this Sir John's servants and chief dependants were encouraged to enter his room to 'take their last look at him', with 'many a tearful eye', and William brought the children in. During the final sixty hours the family did not go to bed, but 'sat or lay' about Sir John's room or the adjoining hall. This was a more crowded and more prolonged vigil than most because Sir John was head of the clan and of a large estate. The old man's body 'heaved and wrought like a blacksmith's forge' as he struggled for breath, though he seemed unconscious except for an occasional cough. This last stage seemed to William long and hopeless, except for the fact that the forefinger of his father's left hand pointed upwards throughout: 'it was a striking symbol for us, the finger of a dying Father pointing up to heaven'.[28] William seemed to be clutching at a straw in his search for a sign of salvation in the absence of Holy Communion or edifying last words.

To the modern reader this memorial seems more protracted than all the others, even the far longer account of Mary Lyttelton's death. Its outstanding characteristic is its clinical realism, with its detailed record of calomel and scammony pills for the bowels, declining rates of pulse and respiration, and the amount of egg or beef tea which could be swallowed. The abrupt switch after the death from the prosaic medical account to a religious discourse of angels and heaven comes as a shock: 'And were there not other watchers there, heavenly messengers who filled the air?' William Gladstone saw it as a day of parting but also a day of meeting: 'He is gone to those whom he loved the best: to his angelic daughter now twenty and seven years old in the peace of God, to his high and noble hearted wife.'[29] But this spiritual discourse was unusually abbreviated, especially by comparison with the clinical detail which preceded it.

William Gladstone composed this memorial in the few days between his father's death and his funeral, when the grief was acute and the memories were vivid. Yet it has far less emotional impact than his poignant account of Jessy's death in 1850, and carries less spiritual conviction than his brother-in-law's account of Mary Lyttelton's death six years later. Sir John's death was, of course, to be expected at any time, given his 87 years. William Gladstone was inevitably disappointed at the great gulf between his own youthful ideal of a good Christian death and the reality of slow mental and physical decay. But he made little attempt to represent his father's death in idealized Evangelical terms, nor did he try to orchestrate the event itself, as he did his mother's death in 1835. Possibly this was a reaction to his little daughter's dreadful death from meningitis only twenty months earlier. That death had undermined for ever William Gladstone's idealized expectations of the good Christian death, and there is evidence that Jessy's death was vividly present in his mind as Sir John lay dying. In recounting his father's symptoms he noted a minor similarity with those of Jessy: 'but the illness of that little angel was infinitely more painful and distressing'. This comment reflected not only the differences relating to the stage of the life-cycle, and the cause of the death, but Gladstone's own degree of emotional involvement. Again, when he mentioned his father's convulsion just before he died, he noted how faint it was compared to little Jessy's suffering 'for hours before her frame was composed into the peace of her angel spirit'.[30]

Lady Lyttelton's death in 1857 approached most closely to the Christian ideal and demonstrated the continued influence of Evangelicalism, even in two families who were predominantly High Church. The account itself was Evangelical in purpose and in some features, but lacked the intense earnestness and extreme piety of Gladstone's memorial to his mother. It was forty-six double folio pages long, of which thirty-two dealt with the final three days, identifying the twelve contributors by initials and including accounts of all conversations, medical attention, food and drink, and spiritual hopes and fears, in a very frank manner.[31] Most memorials were written by only one family member, but the 'Hagley Record', as it became known, was a highly unusual joint effort. George Lyttelton asked four children and seven relatives and close friends who were present at various times to write down their recollections, which he then integrated by hour and day, giving handwritten copies to all participants. That so many contributions were most unusual is evident from Caroline Talbot's 'dread of it being shown to people'; clearly such accounts were considered highly personal.[32] George Lyttelton sought to enshrine every detailed memory of his wife and her last days in a written memorial, to help him through the worst weeks of intolerable grief, and to pass on those memories to those children who were too young to understand at the time. George Lyttelton, William Gladstone, and several of their many children habitually kept a daily diary. William Gladstone and his niece Meriel Lyttelton simply copied out the relevant sections of their private diary entries for the 'Record', almost word for word, and probably other contributors did the same. This was not a deliberate attempt to reconstruct an idealized mother's death after the event.

Mary Lady Lyttelton, Catherine Gladstone's beloved sister, died of heart disease on 17 August 1857 at the age of 44, having borne twelve children in seventeen years. Dr Charles Locock, the leading gynaecologist of the mid-Victorian period, believed that a twelfth pregnancy would be a grave risk to Mary's life, particularly as she was very ill after the eleventh confinement. Locock expressed his fear to one of Mary's female relatives, probably her sister Catherine Gladstone, but not to Mary's husband. The women in the two families concealed the danger from George Lyttelton, feeling that he would crack under the strain if he knew the truth, in view of his manic-depressive tendencies. The twelfth baby was born in February 1857 'after a time of the greatest anxiety' which left no doubt that Mary's heart had been progressively weakened. The first serious heart attack took place on 8 May 1857 and from 15 June Mary spent her final two months in her bedroom at Hagley Hall in Worcestershire in steady decline. By July she retired permanently to bed, with intermittent bilious attacks and increasing difficulty in breathing.[33]

The Hagley Record places far more emphasis on the medical and physical details of Mary Lyttelton's illness than on her spiritual state, because the family took her religious preparation for granted and because High Church deathbed piety was sincere but restrained. The medical information in the Record is difficult to interpret because George Lyttelton's voice was predominant, and the family's conspiracy of silence about the extreme danger of Mary's case kept him in ignorance until the final three days. At the time

George sought to avoid the implication that Mary's death was caused by excessive child-bearing, blaming instead Locock's stimulating treatment for over-exciting Mary's circulation, though he later admitted it was a hopeless case from a very early date.[34] Dr Giles, the local family doctor, was assisted intermittently by three consultant physicians—Evans, Williams, and Locock—who insisted that 'the case was one of much obscurity and compli-cation'—a characteristic response in such a case. On 19 July the physicians agreed that the heart complaint was now well advanced, 'yet nothing serious was pronounced', at least to the patient's husband. George's optimism was still so great that, only five days before his wife's death, he kept a two-day engagement in Birmingham with the agreement of the doctors. Finally, on 14 August, observing the fatal symptoms of difficulty in breathing, cold lips, and a fixed look in the eyes, he acknowledged that the end was near. Next day Evans and Giles warned the family and the sufferer that she was in great danger, though there was still a faint hope.[35]

There was little attempt to glorify or sentimentalize Mary Lyttelton's death. Lord Lyttelton noted that until her last few days his wife had always been rather afraid of death; unlike most of their contemporaries, the two Glynne sisters preferred not to talk about their dead relatives or cherish their portraits. There were few significant spiritual statements or meaningful last words at Mary's deathbed. Indeed, George avoided long conversations in his wife's final days: 'Human nature may be forgiven, if a thought so inexpress-ibly overwhelming as her death was kept at bay, as long as we could do so.' He also wanted Mary to sleep as much as possible and sought to avoid distressing her by giving way to his emotions in her presence. He preferred at the time not to dwell on 'last words and looks' (though he rather regretted this later), because he 'shrank from the misery of such a parting as I dreaded', fearful of Mary's possible suffering at the end.[36]

The family did not set out to construct the good Evangelical death, yet Lady Lyttelton's death approximates to the ideal more closely than most. The direct references to Mary's religious assurance were unusually few, but vitally important. Her family believed that Mary Lyttelton had always led a devout Christian life, the best preparation for a good death, and George was com-forted by the knowledge that 'she left nothing unsaid that she would have wished to say'. On 15 August he assured Mary that she had nothing of which to repent: 'In her behaviour to me and to the children, as far as man can speak, she had ever been as an Angel without spot.' He explained why she had no need of conventional deathbed speeches of spiritual justification: 'On direct religious matters, her faith was peculiarly simple and entire, and she was not fond of dwelling on details. But it was also the result of the untrou-

bled serenity and trustfulness of mind in which death found her.' George
Lyttelton reassured his wife on 15 August that after death she might still watch
over and possibly even influence her family 'while unseen'.[37]

In addition to Mary Lyttelton's devout life, certain circumstances of her
final illness made an unusually good Christian death possible. She had more
than sufficient time for preparation, for she had long known she could not
recover, and no longer wished to do so. The prolonged decline in strength
had led her gradually to accept that she might die, and in the last few days her
fear of death left her. Her mind was extraordinarily clear throughout the
illness, even in the last few days, leaving intact her cheerfulness and optimism. The day before her death Mary expressed surprise at still feeling her
'faculties so clear', for she was lucid until the end and able to converse
throughout. She was also relatively free from pain during most of the illness,
except for a 'fearful spasm' in the heart a few hours before she died. Considerable discomfort from restlessness and breathlessness was treated with occasional doses of morphine.[38]

Mary was also comforted by the nursing care and the physical warmth and
touch of her close and loving family. The nursing was shared between her
sister Catherine Gladstone and her close friend Mrs Talbot, assisted by her
two eldest daughters, Meriel and Lucy, aged 17 and 16. No paid nurses
participated, in part because the Lyttletons were always short of money,
despite their social rank, though no doubt the servants helped with some of
the menial tasks.[39] George commented on 15 August that 'There was this
blessing, in the constant power of alleviating and even producing pleasure, by
rubbing, petting, moistening the lips and mouth with a brush: and such a
smile was ever ready, as if to reward.' George or Catherine often lay beside
Mary on the bed to provide these little comforts and give companionship. On
her last day she said she would like to be warmed by sleeping in her sister's
arms, where she lay during the great spasm of pain.[40]

The last Communion was a most important sacrament for a High Anglican family, and Catherine discussed this with her sister on 15 August, after the
doctors' warning that Mary's death was imminent. The timing of the final
sacrament was important but problematic, because it should take place while
the dying person was in a fit state to receive it, yet sufficiently close to the
hour of death to be appropriate. Mary chose to postpone the sacrament until
the next day, when she hoped to feel stronger, evidently daunted by the
prospect in her weakened condition.[41]

The formal farewells and Holy Communion both took place on 16 August
1857, the day before Mary Lyttelton's death, and the only occasion when the
entire family gathered together in Mary's room. Fictional and artistic repre-

sentations of such family farewells have tended to leave the impression that they lasted longer than they did. This one lasted less than an hour, between 5.30 a.m. and 6.30 a.m. Lucy Lyttelton, Mary's 16-year-old daughter, described the scene in the Hagley Record: 'The room got full; most of the children were there, some half awaken, with their night gowns on, and much moving about and confusion. But that she did not seem to mind. She wished to say goodbye to us all, so one by one went up to her. She said very little: "Bless you, dears, Mammy is going away".' Mary told little Arthur that she hoped she was going to heaven, and Lucy noticed a 'heavenly look on her face, quiet and beautiful'. Also present for this one formal scene were Mrs Newman, the children's nurse, Mrs Ellis, the Hagley housekeeper, and Miss Smith, the governess, who were all requested by Mary to do their best for her children. Then the family doctor, Giles, asked for the room to be cleared to avoid exhausting his patient.[42]

Immediately afterwards, at 6.45 a.m., Revd Billy Lyttelton administered Holy Communion to his sister-in-law, together with Catherine Gladstone, Mrs Talbot, George Lyttelton, Revd Henry Glynne, and the three adolescent girls Meriel and Lucy Lyttelton and Agnes Gladstone. The rest of the family knelt in the next room, where they could hear the service. George Lyttelton noted: 'From that time to the end, all fear and reluctance were gone . . . All of us believed the blessed Sacrament was visibly powerful to the strengthening and refreshing of her soul.' Catherine Gladstone thought her sister seemed more of heaven than of earth after the Communion: 'nothing agitated or distressed her: the weeping around caused no excitement. "She is already half an Angel" was William [Gladstone]'s expression.' Several family members reported in the Record for 16 August that Mary expressed happiness 'at the prospect of seeing our Lord, being with Him'—one of her few references to heaven. She talked to them individually of the 'approaching change', saying she thought the family prayers were helping her to pass safely 'through Death'.[43]

Only two matters marred Mary's peaceful composure in the final two days. She would have liked the final Communion and farewell ceremony to be closer to the actual hour of her death. A few hours after the sacrament on 16 August 'she seemed puzzled what to do, as she became conscious that the actual approach of death was not so close as she had thought it'. Mrs Talbot and Catherine Gladstone suggested she should proceed as usual and as was most comfortable. Secondly, after the last Communion, Mary Lyttelton suffered intense grief at the impending loss of her family. She asked to see the boys a second time, speaking to each of them briefly, and then saw them all again a few hours later. She talked to Mrs Talbot and her sister Catherine

Gladstone about how much they would miss her, and of her anxiety about Lord Lyttelton's grief. She contemplated all that the survivors would have to endure and how they would cope, and felt sad to think of her children dressed in mourning. But on 17 August, the last day of her life, she was resigned and prepared, and died quietly in the presence of her husband, her sister, her friend Mrs Talbot, and Dr Giles. Her daughter, Lucy, noted that 'it would be in Paradise that her dear eyes would open . . . She was looking on the face of her Saviour.'[44]

Mary Lyttelton's death was the closest to the Victorian Christian ideal of the good death in these two families. It demonstrated how nearly a High Church death could approximate to the Evangelical model, when the sufferer was considered by all to have lived a good Christian life and when the assurance of salvation seemed certain. Mary was a central mother-figure, beloved by all, apparently leaving no ambivalent feelings, except possibly some delayed guilt on her husband's part. The deathbed scene was less contrived than many. The family's deep grief seemed genuinely to be mitigated by their sense of Mary's spiritual preparedness and worthiness, as she died in 'marvellous peace' with God. No anger was expressed at the loss of a mother of twelve, only a resignation to the will of God.

Late Victorian Changes

The 1870s marked a turning-point in the history of death in these two families. Mary Gladstone's memorial on her cousin's death in 1875 was the last to follow the tradition of the Hagley Record, except for Mary's account of her father's death in 1898, which was a special case. Moreover, during this period the two families were traumatized by the suicide of George Lord Lyttelton in 1876 and the political assassination of Lucy Cavendish's husband, Lord Frederick, in 1882—both will be considered in a later chapter. These were shocking, violent deaths, outside the normal range of deaths in most families. While the assassination could be represented as a heroic sacrifice, the suicide was the negation of the good Christian death. These affected the families deeply, shattering the familiar pattern of responses to death and disinclining them to make the usual record. Lord Lyttelton's suicide was not even mentioned in the Hagley Record, which had as its focal point his own account of his wife's death. Even Lord Frederick's murder was noticed only in an inferior poem by the Prime Minister, W. E. Gladstone.

The younger generation of the two families did not cease to be committed Anglicans in the late Victorian period, but they shared in the decline in Evangelical fervour in the nation at large. Colin Matthew has suggested that even W. E. Gladstone recognized from the late 1860s that 'the intellectual tide had turned against Christianity', and his own spiritual experience may well have become less intense.[45] Mary Gladstone's account of the death of her cousin May Lyttelton in 1875 already showed significant signs of change. It was composed by the younger generation, chiefly by Mary Gladstone, drawing on the diary accounts of May's sisters and brothers. It is worth remembering that in 1875 Mary Gladstone, at 28, was already two years older than her father, W. E. Gladstone, had been in 1835 at his mother's death. Mary's account demonstrated little of her father's anxious Evangelical expectations of the good death, or his extreme concern with the state of the soul and spiritual preparedness, though father and daughter were equal in practical piety. On the whole it was the older generation of Gladstones and Lytteltons who dwelt on the burden of sin and the divine purpose of suffering and death in purifying the soul. Moreover, the comments of Mary Gladstone, Meriel Talbot, and Spencer Lyttelton all hint at a new uneasiness in the face of an unpleasant and unexpected death. Mary was 'frightened to death' by her cousin's appearance, while Meriel was relieved that 'nothing painful or dreadful' disturbed the final hours—such comments would have been more unusual in the early Victorian period.

May Lyttelton, eighth daughter of Mary and George Lyttelton, died of typhus fever at the age of 25 on 21 March 1875 after nine weeks' illness.[46] May had a reputation as the charming rebel of the family, as more restless and less austerely religious than the Lyttelton norm.[47] She twice fell in love with unsuitable free thinkers, each of whom died, leaving May devastated. Arthur Balfour, the future Conservative Prime Minister, had long been in love with her, and may have come to the point of a proposal shortly before her illness began.

It would be almost impossible to construct an idealized Christian deathbed scene out of a lingering death from typhus, even under the best conditions. But in May's case, management of her illness was the more difficult because the doctors avoided a diagnosis until very late. The family doctor, Dr Giles, initially pronounced it an 'eight days fever', while the consultant, Wade, called it a 'common fever', which he claimed was unlike typhus in character. Despite this uncertain diagnosis, the family greatly valued the advice and support of the two doctors.[48] A good professional nurse was obtained called Halliday, who 'nursed her so tenderly' at considerable risk of infection to herself, and was liked by May and the family. The care of a professional nurse marked a major change from the earlier family deaths. Halliday was assisted by Mrs Newman, the old family nurse, and by the indefatigable Catherine Gladstone, who was 'just like Mamma' to the Lyttelton children throughout.

The physical conditions of the deathbed scene also left much to be desired. May fell ill on 16 January 1875, retiring to bed next day at Hagley Rectory because the roof of the main family home, Hagley Hall, was being repaired. The tiny rectory was overcrowded, with little or no thought devoted to the danger of infection, until Revd Billy Lyttelton's wife, 'Aunt Emy', also caught typhus.

The first five days of intense suffering were probably the most miserable for May, as she was fully conscious of the fever, headache, nausea, and insomnia, but she was delirious from 25 January. 'Mischief in the lung' appeared on 3 February, with acute head pain and confused mind, followed two days later by 'a kind of a "brain storm"'. The next four weeks saw 'ups and downs— hopes and fears', until Dr Wade diagnosed a huge abscess on May's lungs on 29 February, followed by utter prostration on 3 March.[49] A week later May's closest friends, her brother Spencer and cousin Mary Gladstone, were shocked when they saw her through the screen, erected belatedly around May to 'protect' more recent visitors from infection. At 28, Mary had never before seen anyone so ill and was appalled by the sunken cheeks and eyes, the utterly altered voice and appearance. By 18 March May's strength was finally exhausted; she suffered dreadful pain in her side, she lacked the power to swallow, and the rattle in her throat frightened her. She had no pain during the last few days and died peacefully on Palm Sunday, 21 March.[50]

May Lyttelton's death was far removed from the Christian ideal of the good death as epitomized by the death of May's mother. May had not prepared for an unexpected death in her twenties, lacking the instinctive piety of Harry Goulburn, Dorothea Palmer, or her own mother. The fever left her in no fit mental condition to repent of her sins, while family farewells and appropriate last words were out of the question. However, Mary Gladstone did her best to idealize the last hours: 'I seem still to see her eyes fixed on the ceiling as if it was a bit of Heaven very far off—and then she looked so soothed when with the bright morning sunshine one after another of those she clung to most in life passed before her and were close to her to the end.'[51] May's brothers and sisters took turns watching the slowly fading life, reading aloud prayers, psalms, and hymns, including Keble's evening hymn. Meanwhile Catherine Gladstone lay by her side, 'stroking and soothing her', bringing what comfort she could despite fears of the danger of infection. Most of May's siblings were in the room when Revd Billy Lyttelton read the Commendatory Prayer and administered Holy Communion shortly before May died.[52] Her sister Meriel described the scene in her diary: 'There was not the slightest struggle or pang, so we have much to thank God for, nothing painful or dreadful disturbing the deep calm of the end.'[53]

The family tried to take comfort in the Christian consolation that 'her spirit and purified soul is safe in God's keeping right away from us'.[54] But as Mary Waldegrave, a close family friend, noted, 'it is difficult when it is anyone so young and strong'.[55] Mary Gladstone found it especially hard in May's case to say 'Thy Will be done.'[56] His niece's untimely death aroused in W. E. Gladstone some of the questions of faith stirred so strongly by Jessy's death twenty-five years earlier. He wrote to May's father, Lord Lyttelton, 'I have never known a sorer and sadder event than the eclipse through a course of so much pain, and suffering of that bright and brilliant spirit.'[57] To his wife, he confessed:

This is no ordinary death . . . I must own that events like this bring the greatest shock and strain of faith. That she should have died, and that for her this long struggle, those pains, those continued or returning wanderings should have been appointed— How and why is all this? I can find no answer, but in remembering my own weakness and incapacity to judge.[58]

May's brother-in-law Revd Edward Talbot was convinced that the better side of her character 'was refined and purified in God's discipline of suffering'— a sentiment which other, younger members of the two families found less helpful.[59]

The break with the past was marked even more sharply by the death of 23-year-old Laura Lyttelton on 24 April 1886—eight days after the birth of her first child and a year after her marriage to Alfred Lyttelton, the youngest of Mary's twelve children. This death came only eleven years after that of May, but it seemed longer than that, and very far distant from those earlier deaths of Anne Gladstone and Mary Lyttelton. Laura's death was not noted in the Hagley Record, nor did it receive a memorial account from any family member. Indeed, so remote was it from the Evangelical ideal that religious faith was scarcely mentioned by any of the family, though they were deeply affected. The story of Laura's death has to be reconstructed from family letters between the younger generation, from Mary (Gladstone) Drew's diary, and from brief subsequent accounts by Laura's sister Margot Tennant.

Laura Lyttelton died in childbirth—a regrettably frequent event in Victorian family life, since an average of five mothers died for every 1,000 children born alive. This was a death sometimes idealized in Victorian fiction or Evangelical literature. A novelist might have found Laura an interesting subject for a deathbed scene, for she had already bewitched all who knew her and created for herself a reputation as a charismatic woman of wit, charm, and brilliance. She was considered tiny and frail and may have been in the early stages of consumption, like her sisters Pauline and Charty Ribblesdale.

She experienced strong premonitions of death during pregnancy, illustrated by a letter to Alfred's brother Edward Lyttelton: 'I don't think I have done anything quite wicked enough to deserve such an awful punishment as to let the little thing live and me die . . . I think a great deal about [death] now, and often find myself arranging everything, so as to leave all things neat and well.'[60] Laura wrote her informal will two months before her baby was born, confessing that 'the sadness of death and parting is greatly lessened to me by the very fact of my consciousness of the eternal, indivisible one-ness of Alfred and me'.[61] The twin themes of love and death punctuated her correspondence, but it was love for man, not for God. A week before her confinement, Laura told her sister Margot Tennant that she was fairly sure she would die with her baby. Margot was reluctantly persuaded to swear to read Laura's will aloud to the family gathered around her deathbed.[62]

Laura's death was neither Evangelical nor romantic, nor was it in any sense a good death. Laura's large baby boy was born on 16 April 1886, 'after a time both terribly long and dangerous' involving 'an hour's work with instruments'.[63] The bleeding and vomiting continued for five days, despite the efforts of two eminent but puzzled doctors, Sir Andrew Clark and Dr Matthews Duncan, who blamed a 'bad liver illness', and cited exhaustion and haemorrhage as causes of death on the certificate.[64]

Laura's deathbed scene was harrowing, and nobody attempted to idealize any aspect of it. Margot Tennant was appalled by her sister's pitiful appearance and 'ice-white face'.[65] There were no tender farewells, and the only recorded last words were scarcely intended for posterity. Before she finally became unconscious, the dying woman said to her sister Charty Ribblesdale, 'God has forgotten me.'[66] Margot Tennant described the final scene without religious language:

I lay with my arm under my darling . . . Alfred was kneeling with one of her hands on his forehead, and Charty kneeling at her feet . . . For a minute or more we lay quiet with the sun playing on the window blinds fresh from the dawn—then her breathing stopped. She gave a little shiver and died—the silence was so great I heard the Flight of Death and the Morning salute her soul.[67]

Afterwards, Margot read her sister's will aloud to those gathered around the deathbed, as she had sworn to do, while Alfred looked suffocated and efforts to deter Margot failed.[68]

Few people could conjure up any comforting words of condolence after this death. Mary (Gladstone) Drew felt 'indescribable sadness', despite her deep Christian faith: 'Impossible to exaggerate the tragedy-pathos of this event. . . . What a crushing of hopes, what a light gone from a shady place.'

Mary travelled to the Tennants' home, the Glen, in Scotland, for the funeral, but found the days there 'rather ghastly': 'The [Tennant] parents were curiously unsuited to days of mourning, their own idea being to cheer up and behave as if nothing had happened'[69]—very different behaviour from that of the Lytteltons and Gladstones, but another significant indicator of changing times. Most mourners were stunned. The funeral was simple, with little attention paid to mourning etiquette, as Mary Drew observed: 'They have not got their mourning yet and are dressed just in anything, so also there was no pomp or ceremony.'[70] Mary found Alfred 'desperately wounded' and she was herself clearly still in shock: 'No dream was ever so unreal, I could not believe it; but felt quite cold and hard . . . It seemed too much, the little white bride, inside the coffin, and all the broken hearts around.'[71] The response to Laura's death marked a real change of attitude. Despite the deep grief, there was little or no concern about the state of Laura's soul or the spiritual consolation of the mourners, while the Tennant family was clearly incapable of communicating and sharing its sorrow. Part of this response was the effect of shock at the sudden death of a young mother, but part reflected a profound cultural change, as Evangelical influences were slowly displaced by the forces of secularism, indifference, and unbelief.

The death in 1891 of W. E. Gladstone's eldest son, also named William, aged 51 and master of the Hawarden estate, was another sign of change, as he was the first member of the two families to die during surgery, though not in hospital. No deathbed scene of any kind was possible and the family was not prepared for the death. Early in 1889 William appeared to have a 'stroke of paralysis' followed by a series of attacks, marked by depression, weakness, and slow speech. When he had a relapse in 1891, the family consulted a new set of doctors, who diagnosed a possible growth in the brain, and advised an exploratory operation.[72] This was carried out on 2 July 1891 at William's house in Park Lane, London, at his own request, as he could not face 'the grimness' of University College Hospital.[73]

William evidently stood the operation well, but it revealed a large brain tumour which would have caused continuous pain and was set too far back to allow removal.[74] Mary Drew was the only family member to mention explicitly that 'it was the chloroform that killed him. He never recovered consciousness.'[75] But Catherine Gladstone expressed relief that her son suffered no pain at the end and 'fell asleep not knowing the sad result'.[76] Even she seemed to be acknowledging the painless death as the nearest equivalent to the good death in these circumstances. Catherine was nearly 80 and able to acquiesce in the loss of her beloved son more easily than she might have done decades earlier, especially as she hoped for a speedy reunion.

On the day of his son's funeral, W. E. Gladstone wrote a nine-page record of his eldest son's life and death. It was very different in length, form, and tone from his earlier accounts of the deaths of his mother, father, and little daughter. In 1891 he was an octogenarian father who would shortly be joining his son in death, while the nature of William's death eliminated any deathbed scene. Moreover, the account showed that even W. E. Gladstone had been affected by the decline in Evangelical enthusiasm and the reduced emphasis on sin, penitence, and judgement by the end of the century. The chief purposes of this record were to keep William's memory alive for his family, and perhaps also to help the father himself through his loss. He probably felt that it was a traditional family tribute due to his eldest son, though it was far removed from the early Victorian Evangelical accounting for the good life and death. It provided a short and modest chronicle of a modest man's life, fine character, and fatal illness, making little attempt to justify his spiritual salvation.[77] It was totally different from the father's anguished memorial to Jessy forty years earlier, reflecting the gulf between the middle and late Victorian periods as well as that between the death of a young child and a middle-aged man.

The long family tradition of keeping a detailed record of death was briefly revived for W. E. Gladstone's death in 1898, and there it ended. Gladstone's death at the age of 88 was inevitably a special case, involving a return to the values and behaviour of an earlier generation of Victorians, and a temporary breach in the late Victorian pattern of change. Mary Drew's account of her father's death was influenced by her perceptions of what was due to her father's reputation as a great statesman, and her memory of Gladstone's own memorials to loved ones gone before. Gladstone's death was unusual as well as difficult, because it took place slowly and painfully, in the full glare of the publicity which accompanied his fame. Cancer of the mouth caused agonizing pain for over a year, but the doctors did not diagnose it until a late stage, believing he exaggerated the discomfort caused by 'nasal catarrh'.[78]

The Gladstone and Lyttelton families were hoping and praying for a good Christian death, but even the Grand Old Man was not allowed to select his final hour or orchestrate his deathbed scene. In some respects his death bore more resemblance than he might have wished to his mother's death in 1835, since unfortunate timing added to the problems caused by extreme suffering. The first near-death scene took place in Gladstone's Hawarden bedroom six weeks before the end, on 4 April, following the final Communion a week earlier:

He thought the last hours were near, and sent for us all that were within reach, to give us his farewell blessing. This was Holy Week, and the services and the thoughts, specially on Good Friday during the three hours, were almost overpowering. Physically, he seemed absolutely crushed under the dominion of pain—baffled, beaten, conquered, as he often said. But in the soul, the spirit, the Victory was absolute.[79]

Even in pain, he uttered triumphant words of praise and thanksgiving from the psalms or the hymns, and talked to Mary about his death.[80] Three weeks later there was another 'last words' scene, this time in the presence of his doctors, while Mary listened from outside:

He was very clear and definitely raised himself to ask them questions,—generally to bear testimony as to the gratitude he felt for all that was being done for him. He seemed deliberately to pull himself together, and mentioned by name and in what special particulars he owed thanks to Doctors, Nurses, servants, friends, relations and strangers.[81]

In the conventional deathbed scene in fiction or Evangelical tract, this would have been part of the final tableau, with farewells and blessings surrounded by the family. But when the appropriate time for that arrived, Gladstone was beyond making such an effort.

Gladstone's last week featured a series of alarms that the end was at hand. On Sunday 15 May 'a kind of coma' came on, as the Grand Old Man lay in 'profound stillness', but with considerable apparent intermittent distress. On 17 May, two days before the death, there was a dress rehearsal for the final scene when the whole family gathered in his room, 'not thinking life could last much longer'.[82] Next morning at 4 a.m. all the family members who had gone to bed were again called to Gladstone's room, and knelt around the bed, but it was another false alarm. That night Mary and Harry Drew kept watch as her parents lay on the bed, but at 2 a.m. they woke the rest of the family for the ultimate vigil.[83] Gladstone died appropriately on Ascension Day, 19 May 1898. Mary Drew described the final scene as the family gathered around the deathbed, with Catherine kneeling by his side and Herbert holding his frail mother in his arms. After two and a half hours Gladstone's breathing slowed, and Revd Stephen Gladstone read the final prayers. 'During the last words of blessing, the spirit fled without a struggle. It was a moment never to be forgotten—full of mystery, awe and wonder.'[84] Nobody doubted that W. E. Gladstone's was a good death in the most fundamental Christian sense or that his salvation was assured. This was not the easy and painless death which many late Victorians hoped for; it was much closer to the triumph through suffering of the Evangelical ideal, 'bearing testimony through the darkness of the mental and physical agony', as Lady Stepney put it.[85]

If Mary Drew's private account of Gladstone's death drew its inspiration from the Evangelical past, the public version reflected its period more accurately. Five years after Gladstone's death, his daughter Helen advised the biographer, politician, and family friend John Morley about the death scene in his *Life of Gladstone*, urging him 'not to speak of Father's end as "gloomy or clouded"'. Helen then wrote to her sister Mary Drew: 'Of course, if he was going through it in detail there was all that dreadful pain and suffering. But spoken of as a whole, I am sure you and I feel the beauty and the triumph [by] far the most—all the suffering swallowed up in victory.'[86] This response gives us an important insight into the construction of sanitized death scenes in published memoirs, biographies, and memorials, especially those written in the twentieth century. Time and suffering could be telescoped to produce one moving scene of family farewells and edifying last words. Events spread over weeks or even months could be described as if they took place within days of death—whilst all ugliness disappeared. Early and mid-Victorians, by contrast, would have seen the suffering as an essential part of the Christian message.

John Morley obliged the family with his death scene in his *Life of Gladstone*, in a memorable passage: 'On the early morning of the 19th, his family all kneeling around the bed on which he lay in the stupor of coming death, without a struggle he ceased to breathe. Nature outside—wood and wide lawn and cloudless far-off sky—shone at her fairest.'[87] Nearly three weeks were telescoped into one brief paragraph. Gladstone was pictured dying peacefully, 'without a struggle'—six weeks of suffering and uncertainty were not allowed to spoil the public version of his 'good death', illuminated by 'nature' shining at 'her fairest'. The most extraordinary omission, however, was not the failure to mention the suffering, but the refusal to explain the spiritual significance of this death. But Morley was an agnostic who substituted nature for God. An earlier generation of Gladstones would neither have chosen an agnostic as biographer of their most famous Christian son, nor encouraged the representation of his death as free from suffering.

Gladstone's wife, Catherine, died two years after her husband, but hers was a very different death, evidently too terrible for Mary Drew to record. Catherine Gladstone died at the age of 88, but a good Christian death was impossible because senility brought mental delusions of a distressing kind. Catherine rallied during her husband's final illness, but afterwards her health declined rapidly. By 12 May 1900 pneumonia was added to mental incapacity and general weakness, as Mary sadly told her brother Herbert: 'almost uninterrupted intense melancholia, only broken by strong fits of nervous irritation, or long silence—constant delusion[s]'. A week later Mary Drew found the 'saddest delusions' hard to bear: 'Now every hour that she is not crying or groaning is a mercy. If only those delusions might have been happy ones! That they should be so fierce and so agonising makes it all so tragic.'[88] For the first time Mary Drew found herself 'longing and praying for the end of the pitiful death-watch', since it was 'heart breaking' to watch the mental agony which they were powerless to alleviate.[89] Catherine died at last on 14 June 1900, and the family thanked God 'that the end was peace' after so much suffering. None of the condolence letters pretended to sorrow, only thankfulness for Catherine's sake 'that the waiting is over', and the two old people would be again united in the life to come.[90]

The volume of evidence on death for these two families declined dramatically after the death of W. E. Gladstone in 1898, the occasion of the last lengthy deathbed memorial. It is significant that Gladstone's daughter, Mary Drew, who had composed the memorials to May Lyttelton in 1875 and to her father in 1898, and who copied out much of the Hagley Record, kept no such account of her own husband's death in 1910. Admittedly Revd Harry Drew died suddenly after an unexpected operation, but that scarcely explains Mary's failure to memorialize his death. Mary had kept a diary all her life and produced detailed records of other deaths in her family, yet she managed no more than a brief entry in her diary on Harry's death. Moreover, unlike the Victorian widows in her own and the Lyttelton families, she was very angry at Harry's death, as we will see in a later chapter.

The member of the two families who wrote the most about death in the period between 1900 and the First World War was Alfred Lyttelton's second wife, Edith. But Edith sought comfort on the deaths of her son in 1902 and her husband in 1913 not through the traditional Christian consolations, but rather through spiritualism, as the last chapter will show. Another symbol of change was the fact that Alfred Lyttelton died in a nursing-home after a failed operation, whereas even in 1891 William Gladstone had been operated on at home.

The sense of the total break with the past was most emphatically marked by the violent deaths of young men from the two families in the Great War, including two grandsons of W. E. Gladstone and one of George Lyttelton. The greatest shock was perhaps the loss of Lieutenant William G. C. Gladstone, W. E. Gladstone's eldest grandson and only son of that other William who also died prematurely in 1891. He was a modest man, like his father, and he went into war out of a sense of duty and patriotism rather than any zest or talent for war.[91] Charles Masterman believed William Gladstone had from the start a 'conviction that with his services he was offering his life'.[92] William was shot in the forehead by a rifle bullet at the age of 29 on 13 April 1915 only a few weeks after arriving in France, with only two days' experience in the trenches.

The Gladstone and Lyttelton families were devastated. William's aunt Mary Drew expressed her shock in her diary two days after his death: 'Felt

bowled over . . . Somehow it is absolutely unbelievable; the greatest blow in
the whole war, and by far the greatest loss . . . Tragic and piteous beyond all
words.'[93] That same day, 15 April, Mary confessed to her sister Helen
Gladstone that 'there is nothing to say, is there, about this piteous event'—
an extraordinary admission for any Gladstone on facing a family death. As
Mary noted, 'it is only when they [war deaths] come into our very midst that
one realizes the hundreds of broken hearts and shattered homes'.[94] Lady
Stepney, a close family friend, could see little comfort in such an utter
tragedy, especially because all the Gladstone family 'thought of him as the
future'. The only possible consolation lay in the idealization of Will's death,
imagining him 'transfigured now *for ever*, and wrapt away in a blinding light
of glory and sacrifice'.[95] But the immediate family found no such comfort in
the early stages of bereavement in the glorification of Will's death.

Will Gladstone's death in the trenches in 1915 was sudden, violent, and
anonymous, with little preparation and none of the traditional support
offered by the family around the Victorian deathbed. Even so, the Gladstone
family was more fortunate than most other families bereaved by the war. Will
died painlessly and his body was not blown to bits or lost for ever in no man's
land. Above all, his family had the prestige and influence to gain permission
from the Prime Minister, the King, and the War Office for the rare privilege
of sending his body back home to Hawarden for the normal ritual of funeral
and burial next to his father in Hawarden churchyard.[96] Only a month later
the War Office ordered that all soldiers must be buried where they died,
recognizing the inequity of allowing privileged families who could afford it to
bring bodies home.[97] The practice of writing death memorials was briefly
revived in Will's honour, to compensate for the family's separation from him
at his death and to help the family grieve in the face of violent death on a
foreign battlefield. It is significant that, like many such wartime memorials,
it was not composed until several years after Will's death, whereas Victorian
memorials were written while the loved one was dying or immediately
afterwards.[98] Moreover, Will's memoir was an account of his life written for
the public record, rather than a private account of the death for the family's
edification. Will Gladstone's death was a world away from the Victorian
deathbeds of Mary Lyttelton or Sir John Gladstone.

All these Gladstone and Lyttelton deaths were marked by the unity and
solidarity of these two large families. The two families were deeply devoted to
each other and closely knit. As late as 1891 W. E. Gladstone's eldest daughter
Agnes remarked on the physical and geographical closeness of the Gladstone
family, even when the children were adults: 'I am the only one of the 7
[Gladstone children] with a separate home and life apart.'[99] Mary Drew often

reminded her mother that the sympathy and support of her family helped her to cope with Gladstone's pain during his final illness.[100] Equally the two families helped each other in grief by sharing their sorrow, as Mary noted in December 1913 on learning of her cousin Spencer Lyttelton's sudden death while she was in South Africa:

How gaunt and sad it was to be 7,000 miles away at such a moment. It made me realise how in every one of those Hagley sorrows, the mere fact of not being by oneself made all the difference in the kind of grief one was going through. When May died, Spencer and Alfred and Lavinia and I were so closely bound together. In 1876 [the death of Lord Lyttelton] the same . . . I did not know the extraordinary difference it made being all together.[101]

The Gladstone and Lyttelton family sources over eighty years demonstrate the practical difficulties in applying the Evangelical model of the good death even in the most devout families. So much depended on the nature of the disease and the age of the dying person, even when family support and spiritual preparation could be assumed. Of all these family deaths, only that of Mary Lyttelton approximated closely to the Evangelical ideal and it is significant that Mary's death came in the 1850s, at the peak of mid-Victorian piety.

PART II

GRIEF AND MOURNING

Introduction to Part II

ARCHIVAL EVIDENCE SUGGESTS THAT IN THE NINETEENTH CENTURY
mourning rituals provided opportunities for the bereaved to express
their sorrow in a manner that made the grieving experience easier to endure
and to complete, aiding an ultimate return to a more normal way of life.
Mourning customs offered therapeutic benefits which could outweigh any
attendant disadvantages for those who suffered most in private. Modern
psychologists argue that mourning rituals meet the psychological needs of the
bereaved by structuring death within a coherent system of values, whilst
also rallying the support of family, friends, and community to comfort the
bereaved.

Part II of this book explores the rituals and experiences of middle- and
upper-class Victorians as they mourned their loved ones after death, and as
they attempted to express and understand their grief. Major changes in the
conduct and form of funerals, not least the introduction of cremations, point
to profound cultural and religious shifts in Victorian and Edwardian society.
However, Protestant Christianity still provided the dominant belief system to
console the bereaved, complemented by the solace of memory. Public expressions of grief continued after the week of the funeral in the form of mourning-dress, condolence letters, and the support and sympathy of family and
local community. For most bereaved people there was a normal cycle of
mourning and grief which gradually healed the wounds of their partners' or
children's deaths, in part or in full. But for an unfortunate but tiny minority,
like Lady Frederick Cavendish and Emma Haden, grief became their constant companion, and the death of their beloved the most important fact of
life. In some ways the greatest challenge of death was to the unbelievers, who
could not accept the promise of family reunions in a Christian heaven, and
who found themselves isolated from the usual mourning rituals. These Victorians and Edwardians bridged the religious and family experiences of the
nineteenth and twentieth centuries. Their anguished solitude echoes in our
own time.

✿ 9 ✿

FUNERAL REFORM AND THE CREMATION DEBATE

From Extravagance to Simplicity

Historians have tended to condemn Victorian funeral extravagance as if it were a continuing feature of the entire Victorian period. Bertram Puckle in *Funeral Customs* in 1926 denounced the Victorians in general for the vulgar 'madness' of their ostentatious funerals and elaborate memorials, while conceding that 'a foolish display of wealth to uphold the family honour is a very old human failing' at times of death.[1] John Morley in 1971 devoted two chapters of *Death, Heaven and the Victorians* to funerals, drawing largely on sources from the 1840s and 1850s, including one entire chapter on the excesses of the Duke of Wellington's state funeral in 1852. James Stevens Curl in *The Victorian Celebration of Death* in 1972 claimed that 'ostentatious displays of grief were very much required by Victorian Society . . . [with a funeral] the wealth and power of a family could be publicly displayed'. Julian Litten has recently depicted the 1890s as 'the golden age of the Victorian funeral'.[2]

There is no doubt that the early Victorian middle and upper classes spent a good deal of money on impressive funerals, but this expenditure needs to be placed in a broader historical perspective. Early Victorians were not alone in burial excesses—they were continuing a cultural practice which can be traced back in various forms through the centuries. The most obvious difference in the nineteenth century was that many more upwardly mobile middle-class families had the money to indulge in expensive funerals. Throughout the ages the elaborate tombs of kings, priests, and officials must have consumed a sizeable portion of their family's wealth. Marvellous monuments of the ancient world were devoted to housing the dead, including the pyramids of the Pharaohs and Tutankhamun's tomb. Expenditure on the funerals of the British nobility rose markedly from the late fifteenth century; the funerals of Henry Percy in 1489 and the second Duke of Norfolk in 1524 each cost more than £1,000.[3] Lawrence Stone believes the early-modern period marked the zenith of extravagant aristocratic outlay on funerals.[4] The emphasis on individual glory increased during the Renaissance, with grand displays over the grave, such as Henry VII's chapel in Westminster Abbey. John McManners has shown that it was customary in eighteenth-century France 'to spend more, rank for rank, than was reasonable by any provident standard'.[5] Throughout history people have received the funerals and memorials they were willing and able to pay for.

The extravagant funerals of the first half of the nineteenth century were the culmination of a process which began long before Victoria ascended the throne. Lou Taylor argues that from the late seventeenth century the vogue for grand funerals spread from royal and aristocratic circles to the growing numbers of the middle classes, enriched by trade and later industrialization: 'a whole new section of society threw itself with enthusiasm into the previously forbidden delights of aristocratic mourning etiquette'.[6] Extravagance was well entrenched by the early nineteenth century. A gentleman's funeral recorded in the *Benenden Letters* for 1785 included expenses for eight hearse-pages and a 'feather-man', with his tray of waving black ostrich plumes.[7] An undertaker's bill for a lady's funeral in 1824 came to £803. 11s. 0d., including 'A rich plume of best black ostrich feathers' costing £11. 0s. 0d., and twelve pages with wands (£9. 0s. 0d.), each with black silk hatbands and gloves (£10. 16s. 0d.).[8] The latter sum alone constituted half a year's wages of a domestic servant of the period. Edwin Chadwick's 1843 *Report on the Practice of Interment in Towns* found that the average funeral expenses of the aristocracy in London varied from £500 to £1,500, and those of the upper gentry from £200 to £400. A London undertaker testified before Chadwick's inquiry that an 'ordinary' middle-class funeral would cost from £50 to £70, and that could be reduced by 50 per cent without diminishing the solemnity of the occasion.[9]

The customary cast of attendants in the funeral tableau had changed little by 1837, but the number of middle-class families able to afford them had substantially increased. Chadwick's Report underlined the incongruity of the funeral attendants for the lower and middle classes. A London undertaker called as a witness was obliged to confess his ignorance that funerals were based on the heraldic array of a baronial funeral; thus the man carrying a plume of feathers represented an esquire bearing the shield and helmet of the deceased, the men with wands were the gentlemen-ushers, and the two mutes standing at the doors were supposed to be the castle porters with their staves. The undertaker thought his clients were equally unaware of the incongruity for which they paid, and he admitted that funerals in general were unnecessarily expensive. He explained that families usually asked the undertaker to 'provide what is customary', the term commonly used in giving such orders, even after a dying wish for a simple funeral. It was left to the undertaker, with a direct financial interest in the outcome, to determine what was 'customary', while the expenses were often paid from trust funds by executors of wills.[10]

A relatively modest upper-middle-class funeral of the early Victorian period demonstrates the nature of the funeral trappings found so offensive by the next generation of the same class. A young lawyer, Harry Goulburn, son of the Chancellor of the Exchequer, was buried in 1843 with only one mourning-coach, at a total cost of £130. 17s.—considerably less than the minimum level listed for the upper gentry by the 1843 Report. The undertaker's bill itemized an elm coffin (at £5. 15s. 6d.) inside a strong outer lead coffin (at £7. 7s.), with a rich white silk winding-sheet and silk gloves for the corpse (£3. 17s.). The three men dressed in mourning with wands, to attend and carry the lid of best black ostrich feathers, were an economical item at a mere 18s. 6d., while the lid of feathers was a bargain at a guinea (though the ostrich feathers for the hearse and the one mourning-coach were a further £4). The items which Victorian funeral reformers denounced as most lavish and superfluous were the haberdashery and millinery, which brought easy profits to the undertaker. The total cost of gloves, scarves, hoods, and hatbands was £47. 3s. 6d., almost one-third of the entire funeral bill; this compared with a total of a mere £23. 18s. 6d. for the two coffins, the hearse, and four horses, and the one mourning-coach and four. The nine chief gentlemen-mourners and the clergymen had the best crape hatbands, scarves, and silk gloves for £17. 16s. 6d., which exceeded the combined cost of both coffins. Even the haberdashery items for the six servant-mourners came to £16. A further £7. 2s. 6d. was needed to pay for fourteen rich silk hatbands and gloves for two mutes, six hearse-pages, four coach-and-feather pages, and two coachmen.[11]

To view the question of funeral extravagance in perspective, however, we should distinguish the vast majority of middle- and upper-class private family funerals from the public ceremonials on the deaths of famous people. Critics have tended to condemn the Victorians for ostentatious funeral display mainly on the evidence of ceremonial state occasions. The Duke of Wellington's funeral in 1852 is often cited as the high point of Victorian funeral extravagance; the triumphal funeral car alone cost £11,000, while the *Observer* calculated that £80,000 was spent on seats for the funeral. But Wellington's funeral was remarkable precisely because it was extraordinary and it was intended to be an impressive public spectacle. T. H. Huxley, the agnostic scientist, thought the funeral 'impressive enough' and heard 'the magnificent service in full perfection'. But he considered the whole pageant as 'stage trickery compared with the noble simplicity of the old man's life. How the old stoic, used to his iron bed and hard hair pillow, would have smiled at all the pomp.'[12]

Other nineteenth-century state funerals could also be cited as examples of excessive funeral expenditure, though none was quite so extreme as Wellington's. At the start of the century the statesman Charles James Fox was buried in Westminster Abbey at a cost of over £2,840. The bill included £485. 18s. for a large open hearse 'richly decorated with black, velvet draperies . . . the canopy surmounted with a mass of very rich ostrich plumes and drawn by six horses with ostrich feathers and velvet covering'. The three bands of the Regiments of Guards received £23. 2s. each, and six trumpeters had to divide twelve guineas between them; £190. 10s. 0½d. was paid for the work of carpenters, bricklayers, masons, and assorted labourers inside the Abbey, while seven extra constables received £2. 9s. between them.[13]

Fox's funeral was a state farewell intended to impress the nation, as was the Duke of Wellington's. The Duke of Northumberland's burial in Westminster Abbey in 1865 was another great public spectacle, described by *The Times* as 'an imposing celebration, worthy of the high rank and vast territorial influence of the late peer'. The procession from Northumberland House to the Abbey included numerous mutes on horseback, two pages with a lid of black feathers, a horseman carrying the ducal coronet on a crimson-velvet cushion, a hearse and six accompanied by twelve pages, fifteen mourning-coaches and six, each containing four persons of importance, followed by more than 100 private carriages of the nobility and gentry. Shops were closed along the route, which was thronged with spectators, even at the tops of the houses. Inside the Abbey 'every nook and cranny from which a glimpse of the ceremony could be obtained was occupied'.[14]

However, Victorians were more inclined to private family funerals, even for men of distinction. For example, the decision whether to have a ceremonial public funeral in Westminster Abbey or a private family burial had to be made three times in 1881–2—for a famous statesman, an Archbishop of Canterbury, and the agnostic scientist who transformed human thought on the creation of the universe. The correspondence concerning each of these decisions demonstrates a precise understanding of the distinction in function, style of ceremony, and cost between state funerals for celebrated individuals and private family burials. Hence it is misleading to use state funerals as a guide to nineteenth-century funerals in general.

When Benjamin Disraeli, Lord Beaconsfield, died in 1881, W. E. Gladstone, as Prime Minister, offered the honour of a public funeral as a national tribute to a great statesman. But Beaconsfield had directed in his will that he was to be buried in the same vault as his wife in the churchyard at Hughenden, with the same simplicity as for her funeral.[15] The pomp of a Westminster Abbey ceremony might have seemed more appropriate to Disraeli's flamboyant personality than the simple Hughenden service he received. But his wife's touching farewell letter, written to him twenty-five years earlier, convinced his advisers, when they found it in his dispatch-box. Mary Anne Disraeli had written in 1856, 'You have been a perfect husband to me, be put by my side in the same grave.'[16] The original of this letter was placed next to Lord Beaconsfield's heart in the Hughenden vault.

On the death of A. C. Tait, the Archbishop of Canterbury, in 1882, the Church of England put a powerful case to the Archbishop's family for his burial in the Abbey. The representative of the Church, W. M. Sinclair, argued that while a great Dissenting minister might be exclusively claimed by his family, 'the remains of the great Patriarch of the Anglican Communion . . . should be generously yielded to the nation'. Public burial at Westminster 'amongst the heroes of past ages and the scientific and historic lights of the present generation' would create an invaluable 'public impression in favour of the Church of England and of the Establishment'.[17] The family wanted a private burial at Addington churchyard beside the Archbishop's beloved wife and only son, who had both died four years earlier; reluctant to veto Queen Victoria's expressed wish for a state ceremony, they asked her to make the final decision. Victoria allowed the private burial at Addington, subsequently described in the parish magazine as 'simple and unostentatious and happy', with a 'bright' service led by the village choir.[18]

The powerful wish for a simple private burial alongside beloved family members decided the families of both statesman and Archbishop against the great honour of a state ceremony in the Abbey. It is ironic that Charles Darwin, the agnostic scientist, whose theory of natural selection contributed much to the spread of scepticism, was the only one of these three to be buried with Christian pomp in the Abbey. Even the Bishop of Carlisle, who preached the funeral sermon on 3 May 1882, noted the paradoxical character of the occasion; applauding the decision to bury the 'most conspicuous man of science in this generation with the fullest expression of Christian hope'.[19] Sir John Lubbock, politician and naturalist, was the prime mover in sending a letter to the Dean of Westminster requesting this privilege for Darwin, signed by twenty Members of Parliament. Press, government, and public were largely agreed that the Abbey was appropriate, and many Church leaders sought to show that God and science could be reconciled. Not all Darwin's family, colleagues, and friends shared this enthusiasm for a funeral of religious pageantry for an unbeliever who disliked such pomp. His wife, Emma, although herself a committed Christian, opposed funeral extravagance and declined to attend her husband's state funeral, for which full mourning was required. She would have preferred him to be interred simply in the family vault at Down amongst his family.[20]

Wealthy early and mid-Victorians would appear to have been no better and not much worse than their predecessors in the matter of funeral extravagance, but the Victorians were themselves responsible for significant funeral reform. As early as 1843 Edwin Chadwick's Report made a strong case for the reform of funeral ceremonies and for the creation of new suburban cemeteries. The awakening concern for public health was reinforced by the revelations of the 'putrid emanations' from the overcrowded and insanitary churchyards of the 1830s and 1840s. The first of the new London cemeteries, Kensal Green, was opened the year before Chadwick's Report, which implicated graveyards in spreading fever. The case for burial reform was readily accepted on public-health grounds and eight new metropolitan cemeteries were built by joint-stock companies—a process already begun with Kensal Green. The 1850 Metropolitan Interments Act prohibited intramural burial and further interments in churchyards, closed old burial grounds, and stipulated that a Board of Health should provide for funerals in cemeteries at fixed charges. This marked the turning-point for funeral and burial reform, especially as the legislation was extended to the rest of England and Wales in 1853.[21] Societies such as the National Funeral and Mourning Reform Association were established to encourage moderation and simplicity. Wellington's 1852 funeral was widely criticized, and *The Times* correspondent condemned the ostentation of the funerals of the Duke of Northumberland and Cardinal Wiseman in 1865, ridiculing in particular, '[the] mutes on horseback, lids of feathers, long cloaks, long velvets, frowsy plumes, and all the undertaking millinery of the grave. These unmeaning traditional adjuncts of death were the attractions in both cases, and drew thousands to witness the procession of mutes, which are as senseless now as they were 200 years ago.'[22]

By the 1870s the complex mourning conventions were being relaxed and many more people were asking for more modest funerals. *Cassell's Household Guide* of 1869–71 outlined eight classes of funerals offered by a large London undertaking firm with prices ranging from £3. 5s. to £53. Their cheapest included a carriage with one horse, a lined elm coffin, and the use of a pall, bearers, coachman and attendant, complete with black hatbands and gloves. The most expensive funeral secured a hearse and four horses, two mourning-coaches with four horses, twenty-three plumes of rich ostrich feathers, a strong elm shell with stout outer lead coffin, two mutes, and fourteen men as pages, feathermen, and coachmen, complete with truncheons and wands.[23] The upper price levels still allowed for traditional trappings, but at much less than half the cost of Harry Goulburn's relatively modest funeral. By 1894 the *Lancet* rejoiced that funeral reform had been achieved and that the cost of funerals had been greatly reduced among the upper and upper-middle classes:

It is found that the expenditure of £10 to £15 will allow of everything being completed in good taste and reverence, but without any excess . . . It is unnecessary now to attack burial on the grounds of its expense in funeral paraphernalia. Funeral reform is an accomplished fact in most parts of the Kingdom, and the funerals of the past generations are almost as extinct as the dodo.[24]

Lady Colin Campbell advised in her *Etiquette of Good Society* in 1893 that 'the love of parade and show' which used to attend funerals had been largely abolished by good taste, though it was still necessary to restrain enthusiastic undertakers, whose interests were served by ostentation rather than simplicity.[25]

The overwhelming evidence from the family archives of these middle- and upper-class families shows that they whole-heartedly agreed with the aims of the funeral reformers throughout the Victorian period. Far from seeking ostentatious funerals to display their wealth and rank, their burial requests reiterated a common desire for simple and dignified ceremonies. Chadwick's Report of 1843 noted the admission of undertakers that the respectable classes were increasingly expressing in their wills a wish to be buried plainly and at moderate expense, sometimes fixing an upper limit. Objections to the use of feathers and the general display were already common, and more funerals were performed according to a written contract.[26] As early as 1823 Margaret Lady Fairfax left a memorandum requesting that her funeral should be conducted 'in a decent frugal manner'.[27] In 1842 the funeral of Elizabeth Fox, widow of Charles James Fox, was 'simple and unostentatious in outward circumstances', following her request.[28] The third Baron Holland left a direction to have 'this last Duty done quietly as possible', so the family admitted to the 1840 funeral only three outsiders in addition to relatives who had requested to be included.[29] Sir John Dashwood King left a codicil to his will instructing that his burial be conducted 'with as little expense as possible', and without a monumental inscription over his grave.[30]

Reports in *The Times* for 1845 illustrate the frequency of requests by men of high status for private funerals free of ostentation. The funeral of the Marquis of Westminster in February was conducted 'in as private a manner as was consistent with the rank of the deceased nobleman'. He had expressed opposition to a public funeral, so private carriages of the nobility and gentry were not allowed to join the procession of seven family mourning-coaches.[31] A week later the Earl of Mornington's funeral in London was conducted, according to his wish, in 'a strictly private manner', with only immediate relatives present; 'the customary pageantry on such occasions was in great measure dispensed with', and the cavalcade was reduced to four mourning-coaches.[32] *The Times*'s account of Earl Spencer's funeral at Althorp in October 1845 noted that 'the funeral obsequies were distinguished by the absence of parade or ostentatious ceremony', following the Earl's wishes. The hearse was drawn by six horses, accompanied by only one mourning-coach, followed by several estate employees on foot and twenty Althorp tenants on horseback.[33] Such reduced pageantry is evident in reports of aristocratic funerals from the 1840s onwards.

The evidence from the 1850s and 1860s and from further down the social scale tells the same story. The extravagant Victorian funeral, which critics so loved to condemn, was chiefly a feature of the first half of the century, and was already under attack and in decline during the first two decades of Victoria's reign. Sir John Gladstone was worth £746,000 in 1848, but his funeral in 1851 cost only £88. 3s. 7d., an economical sum for the head of his clan, following the baronet's decree that the funeral be conducted in a plain and unostentatious manner.[34]

In the thirteen years since the funeral of his son Harry Goulburn, described above, Henry Goulburn, MP, evidently decided that a funeral cost of £130. 17s. was too much, even for a former Chancellor of the Exchequer. Harry's brother Frederick reported among his father's last words on the day of his death in 1856: 'Let me not be buried with any funeral pomp—no hearse no mourning coaches—let me be simply carried from the house into the church and laid by the side of Harry.'[35] His funeral bill has not survived, but it was doubtless less than Harry's.

The Palmer and Wood family archives tell a similar story, though their desire for frugal funerals may be traced back further, to the 1830s. Revd William Wood, vicar of Fulham, was the father-in-law of Eleanor Wood (née Palmer), sister of the first Earl of Selborne. As early as 1832 Revd Wood requested in his will that his funeral 'may be as private and plain as possible consistently with propriety and decency', and no monument should record his name or memory.[36] In 1852 Eleanor Wood's father, Revd William Jocelyn Palmer, rector of Mixbury, shared these modest testamentary sentiments, asking for the 'least expensive' funeral, with no tablet or other monument erected to his memory in the Mixbury church.[37] The funeral costs for Revd William Palmer's wife, Dorothea, and three of his daughters were in keeping with his views on funeral frugality. The funerals of his two unmarried daughters, Mary and Emma, in 1859 and 1874, cost £38. 7s. and £36. 2s. 3d. respectively, well below the top of the range of the eight classes cited by *Cassell's Household Guide* in 1869–71. This providence did not reflect limited means, since Mary Richardson Palmer left £7, 371. 3s. 7½ d. at her death in 1859. The funeral of the married sister, Eleanor Wood, in 1873, was in the same range at £42. 12s. 7d., also moderate for an earl's sister. The funeral of their mother, Dorothea Richardson Palmer, in 1867 was the only one of the four which went somewhat above *Cassell's* top of the range at £66. 17s., but perhaps the family believed this more appropriate for the mother of eleven, including an earl.[38]

By the 1870s simple funerals had become *de rigueur*. The funeral of Mary Vivian, Rose Horsley's aunt, was conducted at Highgate Cemetery in 1875 as quietly as possible, reflecting the family's opposition to 'funeral parade', mourning-scarves, and hatbands.[39] Mrs Hugh Childers's funeral service in 1875 was a plain ceremony lasting one and a half hours, with no plumes, hatbands, scarves, 'or other usual insignia of grief'. The mourners were intended to walk, but mourning-coaches were reluctantly used because of the deep snow.[40] The evangelical clergyman Canon William Conway was buried in a simple ceremony at Rochester in 1876 with no mourning-coaches, feathers, cloaks, or hatbands, following his expressed wish.[41] Egerton Harcourt's will in 1880 asked for his funeral to be 'simple and inexpensive with no procession and without scarfs and large hatbands'.[42] In 1892 Agnes Anson described the funeral of her grandmother Lady Acland: 'There will be a simple bier—and some plain carriages (sort of flies). No undertakerism at all—and very little crape about our clothes.'[43]

By the late Victorian period the funeral reformers had made their point about simple funerals, and turned their attention instead to the sanitary argument for lightweight, 'perishable' coffins, rather than strong coffins of wood or lead which allowed the earth no direct access to the bodies. Sir Francis Seymour Haden, a burial reformer and Rose Horsley's brother, even argued in 1900 that bodies without coffins should be placed directly in the earth, where they would disappear rapidly without pollution or spread of disease.[44] Many members of these upper- and middle-class families were aware of the debate and sympathized with the aims of the burial reformers, while not going quite so far in zeal as Haden. Indeed their repugnance at the new proposals for cremation from the 1870s probably contributed to their enthusiasm for burial reform, to counter the sanitary arguments of the cremationists. As early as 1852 the will of Revd William Jocelyn Palmer, rector of Mixbury, directed that 'my body may be buried in the Church Yard at Mixbury, in the plainest, commonest, and least expensive way, in a single coffin, made of elm board, and in a common grave, as near as may be [to] that of my dear son Thomas; without brick and mortar, except so much as shall be sufficient to give stability to a common head and foot stone'.[45]

Twenty-five years later, a press reporter welcomed Archbishop Tait's decision to bury his son Crauford in a common grave in the earth rather than a vaulted or brick grave.[46] Countess Morley noted in her diary in 1877 the problem caused at her mother's funeral by the doctor's insistence on a lead coffin: 'it was all done very well except having a lead coffin, the weight terrific'.[47] Mary Drew was quite specific in her instructions in her informal will, written when she was seriously ill in 1890: 'If I should die, I specially wish not to be put in a heavy lead and wood coffin, but in a wicker one lined with moss, to avoid the jar and struggle at the funeral, when all should speak only of peace and hope.'[48] Two years later, Lord Sherbrooke was buried in one of the perishable coffins promoted by the burial reformers as 'earth to earth' or 'pressed pulp' coffins.[49]

Even the major ceremonial funeral of the later nineteenth century, that of W. E. Gladstone, the great Liberal statesman, in 1898, showed a concern for dignity and simplicity which contrasted markedly with Wellington's state funeral nearly half a century earlier. Gladstone had expressed the wish that his funeral should be modest, and his son Herbert organized the event in Westminster Abbey accordingly, as John Morley's biography recorded: 'Even men most averse to all pomps and shows on the occasions and scenes that declare so audibly their nothingness, here were only conscious of a deep and moving simplicity, befitting a great citizen now laid among the kings and heroes.'[50] Gladstone's funeral dispensed with the black shoulder-scarves, the weepers, mutes, and feather-men of Wellington's funeral, and even the pall-bearers wore simple frock-coats, black gloves, and plain top hats.[51] Lady Battersea was eloquent in her approval: 'Wonderful, striking in every detail; simple, impressive, dignified, grand, real emotion displayed.'[52] Gladstone's grandson William Wickham expressed the intentions and evident achievement of the family when he wrote to congratulate his uncle Herbert Gladstone: 'I felt that everything was perfect and quite ideal. Not only was it grand, solemn and impressive but it was also *simple*. It made one feel that though many were there to mourn, no one was there to gaze as at a show. It was too simple to be tawdry and too grand to be unworthy.'[53]

The Cremation Debate

During the 1870s cremation societies were formed in Italy, Germany, Holland, Belgium, and America; only ten officially recognized cremations were performed in Europe before 1877, when they were first permitted in Italy.[54] Sir Henry Thompson, surgeon, artist, and President of the British Cremation Society, opened the debate in Britain with a powerful and well-publicized article in the *Contemporary Review* in January 1874, proclaiming the sanitary and utilitarian case for cremation. He argued that cremation was necessary to eliminate the 'repulsive offensiveness' of graveyard pollution of air and water which propagated infection and raised the death-rate. Sir Henry also presented the economic argument that cremation offered an escape from the costly ceremonial of burial and the wastage of land. An additional advantage was that cremation would make the destruction of the body instantaneous, reassuring those who dreaded premature burial, a common anxiety not confined to the Victorians.[55]

Sir Francis Seymour Haden, another prominent physician and Thompson's chief antagonist in the thirty-year debate, established the Earth to Earth Society in 1875 to promote the reform of earth burial in opposition to the Cremation Society. Haden was a foe worthy of Thompson, an even more prolific propagandist, who fuelled the debate in the weekly periodicals, and in the correspondence columns of _The Times_ and the _Lancet_. Like Thompson, Haden was interested in material rather than religious arguments and his chief concern was to undermine the cremationists' sanitary case. He argued that expert evidence abundantly disproved the charge that burial spread infection and increased the death-rate. Haden's major proposal was to abolish current burial abuses by reform of the burial system rather than by cremation. Sanitary problems should be removed by safe and proper burial in the earth, which was the best known disinfectant, transforming putrefaction into inoffensive organic matter with no pollution or spread of disease. Haden condemned the widespread use of imperishable wood and lead coffins, brick graves and solid vaults which prevented decomposition, and caused the accumulation of 'a vast quantity of human remains in every stage of decay'. Instead the dead should be buried as quickly as possible in perishable 'earth to earth' coffins made of material, such as wicker, which allowed access by earth and air. He conducted experiments to show that animals as large as calves, buried at a depth of four feet, were completely dissolved in the earth within four and a half years.[56]

Haden met Thompson's financial argument for cremation with the rejoinder that enormous expenditure would be required to destroy bodies by such a cumbersome procedure as cremation. He produced medical evidence to demonstrate that premature burial was never a serious risk in the first place, avoiding the crude response that burning alive held no more appeal. Haden introduced the new argument that cremation encouraged crime by wholesale destruction of all evidence of murder.[57] Thompson responded to this legal point in his subsequent work, maintaining that crimes such as poisoning were rare and could be prevented by a more careful system of post-mortem examinations and death certification.[58]

The debate became more heated in 1879 when Thompson and the Cremation Society constructed a crematorium at Woking, where they successfully cremated a horse. The community outcry which followed the news that they planned next to cremate a human corpse was so fierce that the Home Secretary was obliged to threaten to prosecute the Society. The experimental burning of bodies temporarily ceased. However, in 1884 Sir James Stephen advised the jury in an unsavoury case of attempted cremation that the practice was not illegal in England, so encouraging the Cremation Society to offer its services on request. Crematoria were then established in various places, including Woking in 1885, Manchester in 1892, and Scotland in 1891. Finally, the Cremation Act was passed in 1902, legalizing and regulating the practice of cremation in England, Scotland, and Wales, indicating that public opinion by then at least tolerated it. But the pace of change was still slow after the 1902 Act with only 105 cremations in London in the first five years and about 800 per year in Britain by 1908. Not until the 1960s were half of those who died cremated.[59]

The reasons for this slow acceptance of cremation are revealed by a study of the debate in the *Lancet*, which, as a leading medical journal, might have been expected to support cremation on sanitary and medical grounds. The two chief protagonists, Haden and Thompson, both surgeons, concentrated on the sanitary, utilitarian, economic, and medical aspects of cremation, failing almost entirely to explore the religious dimension. Up to 1879 the *Lancet* did likewise, pronouncing Thompson's public-health argument cogent and concluding that cremation was 'safe, speedy, wholesome and economical'.[60]

The *Lancet* appeared to be so mesmerized by the sanitary arguments in the 1870s that it failed entirely to consider the influence of 2,000 years of Christian burial tradition. An editorial of 1874 briefly acknowledged that the main objections to cremation rested on 'the sentiment so impressively expressed in our burial service that these our bodies shall rise again in an incorruptible state'. But though the *Lancet* noted the influence of Christian beliefs in opposition to cremation it still found in its favour during the first decade of the debate.[61] In 1874 the *Lancet* published but did not comment on the letter of a disapproving reader who pointed out that the journal's case for cremation was entirely based on the sanitary question: 'It is, I believe, a heathenish custom, and one not likely to be adopted by Christian people, or any who believe in the Bible. The Bible tells us we shall return to the ground from whence we were taken (Genesis iii, 19).'[62] More significantly, that same year the *Lancet* also brushed aside condemnation of cremation by Dr Wordsworth, Bishop of Lincoln, as 'barbarous and unnatural'. The Bishop believed that the heathen practice would undermine popular faith in the resurrection of the body, leading to disastrous social revolution and widespread immorality. In response the editor pointed out that belief in the actual resurrection of the material body was inconsistent equally with cremation or burial, since it was just as difficult to raise up a material body from bones in the earth as from ash in an urn.[63] The Bishop was dismissed as a cloistered cleric, trying to prejudice an impartial discussion by introducing irrelevant religious issues.[64]

Suddenly in 1879 the *Lancet* changed sides, evidently in response to the public outcry over the erection of the Woking crematorium, which led to belated recognition of popular support for the religious argument. Editorials in 1879 for the first time dwelt on the religious aspect of the question, and the journal began to argue that the sanitary problem could be solved by 'earth to earth' burial reform rather than cremation. The burning of the dead was now represented as unnatural and 'antagonistic to the genius of Christianity' and its fundamental doctrine of resurrection. The Woking experiment was denounced as offensive to the public's sense of decency, since 'nothing so imbecile as an adoption of the heathen practice of burning the dead will be tolerated in England'.[65]

The *Lancet* seemed relieved to climb down from this high moral ground in 1885 after Stephen's verdict that cremation was legal when decently performed; the journal declared that the permissive stage of individual choice had been reached after full discussion and hoped that Haden's burial reforms would be more widely adopted to solve the sanitary abuses.[66] It was noted in 1892, however, that, though some clergy favoured cremation, the majority continued to prefer burial, which 'still holds the public mind with a power little if at all abated'.[67] By 1902–3 the *Lancet* felt compelled reluctantly to support the Cremation Act in the interests of public health, ignoring the religious dimension except to note that it had been necessary to move slowly with this reform in order to educate public opinion.[68]

In the end the political decision in favour of cremation in 1902 was exclusively based on sanitary arguments. But though the sanitary case swayed the legislators and doctors, it did not succeed in persuading many people to choose cremation. Christian tradition and an emotional distaste for the concept of cremation still strongly influenced the attitudes of the majority of the population, even those who no longer attended church services. A diffuse, residual religious sentiment led to passive resistance to cremation and a contrary preference was indicated by the vast majority of the lay population up to 1914.

The discussion in the *Lancet* was significant because it illustrated that popular religious sentiment against cremation was powerful enough to influence even the attitude of the medical profession, despite its natural predisposition towards the sanitary case. This sentiment largely explains the strength of middle- and upper-class hostility to cremation and its exceedingly slow acceptance. It is not surprising, then, that these middle- and upper-class families scarcely mentioned the cremation debate in their family papers, and that the overwhelming majority were buried according to the rites of the Church of England. It is possible that they preferred not to discuss cremation in their letters or diaries since it fell into the taboo area occupied by such issues as contraception and suicide. But, for most people, cremation was never an issue worth contemplating, for their religion and family tradition both supported burial.

The limited direct evidence about cremation in these family papers relates to the tiny minority who usually made their choice for particular reasons such as fear of burial alive. Among the eminent aristocrats who supported cremation was the Duke of Westminster, while the Duke of Bedford even established a private crematorium for his family, first used at his own death in 1891.[69] The council of the Cremation Society included at various times Anthony Trollope, Herbert Spencer, Sir Leslie Stephen, John Everett Millais, and Frances Power Cobbe, as well as other literary and professional people, including lawyers, scientists, doctors, and even clergymen.

The first cremation mentioned in these family archives was that of Katherine, the first Lady Dilke, on 10 October 1874. She had an extreme horror of burial in the earth, presumably from fear of burial alive, and expressed a wish to be cremated. Since cremation was still generally believed to be illegal in England, where Sir Henry Thompson had only just opened the debate, Sir Charles Dilke made arrangements to cremate his wife in Europe with the help of the Cremation Society. Since the business of gaining permission to cremate Lady Dilke in Dresden was difficult and prolonged, Sir Charles had his wife's body embalmed at their London home on 23 September and hermetically sealed in a lead coffin.[70] Permission was finally obtained for the Dresden cremation only on condition that twelve officials were present as witnesses, including a number of clergymen, and the furnace was to be left partially open to allow inspection. The attendant officials were not told the name of the deceased and were requested to maintain silence about the cremation. Unfortunately for the Dilke family, one of the officials misrepresented the story to the press as a deliberate experiment to which the family had chosen to invite a large number of scientists. Macabre details were published of the timing of the process of disintegration—six minutes for the coffin to burst, twenty-one minutes to strip the skeleton bare, and so on. The *Lancet* regretted that the fulfilment of a wife's last wish, 'carried out at great trouble and sacrifice of private feeling', was falsely depicted as a 'coarse

experiment'.[71] Such were the tribulations of a family seeking to cremate a
loved one in 1874.

After Stephen's ruling in 1884, those few who adopted the practice were
likely to be unbelievers. Arthur Galton, a relative of the scientists Francis
Galton and Charles Darwin, had been ordained a Roman Catholic priest, but
left the Church at the age of 33 in 1885. Later that year he inserted a postscript
to the elegy he composed in his grandmother's memory: 'As I am strongly in
favour of cremation, because it is more cleanly than burial, and removes the
chance of a living burial; I should like my body to be burned, and the ashes
gathered into a small urn, of a Greek shape, and placed by my Grandmother's
coffin, in the vault at Hadzor.'[72] It is worth noting that motives for cremation
could be mixed and that fear of burial alive was not confined to the ignorant
and uneducated. In some cases the decision was made primarily on sanitary
or aesthetic grounds. Dyson Williams, brother-in-law to Beatrice Potter, was
cremated at Woking in 1896 in the presence of only three family members.
Since he had died of syphilis after several years' invalidism it seems probable
that the family chose cremation on public-health grounds.[73] Later that year a
doctor wrote to the *Lancet*, describing the recent cremation of his invalid son
in Manchester, evidently satisfied that this had been the most appropriate
mode of disposal of his disabled child's body. The doctor found great
comfort in knowing that 'the poor earthly shell in which his suffering spirit
was so long imprisoned has returned to its primary elements'. The parents'
thoughts were not restricted to a particular grave in an overcrowded cemetery, nor depressed by the 'slow and horrible process of putrefaction'. Dr
Martin reassured readers that the cremation procedure was peaceful, reverent,
and soothing, most unlike that at the graveside in a cemetery.[74]

The most explicit sanitary explanation for the choice of cremation was
offered by William Rathbone of Liverpool, who died in 1902. He directed
that his body be cremated, believing that 'the burial of a large number of
persons in the midst of populous districts was endangering the public health'.
It should be done as simply and inexpensively as was possible without
eccentricity, using an alabaster casket. None of his friends was to attend if
there was any risk to their health, nor to uncover their heads in the open
air. William Rathbone took the sanitary arguments of the cremationists to
heart, so it was fortuitous that he died in the year of the 1902 Cremation
Act.[75] The following year Kate Courtney reassured her sister-in-law that
Herbert Spencer's cremation was less unpleasant than expected, though
'English society' ignored it: 'I wish you had been there, for there was nothing
repellent as I feared about the business part of the ceremony—it was
simple and reverent.' The little chapel was full of friends and admirers,

impressed by the ceremony and evidently undeterred by the unusual prospect of a cremation.[76]

This family evidence does challenge Jennifer Leaney's contention in 1989 that 'religious objections to cremation were not in Britain, however, particularly potent'.[77] Support for cremation was undoubtedly strongest among the upper-middle and upper classes, especially among the scientific and literary intelligentsia, and weakest among the working classes. But the evidence from the archives in this study suggests that it was weak even amongst the very classes from which it drew its support, and very slow to grow. The reason was almost certainly the continued strength of Christianity among the middle and upper classes until the end of the nineteenth century. Leaney argues that the success of cremationist propaganda and the growing popularity of the practice from 1884 was due to 'the unease experienced by the middle and upper classes at the process of physical decay'. Undoubtedly some cremationists did express their repugnance for the process of putrefaction, but there is little evidence that this extended to the middle and upper classes as a whole, or that this was an 'antecedent of the modern attitude of death denial'. The Victorian middle and upper classes may not have been quite so familiar with death as the working classes, but they were very much better acquainted with it than we are today, and practical rather than uneasy in their dealings with it.[78] Moreover, apart from a few people anxious about premature burial, that minority who supported cremation was chiefly influenced by the public-health argument rather than by an 'intense loathing for the physical remains of the dead'. Indeed, cremation was still far from popular by 1914. Even though it was legalized, it was only very reluctantly tolerated and still generally regarded as heathen and unnatural.

‎⟨❦⟩ 10 ⟨❦⟩

THE FUNERAL WEEK

THE WEEK OF THE FUNERAL BEGAN THE PROCESS OF WORKING THROUGH grief with the help of a supportive structure of public mourning rituals and family unity. John Hinton argues that mourning ritual provides a 'socially approved catharsis of grief' in the first weeks of bereavement:

It insists that the death has occurred, repeatedly demonstrating this fact in various ways over a few days so that the bereaved, whatever their state of mind, accept the painful knowledge, assimilate it and can begin to plan accordingly. Viewing the body and taking part in the funeral emphasize beyond all doubt that the person is really dead. The condolences, the discussion of the deceased in the past tense, the newspaper announcements, the public recognition of the death, all affirm the loss.[1]

Beverley Raphael also notes the importance of the funeral in providing 'an opportunity for reestablishment of the social group, for a reinforcement of its life and unity'.[2] Of course most families were unlikely to be as geographically dispersed in Victorian times as they may be today, and many had already gathered together before the death finally occurred.

The week of the funeral was a hiatus between nursing the dying and the prolonged period of individual grieving. Psychologists observe that the immediate reaction to a death is usually a sense of numbness which may last for several days, temporarily limiting the full impact of the loss.[3] At first the bereaved often find the whole situation unreal, and may need help with the practical arrangements. After the initial shock has worn off, the second stage of acute pangs of grief and severe anxiety usually begins a few days after the death, reaching a climax within five to fourteen days.[4]

Numerous family archives testify to the Victorians' understanding of the need for family unity and sympathy during the week of the funeral and throughout the process of grieving. The experience of the Unitarian Sharpe and Reid families of London was characteristic, as they faced the death of 17-year-old Laetitia Reid in October 1844. Letty's sister Lucy Sharpe found consolation in the gathering of the family for the funeral:

This sorrow draws us closer together and seems to open our hearts to one another . . . The day tho' one of sorrow had in it many gleams of happiness. The loss of one in the circle makes the rest draw closer together and there seemed in the whole band of brothers and sisters yesterday a softness and affection one toward another that was to me very delightful—I would not have been away at such a time.[5]

Letty's father, Thomas Reid, was pleased that all his four sons would come to Exeter for the funeral: 'it will be gratifying to have them around the remains of their loved sister and [that] we may all be in love together'.[6] Relatives understood that Letty's mother, Mary Reid, would find 'the greatest balm to your sorrowing heart in the bosom of your affectionate family'.[7] When Thomas Reid followed his daughter only five months later, Lucy Sharpe told her husband that while the chief link of their family chain was gone, 'we all should draw closer to maintain some of its strength'.[8]

Most family members seem to have been similarly comforted by the support and sympathy of relatives, friends, and neighbours who were brought together for the funeral. Lord Holland remarked on a funeral in the Carlisle family in 1840: 'They are so many, so affectionate and so united that they soothe and sustain one another.'[9] Mary Somerville, the scientist, wrote to her daughter-in-law Agnes Greig after the funeral of Agnes's sister in 1867: 'It must have been a great comfort too to see how much she was beloved and respected by all who knew her, the funeral was a sad but pleasing testimony of that . . . I like Sir William Gordon for coming so far to be present. He is indeed a true friend.'[10] On the funeral of his wife in 1878, Archbishop Tait derived some comfort from 'the kind gathering of neighbours and of so many Bishops', as well as family and numerous friends at Addington churchyard.[11]

The most urgent task immediately after death was the laying-out of the body—a service usually performed in upper- and upper-middle-class families by the nurse attending the final illness or by faithful family servants. A rare direct reference to the laying-out of the body was made by Miss Cameron, the maid of the dowager Duchess of Atholl, after the Duchess's death in 1897. Miss Cameron noted in her diary that very soon after the death occurred, the nurses and Miss Macgregor, the Duchess's cousin, commenced the first part of the dressing, 'but they could not put her teeth in, then I put her nightgown on and smoothed her hair and put the best ironed nightcap on—just the ordinary things she always wore—she looked very sweet and pleasant'.[12] This servant's diary provides a vivid glimpse of the first practical duty between death and burial.

Nurses and servants were usually familiar with the procedure for laying out bodies since nurses were taught as part of their training and maids were instructed by nurses. W. J. Butler, Canon of Worcester, edited a pamphlet for nurses in 1881 which provided special prayers before laying out the dead, to encourage nurses to carry out this last service for Christians with care and reverence, 'rather than in the heartless mechanical fashion' which often prevailed.[13] Nurses were cautioned to remember that the lifeless body they laid out would one day be raised from the dead.

A small pamphlet published in 1910 by two anonymous nurses set out clear, simple instructions for the task of laying out the dead, based on 'the usage of many generations'. It was written for the 'untrained person who may find herself unexpectedly called upon to care for the Dead', suggesting that this task almost always fell to women. The nurses explained that immediately after death a handkerchief folded into a three-inch-wide band should be placed under the chin and fastened at the top of the head to keep the mouth closed until rigor mortis set in. The eyelids should be closed with small pads of wet cotton wool. The nightclothes must be removed and the limbs straightened out, exercising great care 'not to expose the body more than in life'. An hour later the body should be washed all over with soap and water 'under a blanket or sheet', using old linen, which should be burned afterwards. Then the body from the waist to the thighs should be firmly bound with clean, strong calico about half a yard wide, again without exposing the body, and a firm packing of cotton wool or clean rags placed in the body's orifices. A white nightgown should be put on, with white socks, the ankles firmly tied together with white tape, the hair brushed neatly and the arms folded across the breast. The eye-pads and headband could be removed after a few hours. The two nurses emphasized the sanctity of these last offices, which should be carried out in silence, with no one present but those actively involved, observing reverence and care in preparing the deceased for '"sleep" until the judgment day of God'.[14]

Family archives generally pass silently over the laying-out procedure, but they have more to say about viewing the body and final family farewells. Lady Anne Blunt's diary reveals only that her sister-in-law Alice Blunt was laid out by two female family friends, rather than servants, on her death in 1872. Anne Blunt later went to say farewell: 'I kissed her hair on her forehead that I might once more say goodbye to her. I thought it was not wrong just once to touch her face.' Alice was placed in the coffin two days after she died, when the coffin was closed.[15] In 1865, on the death of Woronzow Greig, son of Mary Somerville, his widow Agnes found comfort in physical proximity to his body:

I kept on his bed as long as they would let me and then on Saturday evening he was placed by loving hands in the shell—but they kept it open as long as possible for I could not bear to part with what was so dear to me and then they closed all up. Oh it was dreadful. Still I had my dead to pray by. Till Friday night I felt as if he were not quite gone so long as they would let his earthly form be near.[16]

The family papers of John Callcott Horsley, the artist, demonstrate the significance for Victorians of viewing the body, and their realistic awareness of physical deterioration. They preferred to see their loved ones immediately after death, before the features stiffened, and while the relaxed facial muscles presented a more serene appearance. On the death of John Horsley's sister Fanny in 1849, her husband, Dr Seth Thompson, 'hardly leaves the room and it is becoming almost necessary he should'. As Fanny's mother, Elizabeth Horsley, pointed out, 'the change is so rapid . . . already the mouth is so changed [a drawing] cannot be finished'.[17] When Elizabeth Horsley's husband, William, died on Saturday 12 June 1858, she slept in the sitting-room but spent considerable time in her bedroom on the Sunday with her husband's corpse, while John made a drawing of his father's body on the bed. She attempted to view the body again on the Monday morning but 'could not stay a moment and it was no comfort, the whole was so changed'. Decomposition began more quickly than usual because of the intensely hot June weather, necessitating the early closure of the coffin and advancement of the funeral date.[18]

Occasionally the family judged it prudent to discourage the viewing of the body on aesthetic grounds. Rose Horsley's cousin Mattie Vivian dissuaded her elderly, confused father from seeing his wife again after her death in 1875: 'for she was much altered and would have alarmed instead of pleasing him'.[19] It must be emphasized that attitudes towards viewing the body varied according to class, as well as climate and personal taste. Edwin Chadwick's 1843 *Report on the Practice of Interment in Towns* noted that a corpse generated feelings of respect and awe only among the comfortable classes. Among the lower orders it was often treated 'with as little ceremony as the carcase in a butcher's shop', due to the familiarity and even disgust induced when bodies were retained in overcrowded living-rooms for over a week.[20]

Business matters relating to the death had to be attended to in the first week after the bereavement, distracting the family from their loss. Within five days, one of those present at the death had to notify the registrar of the district of the date and cause of the death, as well as the name, sex, age, and profession of the deceased. The minister officiating at the burial was required to see the certificate of registry before interment. Emily Harcourt was able to help her brother Sir William Harcourt on his wife's death in 1863 by sorting through her sister-in-law's clothes and personal effects. Emily left these in safe keeping for the child, Lewis, in two boxes, together with a green velvet work-box and a small leather desk. She advised her brother to dispose of the seven made-up silk dresses and the sealskin, enclosing a detailed list of Thérèse's clothes. She confessed that the letter was painful to write, as it would be to read, but it was better done earlier than later.[21]

Lord Carnarvon dealt with his mother's affairs after her death in 1876. He examined all the drawers of her dressing-room for any papers which required urgent attention, taking account books and bank-books, but leaving a mass of old family letters to peruse later.[22] The following year Lady Morley inherited her mother's property and household on her death. She told the servants of the legacies left for them and informed four servants she wished them to leave. Five weeks after the death she paid £675 probate duty, disposed of the family coach for £25, and commenced her own improvements to the estate.[23]

John Horsley's diary provides a vivid and poignant account of the pressures and duties of the week following the death of his first wife, Elvira, on 1 December 1852. The day after she died he visited the cemetery with his brother-in-law Dr Seth Thompson to select the burial-plot. On 3 December he and his sister Sophy 'decked the Dearest's bed with flowers', pleased that the only change was that Elvira became 'more like herself'. They also invited several close friends and relatives to view the body, including Rose Haden, subsequently John's second wife, warning them not to delay beyond that evening. John noted the names of more than a dozen friends who 'saw the dearest's form', which still 'looked beautifully'. On 4 December the body was carefully moved from the bed into the coffin by the nurse, the cook, and Martin, the upholsterer, who had fitted out John and Elvira when they were married, and was now acting as undertaker. Later, after the children were in bed, John and Sophy placed Elvira's wedding bouquet on her breast, finding it still in the same box in which it came from Covent Garden on their wedding morning. They hung round her neck a little red velvet bag containing locks of hair from John and the children, so that she could take to the grave some earthly reminders of her family. John recalled in his diary how his dying wife had planned this a month earlier, calling in the children one by one, cutting off locks of their hair, wrapping each in a note stating the name and date. Finally John placed in the coffin, at his wife's request, a pine box containing his letters to her. He spent all day with the body on 6 December, Sophy sharing his vigil, joined briefly by Seth and their mother. Almost a week after Elvira's death, John's sister Mary Brunel arrived from Devonshire and was pleased to see Elvira's body, despite signs of 'change'. John looked for the last time at his wife's face, before placing a 'cloth' over it, and watching the closing of the coffin.[24]

Some people left specific instructions about their burial, either in a will or in informal written or verbal wishes, if they were married women without the legal right to make wills. When she was dying in 1852, Ada Lady Lovelace elaborated plans for her own burial to her husband and mother in a series of notes and oral directions. Ada was determined to be buried in a romantic resting-place at Hucknall Forkard, near Nottingham, in the same vault as her famous father, the poet Lord Byron. She wanted a 'simple but yet pretty little marble monument' erected with an epitaph, which was to include a biblical text from St James's epistle and a poem she had herself composed. Similar monuments to her memory were to be erected at four other specified locations. Ada was extremely fearful of burial alive—dreaded as much in the nineteenth as in earlier centuries—and insisted that her husband and Dr Barwell take all precautions to prevent it.[25] Lord Lovelace followed his wife's instructions to the letter, burying her by Lord Byron's side in an elaborate ceremony.

Ada Lovelace's last wishes were romantic, expensive, and most unusual. Most Victorians confined themselves to requests to be buried next to their loved ones and sometimes also for simple funerals. Sir Thomas Acland was buried in 1871 by his wife's side in the same grave, following the wish he had often expressed.[26] In 1878, eight years before his death, Frank Rogers sent instructions to his brother: 'You must always remember that I am to be buried by my late wife in the same grave made expressly large enough to hold us both.' He asked that a headstone be erected with an inscription expressing his regard for his wife.[27] There were occasionally more unusual requests, such as that of Blanche Cripps, who committed suicide in 1905, leaving directions 'that she was to be buried with her head on a Bible and her feet on a Shakespeare'.[28]

The selection of the burial-plot was an immediate duty for the family on the death of a baby, child, or person who had expressed no preferences. The day after the death of Seth Thompson's wife, Fanny, in 1849, her mother, sister, and husband visited the cemetery 'to choose her last resting place', which her sister described as 'a lovely spot [with] a full view towards the gardens and Notting Hill'.[29] Bereaved families often chose burial-plots in places of beauty, sometimes even with views, as if these mattered to the souls sleeping below. On the death of his baby son Julian in 1862, Sir William Harcourt sent a request to his spinster sister Emily: 'I wish you to choose for him in the churchyard on the south side the prettiest and freest spot you can find for our darlings grave where we may grow flowers over his bed . . . let there be space enough for his father and mother one day to sleep by his side and to put up the monument I mean to design.'[30] Emily obligingly made two visits to the Nuneham churchyard where she settled on 'the brightest spot on the south side', leaving ample room for two other graves.[31] In a letter of condolence to his son the next day, the bereaved grandfather Revd William Harcourt was moved to express his own burial preference: 'Tho' no one cares less where his bones may lie, if I die here [at Nuneham] I shall be buried in this Church yard, and may perhaps not be long in following my dear grandchild.' He had already selected a spot above an ancient vault near the church entrance.[32]

Undertakers rarely appear in these families' correspondence or diaries. They were simply regarded as tradesmen with a particular job to do, like the seamstresses who made up the mourning-clothes. Where mentioned, it is rarely by name, unless there was an unusual personal association, as with John Horsley's upholsterer, who fitted out the family in marriage as in death. Horsley observed after his wife's funeral in 1852 that Martin had performed his alternative duty as an undertaker with appropriate order and reverence.[33] The very few archival references suggest that these families usually hired the local undertaker who had looked after previous family funerals. No undertaker is cited as providing personal advice or sympathy beyond the role of tradesman. Though archival silence eliminates possible criticism as well as praise, a general hostility to the undertakers' role in excessive commercialization of funerals was implicit in the support of these families for the funeral reform movement.[34]

Funeral services varied according to religious affiliation, but the burial-service of the Church of England was used fairly widely by many sects, and was by far the most common among these Victorian families. In 1858 the Society for Promoting Christian Knowledge published a short pamphlet advising mourners on conduct and consolation at funerals:

There is much of instruction as well as consolation in the office appointed by our Church for the Burial of the Dead; in which, as in all other parts of The Book of Common Prayer, it is edifying to observe how strict an agreement with Holy Scripture the Church Services maintain. Of the whole Burial Service, three-fourths at least are the very words of Scripture itself. The selection has principally been made from those portions of it which relate to the Resurrection. And, it may be asked, what doctrine is so well calculated as to dry the mourner's tears?

The Society evidently had some doubts that all its readers would find the burial-service as elevating as they were supposed to. While advising readers to join in the service 'soberly and devoutly', it was thought necessary also to admonish them: 'you will not look about you, nor whisper to your acquaintances, nor stare at the mourners'. After the funeral, they were warned to heed the words of Jeremy Taylor: 'Go home, and think of dying, and do that daily which you would wish to be found doing whenever death shall overtake you.' The funeral service should in this way be employed to bring 'benefit and consolation to your own soul'.[35]

It is difficult to evaluate mourners' responses to funerals, and to assess their therapeutic value or spiritual significance, because family comments on funerals in letters and diaries were surprisingly few and brief, in sharp contrast to the lengthy accounts of dying and the deathbed. It is as if the week of the funeral marked a quiet interval between the business of dying and the months of grieving. Certainly family and friends were gathered together for the funeral and had no need of letters, while they were often too preoccupied to maintain their daily diaries in any detail. It is also likely that for many mourners most closely related to the deceased the funeral came too soon after the death for them to respond in writing, since they were still too shocked. Agnes Greig was desolate in 1865 as her husband's coffin was carried away: 'and they put my widow dress on me. I seemed a sort of machine.'[36] The shock left many mourners too disoriented to record personal responses to the funeral, noting instead random, bathetic, and seemingly irrelevant details. In 1898 Mary Drew was unusually restrained in her description of the burial of her father, W. E. Gladstone: 'a wonderful scene which one had hardly presence of mind to take in. The grave is very deep and full of sea sand.'[37] Press reports of funerals often provide more information than the letters and diaries of the families involved, though the newspapers reveal nothing of personal responses.

Florence Herbert was unusual in attempting to describe in writing the shock of early grief. She wrote to her brother Lord Cowper in 1882, four days after the death of her 10-year-old son, Rolf, saying she would like to see him later on, but not just at present. 'Now I am too sick and sorry, like a wounded beast longing to creep into a hole quite alone, "so tired" (as he used to say in his illness) in heart and spirit and mind.' 'Dolly' Herbert wanted a week or two of 'perfect rest and silence, when I shall be able to pull myself together and start again'. In this sombre frame of mind, she wrote of the funeral: 'We laid his poor little body ourselves in the coffin yesterday and brought it down with us. One's poor brain playing one all sorts of tricks—of still expecting to find him hopping and springing about in his blue pilot jacket and cap when one arrived here. The body and the funeral and all that feel so strangely away.'[38] Many mourners must have felt as sick at heart as Dolly Herbert, but few testimonies to such feelings have survived.

Some more devout Christians found spiritual edification or consolation in the funerals of their loved ones. For John Horsley, the funeral of his wife, Elvira, on 8 December 1852 was a day of prayer and contemplation. The day began with the early-morning visit of his children to his bedroom, dressed in black, to say their morning prayers. Later John and his sister Sophy knelt in prayer by Elvira's coffin, which was covered with a velvet pall:

I prayed as I have ever done of late, that this heavy trial may be a purifying one to me, that the memory of my dearest Elvira may by God's grace be an additional incentive to the performance of my duty and most fervently did pray that that duty might be so performed that I might have a reasonable hope ere I died of joining my dearest wife for eternity.[39]

For John Horsley the funeral service was primarily a religious ceremony of continued prayer for the purification of his own soul, to enable him to join Elvira in heaven. Even the 'wet mizzling and wretched' weather had its advantage, in that it 'diminished the number of the starers and gapers' at the small funeral cortège of three carriages carrying twelve mourners. The clergyman read the service 'most simply and beautifully', and later John knelt at his wife's graveside as the Lord's Prayer was said. But his faith and prayer did not prevent a powerful emotional reaction immediately after the funeral: 'I am thoroughly broken up, feeling as though I had been kneaded like dough, or pummelled for a week.' For John Horsley the week of the funeral was an intense and valuable religious experience, while the attempt to represent it in his diary carried its own consolation.[40]

Other Christian mourners found similar solace in the funeral service. Emily Palmer was consoled by the funeral of her sister Dorothea in 1852: 'The Burial Service seemed to give me so *much* comfort and yet more still for it seems to stir up all one's longings after holiness.'[41] Meriel Lyttelton's diary entry on the funeral of her mother, Lady Lyttelton, in 1857 noted: 'God grant that we may remember, and act upon the remembrance of that day and service.' It was obviously important to Meriel that all nine older children attended the service and received Holy Communion together afterwards, with friends, relatives and neighbours.[42] Sarah Acland experienced a sense of peace and joy during the 'walking funeral' in 1866 for her 80-year-old father, William Cotton. She walked near the front of the family procession, behind her father's coffin, from the house to the churchyard: 'It gave me such a wonderful feeling, walking so slowly and silently along: as if I might have walked on always and found myself at last, in another world.' Sarah gained some comfort from the beautiful words of the burial-service, though she missed the opening sentences because the wind was strong at the churchyard gate.[43] On her husband's death in 1883 Laura Harcourt found every word of the 'last Solemn Service . . . so applicable and therefore so comforting to hear'.[44]

However, positive responses to funerals were almost equalled in number by the more critical comments of mourners who experienced them as ordeals. George Dashwood, MP was profoundly depressed by the funeral in 1846 of his brother Revd Henry Dashwood: 'I never passed a more miserable melancholy day than yesterday. Everything reminded me of poor Henry and his unfortunate career.' Their father, Sir John Dashwood, was becoming senile and probably did not even realize his son's loss, so that he did not appear the least affected and was even laughing.[45] After attending her father's funeral in 1858, Sophy Horsley commented that she would always wish to fulfil such a duty towards those she loved, 'but excepting witnessing their death I can conceive nothing so painful'.[46] Augusta Touzel observed her uncle's reaction to his wife's funeral in 1856: 'he nerved himself for the morrow's trial, and got through it as well, if not better than he expected', though Augusta's husband considered it 'a most trying day'.[47] Even the devout fourth Earl of Carnarvon was negative about his mother's funeral in 1876: 'the painful ceremony is over with as little pain as could be expected'.[48]

Non-Anglican funerals could vary greatly. At one end of the Christian spectrum, Wilfrid Scawen Blunt's brother Francis, the devout Catholic squire of Crabbet in Sussex, was buried in 1872 according to the rites of the Roman Catholic Church. The family was determined on an appropriate Catholic ceremony for Francis, in part because he was a tertiary of the Franciscan monastery he had founded at Crawley. They were probably also influenced by unhappy memories of their mother's funeral nearly twenty years earlier. Though their mother, Mary Blunt, was a converted Catholic, the law required her to be buried in a Protestant graveyard in 1855, an indignity aggravated by the 'port-drinking parson' who read the Anglican burial-service.[49] Before Francis's funeral in 1872, the family arranged the crucifix and the candles on the table in the little room where the coffin lay, hanging a picture of the Madonna of St Sixtus up above. Wilfrid and his wife, Lady Anne Blunt, discussed with their lawyer the legal arrangements for the foundation of an anniversary mass for Francis, learning that a special trust was necessary 'so as to avoid being illegal as a "superstitious practice"'.[50] The funeral on 29 April 1872 began with the Mass, followed by Casciolini's Requiem sung by a group of unaccompanied singers, 'very fine and all of it strong and serious'. The mourners in the body of the church were all men, the four women being obliged to observe it from the gallery, where they could see little beyond the altar, and they left before the burial. Francis Blunt was buried in his Franciscan robes in a vault in a small side-chapel at the Crawley monastery church.[51]

Some mourners found comfort in the elaborate ritual of a Catholic funeral, such as that of Peggy Talbot held at Arundel Castle in 1899, described by Gwendolen Cecil:

I am down here for my darling Peggy's funeral. . . . It has been a beautiful service today;—last night was the most striking perhaps and the most touching. The coffin was in the chapel and at seven o'clock we had a service, and then, with a long procession of choir and clergy singing, with torches and candles, they carried her out through the Castle court and grounds, and then along the street to the church where, after another service, we left her till today. . . . Today they had High Mass before the burial, and one realized the other side—the spiritual mystery, the beauty and awfulness of Christian death.[52]

But not all mourners appreciated the 'spiritual mystery' of a Catholic or a High Church funeral. In 1890 Evan Thompson described 'the terrible ordeal' of the High Church London funeral of Margaret Luckock, a wife and mother who had died of typhoid aged 46. A Communion service was held after the first part of the burial-service, accompanied by 'a great deal of intoning and singing, some of it very beautiful'. He believed Herbert Luckock, the widower, 'derived some comfort from the elaborate ritual, but to everyone else I think the effect was painful. But poor Maggie liked that sort of funeral.'[53]

At the other end of the Christian spectrum was the plain burial of the Quakers, described by Basil Montagu in *The Funerals of the Quakers* in 1840. A plain coffin was used without a pall, which was carried to the grave attended by mourners who did not wear any special mourning-dress. After a silent burial, they retired to a meeting for worship, 'when any friend who is moved to speak addresses the meeting'. Graves were dug in rows according to the order in which people happened to die, rather than in family groups, and with no use of sepulchres, underground vaults, tombstones, monuments, or epitaphs. They judged it more reasonable and pious 'to assist than to oppose the laws of Nature'.[54] Mary Lady Pease was buried in 1892 at the Friends' Burial Ground at Darlington, to which her body had been carried on 'a plain unplumed hearse'. Two mourners broke the impressive silence at Lady Pease's graveside by softly chanting hymns after the coffin had been lowered. Mourners then proceeded to the meeting-house where four friends delivered addresses, prayers were offered, and a female friend of the deceased sang 'Rest in the Lord'.[55]

Christian funerals were religious ceremonies which could make unbelievers feel uncomfortable, with their emphasis on resurrection and atonement, and their implications for the unhappy fate of unrepentant sinners. As an agnostic, Charles Darwin disliked funerals, which tended to aggravate both his grief and his ill health. He did not attend the funerals of his father, his daughter Annie, or his old friend Professor J. S. Henslow, usually citing his poor health as justification. He declined to be a pall-bearer at Charles Lyell's funeral in 1875, 'as I should so likely faint in the midst of the ceremony and have my head whirling off my shoulders'.[56] Perhaps he was able to attend the

1856 funeral of his 78-year-old aunt Sarah Wedgwood because he felt less emotionally engaged or better prepared because of her age. Darwin's account of Sarah's funeral was prosaic, unemotional, and devoid of the familiar religious references; the only personal notes were his comments that the clergyman read the service badly and his aunt's three servants cried profusely.[57]

Women did not usually attend upper- and middle-class funerals in the early and mid-Victorian periods, on the grounds that allegedly they could not control their feelings. An 1849 guide to court etiquette directed that women should never be seen in the funeral cortège of the gentry. If 'eccentric people' broke this rule, the women present must take their seats in the church before the service, but must not participate in the funeral procession.[58] It was cause for comment if women chose to attend a funeral, as when Lady Carlisle insisted on attending her husband's funeral in 1840, 'as calm and composed as could be expected'.[59] Marie-Thérèse Harcourt did not attend her baby's funeral in 1862 because her husband thought 'the service would be too long for me'.[60] Roundell Palmer dissuaded his wife from attending the funeral of his sister Dorothea in 1852; his family considered she was already 'at your post' as she had children to care for.[61] When William Horsley died in 1858 his adult children spared their mother, Elizabeth Horsley, as much of the bustle of the funeral week as they could. She did not attend her husband's funeral, feeling exhausted and 'unequal to it in mind and body', especially as the heat was so intense.[62] Even as late as 1870 *Cassell's Household Guide* opposed the tendency among the poorer classes for female relatives to attend funerals: 'This custom is by no means to be recommended, since in these cases it but too frequently happens that, being unable to restrain their emotions they interrupt and destroy the solemnity of the ceremony with their sobs, and even by fainting.'[63] By the 1870s a compromise was sometimes reached whereby the grieving widow might attend the funeral service in the church, but retire home before the burial ceremony without speaking to relatives and friends, as Laura Harcourt did in 1883.[64] Lady Colin Campbell noted that by the 1890s it was becoming rather more common for female members of the family to attend the funeral: 'If they feel strong enough, and can keep their grief within due bounds, let not the thought of what is customary prevent them from following their lost one to the grave.'[65]

The custom that mourners should control their grief at funerals and be seen to behave bravely could turn a funeral into an ordeal of self-control for those in deep sorrow. This custom can be traced back to 1651 to Jeremy Taylor's *Holy Dying*, which condoned the need to weep 'awhile' before the burial, but cautioned the good Christian, 'if the dead did die in the

Lord . . . it is an ill expression of our affection and our charity to weep uncomfortably at a change that hath carried my friend to the state of a huge felicity'.[66] It was considered permissible for early and mid-Victorian males to express their grief openly, but restraint was expected at funerals and in public. Male mourners often mentioned their efforts to restrain their emotions for the sake of the women in the family. On his father's death in 1856, Frederick Goulburn wrote to his brother, 'God give us strength to do our duty and restrain our feelings for the sake of my poor mother and Jane.'[67]

Courageous control of sorrow at a funeral could be particular cause for congratulation in the late Victorian period, when emotions were expected to be kept under far tighter rein than a generation earlier. Revd Edwin Palmer was pleased that his sister Eleanor 'bore up well' at her husband's funeral in 1870, though it was clearly 'a perpetual effort to keep her emotion from overflowing'. However, the family and their doctor recognized that it had been therapeutic for her to 'give way freely and fully' soon after Cyril's death.[68] Again the contrast is clear between the desire for emotional restraint at the funeral and the recognition of the value of weeping in private. In 1898 H. M. Stanley wrote to Elsie Pease after her father's funeral, 'I turned away from you at the station with a very high respect for the brave way you bore yourself at such a trying time.'[69] In 1897 the Chamberlain family was concerned that both Agnes and Walter Chamberlain would have difficulty controlling their emotions during the funeral of their schoolboy son. The Church of England service was conducted for this Unitarian family at Joseph Chamberlain's house at Highbury, making it as easy as possible for the bereaved parents—it was 'solemn but not gloomy'. Mary Chamberlain noted that her sister-in-law Agnes 'went through it bravely', but after the service was over and the men went to the churchyard for the burial, she joined two female relatives in the drawing-room: 'Of course she had to break down but she controlled herself soon again. All unite in thinking she has shown much character and strength.'[70] It was not only female mourners who occasionally failed to control their feelings at funerals. On the death of his wife in 1890 Herbert Luckock was considered 'most terribly broken—they all say they had never seen a man in so hopelessly wretched and unmanned a condition'—by contrast with the children, who were 'very good and brave'.[71]

The evidence suggests that some late Victorian and Edwardian families derived almost as much comfort from the natural beauty of the countryside surrounding the graveyard or from the church music or the flowers scattered on the grave as from the religious message of the burial-service. Comments to this effect increased from the 1880s. As funeral ceremonies became less elaborate, so the fashion for sending wreaths to cover the coffin gained popularity.[72] When her mother was buried in the Lake District in 1888, the novelist Mrs Humphry Ward, an undogmatic Unitarian, derived most consolation from the beauty of the 'everlasting hills', reinforced by the loveliness of the music and the flowers. The Ward family called upon the services of a group in Ambleside 'who form a little society for providing music at funerals' to play a hymn, some organ music, and the 'Dead March'. The grave was lined with ivy and moss, so that the mourners saw 'nothing but the beautiful mass of white flowers among the green', as the coffin was lowered. Mary Ward thought the ceremony and burial beautiful, peaceful, and simple.[73] Similarly, Victoria Dawnay arranged for her husband to be buried in 1910, at his request, in the quiet little churchyard at Ranmore which they first visited on their honeymoon. Afterwards she reported to her sister that the funeral was 'all perfect', just as her husband would have wanted: 'Just back again after the most beautiful service, having laid him in the little churchyard which he loved, under a large oak, a real bank of glorious flowers near the grave. And the surroundings were so perfect—glorious sunshine—all the trees in their greatest beauty and the little church filled with the people he loved best.'[74]

There is little evidence in upper- and upper-middle-class family archives about the survival of the funeral feast. Clare Gittings has demonstrated that the feast was a vital component of sixteenth- and seventeenth-century funerals, amounting to about half their total cost and justified in social terms as 'a form of communal therapy and social restoration for the bereaved and their immediate social group'.[75] J. S. Curl has perpetuated the myth about Victorian funeral feasts in *The Victorian Celebration of Death*. 'Feasts in mid-Victorian times became status symbols, and families of all classes vied with their neighbours in terms both of display of funeral magnificence and of the provision of victuals.'[76] Certainly the working-class culture of death still made much of the feast, as Ruth Richardson has shown.[77] But the significance of the funeral meal was greatly diminished among these nineteenth-century professional and upper-class families, and it was not even mentioned in the funeral entry in *Cassell's Household Guide* for 1860. An 1849 guide to court etiquette for funerals of the gentry instructed that all mourners must take their leave almost immediately after the carriages returned to the family house, except for those requested to remain to hear the will read.[78] Hospitality would be provided for the chief mourners, especially those who had travelled some distance to the funeral. Usually such hospitality would include the provision of a meal or refreshments at the family home immediately after the funeral, but these seem to have been quiet, restrained affairs which received little notice. After Elvira Horsley's funeral in 1852, only the doctor and one other mourner returned to the house, and they stayed only a few minutes.[79] Six years later, after the quiet funeral of Elvira's father-in-law, William Horsley, all mourners at the funeral returned to the family home afterwards to have breakfast and hear the will read.[80] In 1875 after the funeral of Mary Vivian, her two nephews and her doctor returned to the family home for some hot soup, as they were 'chilled to the bone'. The visitors admired the cat, who paraded before them wearing a black ribbon, as his dead mistress had wished.[81] In 1872 the Blunts left instructions with one of the servants 'to ask anyone to come to Crabbet who would' after Alice Blunt's funeral.[82]

The funerals of clergymen and their families usually included refreshments for the tenants at the vicarage after the ceremony. William Jocelyn Palmer, vicar of Mixbury, directed in his will in 1852, drawn up eighteen months before his death, that on the day of his funeral the poor families in his parish should be provided with a good meal of fresh meat in their own homes at his expense.[83] John Keble's funeral expenses in 1866 included £2. 10s. for the provision of 'Refreshment at the Old Vicarage for the Tenantry including Beer'.[84] Archbishop Tait mentioned in his journal 'the hurried visit to the Vicarage' after the funerals of his wife and his son, both in 1878.[85] There is no evidence here of ostentatious funeral feasts intended to impress neighbours and community with a family's status and wealth.

Wills

Ralph Houlbrooke has suggested that English wills were slowly secularized in form and content in the three centuries before 1900, reducing their value for historians interested in contemporary views on death. Pious bequests disappeared from wills during the eighteenth century, as did the introductory clauses on the state of the soul. Increasingly wills were made at an earlier stage in life, ending the medieval association with the deathbed scene.[86] By the nineteenth century wills were devoted to the disposition of worldly goods, revealing little or nothing of value about the testator's attitude to death, while spiritual or affectionate messages were often delivered separately.

Victorian and Edwardian wills were usually concerned exclusively with land and property, and were expressed in legal language which largely eliminated sentimental or religious expressions. The average will was short, usually between one and two pages. Even the most devout Victorians usually excluded religious exhortations and pious phrases from their wills, or reduced them to the minimum. Religious references in William Horsley's 1843 will were restricted to two formulaic final sentences, which were fairly typical for early Victorian Christians. He commended his soul to God, asking forgiveness for his sins, and praying for his guidance so 'that after this life I fail not to enter the eternal kingdom'.[87] By the end of the century such clauses were still further reduced or disappeared entirely; even W. E. Gladstone, not renowned for brevity in such matters, confined himself to one terse sentence commending his soul to the infinite mercies of Christ. Apart from such rare religious references, the only clause of a more personal nature which appeared in some early and mid-Victorian wills was the expression of a wish for a simple funeral or burial in a particular spot. Even these requests disappeared from most wills at the end of the century, as anxiety about funeral extravagance abated. Wills were composed at the deathbed only in the most unusual circumstances; Revd Harry Drew's premature death following surgery in 1910 allowed him to leave only a simple statement of eight lines bequeathing everything to his wife. Wills usually listed bequests in the briefest of terms, with none of the personal explanations sometimes found in women's informal wills.

The few longer wills were usually prepared for family patriarchs with money and property to distribute among large families. Richard Potter, who died in 1892, required a seventeen-page will dated 1883, which was carefully drafted and sectionalized, with four codicils dated between 1884 and 1888, to divide his estate of just over £13,000 between his eight daughters. Lord Lyttelton, who died in 1876, left a tortuously constructed will of twelve pages, not that his estate was extraordinarily valuable (less than £20,000), but because he wanted to be fair to all fifteen children of two marriages.

If a personal explanation of the will's clauses was considered necessary, this was sometimes provided in separate, confidential statements, usually addressed to the wife. A few letters survive in the Stanhope archive from a much longer correspondence in 1894 between the sixth Earl and his wife regarding the contents of his will. Lady Stanhope expressed concern in December 1893 that there was some bad feeling between their sons about the distribution of property, and she advised her husband not to select their younger son Philip as a trustee: 'he has always been disposed to feel that he and Harry were injured by being younger sons, and perhaps this feeling would be revived if he had much to do for us'. She concluded that it was exceedingly difficult to be fair to all parties.[88] Over ten years later, on her husband's death, Lady Stanhope wrote about family finances to her eldest son, the seventh Earl, on his assumption of the title and estate responsibilities. She informed him that the contents of their family seat, Chevening, had been valued at just over £22,000, presumably an undervaluation with death duties in mind, for she added: 'I hope they won't question the last; after your appeal the authorities may think it inadequate, as of course it is.'[89]

The fourth Earl of Carnarvon left a series of letters for his second wife, Elsie, as a guide to his finances to be opened after his death. These explained, in more detail than the will permitted, his wishes for the disposition of his books, manuscripts, correspondence, pictures, and various keepsakes and personal bequests. The most significant memorandum, dated 1889, was a justification of his stewardship of the estate he inherited and his views as to its disposition on his death, 'desiring to avoid those misconceptions and misrepresentations which so often arise in the distribution of a considerable landed property'. Though he accepted the principle of primogeniture, Lord Carnarvon believed it was wise to provide for younger sons where the estate was sufficiently large, and he intended to leave one of his properties to his second son.[90]

Personal and sentimental messages were also reserved for informal wills or separate letters addressed to the spouse. Lord Carnarvon, for example, expressed his love for his wife and his children in separate letters and asked his wife to continue to care devotedly for their family. He assured her 'how happy and more than happy you have made me and with what absolute trust I leave everything that I can in your hands'. Lord Carnarvon also warned her that, given the uncertain economic and political climate of England during the agricultural depression of the 1880s, she should be prepared to establish a new home overseas if necessary; Canada, in his view, had a better 'moral atmosphere' than Australia, but she should acquaint herself with the family properties in both countries, keeping their securities divided in many 'baskets'.[91]

The reading of the will generally received little mention by family members during the week of the funeral, and did not usually seem to provoke discord at a time when family unity was considered essential. The experiences of the fourth Earl of Carnarvon and the Potter family seem to have been representative. In 1876 Carnarvon dealt with the uncomplicated business details of his mother's death. He opened the will with the lawyer, to find that 'it was a formal document only. With it however was a paper of instruction though not so full as I had hoped.'[92] In 1892 the Potter family assembled at Standish, the family home near Gloucester, for the funeral of their father, Richard Potter. The seventeen-page will was read in the lawyer's office, carefully dividing the father's estate equally between the eight daughters, who then agreed on the presents they should give to their father's elderly servants. A touching scene followed when they told Mrs Thompson she was to receive £500 as a recognition of her devotion and care of their father for six years. When the old servant recovered her composure she said she would like to have Mr Potter's razors to remember him by, and then burst into tears, as did the sisters. Kate Courtney concluded her account of their father's funeral on a positive note: 'Happily too all our family arrangements and all money matters have passed off without a single moment of friction between any of us; all the sisters have been as nice as they could be.'[93]

If a man died intestate, however, the complications could be stressful and time-consuming, as Woronzow Greig's widow discovered to her cost in 1865. Agnes Greig and her mother-in-law Mary Somerville were shocked to learn that Woronzow's will could not be found, assuming that a lawyer of 60 must have made a will and that his bankers had carelessly lost it. Both women placed the matter in the capable hands of Agnes's brother James Graham, another lawyer, since they were 'so totally ignorant in all matters of business'.[94] As James Graham explained, even under normal circumstances, 'The forms to be gone through in the case of persons dying without leaving a Will are harassing beyond conception,' but in Agnes Greig's case the trauma was vastly increased. The lack of a will prevented her from inheriting any of her late husband's property and estate, all of which would go to his mother and sister. Usually the law determined that if a man died intestate, his widow would receive half his estate and his mother and sisters the other half. But a clause in Agnes's marriage contract prohibited any interest for Agnes in Greig's property beyond the provision of that contract, unless it was specified in his will. Thus, the mother and sisters were regarded as next of kin and so inherited the whole estate. Moreover, without a will, even the capital sum of £8,000 invested for Agnes's marriage settlement would also go to his mother and sisters on Agnes's death. At least the poor widow was spared the 'distressing annoyance' of having government valuers invading her privacy to make their inventories of her household furniture, since that was secured to her by the marriage contract.[95]

A far greater shock to the widowed Agnes Greig was the discovery of an unproved will revealing the existence of her husband's natural daughter, now named Mrs White and aged 40. She was born the daughter of a Swiss maid who worked in Mary Somerville's house when Woronzow was about 20, and was now married and living in Australia. Woronzow believed the child to be his and had secretly sent money to the Whites for many years. It was his 'lifelong secret', which he had concealed from Agnes, despite a very close and loving marriage. The discovery was an 'awful blow' to Agnes, and for several days her brother 'feared lest she should have sunk under the shock', which compounded her great grief.[96]

Though most wills seem to have provoked little family discord, there were inevitably exceptions. The aristocratic Fox family at Holland House was unusual in this respect as in others, including their secular attitude to death and dying, their lack of any religious 'enthusiasm', and their distant and often hostile family relationships. The major quarrel over wills and property in the Fox family erupted over the decision of the third Baron Holland to change his will in May 1837; he was influenced by his manipulative wife, Elizabeth Lady Holland, renowned hostess of the glittering Holland House salon. The new will left Lady Holland, aged 66, as sole executrix, with extensive powers over the family properties as tenant-for-life, and owner of the contents of the two main houses, Holland House and Ampthill. She had no love for the heir, her son Henry, who rightly feared that, though he would succeed to the title if his mother outlived his father, he would lack the means to support it. The new will left the heir the absolute minimum the law allowed, while every-thing else was in his mother's control. Even the indulgent Lord Holland had admitted that his wife had become 'irritable and peremptory and even a little selfish'; Henry amplified this understatement, for his own wife's benefit, adding that his mother 'has *grown* besides most avaricious and grasping'. Henry feared that this new will was the death warrant for Holland House and its library. He was relieved that he and his wife, Augusta, lived and worked in Italy, away from his mother's 'thraldom' and from the 'selfish contaminating corrupting atmosphere' she generated.[97]

Henry Fox had painful scenes with his mother, but refused to remonstrate with his father about his proposed redistribution of his property, deeming such conduct 'indelicate and offensive' in a son. Henry regretted that his mother and elder (illegitimate) brother Charles did not share his scruples, but waited like vultures to tear his father's fortune to pieces. He fervently hoped his father's good health would continue, so 'the most hungry will never have an opportunity of satiating her appetite': 'All these scenes and heart burnings about pictures—coffee pots—etc. etc. are quite hateful. It may and I believe will be injurious to my interests to live away from these struggles but I think the sacrifice of a picture or a coffee pot small if one can thereby buy ignorance of the business and rapacity of our best and dearest relations.'[98] Between 14 and 23 May 1837 Henry Fox had a series of distressing conversations with his father, which reassured him that the new settlement was dictated by his father's 'weakness and submission to the most selfish of human beings', rather than by unkindness towards himself. Lord Holland asked his son's pardon, which Henry gave out of 'submission and compli-ance' to a loving father; 'I would rather lose my whole birthright than embitter any of his declining years with such bare and cruel contests.' Henry felt he was treated as if he had been the most extravagant and worthless of sons and he dreaded the bad blood that must follow should his father not survive his mother.[99]

Henry Fox's worst fears were realized when his father died in October 1840, while his mother survived until 1845, leaving her son without the property or income to support his new title. As fourth baron Holland, Henry had no family property and only £2,000 per annum, while his mother sold off Ampthill to pay off estate debts and also sold family paintings, china, furniture, and books. Anger, mistrust, and dislike between Lady Holland and her two elder sons increased, though the sons initially tried to be sympathetic to their mother's bereavement. But in May 1842 Henry condemned her conduct 'towards my father's children—children he dearly loved and who loved him'.[100] It came as no surprise to them, when Lady Holland died in 1845, that 'her will was unnatural, her children being almost excluded',[101] though the fourth Lord Holland at last succeeded to his father's property and estate.

Henry Fox's experience of family discord about his father's will was unusual, as was Agnes Greig's financial predicament when her husband died intestate. Both cases demonstrate how the immediate problems of coping with a close family death could be complicated by personal differences and by any unfavourable economic consequences of the death. But even in these unfortunate cases the rituals of the funeral week were retained, and the material difficulties were addressed subsequently. The funeral week was a period of entr'acte between death and the prolonged process of grieving, which required the initial observance of the customary rituals for its normal progression.

✑ 11 ✑

WIDOWS:

GENDERED EXPERIENCES OF WIDOWHOOD

V ICTORIAN WIDOWS' EXPERIENCES OF THE PROCESS OF GRIEVING, AS WELL
as their sources of consolation, differed significantly from those of
widowed men in the nineteenth century and also from widows of the present
day. Middle- and upper-class widows generally had a tougher time than
widowers, with no paid occupation to divert their time, more practical and
financial hurdles to overcome, and little expectation of remarriage, except
for the youngest and prettiest. This chapter examines the normal range
of experience of sorrow for Victorian and Edwardian women who lost a
husband.

The high rates of mortality in the nineteenth century produced high rates
of widowed people. Michael Anderson estimates that about 19 per cent of
marriages in the 1850s would have been shattered by death within ten years,
and about 47 per cent within twenty-five years; those figures would have
declined to 13 per cent and 37 per cent respectively for the 1880s, with a more
rapid reduction after 1900. The majority of these widowed people were
women, because of the mortality differential favouring women and the higher
rates of remarriage for widowed men. After 1850 the number of widows over
35 in England and Wales was more than double that of widowers. Anderson
calculates that 14 per cent of men aged 55 to 64 were widowed compared with
30 per cent of women. This differential increased with age, resulting in a large
surplus of widowed women in old age.[1]

Marriage was the most important social institution for the vast majority of
middle- and upper-class women in Victorian and Edwardian Britain. Their
society emphasized the 'natural' separation of the spheres on a gender basis,
and young girls were brought up primarily to be good wives and mothers.
Protestantism reinforced traditional views of the female role as dutiful wife
and guardian of the family. Few alternatives existed for middle- and upper-
class women, other than teaching for a pittance, and spinsters were often seen
as human failures. Widowhood, as the end of marriage, was a devastating
experience, entailing the loss of the central role of wife, which defined the
identity and sense of worth of so many women. The role of widow was

stigmatized less than that of spinster, but it was considerably inferior to that of wife. It signified the probable end of the social recognition and responsibilities which flowed from the husband's work, wealth, and status. Widows were set apart from society, and yet starkly identified by their sombre weeds. For most women, there was no escape from this new condition, since few widows remarried and there were few opportunities for meeting new partners or taking on different challenges through a career. Widowhood was a final destiny, an involuntary commitment to a form of social exile.

Stages of Grief

In many respects the emotional trauma of widowhood and the 'stages of grief' for widows in middle- and upper-class Victorian families followed the patterns described by modern psychologists such as Colin Murray Parkes, John Bowlby, and Beverley Raphael. Parkes's widely accepted conclusions are based on a number of studies of the process of grief among randomly selected groups of widows. These include his own 1970 study of twenty-two London widows under the age of 65, and a Harvard study of sixty-eight Boston widows and widowers under 45. Parkes and Bowlby note that the immediate responses to a spouse's death varied greatly, but there was often a sense of acute anguish at the moment of death, followed by a feeling of numbness, which blunted the senses for a few days, and a refusal to accept that the death had taken place. Often this defensive numbness lasted until the funeral, which first brought home to some widows the reality of the death.[2]

The second phase is characterized by yearning and searching for the lost person, accompanied by 'pangs of intense pining', restlessness, insomnia, and preoccupation with thoughts about the lost husband. This stage is distinguished not so much by prolonged depression as by 'episodes of severe anxiety and psychological pain', known as the 'pangs of grief'. Most of the London widows in Parkes's study were afflicted by panic attacks and a generalized restless anxiety which left them feeling irritable and tense, behaving at times in a 'thoroughly disorganized and fragmented manner'. This second stage was also usually marked by varying degrees of anger, as the surviving spouses sought some person or event to blame for their distress, and expressed frustration that the search for the loved one was so futile. Some also felt guilt and blamed themselves for real or imagined failings in their relationships with the lost husband. As the intense pangs of grief diminished, the third stage, of apathy often accompanied by depression, slowly replaced it. In time the mourner was normally able to reorganize her life and establish a new social identity.[3]

The experiences of grief and mourning among Victorian and Edwardian widows included many of the characteristics noted by Parkes and Bowlby. Most recorded an initial stage of numbness, shock, and disbelief. Harriet Baroness de Clifford lost her husband suddenly in 1877 after twenty-four years of marriage:

My dearest was taken from me with scarcely time for me to take fright—it was all [so] awfully, awfully sudden that even now when I *know* it is true I don't in the least believe it and try in vain to wake up from what I hope is some horrible dream . . . the future looks blank but I will try to bear it.[4]

In 1910 Maggie Cowell-Stepney sought to comfort her friend Mary Drew the day after Mary's husband died: 'There is a merciful *dazed* feeling sometimes, when one can't suffer any more—I hope it may come and help you.'[5]

In the second stage most widows experienced the intense psychological pain of acute pangs of grief in the early months. The death of her husband in 1856 plunged Blanche Balfour into such extreme grief that her relatives feared for her sanity, as she lay 'ill and distraught' for several weeks.[6] In 1865 Agnes Greig experienced 'unspeakable' desolation on the unexpected death of her beloved husband Woronzow: 'I am so bewildered and crushed and bowed down—he used to do and arrange all for me.' She had no idea how she endured her first days of despair. After two months she still broke down frequently at night, and the sleeplessness made her feeble and listless, while the smallest tasks exhausted her. 'My loss meets me at every turn, our lives were so bound up together, I feel as if only a shred of myself remained.' Agnes wrote that her brain often felt 'as if in a whirl' every time she realized afresh that she had lost her husband for ever and that she must learn to live alone, 'without his constant aid'.[7]

Twenty years later Alice Latham described the terrible sorrow which afflicted her daughter Emily Ampthill following her husband's death two months earlier: 'When you talk of her "anguish" you use quite the right word for really I never saw such overwhelming grief and desolation as that which has fallen upon her, and at present she cannot, poor darling, bow her head to the cruel blow or feel anything like resignation.' Her mother believed that her daughter's life would continue to be a painful and apparently hopeless struggle for a long time, but that she would ultimately learn to face her sad future with courage for the sake of her children. At present, however, it was heart-breaking to watch her yearning for her lost husband's presence and his 'dear voice and touch'.[8]

In 1914 Mary Countess Minto vividly described the pain of the pangs of grief accompanying her futile search for her lost husband:

I have been here [at home] five weeks and have gone through hours of intense anguish. It was terrible arriving and walking straight into my bedroom and seeing him in my mind lying suffering in my bed or in my chair by the fire—The agony of the loneliness is almost more than I can bear. His sitting room is just the same as if he was going to his writing table that minute. The cushions on his sofa smell of the stuff he put on his hair. I go and bury my face in them many times a day and try to feel him there. I am so miserable—God help me, I was so happy . . . He speaks to me from every nook and corner and the beauty of the place stabs me 1000 times per day . . . His presence is everywhere.[9]

Many widows endured this characteristic search for their lost husbands, the attempt to locate them in favourite chairs, and the illusions that they had seen or heard them. Familiar domestic items, like the cushions on Lady Minto's sofa, could readily evoke a sense of closeness to the dead person, even without the aid of the scented hair-oil.

Some widows experienced severe panic attacks during the first three months and felt the trauma was too hard to endure. About a month after Alfred Lyttelton's death in 1913, his widow, Edith, wrote to her friend Arthur Balfour, 'Sometimes I wonder, Arthur, how I *can* go on without him—I suffer every now and then from a storm of panic . . .'.[10] In the first week of Edith's bereavement, her sister-in-law Lavinia Talbot noticed that Edith grew increasingly 'conscious of the ache and longing for him' as each day passed and she could no longer seek protection in disbelief.[11]

A number of widows visited one or other of their children in the early days or weeks of bereavement, and subsequently found the return to the home they had shared with their lost husband a devastating experience. Victoria Dawnay stayed with her daughter after her husband's death in 1910, returning four weeks later: 'Coming back home last Thursday was worse than I expected—quite heartbreaking . . . Then his empty room. There is such desperate desolation about that.'[12] Emily Yates suffered similarly on returning to the Lake District in 1919: 'The homecoming was the worst. This Rydal seems *his*.'[13]

These stages of grief are clearly marked in the family correspondence concerning the first eighteen months of Gertrude Gladstone's bereavement in 1891, following her husband's unsuccessful operation for a brain tumour. Her mother-in-law, Catherine Gladstone, was sympathetic and supportive, relieved in August 1891 to find Gertrude 'not worse, and I think this is something to say, for I had expected the 2nd month to be worse in all its reality, all its trial'.[14] Later that second month, Catherine was briefly reassured to find Gertrude able to discuss matters calmly; but she soon collapsed again:

Then came a sudden touching of a chord—poor thing she quite broke down. She thought of having had no last word with Willy . . . There was nothing to do, but to give her time—and she recovered—on the whole I see some progress. Then her moving and walk is better . . . In the meantime she says she can keep no account of time—and feels as we do [that] we have lived months and months—I see returning interest as to the children.[15]

By the fifth month of bereavement Gertrude felt 'very helpless still in my misery—so lost without Him who was everything to me'.[16]

Like most widows, Gertrude Gladstone found special anniversaries particularly hard to bear, reminding her too vividly that William was no longer there to share the family occasion, while marking a further stage in the journey away from him. Five months after her husband's death, Gertrude thanked her father-in-law, W. E. Gladstone, for his birthday greetings: 'Any special day now seems only to make more vivid, if it were possible, the overwhelming greatness of the blank He has left amongst us.'[17] Gertrude noted six weeks later, 'Christmas Day was intensely sad, marking the great blank more than ever.' But at least, after six months of grief, she had more capacity to remember the happiness they had shared in the years before his 'trying illness', instead of recalling only the final misery.[18] Even so, eighteen months after his death, Gertrude considered avoiding her second family Christmas at Hawarden without William, and removing 'my wretched self', leaving the children with their grandparents: 'For it is just especially in Church that utterly breaks one down, the empty place when *all* the rest are there.' But she knew she must stay, 'and strength will be given if I ask aright'.[19]

Most widows believed they should endure the suffering bravely and stoically, for the sake of the family and the dead husband. The response of Alice Lubbock, Countess Avebury, on the death of her husband in 1913, was characteristic:

I go on day by day. I try to do the right thing and what I ought to do—but at present all is a terrible effort and I only feel half alive—I miss my darling more intensely every day—and oh, it's so terribly dull without him. I never wanted anything but him and we were always happy together—If there were worries and anxieties we shared them but now the desolation and the longing for the past again and fighting against the inevitable sometimes overwhelms me [so] that I feel I have no strength left to go on with—But I must bear it and bear it bravely as he would do or would have done— if he had been able—only he could not latterly.

Six months later Alice's life continued 'all very ghastly and lonely', but she persevered, taking one day at a time, trying to cope as well as she supposed her husband might have done had the situation been reversed.[20]

Most of these nineteenth- and early twentieth-century widows endured severe anguish, to varying degrees, during the first year of bereavement. Most, like Countess Avebury, found it a 'terrible effort' exacerbated by inadequate food and sleep, and the inability to concentrate or keep account of time, which seemingly passed so slowly. They gradually learned how to survive independently of their partner of many years, living from day to day, as depression or apathy turned reluctantly into acquiescence. Lady Wantage warned the newly widowed Evelyn Lady Stanhope in 1905: 'the hard time comes when one has to begin to tread the path of life alone', but she already knew from her own experience that 'one must fight the battle alone'.[21] These widows usually coped with loneliness and practical problems more effectively during the second year of bereavement, when 'the numbing sense of utter indifference' faded, and an attempt to build a new life began.

Special Features of Victorian Widows' Grief

Many of these symptoms and behavioural characteristics of grief seem to have been similar for middle- and upper-class widows in the nineteenth and later twentieth centuries, but two significant differences between the two periods stand out. First, the Victorian and Edwardian widows usually suffered a greater sense of the total disintegration of their lives, which for most were dependent on the financial means, social status, and professional careers of their husbands. Much of this dislocation was caused by their reduced financial circumstances, especially when marriage settlements were non-existent or inadequate. *The Times* reported in 1845 that Thomas Hood, the poet, left a widow and two children 'in straitened and precarious circumstances, with no other means of subsistence than a small pension', barely adequate for the basic necessities of life, let alone the children's education. Even that tiny pension had been diminished in the last five months of his life to meet heavy medical and funeral bills.[22] Reduced means were, of course, relative to the widow's earlier living-standard. When Lady Wellesley was widowed in 1842 her husband left no money or property, so she had only an old pension of £300 p.a., but 'her health and habits make this but a sorry pittance'.[23] That same year Henrietta Phillipps was also painfully aware of the financial insecurity of widows, as she questioned her fiancé about the economic implications of marriage without her father's consent and, therefore, with no dowry: 'In what situation should I be if I have no security from you of a settlement on me in case I should be left a widow. I could not return to my Father having married without his consent, and as I have no fortune of my own, just consider in what a destitute condition I should be.'[24] This was

Agnes Greig's predicament in 1865 when her husband's will could not be found: 'you know I shall only have just what was settled on me when I married to live on'. Annabella King noted that without a will Mrs Greig would be very 'narrowly provided'.[25]

It was much harder for impecunious widows left utterly dependent on their families, on charity, or on the Poor Law. They faced destitution as well as dislocation. Their plight is revealed in family papers through the letters of supplicants. Ada Burlingham wrote in 1901 to seek Lord Aldenham's help on behalf of her mother, who was old, ill, and penniless. After Lord Aldenham obliged with a small annual allowance, the old lady thanked him, explaining that she had lived with her daughter through years of widowhood: 'My position was a most painful one, entirely dependent for everything upon a Son-in-Law by no means well off.' His recent death had rendered her position intolerable until the receipt of Lord Aldenham's generous gift.[26]

In the Victorian period many widows suffered from alarm or panic at the loss of security and protection, and the fear of the new circumstances reduced some to utter helplessness, both actual and emotional. Most of these women had not been helpless before bereavement, but their skills were largely confined to the domestic sphere where they had been capable household managers, mothers, philanthropists, and hostesses. But their financial vulnerability, inexperience in business affairs, and lack of a paid occupation compounded their problems in this period of bereavement. Lady Rice was most anxious about her newly widowed sister-in-law in 1891: 'Poor Susan! I can't imagine how she can get on alone. He thought and did every single thing for her always.'[27] May Harcourt found George Bentinck's widow in a 'dreadful state' after his sudden death in 1909: 'Poor, poor woman—What will she do? She has no interests and no occupation,' after a life devoted to her husband's career and well-being.[28] Marion Montagu's father died in 1911, having been the mainspring of family life for years: 'All dear mother's actions were dependent on him.—It is very, very hard for her and she feels so alone—but she is wonderfully brave.'[29] Most widows felt dislocated, disorientated, and unutterably alone, as Lady Wantage did in 1905: 'One's whole past life seems, as it were, swept away; nothing can mitigate the feeling of solitude and desolation.'[30]

Such feelings of dislocation and insecurity were exacerbated if the widow was obliged to move out of the family home as a result of the husband's death. Even at the more prosperous levels of society, widowhood could involve displacement and the search for a new home as well as the loss of a lifelong companion. On the death of Canon William Harcourt in 1871, his elderly widow, Mathilda, was obliged to leave the family home at Nuneham, near Oxford, to her eldest son, and move in for a while with her daughter. A week or so after her husband's death, Mathilda admitted to her second son, William, how deeply she felt the parting from 'this happy home'. A year later she doubted that her income would pay her way for the current year, confessing that 'all I desire is to be as free *as possible* from money considerations or at all events from misunderstandings'.[31]

Like Mathilda Harcourt, many widows sought to be as independent of their family as means permitted, despite restricted circumstances. At 65 Elizabeth Horsley had to leave her family home on her husband's death in 1858. She had to find a new home for herself and her spinster daughter Sophy, but rejected an invitation from her eldest daughter, Mary Brunel, to live with her family in Devon. Elizabeth Horsley believed it would be irksome for Mary and her husband, Isambard Kingdom Brunel, to take on two more dependent family members in view of Isambard's failing health. Moreover, she added, 'at my age and with my habits I must be a great trouble to anyone', so that she would seek 'a respectable unfurnished lodging' near her sisters, which would suit her and Sophy. As to her income, 'I should never be happy to feel in the slightest degree *dependant*, I mean that I must make my general expense meet my income (certain), so that come what may we should feel secure.' When the insurance policy was paid and the bills were settled, she reckoned on £200 per year on which she and Sophy could live comfortably in their lodging-house.[32]

The second major difference between the nineteenth- and later twentieth-century experiences was that most widows in these Victorian and Edwardian families did not seem to undergo or express the stage of anger, seen by experts today as a typical and normal behavioural response to grief. According to Bowlby, 'Another common feature of the second phase of mourning is anger . . . it has been reported by every behavioural scientist, of whatever discipline, who has made grieving the centre of his research.'[33] In his 1970 study of twenty-two randomly selected London widows, Parkes found strong anger in one-third at the first interview, one month after bereavement, while the majority admitted feeling anger at some point during the first year. The anger was directed against anybody who could be held partly responsible for the death, including relatives, clergymen, doctors, and the God who removed their husbands.[34]

In marked contrast, Victorian and Edwardian widows almost never expressed anger in writing in response to the loss of a spouse, though widowers were less reluctant to do so, and parents more often did so on the deaths of children. Mary Drew, a devout Anglican, was the only widow among many dozens to articulate anger on the sudden death of her clergyman husband Harry in March 1910, and the singularity of her case renders it worthy of closer scrutiny. The day before he died Harry was 'absolutely well, in the best and brightest state of health and spirits', but a sudden, excruciating, internal pain forced the doctors to operate immediately, though they admitted the operation was 'nearly hopeless'. After the operation Mary knew from his state of total collapse that she 'had to give him up then to God', though 'it has *seemed* so cruel, the rending agony'. She suffered acutely from the pangs of grief, but no more so than most other widows of the period. Nine days after Harry's death, Mary felt 'utterly incapable of facing life without Harry . . . It's far worse losing a husband than I ever dreamed.'[35] Two weeks later she described the 'awful emptiness' when 'half of me has been taken away', surrounded by a silence which grew deeper every day.[36]

Seven weeks after her bereavement, Mary confessed to her closest friend, Maggie Cowell-Stepney, that she felt angry at Harry's death: 'Sometimes I feel . . . so angry that he has been torn away from his full busy useful life. If one might kick and swear I sometimes feel as if one would be relieved from the sore tension.'[37] Mary's anger was expressed on Harry's behalf as well as her own, and seemed to have been aimed at God. Three weeks later the anger persisted, combined with guilt that she should harbour such unusual and self-indulgent sentiments, as she confided to her cousin Lavinia Talbot:

I am rather oppressed with the sense of the weakness and selfishness of my nature. I remember Lucy [Cavendish] all through her bitter grief [at her husband's death] so loved all nears and dears and felt so soothed and comforted by them. She had none of this numbing sense of utter indifference to things and people, events and books . . . People say 'How good and brave you are!' But you can't kick and scream! and if one doesn't do that sort of thing, they imagine one is all right, instead of being filled with wild rebellion.

It is difficult to imagine either of these letters being written by an early Victorian widow of strong Christian faith. Mary went for a spiritual retreat to the Clewer Sisterhood a few days later, hoping in part that 'perhaps it may make me a little less wicked'.[38] It is significant that she interpreted her feelings of anger as selfish and sinful, recognizing only too well the implicit lack of faith in God. Mary Drew spent the first half of 1911, her second year of widowhood, with her brother Lord Gladstone at Government House in South Africa. She coped with life more effectively again on her return to England, though she did not finally settle in a home of her own until 1913.

It is easier to understand why the majority of Victorian widows in this book did not express anger than to explain why Mary Drew should be the exception. In many cases, religious faith may have consoled widows sufficiently to overcome anger, or encouraged them to repress it in resignation to God's will. They were also better prepared to deal with death than many people are today and, if they were able to discuss impending death with their husbands during the final illness, then feelings such as anger and guilt may have been reduced. It is also likely that some nineteenth-century widows experienced anger but believed it was an unacceptable response for Christians, and so refrained from mentioning it in correspondence or diaries.

Mary Drew herself felt it was weak, selfish, and wrong to protest against the will of God. That she did so in confidence to a few close friends was probably due to a complex combination of reasons. She was always open and direct by nature, and accustomed to commit her feelings to paper more freely than many. Though she was herself deeply religious, she found it difficult to reconcile a God of love with the unexpected and extremely painful nature of Harry's death, while he was still young and healthy enough to continue doing God's work. The suddenness of his death allowed Mary no time for preparation and deprived them both of the good Christian deathbed scene. Moreover, Mary regretted that her own selfish and angry response to Harry's death fell so far short of the model of widowhood established by her cousin Lucy Cavendish, who had responded in a sacrificial manner to her husband's assassination in 1882, at great cost to herself. Lastly, it is also significant that Mary Drew's anger came in the early twentieth century—another sign that attitudes towards death were gradually changing, making it more permissible to express anger, even among devout Christians.

There is also little evidence of guilt in the response of these nineteenth- and early twentieth-century widows. Psychologists argue today that widows are particularly prone to suffer from feelings of self-reproach if the married relationship was ambivalent or poor, and they link guilt with anger, or 'anger turned towards the self'. Thirteen of the twenty-two widows in Parkes's London study expressed self-reproach during their first year of bereavement, retrospectively focusing 'on some act or omission which might have harmed the dying spouse', or castigating themselves for not doing more to help or not bearing the strain of the terminal illness more readily.[39]

There is little evidence that Victorian and Edwardian widows suffered guilt to this extent, and there are few examples of widows expressing self-reproach. Rosie Dyson's husband died of venereal disease in 1896, leaving 'poor Rosie in despair and full of morbid self reproaches' for a disappointing life and an inadequate marriage.[40] Such ambivalent relationships doubtless encouraged self-reproach and complicated the grieving process. Lady Minto's journal illustrates a milder form of self-reproach: 'My shortcomings overwhelm me and countless regrets about things that I would have done differently.' She dwelt obsessively on the details of Lord Minto's terminal illness in 1914, wondering how she could have altered things for the better: 'I kept thinking, could I have made more of each day.' In more rational moments Lady Minto was able to reassure herself that her husband was so easily tired, and slept so much of the time, that she could have done little more.[41] But most of these widows do not seem to have reproached themselves, even mildly, for the real or imagined shortcomings of their marriage or their roles in their husband's last illness. Their religious beliefs assisted them, as did their more limited expectations of married life. They were mostly well prepared for deaths which usually took place at home, and which involved them fully.

The Consolations of Widowhood: Religion, Memory, and Family

Three sources of consolation and support were absolutely vital for widows in their grief—religious faith, memories of their husbands, and the love of their family and children. For Christian widows, spiritual comfort was usually the most helpful and though this is discussed elsewhere, it also merits brief attention in the context of widowhood. These three sources of comfort helped men as well as women, but they were generally even more significant for widows because they could not seek refuge in work, nor did they have much prospect of remarriage.

Faith offered Christian widows several rather different forms of consolation, some more helpful than others. As for all Christians, the belief in an afterlife and the hope of reunion after death were the paramount spiritual solaces. Mary Somerville represented many sorrowing widows when she wrote in 1860 that the greatest of all her sources of consolation was 'the blessed hope of meeting again', since her husband William had been a truly good man and a sincere Christian.[42] When Lord Stanhope died in 1905, the Duchess of St Albans prayed that his widow, Evelyn, might be given 'the *certainty* of being reunited in his own good time. *That* is the only comfort. Everything else is hollow and empty.'[43] Mary Countess Minto found comfort in the fact that she was taking Holy Communion during the operation which killed her husband: 'I knelt then and prayed to be able to lead my life as he would wish me to do and to be reunited with him ere long.'[44]

Almost equally influential were the associated Christian beliefs that all deaths were the will of God, and that he would send the strength and courage to bear the sorrow and pain with calmness and resignation. There are countless surviving testimonies to Victorian widows' acquiescence in these tenets of their faith. J. D. Coleridge admired the Christian response of the widow of his uncle Henry Coleridge in 1843:

His poor wife is supported in her trial in a way that seems quite marvellous—I never saw such perfect calmness combined with a thorough realising of her desolate state. People, I suppose, often enough contrive not really to bring it home to themselves, or get rid of it by means of business or pleasure, but this is a very different thing indeed.[45]

This was a clear acknowledgement that while some mourners tried to evade facing up to their grief by submerging themselves in other preoccupations, including work, widows were less likely to have those options. The elderly Sarah Cotton was equally resigned to her bereavement in 1866: 'My Merciful Heavenly Father greatly sustains me, and tells me that He will be my Husband.'[46] On the death of her husband in 1887, Winifred Byng was grateful for the strength she received from prayer: 'Yes, indeed, God is the only refuge in such misery as this. He alone can send the comfort and He does.'[47]

Agnes Greig's response to bereavement in 1866 was typical of other devout Anglican widows, illustrating her firm belief in a future reunion with her husband, and her search for calm submission to God's will through prayer and faith. Agnes believed that she only endured her first day 'of desolation' after Woronzow's death because of her 'perfect sureness of his spirit having gone direct to Heaven'.[48] Ten weeks after her bereavement, she assured her cousin Captain Henry Fairfax that God had given her strength to cope with her grief: 'Do not think that I do not fight against my sorrow for God has been very good to me in at times giving me a great measure of calmness in immediate answer to prayer and he has indeed fulfilled his promise in a remarkable manner to me in being the "widows stay".'[49] In many letters Agnes insisted that 'I pray so strenuously for calmness and strength to bear all,' and that she was struggling hard to find the courage to 'bear up in my great sorrow' and 'God helps me so wonderfully.'[50]

The majority of these Victorian widows seem to have been able to find sufficient strength through prayer to resign themselves to the will of God in accepting the loss of their husbands. In most cases some degree of struggle for submission was necessary, and the family archives reveal fragments of that struggle by devout widows who sometimes found that spiritual consolation failed them. Harriet Baroness de Clifford lost her husband in 1877 after twenty-four years together. She confessed that 'God alone knows what I am suffering tho' he seems to have turned his face from me so I can't pray.'[51] Lady Musgrave also found that prayer could not help her on her husband's death: 'I am so bowed down with grief and overwhelmed with distress that I find it difficult to derive any consolation . . . I try to read, I earnestly try to pray, but some sad melancholy thought takes possession of me night and day.'[52] Maggie Cowell-Stepney feared that religion might bring only partial comfort in Mary Drew's 'utter desolation' at the death of her husband, Harry, in 1910: 'Of heavenly consolation there is an *unending* amount. But, oh, how hard to keep wound up to it—and how one falls to earth again.'[53]

In most of these cases, the widow's struggle seems to have ended in Christian resignation and acceptance. Laura Harcourt's case was typical. Her family considered her 'utterly desolate' on her husband's death in 1883, 'and yet she is so unselfish she will struggle with her grief, for the sake of others— and has found strength and cheerfulness out of her numerous great trials'.[54] It is scarcely surprising that few widows expressed anger and that most managed to accept the loss of their husbands as the will of God. Religious training as well as cultural conditioning taught them that good wives were obedient and submissive; if they could generally maintain this role in their relationship with a husband, they could surely sustain it on his death, in their relationship with their God. Women were trained from an early age to sublimate feelings like anger through the channel of religion, and during widowhood they had abundant time to work through such responses in prayer and religious contemplation.

The memory of the beloved husband and of a contented marriage was also helpful to many widows, particularly when they anticipated a continuation of marital bliss in heaven. On the death of Captain F. F. Hervey in 1861, Elizabeth Rathbone commented that for his widow, 'the fulness and com- pleteness of the union, I think, must be the greatest support in the separa- tion'.[55] Constance Shaw-Stewart in 1900 found consolation in the remembrance of her husband's 'beautiful life and holy example'.[56] Alice Lubbock, Countess Avebury, was helped by the memory that 'he loved me— as no woman has ever been loved before, with such tenderness, such con- stancy, such consideration . . . I will always love and adore him—and feel he is here.'[57] Such memories were often most vivid in the home where the couple had lived together. Even when the return to the family home was initially painful after the death, the memories it held could become a consolation, as Emily Yates discovered in 1919: 'His love must be here in this home he adored and where he only seemed really to *rest*. . . . How more and more, we live in our memories! They grow to seem the only realities.'[58]

The support of their families, combined with love of children and grand- children, also helped to provide a positive purpose in life for many widows, especially in the weeks immediately following their husband's death. Many widows found real consolation in children and grandchildren, who helped them to recover a degree of enjoyment in life. When her husband died in

1856, Anne Lady Cowper wrote to her son, the new 22-year-old Earl: 'with such a child my heart cannot remain quite desolate . . . Thank God that he lived to see you grow up; and if he sees us now, he knows that I have a help in time of need.'[59] On his father's death in 1860, Woronzow Greig reassured his mother, Mary Somerville, that she still had the abundant love and support of her children:

No! My Beloved Mother *not* alone whilst your four devoted children are spared to you—*not* alone whilst *one* of these children survives! . . . While one drop of Christ's blood remains to any one of us, you must continue to be the chief object of our attention and care. As the circle narrows the bonds which unite the survivors increase and strengthen. We five must hereafter be as *one*.[60]

Two weeks later Mary Somerville left no doubt that her son's emotional promise of support was fully appreciated. In the midst of her grief, God had been merciful in 'the care, the affection and tenderness of beloved children', especially her daughters Martha and Mary, who cared for her day and night with devoted affection.[61] Six years later, the recently widowed Lady Lansdowne reported that she was stunned and miserable, but deeply grateful for the affection and support of her children, which she found very soothing in her grief.[62] Baroness de Clifford wrote on her widowhood in 1877: 'My children are angels of goodness to me—they are all here and we have the comfort of being united.'[63] Victoria Dawnay was 'deeply thankful for my children' when her husband, Lewis, died in 1910.[64]

Under the circumstances it was scarcely surprising if some widows became overly dependent on their children. Emma Lady Ribblesdale, for instance, was widowed in 1878, while still in her forties, though her diary entries read as if she was already elderly. She then lived vicariously through her children and grandchildren: 'I now live on in the life of others; waiting on, hoping on, for them, and praying for blessings to come to them.'[65]

Concern was expressed if widows were left childless or with few or none of their children around them during the first year or more of bereavement, and female children were considered to provide more support than their brothers. Lavinia Talbot was worried about Edith Lyttelton's health seven months after Alfred died in 1913: 'How I wish there were several *more* children to be round her. It is so un-natural for her and very young Mary to be the only company to each other. Of course Oliver makes an enormous difference when he comes home, but no men can be depended on to be home birds in the same way as one or two girls.'[66] The worst situation of all was to be left childless. Lady Stepney, Mary Drew, and Lady Aldenham were each widowed with one child, and Lady Stepney commented in 1910: 'Well, let us all three be very thankful for our children. We have each got an immense blessing in them. Fancy if we were three "childless widows".'[67]

Widows lost husband, status, and occupation simultaneously, with little prospect of paid employment, and many were left feeling helpless and vulnerable, with every aspect of their previous life destroyed. Yet many learned to cope, and some responded remarkably well to their new roles. For Mary Haldane, widowhood brought the challenge of independence. After her husband died in 1877, she took her daughter Elizabeth and a maid for a winter in Paris and, as Elizabeth remarked, the visit 'was admirable for my mother, who was able to do many things that she could not do before and to give expression to faculties hitherto latent. The main one was painting.'[68] Lady Battersea also responded to the unexpected challenge of new responsibilities on her husband's death with energy and initiative. She had previously been unaccustomed to business but, finding that Lord Battersea's love of building and art had placed his estate in considerable financial straits, she immersed herself in the business and cleared the debts with the Rothschilds' help.[69]

At a less spectacular level, many widows were obliged to take on unaccustomed business and financial duties in organizing funerals and settling their husband's estates. This extra responsibility helped some to deal with the shock of early grief by keeping them occupied. It also aided the process of reorganizing their lives to include the public sphere, which had been the husband's. William Gladstone's widow, Gertrude, proved herself capable of dealing with the financial and estate matters which had been her husband's concern before his death in 1891. William Gladstone was the eldest of W. E. Gladstone's sons and owner of the Hawarden family estate, which was transferred on his death to his young son William. Anxious to understand her husband's will thoroughly in order to safeguard her son's inheritance, Gertrude wrote copious letters to both brothers-in-law, Herbert and Henry, regarding the implications of various clauses in the will and matters of inheritance law.[70] She wrote to them as equals, growing in confidence as she became more familiar with the estate affairs and the legal complexities which had previously been her husband's responsibility.

On the death of her husband, Lewis, in 1910, Victoria Dawnay was kept exceptionally busy, so that after two weeks she was feeling 'overwhelmed, tho' perhaps it is a good thing to have something definite to do'. She methodically answered the mountains of condolence letters, and held discussions with her lawyer before her meeting with the valuer for probate. Six weeks after Lewis's death, Victoria found it heart-breaking to return to the family home without him: 'but God always helps one and I find such an immense amount to do

PLATE 1. Emma Haden in mourning dress *c*.1858

PLATE 2 Death of a young woman from tuberculosis: *Fading Away* by Henry Peach Robinson, 1858. This was very popular at exhibitions

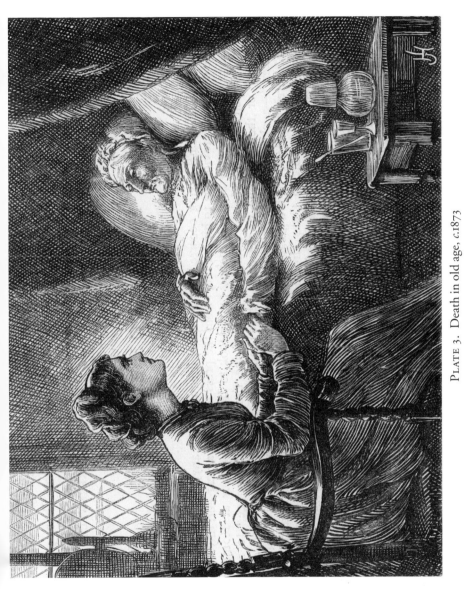

PLATE 3. Death in old age, c.1873

PLATE 5. Henry Rogers' grave in Oxford

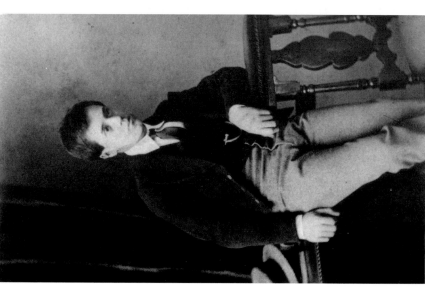

PLATE 4. Henry Rogers, who committed suicide
at seventeen in 1876

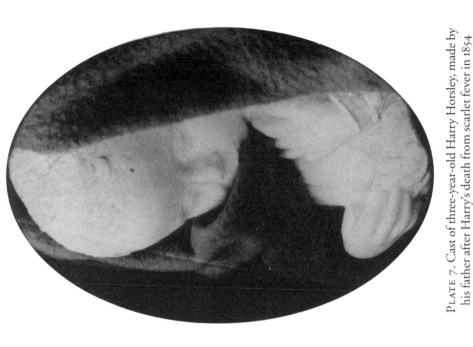

PLATE 7. Cast of three-year-old Harry Horsley, made by his father after Harry's death from scarlet fever in 1854

PLATE 6. Mary Ann Rogers in her bath chair c.1870

PLATE 8. Assassination of Lord Frederick Cavendish, 1882. 'The dear beautiful photograph of sleeping Freddy' taken in the Dublin Hospital immediately afterwards and sent by his widow to relatives and friends

PLATE 9. Lord Frederick Cavendish lying in state at Chatsworth, 1882

PLATE 10. The Gladstone Family at Hawarden, 1894. *Back row, left to right*: Stephen and Annie, Mary and Harry Drew, Herbert, Helen. *Front row*: Catherine and William with their grandchildren

PLATE 11. The room in Hawarden Castle in which W. E. Gladstone died, as it was at the time of his death in 1898

PLATE 12. 'The Old Dozen' — the twelve children of the fourth Lord Lyttelton by his first marriage. *Back row, left to right*: Neville, Charles, May, Spencer, Albert. *Second row*: Alfred (*seated*), Lucy, Arthur, Meriel (*seated*), Edward, Lavinia (*seated*), Bob

PLATE 14. Margaret Gladstone (neé King), who died of puerperal fever in 1870, four weeks after the birth of her only child

PLATE 13. Mary, Lady Lyttelton, who died of heart disease in 1857, having borne twelve children

CERTIFIED COPY OF AN ENTRY OF DEATH

GIVEN AT THE GENERAL REGISTER OFFICE, LONDON

Application Number. 8730 B

REGISTRATION DISTRICT Marylebone

1876 DEATH in the Sub-district of Cavendish Square in the County of Middlesex

Columns:— 1	2	3	4	5	6	7	8	9
No.	When and Where died	Name and surname	Sex	Age	Occupation	Cause of death	Signature, description and residence of informant	When registered	Signature of registrar
457	Nineteenth April 1876 18 Park Crescent	George William Lyttelton	Male	59 years	Baron P.C.,K.M.Q. D.C.L. &c &c F.R.S.	Internal Injury insufficiently known & fall Suicide Temporary unsound mind	Certified code received from Geo. Danford Thomas Coroner for Middlesex Inquest held Twentieth April 1876	Twenty Second April 1876	Wm. Tickey Registrar

CERTIFIED to be a true copy of an entry in the certified copy of a Register of Deaths in the District above mentioned.
Given at the GENERAL REGISTER OFFICE, LONDON, under the Seal of the said Office, the 30th day of July 19 82

DX 266831

This certificate is issued in pursuance of the Births and Deaths Registration Act 1953. Section 34 provides that any certified copy of an entry purporting to be sealed or stamped with the seal of the General Register Office shall be received as evidence of the birth or death to which it relates without any further or other proof of the entry, and no certified copy purporting to have been given in the said Office shall be of any force or effect unless it is sealed or stamped as aforesaid.

CAUTION:—Any person who (1) falsifies any of the particulars on this certificate, or (2) uses a falsified certificate as true, knowing it to be false, is liable to prosecution.

Form A504M Dd 8254413 10M 12/81 Mcr(3017)

PLATE 15. Copy of the death certificate of Lord Lyttelton, who died in 1876. The cause of death reads: 'Internal Injury and Shock from a fall. Suicide. Temporary unsound mind.'

PLATE 16. The Duke of Wellington's triumphal funeral car, which cost £11,000 in 1852

PLATE 17. An exhibition of perishable coffins at Stafford House, 1875. The caption reads: "Mr Seymour Haden's coffins are of wicker, with their meshes filled only by mosses, willows, fragrant shrubs and evergreens. Accompanying each of them is a narrow leaden band or ribbon, pierced with name and date of death, to be passed round the chest and lower limbs, for identifying the bones."

PLATE 18. New mourning gowns; advertisement featured in *The Girl's Own Paper* in 1887

PLATE 19. The London General Mourning Warehouse, Regent Street; advertisement featured in *The Art Journal* in 1849. The caption reads: MOURNING:- COURT, FAMILY AND COMPLIMENTARY. The Proprietor of the London General Mourning Warehouse begs respectfully to remind Families whose bereavements compel them to adopt Mourning Attire, that every article (of the very best description) requisite for a complete outfit of Mourning, may be had at his establishment at a moment's notice. Widows and Family Mourning is always kept made up, and a note, descriptive of the Mourning required, will ensure everything necessary for the occasion being sent immediately, either in Town or into the Country, and on the most reasonable terms"

PLATE 20. *The Father's Grave*. Engraving by W. Egleton
after a painting by John Callcott Horsley

that there is hardly time for thought—and at night I am too tired not to sleep! So this is an untold blessing . . . We are all dividing, sorting and destroying [his] things.'[71] Victoria Dawnay was also left to solve estate and financial problems inherited from Lewis, finding to her surprise that she was obliged to question his judgement: 'In looking through my account books I cannot help rather regretting dear Lewis' intense generosity and for the first time grudge the gift of land, nearly 1400 acres, to Bill. He gave many rather large gifts.' Her son Guy was obliged to sell a large piece of land to meet 'these appalling death duties', and let the house for several years to fund the financial deficit, while she had to move out of her home after two months.[72] Victoria dealt with new and complex problems bravely and efficiently, proving to herself as well as to her family that she was capable of operating beyond the usual realm of the woman's domestic sphere.

A Most Unusual Widowhood

The widowhood of the third Lady Holland was the exception which proves the general rule. She had no intention of becoming submissive, resigned to her fate, or socially marginalized, like most widows. Her responses to bereavement were influenced little, if at all, by religious beliefs, while the conventions she observed applied more often to men than to women. The shocked reactions of her family demonstrated the degree to which she disregarded the customary behaviour expected of a Victorian widow.

Most widows found some comfort in their family, their faith, and their memories, but Lady Holland was most exceptional in her response to the death of her husband in 1840, when she was 69. Her unusual case deserves inclusion here to demonstrate the range of responses and remind us that the saintly widow was not universal. Her relationship with Lord Holland had an unconventional start, for she was already married when she met him in 1794 and their eldest son was born out of wedlock before her divorce. She became an influential society and political hostess, with friends in high places, respected by many and feared by some. Her famous salon in Kensington attracted a dazzling circle of social, literary, and political talent, drawn by Lord Holland's political importance and genial charm, combined with her own beauty, wit, and personality, which became more autocratic with advancing years.[73] She was unorthodox as a mother as well as a wife, showing little or no affection for her children, to the extent of largely excluding them from her will. When Lord John Russell protested at her bequest of a family estate in Kennington, which enriched him for life at the expense of her legitimate children, she replied, 'I hate my son; I don't like my daughter.'[74]

Her husband, the third Baron Holland, nephew of Charles James Fox, died unexpectedly in October 1840, and the first two months of her widowhood were not unusual. She spent much of the second day in floods of tears, suffering from 'sheer fatigue of Mind and Body', following the advice of her daughter-in-law Lady Mary Fox to give way to her tears.[75] Her illegitimate eldest son, General Charles Fox, made her welcome immediately at his home, where the family shared their misery, 'feeling a great comfort at being together assembled under the same roof'. Their differences over property and wills were for a short time submerged in their common grief.[76] Lady Holland's two sons Charles and Henry and her daughter Mary Lady Lilford set aside all resentment at their mother's earlier lack of maternal affection and made the utmost effort to devote themselves to her needs. For a few weeks the widow seemed to appreciate this family support, finding especial comfort in the kindness of the Lilfords, with whom she stayed for some time.[77] She was also glad of the sympathy and companionship of her unselfish sister-in-law Caroline Fox and the devoted Dr John Allen, formerly her husband's private secretary.

Unfortunately for all concerned, this unaccustomed family affection and solidarity lasted only about two months, as the grieving widow soon reverted to type. Six weeks after Lord Holland's death, Caroline Fox warned her nephew Henry, the new Baron Holland, what to expect on his return from Italy: 'We must not forget that the passion of Grief, like any other passion, tho' deep and sincere, will in its manifestations take a tinge from the natural character and habits.'[78] Lady Holland's particular manifestation of grief had two primary characteristics which differentiated it from the responses of most other widows of her class. First, it was profoundly secular, as was the response of most of her family. The Holland House correspondence relating to family deaths ignored Christian faith almost entirely, striking a strange note in the early Victorian period in using no religious language and offering no spiritual words of comfort. Thus the new Lord Holland's words of condolence to his mother were bleak and sparse: 'I can offer no consolation for I feel none. We must all cling together and as we can, try to support each other.'[79] This great Whig family appeared untouched by the mighty fervour of the Evangelical revival or the Oxford movement, and the subject of religious belief was seldom mentioned in family conversation or correspondence.[80]

Secondly, after about two months, the widowed Lady Holland required the stimulation and support of a busy social life far beyond the narrow confines of her family. Only three weeks after Lord Holland's death, Aunt Caroline Fox was already warning her nephew Henry that his mother 'complains sadly of the dreariness of this place [Putney], and fancies vainly that a change of place or the neighbourhood of a great town or the being in it would relieve her from that weariness which *now* being the weariness of sorrow, will cling to her alas, wherever she goes'. Within three months of her bereavement her dinner-parties recommenced, dominated as before by influential male guests. That on 21 January 1841, described by Charles Greville, was attended by eight men, including Lords Macaulay, Melbourne, and Morpeth: 'Everything there is exactly the same as it used to be, excepting only the person of Lord Holland, who seems to be pretty well forgotten. The same talk went merrily round, the laugh rang loudly and frequently, and, but for the black and the mob-cap of the lady, one might have fancied he had never lived or had died half a century ago.'[81]

Lady Holland's family became exasperated by her self-centred grief and outraged by her total disregard for the conventions of mourning. Her eldest son, General Charles Fox, was sufficiently angry and distressed after a nasty argument with his mother in May 1841 to send her a stern letter. He reminded her of her unnatural behaviour over the years to all her children, and her unpleasant attacks on them, even during the first four months of widowhood, prompted entirely by anxiety for her own comfort: 'Let me hope to see you gradually becoming resigned, more cheerful, and less dependent upon the casual feverish nonsense of acquaintances of the Day.'[82] But even this most unusual admonition from a son to a widowed mother failed to have the desired effect. In March 1842 her second son, the new Baron, told her that he was not surprised her health and spirits failed to revive: 'A numerous acquaintance and general society will, I have no doubt, give you momentary excitement but cannot completely ward off painful reflections.'[83] Her family considered the widow's frantic social life lacking in feeling and decorum, as she continued to hold her salons, dine out, and meet the leading politicians of the day. More pointedly, Henry told his mother that her salons would always be 'flat stale and unprofitable' without his father's presence, which 'made its charm and gave it life and animation'.[84]

Lady Holland complained incessantly about her ill health and her depressed state of mind. On her seventieth birthday in March 1841 she sent a self-pitying letter to Henry asking for the tenderness and protection of her children in her affliction and despair: 'my health quite impaired, my spirits fled, so it is not probable that my claim upon compassionate feelings can be of long duration'.[85] Two months later she sent an indignant response to family criticisms of her social life: 'The anguish at times is insupportable. My eyes from weeping are very tender . . . In short my life is a blank.'[86]

The sympathy of Lady Holland's children was not engaged by her constant complaints. They had always regarded her as a hypochondriac, spending much of her time in a wheelchair even before her bereavement, which seemed merely to accentuate her maladies. Six weeks after Lord Holland's death, three doctors diagnosed a kidney complaint, but shared Caroline Fox's view that it was 'greatly aggravated by the state of her nerves and mind. She refuses to be comforted, and aggravates all her essential sufferings by fretting about worldly affairs—imagined poverty with £5000 a year.' Caroline considered this sum more than ample for a single woman 'provided with everything'.[87]

Instead of improving with time, Lady Holland's suffering was intensified in April 1843 by the death of John Allen, her devoted companion since her husband's death. Her immediate response to this second loss was to move out of Caroline Fox's house, where she had been staying, into apartments kindly offered her at Stafford House, 'more à partie for the visits of friends'. But she continued to complain of loneliness, depression, and pain: 'I am sick at *Heart* as well as bodily ailments and these denote more a lingering malady than a speedy end, the most to be dreaded to one so solitary and forlorn, what Aeons of dreary suffering awaits me!'[88]

Henry generally believed that his mother's distress was never powerful enough to make her lose sight of 'all that can contribute to her own comfort or amusement'.[89] But her melancholy letters on Allen's death caused him temporarily to view her situation more tolerantly, as he confessed to Aunt Caroline Fox:

Everyone in grief feels so differently that there is no calculating upon what a loss like this may produce upon her mind . . . It is only in society—in crowds of visitors and in a full dinner table that her losses can be forgotten and it is not in the devotion or affectionate attentions of near and dear relations that she can for an instant find any consolation. That at such a moment she should leave you—your quiet home and all her nearest and dearest relations to return immediately to the bustle and excitement of general society shews what I always was convinced of that it is from the world alone she can derive comfort or amusement.[90]

The Fox family condemned Lady Holland for her disregard of the normal mourning conventions on her husband's death. They were all, of course, judging her by the standards set for other widows of her class, and by those standards she failed abysmally, seeking a public role in the world of society above the affectionate company of a grieving family. If she were to be judged instead by the standards set for men, she would emerge with more credit. Her salon was her career and as a political hostess she was inordinately successful. As the next chapter demonstrates, had she been a male, she would have been encouraged by society to return to that occupation within a month or six weeks of bereavement; but when she chose that path as a woman, she was condemned as a heartless, selfish socialite. Henry seems belatedly to have understood this, though with considerable reluctance.

When Lady Holland eventually died in November 1845, her son Henry made no attempt to manufacture false sorrow. The doctors professed astonishment that the old lady lived so long, since she had a stone in the bladder, an exceedingly diseased liver, and 'her heart was a perfect stone!!!' As Henry noted sardonically, this last might account for many things. Any guilt the family might have felt on learning of the genuine medical basis for their mother's complaints was undoubtedly dispelled by her highly unusual and vindictive will. She had already sold off family assets and property without their permission, and her will left Henry with slender means to maintain his title. Her will detailed an immense list of legacies and annuities, chiefly to those outside the family, as well as £300 to her executors to pay for her own monument. As Henry remarked, the malevolent spirit of the will was the same that she had invariably shown her children: 'she was always tinkering at the will—it is bad for me but might have been worse had she lived on and added every month some fresh legacy, annuity and bequest'. Two children by her first husband were not mentioned at all, her illegitimate son Charles received only £1,000, and Henry, his father's pictures, together with two further paintings she believed he disliked.[91]

Charles Greville concluded that Lady Holland's death would generate no grief because she was a woman who inspired no affection, though the closing of her brilliant salon would be a serious social loss.[92] Henry was relieved to have no heavy debt of gratitude to a mother who 'has been invariably so unkind towards me' for the last twenty years. The will finally proved 'the very slight regard she entertained for me', so his loss could not be deemed very great. The widowhood of the third Lady Holland can only be categorized as extraordinary, but it serves to remind us that not all widows fitted the stereotype.[93]

If we exclude an unusual minority represented here by Lady Holland, several conclusions can be reached about the experience of the majority of Victorian upper- and middle-class widows. Widowhood signified the permanent loss of the status of wife, which was expected ideally to give economic security and social position, as well as personal contentment and companionship. The loss of their position as wife relegated widows to a lower level of the social hierarchy. The elaborate and uncomfortable widows' weeds which they were obliged to wear identified them as members of a distinct, inferior group to which they usually belonged for life. There was, however, a more positive dimension to this apparently bleak picture, for many Victorian widows demonstrated a remarkable capacity to cope with the collapse of their former lives. The lack of available diversionary options such as paid work and remarriage obliged them in general to face up to their grief and work through it. Many widows found consolation and strength through their Christian faith, which taught them resignation to the will of God, and offered the prospect of a future reunion with their dead husband. Widows were also helped by their family and friends, who generally recognized that the need for support extended well beyond the early weeks of bereavement.

⚜ 12 ⚜

WIDOWERS: GENDERED EXPERIENCES OF
WIDOWHOOD

T HE IMMEDIATE PSYCHOLOGICAL AND EMOTIONAL RESPONSES TO THE
loss of a spouse were broadly similar for men and women among the
Victorian middle and upper classes, but attempts to cope with their disrupted
life varied markedly according to gender. The findings of modern psychologists on gender differences in widowhood are again instructive, though
comparisons over two centuries must be treated with caution since there are
many variables. Colin Murray Parkes comments that loss of a husband in
contemporary society is more likely to cause psychological problems than is
loss of a wife: 'One way and another women usually come out of bereavement
worse than men . . . Husbands occupy a larger part of the life-space of their
wives than the wives do of their husbands. The wife's roles, plans and
problems tend to be husband-centred and she is reliant on him for money,
status and company to a greater extent than he is on her.' Parkes outlines
various studies of comparative gender responses which substantiate these
conclusions, showing that women's 'psychological and social adjustment a
year [after bereavement] was less good than that of the widowers'. However,
when individuals were followed up two to four years after bereavement, the
men had taken longer to recover than the women.[1]

John Bowlby also concludes that the methods of coping with grief in
widowhood vary according to gender. He examines a 1974 Harvard study by
Parkes of forty-nine widows and nineteen widowers in Boston under 45.
The widowers were found to be more pragmatic in coming to terms with the
reality of their spouse's death. Widowers 'tried deliberately to regulate the
occasions when they allowed themselves to grieve', avoiding memories of
the past except at those times. They were also far more likely to consider
remarriage, a majority contemplating it quite soon after bereavement. A year
after their spouse's death, half the widowers had either remarried or seemed
likely to do so shortly, compared with only 18 per cent of the widows. Two
or three years after bereavement, the majority of widowers had established
new lives, though four out of the twenty-two had failed to do so, continuing
to be depressed or alcoholic.[2]

It is more difficult to trace the basic patterns of grief for Victorian widowers than widows because less evidence has survived of their emotional responses. In part this reflects the fact that widowers usually returned to work fairly soon after bereavement, leaving less time to think and write about their loss. It also suggests that the men were more restrained in describing their feelings of loss, especially towards the end of the century when they were socially conditioned to believe that strong men controlled their emotions. When J. Horsley Palmer was widowed in 1839, 'it costs him a strong effort to keep his feelings under restraint:—but he does so, and his example contributes to support his children'.[3] Women were also commended for emotional control, but it was assumed that they were less likely to achieve it.

Frequently the accounts of female relatives provide the only fragmentary descriptions of widowers' grief, whereas widows were more likely to leave direct evidence of their own experience. On his wife's death in 1857, Sarah Disraeli regretted that her brother James was 'very dejected indeed and I fear must get worse every day for a long long time—he dreads the return home'.[4] In 1875 Eveline Lady Portsmouth told her recently bereaved brother Lord Carnarvon of another widower's experience of sorrow: 'Poor old Mr Russell, who after 49 years of marriage has just lost his wife, came to me yesterday and sitting over the fire, cried like a child. "I thought", he kept saying, "I was too old to have felt anything again so strongly, but I shall never never get over it—I am so desolate".'[5] Loneliness could be just as intense for widowers in the early months of bereavement as for widows. In 1911 Katharine Bruce Glasier wrote that Jim Middleton was suffering extreme loneliness and grief after his wife's death from cancer: 'When I think of his loneliness now I can't *see*. There are some awful darknesses in life.'[6]

The two major differences between widows and widowers related to the possibility of remarriage and the consolation of a professional occupation. Young and middle-aged widowers were strongly encouraged to return to work at an early date, and later to seek solace in a second marriage. Members of the Holland House circle were quite certain that Lord John Russell should return to work as quickly as possible after his first wife's sudden death in 1838. Caroline Fox remarked, 'What will become of poor Lord John? His plunging into business at once is his best chance of struggling against the sadness.'[7] Mary Ann Rogers wasted no words in advising her son Richard Norris Gandy on how to cope with his wife's death in 1865: 'get out and occupy yourself'.[8] Sir Warwick Morshead's response to his wife's death was to 'throw myself into everything that I can, which distracts thought, and now I am busy about setting up a workman's club in the village'.[9] In 1878 A. W. Roffen advised Archbishop A. C. Tait that 'Coming back into the world and facing your duties will be very hard,' but God would support him and his work would help him through the ordeal of the loss of his wife and eldest son.[10] When Lord Cromer heard of Lady Grenfell's death in 1899, he wrote, 'Poor Francis. I hope he will stick to his work, though he will find it a hard struggle particularly at first.'[11]

The second significant difference was that widowers were far more likely to remarry than widows, especially those over the age of 30. Studies of earlier periods have demonstrated that prospects of remarriage for widowed people varied greatly according to gender and age. Margaret Pelling found that the numbers of elderly men without women in late sixteenth-century Norwich were extremely small (only 5 per cent of her sample), reflecting a 'studied avoidance' by men of being left alone. Men overcame their fear of loneliness by remarriage, often at mature ages and to much younger women, aided by the accident of the unequal sex ratio among people over 50.[12] Pelling concluded that life was often much harder for widows than widowers, whether they were aged 40 or 80, and they could expect to live alone for long periods after bereavement. S. J. Wright showed that in the first half of the eighteenth century only 10 per cent of widows in Ludlow remarried, compared with 40 per cent of widowers. Whereas poverty encouraged men to remarry, poverty and age both limited women's prospects of remarriage. Older widows had even fewer prospects in the marriage market as the mortality differential favouring women increased from the sixteenth century.[13]

In the nineteenth century, also, widows over 30 had far less hope of remarriage than widowers, and, after 40 their prospects were negligible, as William Farr's tables of marriage rates for 1851 and 1870–2 suggest. While the annual marriage rate for widows in 1851 per 1,000 of population sank from 19.649 at 20 years of age to 11.611 at 30, 4.333 at 40, and 1.298 at 50, for widowers the rates remained much higher—30.766 at 20, 28.627 at 30, 14.075 at 40, and 5.711 at 50.[14] Michael Anderson estimates that about 14 per cent of all males who married in England and Wales by about 1850 were widowed, compared with 9 per cent of females, but the proportion of women remarrying was much lower at older ages.[15]

Family archives richly substantiate the message of Farr's statistical tables. Marriage prospects for spinsters depended on their wealth, youth, and beauty, but these assets were even more significant for widows. Young widows who were fortunate enough to boast either looks or means were the target of malicious gossip from such women as Lady Holland. In 1835 she reported society's latest 'buzz', that the 43-year-old bachelor politician Lord John Russell was to marry Lady Ribblesdale, 'a very pretty widow of 27 years old with *four* children'. While Lady Ribblesdale's age, her temperament, and

TABLE. *Annual marriage rates of widowers and widows at different ages, 1851, and 1870–1872 (per hundred of population)*

Age	1851		1870–2	
	Widowers	Widows	Widowers	Widows
15–19	—	5.000	1.149	4.235
20–4	30.766	19.649	22.917	17.064
25–9	35.790	14.906	30.296	15.678
30–4	28.627	11.611	27.943	10.806
35–9	20.313	7.253	21.872	7.116
40–4	14.075	4.333	15.337	4.459
45–9	8.858	2.672	10.739	2.809
50–4	5.711	1.298	7.323	1.513
55–9	3.201	0.731	4.519	0.820
60–4	1.745	0.241	2.735	0.393
65–9	0.862	0.068	1.185	0.133
70–4	0.316	0.025	0.538	0.047
75–9	0.100	0.015	0.190	0.013
80+	0.067	0.011	0.061	0.002

Source: William Farr, *Vital Statistics* (1885), 78–80.

even her figure were all in her favour, her four children and her poverty weighed strongly against her in the Holland House scales of marital merit.[16] Six years later, Lady Holland remarked of a widow with youth, beauty, and means, 'What a marriage for Dr Kaye! a beautiful widow of £8,000.'[17] Victorians were well aware that the consequences of widowhood varied with age. Evelyn Stanhope remarked in 1887 on the recent widowhood of Lord Carnarvon's young daughter Winifred Byng married for less than a year: 'What a short era of happiness, but she is young and buoyant and will recover. I always think such a calamity is much more crushing to middle-aged people than to the very young: the power of recovery is less, the responsibilities probably heavier, and there is not the consolation of the old: that the loneliness can last but a short time!'[18]

There is ample evidence to show that widowers tended to marry again quite soon and usually to considerably younger women. Mr Baugh, a widower of 50 with two sons, remarried almost immediately in 1841, to an heiress, Lady Jersey, a single lady of 36, considered suitable in age and wealth.[19] Only six weeks after Ada Lovelace's death in 1853 her friend Mary Somerville was sceptical about the depth of Lord Lovelace's sorrow: 'Lord L. will be married again before a year, such violent grief never lasts and that you will see.'[20] Lord Lovelace did not remarry until 1865, but Mary Somerville's assumption reflected social expectations. That same year General Charles Fox married 'an old flame of his', who was considered very pretty, only a year after the death of his wife of forty years.[21]

George Lord Lyttelton was widowed with twelve children on the death of his beloved wife, Mary, in 1857. Four years after Mary's death he was still desperately lonely and he sought a second mother for his large family. In 1861 he wrote to Lady Canning, expressing interest in marrying her wealthy widowed sister Lady Waterford, whom he scarcely knew. Lord Lyttelton was relatively poor for a man of his position and he honestly admitted, 'I *could* not marry any one without any fortune.' Not surprisingly nothing eventuated. But his 'extreme longing for a companion' continued: 'There are few men of my age to whom long years of widowhood are not "a sore burden too heavy for us to bear".' At last in 1869 George Lyttelton at 52 married Sybella Mildmay, a prosperous widow of 33, but their apparently contented union only lasted until his suicide seven years later.[22]

Dying wives and their friends encouraged husbands to remarry in the interests of motherless children, and to satisfy the assumed male need for sympathy and support. Deborah Reynolds of Liverpool died of puerperal fever in 1803, leaving several children as well as the new baby. She told her husband on her deathbed that if he should marry again, she hoped he would choose a woman no less worthy of him than herself.[23] Fifty years later Elvira Horsley died of tuberculosis at the age of 31, leaving three young sons under 5 years of age. At her deathbed husband and wife talked freely of the consequences of her death: 'She spoke (having done so frequently before) of my marrying again, how she wished me to do so if it was for my/and the children's comfort and good.'[24] Her husband, John Callcott Horsley, the artist, took his first wife at her word and, less than two years later, married Rose Haden, a friend of his sister's, to start a new family of seven. The engagement to Rose Haden was kept secret for many months, but the Haden and Horsley families seem to have welcomed it.

A year after his wife, Margaret, died in 1911, Ramsay MacDonald was advised by Katharine Bruce Glasier that his wife would have wished him to remarry, to 'love and live again in all fulness'. Margaret had known her husband's need of the love and sympathy of a 'true woman', and would want him 'to seek, and soon, another woman who would "mother" both him and the bairns'.[25] The Count de Franqueville, well over 60 years old, wrote to Lord Selborne in 1916 to justify his second marriage, only a year after the death of his first wife, Selborne's sister, from cancer. The Count confessed that he was becoming depressed and neurasthenic, living alone in a big house with none of his children able or willing to live with him: 'Such being the case, I asked a lady friend to become the companion of my last days . . . she is quite free and able to take care of me.' The letter made no reference to affection but stressed his need of this 'very kind, very holy' and most respectable lady of 60 years to look after him in his old age.[26] A middle-aged or elderly widow could scarcely expect to justify a second marriage on the same grounds. There is no evidence of encouragement to widows to 'love and live' again—rather the reverse. Lady Randolph Churchill, for example, shocked society in 1900 when she married the much younger George Cornwallis-West, and again in 1918 when she married for the third time at the age of 64.

Four case-studies of Victorian widowers are presented in this chapter to illustrate the experience of widowhood for men. They are better documented than most, and are probably not unrepresentative of professional middle- and upper-class males in general, though these four men were perhaps exceptionally devout. At the time of bereavement Seth Thompson was a doctor, William Harcourt and Alfred Lyttelton were lawyers, later to become politicians, and Lord Carnarvon already an established politician. Dr Seth Thompson lost his wife, Fanny, suddenly and unexpectedly in 1849. They had no children but he found comfort in the support of the Horsleys, his wife's family, and relied chiefly on the consolations of religious belief, professional work, and his wife's memory. In the early stages of bereavement he had to struggle hard to achieve the submission to God's will and the patient resignation he knew he ought to feel. Six days after Fanny's death, Seth wrote to his brother-in-law, John Callcott Horsley, explaining that the sudden nature of her death made acceptance far harder: 'I thank God that today I am altogether calmer and better and trust by his help to feel more and more as I know I ought but at times it is too hard for me . . . I hope that earnest prayer has given me the relief I feel today and that by God's grace this may be continued to me.'[27] A week later, constant prayer and a strong faith were overcoming his resistance, and he was becoming more resigned. He commented that there was 'a good deal of might in the Church Service and I could look back on what had passed a fortnight previously better than on the first Sunday'.[28] The hope of reunion with his wife in the next life contributed to his growing calm and acquiescence: 'Fanny left us to go where, may God grant, I may be permitted to see her again.'[29]

Religious faith was Thompson's primary consolation, apart from his work, but he also found comfort in contemplation of Fanny's memory. As he told

John Horsley, much of the time he felt as if she was still living with him: 'She is at every moment before my eyes when I am at home and alone. I do not always feel as if I had lost her . . . I feel more and more as I now gradually get in to what will be my solitary life, that my only real comfort is in dwelling on her memory.'[30] Thompson was especially grateful for the more tangible reminder of his dying wife provided by Horsley's deathbed portrait. The family feared that this portrait would be marred by the 'additional fatigue' of approaching death but, after the initial shock, Seth was soothed by the 'beautiful recollection of what she was in her last days'. He intended to have a case made for the portrait with folding doors, to be kept locked in his absence, for it was his greatest consolation 'and will be as long as I live my comfort day and night': 'Without this drawing I should be infinitely more wretched than I am now for it brings her back to me with such reality that a short time spent in looking at it and praying by it has always a wholesome effect upon my mind.'[31] Elizabeth Horsley believed that her son-in-law's 'greatest happiness is in the portrait . . . it will contribute more than anything else to calm and soothe him'.[32]

But his family had little fear that Dr Thompson would dwell too much on his recent loss or devote too many hours each day to prayer. His sense of duty called him back to his medical practice within a fortnight of bereavement, although he was so 'thoroughly unhinged' during his first hospital visit that he wondered whether it was too soon. However, he resolved to act 'rigidly and firmly up to what I know is my duty', to continue his work 'which is now my only real source of consolation'.[33] This decision made him feel stronger in mind and more able to encounter the succession of painful thoughts which beset him at home and at work. For a man it was thought unwise and self-indulgent to dwell for too long on the recent loss, whereas a woman was given little alternative but to confront her loss day by day for months on end. The primary sources of strength and support were the same for Seth Thompson as for most widows in the first two weeks of bereavement, but thereafter the demands of medicine helped distract his mind and pass the time. The family was relieved and gratified to see 'how admirably he bears this most heavy loss'.[34] He died only twelve years later, still probably in his forties.

On 31 January 1863 William Harcourt lost his first wife, Thérèse, at the birth of their son Lewis, only a year after the death of their first son, Julian. William Harcourt was a brilliant scholar who would rise to the highest levels of the Liberal Party, though in 1863 he was a successful barrister aged 36 who had not yet entered politics. He came from a deeply religious Anglican family who felt assured that he would find solace in his faith. Mathilda Harcourt comforted her son with the hope of reunion in the next world, reminding him to keep his mind 'so fixed upon the Heaven to which She has fled as to join Her there', and praying 'that God's holy spirit may comfort you'.[35] Harcourt was also consoled by the affection and sympathy of his family, as he assured his mother: 'I need not tell you what your aid and comfort and support has been to me in this awful time . . . Everything that tenderness and affection can do for me has been and is being done.'[36] The first days and weeks of his bereavement were agonizing: 'Indeed I do very badly without her. The desolation of this house is quite unbearable to me. I find I am quite unable to form a concise plan of the future. My existence was so mixed up with hers. I have to endure as I can from hour to hour and I cannot decide what I shall do 24 hours hence.'[37]

William Harcourt determined to immerse himself in contemplation of his wife's memory at the family seat of Nuneham, near Oxford, where she and their son Julian were buried. For a few weeks he found temporary solace there, paying daily visits to his loved ones' graves and remembering, 'I have been wandering in the woods and collecting some primroses to plant upon her grave. We have made [it] so nice and pretty. I am as happy as I shall ever be able to be again here. This place is inexpressibly soothing to me. Every spot of it is consecrated by some recollection of the origin and progress of our love up to its end.'[38] But his mother and mother-in-law, Lady Lewis, were most concerned at the potential ill effects of his daily 'sad contemplation of the two graves'. Lady Lewis considered grave-visiting morally uplifting for those whose grief was superficial, but a broken-hearted man like William 'needs all the support moral and physical that he can have . . . Nobody who *really* grieves as he does, could go every afternoon to those sad spots and dwell on all that made life most precious to him with renewed emotion with impunity.'[39]

Indeed William Harcourt seemed so pale and unwell that his mother-in-law sent for Dr Cumberbatch to make sure there was no physical illness. The doctor satisfied her that William's 'state was chiefly mental', despite liver decay, and his primary prescription was a speedy return to work—the sovereign remedy for widowers' grief: 'Cumberbatch is most anxious in spite of any fatigue at first that he should be got into harness and be forced to work in his profession as the *only* remedy or rather palliation to his present state.'[40] Lady Lewis concurred: 'We shall now watch with painful interest the next phase in his desolate existence—the return to work. God grant it may bring some relief to his broken heart.'[41] Other family members also expressed their view that three weeks of grave-visiting at Nuneham were quite enough; any more would be self-indulgent and detrimental both to mental and physical recuperation. Three weeks after Thérèse's death, her brother Thomas Villiers Lister was both concerned and outspoken:

I hope your clerk will soon call you to work, for Nuneham will ere long cease to be the best place for recovering health and courage and there will be most danger there of your learning to love your sorrow instead of bearing it. You will not think me unkind in saying this: our darling Thérèse was my idol and had I been still unmarried I should have been quite crushed by her death . . . But we have in this world to rub so much against our fellows that we must get our wounds healed as quickly as we can and I cannot but fear lest you should injure your health or diminish your fortitude by lingering too long by our dear one's grave.[42]

William himself accepted this advice, telling his mother, 'I shrink from London but I must face it the first week in March . . . I feel I must not indulge myself too long in this luxury of grief.'[43]

Thomas Lister's forceful advice on grief represented the views of both the Harcourt and Lister families, illustrating the stark contrast between the counsel given to a man and a woman. Victorian widows were never advised to 'get our wounds healed as quickly as we can', nor warned of the danger of 'learning to love your sorrow instead of bearing it'. Widows were usually advised to pray, to rest, and to resign themselves to the will of God; if that prescription took many months of sad contemplation and grave-visiting, their families did not find it necessary to sound the alarm. What was considered self-indulgent for men was required therapy for women, for many of whom it seems to have been more helpful than not. Possibly families believed that men were in greater danger of prolonged and unhealthy grieving, and so sought to sublimate it in work as early as possible. A more practical explanation for the gender difference was that men were usually essential to the family economy, so prolonged grief was an indulgence which was simply too expensive.

If the Harcourt family believed work was a necessary therapy for the grieving widower in the short term, they were also convinced that William's baby son should be his primary comfort in the longer term. The baby was cared for by his grandmother Lady Lewis during the early months of bereavement, and William saw the child only once in the first two months. The family made little reference to the boy in their letters to the grieving widower in the early weeks, rightly fearing that it would remind him too harshly of the cause of his wife's death. A week after Thérèse's death, Edward Harcourt, William's brother, sent him a brief, sensitive report on the baby's welfare, ending: 'Of course the life of a Baby is always precarious, but I cannot help feeling that this child is meant to live and comfort you.'[44] William's uncle Egerton Harcourt believed the infant was left to his nephew as a pledge of Thérèse's affection.[45]

On 27 February 1863, nearly a month after his wife's death, William Harcourt saw his baby for the first time, but the sight induced 'terrible

agony'. His mother-in-law recognized that this first visit was 'but an aggravation of his sorrows'. Both families must have been worried that William
might reject the baby, though Lady Lewis denied any fear that he might not
love it.[46] Six weeks after her daughter's death, when William had been back
at work for two weeks, she sent him a stern warning that he must struggle
against overwhelming grief in his baby son's interests:

I cannot but feel that your whole energy and power of motivation are required to
help you through this misery and desolation that you now feel—but you *must*
struggle with it or there is a worse price to be paid than death—When grief obtains
mastery mind or health may give way and not life, and you must think how earnestly
she would have wished you to live to take care of her little child![47]

Two weeks later, exactly two months after his bereavement, William was
contemplating 'making over' his child to his sister Lady Morshead. Lady
Lewis hoped that this idea would disappear with time, for such a solution was
quite foreign to her concept of parental obligation: 'that Child's home ought
to be with its only parent—and will have a softening and wholesome influence on his grief'.[48]

In the months that followed Harcourt's ambivalence towards his son was
transformed into the strongest bond of affection. As his biographer noted, in
Lewis 'the shattered affections of Harcourt centred with an intensity that
continued unbroken to the end of his life, and became a legend in the social
and political world'. William became devoted to the son 'who embodied the
memories of his brief domestic happiness' and who accompanied his father
on most of his leisure pursuits. When Lewis was 11, William (now Sir
William) consoled Sir Charles Dilke on the loss of his wife with the hope that
his child would 'live to be to you what mine has been to me. Make an effort
to transfer to it the wealth of your loving heart which has been so terribly
lacerated.'[49] Only when Lewis was 13 and away at Eton did Sir William marry
an American widow, Elizabeth Cabot Ives. The boy acted as his father's best
man, most unusual for a child so young, as well as accompanying the couple
on their Paris honeymoon. The mutual affection between father and son
demanded many years of Lewis's adult life, when he unselfishly acted as his
father's private secretary and constant companion; he devoted a decade to his
quest to make his father Prime Minister, at considerable cost to his own
career.[50]

A third case-study is provided by the fourth Earl of Carnarvon, who
recounted in his diary the death of his first wife in childbirth on 25 January
1875 and his experience of bereavement. Many diary entries immediately
before and after her death have been cut out, probably by the Earl's second
wife after his death, presumably because they were considered inappropriate

for later readers, but glimpses of his experience have survived. Like William Harcourt, Carnarvon consulted a doctor about his ill health during the first month of bereavement, though in his case the complaint was heart pain. But the medical diagnosis was the same, namely 'the result of nervous depression in consequence of what I have gone through, not of any organic mischief'.[51] A month after his bereavement, his sister reassured him that these early weeks and months were the hardest, so they must not be too anxious about his progress.

Like Dr Thompson and William Harcourt, Lord Carnarvon returned to work in the very early stages of bereavement—in his case to arduous labour as Secretary of State for the Colonies in Disraeli's government. Nearly a month after Evelyn's death, Carnarvon's devoted sister Eveline Lady Portsmouth began to fear she had been premature in her initial encouragement of a speedy return to work:

I think very continually of you—for I often feel how very hard and burdensome, how little spring in it your working life must be—And then I wonder if returning to it will bring the good fruits I, like so many of your friends believed. But as you would not shrink from the duty so at least you will always feel should you hereafter decide to retire that your judgement is backed by real experience and has nothing hasty in it. But just as I rejoiced at one time that you persisted in a return, so I now earnestly hope you will not force yourself after the trial to any unnecessary prolongation of Official life should your strength seem in the least failing or even this great craving for repose continue.[52]

Many references remain to the sympathy and support of his sister, as on a visit to her home on 23 March 1875: 'What has she not been to me and mine these last sad two months. Her courage, and faith, and sympathy and wise counsel in every difficulty have carried me on when I must I think have either broken down or miserably failed.'[53] Throwing himself into his work did not resolve the grief and he still needed time to think and relax.[54] Three and a half months after his bereavement Lord Carnarvon badly needed a 'change of air', so he took the children to the Isle of Wight, establishing them in a nearby house and himself on board his new yacht, which carried no memories of the past. Otherwise he found each social visit to a familiar place a strain: 'it has cost me something to go anywhere again—indeed each new thing that I do seems an effort—and Hatfield [House] particularly has many memories which are very saddening to me'. But he gained increasing pleasure from taking the children with him on these visits and watching their enjoyment.[55] Indeed, by November, he was able to place the children's health and happiness above his own political advancement in a decision to refuse a senior position in India. His sister could see no advantages in such a move for the children: 'as things are I feel the overpowering claim of the children upon you to outweigh all other claims . . . With the great loss your children have sustained I think your presence in England or at least with them is the first.'[56]

The extant diary entries indicate that Carnarvon's chief consolations came from his children and his work at the Colonial Office, which he regarded as a duty. He was 44 when his first wife died, and three years later he married his cousin Elizabeth Howard, aged only 22. Again it is worth noting that a widow of 47 would have had little prospect of remarriage and almost none to a partner less than half her age. Given Carnarvon's strong religious beliefs, he undoubtedly gained far more spiritual consolation than the surviving diary entries suggest; it is possible that such references were among those deleted as being too intimate, too emotional, and perhaps inappropriate for a late Victorian male.

Alfred Lyttelton's beloved first wife, Laura Tennant, died on 22 April 1886 after a difficult labour and only a year of idyllic married life. His cousin, Mary Drew, thought Alfred 'desperately wounded. He can never be quite the same again,' but she believed there was no alternative but to work through the suffering.[57] Alfred tried to cope day by day through work and routine, as he admitted to Mary Drew two weeks after the funeral: 'I can't write at all tho' I can work, and have got to a certain extent back into routine . . . The silence grows so intolerable.' He found some comfort in the numerous condolence letters which reminisced about Laura's life and kept her memory vividly alive, even though he found replies difficult.[58] The first few months of widowhood were extremely painful, though he tried to submerge his grief in work. As he later admitted: 'The quick return to work after April, though the right thing to do—I would do it again—was a frightful strain in my state of mind then, but it was absolutely necessary to have the obligation of other men's affairs to look after in order that part only of the day should be spent in the agonising thoughts of fresh grief.'[59]

Three months after Laura's death he felt no better and wrote a 'very miserable' letter to his brother-in-law Edward Talbot, which he immediately regretted, and he wrote again to reassure him:

I get along pretty well when I have active work, and when I am with others—but for me who used to love a good deal of solitude, it is strange and sad enough to dread my own company. For when I am alone I feel sometimes almost despair . . . I feel myself, not as I should be, strengthened and refined by the intense suffering I have borne, but rather the reverse.

Alfred decided to take a holiday abroad in the hope that a complete change might do him good, since part of his present condition might be due to 'mere bodily depression'. Yet he dreaded the effects of such a break in his routine: 'It is my unalterable conviction that there is strength, and beauty, and glory, to be won from these awful events, if only one is man enough to struggle bravely, and if the body only can be subdued to the spirit.'[60] Talbot, an Anglican clergyman, replied that great troubles brought 'a kind of exaltation' and inner strength, and that God had shown in Alfred the strength of the Cross, 'in the instinct which enabled you to discern, and accept, the truest meaning of a great sorrow as Sacrifice'.[61] Earlier chapters have suggested that a prolonged spiritual struggle for submission to God's will was probably more common in men, whereas women had more social conditioning in patience and submission. Late in August Alfred visited Laura's family at Glen. They often spoke of Laura 'and it doesn't jar', but the little grave in the wind-swept churchyard filled him with 'unutterable longings'.[62]

Six months after Laura's death, Alfred returned from his American holiday far more at peace with himself:

I *am* the better for [the holiday] in all ways . . . As you get a little bit away and the wounds begin to close a little, it is good to have the long days to oneself and to books, when one can travel back over every day of the sunny time, and when one can find in beautiful poetry above all, deeper and more hidden beauties, which no one can quite appreciate without experience of their truth.[63]

His Lyttelton and Tennant relatives 'spoiled' him, especially Lucy Cavendish and Charty Ribblesdale, who looked after his baby, Christopher, in the early months. Alfred discovered that 'the infant makes a large difference in the feeling of isolation' which he experienced on his return to his London house: 'He has got to know me a little, and he is beginning to throw a gleam upon my life.'[64]

But just over two years after his mother's death, in May 1888, Christopher died of tubercular meningitis. He was buried at Glen with his mother, on his parents' wedding anniversary. Alfred found some comfort in the thought of 'his being with my little Darling', as 'an unspotted little messenger from me'. Even the funeral service helped him, 'for unlike almost every other funeral I ever recollect, not one jarring note struck on the utter pathos and beauty of it all'. But Alfred was oppressed by 'the dreadful thought [of] the future, without the point and centre which he would have made . . . I don't think that I can face living in the poor little house any more—or the domestic life which has now lost its *raison d'être*.'[65] Mary Drew could find no comfort in the situation at all, as she confessed to Alfred on the day of the funeral:

I felt knocked over somehow, it seemed to me I could see nothing but the intense sadness and apparently utter waste of it all: it revived all the keen misery of 2 years ago and without its hope and possible kind of explanation, it made her death seem so hard and as if it were in vain . . . I had always looked upon this darling baby as such a humanising help and comfort for all your life. I had never dreamt that he could die . . . I know it must feel today as if Laura had died again. The wounds must be so torn open and bleeding . . . But that short year of marriage, so brilliant and beautiful, *did* give you some things to hold on by, and which will not fail you now.[66]

Alfred Lyttelton married again six years after Laura's death. His second wife, Edith Balfour, had initially seen him as a man set apart, sanctified by the loss of both wife and child. Edith had not expected love in return, 'only that it would fall to me to give him back a home and some happiness'. But she was delighted to discover that 'love of the dead need not be lost in love of the living'.[67] Alfred's grief for his wife and child was intense, but it was never obsessive. He endured his bereavement with resignation and courage, aided by a deep religious faith and disciplined adherence to his professional occupation.

These four case-studies suggest that gender made a decisive difference in coping with the experience of loss of a spouse. Nineteenth-century Victorian widowers had access to two important sources of consolation which were largely closed to upper- and middle-class widows—work and remarriage. All four widowers examined in this chapter resumed professional work between one and four weeks after bereavement. Three out of the four remarried, after intervals varying from three years in Lord Carnarvon's case, to six years for Alfred Lyttelton and thirteen for William Harcourt. Only Dr Seth Thompson failed to remarry and he died comparatively young, twelve years after bereavement. Opportunities for professional work and remarriage were restricted in most cases to men, while widows usually had to rely on family, friends, and faith for sustenance, if they were fortunate. However, Victorian widowers were expected to repress their feelings during bereavement, at least in public, and to recover from grief relatively rapidly. The dichotomy between the public and the private sphere could become intolerable for some sensitive widowers, but at least there were real choices available to begin a new life with challenging work and a new partner's support.

13

CHRISTIAN CONSOLATIONS AND HEAVENLY REUNIONS

GRIEF AT THE DEATH OF A BELOVED FAMILY MEMBER WAS TRAUMATIC for unbelievers and believers alike, but Christians trusted that their faith offered consolation, support, and hope for the future. The supreme comfort offered by the Christian religion on the death of a loved one was the belief in the resurrection of the soul. Christianity advanced the hope of Christ's atonement and resurrection, with its promise of life after death for contrite Christians. Most Victorian Christians extended this doctrine to mean that they would be reunited with their departed family and friends in heaven. This belief in immortality, with its associated hope of heavenly family reunions, is the chief subject of this chapter. Many devout Christians also believed that sorrow had its own spiritual value, like other forms of suffering, in purifying the soul and bringing it closer to God. In 1878 Revd William Benham reminded Archbishop A. C. Tait of the utility of sorrow on the death of his son Crauford:

A man feels then that the sorrow has brought him closer to God than he ever was before. And not only so but he sees as he never saw before the *reality* of God's love and goodness. I know that the doctrine which I had so often preached, namely that God is not a tyrant or task master but a Father, never came home to me with such power as in the weeks that followed my wife's death, and at the very time when I seemed not to care whether I died or lived, I still could fall back on that faith and find peace.[1]

But Benham acknowledged that the supreme solace of Christianity was the belief in an immortal life which could reunite separated families: 'the faith in the great *forever* swallows up everything else'.[2]

Yet other features of Christianity were less helpful in dealing with grief. The fundamental difficulty of explaining how a just God of love could ordain suffering and death troubled many bereaved people. This problem was aggravated in the case of a premature death of a child in a pious family, as we have seen. The conviction of some devout parents that the death of a child was a punishment from God for their own sins immeasurably increased the burden of grief. The common belief of pious Christians that anger and depression represented rebellion against God's will further complicated the grieving process. Yet most Victorian Christians believed that the consolations of their faith more than compensated for these limitations.

Perceptions of Heaven: 'Unspeakable Bliss' or 'Fruitful Sunlit Activity'?

Geoffrey Rowell and Michael Wheeler have documented the decline during the nineteenth century of literal belief in hell as everlasting physical punishment. This helped to resolve the dichotomy in Christian theology between the concepts of judgement and resurrection. It also helped to remove the dilemma caused by the abolition of purgatory at the Reformation, which left Protestants with a stark choice between heaven and hell, though most souls were presumably better suited to somewhere in between. From the seventeenth century some theologians saw the concept of everlasting torment as incompatible with a just and loving God, and the doctrine of hell slowly began to be eroded. By the nineteenth century many Protestants believed in some sort of intermediate state, rather like the Catholic purgatory, where spiritual progress was possible before the Last Judgement. Protestants increasingly interpreted hell as meaning the absence of God, while a minority of liberal Protestants argued that all would ultimately be saved.[3] Indeed the doctrine of hell had so far declined that it was mentioned in few of these Victorian family archives, except by a lapsed Catholic, Wilfrid Scawen Blunt, and a dying free thinker, Ada Lovelace.

The focus of these Victorian Christian families was rather on the prospect of immortality in heaven, while the declining influence of the doctrine of hell increased the expectation of a blissful future. Colleen McDannell and Bernhard Lang argue in *Heaven: A History* that beliefs about heaven were transformed in the West in the nineteenth century. They claim that the traditional, static, theocentric view of heaven as a restful place for psalm-singing saints engaged in the eternal worship of God was rejected by the Victorians by the 1860s, except in popular hymns. Heaven as worship was allegedly displaced by two quite different anthropocentric models of heaven: 'late nineteenth century Christians, for the most part, imagined a heaven of growth and activity . . . During the nineteenth century, service and education replaced worship as the primary activity of the Protestant heaven.'[4] McDannell and Lang depict the Victorian work ethic and passion for progress as extending to the afterlife, as did contempt for idleness. In the second new model the family in the home became the basis for heavenly life, as Christians moved from one loving home to another, to meet departed loved ones in the next world.[5] The next section will test the views of McDannell and Lang against the arguments of Victorian theologians and the historical evidence of family experience.

It is important to distinguish between coherent theological doctrine and the more diffuse beliefs of ordinary people—even educated middle- and upper-class people—and to consider both perspectives. A symposium in the leading periodical the *Nineteenth Century*, in 1877, on 'The Soul and Future Life', provides a revealing insight into the views of intellectuals and theologians, at a time when the advance of science was raising new questions about immortality. R. H. Hutton, Anglican theologian and editor of the *Spectator* from 1861, offered the traditional theocentric concept of heaven, as a future of eternal praise and veneration of God: 'a life absorbed in the interior contemplation of a God full of all perfections . . . What a Christian desires is a higher, truer, deeper union with God for all, himself included.' Hutton defined the soul as the spiritual core of the sense of personal identity, and stated that, in his view, immortal life perpetuated the personal affections and the human will.[6] Dr W. G. Ward, a Roman Catholic, provided a similar traditional interpretation of the Christian heaven: 'Christians hold, that God's faithful servants will enjoy hereafter unspeakable bliss, through the most intimate imaginable contact with Him whom they have here so tenderly loved.' They would see God face to face in his 'most exquisitely transporting beauty'.[7] The heaven of Hutton and Ward was centred on God, rather than man, and it contained no references either to hell or to idyllic family reunions in the next world.

By contrast the progressive view of heaven was affirmed by Baldwin Brown in the *Nineteenth Century* symposium, and by Edwin Arnold in the *Fortnightly Review* in 1885. The Revd James Baldwin Brown, a liberal Congregationalist, was critical of Hutton's 'lofty view of adoration', and believed that this traditional 'restful and self-centred vision of immortality' continued to exercise an unfortunate influence on popular notions of heaven. This 'poor, narrow, mechanical' view of heaven as a passive place of eternal praise was not a defunct, medieval monastic ideal, because it still featured prominently in the favourite hymns of the Evangelical school. One particularly trite verse attracted Baldwin Brown's strongest censure: 'There on a green and flowery mount, Our weary souls shall sit, And with transporting joys recount, The labours of our feet.' These selfish souls 'mooning on the mount' deserved a vigorous shake, in Baldwin Brown's opinion, and they should be set instead to 'some good work for God and for their world'. But while the notion was easy to ridicule, it was harder to compose a convincing substitute consistent with Victorian ideals of useful activity and moral elevation. Brown's alternative concept was lacking in imagination: 'It is the life which is lived here, the life of the embodied spirit, which is carried through the veil and lived there . . . The risen Lord took up life just where He left it.' Heaven promised a new career of 'fruitful sunlit activity', based on truth, righteousness, and love.[8]

Edwin Arnold, a poet and journalist, was another exponent of the progressive view of heaven. In the *Fortnightly Review* in 1885 he sought to reform heaven rather more rigorously than Baldwin Brown, positing a dynamic, evolutionary, and morally uplifting view of the next life, whereby the 'ethereal body' would find an enriched and higher existence: 'art divinely elevated, science splendidly expanding; bygone loves and sympathies explaining and obtaining their purpose; activities set free for vaster cosmic service . . . Everywhere would be discerned the fact, if not the full mystery, of continuity, of evolution, and of [the] never-ending progress in all that lives towards beauty, happiness and use without limit.'[9]

These learned papers on the nature of the afterlife accurately reflect the continuing influence of the traditional theocentric model of heaven in the Anglican and Catholic Churches. Revd Richard Baxter's *Saints' Everlasting Rest*, first published in 1650, portrayed heaven as 'an eternity of holy repose' in the presence of God, and remained popular in the nineteenth century.[10] Indeed, as Wheeler points out, both the Evangelical and Tractarian movements conceived of heaven as 'the eternal sabbath; as the future blessedness of which holiness in this life is an earnest'.[11] The *Nineteenth Century* symposium suggests that the traditional view of heaven as a place of eternal worship persisted among Anglicans and Catholics, and that the concept of heaven as a place of dynamic progress was more influential among some Nonconformist liberal theologians than heaven as a happy home. If these essayists largely overlooked hell, they also failed to mention reunions of family and friends in the next life, while vaguely hoping that personal affections would be perpetuated.

The correspondence, diaries, and death memorials of our Victorian and Edwardian middle- and upper-class families reveal a number of important features about their perceptions of heaven. In some respects these are at variance with the views of McDannell and Lang and also with the late Victorian theologians. One important point common to all, however, was the lack of any clear definition of heaven. Wheeler has underlined the absence of coherent New Testament teaching on heaven, with no detailed descriptions outside the Book of Revelation.[12] This allowed scope for the imagination of poets and preachers, but it gave no direction to those less well endowed with creative and literary skills. The Church of England, however, gave less encouragement than some Nonconformist churches to speculation about the actualities of the afterlife, taking refuge in metaphors and symbolic language. The general assumption was that earthly descriptions would be utterly inadequate in depicting the perfection of heaven. Lucy Sharpe's remarks in 1862 on the ill-defined scriptural basis for heaven applied to Anglicans and Unitarians alike:

One can hardly walk thro' a village church yard and see the various epitaphs, without feeling that few people have a very *definite* idea of the resurrection,—some say their friends are *now* with God—some that their *spirits* only are there, some that body and soul await the sound of the last trumpet here below. And it seems to me that the form and the manner of our last change is one of the subjects that our Heavenly Father has left undefined, that each child should adopt that view most consoling to his spirit.[13]

The second significant point is that these voluminous Victorian family papers contain very few specific references to the afterlife as a dynamic place of busy moral progress. The references to 'God's kingdom' were overwhelmingly passive, defining heaven as a place of peace and everlasting worship. This evidence challenges McDannell and Lang's conclusion that late nineteenth-century Christians mostly conceived of 'a heaven of growth and activity'. The only evidence in these archives to support this view derives from one mid-Victorian free thinker and two clergymen, hardly a representative sample of Christian laity. Three months before her death in 1852, Ada Lady Lovelace, mathematician and free thinker, imagined the afterlife not as 'one of simple beatitude but rather one of progress. That all mankind had some appointed task set to it and some eventual destiny to accomplish.'[14]

The only other references to a progressive heaven came from the later period and from clergymen rather than laity. The Bishop of Madras consoled Archbishop Tait in 1879 on the death of his wife with the thought that God had long been preparing her for 'His own blissful presence and for some heavenly service throughout eternity'.[15] Even this reference to 'heavenly service' need not have been very active, since it could also mean worship. Thirty years later, in 1910, a sermon by Revd Harry Drew, an Anglican clergyman and W. E. Gladstone's son-in-law, provided more information on this progressive view of heaven, with some insight into the ideas disseminated to Anglican churchgoers in the Edwardian period. Drew described an afterlife 'of endless bliss and infinite possibilities and capacities . . . where every power and faculty shall have free and unimpeded development'. But there was some contradiction in his vision, since heaven was also 'the land where all shall be peaceful and harmonious'—as if he made some allowance for the preferences of his own congregation.[16] There were no such references from the laity, suggesting that ideas of this sort were largely confined to more progressive clergymen and Nonconformists, and were perhaps more influential in America, the source of much of McDannell and Lang's evidence.

The third outstanding feature of the heavenly references in these family archives was the continuing influence up to 1914 of the older, theocentric model of heaven as a peaceful place of worship 'in God's presence'. Heaven as worship was not displaced by heaven as dynamic progress from the 1860s. Undaunted by the prospect of joining the souls 'mooning on the mount', these families showed little desire for the dynamic vision of a future life of perpetual progress. Mary Flounders of Newcastle was consoled on the sudden death of a beloved aunt in 1838 by the belief that her aunt 'exchanged a world of much trial for joy unspeakable in the presence of her Saviour whom she so truly loved and served on earth'.[17] Easter services in 1843 led Mary Palmer to think about the future life, 'where we may offer a more acceptable service of prayer and praise, and progress in virtue and knowledge, without fear, sorrow or separation'.[18] This reference suggests the mild possibility of spiritual progress within a heaven dominated by worship. Dr John H. Gladstone, a professor of chemistry, felt sure that his first wife, Jane May, a Presbyterian who died in 1864, was thereafter 'in the unclouded enjoyment of God's love'.[19] Mary Waldegrave was certain in 1885 that her dear sister, Lady Selborne, was 'recalled to His own treasure house . . . "She is safe at home for ever"—and what a joyful surprise to find herself in the Saviour's presence.'[20]

This traditional, theocentric concept of heaven as union with God was a constant feature in the writing of many Victorian and Edwardian Christian families right up to 1914. Their references were prosaic and conventional, drawing on traditional symbolic Christian language which was generally restrained as well as derivative. The major themes sprang primarily from faith in the message of hope provided by Christ's resurrection, and they focused on eternal union with God. The simple metaphors derived chiefly from the Scriptures, especially Paul's epistle to the Corinthians (15: 1–8, 35–57), from the Psalms, the Gospels, and Revelation, and from popular hymns. Devotional literature, such as *The Pilgrim's Progress*, was another common source, sometimes difficult to distinguish from biblical references to St Paul and the Book of Revelation, which were themselves sources for *The Pilgrim's Progress*. Some references were drawn from anthologies such as Priscilla Maurice's *Prayers for the Sick and Dying* and *Sacred Poems for Mourners*, published in 1853 and 1846 respectively. The extract Maurice recommended, from Revelation 21: 3–4, starting 'And God shall wipe away all tears from their eyes', appeared countless times.[21]

On the day his mother died in 1876, Lord Carnarvon believed she was 'safe and at rest', having crossed the river 'to reach the Eternal City'.[22] Mrs Benson consoled Laura Ridding after her husband's death in 1904: 'the dark River is past, and they have led him to the Celestial City . . . O what a noble rest for the happy Warrior!'[23] The occasional imagery of pearly gates and a heavenly city wall garnished with precious stones was drawn directly from the Book of Revelation, and merely described the ornate architecture of the holy city. There was little speculation about the precise nature of this future life of 'eternal bliss with God'. Hugh Cecil was unusual in his philosophical reflections on 'the next life as an obvious reality' when writing to console Lord Selborne on his sister's death in 1915: 'What are they all doing? Is the life contemplative or active?—And again, which of our qualities are really personal and permanent, and which are corporeal and die? I used to discuss these points with Harry Percy constantly. A sense of humour is an obvious illustration . . . I think it is a very personal quality and lasting.'[24]

Family Reunions in the Heavenly Home

The fourth significant feature of these Victorian and Edwardian family references to heaven was the general agreement that its primary consolation was the reunion of earthly families divided by death. Wheeler notes that theoretically the two models of heaven as worship and heaven as home appear to be contradictory,[25] but this did not seem to worry these families. Domesticated images of happy families in heaven were indeed the characteristic feature of the Victorian heaven which attracted the most detailed attention, especially from the 1860s. References to happy reunions and family love in heaven were usually brief and often oblique before the 1860s, perhaps reflecting a greater recognition of the New Testament injunction that marriage did not exist in heaven. Indeed the early nineteenth-century references to heaven are so vague and brief that heaven could have been a state of mind rather than a place. When Emma Wedgwood (later wife of Charles Darwin) lost her beloved sister Fanny, aged 26, in 1832, she left a prayer in her papers: 'Grant that I may join her with Thee never to part again . . . What exquisite happiness it will be to be with her again, to tell her how I loved her.' Emma wrote to her aunt that Fanny's death made 'the next world feel such a reality'.[26] The prose was often biblical and the metaphors sometimes mixed, as in the earnest letter sent by the young William Sidgwick to his fiancée, Mary Crofts, in 1833: 'Though death may separate us for a few years still the one who last reaches that bourne from which no traveller returns will find the other's spirit to welcome its approach to the shores of bliss, and after the day of resurrection both our souls and bodies will be for ever united in glorious presence and possession of Him who died to save us.'[27]

Most of these early and mid-Victorian families were diffident about their hopes of meeting their loved ones again in heaven. Their brief references to the afterlife were usually framed in the conditional tense, expressing hope for reunion only if their behaviour in this world merited it. At the age of 71 in 1831 Lady Anne Harcourt, wife of the Archbishop of York, wrote a farewell letter to her sixth son, Henry, a Colonel in the Guards, whom she considered too preoccupied with worldly affairs. She did not expect to meet Henry again in this world and this letter anticipated her own death, which took place nearly a year later:

I, on parting with you, feel intense anxiety to cherish a well-grounded hope of our enjoying a happy immortality together with your best of fathers and our ever-beloved children . . . Wherefore I hope you will pardon the over solicitude, perhaps, of a fondly attached mother for your temporal and eternal welfare . . . The greatest pang I could feel on my death-bed would be to apprehend that any of my children had a less lively faith in the Divinity of Christ than I have, or that their hopes of salvation through His merits and mediation alone were less strong than my own . . . Oh! my dearest Henry, I entreat you to pray continually for the assisting influence of God's Holy Spirit . . . so that . . . the religion of *the heart* may be manifested in all the future actions of your life.[28]

References by early and mid-Victorians to their hopes of heavenly reunion were frequently accompanied by such exhortations to spiritual reform which would increase their prospects of meeting again. Mary Palmer's Easter message to her nephew in 1843 looked forward to a 'joyful meeting in a future life', but emphasized that this would be dependent on good behaviour on earth: 'the time here is short, although everything depends upon our manner of using it'.[29] Mrs Sarah Acland's comment on her aunt's death in the mid-1850s was similar: 'it is blessed to think that she has gone before us, and that if we diligently walk in her steps . . . we shall not always be parted from her'.[30]

In the mid-Victorian period more questions were asked about the nature of heaven, particularly whether souls would retain their identity and their earthly memory, allowing them to recognize their loved ones. The traditional, theocentric model stressed heaven as worship in the presence of God, where marriage was not possible and earthly loves were irrelevant. However, an anthology by theologians entitled *The Recognition of Friends in Heaven* in 1866 concluded that those who were saved would have a continuing identity in the next life which would allow them to recognize their families.[31] This theological debate about identity and family recognition in heaven was reflected in a number of passages in family archives, chiefly between 1850 and

1860. The one reference of an earlier date was made in 1832 by Edward Harcourt, Archbishop of York, when, as an old man of 75, he was mourning his wife's recent death. In a private letter to his nephew, he expressed his confident belief that his wife's spirit had been 'received into the Divine Presence', and he hoped he would be found worthy of the same fate: 'Though there are no *positive* intimations in Scripture on the subject of future recognition, it is a prospect which she was always fond of cherishing, equally with myself.'[32] Nearly thirty years later, Mary Morice, a friend of the Keble family, indicated her awareness of the debate on future recognition on the death of John Keble's sister Elizabeth: 'Should recognition of those that are dear to us be one of the rewards of the faithful in the separate state, what joy there must now be among many dear friends of yours and mine!'[33]

Not surprisingly, Ada Lovelace, as free thinker and scientist, took the pessimistic view in this debate about heaven, even on her deathbed in 1852, when she might have appreciated reassurance about continuing personal identity in the afterlife. In theory Ada believed that only death itself could resolve the momentous question about immortality; but in practice even death was not decisive because 'there will be no memory or identity in the future and therefore nothing to feel solved *then*, as to our past doubts'. She speculated that 'in some future condition' there would be no actual consciousness or exact recollection of the previous earthly life, though there might be a general sense that current happiness or misery was largely determined by endeavours in an earlier existence.[34]

From the 1860s and 1870s consoling references to heavenly family reunions became more explicit and less conditional. Theologians in the late Victorian period placed more emphasis on the incarnation than the atonement, and less on sin, judgement, and hell, and this was reflected in lay views of heaven. It was usually taken for granted that Christian families would meet again in the next life, without the earlier need to justify salvation by a detailed account of pious behaviour in this life.

Where heaven was sometimes perceived as a state of mind in the early Victorian period, from the 1860s it was increasingly depicted as a 'Heavenly Home', often in a more sentimental way than hitherto. The concepts of heavenly love and marriage were increasingly condoned by clergymen, while Charles Kingsley, influential liberal Anglican and Christian socialist, even encouraged belief in a sexual life in heaven. A number of popular religious books and tracts catered to this growing interest in heaven, including *Heaven our Home*, published by Revd William Branks in 1861, which emphasized that personal recognition of family in heaven would be combined with a continued affection for those remaining on earth. Branks described a social heaven of 'saint-friendship, and social intercourse among those who are in glory . . . a home with a great and happy and loving family in it . . . We have a home for eternity, and that home is heaven.'[35] The most popular work on heaven was the 1868 novel *The Gates Ajar,* by the American writer Elizabeth Stuart Phelps, which sold 100,000 copies in England by 1900. She ridiculed the theocentric heaven of psalm-singing saints, painting instead a portrait of contented families in a superbly landscaped social community.[36] As Boyd Hilton puts it in *The Age of Atonement*:

Hell departed into metaphor, while Heaven retained its felicitousness, as indeed it had to do if it was to attract mankind once Hell had shed its terrors, but at the same time it became domesticated. The strategy now was not to frighten sinners into Heaven but to beckon them there by promising more of the good things they had enjoyed in life. So as Hell ceased to be a fiery furnace, Heaven became a cosy fireside where long-lost loved ones congregated.[37]

Revd John Stoughton of Kensington was more than usually confident about the social structure of heaven in his 1865 contribution to an anthology of sermons, poems, and essays on heaven. He believed that the New Testament represented heaven as a social state which would preserve the distinctive features of human nature. Christ's veto on marriage in heaven merely referred to the legal relationship, but did not preclude 'special loving bonds' in heaven between those who had been married on earth. Stoughton had more difficulty with the common assumption that everyone would be 'loved alike' in heaven. He conceded that 'all the excellent of the earth will form one family', but was repelled by the prospect of 'a sort of perfected socialism hereafter—a cosmopolitan kind of existence' in which everybody would seem the same. Evidently some souls would be more excellent than others: 'we shall love and delight in some more than others'. In Stoughton's heaven all such conflicts would somehow be resolved: heaven 'is a state of repose, yet a state of activity . . . In heaven the affections will be balanced. Friends will be loved, but not supremely. God will be the chief object of regard, and gratitude, and praise.'[38]

Heaven as home was the dominant metaphor in the references to the afterlife in these late Victorian family archives, which lack the topographical detail of the popular published accounts, and primarily emphasize the joy of family reunions. The simple fundamentals of family reunion in the heavenly home were similar in the 1870s for a young Unitarian woman, an elderly Presbyterian mother, and two eminent Anglican churchmen. Emma Lee, a Unitarian aged about 19, wrote to console her friend Maria Sharpe on her father's death in 1870:

It takes away all the mystery and horror of the grave, to think that when we die we shall only pass from the loving hearts and arms here, to the arms of those who have gone before us. I am sure I often feel, even while talking and laughing, as if I could turn round and clasp my arms round my darling sister at my side, who has stepped across those awful shores, to take my hand and kiss me.[39]

After the loss of both a son and a daughter within four years, Elizabeth King, a Presbyterian, confessed to her widowed son-in-law in 1874 that she had no desire to live: 'If I dared to wish for anything it would be that we might all be quickly taken up to join them—How beautiful David's sweet young face must look among the heavenly throng . . . Surely our love cannot perish. He loves me still as I love him.'[40] Churchmen as well as laity were at pains to underline the concept of heaven as home, allowing the continuation of family love and care. When Archbishop Tait's wife and son died in 1878, he was consoled by the thought of 'that happy meeting between Mother and Son'. He described the afterlife as 'a better land through Christ, changed, with all our imperfections and stains removed, but still the same'.[41]

The Bishop of Gloucester wrote to Archbishop Tait in 1879 expressing his deep trust in 'the abiding nature of the blessed family bond', which, in his view, was not emphasized enough in the Church's consolatory teaching. In a letter of condolence on the death of the Archbishop's sister, the Bishop of Gloucester stressed that the intermediate state was not a place of seclusion, for the Bishop was sure of the 'practical reality of the Communion of Saints. Surely those whose souls have been bound up in love and prayer with us here—below,—surely they cannot be far from us in our holier musings and deeper prayers.' He fervently believed that since 'the home is of God, and especially the Christian home, it must be a permanent bond between family members in this world and the next'.[42] These sentiments were close to those of the young Unitarian woman, the Presbyterian mother, and the Anglican Archbishop, despite differences in gender, age, status, and sect. None of them had any difficulty in reconciling the vision of the reunited family in heaven with the concept of heaven as worship, where all members were 'united in Christ's presence . . . in Everlasting bliss'.[43] The heaven of contented family and social community was united with the traditional heaven of worship.

By the 1880s anticipation of such family reunions in the heavenly home became the primary consolation for many mourners. On his wife's death in 1880 Lord Selborne saw the prospect of reunion as one of the paramount consolations:

I have, in looking forward, the sense, which I hope God will enable me to realise, of communion with her, as well as with our parents and brothers and sisters, on both sides, in that Communion of Saints which the epistle to the Hebrews sets before us;

and the trust that, by this most unmerited mercy in our Lord Jesus Christ, I may be reunited with them, and with her, in the eternal world.[44]

The letters of condolence which Lord Selborne received conveyed the same message, such as that from Lady Cairns: 'The best of all comfort is *reunion* and how *soon* that may be for *us* all.'[45] Lucy Stanhope recognized in 1886 that the approaching death of her stepfather, General Hankey, '*must indeed* be heart breaking but for the hope which keeps the old so brave—the hope of a short parting and a meeting again for ever—What should we do without that faith? My dear—One would lose heart at the very first start—with one's first loss.'[46]

Occasionally the bereaved sought more precise explanations from the clergy as to the nature of the future life, as did Louisa Antrim on her mother's death in 1890. Revd Paget's response seems to have been typical in its ambiguity, though it reassured Louisa: 'If we are not reunited in the way we wish—it can only be because God's reunion of those who care for each other is so far happier, better and more satisfying than anything we can possibly imagine.'[47] Revd Harry Drew's sermon, nearly twenty years later, was little more revealing, though it would have pleased those who sought confirmation of a continuation of earthly emotions and relationships in the next world: 'Death "in Christ" is the true entrance to a land where partings are no more . . . We shall meet again those we have loved here, and we shall both know and love them as we have neither loved nor known them before. Every pure earthly happiness and love shall be perfected and made eternal then.'[48]

Several reasons may be suggested for the increasing emphasis on family reunions in the afterlife from the 1860s. McDannell and Lang attribute it primarily to what Lawrence Stone has termed the 'affective revolution', whereby family relationships were increasingly determined by affection from the seventeenth century, and love within the family was idealized. Stone's argument certainly has weight, but we must not neglect the impact of both the decline of Evangelicalism and the reduced emphasis on hell. Moreover, in a Christian world rendered increasingly insecure by the perceived challenge of 'science', biblical criticism, and agnostic versions of Darwinism, families sought greater reassurance of their domestic immortality, seeking safety in a peaceful afterlife which promised continuities between this world and the next.

Christian Consolation in Practice

In this section I will examine the actual process of grieving in an early Victorian family, to illustrate the complex way in which Christian faith and consolation operated, when the Evangelical religion of the heart was at its most powerful. As we have seen, Harry Goulburn's death from tuberculosis at the age of 30 in 1843 was a model of the good Evangelical death. Harry was the eldest of the four children of Henry Goulburn, Chancellor of the Exchequer in Peel's cabinet from 1841 to 1846. The response of his devout Anglican mother, Jane Goulburn, to the untimely death of her beloved adult son reveals one of the most distressing and painful grieving experiences.[49] The grief of Victorian parents for adult children may have exceeded that for very young children, because such deaths were not expected beyond the age of 10, and the emotional investment was far greater.

Modern psychologists' findings on the role of religious rituals and beliefs in helping the bereaved to work through grief in today's society have been tentative but generally positive. Beverley Raphael notes that religion may provide a ritualized system and a supportive framework which helps people to come to terms with death, offering comfort and giving meaning to the trauma.[50] Colin Murray Parkes is more cautious, warning that the relationship between religious belief and adjustment to bereavement is very complex. However, he recognizes that a number of psychological studies have demonstrated the value of religious belief in providing some explanation for death.[51] Jane Littlewood is more sceptical, noting that the evidence is by no means clear, while her own 1983 study illustrates the problem created when the majority of twentieth-century participants report relatively low levels of religious commitment.[52] It is difficult to measure levels of intensity of belief, for church attendance alone is not a sufficient indicator, and it is impossible to measure faith itself.

The letters of condolence which poured in to the grieving Goulburn family in 1843 placed their overwhelming emphasis on the consolations of Christian faith. Those friends and relatives who had known Harry well were genuinely convinced by his Christian life and devout preparation for death that he enjoyed the 'sure and certain hope of . . . eternal blessedness'. For most sympathizers this implied a traditional, theocentric afterlife for Harry: 'he is now in the glorious presence of his Saviour'. The references to a heavenly family reunion were brief, but confidence was expressed that Harry's spirit was 'more fit for heaven than earth' and that his bereaved parents had a 'well grounded hope of a happy reunion with him who has entered into peace'.[53] The evidence of Harry Goulburn's life suggests that these tributes and expectations were more than usually well deserved.

Harry Goulburn died on 8 June 1843, resigned to his fate and well prepared to meet his Lord, leaving his mother to confront her own crisis of faith at the loss of a brilliant young son in his prime. Jane Goulburn kept a detailed daily diary for seven months after Harry's death—rather like that of A. C. Tait on his little daughters' deaths—in which she expressed her sorrow and described her devotional responses, as in her entry two weeks after bereavement: 'Grant that when my hours of agony begin, I may find thee [God] an all sufficient support, as he [Harry] did, and do thou maintain my faith and my patience as thou didst his . . . [let me] be admitted into thy presence, altho' in the lowest of all thy heavenly mansions . . . Suffer me not to lose the benefit intended for me by this heavy chastening.'[54] Like Archibald Tait and John Horsley, Jane Goulburn saw her child's death as a punishment from God which would cause an agony of grief and a trial of her faith. Her conviction of the saintliness of Harry's life and death, compared with a much humbler view of her own worth, must have increased her sense that his death was punishment for her own sins. The belief that a child's death was God's punishment was hard to equate with a God of love, adding an immense burden of guilt to the already heavy weight of grief. However, this was to some extent balanced for Jane Goulburn by the conviction that God, who sent the ordeal, would provide the strength to survive it, and would ensure that she and her remaining children would benefit from it spiritually.

Jane Goulburn's grieving process was a constant trial of her faith, as she recorded in her diary. A number of entries towards the end of the first month of bereavement recorded that her heart was wretched and her faith declining: 'still unable to regain the feeling of lively faith in his [Harry's] present happiness which supported me so much at first. Oh Lord increase my faith which is too feeble to combat the overwhelming sense of what I have lost.'[55] This underlined another dilemma for grieving Christians in the early stages of bereavement. They felt that good Christians should rejoice at the heavenly fate of their loved one, whereas their own deep sorrow was a sign of a weak faith and rebellion against God's will. A minority of mourners found this an insurmountable obstacle to resolution of their grief, as did Mrs Acland on the death of her son Herbie.

Jane Goulburn's ordeal was aggravated by the death of her niece Ellen Fazakerley on 9 August 1843, only two months after Harry. Both Jane and her sister Eleanor Fazakerley saw their ordeal as a 'trial directly coming from God' and were at least able to empathize fully with each other's struggle. This second blow was the more stunning in that it followed the death of their nephew Lt.-Col. Robert Ellison only a month earlier, increasing their fear of divine retribution for the family's sins. The two bereaved mothers interpreted as a weakness of faith their overpowering regrets for lost happiness, their yearning to see their dead children again, and their inability to take full pleasure in the present heavenly state of their children.[56] Like her sister,

Eleanor Fazakerley also had to struggle against 'the evil heart of unbelief' and the 'clouding of that spiritual hope which can alone give us strength'. Yet she recognized that this spiritual anguish was partly a product of the poor health which accompanied bereavement for them both. Eleanor was certain throughout the ordeal that her faith sustained her, insisting that 'God supports me wonderfully', and prayer kept her calm. Her most important consolation was her belief that her daughter was reunited with her cousin Harry in a happier life everlasting: 'The idea of my Ellen's glad spirit joining dear Harry's, has supported me through many a sad hour of the dreadful nights, and will often soothe me in those which are to come.' As the months passed, Eleanor's bouts of anguish and spiritual torment diminished and her faith in God's love and her hope of future reunion triumphed. She was sure that God would 'sanctify our sorrows, and let us be where He is, and where our treasures now are'.[57]

Mourning for her child involved a more prolonged, uncertain, and complex period of penance for Jane Goulburn than for her sister, and she had to struggle harder for submission to God's will. Her degree of resignation varied from day to day, for shifts of mood were frequent for both women, especially in the earlier months of mourning. Four weeks after Harry's death a particularly uplifting church sermon helped Jane to 'acquiesce entirely in God's will in removing my blessed Harry from serving him on earth to serving him, as I trust he is permitted to do, in Heaven'. But many more entries recorded that she was listless and lacking in spiritual comfort. On 18 August, for instance, she felt her loss more intensely than ever: 'alas my heart is sunk in sadness and despondency as everything reminds me of happiness gone for ever'.[58] Normal responses in the grieving process, including anger, bitterness, and depression, could be interpreted by the devout as rebellion against God's will and a failure to rejoice in the heavenly fate of the deceased. In October Jane was deeply depressed: 'many very painful struggles to subdue my constantly increasing longing to see my blessed loved one and to hear his voice'. She found it impossible to bear the prospect of the lengthy period she might have to wait until she saw Harry again, and 'yet I feel utterly unfit to rejoin him'.[59] Unlike later Victorians Jane always referred tentatively and conditionally to the possibility of family reunion in the afterlife.

Six months after Harry's death Jane Goulburn was beginning to come to terms with her loss, helped by the prospect of ultimate reunion with Harry in heaven. By November 1843 she resolved to cease recalling so constantly all the harrowing circumstances of her son's death. Instead she endeavoured to remember more often that Harry was happier in heaven: 'to think of him as free from all pain and sorrow and associated with all the blessed spirits of the just made perfect', admitted to Christ's presence. The struggle to reconcile her loss with her faith was similar to that endured by the Taits, John Horsley, W. E. Gladstone, and other devout Christians who suffered a particularly grievous and untimely loss. Familiar Christian arguments of consolation and support took several months or more to achieve a soothing influence.[60]

On New Year's Eve 1843 Jane Goulburn drew up a Christian balance sheet, accepting for the first time in seven months that God's mercy in taking Harry and his two cousins was greater than his need to punish or judge: 'On the retrospection of the past year, in which so many awful events have followed in rapid succession, in spite of all the agony of mind which I have undergone and the loss of my best beloved Harry, which I must feel ever now and more until it pleases God to put an end to my own existence in this world, I am constrained to acknowledge that mercy has predominated over judgement.' She convinced herself that God was merciful in taking Harry rather than his mother or brothers, because they were too worldly and he alone was in a fit state of spiritual preparation for death.[61] Jane Goulburn's experience illustrates that for many Christians the primary longer-term consolation on the death of a child came through faith, with its accompanying hope of family reunion in heaven and its suggestion of divine purpose in suffering. Yet even for the most devout, reconciling faith with bereavement could involve a long struggle for submission to a seemingly harsh divine judgement. Jane Goulburn died in 1857, fourteen years after Harry and just a year after her husband, Henry. The commemorative inscription for all three on the tablet in Betchworth Church appropriately said of the mother, 'A simple faith a true devotion prepared her for hours of trial and united her to Her Redeemer.'[62]

In the end it was faith that triumphed for Jane Goulburn, especially faith in God's greater wisdom and mercy, and faith in the ultimate heavenly reunion of her family. Her Christian beliefs seemed to add doctrinal burdens to her ordeal in the early months of intense grief, but Jane's conclusion was that the benefits of her faith outweighed the disadvantages. Faith is neither logical nor rational, and is not readily amenable to measurement. We are left with the personal statements of many Victorian mourners that their faith provided comfort and strength to endure the grief and assist them to return to a useful life.

Christian Devotional Literature as an Aid to Mourning

The Goulburn family's experience on Harry's death illustrates the widespread use of Christian devotional literature as an aid to mourning, in addition to the prayer-book and the Bible. Numerous anthologies of verse, Scripture, and sermons were compiled in the nineteenth century to console families around the sick and dying, to soothe mourners, or to help particular bereaved people, such as widows or parents who had lost children. Priscilla Maurice's anthologies of sacred poems and prayers were widely read, frequently aloud within the family.[63] In 1843 Archdeacon Samuel Wilberforce sent Jane Goulburn a volume of elegiac poems by Revd Richard Chenevix Trench to soothe her mind while mourning the death of her son Harry. Wilberforce commented on the value of such poetry as an aid to mourning: 'Trench has known indeed the deep heart of sorrow and its sacred free masonry admits his moods readily into the hearts of other mourners.'[64] After his five children died at Carlisle in 1856, A. C. Tait sought solace in Trench's introduction to Maurice's *Sacred Poems for Mourners*, as well as in the anthology itself. Over twenty years later, when his son Crauford was dying, Crauford read through Jeremy Taylor's *Exercises of Holy Dying* to aid his preparation for death in appropriate contemplation and prayer.

Condolence letter writers frequently recommended particular devotional books, poems, or verses of hymns which they had found helpful in grief. Louisa Cane suggested in 1843 to her friend, the young Jane Goulburn, on her brother's death, that she read a particular chapter of Philip Doddridge's *Rise and Progress of Religion in the Soul*, a favourite of many Evangelicals seeking spiritual edification, including William Wilberforce. Louisa Cane especially recommended a chapter on affliction, which she found most soothing with its 'assurance of the Almighty that he chasteneth whom he *loveth*'—addressing one of those paradoxes of Christian consolation which had particular meaning for the Goulburn family. Louisa also suggested a hymn by Newton, 'In vain our fancy strives to paint the moment after death'.[65] Louisa's sister Caroline sent Jane a devotional book which 'is written in a very feeling manner by one who had experienced much grief', though she did not identify the author.[66] Many Victorian mourners compiled their own devotional commonplace books, as did Emma Haden in 1858 in her 'Book of Meditations on Bereavement', in which she copied out verse and Scripture she found consoling after her daughter's death, including some of her own composition.[67]

The most popular consolation poetry of the early and mid-Victorians was John Keble's volume *The Christian Year*, published in 1827. Indeed it was the most popular volume of verse of the century, selling 265,000 copies by 1868,[68] though its astonishing success disconcerted its modest and saintly author. As David Newsome comments, 'In his silent adoration of the holy mysteries . . . [Keble] made an appeal to the hearts of countless men and women in his day,' touched by a spirit in part pietistic, in part romantic.[69] In the late 1830s George Cornish suffered the loss of his daughter from scarlet fever, but assured his friend John Keble, 'The comfort which your dear Book gives would of itself make me eternally turn to you.'[70] Favourite verses of *The Christian Year* were recited in numerous letters of condolence, especially stanzas from poem 85, 'St Barnabas the Apostle', and poem 101, 'Burial of the Dead', including the lines:

> Yet is the voice of comfort heard,
> For Christ hath touch'd the bier . . .
> 'The Resurrection and the Life,
> Am I. Believe, and die no more'.
>
> Unchang'd that voice—and though not yet
> The dead sit up and speak,
> Answering its call . . .
>
> Far better they should sleep awhile
> Within the church's shade,
> Nor wake, until new heaven, new earth,
> Meet for their new immortal birth
> For their abiding place be made.[71]

While *The Christian Year* continued to hold its appeal, from 1850 it was challenged in popularity as consolation literature by Alfred Lord Tennyson's great poem *In Memoriam*, published nine years before Darwin's *Origin of Species*. Most committed Christians were not fundamentally threatened in their faith by the discoveries of the geologists and the theory of natural selection, but mourners were all too familiar with the doubt aroused by the suffering and death of a blameless loved one. As Revd W. V. Harcourt observed in 1853, 'Many more than own to it are often perplexed with doubts and apprehensions respecting their condition after death.'[72] Though religious doubt among Christians was familiar before 1850, the numbers afflicted by it increased considerably thereafter, and they were reassured to know that Tennyson's search for faith finally triumphed over doubt.[73] Owen Chadwick elegantly encapsulates the main themes of *In Memoriam*:

Loving the dead Arthur Hallam with a pure affection beyond the wont of men, Tennyson rested upon faith that a being so noble could not be destined to extinction, that a love so profound must reach to eternity. Then science stepped in to criticise, with fossils and bones showing countless types extinguished, cast as rubbish to the void; dragons tearing each other in the slime, nature red in tooth and claw, shrieking against his creed. The poet represented his soul as coming through to faith in the purpose and design of the universe. But his faith, which had once firmly trod, now faltered—

> . . . I stretch lame hands of faith, and grope,
>   And gather dust and chaff, and call
>   To what I feel is Lord of all,
>   And faintly trust the larger hope.[74]

In Memoriam held deep meaning for many Victorians in mourning, not least W. E. Gladstone's daughter Mary Drew, who made special bequests of her two copies of the poem in her informal will. In her 1886 will, dedicated when she believed she was dying, she left to Sibell Grosvenor her white vellum edition, a precious gift from the poet's son Hallam Tennyson, who had once been in love with her. Her bequest to Berthe Drew in the amended 1890 will helped to explain the poem's special significance for Mary:

My little old blue morocco 'In Memoriam', very shabby and all the things I had first written on it cut out. I tried to write down all that it meant to me when I was in trouble—it is almost necessary if you want its real interpretation to read it when you are in trouble—being literally the pouring out of the man's soul, even tho' his friend had been dead more than twenty years.[75]

Nearly a quarter of a century later Countess Avebury expressed the feelings of so many mourners over the previous six decades when she found consolation on her husband's death in Tennyson's great poem. As she wrote to Kate Courtney in 1914, 'Do you love "In Memoriam"? I do. It just expresses all one feels at different times—wanting to believe oh so much—doubting terribly and yet feeling trust in a power that seems to have made us believe in immortality and therefore could not annihilate affection.'[76]

The central consolation offered to Victorian and Edwardian Christians was the concept of immortality in an afterlife shared both with God and also with the beloved earthly family 'gone before'. Academics and theologians might find some conflict in this juxtaposition of the theocentric and anthropocentric models, but for Victorian Christians it was natural to hope for a heavenly reunion in which their families would join the angels around God's throne. There was no tension between heaven as home and heaven as worship. Christianity imposed additional doctrinal burdens on its followers, with such tenets as judgement and punishment for past sins. But most middle- and upper-class Christian families seem to have found a comforting assurance in their faith in confronting the harsh realities of the process of dying, and coping with loss on the death of a loved one. For these Christians, human life could begin, and could end, with that most reassuring of all human emotions—hope, based on faith.

๑ 14 ๑

THE CONSOLATIONS OF MEMORY

The Role of Memory in the Grieving Process

The memory of the deceased was central to the grieving process for Christians and unbelievers in the nineteenth century. The psychiatrist Beverley Raphael has emphasized the importance of memory in the dynamics of grief, noting the mourner's initial absorption in memories of the lost relationship. Early hopes that the deceased may somehow be restored to life are increasingly countered by public mourning rituals affirming the death and by recognition of the finality of the loss:

The psychological mourning process involves the review of [all] aspects of the lost relationship in order that the bonds binding the bereaved to the dead partner may gradually be relinquished, freeing the emotional investment for ongoing life and further relationships. Thus the bereaved reviews, piece by piece, memories, thoughts, and feelings associated with the image of the dead partner. Sadness and other feelings relevant to each of those memories are experienced intensely as each is faced, treasured, and reluctantly put aside. The process is inevitably painful, yet must progress.

In the first stages of this review the mourner idealizes the deceased as a perfect man or woman, but in time he or she is usually remembered in more realistic terms, as the negative qualities also surface and are accepted. Prolonged idealization and distortion of the memory are often caused by ambivalent feelings, such as guilt and regret, which interfere with the successful resolution of the mourning process. Where the relationship was essentially affectionate and positive, and support is forthcoming from family and friends, the ambivalent feelings are usually worked through effectively. Raphael underlines the importance of such social support in the resolution of grief, especially in responding to the mourner's intense need to talk through memories at length, and repetitively, with relatives and friends.[1]

Victorian archives provide abundant evidence that Raphael's analysis of the role of memory in the grieving process applied equally then as now. William Somerville understood this process well when he wrote to his recently widowed sister Janet Elliot in 1841:

I am very sure that however painful the return to your once happy house may be, you are right in going home—A thousand recollections will rush upon you at first which time will convert into objects of pleasing recollection—how different the case would have been if you had anything to forget—On the contrary you will call up every circumstance you can from your memory and cherish the ideas they recall.[2]

When Lucy Sharpe's father, Thomas Reid, died in 1845, her relatives felt sure that his memory would console her, as well as her Unitarian faith. As her cousin assured her, 'After the first agony of separation is passed the recollection of your beloved father's many virtues will fill your heart with soothing thoughts . . . The memory of the just and good is indeed a blessing to the survivors.'[3] Two months after her father's death Lucy Sharpe wrote to her husband from her parents' home, telling him that 'this place . . . is full of precious recollections that are so pleasant yet so mournful'. She had an unusually sensitive perception of the power of memory:

I feel a sacred pleasure in strengthening the impressions of these happy times because I hope that the vivid recollection of what his influence was over me may enable me to supply in some measure the loss I feel our children have in him . . . Anything that will aid me in promoting the happiness of those around me with the activity and energy so remarkable and beautiful in his character I shall indeed esteem a blessing.[4]

The Quakers placed even more emphasis on memory than most Protestant sects because they rejected all external forms of grief, including mourning-dress, monuments, and their inscriptions. They understood the human need to perpetuate the memory of deceased loved ones, to communicate grief, and to express affection, but they believed all this could better be achieved through memory than monuments: 'If you wish to honour a good man who has departed this life, let all his good actions live in your memory. Let them live in your grateful love and esteem. So cherish them in your heart that they may constantly awaken you to imitation.'[5]

The memory of worthy people was seen by Christians to have a positive power in influencing their survivors for the good. In 1879 Archbishop Tait returned to the churchyard where his wife and his son Crauford had been recently buried. During Holy Communion he 'felt the presence of the beloved ones very near' and found comfort:

Never since [Crauford's] death have I had so distinct a vision of my dear son in his manly beauty as today in Church and his beloved Mother also was clearly manifested to the minds eye in all her motherly sadness as I last saw her in that Church, on the day when Crauford's [memorial] window was put up . . . It is scarcely possible to realise all that has passed since. But my lonely bedroom and her deserted dressing room and what used to be her bright busy morning room now closed and the dear picture of mother and son in the dining room and a thousand other things full of memories—stir the heart . . . Here [at Addington] there is less to distract the thoughts and the grief at times is overwhelming.[6]

The emphasis on the value of memory as a source of consolation in grief was increased for some by the growth of religious doubt. Agnostics often placed primary emphasis on memory in the absence of other significant sources of comfort, as a later chapter will show. One example will suffice here. On learning of the death of his friend and tutor the botanist John S. Henslow, Charles Darwin's condolence letter to his colleague J. D. Hooker was exceedingly brief. Darwin expressed gratitude that Henslow's suffering was over, sympathy with Hooker's grief, and respect for Henslow's 'noble character'. But the only source of consolation he recommended was memory: 'It will ever do one good to think of him.'[7]

Middle- and upper-class Victorians seemed to understand the value of reliving their memories of the past and talking about their dead loved ones as an aid to mourning. Even the Fox family of Holland House, unusual among early Victorians in writing little about either religion or death, acknowledged the soothing power of memory. In 1843 the worldly political hostess the dowager Lady Holland was afraid that a return to her marital home, Holland House, would 'foster morbid feelings' after her husband's death. Her son Henry Lord Holland, not usually prone to discussion of feelings such as sorrow, reassured her that it would almost certainly be consoling to revisit the memories of her marriage:

I am convinced that it is a great misfortune to indulge and foster morbid feelings such as you describe and that after the first struggle against them the objects which at first were painful and almost hateful become endeared and even more highly prized by the recollections they revive. Time which does so much in this world will I am sure make you feel this and tho' the pleasure is a melancholy one yet there is a pleasure to those who really have loved to look at and enjoy the scenes of former happiness—at length they impart some of the happiness of other days and are sanctified and sometimes perhaps even childishly worshipped for the sake of such reminiscences.[8]

Two weeks after the death of Ada Lovelace in 1852, her 15-year old daughter Annabella King observed that her father talked a good deal about his dead wife: 'he seems to feel pleasure in recollecting and thinking of those spots where *she* has walked, and what *she* liked and thought'.[9] On the death of her sister-in-law Caroline Wedgwood in 1888, Emma Darwin was saddened that she had lost the last surviving close female relative of her own generation and the remaining link with old times. She did not count her brothers because she believed that most men 'do not like remembering'.[10] Emma Darwin's view of gender differences in relation to memory probably reflects the fact that

Victorian society encouraged females to work through their grief, while males were expected to return to public duties far more rapidly.

Many Victorian mourners found consolation in writing about their dead loved ones, as well as thinking and talking about them. Earlier chapters have drawn on the numerous Evangelical written family memorials on the life and death of the deceased, intended as spiritual accounting to God, and for Christian edification and moral example. Most written memorials were also intended as a precious recollection of the life and death of the deceased, either for the writer alone, for immediate family members, or, more rarely, for a wider audience of local congregation and community. Some memorials were intensely private outpourings of grief, such as W. E. Gladstone's account of little Jessy's death, and these often served incidentally as therapy for the writer. Lawrencina Potter's detailed account of the death of her only son in 1862 was another personal expression of grief which helped relieve pain.

Numerous Victorian testimonies have survived to the therapeutic value of recording personal memories soon after the death of a loved one. In the week after his wife's death in 1852, John Horsley felt 'thoroughly broken up', but found that committing his experience and emotions to his diary was beneficial: 'while I write I feel better'.[11] Lady Minto suggested to the recently widowed Katharine Elliot in 1865 that she write a short memoir of her husband to provide 'some little occupation' in her loneliness and to reflect her feelings.[12] In 1895 Lucy Smith was deeply distressed at the death of her mother, Lady Tennant: 'she is my life, my chief pleasure and only comfort'. To ease the pain of her grief and supply a measure of peace she wrote a short record of her mother's life, chiefly from her own recollections, since little evidence survived from diaries or correspondence.[13] In 1910 Edward Talbot was crying as he composed his memoir of the life and death of his beloved brother John. As Edward's wife, Lavinia, wrote to her sister Meriel, John's widow, 'I know how much comfort and thankfulness will come to you, my old dear, to have the wonderful account put before you of recognition of Johnny's life and character, of deep respect and love.'[14] To the families who treasured these accounts, they were not sentimental effusions but consoling memories which sustained their sense of closeness to the deceased as well as helping them through the grieving process.

A number of family memorials which were initially intended for the family alone were eventually published. One of the most famous, already discussed, was the volume recording the deaths of Archbishop Tait's five children and his wife which appeared in 1879. A letter from Alec Macmillan, its publisher, provided evidence of its popularity, revealing that 12,100 copies had been printed within the first year, when the Archbishop's profits reached

£1,547.4.5.[15] The public demand for this commemorative volume and the many letters of thanks which poured in to Archbishop Tait demonstrated just how therapeutic it was considered to be. Revd A. G. Butler, headmaster of Haileybury School, wrote to thank Tait for the 'wonderfully touching Memoir' of Catherine Tait, who had been well known to him when he was a pupil at Rugby, noting that 'old times and memories become so precious as we move on in life'. Butler considered the sad account of the five daughters' deaths would be a source of comfort to thousands of bereaved parents all over the world.[16] The simple faith and loving courage of the Tait parents had similarly helped Agnes Moore, who had also sent copies of the book to a number of people who had affirmed that 'it has done them good'.[17] Joseph Parker was soothed by the Archbishop's quiet confidence in God: 'Your memorial book must find its way into countless chambers of sickness and households of bereavement, and through many generations it must sanctify and lessen the sorrow of Christian families. Viewed in this light how sublime are the uses of such sorrow!'[18]

Memorial Likenesses of the Dead

Unlike the Quakers, most Victorians felt the need for external symbols of remembrance, in addition to recalling their loved ones in thoughts and conversations, and in writing. The psychological explanation for the value of material memorials and likenesses is straightforward since the physical memory of the deceased is particularly important in the 'searching' period of grief, following the shock of the death.

In the initial period of deep grief and 'searching' for the lost person, and often for long afterwards, Victorian mourners sought to keep their loved ones' memory alive as vividly as possible through paintings, drawings, photographs, busts, and death-masks. The wealthy could afford to pay portrait painters to memorialize them in their final years or months, while the less fortunate had recourse to drawings or photographs. Dr Samuel Beckett, a provincial surgeon, commenting on his young sister's death in the early 1850s, regretted that the family had only a black silhouette profile as a reminder, despite their family weakness for memorial portraits.[19] The death of their mother in 1855 prompted the Leakey family to consider having portraits painted of her two more delicate daughters, especially the consumptive Sophia, who died three years later: 'In her weak state of health should we not provide against the spoiler? Should we not immortalize our sister?'[20] Three months before Ada Lovelace's painful death from cancer in 1852, her husband arranged to have a portrait painted, even though she was already 'wasted almost to a beautiful shadow'. This seemed to please Ada's young daughter Annabella (later Anne Blunt), who told her brother, 'Mr Philips, the artist, is taking Mama's likeness, and I think it will be very good . . . She is *so* beautiful now, and so gentle and kind. I think her like what I should imagine an angel to be.'[21]

Photographs, drawings, or portraits of the recently deceased, sometimes lying in the coffin, were another common form of remembrance which brought comfort to the bereaved family, however macabre they may seem to late twentieth-century eyes. The Horsley family archives are especially interesting in this regard because John Callcott Horsley was himself an artist. His diary for 1852 demonstrates the importance he attached to record-ing the likenesses of those recently dead, especially when they were children of less wealthy families. On 24 April 1852 he noted, 'In the afternoon I went to make a drawing of a dead child, thinking it a duty so to do, indeed had I not done it it would not have been done—the child the only son of Mrs Hodge.'[22] John Horsley preferred to make his drawings as soon as possible after death occurred, while the facial muscles were still relaxed and the expression serene, before the features stiffened. He spent the afternoon im-mediately after his father's death in 1858 making a drawing, before his father's body was placed in the coffin. His mother commented to his sister, 'the likeness is perfect, and we are so happy you should see exactly how he looked . . . The peace and beauty of his expression is not to be described.' John's sister Mary Brunel was abroad, and had difficulty in accepting the reality of her father's death. Mary initially requested a photograph of John's drawing, but was persuaded to wait until she could see the drawing itself, to her mother's relief: 'I am so glad you decide not to have the Photograph. It is so inferior to the drawing that I should be sorry you saw it first. I almost always go to look at it on my way to the parlour in the morning and it is really like looking at him in his bed for it has not to me the look of death but of a calm sleep.'[23]

Another artist, the poet Wilfrid Scawen Blunt, was anxious that likenesses should be made of his brother Francis and sister Alice, when each died of tuberculosis in 1872. Wilfrid made a number of sketches of Francis during his illness and immediately after death. Wilfrid's wife, Anne Blunt, remarked in her diary on her brother-in-law's face just after he died, when she and Wilfrid attempted their drawings, 'His face was beautiful like the face of a saint as I imagine it to be . . . Death is horrible but at the first moment there is something beautiful in it too.' Wilfrid also arranged to have a photographer take two pictures only four hours after Francis died. In the following weeks Wilfrid modelled in clay a larger-than-life recumbent effigy of Francis in his

Franciscan habit, based on the sketches. The completed effigy in alabaster, his only attempt at sculpture, was judged a 'brilliant achievement' by Wilfrid's biographer, and was placed above Francis's grave at the Crawley monastery he founded.[24] Three months later Wilfrid and Anne invited an artist, Mr Moloney, to make a sketch of Alice as she was dying, which was later framed and presented to her husband.[25]

Such paintings and drawings were often kept in positions of prominence in mourners' houses as a vivid reminder of their loved ones. William Burdett-Coutts mourned his wife's death for the rest of his life and sought to remember her for ever through the life-size painting on his dining-room wall: 'he often dined at home alone to feel she was with him once more'.[26] From the 1850s the less wealthy were likely to use photographs to fulfil the same purpose. On her husband's death in 1860 Mary Somerville thanked a relative for sending photographs, 'valuable before—how precious now; they are good, very good and give the most agreeable impression of my dearest husband in his extreme old age'.[27] After the death of Archbishop Tait's wife and eldest son in 1879, his surviving children gave him 'four sweet photographs of the two dear ones we are mourning'. He kept them on the table of his living-room, 'and the sight of them comforts me'.[28]

It was not uncommon for wealthy Victorians to perpetuate the memory of loved ones through death-masks, either alone, or as the basis for effigies and busts. A plaster-cast was made before the features stiffened, with the plaster carefully applied to record the details of the face, and usually removed in three pieces.[29] John Horsley made a cast of the head and shoulders of his 3-year-old son Harry, who died of scarlet fever in 1854.[30] Even though the lower part of Harry's face was unrecognizable, the father kept the cast on a table in the corner of his dressing-room. Three months after Harry's death, John's mother showed the cast to Harry's brother Frank: 'he knew it very well and said it was like dear Baby'.[31]

Widows appear to have derived special consolation from death-masks. On the death of Woronzow Greig in 1865, his widow, Agnes, found some comfort in the appearance of his face in death, 'his Countenance having the calm of Heaven in it . . . so dignified, so refined, so grand'. A death-mask seemed crucial to her: 'I am so thankful I got a cast taken of it. All were struck with it. Never had they seen anything so calmly beautiful.' Her brother and sister 'hardly dared to ask me', but shared her view that it should be done.[32] Casts were sometimes taken of the head and shoulders, and of the hands. Lady Charlotte Phillimore reported on the death of her husband in 1885, 'I have had a cast taken of his beautiful face and hope for a successful Bust.'[33]

Busts of family members were sometimes among the bequests made at death. Egerton Harcourt in his 1880 will bequeathed the marble busts of his father and a brother to his niece Cecilia Rice.[34] Casts were taken of Ada Lovelace's hand in 1852, while her portrait was being painted.[35]

In the late nineteenth century mourners also favoured commemorative objects which were useful as well as aesthetically pleasing, with memorial church windows high on the list. Lord Frederick Cavendish's assassination inspired several such windows, including one erected by iron- and steel-workers in St James's Church, Barrow-in-Furness, and another imposing window in St Margaret's Church, Westminster. In 1901 Mary Drew was practical in her plans for a memorial to her mother in Hawarden Church, as she wrote to Lord Rosebery: 'Will you help me with £50? Do you remember the Tower of our Church? I was about to build a Baptistry underneath it as a little memorial to my mother but it was discovered to be crumbling to pieces.'[36]

Grave-Visiting for Remembrance

For many families in the nineteenth century the grave in the cemetery became a site for remembrance and for meditation. It helped them to evoke a sense of closeness to the dead person, by associating him or her with a particular place. Graves could thus become shrines which mitigated grief during a temporary period of intense anguish by keeping alive the memory of the dead person in a particularly vivid manner.

A tombstone was chosen carefully as a memorial which would mark the burial place of a loved one and provide a site for remembrance in the future. Considerable family discussion took place in deciding on the most suitable gravestone. On the death of their sister Elizabeth Keble in 1860, Thomas Keble left the choice of gravestone to the 'taste and discretion' of his brother John, after perusing a series of numbered gravestone drawings, presumably provided by a stonemason.[37] When her father died in 1861, Martha Somerville consulted her brother Woronzow Greig about a suitable monument, expressing her own preference for a simple, solid, yet handsome stone, which happened to involve the least expense.[38]

Financial concerns and family indecision caused a five-year delay before a tombstone was erected over the grave of Louisa Rogers, a spinster who died at the age of 59 in 1865. Her aged mother, Mary Ann Rogers, frequently expressed her anxiety about this gravestone in her letters to her son Richard Norris Gandy. In August 1865 she enquired, 'Have you seen about poor

Louisa's stone yet?' Mary Ann supposed that any design must first be submitted to their rector, and she hoped the stone would be laid before the frost set
in. Her agitation was increased by a monument recently erected to the late
village blacksmith. Not only was it taller than any others in the churchyard,
but it was in the form of a cross, 'rather out of character when we know what
the poor old man was, something less pretending would have been better'.
Mary Ann composed a simple inscription for Louisa's stone, merely the
names of daughter and parents with Louisa's birth and death dates. After
nearly four years' further delay, the installation of Louisa's gravestone was
marred by trouble with the rector, who had not been consulted before he
discovered the masons at work, and by an untoward error in Louisa's death
date (two days out) on the stone.[39]

Victorian families usually took great care in their choice of gravestone
inscriptions, sometimes to impress, but more often because they wanted their
choice to be appropriate. In 1841 Janet Elliot requested the assistance of her
brother William Somerville in devising a worthy inscription to the memory
of her husband. William had strong views 'on so sacred a subject': 'To be read
it should be short—and to claim respect for the living as well as the lamented
it should not be as these monumental inscriptions often are—gross tho'
misplaced flattery—In your position you have no need of anything but
truth . . . something very short and expressive if we can achieve it of his
virtues as a man and his merits as a soldier.'[40] In 1866 Thomas Lister thanked
his brother-in-law Sir William Harcourt for his assistance in drafting the
lengthy inscription for his mother's monument; this now included a reference to the family's 'happiest days spent amidst these Hills which she loved
so well'.[41] Inevitably some mourners were much concerned with their own
status on any family inscription. Dr John Gladstone composed the text for
the stone of his second wife, Margaret, in 1871, 'the result of much thinking
and consulting with others'—and also of studying other monumental inscriptions in Kensal Green for ideas. Margaret was described merely as the
'second beloved wife', whereas the titles and qualifications of her father and
husband were given in full, as was often the case.[42] The higher status of males
was affirmed even in the cemetery.

Visiting the graves of family members was an important source of consolation and a vital part of the process of mourning for many bereaved. Visits
were usually more frequent in the first year of loss, gradually diminishing
thereafter to weekly or monthly visits and anniversaries. The nineteenth-
century garden cemeteries established outside city centres, starting with
Kensal Green in 1832, provided a peaceful rural setting which was very
different from earlier overcrowded and insanitary city graveyards.[43] Two

weeks after her father's death in 1850, Catherine Ellen Taylor explained the importance of her visits to his grave, which she saw as 'a sacred home':

The lovely burial ground at Gosfield is often in my thoughts—not as it was on that painful day when its silence was disturbed by the trampling of horses and many feet—but as it looked on Saturday morning when we went there—the wind in the trees—the sunshine on the grave—the cawing of the rooks—the repose and peacefulness of the scene. I shall never forget—it is a sacred home to think of when the burden of life is too heavy, the years too long.[44]

Ten months later, Catherine Taylor's mother enclosed a violet from her husband's grave with a letter to her sister, explaining the consolation offered by her visits to his 'resting place'. In the early months she went more frequently: 'By the grave my soul hovered ever—mournful as was the feeling—there to me was my life and hope—or rather the sad end of both.' But she felt more hope and peace by his grave as the months passed.[45] Lady Anne Blunt's diary recorded her visits in 1872 to the little graves of her three babies—her first-born son and female twins—who died soon after birth. The visits helped her to grieve for children too young to be mourned by anyone else—even the father in the case of the little girls.[46]

Keeping the anniversary of a death with a visit to the grave was a common form of remembrance. Rose Horsley's diary recorded grave-visits on the first and second anniversaries of the death of her sister Emma Bergeron in 1858; on the second anniversary she went to the cemetery with the Bergeron family and they lunched together afterwards in Rose Horsley's home.[47] The memory of the loved one was recalled most vividly on a number of anniversaries, including weddings and birthdays, but especially dates of death. Lucy Sharpe shared this ritual of remembrance with her mother in 1846, on the first anniversary of her father's death:

Tho' our sad loss can never be absent from our minds yet this recurring season must bring to our minds in a more lively manner the sorrows of the last—every day every hour of this particular week has its feeling its hope or its fear never to be forgotten and every now and then memory brings so vividly before me an expression of my dear Father's most benevolent countenance that comforts me tho' it makes me feel more deeply what we have lost.[48]

James Thorold Rogers noted in his diary in 1854, on the first anniversary of his first wife's death, 'The first anniversary of the saddest day I ever had or can have, as far as this life and its persons are concerned'. A year later he noted: 'Sad day to me and I was dull, very dull the whole day. It cannot not be, that this the most unhappy anniversary of my whole life, should even now grieve and shock me.' But like many widowers he remarried, just seven weeks before this second anniversary, which may explain his failure to mention the third anniversary in 1856.[49] In May 1877, on the anniversary of his mother's death, Lord Carnarvon noted in his diary, 'It has been all the day through in my mind.'[50]

Given the memorial significance of the grave, families were concerned to maintain the plot as a pleasant place of remembrance, planting shrubs, renewing flowers, and keeping it tidy. The Horsley family was typical. After Fanny Thompson's death in childbirth in 1849 the Horsley family visited her grave at Kensal Green Cemetery soon after the funeral to place several plants in pots as a temporary measure, intending to undertake a more permanent planting in the ground once the weather permitted.[51] Two days after the funeral of his first wife, Elvira, in December 1852, John Callcott Horsley found that her grave was still in the same 'rudely formed' condition owing to the wet weather. As a symbolic gesture he plucked a rose from his sister Fanny's grave for Elvira's, planning to plant evergreens until the weather improved. Eighteen months later Mrs Elizabeth Horsley described Fanny's grave as a 'perfect bower of white roses', while the turf on Elvira's grave was flourishing and the roses were starting to bloom; she enclosed two roses from the grave for Rose Horsley, Elvira's successor. Both graves looked in good order, and Mrs Horsley liked the inscriptions on the gravestones of John's two 'dear children' who had died earlier in the year.[52]

The physical importance of the grave as a site for consolation and remembrance was emphasized by Gertrude Gladstone in writing to her brother-in-law Herbert Gladstone, who managed all the funeral arrangements on her husband's death in 1891:

I think all that you are doing at my Dear One's Grave, dearest Herbert, sounds quite what I shall like—if you will get the shrubs thick enough, I mean planted as close together as they can be—I like the cross to stand out rather higher than the surroundings—I find the photo of it a great comfort to me, it looks so quiet and peaceful, and makes one long so to be lying there too, with all one's great misery ended.[53]

In a similar vein, Victoria Dawnay commented in 1892 to her sister Mary Countess Minto on the delightful appearance of their mother's grave almost two years after her death, with fresh gilt letters for the simple inscription, and a border of golden yew inside the newly painted railings.[54]

Many families were concerned about the possible neglect of family graves, especially if their relative was buried far from home. In 1911 Mary Chamberlain, third wife of Joseph Chamberlain, urged her stepson Austen to make a pilgrimage to Adelboden in the Bernese Oberland, where his youngest sister,

Ethel, was buried in 1905.[55] A few days later, Austen's sister Hilda was delighted to learn that Austen would make that 'pilgrimage of love and remembrance' to see that the grave was not neglected, and to 'make it rather less lonely' for Ethel, buried so far from home; 'Though it is perfectly true that Ethel lives and will always live in our hearts and lives, so that it is unthinkable to talk of neglect of her memory, yet somehow one's sentiments cling to the spot where the one we loved so much is buried, and I have felt unhappy at the thought that it might look as if no one cared for her.'[56] Mary intended to keep Austen's photographs of the grave to give to Ethel's daughter, along with other mementoes, when she was old enough to cherish them.[57] Photographs of the grave were often sent to family members and close friends, especially if they were unable to attend the funeral. Maggie Cowell-Stepney was grateful for the photograph of Harry Drew's grave in 1910: 'The great White Cross is too lovely—I never saw a more beautiful grave picture.'[58]

Commemorative Bequests, Keepsakes, and Mourning Jewellery

The bequest of favourite possessions of the deceased assumed an emotional importance disproportionate to their everyday value because of their associations; they continued the links with the lost loved one and might even, as Raphael notes, 'symbolically represent the dead person'.[59]

Nineteenth-century formal wills usually tell us little about commemorative bequests since they were entirely concerned with specific bequests of money or property and composed in legal language. Women's informal wills, however, were often more revealing about commemorative bequests, particularly as they were likely to be composed closer to the time of death. Before the Married Women's Property Acts of 1870 and 1882, wives had no independent legal rights, including the right to make a will, since 'by marriage the very being or legal existence of women is suspended', as Blackstone put it in 1765. As a partial substitute many women in wealthier families made informal wills itemizing all their personal belongings such as clothes, jewellery, paintings, books, and small pieces of furniture, stating who was to receive them and sometimes explaining why.

At the age of 81 in 1865 Mary Ann Rogers, mother of Professor James Thorold Rogers, filled a notebook with bequests to be distributed after her death, though she lived another eight years. By 1865 she had already lost her husband and ten of her sixteen children, so that many pages of the notebook had lines or paragraphs deleted or altered accordingly. Mary Ann had little of great value to leave, so that much of the notebook concerned the disposition of clothes, linen, furniture, china, and kitchen utensils, with frequent references to their particular links to relatives now dead. For example, her granddaughter Annie, aged 9, was to have a brooch containing the hair of her own dead baby brother. Mary Ann initially bequeathed to her son William a barometer, a looking-glass, and an easy chair purchased by his father before his birth; 'the first sleep he had in the world was in it'. But as a result of William's death in 1866 at the age of 62, she was obliged to amend the item, 'since his Death to his son Murray'. Her granddaughter Emma was left a rosewood tea-caddy, her linen sheets, and all her shifts, nightgowns, and under-petticoats, as well as any money remaining after payment of funeral expenses. Her granddaughter Alice received Mary Ann's Chinese work-box, a fender and hearth-brush, and 'a little tea cup which was promised her poor Mother', Elizabeth, who died that same year aged 52. Mary Ann's constant awareness of mortality was evident from her note that if Alice did not live, her brother Vining should inherit those bequests, in addition to a wash-stand and foot-bath.[60]

Two months before she died in childbirth in 1886, Laura Lyttelton wrote her informal will, a romantic essay which was very different from Mary Ann Rogers's utilitarian list. Laura said of her husband, Alfred, 'all I have in the world, and all I am and ever shall be belongs to him. . . . So few women have been as happy as I have been every hour since I married.'[61] Surviving extracts show that Laura left Arthur Balfour her copy of Boswell's *Life of Samuel Johnson*: 'He taught me to love that dearest of men . . . If he marries I should like him to give his wife my little red enamel harp. I shall never see her if I die now.' She left her Plato to Arthur's brother Gerald Balfour, together with the wish that he would marry: 'he deserves a beautiful and noble woman'.[62]

W. E. Gladstone's daughter Mary Drew left one of the most comprehensive examples of a woman's informal will, totalling fifty-six pages. Most of this will was composed in September 1886 when Mary was childless and close to death after a miscarriage, and was dictated to her husband, Harry, who acted as scribe.[63] It comprised a long list of bequests of particular items of clothes, jewellery, personal belongings, and books, sometimes with requests to transmit items to specified people after legatees in turn died. Mary's bequest to her sister Helen was typical: 'Diamond star earrings and pearl and diamond Cross (only will she please leave the Cross to Katie Wickham) and my Lacaita coral necklace (to be handed on to Margaret Wickham)'. Her sister-in-law Annie Gladstone was to have her picture *The Good Shepherd*, which Annie had originally given Mary for the nursery of her stillborn child.[64]

Mary Drew's bequests spoke powerfully of relatives and friends since dead and of the value these families placed on the exchange of keepsakes, for many items had themselves been bequeathed to Mary. Kathleen Lyttelton was to have the diamond and sapphire brooch given to Mary by Kathleen's sister-in-law Laura Lyttelton, who died some months before this will was written. Laura's brother-in-law Spencer Lyttelton received '*The Imitation* [*of Christ*, by Thomas à Kempis] which Laura gave me the night before her wedding. Also Laura's little honey-moon letter to me.' Sir Edward Burne-Jones was to have 'Laura's corner cupboard in keeping for his Margaret'. Lord Pembroke had an odd keepsake: 'An ugly little black enamel locket with centre pearl which I had made for him soon after Reggie's death [Reginald Herbert, drowned in 1883] with Reggie's hair but didn't give him as he had left off being my great friend'. This black enamel hair locket had been specially made as a commemorative gift, but Lord Pembroke might not have welcomed the accompanying message. Edward Hamilton was to receive Mary's 'print of Freddy'—possibly a print of Lord Frederick Cavendish in his coffin. Significantly, Arthur Balfour received Mary's Hagley Record, which was May Lyttelton's handwritten copy of family death memorials, including the extensive account of the death of her mother, Lady Lyttelton; Mary herself had since added an account of May's own death. Since Arthur Balfour had hoped to marry May Lyttelton, this gift was especially poignant.[65]

Four close friends, including Hallam Tennyson, were mentioned as recipients of curls of Mary Drew's hair, and a brown curl tied with blue embroidery thread was included in the 1886 will. Revd Edward Ottley, who had boosted Mary's confidence greatly by his proposal of marriage in 1879, received a little Russian silver crucifix to wear round his neck, with the comment, 'I owe much more to him than he knows.' John Ruskin was to have her old volume of poems by Frederic Myers because that was the first book Ruskin discussed with her in letters and conversation, and therefore 'the beginning of much, very much that is valuable and precious to me'.[66]

Many Victorians attempted to explain the meaning of these remembrances, often in letters sent to the recipients of bequests. On Christmas Day 1848, signing herself 'Old Gran', Theresa Villiers sent her granddaughter a precious bracelet because she thought it would bring more pleasure to give it directly rather than leaving it in her will: 'you must keep and wear the accompanying bracelet for my sake as long as you live, and in remembrance of *me*'.[67] Shortly after his wife's death in 1849, Dr Seth Thompson sent a teapot to his brother-in-law John Horsley: 'when you are happy with your children and grandchildren about you I feel sure you will think of dearest Fanny and of by gone days'.[68] Ada Lovelace in 1852 left her former lover John Crosse her much-used shabby leather writing-box, to be delivered with its contents of seals, minerals, and paper exactly as they were found on her death: 'Its value would cease if it and its contents were in any way altered after

I had last used it.' This intimate bequest was designed to remind Crosse on a daily basis of their 'many delightful and improving hours' together in literary pursuits.[69] These bequests were intended as reminders of their original owners, particularly when they had been much used by them. As Lady Lewis noted, soon after her husband's death in 1863, when she sent her son-in-law a paper-cutter which was always on her husband's table: 'it is a trifle but nothing seems a trifle that has associations'.[70]

All such bequests were intended 'in remembrance of *me*', and were usually valued and sometimes passed on again when the recipient also died. The practice of giving such keepsakes at death was evidently comforting to the bereaved, who themselves sometimes requested a lock of hair or a keepsake. When Harry Goulburn died in 1843 a friend wrote to his brother, 'It would be a great satisfaction to me, if I am not asking too much, to possess some trifle which your brother has left behind as a memorial of our friendship.'[71] Usually recipients of commemorative bequests seemed genuinely pleased and grateful, as was Constance Villiers in 1863 when her cousin-in-marriage Sir William Harcourt sent her a bracelet and circle of hair belonging to his recently deceased wife. Constance assured him how much she would value anything belonging to his 'lost darling', especially the 'dear pretty bit of hair'.[72]

Mourning-rings, brooches, and lockets were commonly worn as commemorative jewellery during and after formal mourning. Mourning-rings were sometimes designed before death and left to particular relatives in the will, usually engraved with an appropriate inscription.[73] For example, two months before she died of cancer in 1852, Ada Lovelace drafted inscriptions for memorial rings for her family. For her manipulative and domineering mother Lady Byron it was 'Malgré Tout'; for her long-suffering husband, Lord Lovelace, 'in token of my earnest and humble hopes of our eternal union!'; for the serious young daughter who had seen little of her mother, 'with earnest exhortation to unvarying sincerity and truth!'[74] In 1847 Isaac Disraeli's will left twenty-five guineas to each of two sons to purchase rings as a 'token of regard for my memory'.[75]

Memorial rings, brooches, and lockets containing locks of the deceased's hair were favoured in the eighteenth century as well as the nineteenth, the lock of hair being a tangible reminder of the person in life. In 1852 Emily Palmer explained the significance of wearing a mourning-ring containing the hair of her recently deceased sister Dorothea:

Dear Laura [her sister-in-law] has given us each a ring of our Do's hair with a small pearl in the middle. I am so fond of it. We chose a ring—and I am glad for 3 reasons. First because always wearing it—helps me always to think of her—2nd because a ring seems to be bond of love—3rd it being round—a circle reminds one how one's love and communion with her may and will last for ever if we don't lose it by our own fault. Then the Pearl 'Purity' pleases me so much.[76]

Captain G. H. Gildeas wrote a condolence letter from the regiment on the death of Mrs Sneyd's son in 1864, enclosing a lock of 'dear Clement's hair', which he cut for her just before Clement was placed in his coffin.[77] As a deathbed bequest in 1852 Ada Lovelace left to Mary Millicent Montgomery a red cornelian brooch which she had worn frequently, with a lock of hair added 'in token of my great esteem and respect for her'.[78] On the death of Lady Selborne in 1885, Lady Cardwell asked Lord Selborne if he would 'keep a little bit of my blond friend's hair for me'.[79]

Apart from commemorative pieces and diamonds or pearls set in black, jewellery was not worn in the first stage of deep mourning, but jet jewellery or special pieces could 'slight' or offset the mourning at a later stage. This was clear in a letter from Lavinia Talbot in 1882, when her newly widowed sister Lucy Cavendish was disposing of all her coloured clothes and some of her jewellery: 'Don't let her [Lucy] distribute *all* her poor little trinket things— I mean anything which could brighten up her black further on I want her to have. Don't you know the look of Concy Lothian in the deep black but with one or two precious things which make her look so dignified.'[80]

Grave-visiting, memorabilia, and likenesses of the dead were vitally important for Victorians as therapeutic aids in the process of grieving. They are sometimes perceived in the later twentieth century as morbid and distasteful, and as symbols of 'exaggerated grief'—as in John Morley's 1971 critique: 'The congealed romanticism that encapsulated Victorian family life, that produced the keepsake and sentimental ballad, and that effloresced in the Valentine, found its reverse expression in objects, poems, ceremonies, and clothes in remembrance of the defunct.'[81] Such criticism tends to judge surviving Victorian artefacts by later twentieth-century standards and assumptions. It neglects the significant role of visible symbols of remembrance in the natural dynamics of grief. We can only begin to understand the value of these commemorative symbols in nineteenth-century terms if we consider them in the context of the evidence for the Victorian family's experience of grief and mourning.

⚜ 15 ⚜

RITUALS OF SORROW
MOURNING-DRESS AND CONDOLENCE LETTERS

Mourning-Dress

Modern observers of nineteenth-century mourning rituals have tended to assume that all were of equal value and that mourning-dress was representative. The archival evidence suggests, however, that mourning-dress served a less useful purpose than many other rituals for the bereaved, and perhaps for that reason it has been an easy target for later critics. Its real value has been difficult to assess because far more evidence survives about the formal requirements of dress than about people's actual behaviour and attitudes; moreover, twentieth-century censure has distorted our view of the Victorians' own experiences and responses to bereavement.

The therapeutic value of Victorian mourning customs naturally depended on the nature and degree of the consolation they offered to the bereaved. Mourning-dress rules were based in part on traditional customary judgement regarding the most appropriate time required to work through grief. It was assumed that normally the period of mourning dictated by society would approximate to the period of personal grief. The dress regulations derived from the royal court procedure, which percolated down the social hierarchy during the eighteenth century when the code became more formalized and widespread in its social application. The strict dress code of the eighteenth and nineteenth centuries was applied most rigorously to widows, who were required to wear full black mourning for two years—non-reflective black paramatta and crape for the first year of deepest mourning, followed by nine months of dullish black silk, heavily trimmed with crape, and then three months when crape was discarded. Paramatta was a fabric of combined silk and wool or cotton; crape was a harsh black silk fabric with a crimped appearance produced by heat. Widows were allowed to change into the colours of half-mourning, such as grey and lavender, black and white, for the final six months. After 1820 the family firm of Courtaulds established a virtual monopoly of the manufacture of crape. From the 1840s to the 1880s Courtaulds exploited the commercial potential of crape to the full, aided by the introduction of fashion magazines for middle-class women, in which mourning costume was updated according to the latest season's fashions. Courtaulds' profits were increased by the belief that it was unlucky to keep crape in the house, which explains why many women kept renewing their mourning wardrobe and so few specimens of widows' costumes have survived.

Lou Taylor has argued, with some justification, that the harsh restrictions governing widows' clothing reflected the view of the wife's role held in nineteenth century middle- and upper-class British society. The drab, uncomfortable attire symbolized the perception that a wife's identity and sexuality were subsumed in her husband's and died with him.[1] It helped to place her beyond the marriage market. This was reinforced by the fact that the wearing of mourning-dress implied social isolation, since a widow could not accept formal invitations in the first year, except from close relatives, and had to avoid public places. By contrast with the rigid, formalized code for widows, men's clothes were not substantially altered by mourning requirements; in addition to their usual sombre suits, until about 1850 men had only to wear black mourning-cloaks, while black gloves, hatbands, and cravats were sufficient thereafter. The time of mourning was reduced for the bereaved other than spouses—the mourning period of a parent for a child, and vice versa, was twelve months, while six months was conventional for a brother or sister. Inevitably most of the evidence on mourning-dress relates to widows, who experienced the code in its most severe form.

Extravagance and social emulation were not uncommon in the mourning rituals of the expanding middle class, but it is important to view this question in a balanced manner, with an eye to the bias of the sources. The leading authorities on mourning etiquette, such as the journals *Queen* and the *Gentlewoman*, together with prescriptive advice manuals, were capable of absurd refinements; they could leave the impression that all Victorian widows were either social outcasts, subject to ancient taboos, or superficial and socially ambitious hypocrites. Victorian novelists, notably Charles Dickens, tended to ridicule extremes in mourning etiquette, enhancing the impression that widows were motivated more often by social emulation, convention, and vanity than genuine sorrow.

Twentieth-century psychologists and sociologists have generally agreed that most mourning rituals assist in providing a helpful rite of passage for the bereaved. Geoffrey Gorer concluded in his 1965 study that the wearing of mourning clothes identified the recently bereaved, thereby stimulating support and sympathy from the community. John Hinton argued in 1967 that mourning rituals were usually helpful in relating social customs to the feelings of the bereaved: 'During mourning the instinctive withdrawal from conviviality is fostered, with an expectation that social engagements will be limited. If not dressed in the black of deep mourning, the bereaved are expected to choose sombre garments which reflect their mood. Gay clothes which enhance the appearance would seem disrespectful or adjudged so symptomatic of human vanity as to be callous or near to wickedness.'[2] Parkes commented that it might help mourners if their clothes remind society that they feel 'heavy-hearted'.[3]

David Cannadine, a leading social historian, is more sceptical and takes issue with the modern consensus of psychologists and sociologists: 'it remains undemonstrated exactly how—if at all—the elaborate rituals of [Victorian] mourning actually helped to assuage the grief of the survivors'.[4] Some Victorians certainly shared Cannadine's view in relation to mourning-dress, which they criticized as a useless religious trapping. For example, an agnostic doctor, Keith Norman MacDonald, wrote a pamphlet in 1875 *On Death and How to Divest it of its Terrors*, attacking the misery inflicted by the Christian belief in a future of eternal punishment. He rejected the wearing of mourning-dress as 'a silly custom' which 'adds to the embarrassments' of mourners.[5]

The primary functions of mourning-dress in the Victorian period were to identify the mourner, show respect for the dead, elicit the sympathy of the community, and match the mourner's sombre mood. Basil Montagu recognized in 1840 that visible symbols of grief expressed the desire for sympathy in times of sorrow: 'In the mourning dress, the outward sign of sorrow, we call for the solace of compassion, for the kind words and looks of friends and for the chastened mirth of strangers, who, unacquainted with the deceased, respect our grief and recognize in silence the suffering that has been or will be theirs, the common lot of all the children of mortality.'[6] Victorian advice manuals on etiquette tended to highlight the argument that it soothed the sorrow of mourners to express it outwardly. Mrs Fanny Douglas insisted in 1890 that mourning-dress permitted those in genuine grief to express their feelings in a manner which might afford solace. Mrs John Sherwood maintained in *Manners and Social Usages* in 1884 that wearing black was a customary mark of respect for the deceased and afforded protection from unwanted intrusion on private grief: 'A mourning dress does protect a woman while in deepest grief against the untimely gayety of a passing stranger. It is a wall, a cell of refuge.'[7]

Undoubtedly the conventions of mourning-dress imposed a heavy burden on the women in early and mid-Victorian families, even when they could afford to pay dressmakers and to purchase materials from Courtaulds. Two examples from the Horsley family's experience in the 1850s will serve as illustrations, since the history of Victorian mourning fashion has been examined elsewhere.[8] The Horsleys were devout Anglicans who suffered deeply in this period on the family deaths of two young women, an elderly man, and three children. They were not particularly concerned with fashion for its own sake, but were anxious to follow the proprieties to show respect for their dead. Putting the family in mourning-dress was regarded as one of the necessary formalities to be dealt with at a time of death, like organizing the funeral, settling the estate of the deceased, and responding to condolence letters.

In 1857 John Horsley, the artist, lost his third son, Frank, from scarlet fever at the age of 7, as we have seen. John's mother, Elizabeth Horsley, looked after the three remaining children, while her son and daughter-in-law organized the funeral. Elizabeth Horsley corresponded with her daughter-in-law Rose about the arrangements for putting the children into mourning. They agreed that Walter and Hugh, aged 2 and 1, should wear their coloured 'common dresses' until proper black could be made up. Their frugal plan to utilize the children's existing clothes, where appropriate, was frustrated because the black merino dresses had been hanging in the sick-room when Frank died, and could not be used until the room was fumigated. However, Walter was to wear his cousin's black frock if it fitted. The boys' grandmother settled on black straw hats trimmed with plain black ribbon, but found it more difficult to reach a decision on the baby's cap border and trim.[9] If Elizabeth Horsley's three letters on the children's mourning clothes were read out of context it might appear that she was obsessed with the minutiae of mourning fashion; but other evidence shows that she was a capable 64-year-old grandmother trying to relieve her bereaved son and daughter-in-law of some of the necessary mourning duties.

Only a year later the family again suffered bereavement on the death of Elizabeth Horsley's 84-year-old husband, William, a composer of glees. The widow had her black paramatta dress, made up for Frank's death a year earlier, 'done up' and retrimmed with crape, so that it looked almost like new. A new best dress of paramatta was also made up by the dressmaker Miss Springer, its body covered almost entirely by deep black crape. Elizabeth's outdoor mourning costume included a shawl of paramatta deeply trimmed with crape, which must have been very warm in June. Her 39-year-old spinster daughter, Sophy Horsley, had a new black dress made up, with deep crape on the flounces and sleeves, and her pretty new bonnet was dyed black and trimmed with a crape veil. Her mother was horrified at Sophy's treatment of the new coloured bonnet, but Sophy insisted there was no point in not wearing it during her year of full mourning. Sophy borrowed a black dress covered with crape from her sister-in-law for her father's funeral, while she waited for Miss Springer to finish the new black dress. But she was only able to tolerate the hot paramatta and crape until the funeral tea, when she told her mother she could endure it no longer and changed into a cooler, if less appropriate, black costume. When Sophy's best black dress finally arrived from the dressmaker late on Saturday night, five days after the funeral, it was several inches too short, preventing Sophy from attending church the next day, since the borrowed dress had been returned. Such were the frustrating practical problems for bereaved women in the 1850s.[10] No doubt the Horsley women would have found the early weeks of grieving a little less difficult without the additional strain of concern about black costume.

Even at the height of Victorian extravagance in mourning ritual in the 1840s and 1850s some effort was made to economize where possible, as the Horsley archives indicate. The Sharpe family demonstrated a similar concern to be sensible and frugal. On the death of a cousin in 1848, Mary Reid advised her daughter Lucy Sharpe that, in view of the close family relationship, Lucy's sisters would wear slight mourning for a few weeks, but she added, 'We are busy looking out what can be altered and worn.' Five years later, on the death of Lucy Sharpe's elderly stepsister by marriage, Mary Reid helped organize her grandchildren's mourning clothes. She chose jackets that would serve once mourning was over, and sent off their old hats to be cleaned. Some new clothes must be bought, but she insisted that 'all things [should] be simple and good, no extra trimmings or fripperies'.[11]

The later Victorians presided over the reform of the worst excesses in mourning-dress through the efforts of the two Funeral and Mourning Reform Associations established in 1875 to simplify mourning ritual and reduce its expenses. Their aims were not to abolish the 'outward and visible signs of grief' for close relatives, but to abandon expensive material such as crape.[12] Even the *Queen* admitted in 1875 that mourning expenses were excessive, advising less wealthy women to 'use their common sense and discretion . . . a plain black dress is by no means inordinately costly'.[13] By the late Victorian period, advice manuals placed their emphasis on moderation, expressing impatience with the 'ghoul-like ghastliness of "ornamental" mourning, with its exaggerated absurdities and affectations'. As Mrs John Sherwood remarked, 'People of sense, of course, manage to dress without going to extremities in either direction.' She favoured simplifying mourning-dress and replacing the ubiquitous crape, so ugly and expensive, with more comfortable and economical black fabrics.[14] By the 1880s the decline in the demand for crape affected Courtaulds' profits, and the more rigid conventions began to relax.[15] Once more the 1870s and 1880s can be seen as a transitional period in relation to death, grief, and mourning.

From the 1860s the detailed references to mourning-dress in Victorian family archives are vastly reduced, indicating the success of funeral and mourning reform in relaxing the strictness of the social rules. It has to be said, however, that such references to mourning-dress are fewer than might be expected throughout the entire Victorian period. Black dress was generally taken for granted and was usually the least of the concerns of people suffering intense grief. Few women had both the money and the inclination to follow the dictates of the fashion plates, and many had the common sense to modify them according to their needs and pockets.

There are many more examples of moderation, common sense, and 'making do' in the family discussions on mourning-dress than of fashionable extravagance. Recently widowed Agnes Greig advised her sister-in-law in 1865 that she would be making little fuss about mourning clothes: 'we mourn in our hearts too deeply to make any parade'. She was 'living in a merino gown', though she had purchased 'a proper worsted one with crape' for formal occasions; she thought her sister-in-law Martha Somerville might prefer a dark navy-blue serge, with crape round the arm, which would look 'longer nice' than black serge.[16]

The late Victorians and Edwardians were even more modest and economical in their concessions to mourning fashion. Agnes Anson had to wear black in 1888, 'as public mourning is desired, but I can so manage that it will not cost us much'.[17] Victoria Dawnay had 'no black whatever' on Uncle Harvie's death in 1887, but did not think that would matter—'my clothes are all dark'.[18] On the death of her Aunt Margaret in 1889, Elizabeth Haldane thought her mother already had sufficient 'black things', except for a new black bonnet. Elizabeth had sent her own 'black dress body' for alteration, presumably because she had gained some weight since she last wore it.[19]

Mourning-dress performed a useful function in reminding friends and relatives that those most closely affected by the bereavement were likely to be in a state of depressive withdrawal for a number of months, not just the funeral week. For example, in 1896 two elderly spinsters, Elizabeth and Agnes King, were in deep mourning for their mother, who died two months before their niece's wedding. They wished to attend the wedding ceremony, 'black dresses and all', but did not feel 'quite up to joining any gathering of friends' afterwards. Their thoughts would be with the bride's dead grandmother, so that 'I think we should either break down altogether or else be too cold and quiet, like dampers on the happiness of others.'[20] In similar circumstances Mary Ann Rogers declined to attend a wedding in 1864 because she was in mourning for her daughter Louisa.[21] Weddings were often postponed if a close relative of bride or groom died, as when Elsie Blunt's wedding in 1884 was put off because the groom's mother died.[22] But other families sometimes decided the circumstances merited continuing with a small, quiet ceremony. When Harry Acland's mother died in 1878, three weeks before his wedding to Maggie Rogers, his prospective mother-in-law suggested that they continue as planned:

I feel you need Maggie more than ever now to help and comfort you—and to her too it would be very trying to be parted from you at this time. I think we must give her to you quietly, with no gathering even of the family—and you must take her away from the Church and be comforted in calling her your wife, though we cannot make a marriage feast as we had planned, our thoughts are all too heavy for that.[23]

Mourning customs undoubtedly restricted normal social activities, but the degree to which this was irksome depended on the proximity of the relationship, the social status of the mourner, and the depth of the sorrow. Sarah Acland did not go out at all while mourning her father in 1866, and had no regrets at declining invitations to dances and other social gatherings.[24] But families were often more reluctant to curtail their social activities following the deaths of those relatives further removed from their immediate circle. In December 1872 Lord Cowper told his mother about a ball they were planning at Panshanger, and asked whether they should cancel it because of the death of a cousin, Lady Constance Ashley. Lady Cowper's response was reminiscent of Jane Austen's concern for the social niceties. She was sorry that she herself could not attend the ball, 'but I think being so very intimate in with [Lord] Shaftesbury, I had better not. With respect to you and Katie it is quite another thing; and I don't think any one could expect you to put it off. They are not the same county, and she is only a cousin.'[25]

The chief expressions of criticism or of irritation about the etiquette of mourning were usually reserved for public ceremonial mourning required for royalty. Since such official ritual mourning was usually unrelated to private grief, it could be an imposition or an excuse for the kind of fashionable excess so often condemned. In 1857 Augusta Touzel warned her sister that the Duchess of Gloucester was rumoured to be dying: 'I don't know if you will take the trouble, but I intend taking a black Dress for if there should be a general mourning it would be very awkward not to have any wherewithal to appear respectable.' Two days later she saw the report of the Duchess's death in the paper with a notice of ten days' general mourning, so would appear in 'decent black'.[26] It must have been frustrating for Lady Lincolnshire's children to be forbidden to skate on the ice as usual in January 1892 because of the death of Queen Victoria's son Prince Eddy. Mary Chamberlain noted in her diary on the same occasion, 'all engagements given up'.[27] When King

Edward VII was seriously ill in May 1910 Audrey Wallas hoped he would not die at an 'inconvenient moment', though she had no intention of wearing more than 'a little black' whenever that moment came.[28] Even more tedious was the business of court mourning for foreign royalty; Lady Lincolnshire noted in her diary in June 1880 that they all had to go in mourning to Ascot because the Empress of Russia was dead.[29]

The value of mourning clothes to the recently bereaved is difficult to evaluate. The evidence suggests that wearing mourning-dress was not necessarily an intolerable burden for those in deep sorrow, nor did they view themselves as social pariahs, for black clothes often matched their sombre mood. None of these widows protested against the rigid and excessive demands of the ritual, though widows were undoubtedly the most strictly regulated. On the other hand, no widows explicitly stated that wearing weeds was helpful, except for Lady Stepney, who appreciated 'the outward acknowledgement of the inward mourning'.[30]

Condolence Letters

The evidence for the therapeutic value of condolence letters is far more positive than that for mourning-dress. Together with the funeral, these letters were a vital part of the important process of rallying the support and sympathy of friends, family, and community. Middle- and upper-class Victorians usually took trouble to write considered letters which would give comfort and show sympathy, and they assigned such letters priority in the time set aside each day for correspondence. They were often accomplished in the art of writing letters, not least condolence letters, though the modern reader may have some difficulty in evaluating them. The religious discourse which was such a fundamental part of Victorian consolation literature may seem sentimental or formulaic to modern eyes, but to Victorians it conveyed genuine meaning and comforted believers. As Lord Ilchester admitted on the death of his mother in 1842, 'the most heartfelt expressions become banal by repetition—though under present feelings the most commonplace ones are literally true'.[31] A high level of sensitivity and understanding of the process of grief, often founded on personal experience, characterized a large proportion of the thousands of condolence letters in these family archives.

Some of the most valued condolence letters were simple, brief, and written from the heart by people who knew and loved the deceased—people who shared the family's grief, and felt some relief in expressing their own sense of loss. They drew on one or more of the consolations of Christian faith, memory, time, sympathy, and love. Lady Cardwell's soothing letter to Lord

Selborne on the death of his wife, her dear friend Laura in 1885 was characteristic:

I know that nothing I can say can comfort you—I can only commend you to God— he will be to you a strong tower—in this dark hour. Surely no one was ever so blessed in a wife—and no one ever made another so happy as you did her.

The light that is quenched in her love—her wonderful interest and sympathy in one sore afflicted will make this world dark indeed to me now . . . Dear Lord Selborne you are much blessed in the children she has left you—They are like a part of herself. May God bless and comfort you all . . .[32]

This short letter chiefly offered spiritual consolation, powerfully reinforced by the memory of 'so blessed' a wife, and the comfort of the children who would always keep his wife's memory alive. It might be argued that this was a conventional letter using well-worn phrases, but it expressed genuine sorrow and sympathy, and its simple words carried conviction.

Many writers had themselves suffered bereavement, and their own experience provided an added dimension of understanding and sympathy. Such was the letter from Amelia Villiers on the death of Sir William Harcourt's wife, Thérèse, in 1863. Amelia had lost her husband, Henry Villiers, Bishop of Durham and uncle to Thérèse, two years earlier, and was certain that only those similarly afflicted could understand the 'utter desolation, the complete blight' of the loss of a spouse.[33] Sometimes the recently bereaved were still too immersed in their own sorrows to look outside themselves and offer positive consolation to others. George W. E. Russell wrote to A. J. Balfour on his brother's death in 1882 in the belief that his own great sorrow 'fires a kind of passport to the inner feelings of fellow-sufferers'; beyond sharing his own pain at considerable length he did little to alleviate Balfour's.[34]

The primary function of condolence letters was the offer of affection, sympathy, and support from family, friends, and community, complementing the rally of sympathizers at the funeral. In 1843 Jane Goulburn poured out her grief on her brother Harry's death in letters to her friend Louisa Cane, while restraining the expression of her feelings at home for the sake of her mother and immediate family. Louisa's responses conveyed a warm and supportive understanding of the agony of such a bereavement and the need to express this openly:

Never my darling Jane ask me to forgive you for pouring out your feelings to me. It is what I like. Indeed always do so without limit for I am sure it must be good for you. They must have a vent sometimes and I am sure for your dear Mothers sake you keep a great control on them. Besides we have the countenance of our blessed Saviour's example to weep for those we love so why should we not do so with our friends.

Louisa believed that 'it seems to soften grief and afford relief and comfort to the mind' to talk and write about it with friends and family. Early Victorian Evangelicals, schooled in the religion of the heart, were accustomed to the open expression of their deepest beliefs and feelings, to a greater degree than their grandchildren. However, Louisa did add that such intense grief should not be indulged to an 'undue degree', for 'it is not right to be always melancholy'.[35]

Victorian condolence letter writers offered affection and sympathy in abundance. Henrietta Martin, a beloved family governess, promised Dr Henry Acland all the help and strength 'that the love and sympathy of hundreds of friends can give you' on his wife's death in 1878.[36] Constance Leconfield comforted Evelyn Stanhope on her stepfather's death in 1886: 'Please remember that there is one whose heart is with you in deep affection and sympathy, far more than there are words to express.'[37] Many writers offered to spend time with the bereaved. William Somerville told his daughter in 1837 that he was pleased she would stay with their grieving friends: 'altho' one can do or say nothing to alleviate sorrow even the silent presence of a friend is a source of comfort'.[38] After the death of William Harcourt's first wife in childbirth in 1863, his sister Emily promised 'I shall be there when sent for . . . I can sit bye you and be there, as I know she would like it.'[39]

In addition to the promises of love and support, most condolence letters usually highlighted the two significant consolations of Christian faith and the memory of the loved one examined in earlier chapters. Spiritual comfort was offered by the majority of these correspondents, especially in the early and mid-Victorian periods, with an assurance that the familiar pieties would be soothing.

The condolence letters in 1856 on the death of 72-year-old Henry Goulburn, former Chancellor of the Exchequer, illustrate the common use of a religious discourse which drew on well-known Bible passages, devotional texts, and popular hymns. Many mourners wrote from the heart, offering the promise of solace based on the confident mutual Christian faith of writers and recipients. Richard Cane, for example, had recently been widowed, and mourned simultaneously for Henry Goulburn and his own young wife: 'Both are gone to that land where there is no more tears nor sorrow. Both have fallen asleep on the bosom of that Saviour, who lent them for a while to us. What a consolation is this to those who are left behind. I at least find it so.'[40] Whatever a modern reader may think of these words, a simple faith shines through them. All writers shared Lady Ripon's conviction that Henry Goulburn had 'gone to everlasting rest and peace', freed from human sorrows. Some wrote that he had 'gone to a better world' or to a 'World of eternal happiness'; others that 'he is with the God and Saviour whom he is known to have adored sincerely and served consistently'. Most justified their assurance of Henry's present blessedness by a reference to his good life and death, for he was 'in every respect a Christian'.[41] Again, where later Victorians placed greater emphasis on happy family meetings in the next life, early and mid-Victorians concentrated more on the union of their loved one with God.

The condolence letters conveyed to William Harcourt by his family and close friends in 1863 also promised that God alone could provide him with the strength to endure the loss. His sister Lady Rice was sure he would be given support from heaven to bear the terrible blow, reminding him that Thérèse's 'pure bright spirit' was now in heaven, 'freed from all suffering and sorrow', so that they should envy rather than grieve for her.[42] A characteristic example of Christian consolation was offered by his sister-in-law Lady Susan Harcourt:

One can only say God's will be done—and it is God's help *alone* that can be a support to us at such a time—but we have a firm trust and belief that *all* that God *sends* is for the best . . . and that he is a merciful and loving Father who does not afflict any of His Children except for some good end . . . As for *her*, now happy and at peace for ever, how can one grieve for her. The change to one so ready to go can only be to such joy that surely we could not wish her back in this world of trial and trouble . . . [She is] the happy Spirit at rest with God and out of the reach of Sin and Sorrow.[43]

Memory was also an important source of consolation for the bereaved, irrespective of their faith, and it was given prominence in most condolence letters. The day after the death of Lord Holland in 1840, Lord Lansdowne assured the widow that he had long loved her husband, 'whose memory I shall ever cherish near to my heart while I live'.[44] Mary Gladstone wrote in 1875 on the death of her young cousin May Lyttelton, 'All the bright memories of her will, as time goes on, stand out with ever increasing brilliancy and will soothe and soften the future for all who miss her so terribly.'[45] Many condolence letters promised to cherish the loved one's 'dear memory' and thankfully recalled shared experiences and the last meeting with the departed, especially if that was at the deathbed.[46] A sad letter from Auberon Herbert to his sister-in-law Lady Carnarvon on the death of his brother and her husband in 1890 underlined the comfort to be gained from the memory of a happy marriage: 'Your two lives have been so happy, so close, so true to each other, that you of all people, have no need for unhappiness. The only real unhappiness is where love has failed,—then I think death is a very very bitter thing. Nothing can take from you what you have been to each other, that remains the one the truest of all possessions.'[47]

The memories of the deceased which these letters evoked were uniformly favourable. Victorian writers of etiquette books, such as Mrs John Sherwood, explained that it was a necessary part of the process of mourning to idealize the deceased immediately after death:

It is a very dear and consoling thing to a bereaved friend to hear the excellence of the departed extolled, to read and re-read all of the precious testimony which is borne by outsiders to the saintly life ended—and there are few so hard-hearted as not to find something good to say of the dead: it is the impulse of human nature . . . and it comforts the afflicted.[48]

Modern psychologists, such as Beverley Raphael, share the view that idealization of the dead is essential in the early stages of mourning:

The bereaved may sincerely express warm sentiments and idealized views of the deceased, opinions which can on occasions contrast pathetically or ludicrously with an antipathy that had existed during life . . . If grief is deep, it may be some while before the deceased can be sincerely mourned for the imperfect person he truly was.[49]

Most of the Victorian tributes to the life and character of the dead were highly selective eulogies. For example, in 1844 Mary Somerville consoled her brother that his young wife, Montgomerie, 'has been perfected by suffering and has died the death of the righteous'.[50] Young wives and children were often remembered as angels, particularly in the early and mid-Victorian periods. On the death of Thérèse Harcourt in 1863, Constance Villiers insisted that '"perfection" is the only word to give to the Angel so lately on earth and now looking down on us from Heaven'.[51] In 1872 Agnes Greig mourned her mother-in-law, Mary Somerville, 'who was so lovely, so graceful, so elegant, and so full of love and affection for us all, and with the highest powers of intellect and cultivation united to all that is most to be prized in woman'.[52] Lady Iddesleigh's tribute to Lord Stanhope in 1905 was characteristic: '[Your husband's] goodness was so unpretending and his abilities and energies so steadily used in every good cause that I feel the world is poorer without him . . . An honored and a useful life is a great blessing to look back on and you will always have that memory to comfort you.'[53]

Only in the later months of the grieving process did the bereaved usually reassess their relationship with the deceased, considering the negative as well as the positive aspects in a more balanced way.[54] Kate Courtney's immediate response to the death of her brother-in-law Robert Holt in 1908 was honest but most unusual, and it was confined to the privacy of her diary: 'The papers—Liverpool especially—are full of Robert's virtues as a citizen and speak of him as a "leader" in politics which he was not . . . Husband of a woman far abler and bigger than himself but not gifted with calmness or adaptability he rather broke down amid ill health and elderly life.'[55]

The content and tone of condolence letters obviously varied greatly, according to the age of the deceased, the period in which they were written, and the faith of writer and recipient. It is instructive to compare the condolence letters received by the Goulburn family on the deaths of 30-year-old Harry in 1843 and his father, Henry, at 72 in 1856. Religious consolation was the overarching theme of both sets of many dozens of letters, but those for Harry were far more intensely emotional, even at times desolate and strident, than those for his father. Letters of sympathy on the death of the elderly politician found much to say of comfort to the family about his service to the nation. Friends were able to accept Henry's death more calmly than Harry's in the light of his long, worthy, and fulfilled life. The family doctor, for example, wrote, 'Pray remember, for your consolation, that his age was ripe—that he had fought a good fight—and that, if of any one, we may express a confident hope and belief that *he* has passed to a better world.'[56] Many writers emphasized that Henry Goulburn had a long lifetime of Christian preparation for his death: 'his preparation for the great change was not a matter of yesterday, but the work of many years in the laborious performance of his duty to his God and country'.[57] One friend reminded the family that Henry Goulburn died 'full of years and honour', and must have been looking forward to the end for some time, since no one desired extreme old age.[58]

But the condolence letters which had poured in to the Goulburn family thirteen years earlier on the death of a brilliant son in the prime of life were very different. Deaths of adult children between about 20 and 50 were untimely and unexpected, while they could be harder to cope with than deaths of younger children because of the years of emotional investment. Lady Ripon, a close family friend, sent wise advice to Henry Goulburn on his son's death. She acknowledged the parents' preparation during Harry's illness and their certainty of his 'present happiness'. But she understood that resignation to such an appalling blow took time: 'In the first bitterness of grief, these [sources of consolation] will not avail, as they will do some little time hence.'[59] Presumably she recognized that un-Christian responses, such as anger and bitterness, were possible in the early months, even on the part of the most saintly parents.

Several parents who had also lost children offered mutual condolences. John Thornton of Clapham thanked God that Harry Goulburn, like his own son, had attained at an early age all that the longest life might have secured for him 'in the world beyond the grave'. Thornton concluded, 'May God grant that when you and I are called to give up an account we may be as well prepared as he was!'[60] In Harry's case such sentiments appear to have been rather more than the usual exaggerated idealization of the dead person's earthly perfection. Another friend, H. V. Elliott, had also 'trodden your path of tribulation and well nigh sunk in it'. He understood the extremity of the Goulburns' grief because of his own loss, as well as his love and admiration for Harry. In a very emotional letter he requested permission to join the Goulburns in the weeping, intending to visit them next day: 'May the God of all comfort bind up your bleeding hearts.' Such language may seem ornate and extravagant today, but it conveyed real meaning for early Victorians, so familiar with the Bible and the hymnal, particularly when it was so evidently written from the heart.[61] It reminds us that early Victorian men were not afraid of expressing their emotions. Lord Bathurst also knew from sad personal experience that 'one is never as much prepared to meet a Calamity as one thinks one is'.[62]

More than any other death, that of a promising young adult reminded friends and family of their own mortality, inviting them to contemplate their own preparedness if death struck prematurely. Harry Goulburn's death provoked many such intimations of mortality, particularly from other males in his own family. Serjeant Edward Goulburn, barrister and brother of Henry Goulburn, was strongly affected by his nephew's untimely death, which led him to contemplate Harry's greater piety despite his relative youth:

I wish my dear brother that these warnings may make upon my cold and worldly heart an impression not to be erased; but alas! I find that as I advance in Life and get nearer and nearer to my long home my thoughts of Eternity are less vivid than they used to be when I was almost at the starting point of Existence . . . Help thou mine unbelief is my constant prayer.[63]

Most of all, Harry's cousin Revd Edward Meyrick Goulburn pointed to the didactic value of this death. Revd Goulburn was a pompous theologian, whose condolence letter from Oxford might have come straight out of one of his theological treatises, and certainly owed something to Jeremy Taylor's *Exercises of Holy Dying*. He thought no family could have sustained a more severe loss, but 'it may prove salutary in proportion to its bitterness', encouraging the family to strengthen their prayer and devotional exercises. All Christians needed to be solemnly reminded that time was short and that a sick-bed was not the place for 'working out our salvation'.[64] This kind of edifying lecture was never prompted by the death of a baby or very young child, who were assumed to be almost free of sin, and it was less frequently called forth by the death of an old person, who had more time to prepare for death. But it was a common response to the untimely death of the adult child: *memento mori!*

Condolence letters on the death of a baby or very young child also had their special features. Charles Horsley's letter to his brother John on the death of his young son Edward in 1854 was characteristic: 'For the dear child one can hardly grieve, as he has been taken at a time of life when hardly any responsibility can attach to his actions, and is at rest and doubtless *happy*, and *saved many* a struggle and temptation.'[65] Three years later, on the death of his third small son, Frank, John Horsley's sister-in-law Mary Haden was 'quite stifled with my tears in remembering the dear little bright form' who once played so happily with her own children. As a mother, she understood how difficult it was, on the death of a young child, to pray honestly that God's will be done. But she knew John was a true Christian who accepted that 'whom He loveth—He chasteneth'. When time had soothed and sanctified his grief, once again he would see this death, like the other two, as 'a disguised mercy . . . He is now with spirits as loving as your own, freed from the ills of life and mortality.'[66] Most writers mentioned the importance of family support, but their chief focus was on spiritual consolation—John's faith in God's mercy and his Christian resignation to God's will, 'for his is a truly Christian heart and spirit'. The ultimate consolation for the father was the knowledge that 'his little one is safe with its mother in the merciful care of God'.[67]

Condolence letters also varied greatly according to whether they were written in the early Victorian years or later. The Horsley, Harcourt, and Goulburn condolence letters demonstrate the central reliance on Christian consolation in the earlier period, but the content, emphasis, and tone of such letters of sympathy underwent a slow but significant change in the later Victorian and Edwardian periods. The major causes of this change were the decline in Evangelical fervour and the increase in secularism and agnosticism. Most writers no longer expressed the pious certainties of those who consoled the Goulburns, Horsleys, Taits, Gladstones, Lytteltons, Harcourts, and Aclands in earlier decades. There were many more short notes, trite phrases, and platitudes from writers who often seemed to lack faith but had found no adequate consolatory substitute. The Marquess of Donegall wrote to Lady Stanhope on the death of her father-in-law in 1875, but his only consoling thought was that death 'alas! must happen to us all, sooner or later'.[68] On the death of Ramsay MacDonald's son David in 1910, several writers offered love and sympathy and any practical help possible, but regretted that 'there *are* no words' to offer any genuine consolation.[69]

This change in condolence letters is further demonstrated by comparing those on the death of 87-year-old John Horsley, the artist, in 1903 with those on the death of his children half a century earlier, or on Henry Goulburn's death in 1856. The Edwardian letters were mostly brief and formal and emphasized the writers' esteem for John Horsley's memory. They paid tribute to his temporal rather than his spiritual qualities, unlike the letters of the 1840s and 1850s; his 'cheery companionship' and 'sweet temper' were highlighted rather than Christian virtues such as resignation and spiritual preparedness. The religious content had disappeared entirely in many letters, and in the remainder its role was much less significant. The few Christian sentiments were usually phrased in formulaic terms, such as 'May God in His mercy comfort you.' Very few referred to hopes of immortality or family reunions in the afterlife. One writer comforted the family with the assurance that 'the parting is only for a short time', with no elaboration. Another reminded the widow that 'the sure and certain hope of everlasting life is the consolation you have'. But in 1903 these Christian comforts were unusual.[70]

Writers of condolence letters seem to have found the task difficult when writing to an agnostic or a former Christian who had moved to more unorthodox beliefs. This may explain the particularly bleak letters which reached Edith Lyttelton, a spiritualist, on the death of her husband, Alfred, in 1913. Even committed Christians appear to have avoided use of their customary messages of Christian consolation, stressing instead time and memory, and taking refuge in commonplace remarks. One writer suggested that Alfred's death was a testimony to 'the great living inextinguishable quality of life itself . . . Life and death are just great opportunities to prove our worth.' A month later, reflecting on the failure of her first letter to offer any comfort, she tried again, but could only suggest that time would help: 'the personal blank is agonising and it just has to be borne and endured till time helps the pain'. Another correspondent in 1913 also suggested that little would help Edith in her 'unbearable' grief but time itself: 'It is true time is the healer. People always say that those who feel very acutely and deeply get over sorrow the quickest . . . Human nature could not bear the agony of desolation indefinitely . . . peace and capacity for life return.'[71] By contrast, early and mid-Victorian writers usually avoided emphasis on the consolation of time, because they appreciated that few mourners wished to be told that they would forget the deceased, while time itself offered no immediate consolation. Mary Barham responded to a condolence letter from a friend on the death of her son in 1870, 'You are quite right Maria, it is no comfort, but actual pain, to be told that time will lessen one's grief.'[72]

Recipients of condolence letters paid warm tribute to their value as a source of sympathy, support, and consolation. Many Victorians, including the Queen herself, seem to have found '*expressed* sympathy very healing'.[73] General Charles Fox testified to the importance of condolence letters on his father's death in 1840: 'If anything under such misery can soothe it is the universal feeling! the Letters that come full of sympathy for poor Mama and of Respect for him.'[74] Caroline Cane found the 'multitude' of letters on her father's death in 1853 'all on the one sad subject . . . a very great comfort', because of both the affectionate sympathy shown to her and the great esteem demonstrated for him.[75] One of the most powerful tributes to the value of such expressions of sympathy came from Aubrey Harcourt in 1876 on his grandmother's death:

The universal sympathy which has flowed in upon us from all quarters, from relations, friends, and in some cases from entire strangers would, if anything could, lessen the terrible blow which we are now doing our best to bear. Many who like yourself have known what it is to lose a loved one, have all agreed in saying that the heartfelt sympathy of friends . . . is the best human consolation that can be offered to the bereaved.[76]

Archbishop Tait noted in his private journal on his wife's death in 1878, 'telegrams and letters of condolence poured in. All felt for us from the Queen to the Mothers' meeting at Lambeth, and the letters soothed our souls.'[77] On her father's death in 1879 Louisa Lane was comforted 'to find how *every one* loved him, such expressions of love and sympathy flow in alike from high and low'.[78] After her husband's assassination in 1882 Lucy Cavendish was sustained and 'protected and wrapped round as with soft cotton wool with the sense of love and sympathy all round'.[79] Constance Flower thanked Marion Bryce for her letter of condolence on her husband's death in 1894: 'the love shown to him does help me . . . I long and cling to those who cared for him.'[80]

   The overwhelming affirmation of the value of condolence letters continued in the Edwardian period. Mary Herbert wrote on the death of her father, Lord Acton, in 1902, 'it *does* help to see how much his friends mourn with us . . . My Mother was made happier by Mr. Bryce's beautiful letter.'[81] On her mother's death in 1903, Mary Bryce wrote: 'We have received over 100 letters and cards together, and there is such a wonderful spontaneity of feeling about the sympathy—a real genuine feeling of admiration and reverence for her that is very touching . . . One does feel grateful for so much sympathy.'[82] Few negative comments on condolence letters have survived. In 1859 Lady Mary Fox considered them tiresome interruptions to the performance of the 'sad painful duties' of the funeral week.[83] Archbishop Tait in 1878 and many others before and after would have argued, to the contrary, that 'reading and answering so many kind letters' was a vital component of those sad duties and one which helped pass 'the gloomy days . . . as well as could be expected'.[84] The critics of condolence letters were overwhelmingly out-numbered by those who paid warm tribute to their therapeutic value. No such testimony survives to the usefulness of mourning-dress, which could undoubtedly be a burden to widows, especially to those of little means.

❧ 16 ☙

CHRONIC AND ABNORMAL GRIEF
QUEEN VICTORIA, LADY FREDERICK CAVENDISH, AND EMMA HADEN

T HE MAJORITY OF BEREAVED MEMBERS OF THE VICTORIAN FAMILIES IN this study seem to have worked through their grief in the first two years after bereavement. They usually achieved some sort of resolution, whether through Christian faith, the memory of the loved one, family support, professional work, re-engagement in family and community activity, or remarriage. Chronic and obsessive grief was very rare among these nineteenth-century families, probably more so than today. It was usually an extreme response to the death of a spouse or an adult son or daughter which took place in extraordinary and acutely distressing circumstances, including suicide and other violent, sudden, or premature deaths. Only four well-documented examples survive in these extensive family archives. Ann Rogers's inconsolable grief and her obsessive visits to her son's grave for many years after his suicide at the age of 17 in 1876 have already been examined. In addition to Queen Victoria's reaction to Prince Albert's death, this chapter will consider Lady Frederick Cavendish's response to the assassination of her husband in 1882, and Emma Haden's prolonged grief after the death of her favourite daughter in 1858.

While the evidence shows that chronic grief was most uncommon, it nevertheless requires exploration, in part to explain the Victorian antecedents to the chronic grief on a mass scale which followed the terrible deaths in the Great War. It is also necessary to examine chronic grief more carefully to correct misleading impressions of its incidence. The image of Queen Victoria as the eternal widow of Windsor has been so pervasive that she has sometimes been seen as representative, rather than the reverse. Lou Taylor describes the Queen as 'the middle-class ideal of Christian widowhood' who turned her mourning for Albert 'into a cult which dominated most of the rest of her life. Her example was admired, respected and copied . . . by many Victorian ladies.'[1] Philippe Ariès also contributed to this fallacious view with his argu-ment that mourning in the nineteenth century became exaggerated and ostentatious, as survivors became increasingly reluctant to accept the death of their loved ones: 'The nineteenth century is the era of mourning which the psychologist of today calls *hysterical* mourning.'[2] David Cannadine has apparently supported this view of Victorian mourning and its consequences in an otherwise valuable scholarly essay on the early twentieth century:

The excessive concentration of [Victorian] mourning did not so much help the bereaved to come to terms with their loss and make a new life for themselves, but actually robbed them of the will to recover, and condemned them to spend their remaining years more obsessed with death than was either necessary or healthy—as exemplified most spectacularly in the case of Queen Victoria.[3]

Cannadine's sweeping claim may be justified only in a minority of extraordinary cases, such as those of Queen Victoria, Lucy Cavendish, Ann Rogers, and Emma Haden, and this chapter will suggest that factors other than mourning rituals were responsible for their chronic grief.

Queen Victoria has been cited as the archetypal Victorian mourner, whose influence on nineteenth-century mourning behaviour was 'supreme'. Her experience of bereavement merits closer analysis to determine how far her grief was either typical or normal.[4] Queen Victoria's father died when she was a baby and her search for a father-figure included Lord Melbourne and culminated in the Prince Consort. Her love for Albert was overwhelming, involving powerful dependency, even in matters of state. Victoria was highly emotional, prone to what Albert called 'combustibles' and temperamental nervousness. Her response to her mother's death in March 1861, aggravated by guilt and remorse, led to a nervous breakdown. She nursed her sorrow in isolation, her 'unremitting grief' arousing rumours that her mind was unbalanced. Victoria had barely begun to recover from her mother's death when Albert died suddenly of typhoid in December 1861. The doctors had concealed the gravity of his illness from the Queen, so 'this frightful blow has left her in utter desolation', as Mary Ponsonby noted. Yet the initial stage of numbness was unusually long, and the Queen's household was surprised at her calm behaviour, instead of the further breakdown they anticipated.[5]

Victoria's mourning involved the 'mummification' of Albert, leaving his rooms and belongings undisturbed, as if he might return from the dead at any time, with his clothes laid out each day together with hot water and a towel. Soon after his death Victoria told the Belgian King: 'My life as a *happy* one is ended! The world is gone for me! . . . I live on with him, for him; in fact I am only outwardly separated from him, and only for a time.'[6] She confessed to Lord Canning:

To lose one's partner in life is . . . like losing half of one's body and soul, torn forcibly away . . . But to the Queen—to a poor helpless woman—it is not that only—it is the stay, support and comfort which is lost! To the Queen it is like *death* in life! . . . and she feels alone in the wide world, with many helpless children . . . to look to her— and the whole nation to look to her—now when she can barely struggle with her wretched existence! Her misery—her utter despair—she *cannot* describe! Her only support . . . is in the firm conviction and certainty of his nearness, his undying love, and of their eternal reunion![7]

Victoria was only 42 on Albert's death, but she continued to grieve for the next twenty years, instead of the two or three years which her subjects would have understood and which the rules of etiquette endorsed. She withdrew from public life and shut herself away with her family and household, seeing her ministers as little as possible. It took her three years to approach a state of spiritual resignation to the will of God. A prolonged depression led her to fear that the pressure of royal business on top of her grief was literally driving her mad. Rumours circulated that she was insane, and the press increasingly condemned her seclusion and neglect of official obligations. The Queen's subjects generally considered her response to death so exaggerated as to be shocking and most certainly abnormal. The campaign against her seclusion reached its peak by 1869–70, eight years after Albert's death, fuelled by yet another refusal to open Parliament. The Queen's gradual recovery in the 1870s was aided by her adoption of the role of matriarch to her enormous family, and encouraged by Disraeli. Yet every move out of seclusion seemed to Victoria a betrayal of her idealized husband, and she felt guilty that her grief was becoming less powerful.

There is no doubt that Victoria suffered intensely during the dozen or so years after her bereavement. She experienced chronic and prolonged depression which left her afraid for her sanity. She was quite literally crippled with grief. The first decade of bereavement was characterized by persistent 'nervous' ill health and physical disorders such as exhaustion, irritability, and gout. Those close to her differed as to the remedy, but agreed about the gravity of her debility. The Queen's physician, Sir William Jenner, maintained in 1871 that 'these nerves are a form of madness, and against them it is hopeless to contend'. Victoria's lady-in-waiting Lady Augusta Stanley considered the Queen self-indulgent and neurotic, rather than mad: she was best when 'taken out of herself—taken out of Doctors and maladies and nerves'.[8]

Psychologists today would conclude that Victoria's was a classic case of chronic grief—an obsessive preoccupation with the dead person, causing severe depression for many years after bereavement. Psychiatrists and anthropologists such as Colin Murray Parkes, John Bowlby, and Geoffrey Gorer have studied chronic grief among random samples of 'ordinary' people, as opposed to psychiatric patients. They conclude that chronic grief is a pathological disorder, characterized by its prolonged duration, intense pining, and severe distress, which are sufficient to impair working capacity and cause social withdrawal. According to Parkes, 'Years after bereavement many of them were still preoccupied with memories of the dead person, pining intensely and severely distressed by any reminder.' Approximately 10 per cent of Gorer's sample and 13 per cent of the London widows studied by Parkes were still in a state of chronic despair and incapacitating depression more than a year after bereavement. Other studies report 'no less high an incidence'.[9]

Such studies suggest that certain antecedent influences help to determine reactions to bereavement. Among the predeterminants of an unfavourable outcome, Parkes includes the loss of a parent during childhood, the death of a spouse in a dependent relationship, and a sudden, untimely death with no previous warnings. He finds that younger women were more likely to experience difficulties in dealing with bereavement, especially if they were 'grief-prone' and had previously responded to death with excessive grief.[10] Judged by such criteria, Queen Victoria should be regarded as an 'exemplar of chronic grief',[11] criticized and misunderstood by contemporaries for her excesses. She was certainly neither the archetypal Victorian mourner nor the model widow. Nor can we blame elaborate mourning rituals for her condition—that is to confuse grief with mourning, and the experience of sorrow with its outward expression. The explanation probably lies in the predetermining influences, such as her lonely childhood, her dependence on Albert, her extreme reaction to her mother's death, and the sudden, premature death of her husband. Jenner's diagnosis of 'a form of madness', ten years after Albert's death, was not far removed from today's psychological verdict.

My study of extensive nineteenth-century family archives has revealed remarkably few well-documented examples of chronic grief, except for Queen Victoria, Lucy Cavendish, Emma Haden, and Ann Rogers, and certainly no incidence as high as Gorer's 10 or Parkes's 13 per cent. Other rare cases which were not so fully documented included a small number of famous men in public life, who were similar to Queen Victoria in certain obvious respects. Lord Aberdeen, for example, had a lonely and disturbed childhood; his father died when Aberdeen was only 7 and he lived with strangers from the age of 11. His beloved wife, Catherine, died in 1812 after seven years of mutual contentment and total commitment. Aberdeen, at the age of 28, was devastated, and grieved for his idolized Catherine throughout his life. He believed that her ghost visited him almost daily and for a year recorded her appearances in his diary in Latin. No woman could replace Catherine in his affections, but he married again after three years for the sake of his three motherless daughters and because of his need for an heir. His second wife's jealousy of these daughters increased his trauma when they all died in the 1820s.[12] There are some similarities with Joseph Chamberlain's experience. He lost his first two wives in childbirth, the first in 1863 and the second twelve years later. Chamberlain was left mourning two wives, with six motherless children. His prolonged sorrow and bitterness evidently exacerbated his cold reserve, acid temperament, and introspection, until his third marriage to Mary Endicott in 1888 finally gave him some domestic happiness, and helped to reduce the bitterness he associated with death.[13]

Ramsay MacDonald suffered similarly after his wife's death in 1911, which left him in a state of shock for some weeks, followed by 'a horrible reaction'.[14] As he explained to friends, he was 'one of those unfortunate people who sorrow alone'. A month after Margaret's death he feared that 'if work will not give me peace I do not know what I shall do', but he was never able to release his grief. As David Marquand noted, 'there was no catharsis; the wound never healed'. The reserved, aloof parts of MacDonald's personality predominated in the absence of his wife's warm companionship. When asked why he never remarried, he replied: 'My heart is in the grave.' This grief and loneliness marred his children's home life, while he tried to find forgetfulness through his work. His son Malcolm remembered his father's grief as 'absolutely horrifying to see': 'This terrible tear-stained agony of grief' haunted the first anniversary of her death, and the twenty-five that followed.[15] Like Lord Aberdeen a century earlier, MacDonald's lonely, insecure childhood, without family life and comfort, made him exclusively dependent on a loving wife and vulnerable to chronic grief on her death. Each functioned effectively enough in public life to become Prime Minister, but both continued to mourn for the rest of their lives, without Chamberlain's consolation of a contented remarriage. The elevated political position of people like Victoria, Aberdeen, Chamberlain, and MacDonald perhaps also left them more personally isolated on the death of a spouse.

Victoria, Aberdeen, and MacDonald suffered chronic and abnormal grief, which was a highly unusual response to death in the fifty-five or so families I have examined. Lady Frederick Cavendish was another widow who suffered in an extraordinary manner, though none of her large family of siblings or cousins were similarly afflicted. Her experience has been selected for a more detailed case-study because the evidence is unusually rich, and because the earlier chapter on deaths in the Lyttelton and Gladstone families has already delineated the contrasting 'normal' experience.

Lucy Lyttelton was born in 1841, the second child of the fourth Baron Lyttelton and Mary Glynne, whose sister, Catherine, married W. E. Gladstone. Lucy had three sisters and eight brothers, besides close companionship with her seven Gladstone cousins. Her childhood seems to have been generally contented; unfortunate episodes with indifferent governesses were counterbalanced by affectionate parents and a deep family commitment to the Anglican Church. The course of her life, however, was profoundly affected by four family deaths—those of her mother in 1857 when Lucy was 16, her sister May in 1875, her father's suicide in 1876, and her husband's assassination in 1882.

When Lucy's beloved mother, Mary, died of heart disease on 17 August 1857, her prolonged illness and death were described in the lengthy memorial examined earlier. Lucy was then an impressionable adolescent, regarded by her family as gentle, sweet-tempered, and devout. She spent countless hours by her dying mother's bedside. Like the rest of the family, she entered in her father's deathbed memorial the daily minutiae of her mother's conversation, her medical treatment, and her growing discomfort. Lucy reported on 15 August: 'it was a miserable uncomfortable day, and she spoke of going from us'. Next day the two eldest children, Meriel and Lucy, were woken with the news that all hope was gone. The girls received their mother's final farewell: 'I am going away from you. I did not think it would have been so soon.' Lucy described the crowded room with the children in their nightgowns amid considerable confusion. Meriel and Lucy stayed while their uncle Revd William Lyttelton administered Holy Communion. Lucy heard her mother say she was not sorry now to leave: 'all fear and reluctance were gone'. Although Lord Lyttelton told Lucy that her mother would probably not suffer much pain at the very end, she clearly found her mother's death an agonizing experience, as she watched her 'breathless and cold, restless and panting'. Lucy was in the next room when her mother had a 'fearful spasm' and heard the 'moaning and gasping' of great pain. Just before she died, Mary Lyttelton said 'goodbye' once again to each child and kissed them one by one 'with icy lips'.[16]

Lucy's experience of her mother's death, recorded in detail in the family memorial, illustrates the ordeal involved for a sensitive 16-year-old girl. It is evident that Lady Lyttelton herself feared that Lucy would suffer more than her other children. The day before her death, Mary asked Lucy to repeat the hymn 'Nearer my God to Thee', but when Lucy broke down she said, 'Poor Locket, it's hard on you.' Later the dying woman spoke to her sister Catherine Gladstone about Lucy, expressing her fear of 'a danger to Lucy of indulging in a sort of luxury of grief'.[17] Other members of the family were aware of this aspect of Lucy's temperament as the years passed. Mary Gladstone, Lucy's cousin, noted in 1881, 'Neville [Lucy's brother] cannot understand anything in the least morbid. He is very impatient with this side of Lucy.'[18]

At first Meriel took their mother's place but when Meriel married in 1860, Lucy in turn became mistress of Hagley and surrogate mother to her siblings, until her own marriage in 1864. Lucy was happily married to Lord Frederick Cavendish for eighteen years, combining a busy life as a politician's wife with numerous philanthropic and church commitments. Her diary shows how much she enjoyed and treasured the precious time she was able to spend alone with 'my Fred', even after many years of marriage. A typical diary entry in 1881 noted, 'Then came the joyful moment of meeting my Fred at the station about 3. Drove off deliciously together.' Days or hours snatched alone together were described as 'honeymoon' days, or 'Darby and Joan' afternoons.[19] Her diary during the years of her marriage portrays a somewhat naïve, serious, and sensitive woman who was deeply religious and genuinely good— in fact the epitome of the ideal Victorian woman.

The second tragic death for Lucy was that of her beloved younger sister May, who died of typhus fever in March 1875. Once again, Lucy contributed substantially to a long family memorial written during May's last illness. After a month spent keeping frequent watch by her sister's bedside, Lucy reported on 4 March, 'After much discomfort, a look like death has come over May's face . . . it was pitiful to hear the altered voice, and see her beautiful tall figure wasted and helpless, and the face hectic, like advanced consumption.'[20] Lucy became severely depressed after her sister's death, though she always endeavoured to conceal this melancholy streak in her nature. Her childlessness was probably a contributory factor to this depression, especially in a year when her sister Lavinia and her cousin Agnes Wickham each celebrated the birth of their children. But her diary leaves no doubt that May's death was the primary cause; a visit to her husband's family home, Chatsworth, in November 1875 reminded Lucy all too vividly of May:

My heart grows heavy with thoughts of May, who came here just this time last year . . . The changes and losses seem to thicken round one, and there is something strangely sad and pathetic in the sort of diligent way one closes up the ranks and goes on and on with the old ways, as if here we had an 'abiding city'; while all the time we hear the clear voices within telling us that everything vanishes away.[21]

Her cousin Mary Gladstone became concerned about Lucy's state that same month, and sent a cry for help to her mother, Catherine Gladstone: 'Do give your mind a little to cheering up Lucy. She must not be allowed to get so low ... She is so bright in company that no-one guesses her wretched depressions.'[22]

But Lucy had little time to recover from May's death before she suffered the far greater shock of her father's suicide in April 1876. The Christian taboo against suicide, based on respect for life and concern for the immortal soul, was still powerful in 1876, as we saw in Henry Rogers's case. The trauma of suicide in a deeply religious late Victorian family was prodigious, despite the mitigating circumstances. Lord Lyttelton had suffered for years from temporary but recurring bouts of acute melancholia which intensified with age, and the ultimate depression may well have been precipitated by May's death. Lucy recounted the tragedy in her diary, exacerbated for her because her father's suicide took place while she was away from home:

It has been God's will to send us a terrible anguish ... it seemed that he had entered upon a different and darker stage: utter lassitude and hopeless distress, with occasional paroxysms of misery. Never any delusion or altered feeling towards any of us, but *true* perplexities all exaggerated ... God only knows what his anguish has been these many weeks past, deepening and deepening upon him ... [On Easter Tuesday] came upon him what we do indeed believe was a messenger of release (God seeing that His true and loving servant could no longer bear the anguish), a momentary and over-mastering paroxysm. Not knowing what he did, he rushed away from the man who was always with him in his room and fell over the banisters: we shall never know if it was in any degree accidental or not, but we *do* know he was as unaccountable as if a lightning-stroke had fallen on him ... And at a little past midnight God took him to His Eternal Peace.[23]

In this account Lucy emphasized the pathological nature of the recurrent bouts of severe depression, her father's inability to control his actions at the end, his continuing faith in God, and the benevolent role of the Almighty in his final release from suffering. She permitted no question about the morality of his death.

Lord Lyttelton remained unconscious after the fall, and died soon after his son-in-law Edward Talbot read the commendatory prayer. Mary Gladstone arrived a few hours later to find 'all in agony of grief; the piteous feeling was, as Edward Talbot said, "that such a Christian life should not have a Christian end"'. Even so, the family's faith enabled them to bear the tragedy with remarkable fortitude, as Mary assured her mother: 'You would be astonished how good and brave and natural they all are ... The horror of it seems lost in the deep faith ... There is nothing morbid or bitter or rebellious in the grief.'[24] For the family it was essential to emphasize the strength of Lord Lyttelton's Christian faith, to counteract the shame of such a death. They dreaded the state of mind of Charles Lyttelton, the eldest son, when he read the newspapers, since they could not contact him. The verdict of the coroner's inquest was stated on the death certificate: 'Internal injury and shock from a fall. Suicide. Temporary unsound mind.'[25] Even in one of that minority of suicides which actually justified the verdict of 'unsound mind', the family found it very hard to shake off the sense of horror and shame which their Church and society still attached to death by suicide. People outside the immediate family, such as the Aclands, were merely informed that Lord Lyttelton sustained a bad fall downstairs which resulted in a 'concussion of the brain'.[26]

Lucy's diary reveals little of her grief, but her eldest sister, Meriel, commented years later that her father's suicide overwhelmed Lucy for a time, even more than her husband's murder.[27] Mary Gladstone considered the prospect of Lucy's grief 'dreadful. Oh, I can't bear to think of her.'[28] Lucy returned from Ireland to London and found some consolation in the numerous letters of condolence which showed how deeply her father was loved: 'Hardly one but calls it a "noble life"; and in the light of it the awful darkness at the end seems to shrink to a point.'[29]

Six years later, when Lucy was 41, Lord Frederick Cavendish was brutally murdered by Irish extremists in Phoenix Park, Dublin, on 6 May 1882, the day he arrived to take up his new position as Chief Secretary for Ireland. Lucy's uncle W. E. Gladstone had committed himself to settle the formidable Irish question when he became Liberal Prime Minister for the second time in 1880. Determined to place the emphasis on conciliation rather than coercion, he chose for the task his niece's husband, a man he loved dearly. Cavendish was widely liked and respected, though not all his colleagues shared Gladstone's high estimate of his political and intellectual capacity. Whatever his merits as a politician, Lord Frederick's assassination raised him to the ranks of martyr and near-saint. Lucy's cousin Revd Stephen Gladstone proclaimed in a memorial sermon, 'Oh, Irish hearts, he died for you, as well as by the hands of cruel men amongst you. Oh, English hearts, he died for the wicked tyranny, the awful selfishness, the bloody cruelty of many of your forefathers. Let both countries be conscience-stricken with a common shame and sorrow.'[30] The day after the murder, the Prime Minister composed and sent to Lucy a sentimental poem of nineteen verses, including the lines:

> O pure true soul! O happy lot!—
> This victim of the murderer's knife
> That bleeding lies, perchance is not
> The prey of Death, but pledge of Life.

> On Reconcilement's altar laid,
> This high peace-offering may await
> The work of angel-hosts to aid,
> And turn to joy a nation's wail.

The widow had to bear the burden of a national sacrifice to 'purge a blot from history's page—To end a tale of woe and sin'.[31]

Lucy's relatives heavily underlined the sacrificial nature of Lord Frederick's death in their personal words of condolence to the widow, as well as in their poetry and sermons. Soon after her sister Meriel Talbot broke the news to her on 6 May, William and Catherine Gladstone came to see her at about midnight. The Prime Minister's first words to his niece were, 'Father, forgive them, for they know not what they do. Be assured it will not be in vain.' Lucy's diary recorded her answer: 'Across all my agony there fell a bright ray of hope, and I saw in a vision Ireland at peace, and my darling's life-blood accepted as a sacrifice, for Christ's sake, to help to bring this to pass.'[32]

Lucy's sacrificial response to her husband's assassination surpassed even the elevated expectations of her family, and confirmed their belief in the strength of her faith. Six months after the murder she wrote her own account during a religious retreat, emphasizing that only her Christian faith enabled her to bear the horror of Freddy's sudden and violent death. She interpreted Gladstone's midnight message as a vital assurance from God that 'my darling's life was not given in vain: thus his death, and my sorrow, might, for Christ's sake, be accepted as a sacrifice'. This first ray of hope never entirely deserted her through 'the dark, blank months emptied of joy':[33]

No word or presentiment of warning was granted me: one minute I was crowned with the fullness of earthly joy and love—my life full to the brim of hope and interest—the next, all lay shattered around me in one dark wreck, and with what circumstances of horror and fear! How was it that reason and faith and nerves did not give way: how was it that I did not sink down into despair? . . . The Eternal God was my Refuge, and underneath were the Everlasting Arms . . . He soothed me, even by the very exhaustion of grief, so that I could sleep.

Even in the first ten days or so, when she woke in the early dawn, vividly conscious of her overwhelming loss, she still had a sense of 'some mighty Protection'.[34]

A deeply religious young woman who was devoted to her family and in a state of shock perhaps had little choice in this terrible situation but to accept the heroic role assigned to her by her family. Mary Gladstone noted in her diary the day after the murder that 'Lucy had borne it wonderfully . . . her splendid goodness and faith had indeed triumphed in this bitter hour.'[35]

Mary reported on 7 May, 'I never saw anything like it, [Lucy] thinking of everyone, counting up her blessings, her 18 years of unclouded married life. She will never get over it, but she is so good she will get through it.'[36] Lavinia Talbot admired her sister's courage and patience, whilst her 'divine strength . . . fills me with almost a joyous amazement that Christ did so manifest Himself in us'.[37] Lucy's cousin Agnes Wickham seemed to take Lucy's 'wonderful state of mind' rather for granted only three days after the assassination: 'Surely such a consistent life of faith and *effort* as hers must bring strength and the power of looking out of self when the hour of trial is come. It would lessen one's belief in religion and Heaven altogether if it were otherwise.'[38]

Lucy's 'wonderful' behaviour continued through Lord Frederick's funeral at Chatsworth House on 11 May, attended by 30,000 people, including half the House of Commons. Her husband lay in state in the chapel, 'one slight cut on his face the only sign of his cruel death'. The reaction of Frederick's father, the Duke of Devonshire, contrasted with Lucy's; at the grave the Duke was 'bowed down with grief, Lucy calm and really the support of all'.[39] Strangely, it seems not to have occurred to Mr and Mrs Gladstone or to Lucy's sisters and cousins that she may have been too calm, still in the numbed state of shock which is usually the first stage of grief. Normal family sensitivity to the pain and shock of grief seems to have been overwhelmed in this case by their perception of the nobility of the sacrifice, which was even compared to that of Christ.

Lucy Cavendish's 'beautiful life of intense religion' perhaps made the loss more bearable in the short term, because she was able to feel that her husband's death had a divine justification. But that did little to ease the pangs of grief, the shock at the sudden, violent murder, and the intense loneliness which followed. After the Chatsworth funeral Lucy stayed for a few days at Keble College, Oxford, with her sister Lavinia Talbot. Lavinia shared the family's pride in Lucy's 'pathetic, patient bearing of grief', but feared a bad reaction once the immediate crisis was over:

We must all face for her a greater *realization* perhaps of the blank loneliness of her life—at least now there is so much to think of, and be proud of in the great honour and feeling about him shown everywhere . . . She feels supported by the prayers all over England for her . . . My heart aches sometimes when one sees nothing can come near her trouble—nothing but her own strength and courage and absolute clinging to God.[40]

Lavinia still found Lucy's widowhood hard to accept: 'It is so extraordinary talking of Lucy's future—what she can or can't do, of all people—and then that frightful [murder] scene at the back of one's mind, and those four men abroad somewhere.' Lavinia seemed to be the first member of the family to recognize that the heroic character of Lord Frederick's assassination was likely to increase rather than diminish the normal pain of widowhood. Lavinia warned her sister Meriel that they must all have infinite patience 'in being near such grief—it is often like being with some one in great physical pain which one can't relieve'.[41] Lavinia seems to have suspected that the violence of the death and the family's elevated expectations might increase her sister's burden. After Lucy left for London, Lavinia reflected that she retained her usual patience, faith, and courage on the surface, but at a deeper level: 'Each day I felt her sadder—the blank I felt was coming very near her, and her dear face has often a wistful, fixed sad look, which makes my heart ache. I am sure it must be so—there must be the grief none can help her in— it must be the "de profundis".'[42]

The matter-of-fact Mary Gladstone, by contrast, concentrated initially on the practical aspects of her cousin's London homecoming. Mary accompanied Lucy back to her London home on 17 May, admitting that the ordeal was wretched, but 'better than she expected. She seems to have faced the dreadfulness of coming home with such growing sadness that it was not quite as bad as she fancied.' The Prime Minister and his wife dined with Lucy on her first evening, seeking to distract her with political news. It seemed to help Lucy to talk over the experience of other widows, while her own widowed stepmother, Sybella Lyttelton, was full of 'sensible talk' about widowhood. The next two days were devoted to working through Freddy's papers, answering condolence letters, and sorting and disposing of Lucy's coloured clothes, which a widow could not wear.[43]

Lucy evidently found some comfort in dwelling on her memories of Frederick and contemplating the photographs taken in the Dublin hospital immediately after his murder, which were organized by Earl Spencer, the Irish Viceroy, as a surprise for her. Lucy and Mary admired 'the dear beautiful photographs of sleeping Freddy' which Lucy found 'such a deep comfort' that she sent copies to relatives and friends. Lord Spencer had cut off a lock of Freddy's hair for Lucy, and she liked the idea of his 'dear hair . . . being enshrined in a beautiful diamond locket'.[44] It also helped Lucy to talk about her past life with her husband: 'she talks freely of Freddy, and loves to hear of people's affection and value for him'.[45]

At a material level, Mary Gladstone was relieved to receive confirmation in June 1882 that Lucy would have a settlement of £3,000 per year, as well as the house at 21 Carlton Terrace. She was also pleased for Lucy's sake that this information would never be publicized since there was no will, so Lucy 'need not be overwhelmed with vampires'.[46] Lucy Cavendish suffered none of the problems of money and accommodation which increased the trauma of bereavement for working-class widows.

But Lucy's emotional burden was abnormally heavy because her family elevated her husband's assassination to the realm of political and spiritual sacrifice, and because of her own temperament and previous experience of death. Even Mary Gladstone was obliged to recognize on 18 May, during Lucy's London homecoming, that practical measures of relief might not reach the depths of Lucy's grief:

> She went on saying she didn't know *what* to do and that the awful part was the utter aloneness for her—people could love and help and soothe and pet and sympathise and sorrow, but nobody could touch her sorrow really, and how awfully forlorn she was . . . She says she feels all bruised and aching and lies in a sort of aching torpor . . . She doesn't know how she can possibly get on without the relief of tears— and the possibility of crying seems to get less and less.[47]

Six weeks after the assassination, Lucy's cousin Helen Gladstone reported that Lucy continued to behave wonderfully, 'but she will never get over it. I mean it will always be a fresh sorrow to her.'[48] By July, Mary Gladstone was concerned that 'the flood of condolence and sympathy is over . . . It is the hardest time when the outside world are beginning to forget and everything goes on as usual.'[49] Three and a half months after Lucy's bereavement, Lavinia Talbot accompanied her sister to Holker Hall in Carnforth, Lucy's favourite among the four Cavendish houses which Freddy would eventually have inherited. The sense of a double loss was painful, as Lavinia reported:

> I do think it is the worst sadness of all, but she is bearing it as she has everything since May with a patience and faith and unbitterness that make one reverence her. Part of the great impression of sadness I have comes I think from the fact of my own realization of it in this dear pretty place. The pathos is beyond what I could describe of seeing her in her lovely sitting room all by herself, with no child like the others, uprooted as it were from the home she and he was to have had together—and she yet so young and full of life. She is never listless, but she says she feels such a wretched indifference compared to former times in the interest over the house and place and that she seems to see Freddy in each turn everywhere, so completely was he bound up in Holker. One comfort is that this is the worst—nothing can ever be so bad again as coming and being here for the first time . . . But her 'raison d'etre' here—oh, how that is altered.[50]

Almost a year after the assassination, Lucy was again staying at Holker Hall with her Cavendish relatives during the trials and executions of her husband's murderers. People wrote expressing their sorrow that Lucy's wound of grief should thus be reopened, but as she later noted in her diary, 'How should that be, when it had never, never for an hour closed?'[51] She wrote to Mary from

Holker in February 1883: 'As you know I am never 10 minutes together without the full and aching consciousness of what has fallen upon me; and my heart is full to the brim of sorrow, so that all these details cannot add anything.'[52]

The sources of consolation and fulfilment open to Lucy Cavendish were necessarily limited because she had been unable to have children. Most widows could find comfort in their children and grandchildren, as well as in their faith and memory of their husband. In 1884 Lucy's response to the news of Lady Ampthill's widowhood underlined this: 'how *can* she fail to be comforted by the children, if only because they are "his"'.[53] Lucy's childlessness, always a source of sorrow, became more poignant in widowhood. Years later, when Mary [Gladstone] Drew and Frances Balfour were both widowed themselves, they agreed that they could share some measure of another widow's grief, but they could not share the particular anguish of the childless widow: 'all those to whom God has given the consolation of motherhood cannot go all the way with the desolation of the childless widow'.[54] Lucy was pleased to care for the baby son of her brother Alfred Lyttelton after his wife's death in childbirth in 1886, but her own grief was renewed on the death of little Christopher two years later.

Had Lucy been a widowed man, the family would have advised her to divert her attention from her sorrow by returning to work as soon as possible. They would have been concerned that the prolonged mourning might encourage unhealthy grief. Since Lucy was a woman such advice was not forthcoming, but the family did consider ways of filling the blank in her life. Paid work was out of the question for a woman of her class. Good works seemed the only solution, as Josephine Butler discovered after her daughter's tragic death in 1863. But Lucy's relatives disagreed about the value of philanthropy as therapy for the recently bereaved. Mary Gladstone and Meriel Talbot were convinced from the first week of widowhood that good works for the poor would distract Lucy, but Lavinia Talbot protested on 15 May, 'I think the active poor people life for the present is distasteful, and she will have a deal to do in writing and sorting and so on.'[55] Lucy's sister-in-law Lady Louisa Egerton shared this view and for the next few weeks was 'moving heaven and earth' to keep Lucy out of London as long as possible. Mary Gladstone insisted in June that Lucy should rehabilitate herself by keeping busy with other people's problems: 'The sooner she gets to some of the old duties, like London Hospital, where she only meets the poor and sick, the better for her.'[56]

Lucy Cavendish did her best to sublimate sorrow in energetic support for all manner of good causes—including education, hospital and workhouse visiting, charitable work for the poor, and a number of political causes dear to her uncle William's heart. In 1884 she refused to be nominated as Principal of Girton College, Cambridge, on the ground that she entirely lacked the essential academic and organizational qualifications. She considered it 'ludicrously out of the question from the outset', and believed she was invited because 'these competent women' had seen her shine on committees; Lavinia Talbot was more inclined to attribute the honour to Lucy's 'beautiful, saintly character'.[57] Lucy's remarks to Mary Gladstone were revealing:

> I used to tell Freddy that I should be inclined to 'take [holy] orders' if I was alone. But not unless God emptied my life of its natural calls and duties, which rather increase upon me than diminish (the little Clives . . . poor people in St. Martin's etc.) I cannot see why, because my sorrow came upon me in that tremendous way, I should conclude that I am called to be dragged up prominent mountain tops. Dear Freddy would wish me rather to be useful in quite natural ways . . . And *nothing* (to speak selfishly) that I can work at, or live for, can be otherwise than deeply sad and drifting—like to me or to anyone, the whole half of whose life is gone from her.[58]

As paid work was out of the question, so also was any prospect of a second marriage for a good Christian widow who looked forward to reunion with her only husband in heaven. She remained very much Lord Frederick's widow and would never contemplate taking another husband, though she was only 41 at the time of the assassination. In 1883 she commented that a particular lady had taken 'more upon her than she can bear' in her second marriage: 'It has convinced me, if I needed convincing, that no desire to devote one's life to another, no idea of unselfish sacrifice from the highest motives, not even when coupled with real affection of the *friendly* type, can ever make it right for a "widow indeed" to try and be a second wife.'[59]

Lucy continued to grieve for the rest of her life, though people outside her family circle would not have guessed it. Her niece Lady Stephenson later claimed that the 'mainspring [of her life] was broken' by Freddy's murder: 'For two years she never slept without desolate tears; no day in the long years of her widowhood passed without a definite thought of her husband.' Late in 1884 Lucy wrote to her sister Meriel, 'You can't think how heavy life is to bear, not from unbearableness, but from the utter vanishing of all my old mainspring of joy and delight.'[60] Yet she never indulged in the luxury of an exaggerated display of sorrow, 'always exerting herself to talk and take an interest in things'.

Ten long years after her bereavement, Lucy visited the Gladstones at Hawarden in 1892 and devoted her recreation time to the design of a memorial window for Freddy in Hawarden church. Mary Drew understood then that the intense grief of early widowhood still remained:

As long as something is going on and she is talking and interested, one is inclined to think her a miracle. Then when she is alone with you and talking about her own condition, it is very wretched and you feel she does not really advance an inch—I mean the wound has not begun to heal in the very least. She is still thankful to get from hour to hour and day to day, but has no grain of pleasure in looking forward. And everything is an immense effort.[61]

Such an analysis by the sensible Mary Drew was a sad testimony to Lucy's state of mind long after deep mourning would normally have ended.

For the next forty-three years Lucy Cavendish responded with sympathetic condolence letters to bereaved acquaintances, as well as close friends, often illustrating how close she remained to her own experience of loss. Twenty-three years after her own bereavement she wrote a characteristic letter to Lady Stanhope on her husband's death:

May I just tell you how I was myself 'comforted by God'? It was not by making great efforts to be good and brave; it was by simply waiting patiently in the darkness, looking all the sorrow, loneliness, and pain quietly in the face, and leaning back dumbly in the Everlasting Arms. It is a time when one learns what God can do for one. I am so very thankful that you have your children to live for.

May God bless and soothe and strengthen you.[62]

Lucy spoke from the heart to Lady Stanhope, who was not an intimate friend, as if her own grief was still fresh. While she assured Lady Stanhope of the value of simple faith in enduring grief, she confessed in 1913 to her newly widowed sister-in-law Edith Lyttelton that the pain of widowhood was intense and continuous: 'I know the weight of sorrow grows harder to bear as the days go on, and what at first comes to sustain one seems to fall away, and one realises more and more what the loneliness is.'[63]

Lucy's belief that Freddy's death was a sacrifice decreed by God made the loss easier to bear in the early months but, over the longer term, it imposed a greater burden. During her early deep mourning in 1883 she wrote in her diary, 'I had the thought sent to me how earnestly I ought to try and not spoil my share in the sacrifice by any repining or want of resignation; but offer up my will with the same single heart as my darling did.'[64] For the next forty-three years she tried to fulfil that pledge. She was, in a very real sense, never able to resolve her grief to allow herself to embark on a new life. The manner of Lord Frederick's death and the nation's response meant that his memory was universally idealized. This made it well-nigh impossible for his widow to review their lost relationship realistically and to proceed beyond the initial stage of intense and exaggerated idealization. Negative memories of Lord Frederick would never have been allowed to surface, so he was never remembered as anything other than perfect, and the process of mourning remained incomplete.[65] This situation was reinforced by the response of acquaintances, such as Margaret MacDonald, who wrote in 1896, 'I always feel a sort of reverence in writing to Lady Lucy Cavendish because of the tragedy in her life.'[66] Like Queen Victoria, though for very different reasons, Lucy Cavendish was elevated by ordinary mortals to a lonely pedestal, as a perpetual widow.

Many of Parkes's suggested 'determinants of chronic grief'[67] seem to have been operating in Lucy Cavendish's case. Her family considered her to be 'grief-prone' and susceptible to 'morbid' events from an early age. She was profoundly affected by the premature deaths of her mother and sister, her father's suicide, and the culminating tragedy of her husband's assassination. Victorian widows could be more vulnerable to chronic, prolonged grief than widowers if they had to confront abnormal circumstances such as suicide and violent or sudden death. In the face of such trauma widowers were far more likely to be protected by their families, ushered back to work to distract their thoughts and encouraged to remarry. It is instructive to compare Lucy's case with that of her brother Alfred Lyttelton, who was widowed four years after Lucy. His loss was great—the death of a lovely young wife in childbirth, followed two years later by the child—but he remarried, had a second family, and a successful political career. Lucy's was the greater tragedy. She was expected to confront her loss starkly, to live constantly with her bereavement hour by hour, day by day, with no children and no career to engross her time, and no prospects of another marriage. Lucy Cavendish's primary consolation was her strong Christian faith. But while religious faith normally acted as a positive source of comfort which encouraged grief to take its course, for her it helped to sustain an intensity of sorrow which prolonged the process of grieving for a lifetime.

So far this chapter has examined chronic grief among Victorian widows and widowers, but parents who lost beloved 'adult children' were a second category of the bereaved who risked an abnormal and prolonged grief process. Psychologists such as Beverley Raphael argue that the untimely death of an adult child is likely to lead to an intense and particularly painful bereavement with a deeply disturbing impact.[68] Jane Littlewood adds that anger over adult child deaths is a common response today to a loss viewed as premature and unnatural. She concludes from recent studies that mothers even more than fathers felt such a loss as 'the most painful experience of their lives'.[69]

In the nineteenth century, parental grief for adult children may have been greater than that for very young children for two reasons. People were well aware that child mortality was highest in infancy and the first five years of life, so that the death of a very young child from an infectious disease was a terrible loss but not one that was entirely unexpected. Over the age of about 10, children were perceived to be out of the dangerous years and more likely to live out their natural span. Deaths of adult children between 20 and middle age were entirely unexpected and untimely, while they were also harder to cope with because of greater emotional investment, a stronger bonding process, and half a lifetime of memories. Elizabeth Horsley in 1858 compared her husband's death in old age with that of her daughter Fanny in childbirth at the age of 34. Her husband's long-expected death 'had none of that stunning overwhelming effect on me that dearest Fanny's death had'.[70] Mabel Allan in 1911 compared the recent death of her baby to a friend's loss of an older child, saying she realized 'how very much greater the sorrow for those who have had to part with older children'.[71]

Emma Haden lost her favourite daughter, Emma Bergeron, in 1858, thirty-four years after the death of her husband, Charles Haden, a surgeon. Her three surviving children included the physician and burial reformer Francis Seymour Haden and John Horsley's second wife, Rose. Emma Bergeron was a favourite with all her family, so that her special place in her mother's affection was accepted as her due. Her sister, Rose, considered Emma 'unselfish and devoted to us all and the very best of us all',[72] while Sophy Horsley thought her 'the delight of all who knew her'.[73] Emma Bergeron died suddenly in July 1858 in Paris, where she was living with her French husband. She was only 38 years old, and appeared to be in excellent health, but she died within a few days of an illness diagnosed as 'rheumatic fever with a mixture of typhoid'.[74]

Emma Bergeron's death was a terrible shock for the entire family, but they all feared especially for Emma Haden, knowing she would feel the loss most deeply. Rose Horsley thought it was a 'terrible blow' for their mother, particularly as she was unable to see her daughter during her brief final illness and was deprived of a 'last look'.[75] The body was returned for burial in Kensal Green cemetery in London, but there is no evidence that the mother viewed her daughter's remains. Emma Haden's ignorance of her daughter's fatal illness and her inability to see her before she died clearly contributed to the mother's long-term failure to accept her loss. As Emma Haden wrote in anguish nearly three years later: 'O my Emma, shall I never see thee again! No more press Thy hand, no more receive thy welcome kiss! Thou didst die far from thy Mother, and she knew not of thy sufferings and death. She was forbidden the last sad farewell of death, but she shall weep over thy grave, and cherish the bright memory of thy sweet form and face till she meets thee in Heaven.'[76]

Emma Haden's grief was chronic, prolonged, and apparently unresolved. She was 64 when her daughter died, but she lived on for another twenty-three years, dying finally at 87. Over an extended period of more than ten years after 1858 Emma Haden recorded her grief in two commonplace books. Most of the entries expressed her feelings and thoughts during bereavement, including some of her own poems, but she also transcribed numerous helpful passages from consolation literature, from the Bible, and from Victorian poetry. The early passages in 1858 describe the experience of deep grief common to most mourners in the early months of bereavement, dwelling obsessively on every detail of the final months of her daughter's life. She found it especially hard to return to the daily routine of domestic duties, which constantly reminded her that her daughter was gone. 'Sometimes it is almost unbearable to me! and I could run into the next room to look for what I cannot find, and cannot see again.' The death of her daughter changed 'the very look of existence' for her. Fortunately she enjoyed her own company, for she was 'a lone woman—all my nearest ties engrossed by nearer ones of their own'—and she found some peace in the solitude of her own home.[77]

We have seen that the memory of the dead assumes an important role for most bereaved people, especially in the first year of mourning. In Emma Haden's case, her daughter's memory continued to have a very powerful influence for many years. An entry in her commonplace book for 1859 stated her view of the significant role of Emma's memory in her own grieving process: 'As every thought of her is pleasing, satisfying, ennobling to my heart . . . I love to let my thoughts rest upon the memories of her life; and though I can behold her no more living, yet I may thus enable myself to dwell with her in the past . . . I live with my lost saint every hour; I call to mind her looks, her words, her gestures.'[78] Four years after Emma's death, Emma Haden found it necessary to justify her prolonged dependence on her daughter's memory, as springing from the love of the soul rather than earthly affection: 'the love that is seated in the soul can live *on long remembrance* . . . The love that survives the tomb is one of the noblest attributes of the soul.' Emma believed that love of the dead was a 'truly spiritual affection . . . purified from every sensual desire', and it sanctified the heart of the survivor.[79]

Idealization of the dead is a natural and common human response to the loss of a loved one in the earlier stages of grief. But for most mourners the process of resolution of grief involves a more realistic assessment of the day-to-day reality of the relationship, including its negative aspects. Such a resolution is impossible if the mourner continues to perceive the deceased as a lost saint in a 'sublime condition of . . . higher existence'. On the fourth anniversary of Emma Bergeron's death her memory was as vital as ever and no less exalted: 'No! there is nothing painful in the thought of you, my departed Emma! . . . Here in my imperfect state I still cling to you with *unchanging devotion* . . . May I not hope, that you in your glorified state though much more perfect than I am, still remember with affection my faithful loving heart?'[80]

Emma Haden's meditations on her bereavement continued throughout the 1860s, with the longest entries on the anniversaries of Emma's death, funeral, and birthday. Her sorrow on the seventh anniversary of Emma's death seemed to remain as painful and fresh as the first, as if Emma had died seven weeks ago rather than seven years: '*How* this death saddens me! It is not that I am in tears, or violent grief, it is a calm *internal* sorrow, a grief that I know not how to describe, but assuredly it is grief. She is always in my thoughts.' After seven years the material memories of Emma's life were as precious as ever—the strands of brown hair and the yellowed letters could still awake a keen regret, while the image of her face still returned with wonderful clarity.[81]

But memories alone did not bring peace or the resolution of anguished grieving. Emma Haden's Christian faith and her belief that she would meet Emma again in a 'blessed Eternity' did rather more to sustain her than memory alone. She meditated on the prospect of reunion with Emma on all her visits to the grave at Kensal Green cemetery. In her first year of bereavement she 'looked with cheerfulness to sleeping beside her. The idea brought closer the prospects of eternity.' She committed herself to spending her remaining years usefully, so that she would be well prepared for her own welcome summons. Advancing age was seen as a blessing since it increased the hope of reunion.[82] The message of Emma Haden's poem on the fifth anniversary was that inward peace would be denied until she could join her daughter in the grave. Like Ann Rogers she continued visiting Emma's grave in anticipation of her own burial, frequently hoping that would not be long delayed.[83]

Emma Haden's struggle for submission to God's will and for complete reliance on faith was long and hard. She viewed her suffering as a trial sent by God and took comfort from his support in her affliction: 'I feel reliance on my Saviour grow stronger every day.' But it was three or four years before that faith conveyed relative peace and acquiescence. Not until 1861 was she able to write, 'We shall be faithful to the dead without a murmur of revolt against God.' Through the gift of faith she trusted 'the bitterness of despair will vanish'.[84] After seven years the reason for Emma's death and her own pain remained a mystery understood only by God. The mystery of suffering 'makes me believe in something to expiate . . . I see in it Jesus Christ, the *Man of Sorrows*.' Like Jane Goulburn, John Horsley, and Archibald Tait, she could only logically explain the death of a child in terms of a trial sent by God or punishment for sin, but she preferred to seek refuge instead in the concept of submission to the mystery of God's will: 'The *reason* of things is hid in God . . . In the act of Christian resignation, which may seem a passive acceptation, a sort of yielding to necessity, I find the most sublime action of the soul. It is entirely of faith, it carries at once from earth to heaven.'[85]

Even at the age of 72, eight years after her daughter's death, Emma Haden was unable to sustain this degree of acquiescence, and her grief was still great. She still visualized herself as a heartbroken, weeping mother, regretting the 'inverted order of events': 'Must then the young be taken and the aged left? . . . Speak to me my child once again!'[86] Emma Haden's response to her beloved daughter's death in 1858 seemed to remain in the acute stage of grief for many years beyond the normal. Her continued exaggerated idealization of her 'lost saint' rendered realistic resolution of her grief more difficult. She suffered such agonies in response to the death of a favourite child of great promise, struck down suddenly in the prime of life for no apparent reason. The grief process was further complicated for Emma Haden because she could not anticipate her daughter's death, nor could she be present at her deathbed. Emma's death in a foreign country added to her distress.

To the extent that Queen Victoria has been represented as the epitome of the Victorian process of grief and mourning, the historical record has to be revised. The Queen should instead be included with those other rare and sad victims of chronic and abnormal grief, female and male, whose lives were blighted for ever by the loss of husbands, wives, or children whose deaths they could not accept. Queen Victoria, Lucy Cavendish, Ann Rogers, and Emma Haden were highly exceptional in their grief rather than representative of the Victorian age, but perhaps in certain unhappy respects they foreshadowed the chronic grief on a mass scale which followed the Great War. It is significant that three of these four cases of unresolved grief in the nineteenth century were reactions to suicide, assassination, and death overseas, which were closer in character to the violence and horror of wartime deaths.

❧ 17 ❧

'A SOLITUDE BEYOND THE REACH OF GOD OR MAN'

VICTORIAN AGNOSTICS AND DEATH

G M. YOUNG PERHAPS OVERSTATED THE CASE WHEN HE WROTE THAT IN .the late Victorian period 'the ethical trenchancy of the Evangelicals was passing over to the agnostics . . . Agnosticism had the temper of the age on its side.'[1] But he was broadly correct over the longer term. From the 1870s church attendance ceased to keep pace with population growth and Evangelicalism had passed its peak by the 1880s. Victorian responses to the combined challenges of geological discoveries, biblical criticism, and Darwinian evolutionary theory varied greatly. They included narrow restatements of orthodox religion and liberal rationalizations of Christian doctrine which abandoned eternal punishment and reduced the emphasis on sin and Christ's atonement. The number of agnostics and atheists among the educated increased from the middle of the century, though the term 'agnostic' was not coined by T. H. Huxley until 1869.

Agnostic views of death were to become less exceptional after 1850. This chapter chiefly examines the experiences of the families of three prominent agnostics—Charles Darwin, Joseph Hooker, and Thomas Huxley—who had to cope with the deaths of their children in the 1850s and 1860s. Their attitudes and responses to death are compared with those of Victorian Christians at a time when Evangelicalism was still extraordinarily influential. This first generation of agnostics had to come to terms with family deaths in a transitional period while they were also confronting the social and spiritual isolation and cultural shock of the loss of faith. The Christian legacy was still immensely powerful and Victorian agnostics were often unable to develop alternative strategies for dealing with grief, unlike some of the early twentieth-century unbelievers who will be examined in the next chapter.

Only Christianity, with its belief in the resurrection of the soul, could reconcile many Victorians to death. For those Victorian agnostics who doubted the existence of a God and were unconvinced by the concept of an afterlife, the trauma of the death of a loved one could be overwhelming. In an age when Christian faith was still so widespread in the political, professional, and scientific establishments, and was an intrinsic part of middle- and upper-class family life, agnostics could feel particularly isolated when confronting personal crises. Henry Atkinson warned Harriet Martineau in 1847 that, as a scientific materialist, she would feel excluded from society: 'the sense of loneliness will accompany you more or less through much of your social intercourse'.[2] Thomas Huxley privately acknowledged in 1893 that his unusual views on life, religion, and death separated him from Victorian society: 'I go into society, and except among two or three of my scientific colleagues I find myself alone on these subjects, and as hopelessly at variance with the majority of my fellow-men as they would be with their neighbours if they were set down among the Ashantees. I don't like this state of things for myself—least of all do I see how it will work out for my children.'[3]

Agnostics could feel especially alone when confronting death, since the Victorian ritual of the deathbed and the funeral, as well as the language of consolation, were heavily dependent on Christian beliefs. Agnostics lacked the church and community support which sustained Victorian Christians, and the system of beliefs and rituals which helped to deal with the process of grieving. Believers held awful fears for agnostics and atheists obliged to face 'the utter grimness of a death unbrightened by faith', as Mary Drew put it in 1895.[4] After her father's death in 1886, Mary Booth concluded that, without belief in immortality, 'life is so meaningless;—and above all the closing years of it, so utterly stale, flat and unprofitable'.[5]

Unbelievers Confront Mortality

Agnostics and atheists confronted the prospect of their own deaths in different ways, but it seems to have been more difficult for the first generation of doubters, cast suddenly adrift from the Christian belief system. Wilfrid Blunt, the poet, was an agnostic who dreaded a death like that of Ada Lovelace and feared the prospect of eternal damnation. Blunt had been converted to Catholicism as a boy and was educated in a Catholic school, but reluctantly lost his faith at the age of 20. He retained from his Catholic childhood 'the wildest pictures which were ever drawn of Hell': 'I am as certain as I can be of anything, that the last thought of every human soul is one of terrible and absolute anguish, of a solitude beyond the reach of God or man.'[6] In 1872 Wilfrid Blunt watched his brother Francis, a devout Catholic, die slowly and unpleasantly from tuberculosis; as Wilfrid put it, 'he looked like Christ dying in his agony'. Wilfrid had nursed a private hope for many months that Francis's death would disprove his own fears; that 'I might catch a glimpse of some other world revealed to me through his dying eyes'. But instead of seeing 'Heaven open' for Francis, he watched his brother being 'utterly extinguished'.[7]

The variety of reactions among free thinkers to the prospect of death is illustrated by Lady Anne Blunt's response to Francis's death. Anne Blunt was Ada Lovelace's daughter and had been brought up by the formidable Lady Byron, her grandmother. By 1872 she was an agnostic, but she became a Catholic in later life, after years of unhappy marriage to Wilfrid Blunt, who was an unfaithful husband. She was very fond of Francis, and her desire to believe in immortality was evident in her diary entry on the day of his death: 'I cannot take in the idea of death as being the soul's death, so that it is not that I doubt a continuance of life though it be invisible and unattainable to us in bodies.' Three days later, when they were preparing for the funeral, Wilfrid asked his wife if she thought Francis was still 'alive'. Anne replied: 'I do. I cannot, I know I cannot, conceive of death, the death of one's self, so that perhaps I am not a fair judge. I would naturally prefer that my soul should live when my body is dead.'[8]

Harriet Martineau, feminist, reformer, and successful author of *Illustrations of Political Economy*, developed a more robust philosophy of scientific materialism than the two Blunts. Martineau never married and gradually abandoned the Unitarian faith of her childhood. She wrote her autobiography in 1855 when she believed she was dying of heart disease, determined to assure her Christian readers that 'I am not miserable about dying,' as they assumed all free thinkers must be. At the time of writing she already had three months' experience of 'constant expectation of death': 'I find death in prospect the simplest thing in the world,—a thing not to be feared or regretted, or to get excited about in any way . . . To me there is no sacrifice, no sense of loss, nothing to fear, nothing to regret . . . I neither wish to live longer here, nor to find life again elsewhere . . . I myself utterly disbelieve in a future life.'[9] As a young invalid, Martineau's years of personal experience of the Christian consolations had not made her happy. Quite the reverse, since she was now convinced that the Christian expectation of immortality was based on flimsy evidence, leading dying Christians to fear the collapse of their 'air-built castle'. Having abandoned 'the selfish complacencies of religion', she was able to face death easily and naturally with the support of philosophy.[10] Harriet Martineau eventually recovered from these earlier illnesses and did not die until 1876, when she expected no future other than annihilation, waiting 'without fear or hope or ignorant prejudice, for the expiration of life'.[11]

Austin Holyoake, atheist, supporter of Bradlaugh and contributor to the

National Reformer, died at the age of 47 in 1874. Holyoake's parents were pious Methodists who taught him 'to dread the wrath of an avenging God, and to avoid the torments of a brimstone hell'. He had attended Sunday School and up to the age of 14 was haunted by fear of the devil, but he gradually 'thought my way to Atheism', emancipated by the ideas of Robert Owen. He was just as firm in his unbelief as Martineau, and equally determined to prove that approaching death did not terrify him or induce him to revise his philosophy. He suffered considerably as he was dying, but in the final days dictated to his wife his 'Sick-Room Thoughts' for publication. He was anxious to test the truth of Christian claims that the principles of free thought collapsed at times of sickness and death, when only the hope of immortality could provide consolation. For twenty years he had not believed in the Christian God or any future state of rewards and punishments: 'I do not believe in a heaven, or life of eternal bliss after death,' for it was a faith founded in selfishness:

Remove this extravagant promise [of eternal bliss], and you will hear very little of the Christian religion. An eternal hell seems to me too monstrous for the belief of any humane man or sensitive woman . . . I have experienced for twenty years the most perfect mental repose; and now I find that the near approach of death, the 'grim King of Terrors', gives me not the slightest alarm. I have suffered, and am suffering, most intensely both by night and day; but this has not produced the least symptom of change of opinion.[12]

Revd Charles Maurice Davies attended Austin Holyoake's funeral in 1874 in pursuit of ideas for his forthcoming book *Heterodox London*. He found a 'motley throng' of advanced free thinkers in the unconsecrated and isolated part of Highgate cemetery, listening to a service written by Holyoake himself, with a brief farewell by Charles Bradlaugh. Davies was impressed, despite himself, by the dignity of the ceremony, but depressed by its utter lack of hope. This was the 'eternal farewell' of the heathen, with no prospect of resurrection. 'The hopeless mourners withdrew, and left him whom, in thought, they had lost for ever.' Davies sat for a while in the cemetery afterwards and concluded his review of the funeral on a sanguine note: 'The utter hopelessness of mere negation seemed to come so forcibly upon me as to carry its own assurance that it could not be true. God would be an austere man, and life the cruel infliction of a tyrant, if all ended in that grave yonder.'[13]

Philosophers could argue with Maurice Maeterlinck, the Belgian writer, in 1911 that body, mind, and memory were all extinguished after death, so there could be no unhappiness and there should be no fear.[14] But it was not so easy for many unbelievers to accept such logic, especially the first generation who had personally rejected the consolation offered by Christianity. Yet there were different individual responses, varying between the uncertainty and ambivalence of the Blunts and the more self-confident unbelief of Martineau and Holyoake. Moreover, though some free thinkers could come to terms with their own mortality, many found it infinitely more difficult to accept the deaths of their children. This chapter will look more closely at the experiences of Darwin, Hooker, and Huxley, as leaders of a Victorian generation of scientists and agnostics who transformed the late Victorian intellectual world.

Charles and Emma Darwin

Charles Darwin (1809–82) was brought up in his mother's Unitarian faith, while his father was a prominent physician and free thinker who concealed his lack of faith from his son. Like his friends Huxley and Hooker, Darwin studied medicine, but unlike them he did not complete the course, moving from Edinburgh to Cambridge with a view to entering the Church. Instead, the famous voyage on the *Beagle* from 1836 led ultimately to his publication in 1859 of the *Origin of Species*, which explained the origins of all animal and plant species through a system of natural selection. In 1838 Darwin's father financed him as an independent scientist, allowing him to marry his cousin Emma Wedgwood the following year. The Darwin family lived a life of rural respectability in the old parsonage in the village of Down, sixteen miles from London. All the family except Darwin regularly attended the village church where they had their own pew.[15]

The development of Charles Darwin's religious views has been extensively discussed by historians and others.[16] Darwin gradually abandoned Christianity in the decade following 1838, though his religious commitment had never been strong. Historical criticism of the Old Testament, with its vengeful God and the 'damnable doctrine' of everlasting punishment, played a part in his loss of faith. He also came to believe that the suffering in the world was compatible with his theory of natural selection, but not with a benevolent and omnipotent God.[17] Unlike Huxley, Darwin was always reticent about his religious beliefs, but when pressed in old age in 1879, he admitted that he had 'never been an Atheist in the sense of denying the existence of a God', preferring to describe himself as an agnostic. As to the future life, everybody must judge between 'conflicting vague probabilities'.[18]

The deaths of his parents profoundly affected Charles Darwin. At the age of 8 in 1817 he was not allowed to see his mother in her final two weeks of terrible suffering from a tumour. His father, Dr Robert Darwin, became deeply depressed and diverted all his time and energy into his medical practice. His father and two elder sisters were unable ever 'to endure speaking about so dreadful a loss'.[19] John Bowlby's biography of Darwin identifies Dr Robert Darwin's response to his wife's death as a more extreme example of his usual avoidance of displays of emotion. Bowlby argues that the family's 'wall of silence' retarded Darwin's emotional development and contributed to his poor health. He stresses the 'strong Darwin family tradition of trying to avoid unhappiness by burying memories and diverting attention to other things'.[20] But Bowlby does not explore how far the agnosticism of father and son exacerbated this inherited family trait in relation to death.

Charles Darwin's sickness, depression, and stomach troubles afflicted him during his father's long final illness in 1848, as they did at any time of unusual strain. He was not well enough to visit his 83-year-old father during his last three weeks, so he recorded no deathbed scene. Charles did manage the journey from Down to Shrewsbury for his father's funeral, but as his four sisters anticipated, he was too distraught to attend the ceremony. Bowlby argues persuasively that Darwin's mourning for his father was inhibited and his grief diverted into a deep preoccupation with his own ill health during many months of chronic depression and recurrent vomiting fits.[21] But we should also consider the impact of Darwin's religious doubts, evidently well advanced by this time. It may be that the responses of father and son to pain and death were inhibited not just by a family tradition of avoidance of suffering, but also by their own free thought. They abandoned the belief system and the set of rituals which their society normally used in dealing with death, and neither found nor constructed an alternative.

Charles Darwin's letters of condolence, as well as his reports on family deaths, indicate his inability to express his own sorrow or to offer much sympathy to others. The letters are terse, stilted, and cold, in marked contrast to the warmly emotional and often fluent letters of so many Victorian Christians. They reinforce Bowlby's view that Darwin preferred to avoid unpleasant personal events and probably found it a severe strain when obliged to write about them. At 33, in 1842, he sent two letters of sympathy to his cousin William Fox on his wife's death. The only consolations Charles was able to offer were relief at the termination of his wife's suffering, and the comfort of Fox's five children (whom Darwin trusted were 'again cheerful', since he assumed children did not mourn for long). Darwin evidently appreciated the inadequacy of his first note, for he apologized in his second: 'I truly sympathise with you, though never in my life having lost one near relation [significantly forgetting his mother in 1817], I daresay I cannot imagine, how severe grief, such as yours, must be.' By 1842 Charles Darwin must have been familiar with early Victorian condolence letters, and therefore aware that he

had lost the language for expressing such sympathy when he slowly surrendered his faith. Writing such letters must have been a particularly difficult
task for the first generation of unbelievers. A year later Darwin sent a letter of
sympathy to William Fox on the first anniversary of his wife's death, expressing some surprise that time had not healed his sorrow: 'I had hoped (for
experience I have none) that the mind would have refused to dwell so long
and so intently on any object, although the most cherished one . . . But I am
writing away without really being able to put myself in your position.'[22]
These were extraordinary condolence letters for the early 1840s, and must
have struck the recipient strangely amidst dozens of conventional Christian
notes of warm sympathy.

Family deaths in the following years enhanced Darwin's personal experience, but they did not alter the tone and brevity of his letters, since he could
still offer 'only sympathy'. Usually he managed a phrase or two in praise of
the deceased, such as that on his sister Marianne Parker who died in 1858: 'she
was an admirable woman'.[23] But the only sources of consolation he ever
mentioned were time, and, if appropriate, the lack of pain. Indeed, Darwin
almost always referred to the degree of suffering involved; given his own
dread of pain, he regarded its absence as one of the few 'miserable consolations' available on death. On a number of occasions, as when his sister Susan
Darwin died in 1866, Darwin noted that 'really death is nothing compared
with much suffering'.[24] He regarded the death of another sister, Catherine
Langton, also in 1866, as a blessing because it ended her great suffering.[25]
Occasionally Darwin made disconcerting observations about the relative
insignificance of individual death in the greater scheme of things, but
he reserved these remarks for his fellow agnostic scientists. He agreed with
J. D. Hooker that Professor Hugh Falconer's slow decline from rheumatic
fever was 'horrid' and 'humiliating'; but 'this slow progress, or even
personal annihilation sinks in my mind into insignificance compared with
the idea, or rather I presume certainty, of the sun some day cooling and we
all freezing'.[26]

Three of Charles Darwin's children died young, but little evidence survives
about two of them. Few references were made to the death of 3-week-old
Mary in 1842, except his wife, Emma's, comment that their sorrow would
have been greater had Mary lived longer, 'though it will be long indeed before
either of us forget that poor little face'.[27] The record of the death of Charles
Waring Darwin, the youngest child, who died of scarlet fever in 1858 at the
age of 18 months, is also slight. Darwin's one-page memorial to the little boy,
who was intellectually handicapped, recorded that the last thirty-six hours
were 'miserable beyond expression', but that his short life was 'placid, inno-

cent and joyful', and he would be spared further pain.[28] Emma behaved 'nobly' throughout, but it was 'wonderful relief when she could let her feelings break forth'.[29] The few surviving extracts indicate that the parents loved and grieved for both children, but the lost children seem not to have been written about in the family any further.

The family death which most profoundly affected Charles Darwin was that of his second child, Annie, his favourite, at the age of 10 in 1851, from 'bilious fever with typhoid character'. Far more evidence survives for Annie's death because the parents were physically separated during her final illness. Darwin's long letters undoubtedly helped release his emotional strain, as he confessed to Emma, 'It is a relief to tell you for whilst writing to you I can cry tranquilly.' After she had been ill for some months, Darwin took Annie to Malvern to try Dr James Gully's water cure in March 1851, accompanied by her younger sister Henrietta, aged 7, and the governess and nanny. Charles returned home to Down for several weeks, but was summoned back to Annie's sick-bed in Malvern when her condition deteriorated in mid-April. Emma remained at home at Down as she was eight months pregnant, but her sister-in-law and close friend Fanny Wedgwood agreed to help nurse Annie and give Darwin support.[30]

Charles Darwin's daily reports to his wife on Annie's condition were remarkably restrained, considering the gravity of the crisis. They described the symptoms and treatment in objective detail, in accordance with Darwin's medical training and his belief that it would not help Emma in the longer term to disguise the bleak reality. There was much medical detail but no Christian consolation as Darwin described Annie's pitiful appearance and Dr Gully's over-sanguine reports. The day after his return to the lodgings at Malvern, his letter reported more than usual about his own state of mind: 'It is much bitterer and harder to bear than I expected—Your note made me cry so much—but I must not give way and can avoid doing so, by not thinking about her. It is now from hour to hour a struggle between life and death . . . Oh my own it is very bitter indeed.' A brief note later that day admitted that Annie's case seemed hopeless after 'four deluges of vomiting'. Yet Dr Gully, who had mastered the medical art of positive thinking, reassured him that Annie was 'not essentially worse', although not out of great danger.[31]

On 20 April, three days before the end of the six-day crisis, Darwin was able to console his wife only with the news that Annie was suffering little and dozing much of the time. Darwin tried not to raise his own hopes, because 'these alternations of no hope and hope sicken one's soul'. Next day the news was worse and starkly described: 'poor Annie is in a fearful mess, but we keep

her sweet with Chloride of Lime'. Despite her plight, their daughter continued to be 'the perfection of gentleness, patience and gratitude'. But on 22
April even the optimistic Dr Gully pronounced Annie in imminent danger.
Next day Darwin sadly told Emma that Annie 'went to her final sleep most
tranquilly, most sweetly at 12 oclock today. Our poor dear dear child has had
a very short life but I trust happy, and God only knows what miseries might
have been in store for her . . . We must be more and more to each other my
dear wife.'[32]

'God' only appeared as a figure of speech in Darwin's deeply repressed
discourse. On reading his letters it is a shock to recall that Annie Darwin died
only a year after Jessy Gladstone, and several years before the Horsley children and the five little Tait girls. Annie Darwin was the same age at death as
Cattie Tait, who also died of fever, five years after Annie. Yet it seems from
Darwin's text as if Annie died a generation or two later, because the contrasts
in discourse are so great, despite the similarities in class. The parental anguish
was undoubtedly intense in all these families, but its expression varied greatly.
There was little or no self-analysis of Darwin's feelings, in marked contrast to
the self-examination of A. C. Tait, John Horsley, and W. E. Gladstone. The
Darwins did not discuss the meaning of death, in theological, philosophical,
or any other terms, nor try to discern any purpose in Annie's death. Unlike
the Gladstones, Taits, and Horsleys, Charles Darwin was unable to find
consolation in the Christian prospect of a happy family reunion in the
afterlife.

However, in certain respects and within his own limits, Charles Darwin
seems to have coped more effectively with Annie's death than with the deaths
of his parents, and perhaps he also coped better than his wife did on this
occasion. Though he lacked the comfort of Christian faith, he had the
consolations of love, sympathy, and family support in abundance. His wife
Emma and sister-in-law Fanny Wedgwood gave him the warmest and most
generous emotional support possible, encouraging him to share his grief with
them and to cry freely. Immediately after the little girl's death, Fanny
confided to Emma that Charles was 'able to find relief in crying much', and
she was sure that was best for him. On Charles's return to Down, Emma
commented, 'We have done little else but cry together and talk about our
darling.'[33] On this occasion Charles Darwin was encouraged to express his
grief far more openly than he had when his parents died, and another
breakdown of health was prevented.

Charles Darwin also gained some consolation from the memory of Annie.
On the day of her death, he told Emma how thankful he was for the
daguerreotype of Annie taken in 1849, which was a good likeness. Four

months after Annie's death he composed a memorial to his daughter written only for himself and Emma—a response not unlike that of William Gladstone, the Taits, and other grieving Christian parents, though his was very much shorter. It was a common mid-Victorian way of expressing grief, as we have seen, and the memory of the loved one was even more important to an agnostic. Darwin idealized Annie's short life, just as Gladstone did Jessy's and Dean Tait his Cattie, though he omitted the deathbed scene. Charles noted that 'in after years, if we live, the impressions now put down will recall more vividly her chief characteristics'. He emphasized her joy in life, her sensitivity, and her affection; her mind was 'pure and transparent', and her conduct in her final illness was 'angelic', always considerate and appreciative.[34]

Sympathy and memory helped Charles Darwin to bear his loss, but he felt bitterness as well as sorrow for a long time. Darwin did not feel well enough to attend his child's funeral in 1851, as indeed he rarely felt well enough for funerals. He gratefully accepted Fanny Wedgwood's generous offer to make the funeral arrangements and to attend the funeral at Malvern in his place, allowing him to travel to Down to support Emma.[35] Darwin never felt well enough to visit Annie's grave. As another daughter, Henrietta Litchfield, explained, 'My father could not bear to reopen his sorrow,' and she never knew him to speak of Annie.[36] Five years after Annie's death, Charles Darwin confided to a cousin that the thought of her illness and death was still extremely painful. He had recently considered two weeks in Malvern, 'but I got to feel that old thoughts would revive so vividly that it would not have answered'.[37] However, almost a decade after the tragedy, Darwin was able to reassure his friend Thomas Huxley, who had just lost his young son, 'that time, and time alone, acts wonderfully'. Darwin well understood how intolerable was the bitterness of grief at the death of a child, but he had found that 'the grief is become tenderer' and he could even recall Annie's smile with 'something like pleasure'.[38]

In this case the death of a beloved child was probably an even more devastating experience for the Christian wife than for the agnostic husband. Emma Darwin remained a committed Evangelical Christian and a regular church attender and cannot have found the difference in faith from her husband easy to deal with, especially as they rarely, if ever, discussed it. Their daughter Henrietta described her mother as sincere and definite in her beliefs—'in her youth religion must have largely filled her life'—and her papers suggested that 'it distressed her, in her early married life, to know that my father did not share her faith'.[39] In 1839 Emma was afraid that Charles's scepticism would cause him to sacrifice his salvation and his prospects of eternal life. It would be a nightmare 'if I thought we did not belong to each other forever'.[40] Emma's views on death and suffering followed traditional Christian lines. As late as 1861 she sent a rare letter to Charles about their different religious beliefs in which she explained her own attitude to suffering: 'I find the only relief to my own mind is to take it as from God's hand, and to try to believe that all suffering and illness is meant to help us to exalt our minds and to look forward with hope to a future state.'[41] Yet her daughter said that Emma spoke little to her own children about her Christian faith, and regretted that it grew weaker in old age.[42]

Emma Darwin made no use of consoling religious language in her letters to her husband on Annie's death. Her silence on the subject of her Christian faith was probably her way of accommodating her spiritual differences with her husband. This habit may well have become so firmly ingrained that Emma maintained almost the same reticence in communicating with those who were Christians. It was difficult to sustain two different languages of grief and condolence. Emma mentioned only two sources of consolation to Charles—to weep together, and to remember Annie's 'happy innocent life'.[43] Moreover, the correspondence between husband and wife while Annie was dying was somewhat one-sided in that the emotional support was mostly going from wife to husband. Emma's letters were full of sustaining messages to Charles and Fanny, rather than lamenting Annie's fate or expressing her own anguish. Emma worked hard to maintain a degree of detachment from Annie's illness in order to support Charles.

No doubt Emma would have found it more comforting to express her sorrow in terms of her religious faith, just as the Taits, Gladstones, and Horsleys did in the same decade. Perhaps she found unspoken solace in private thoughts of reunion in an afterlife with Annie. She seems to have felt a degree of bitterness and anger at Annie's death unusual in Christian mothers of the 1850s, such as Catharine Tait and Catherine Gladstone, who were able to express their grief in terms of their faith. Two days after Annie's death, Charles admitted to his brother that 'Poor Emma . . . feels bitterly and God knows we can neither see on any side a gleam of comfort.'[44] Their daughter Henrietta later said that her mother never essentially recovered from this grief; on the very rare occasions when she spoke of Annie, 'the sense of loss was always there unhealed'. Henrietta also noted that her mother's 'bitter sorrow' was 'terribly aggravated by the anguish of not being able to go to her child's death-bed'.[45]

Charles Darwin evaded public discussion of his religious beliefs so as not to hurt Emma by parading their differences or to prejudice a brilliant academic career which still required respectability. This probably reinforced his natural disinclination to include references to his feelings and religious views in correspondence, even with Emma and his closest friends. All in all, he could find little consolation in facing the deaths of loved ones, and so preferred to divert his mind into scientific channels.

Joseph Hooker and Thomas Huxley

Joseph Dalton Hooker (1817–1911), Darwin's closest friend, was the leading botanist of his generation; he was Director of the Royal Botanic Gardens at Kew for many years and President of the Royal Society from 1873 to 1877. Just as Darwin lost Annie in 1851, Hooker had his share of family grief with the death of his 6-year-old daughter Minnie in 1863, and Huxley lost his eldest son, Noel, in 1860. In imparting the news to Huxley, Hooker said, 'My turn has come at last . . . Ever since your sad loss I have held the like as all but too likely to come to pass here—and so it has—and terrible it is in its realization.'[46] Minnie died very suddenly from obstruction of the bowels and strangulated hernia, after several hours of 'alarming illness'.[47] During the last three hours of her life, Hooker, despite his medical training, was oblivious to the obvious symptoms of approaching death, until the doctor's warning only three minutes before the end. He knew the danger through the night of 'agony and suspense' but preferred to believe she had many hours left. Hooker tried to comfort himself with the thought that she suffered 'comparatively little' and did not know that she was dying.[48] Conversely, Christian parents such as the Taits found some consolation in the knowledge that their children faced death directly and welcomed the prospect of the afterlife.

Hooker's curiously detached description of his favourite child's funeral, written immediately afterwards, also contrasted vividly with many Christian accounts: 'The Funeral service had no more effect on me than on her [Minnie]—the association with her personally snapped as the ceremonial left my door, and oddly enough I felt nothing at seeing the little white coffin go into the vault, my mind was wandering amongst sweeter memories elsewhere.'[49] Darwin and Huxley also had their problems in coping with funerals, since they rejected the Christian doctrines on which they were based. While Darwin's ill health usually allowed him to evade the funerals he dreaded, even those of Annie and his father, Hooker attended in body but not in spirit. Huxley confronted Christian funerals more directly, only to be shocked in 1860 as he listened carefully to his son's funeral service, with its stark reminders of the doctrines of hell and resurrection with their offensive implications for unbelievers.[50]

Hooker's grief for his daughter ran deep, as he confessed to Darwin three weeks after her death: 'It will be long before I get over this craving for my child; or the bitterness of that last night. To nurse grief I hold is a deadly sin, but I shall never cease to wish my child back in my arms as long as I live.'[51] But Hooker's grief for Minnie was acutely lonely, because he had no one, other than Darwin, with whom he could discuss such a 'selfish subject', as he described his grief apologetically. Darwin was hardly the most sympathetic confidant, for he was even more inhibited than Hooker on such a topic, leaving Hooker very isolated indeed, since 'it would make my wife ill if I went on so to her'. Fanny Hooker responded to Minnie's death as Darwin might have done, by taking refuge in illness. But her husband's reaction was very different, as he had a 'greater capacity for feelings which when once aroused, run riot'.[52]

Hooker had no outlet for these feelings of sorrow, except to sublimate them in his work at Kew. He even finished his letter to Darwin on the day of Minnie's funeral, 'And now I must go about my work.'[53] Hooker's botanical work at Kew, normally absorbing, provided inadequate consolation, and time did its healing work too slowly. As the first anniversary of Minnie's death approached, Hooker described to Darwin the anguish of the past year: 'I think we should not keep anniversarys of great sorrows, but as the day draws nearer I feel all the misery of last year crawling over me and my lost child's face and voice accompany me everywhere by day and by night. So that I now dread an attack of what were more the horrors of delirium tremens than the chastened sorrows of a sensible man.'[54] Significantly Hooker told Darwin that 'there is no other living soul with whom I can talk of the subject', underlining the loneliness of a Victorian agnostic scientist at a time of deep grief. The archival evidence suggests that bereaved Christian fathers of the 1860s would not have found it quite so difficult to express their sorrow to friends and family.

Hooker's first wife, Fanny, the daughter of Professor J. S. Henslow, the botanist, and a good botanist in her own right, died in 1874, eleven years after Minnie. Hooker reacted by immersing himself again in his work at Kew, as Darwin encouraged him to do: 'It is very wise of you to exert yourself and face the inevitable as well as you can.' Twelve days after Fanny's death, Hooker returned to work at Kew after spending a few days at Down with the Darwins, but he only hinted at his emotional state: 'I have now to abbreviate those intervals between work, when the utter desolation falls like a black cloud over all my prospects and pursuits.' Darwin, as usual, could suggest no sources of solace other than work and the effects of time.[55] A month after his bereavement, Hooker insisted that he was managing well at Kew, though 'intervals of great depression' still overcame him 'like a whirlwind' and he lived a good deal in the distant past, in a trance-like state.[56] Within two years, however, Hooker found a source of consolation beyond his work in remarriage to a woman who, like his first wife, was gentle, sensible, and involved in his scientific pursuits.[57]

This brief glimpse into Hooker's widowhood suggests that in certain respects his experience was not unlike that of Christian widowers, such as Alfred Lyttelton and John Horsley, in his recourse to work and remarriage as sources of solace. But its spiritual dimension was entirely different, for Hooker had no substitute for the Christian widowers' belief in immortality and a heavenly reunion. Hooker's correspondence on the subject of death was usually brief, stiff, and pompous, though occasionally he ventured a revealing comment of a more philosophical nature. He was more reluctant than Huxley or Darwin to relinquish entirely the possibility of immortality, especially when he was recently bereaved. In 1873 Hooker noted that all scientific evidence suggested extinction on death, but he considered it inconclusive.[58] At times of personal bereavement he sometimes yearned to share the Christian faith in an afterlife, as he did in 1865 after his daughter's death and again on the death of Hugh Falconer, a fellow botanist and friend: 'The inconceivability of our being born for nothing better than such a petty existence as our's is, gives me some hope of meeting in a better world.' But wishful thinking apart, Hooker was usually left with the open question 'What does it all mean?'[59]

More often Hooker attempted to come to terms with death by setting up imaginary utilitarian scales, weighing the pleasures of life against the pains of death. The conclusions differed, according to the degree of his grief and depression. In 1865, on the death of Falconer, he confessed in a melancholy mood to Darwin, 'And when we feel the deaths of friends more keenly the older we grow, we do strike me as being corporeally most miserable, for we have no pleasures to compensate fully for our griefs and pains: these alone are unalloyed.'[60] Two years later, on the death of Sir Charles Lyell, Hooker's utilitarian scales allowed the more positive conclusion that 'the sum of happiness derived from having known and loved Lyell is greatly in excess of the pain felt at his loss'.[61]

Thomas Henry Huxley (1825–95) was the youngest of the three scientists and the least well endowed with social status, family wealth, formal education, or patronage. He came from the lower end of the middle class, born above a butcher's shop in Ealing to a father who taught mathematics at a minor public school. The loss of his father's job left the family without means, and a combination of paternal neglect and poverty left Huxley bitter about a mere two years of formal schooling. He took an apprenticeship in medicine to an East End doctor at the age of 15, studying for his examinations at night, and sailed to New Guinea as an assistant ship's surgeon and naturalist at 21.[62]

Huxley rapidly gained fame for his research in zoology and comparative anatomy, with recognition as a Fellow of the Royal Society in 1851, but unlike most colleagues he had to make a living from science. He was renowned for his public advocacy of the biological sciences, while supporting himself for thirty years as lecturer in natural history at the Royal School of Mines. He was the only one of the three scientists willing to promote and defend his scientific and religious views in contemporary periodicals and on the public platform. He became the eloquent champion of radical Darwinism, gaining notoriety for his defence of Darwin's *Origin of Species* against Bishop Samuel Wilberforce's attack in 1860.

Huxley seems to have been a second-generation agnostic, for his most recent biographer, Adrian Desmond, makes no reference to any family church attendance as he grew up.[63] Huxley's views on religion seem to have been consistent from a young age, seeing himself as an active doubter who must weigh the evidence carefully in his search for moral truth. He repudiated atheism, since he believed it was impossible to disprove the existence of God, while at the other extreme he considered blind faith a sin. His opposition to the Christian doctrine of immortality was clearly stated in the *Nineteenth Century* in 1877: 'If I am not satisfied with the evidence that is offered me that such a soul and such a future life exist, I am content to take what is to be had and to make the best use of the brief span of existence that is within my reach, without reviling those whose faith is more robust and whose hopes are richer and fuller.'[64]

The differences in religious beliefs between Huxley and his wife, Henrietta, were similar to those of the Darwins. Huxley met 'Nettie' in Australia during his naval expedition of 1846 but could only afford to marry in 1854 after years of lonely engagement by correspondence. They subsequently had two sons and five daughters. Nettie was a middle-class woman with a religious background who was disconcerted by Huxley's agnosticism during courtship. Her conventional Christianity was expressed to Huxley in a letter of 1848: 'May we love and grow old together and dying may we meet again in Heaven.' Two years later she was anxious about the insecurity of such hopes for their shared eternal life: 'Oh if I only . . . felt assured that Death would be to us but a dark gate which led us to eternal happiness, what peace would possess me . . .'.[65]

Huxley's attitudes to death and mourning were formed at an early age, and were strongly expressed in his response to the two deaths which affected him while still young. When his mother died suddenly after a heart attack in 1852, he arrived too late to see her alive, and made no attempt to fabricate any arguments of solace for his sister: 'I offer you no consolation, my dearest sister, for I know of none. There are things which each must bear as he best may with the strength that has been allotted to him.' If they were together they might soften the blow by sharing their sorrow and sympathy, but that was all.[66] Huxley also commented to his wife that

This has opened the floodgates, and the whole meaning of existence has sucked out and drowns all other feelings. For me there is neither certainty of faith nor any consolation—but only a stern summoning of all my courage to bear what is inevitable. Belief and Happiness seem to be beyond the reach of thinking men in these days, but Courage and Silence are left.[67]

On the death of his friend the botanist Edward Forbes in 1854, he confessed to his sister that he felt this loss all the more because he had very few true friends and 'there is nothing for it but to shut one's self up again', accepting the inevitable as much as possible.[68]

In 1860, only four years after the Taits' tragedy at Carlisle, Huxley lost his eldest son Noel at the age of 3, also from scarlet fever. Another son, Leonard, later described the impact on his father: '[Noel] lived [nearly] four happy years to be the sunshine of home, the object of passionate devotion, whose sudden loss struck deeper and more ineffaceably than any other blow that befell Huxley during all his life.' Huxley's journal entry on his son's death was very different from those of Gladstone on the death of Jessy, or the Taits on the deaths of their five daughters. Huxley inserted only four restrained sentences, noting that Noel was taken ill on the Friday and was dead within forty-eight hours, but offering no details. He concluded the entry: 'I say heartily and without bitterness—Amen, so let it be.'[69]

The shock of Noel's death was so great that Huxley came dangerously close to a 'complete breakdown', aggravated by the suddenness of the death and the impact of his wife's 'inconsolable grief'. It prompted Huxley to reflect at a deeper level on the meaning of life and death, and the possibility of immortality, in a series of long letters to a new friend, Revd Charles Kingsley, the Christian Socialist:

My convictions, positive and negative . . . are of long and slow growth and are firmly rooted. But the great blow which fell upon me seemed to stir them to their foundation, and had I lived a couple of centuries earlier I could have fancied a devil scoffing at me and them—and asking me what profit it was to have stripped myself of the hopes and consolations of the mass of mankind? To which my only reply was and is—Oh devil! Truth is better than much profit . . . I neither deny nor affirm the immortality of man. I see no reason for believing in it, but, on the other hand, I have no means of disproving it . . . I shall rigorously refuse to put faith in that which does not rest on sufficient evidence.

This letter was written within a week of Noel's death, to a liberal churchman who was not yet a close friend. Nearly three years later Huxley admitted to Kingsley that he was not accustomed to 'open my heart to anybody', and in retrospect was amazed at the manner in which he poured out his troubles to Kingsley 'in those bitter days when my poor boy died'. But the strong and self-contained Huxley needed a confidant at his time of crisis, preferably not one of his scientific colleagues, and perhaps a liberal Christian rather than a fellow agnostic. Huxley admitted that he wrote more openly to Kingsley than he ever had to any person other than his wife.[70]

Noel's death was for Huxley a crisis of faith akin to W. E. Gladstone's on Jessy's death. In Huxley's case it was the strength of his unbelief which was tested, when in many respects it would have been easier to believe in a God and an immortality carrying with it the hope of reunion with his son. In 1860 Huxley was only too familiar with the Christian consolations which he might have enjoyed if his beliefs had allowed. But in his first long letter to Kingsley, he recited and rejected, in turn, all the arguments which could be advanced in favour of immortality. In the end 'my business is to teach my aspirations to conform themselves to fact', not the reverse, and he believed that the various arguments for immortality were mischievous as well as a delusion.[71]

A letter to his eldest daughter on the death of her baby son, twenty-six years later, provides more insight into Huxley's own method of dealing with grief on Noel's death: 'One does not weigh and measure these things while grief is fresh, and in my experience a deep plunge into the waters of sorrow is the hopefullest way of getting through them on to one's daily road of life again. No one can help another very much in these crises of life; but love and sympathy count for something.'[72] Huxley evidently found the painful 'plunge into the waters of sorrow' ultimately liberating, even though it brought him close to the point of breakdown in 1860.

Huxley coped with his grief more directly and openly than Darwin and Hooker, allowing his sorrow its full force at the crisis and thinking deeply about its philosophical implications. He also seemed to find more consolation in sources outside his scientific work than did his two colleagues. Like the Trevelyans later, Huxley loved walking, so his wife and doctor conspired to organize a week's climbing in Wales at the end of 1860. The birth of another son only three months after Noel's death brought more comfort.

Like Darwin, Huxley was soothed by the memory of his dead child, as he admitted to Herbert Spencer: 'As the little fellow was our greatest joy so is the recollection of him an enduring consolation. It is a heavy payment, but I would buy the four years of him again at the same price.'[73] This particular response, like Hooker's utilitarian scales, weighed the joy of life against the pain of death.

Like Emma Darwin, Henrietta Huxley discovered that the loss of a child could be even more traumatic for a Christian mother married to an agnostic. She was unable to share her grief with Huxley in the context of a consoling Christian faith in immortality and family reunion. Moreover, he expected her to battle through the sorrow as he did, accepting distractions where possible and outwardly recovering within a matter of months. But Nettie's initial hysteria was quickly followed by numbness and then by many months of despair, despite the birth of another son. Only three and a half months after Noel's death, Huxley was anxious that his wife 'mends but slowly'. Nettie at last found some relief in her sixth month of bereavement in sharing her grief with a compassionate Emma Darwin during a two-week visit to Down. Emma had herself experienced the same pain on the death of Annie, ten years earlier, and she could offer the traditional Christian consolation which Nettie could never share with her husband. But Huxley was alarmed to find that Nettie was still 'ill and weak from fretting' on her return home, as if seven months was quite long enough to recover from the loss of a child. Huxley's response was first to send his wife and children to recuperate by the sea in Folkestone, and afterwards to move house to break the ties with 'the old scenes' of their house of mourning.[74]

We should not make too much of the three scientists' differences in response to death and loss. They were differences of degree only, reflecting Huxley's more extrovert personality. In general, like Darwin and Hooker, he evidently dealt with the deaths of loved ones in solitary fashion. His son Leonard later noted that he was 'naturally reticent in these matters, and would hardly write of his own griefs unbidden even to old friends'.[75] It is also true that both Huxley and Darwin chose Christians as their rare confidants on the deaths of their children—Emma Darwin essentially performed the same function for Darwin that Kingsley did for Huxley. Moreover, Huxley could be just as inhibited as Darwin and Hooker, even when dealing with deaths which affected him deeply, such as that of his daughter Marion Collier from tuberculosis in 1887, nearly three decades after the death of Noel. Huxley promised Hooker to be 'in fighting trim again before long', even though it was a bitter blow.[76] He told Herbert Spencer in a short letter that he was thankful for the merciful end after three years of terrible suffering; he concluded apologetically, 'Don't answer this—I have half a mind to tear it up—for when one is in a pool of trouble there is no sort of good in splashing other people.'[77] The figurative language recalls his phrase 'deep plunge into the waters of sorrow', but this time he was swimming alone against the tide.

A. O. J. Cockshut observed in 1964 that 'One of the worst dilemmas of the agnostics sprang from the fact that most of them had no alternative system of ethics to take the place of the Christian . . . However unwillingly, they remained dependent upon the Christian tradition.'[78] Agnostics also lacked a substitute for the Christian rituals of death and mourning. Deathbeds for agnostics entirely lacked the consolations of the good Christian death, and their accounts were chiefly notable for their brevity. Agnostics were further deprived of the Christian support network which offered sympathy in its own distinctively Christian language. The consequence for mid- and late Victorian agnostics was a terrible isolation in bereavement, 'a solitude beyond the reach of God or man' in Wilfrid Blunt's resonant phrase. Some agnostics, such as Darwin, were partially sheltered because wives, families, or friends still believed in the Christian consolations and were fully supportive—though in Emma Darwin's case this involved considerable cost to herself. Darwin also protected his health and his work by refusing to think or write about unpleasant subjects such as death, any more than absolutely necessary. Others, such as Huxley, faced death rather more directly, though Hooker found it most difficult to reject the possibility of a life after death. Huxley was the most robust of the three in his unbelief, the only one to attempt rigorously 'to teach my aspirations to conform themselves to fact', and the only one of the three to think clearly about the meaning of the funeral service.

Many people in the twentieth century also seem to have no belief in a positive view of death, but without the cultural context of the Victorian agnostics, surrounded as they were by Christians for whom death was an essential and familiar part of their faith and life. Without a dominant Christianity against which to define unbelief, the meaning of death has largely been excluded from public culture, except for the inherited rituals of the burial or cremation service. But the loss in the meaning of death has also been a loss in the meaning of human life, a cultural problem which post-Christian societies are still trying to resolve.

❦ 18 ❦

EPILOGUE

AFTER THE VICTORIANS
SOCIAL MEMORY, SPIRITUALISM, AND THE
GREAT WAR

THERE WERE TWO MAJOR TURNING-POINTS IN THE HISTORY OF DEATH, grief, and mourning in Britain between 1830 and 1920. Fundamental religious, demographic, and cultural forces were responsible for the first transformation in the 1870s and 1880s, when the decline in mortality and in Evangelical fervour commenced, with profound long-term consequences. As Jose Harris has suggested, religion itself became more secularized in the decades after 1870, retreating into an increasingly nebulous, 'undogmatic "social" Christianity'.[1] The second turning-point was the First World War, which transformed the experience of death in the twentieth century, while also reinforcing and accelerating the more gradual changes of the previous forty years.

David Cannadine applauds the 'inventiveness with which the grief-stricken responded to their bereavement' during and after the Great War.[2] Some people looked to alternative beliefs such as spiritualism to help in dealing with the loss of loved ones, beliefs which could be reconciled with a diluted form of Christianity. Personal and social memory also came to have a new significance as a medium for storing and transmitting past lives, now barred from the Christian heaven by unbelief. But these alternative strategies for coping with death and grief pre-dated the war and can be traced back to an Edwardian generation of unbelievers who were often more resourceful than their more isolated Victorian predecessors. The first two sections of this chapter will consider the ways in which two families—one agnostic and the other still predominantly Christian—tried to come to terms with dying and death after 1900, as a bridge between the cultural world of the Victorians and the post-war generations. The third and final section of this chapter concludes that social memory was turned into new forms of 'civil religion' by the terrible mass deaths of the Great War.

Memory, Nature, and History: The Trevelyans

One important strategy for intellectuals in redefining the meaning of death was the concept that the memory of the virtues and contribution of the dead might inspire future generations and serve as a partial substitute for the loss of faith in personal immortality. This idea of inspirational death was already familiar from the Old Testament and the Catholic practice of invocation of the Saints, but it was developed for non-Christians by Enlightenment thinkers in the eighteenth century and by Comte and the Positivists in nineteenth-century France. As John McManners explains, Diderot rejected the Christian idea of eternal life as part of the secularizing project of the Enlightenment: 'To him, our true immortality consists in the survival of the memory of our deeds in the minds of future generations . . . Thus, religious rewards and punishments in a future life are replaced by the verdict of future generations, a verdict which goes on century after century, accumulating, in the case of great men, at compound interest.'[3] Auguste Comte's 'Religion of Humanity' emphasized that the influence of the dead continued through their 'subjective immortality', as their virtues were recalled in statues and ceremonies designed to inspire the living.[4] Such survival in social memory meant enduring glory for those few deemed truly great, but for the vast majority it seemed to offer rather less than the personal immortality of the Christian heaven.

Positivist ideas had much less influence in nineteenth-century Britain than in France, but they were enthusiastically advocated by Frederic Harrison in the 1877 symposium 'The Soul and Future Life' in the *Nineteenth Century*. Harrison ridiculed the traditional Christian concept of 'a life of vanity in a vale of tears to be followed by an infinity of celestial rapture':

It is not merely that this eternity of the tabor is so gross, so sensual, so indolent, so selfish a creed; but its worst evil is that it paralyses practical life . . . It is an infinite apathy to which your heaven would consign us, without objects, without relations, without change, without growth, without action, an absolute nothingness, a nirvana of impotence . . . You may call it paradise; but we call it conscious annihilation . . . a very place of torment.[5]

The positivist alternative to the 'fumes of celestial immortality' was the theory of posthumous influence, in the tradition of Diderot and Comte: 'Man is so constituted as a social being, that the energies which man puts out in life mould the minds, characters, and habits of his fellow-men; so that each man's life is, in effect, indefinitely prolonged in human society.'[6] Harrison cited Newton as an example of a man whose posthumous influence 'rises into greater activity and purer uses'. But the varieties of inspirational death for

Harrison were infinite. All people left 'influence for good or for evil . . . all continue to act indefinitely . . . The highest part of ourselves, the abiding part of us, passes into other lives and continues to live in other lives.' Harrison promised 'an immortality of influence, of spiritual work, of glorified activity'.[7]

Frederic Harrison's ideas on social memory were criticized by unbelievers as well as Christians. T. H. Huxley believed there was no evidence for the existence of life after death, but even he refused to accept Harrison's concept as a superior alternative. R. H. Hutton, an Anglican theologian, was impressed by the 'imaginative glow' of Harrison's theory of immortality, but pronounced it 'absolutely unverifiable' and, in any case, vastly inferior to the Christian heaven.[8] For most Christians social memory was inadequate without the hope of personal immortality, as Dorothy Stanley observed in 1918: 'We *cannot* live on Memories. We need the assurance of Future Reunion.'[9]

However, Harrison's concept of social memory had a particular appeal for educated agnostics or atheists who had to confront the death of a beloved family member without the consoling rituals and support structure offered by religion. As we have seen, the shared memory of the dead person was a vital consoling force for Christians as well as unbelievers, and in this sense positivism incorporated a widely held notion. The Trevelyan family's experiences exemplify the problem for unbelievers in finding any consolation after the deaths of their children; for them the role of memory became more significant than it was for Christians. Unbelievers could not seek relief in the language of the Bible, in soothing passages from the Psalms or popular hymns, or in meditation on family reunions in the next world. They were forced to explore alternative ways of accommodating death, especially the deaths of children.

George Macaulay Trevelyan, the historian, and his wife, Janet, daughter of the popular novelist Mrs Humphry Ward, lost their beloved 4-year-old son Theodore on 19 April 1911. The loss of a child was even more terrible for Edwardian unbelievers than for Victorian Christians, for the prospect of meeting the child again in a future life was rejected. Janet Trevelyan explained her views on immortality in 1903, before her marriage: 'There is *no* future life for all these millions of individual souls that have ever existed! Each individual has the immortality he deserves *here on earth*.'[10]

Theo Trevelyan died from appendicitis during a family holiday at Swanage, spent with George's brother Charles, the Liberal politician, his wife, Molly, and their children. Theo died the day after an operation to remove his appendix, following several days of fever and occasional bouts of severe pain. There was no detailed family memorial in writing to record Theo's death. Janet Trevelyan's very brief account was reminiscent of John Morley's on the death of Gladstone—eliminating God and highlighting instead the beauty of nature: 'Death called to him with mastering voice, and as the morning sun, on that 19th day of April, flooded with light the little high-placed room where he lay, Theodore slipped from us, all unknowing, and his little limbs lay still.'[11]

Their love of nature helped George and Janet Trevelyan through the immediate ordeal of the funeral and their early grief. Molly suggested to Janet that Theo might be buried in the Lake District, the site of the family's happiest memories of their favourite walking-holidays. They decided to bury Theo in the little churchyard at Langdale, half a mile below Robin Ghyll, the cottage they loved, where the parents would stay on for a while alone together to rest and contemplate.[12] This was also the way in which the Taits had chosen to confront their family tragedy half a century earlier—its appeal was not confined to unbelievers. Besides its natural beauty, the associations of the Lake District with the Romantic poets, and especially with Wordsworth, held a particular attraction for grieving unbelievers.

The Trevelyans buried their little boy on 21 April 1911. They were comforted a little by the beauty of nature in the countryside they loved so well, as Janet told Molly: 'We have come to the end of our long journey now, and laid him to rest among the everlasting hills, and his little grave is one mass of loveliest flowers . . . Now we've said goodbye to him, and I shall never again feel his sweet warm little body.'[13] The shock of the loss was intense, and it was still a very physical deprivation for the grieving mother. Janet's perspective on the burial-service was reminiscent of Hooker and Huxley's, though she was detached about the incongruity of the service where Huxley was angry: 'And the grand, far-away words of the service had a sort of soothing effect— extraordinarily wide of the mark they are in all conscience, but for that very reason one is grateful to them, for one feels that if one had to listen to anything more apt, more poignant, it just couldn't be borne.'[14] Two days after Theo's funeral Janet Trevelyan wrote that 'this dear valley' was the best place for 'two poor souls like us'. Theo's grave in the little churchyard under the fell looked very beautiful, 'and the deep peace of the mountains rests over him. And over us too, it rests, and gives us courage (or *something* does)'.[15]

But the agonies of grief were very great and the Trevelyans needed more consolation than the natural beauty of the Lake District could provide. Husband and wife sought additional solace in different sources, Janet looking to the memory of her son, whereas George found his primary consolation in his work as a historian. For unbelievers the memory of the deceased was often more important than for Christians, since they could only look backwards to recapture their lost children, rather than forward to heavenly reunions. Janet's mother and Molly's father recognized the potential value of the memory of the dead, but they differed as to its significance. Mrs Humphry Ward was optimistic: 'There will come a time, I hope, beyond the first bitterness of grief—when his dear memory will be something of the joy his presence was.'[16] But Sir Hugh Bell, the industrialist, focused on the limitations of memory, which would force Janet in the short term to recall her son's 'dreadful hours of suffering', while in the longer term the dimming of the memory, which carried relief, also reinforced the sorrow. Sir Hugh concluded that the only sensible response was to forget the past as fast as possible and to face life again free from memory's influence—a distinctively twentieth-century reaction.[17]

Janet and Molly Trevelyan, like the family as a whole, shared Mrs Humphry Ward's positive perspective on the value of memory to the bereaved. Molly was relieved that, even the day after he died, her sister-in-law could still talk freely about Theo, and liked to remember little things he used to do. She recognized, however, that 'it will be some time before she can begin to see him again as he was when he was well'.[18] Two days after Theo's funeral, Janet decided to write down all she could remember about her son 'in a continuous story': 'I know that as we get further from the pain of these last days the pure joy and beauty of his little life will shine out more and more, and will be like a light in our hearts to illuminate the rest of our way.'[19] George fully supported his wife's desire to recapture Theo's life, as she read aloud to him letters and stories about Theo collected from all members of their family. As George told his mother, 'It does us good. This is not a case for forgetting, but of remembering until you can bear to remember.'[20] So Janet commenced her account of Theo's short life, which took two years and 133 pages to complete. In her conclusion to her life of Theo, Janet wrote about the significance of his memory in a manner reminiscent of Harrison's 'posthumous influence':

Since neither G.M.T. [George] nor I could derive much comfort from thoughts of 'survival' or of meeting again, we were thrown back more and more on poetry and on the memory of his short life. That seemed to spread out in ever-widening circles, reaching towards the unknown and always inspiring us, through blinding tears, with thoughts of his clear brown eyes, his mischief and his strength. Those at any rate could be known, and could not be taken from us.

Several decades later, Janet Trevelyan published this life of Theo so that 'even the larger world should have a share in him'.[21]

Though George Trevelyan supported and to some extent shared his wife's need to revive Theo in memory, it was not an equally effective therapy for bereavement for him. George shared the need of other bereaved late Victorian spouses and fathers, such as Alfred Lyttelton, Darwin, and Hooker, to seek relief (and possibly distraction) through professional work. Charles Trevelyan told his parents on the day before Theo's funeral that Janet was bearing up well and was unlikely to break down, but that his brother was 'very hard hit'.[22] George scarcely spoke throughout the long journey north with Theo's body, except to say that Theo would never grow up. After the funeral George sent a sad, thoughtful letter to his worried parents, saying that he would never be so happy again as he had been for the past seven years:

I wish, not rebelliously or passionately, but with a quiet preference, that I were lying there instead of him, for the first 35 years are the great ones, not the last 35 . . . I do not mean that I dislike having to live on . . . But the passionately selfish zest at life that every healthy youth has went from me this week. In fact I am suddenly become middle aged, and hope to serve a useful turn so.

Three weeks earlier George had completed his book *Garibaldi*, which represented his best work, but he was 'jealous in my profession' and would find some consolation in it.[23]

In addition to his work as a historian, and his love of poetry and the natural world, George Trevelyan found solace in his remaining children, Mary and Humphry, as did Janet. Charles hoped George and Janet would have more children, 'for that would be the only thing to be any real compensation', though he knew Theo could not be replaced.[24] Molly looked after Mary and Humphry while their parents mourned Theo in the Lake District. George thanked her for the daily letters containing 'the only real comfort—as apart from philosophy—that is the account of the living children'. He believed that Mary would help to 'restore a temperate joy to our house'.[25]

George and Janet Trevelyan reassured their families that they would not allow grief to turn them into perpetually unhappy people.[26] Molly Trevelyan was impressed by the philosophy towards death expressed in George and Janet's 'honeymoon of grief and thought together' in the Lake District. Even on the day of Theo's death, Janet had said that she needed to be able to be happy again and of use to others in the future, and hoped she could achieve this through cheerfulness and through the memory of Theo.[27] Nearly three years later, Molly Trevelyan looked back on Theo's death, and assured Charles that if they were ever similarly afflicted, they too could conquer unhappiness through memory, work, and cheerfulness. She underlined the significant role of memory and a positive approach in overcoming death: 'Death doesn't end such happiness as ours. The remembrance of our times together would go on still, and we should work and play and laugh because the other one would have liked it to be so. WE WILL NOT BE CONQUERED BY SORROW.'[28]

But Molly Trevelyan discovered for herself in 1916 that Janet and George's response to death was tougher and perhaps less efficacious for her than for them. Molly and Charles lost their 13-month-old son Hugh from meningitis in 1916. Molly had kept a diary for many years, confiding in it her joys and sorrows, including even the emotional and physical ordeal of two miscarriages. But she was utterly unable to express her grief for Hugh in its pages, as so many bereaved Victorians had done. Indeed the diary seems to have been terminated for ever with little Hugh's death, acknowledging its inadequacy for Molly at such a crisis.

Molly's daughter Katherine explained years later that her parents went away for a few days' walking during Hugh's final illness: 'in accordance with their beliefs they felt they could be no help to the child in its passage through the Door'. They had reached Durham when they learned of their son's death, and they went inside the cathedral, which offered them some comfort.[29] Victorian Christian parents would have found such a response to a child's terminal illness incredible; for them it was imperative to participate at the deathbed at home, however harrowing, to witness their child's soul leaving for the life with Christ. Five weeks after her baby's death Molly made a brave attempt at a positive response in her diary: 'I can find nothing to regret. In all our baby boy's life there was nothing but sunshine. All the memories I have of him are of a sunny, laughing face . . . I have got a little lock of [his hair] to keep, all I have of my darling except a host of sweet memories.'[30] The diary effectively terminated on that sad note, with its hint that memories alone were not enough. There was just one additional short entry over a year later: 'I am glad to find that the acuteness of the sorrow gets less as time goes on. He is very often in my thoughts, and things suddenly remind me of him, but not with such terrible poignancy as it used to be.'[31] It may have been harder to deal with the death of a child in the bleak emotional landscape of wartime, while the parents' absence from the child's death may have made it more difficult to express their grief openly. It was possibly also harder for Molly than Charles, as she had been a regular church attender before her marriage. She was well aware of the spiritual consolations no longer available to her, and perhaps yearned for something beyond 'a host of sweet memories' and the beauties of nature.

Edith Lyttelton and Spiritualism

Edith Lyttelton was one of the very few members of the families examined in this study who turned to spiritualism as an alternative religion, rather than as a scientific exercise or a parlour pastime. However, Edith represented increasing numbers of people who found spiritualism a comfort in dealing with grief in the period between 1900 and about 1955, since when there has been a steady decline in membership of spiritualist groups. It was a significant sign of the changing times that any member of the Lyttelton and Gladstone families, such committed Anglicans, should need to seek solace in spiritualism.

Spiritualists believed in the immortality of the soul and in the possibility of communication with the spirits of the dead through mediums. The movement began in the United States in the 1840s, and spread in the United Kingdom in the 1850s and 1860s, with private seances, much table-tapping at private 'home circles', some frauds, and little formal organization. Many younger members of these middle- and upper-class families dabbled intermittently in table-tapping and -turning as a leisure-time activity, without taking it seriously. Lady Byron reported in 1853 that six gentlemen had made a table spin at the Athenaeum Club, reinforcing her view that 'table-moving' was the '*credible* part of the Rapping phenomenon'.[32] In this spirit Charles Darwin reported to his friend J. D. Hooker in 1874 on a seance held in his brother's house in London, which was attended by T. H. Huxley incognito:

We had good fun one afternoon; for George hired a medium, who made the chairs, a flute, a bell and candlestick and fiery points jump about in my Brother's Dining Room in a manner that astounded everyone and took away all their breaths. It was in the *dark*, but George and Hensleigh Wedgwood held the mediums hands and feet on both sides all the time.

In characteristic fashion, Darwin found the seance so hot and tiring that he departed before these 'astonishing miracles or jugglery' took place. He did not understand how these activities were carried out but concluded they were 'rubbish', even though Francis Galton declared it a good seance.[33] From the 1890s there was an attempt to organize a national federation of spiritualist societies, whose forty-five affiliated societies in 1892 increased to 141 by 1913.[34] But up to the Great War the spiritualist movement was concentrated in the north of England, had not developed a strong popular following, and had little impact on Victorian social or religious life or even on funeral customs.

The spiritualist movement developed a quite different perspective and clientele with the foundation of the Society for Psychical Research in 1882 by a group of Cambridge philosophers and scientists. Their aim was 'to examine without prejudice or prepossession and in a scientific spirit those faculties of man, real or supposed, which appear to be inexplicable'.[35] The founders and early members included such distinguished names as Henry Sidgwick, F. W. H. Myers, Leslie Stephen, Alfred Tennyson, W. E. Gladstone, A. J. Balfour, and John Ruskin. The membership was chiefly drawn from the upper-middle class, including a strong university element. The Society aimed to use scientific methods to establish the validity of the physical phenomena produced by mediums, such as materialization, levitation, and automatic writing.[36] Many members of the Psychical Society were Christians haunted by religious doubt, such as Henry Sidgwick and Myers, seeking empirical evidence of immortality. Ruth Brandon observes that British spiritualism was marked by a 'feeling of underlying religious yearning', compared with the 'genuine spirit of scientific enquiry' which permeated the European spiritualist scene.[37] Agnostics like T. H. Huxley, who were convinced in their unbelief, felt no need to participate in the serious investigation of spiritualist manifestations. In 1874 Huxley had observed that the only case of spiritualism he had personally examined was 'as gross an imposture as ever came under my notice', and he had no interest in further enquiry as to its 'truth'.[38]

The appeal of the spiritualist movement in the Edwardian period can be explored through the experience of Edith ('D.D') Lyttelton, second wife of Alfred, Mary Lyttelton's last child. This case-study helps us to understand the appeal of spiritualism even within a deeply Christian family. In one sense the supposedly scientific enquiries of the Society for Psychical Research made the spiritualist movement more respectable among the educated social and intellectual élite, but it was rare for a woman such as Edith Lyttelton to adopt it as a religion.

The Lytteltons had some record of involvement in spiritualism before the Edwardian period through their links with A. J. Balfour, Conservative politician, who had been in love with May Lyttelton before her death from typhus on Palm Sunday 1875. A. J. Balfour, his sister Eleanor Sidgwick, and his brother-in-law Henry Sidgwick were early members of the Psychical Society. Balfour and Lavinia Talbot, May's sister, remembered May every year on the anniversary of her death. Spiritualist automatists, who claimed to receive messages from spirits in automatic writing, reported many communications from May, including references to Palm Sunday and to her sister-in-law Laura Lyttelton, Alfred's first wife. Messages were also reported from A. J. Balfour's brother Francis, killed in a mountaineering accident in 1882, and from Henry Sidgwick after his death in 1900.[39]

Spiritualism certainly had an appeal to Christians who doubted their faith but retained a yearning to believe. Edith Lyttelton represented fertile soil in this respect, especially as her interest was already engaged by the family links with the Psychical Society and the knowledge of alleged communications from her predecessor, Laura. Edith Lyttelton was a member of the larger Balfour clan, though not part of A. J. Balfour's immediate family. She was a highly intelligent and articulate woman who married Alfred Lyttelton in 1892, six years after Laura's death in childbirth. She wrote several plays, including one dealing with the issue of sweated labour, and made a significant contribution to philanthropy and public service. Edith admitted to Alfred in 1906 that up to 1902 she had conformed to the Lyttelton family's Anglican beliefs partly out of loyalty to him; she was in some senses an 'unprofessed agnostic' who was always hoping the High Church observances might come to mean more to her. Increasingly Edith felt impatient with the Church's 'want of touch with reality' and was troubled because she could not feel any 'special grace' in the sacraments, and did not find church services spiritually fulfilling.[40]

Edith Lyttelton's dissatisfaction with conventional Christianity combined with her grief over the death of her son Antony in 1902 to lead her to spiritualism. She wrote a very short immediate account of her response to Antony's sudden death, in which the cause of death was not mentioned. Little information was given, except that his death followed several days' illness after an earlier bout of bronchitis. Edith's response was most unusual in that she avoided the sight of her dead child for a complete day. When the agony of loss became intolerable, she finally looked at Antony's face and had a 'wonderful moment by his dead body [which] has been the strongest influence in my life. I can date from it all the belief and hope that have upheld me.' When Edith looked at him, the child appeared to be gone, and she felt him and 'others too, very near to me', and a 'wonderful peace and hope descended upon me'. She believed she could see in the lines of his little face 'the deeply strong and serious character of the man that was to be'. Over three decades later Edith added a note to her short record of Antony's death, emphasizing the significance of this vivid experience: 'Some day far hence the messages which have come through about Antony from another life will be known and will bring proof to many that his life is only a stage in a greater journey . . . This is no credulous dream of a fond mother: I have been allowed to see the evidence which exists of Antony's continuous life as well as that of others.'[41] In 1938, when Edith wrote her memoir, 'Interwoven', she still could not write about Antony's actual death: 'the agony of that parting is still alive and quivering', though the remarkable experience she had then of 'the struggle, the light' helped her later to cope with Alfred's death.[42] After the death of Antony in 1902, Edith experienced a daily, indeed an hourly, struggle to present a courageous front and carry on with life. Her loss never left her mind and 'haunts the hours of talk and social intercourse'.[43]

Edith Lyttelton's grief over Antony's death and her mystical experience by his body led her to accept spiritualism and to join the Society for Psychical Research in 1902: 'the world of the spirit, the communion with something we call God is a living vital reality to me'. She had been 'outside the body' for a moment and had 'realised another place of being', which had led her to her own belief in the soul and a sense of God.[44] In 1910 Edith was continuing her research into psychical phenomena and was impressed by the likeness to life in the communications of the spirits. Her reading in psychical research left her with a 'reasoned intellectual belief in the "soul"': 'I feel convinced that there is a world of spirits with which we have some correspondence *now.*'[45] Edith was an active member of the Psychical Society for many years, becoming its President in 1933.

This belief in an independent life of the spirit after death also helped Edith Lyttelton to come to terms with her husband's death in 1913. Alfred's actual death was not recorded in a private family deathbed memorial in the Victorian manner, but in Edith's public account in her 1917 biography of her husband.[46] Alfred was the youngest of the twelve Lyttelton children, the darling of his family, and a former Colonial Secretary. He was, by all accounts, also a man of unusual charm and vitality, who made numerous friends in his chosen fields of law and politics. Alfred died suddenly at the age of 56, when he collapsed in acute pain the day after he was hit by a cricket ball during a match. On learning that an operation was necessary, Alfred prepared for death, telling Edith, 'One has to be ready, and this is a big affair.' He made his will, and Revd H. E. Ryle, the Dean of Westminster, administered the Holy Communion to Alfred, Edith, and their daughter Mary. Just before Communion, Alfred talked to his wife about the significance of their life together—'unforgettable words, drawn from the depths of his heart and in the light of a clear vision'. Edith did not record these words and was too overcome to respond: 'I had to keep control and to act for him.'[47] Her brief public account in her biography is far removed from the lengthy memorial of Alfred's mother's death in 1857, when every detail was lovingly recorded.

Soon afterwards Alfred Lyttelton went to a nursing-home for the operation—another change, even since 1891, when William Gladstone was operated on at home. Edith described the operation as 'horrible', revealing 'a bad state of things', and Alfred suffered acutely for the next five days. He insisted on being told the cause of the trouble, but was not informed of his 'acute danger', another change in customary practice since the nineteenth century. Alfred could scarcely talk, but asked Edith to read the Psalms and some poetry to him. When he could struggle no longer, Alfred asked to see his children, his brothers and sisters, some Gladstone cousins, and close friends like Arthur Balfour. The farewells lasted an hour or two, at most, and Alfred managed to say a few loving words to each of them. Edith recorded the scene in her biography, knowing that the manner of his dying mattered greatly to Alfred. He said to the doctor, 'I've made a good fight, haven't I?', and he reminded Mary Drew of the wonderful way her father had borne his pain. Edith told him that 'If any of us should be called upon to suffer too, because of you we shall bear it with infinitely greater courage.' Alfred's death was a mixture of the old and the new, combining a nursing-home death and a spiritualist wife with the traditional family farewells, Christian preparation, and resolve to face death with fortitude. Edith thought 'there was a note of triumph in the sorrow, the triumph that a life had been nobly lived and nobly ended, that a spirit had won through its great ordeal'.[48] This hints at the Evangelical ideal of the good death, which had so influenced the Lyttelton family in the nineteenth century, as well as the spirit world which comforted Edith in the twentieth.

Edith Lyttelton's resort to spiritualism for comfort in her grief was a major break with Lyttelton family tradition. Her sister-in-law Lavinia Talbot, wife of the Bishop of Winchester, admired Edith's noble bearing in sorrow, 'and her reality of belief in his Spirit being with her'.[49] Edith told Arthur Balfour that Alfred's death had strengthened her belief in 'another life', though she suffered at intervals from 'a storm of panic' in trying to live without him.[50] Edith kept an account of her psychical contacts with Alfred for six years after his death, recording his 'appearances' to her in a red leather-bound volume, usually when she was most depressed. She provided no specific evidence of his 'existence', and it is easy for a sceptical reader to conclude that Alfred's purported statements emerged from her own wishful thinking. Alfred's responses to her more penetrating enquiries were empty and at times she was close to admitting that she was answering her own questions. On 26 August 1913, for instance, Edith was lying down crying and tried to imagine Alfred beside her, but felt 'the things I could fancy he was saying really came out of my own mind'. But shortly afterwards, 'quite suddenly Alfred seemed to touch both my hands and to *float* beside me', lying slightly above the level of the bed. Edith asked at one point if Alfred was with Laura, his first wife, but his spirit diplomatically refused to answer. He reportedly told her on various occasions not to grieve or be afraid, and reassured her that she would soon join him—though in reality her death was to take a further thirty-five years.[51]

Over the years 1913 to 1919 the intensity and regularity of these psychic experiences declined, as Edith's grief and depression diminished. There is no doubt that she was consoled by Alfred's 'appearances', noting at one point, 'How do people bear sorrow if they are not helped as I am by these wonderful moments?' Even as late as 1939 Edith claimed that she still felt him close to her very often.[52] After Alfred's death Edith began to produce automatic writing under a pseudonym, allegedly even foretelling the sinking of the *Lusitania* in 1915; years later she recorded instances of her work in precognition in her book *Some Cases of Prediction*, published in 1936.[53]

The Great War: The Experiences of the Bickersteth and Charteris Families

The Great War accelerated and intensified trends already in process, not least the decline in religious adherence, all of which profoundly affected families' attitudes and responses to death. Stephen Koss argued in 1975 that the war 'dealt a shattering blow to organized religion. The churches never recovered from the ordeal, either in terms of communicants or self-possession. Thereafter men looked elsewhere, if anywhere, for their moral certainties.'[54] While John Stevenson stresses the longer-term process of slow decline in church membership relative to total population, this is a difference in emphasis only, for all agree on the sharp fall in membership during the war.[55] The Great War also created new strains for the Christian ministry. Alan Wilkinson shows how difficult it was for the Anglican chaplains at the front to offer plausible explanations for the horror or to give adequate consolation after mass war deaths. Their ministry to the dying and bereaved was confused and diluted in these extraordinary circumstances, even capitulating to popular demands for public prayers for the dead soldiers. Moreover, Christian doctrines of immortality, already modified by the late Victorians, were often adapted still further to concede that soldiers killed in a patriotic cause must necessarily go to heaven, irrespective of faith or repentance. Chaplains at the western front also experienced great difficulty in sustaining the religious significance of burial rituals for individual deaths when faced with so many.[56] Clergymen such as Revd Cyril Hudson argued in 1918 that the war had caused 'decreasing indifference to religion in general'.[57] In 1919 Ella Bickersteth was not the only Christian parent to regret the change in her previously devout son Burgon as a result of the trauma of war: 'Burgon just now is unlike himself. He has got very cynical and thinks there is so little real religion in the world. He has lost his keenness for things . . . he says he cares for nothing.'[58]

Whereas organized religion declined during the war, 'religious responses of a less orthodox kind were actually stimulated by the war', as James Obelkevich notes.[59] The spiritualist movement increased dramatically in popularity, despite a hostile press campaign fuelled by fraudulent mediums. Spiritualism was transformed into a movement with mass appeal for many thousands of bereaved relatives eager for communication with their dead. The wartime cause of spiritualism was further enhanced by the very public conversion and advocacy of Sir Oliver Lodge and Sir Arthur Conan Doyle, who refused to accept the finality of their own family losses. Lodge's crude picture of the spirit world in his 1916 memorial on the death of his son Raymond had great impact in reassuring other bereaved families about the reality of the life beyond. By 1919 the number of societies affiliated to the spiritualist movement had doubled since 1913, reaching their peak in the 1930s with about a quarter of a million members.[60]

As Christian faith declined, so also did the mourning rituals which were such an intrinsic part of the Christian community's response to death in the nineteenth century. From 1875 the National Funeral and Mourning Reform Association encouraged funeral reform, simpler mourning fashions, and shorter time in private mourning.[61] D. C. Coleman documents the change in taste away from crape for mourning clothes from the 1880s, with further decline in the home market in the 1890s followed by a dramatic reduction after Queen Victoria's death.[62] The process accelerated during the war, since it was argued that national morale and patriotism would suffer if thousands of widows all wore full mourning-dress, especially after the mass deaths from 1916.[63] Many people commented on the depressing effect of large numbers of families in mourning, even at the Eton and Harrow match at Eton in July 1916, as Lady Gainford observed: 'it was all rather sad and dull, such lots of people in deep mourning'.[64] But others commented on the relaxation of mourning rituals. Soon after the death of her son Morris in 1916, Ella Bickersteth attended the wedding of her younger son Ralph wearing 'black chiffon over apricot with coral embroidery. I could not wear mourning for Ralph's sake, and in any case I am only in black and white.'[65]

Julian Litten has commented on the significant impact of the war on the funeral ceremony:

The greatest influence on the simplification of the English funeral came as a result of the First World War. Primarily, there was a thinning-out of funeral operatives due to war service which, coupled with the requisitioning of non-essential work-horses, led to a reduction in both personnel and vehicles. Secondly, there was a particular undercurrent of public opinion to contend with: the morality of staging a grandiose funeral when those who had died for king and country on foreign fields were unable to be repatriated. At such a time of great national suffering and sorrow, individual displays of funerary pomp and panoply did not sit comfortably on the conscience.[66]

Critics of conventional funeral customs and Christian burial rituals took advantage of the crisis of war to demand the abolition of formal Victorian mourning and to promote cremations. Dr Robert MacKenna argued in 1916 that the 'pageantry of funereal gloom' increased the fear of death by making it 'black, mysterious and awesome'.[67] C. E. Lawrence in the *Fortnightly Review* in 1917 saw the war as the opportunity to replace mourning ritual and 'funeral gloom' with cremations for all, everyday clothes, and 'a sweet and grateful memory': 'The war has greatly helped a tendency which was slowly gathering force. It is only necessary to hasten the certain end and so be done with the odious business of ordered ugliness and dark materialisation of the conventional funerals.'[68] Even Edward Mercer, a theologian and former Bishop of Tasmania, joined in the clamour in 1919 for the abolition of the dismal pomp and unwholesome gloom of funeral ceremonies.[69] Bertram Puckle's book *Funeral Customs*, published in 1926, reflected this post-war enthusiasm for cremation and its condemnation of nineteenth-century funeral and mourning customs.

Condolence letters had already altered in tone, content, and value before 1914, but that process was also hastened. Rituals which were beneficial in peacetime in helping mourners to grieve for individuals sometimes had quite the reverse effect in wartime. Most of the critical comments about condolence letters in the families surveyed since 1830 were expressed during the Great War—in marked contrast to the appreciative remarks of the previous eighty years. William Cecil, Bishop of Exeter, for example, lost three sons to the war between 1915 and 1918. He burnt all the letters of condolence he received, as they 'added so much to his suffering'.[70] Similarly, H. H. Asquith, the Prime Minister, on the death of his son Raymond in 1916, noted 'numberless letters from all parts of the world . . . but I don't know that it helps one very much'.[71] Condolence letters were always ineffectual in that they never restored past happiness; but they had been valuable in expressing and activating the sympathy and affection of support networks. But in the context of mass deaths in wartime, condolence letters seemed to underline the hopelessness of the bereaved and the declining stocks of sympathy and energy among overworked family and community. Moreover, it was necessary that the rhetoric of patriotism and glory continue to be employed in condolence letters long after most people had lost faith in it; recently bereaved families needed reassurance that their loved one had died bravely in a just cause.

The Great War not only accelerated trends already in process, but also dealt a shattering blow to the way families had habitually coped with dying and with grief for more than a century. The war caused a total breach with the Victorian Christian way of death among the middle and upper classes. Between 1914 and 1918 families were suddenly forced to deal with vast numbers of violent and unnatural deaths of adult sons, as though they were the norm. Moreover, this crisis arose when traditional Christian mourning rituals already provided less support than at any time during the previous century. Death was effectively removed from the domain of the family and became instead a communal sacrifice for the nation—death could no longer be readily mourned by individual families.

The Great War combined and far exceeded all those forms of violent, unnatural, and premature death which the Victorians had been unable to resolve effectively even within the conventional Christian framework. The Victorians had been best able to come to terms with certain kinds of death—primarily non-violent deaths of older people which took place gradually within the family home, allowing them to respect the dignity of the dying and the dead. Modern psychologists agree that the untimely death of an adult son or daughter can cause an unusually traumatic and prolonged bereavement, even when it occurs at home and in peacetime. As we have seen, Christian parents experienced considerable difficulty in reconciling their faith with the premature loss of adult children, even when they died peacefully within the family setting. Such deaths were more likely to provoke chronic grief when they occurred overseas and in a violent manner.

The Great War represented a unique combination of vast numbers of soldiers killed simultaneously, together with violence, horror, and anonymity, and the physical impossibility of using Victorian mourning rituals. The war involved slaughter on an unprecedented scale, which nobody had envisaged when war was declared. Jay Winter estimated that 722,785 British servicemen died in the war, and that of the 6 million British soldiers, one man in eight was killed and one in four wounded. Soldiers only had a one in two chance of surviving the war without being killed, wounded, or imprisoned. The well-educated middle and upper classes carried more than their relative share of war losses, as they volunteered readily and were killed more rapidly as officers. This catastrophic loss of younger men helps to explain the powerful myth of the 'lost generation', especially when combined with its disproportionate impact on the influential classes.[72] Most families in Britain experienced the trauma of the death of a son, husband, father, uncle, or cousin, and some lost more than one. Five of Lord Salisbury's ten grandsons were killed in action. Jay Winter concluded that 'the individuality of death had been buried under literally millions of corpses'.[73]

The terrible manner of these soldiers' deaths added greatly to the trauma of their grieving families. Those at home could not conceive the full horror and futility of the western front, while soldiers were often unable to communicate the grim reality, which was veiled by the heroic rhetoric of the early war years. The early idealism perished finally in 1916 at the battle of the Somme, where 400,000 British soldiers were killed to little purpose. 'The fact of mass and meaningless death seared itself on the consciousness of the survivors,' as Wohl observed, describing the front as 'a nightmarish moonscape where men lived underground like rats and died collectively like hordes of swatted flies . . . a desolate hell surpassing Dante's worst imaginings'.[74]

Grieving families were usually obliged to try to confront some level of the new and terrible reality of wartime death, so far removed from the experience of most Victorian families. It was not just that these young men died violently and far from home. Nearly half the total dead of the British Empire in the Great War have no known burial place, and can only be communally commemorated by huge memorials to the unidentified, like that at Menin Gate.[75] Vast numbers of soldiers were blown to bits or left for dead in no man's land, where their bodies could never be recovered. Their corpses were scattered in subsequent fighting, making burial impossible even if the remains could be recovered and identified. Wilfrid Owen wrote of 'unburiable bodies' which 'sit outside the dugouts all day, all night'. Raymond Asquith's last letter to his stepmother in 1916 described the battlefield near Ypres: 'bodies and bits of bodies . . . and a stink of death and corruption which was supernaturally beastly'.[76]

Beverley Raphael and Jane Littlewood offer helpful observations on the impact of war deaths on bereaved families. They note the difficulty for the family in comprehending any sudden and violent death away from home as a reality. This family response can become bitter if the deaths are perceived as serving no purpose, underlining the importance of the wartime rhetoric of patriotism, duty, glory, and honour. The problem in coming to terms with the finality and reality of the death was aggravated by the absence of a corpse which could be viewed and buried by the family.[77] Jane Littlewood's research suggests that the impact of war deaths could be devastating for the parents, who were sometimes traumatized by wartime losses which they never completely accepted.[78] Bernd Hüppauf notes that the lack of a corpse and the remoteness of the front could create doubts in the minds of the bereaved which might continue for years—the foundation for the idea that the dead soldiers somehow still survived, and fertile soil for spiritualism and unresolved grief.[79]

The Great War and its aftermath are largely outside the scope of this book and have already been the subject of excellent work.[80] My final brief case-studies examine the deep trauma caused to the Bickersteth and Charteris families by the terrible wartime deaths, which made the process of grieving so difficult. Since both families were committed Anglicans, their experience allows us to see how little even the more devout Christians were able to retain and find consolation in their traditional mourning customs in wartime.

Lord and Lady Wemyss lost both their sons in the Great War, Yvo Charteris in October 1915, and Hugo (Ego) Lord Elcho in April 1916. Yvo, at 18, only left Eton a few months before he went to France, where he was killed after three weeks' service. His elder brother, Hugo, was realistic about the odds of survival even in June 1915, commenting on the earlier death of their close friend Julian Grenfell, 'I suppose no one has any chance if they go on long enough.'[81] The official letters explained that Yvo died a 'gallant' hero's death, trying to lead his men over the top in an attempt to 'rush a bit of German trench'. The letters reassured the family that he died instantly from four bullets and without pain; and that his body was recovered and buried by his platoon in a village four miles behind the trench, Sailly-la-Bourse.[82] Despite these comparatively favourable circumstances, Yvo's sister Mary described years later how his death affected her:

For some years after his death I was haunted by the most terrible recurring night-mares that he had not been killed but was lost somewhere, insane and helpless, and that I could never reach him, though often he was near. These nightmares were always accompanied by that unearthly depth of sorrow, horror and freezing terror that one only experiences in dreams.[83]

Such sentiments were not usually expressed during the war, because they would be seen as selfish and unpatriotic, but they were probably not uncommon. A few days after Yvo's death, Mary wrote to her mother: 'For days I simply couldn't make myself believe that it was really true that Yvo was dead.'[84] Without seeing his body or participating in his funeral Mary found the reality of her brother's death almost impossible to accept. The memorial service at Stanway church a week after Yvo's death stressed his spiritual preparation, given his recent confirmation, and the 'splendour' of his sacrifice to God. It also emphasized the right of the community 'to look upon him as belonging to all of us in common', reinforcing the concept of the Great War deaths as sacrifices for the nation, and to some extent removing them even further from the orbit of the individual family.

Yvo's only surviving brother, Hugo Lord Elcho, was killed only six months later, but the circumstances of his death were even more difficult for the family to cope with. On 26 April 1916 they learned informally that Hugo had been wounded and taken prisoner at Katia in the Middle East three days earlier. A month later further private sources informed the family that Hugo was not among the prisoners, though one source claimed to have seen him alive at Damascus. As his wife, Letty, observed, 'It is very cruel this waiting . . . it is agony sometimes.' The family endured months of appalling uncertainty before they received informal news in July that Hugo was killed at Katia. But Letty still refused to believe it, since there were no details of his death 'and one knew so well how often mistakes have been made in this war'. At last on 20 August there was official confirmation that Hugo had been killed by a shell and his body left at Katia.[85]

The family tried to accept the reality of Hugo's death, but a new form of torture began, for they could not be satisfied death was instantaneous. Letty was 'on the rack' from July until the end of September, seeking details of his wounds, confirming that he would have been 'rendered unrecognizable'. She wanted to be grateful that Hugo was happy somewhere with that 'glorious host of gallant-hearted men', but the consequences for his bereaved family, including his two sons, were 'unspeakable'. Letty confessed to a family friend: 'There is no *comfort* to give . . . It was a long-drawn-out agony—months of it—and the death-blow badly dealt. And there is more to come! . . . When Peace comes, and just a few loved ones are set free and return rejoicing, then is the time when the full deep measure of the fearful loss will be realized. I dread it too terribly.'[86]

Mary Charteris, Lady Wemyss, the mother of the two dead soldiers, continued to grieve for years. Only in 1932 did she produce 'A Family Record' of over 400 pages in their memory, for private circulation. Lady Wemyss created this record for her surviving children and grandchildren, to remind them of Hugo and Yvo 'in their very happy home life'. The Book of Remembrance at the end listed neighbours and friends who had also died in the war, noting that Hugo's name was engraved with those of 3,000 other soldiers with no known graves on a beautiful 'Memorial of the Missing' on the Mount of Olives in Jerusalem.[87] The anguish caused by such uncertainty and grief as the Charteris family endured had no parallel in the non-violent deaths which took place in Victorian Britain. In these wartime circumstances, the traditional mourning rituals were inadequate, irrelevant, and often impossible, even for Christian families.

The experience of the Bickersteth family was also dreadful, though the details of the ordeal differed and only one son died. Morris Bickersteth was killed on the first day of the battle of the Somme on 1 July 1916, aged 25. His

father, Revd Samuel Bickersteth, vicar of Leeds and canon of Ripon, belonged to a famous Victorian Evangelical family. Samuel and Ella Bickersteth
had six sons, three of whom were fighting at the front, with Julian and Morris
both involved in the Somme offensive. On the first day of the Somme,
20,000 were killed of the 110,000 who attacked, and 40,000 more were
wounded. It was days before the wounded in no man's land stopped crying
out.[88] On 1 July Morris was reported missing, but three days later his brother
Julian learned from survivors that Morris was killed near Serre, gallantly
leading his company in the attack. Morris was struck in the back of the head
by a piece of shrapnel, but his body had to be left unburied in no man's land,
as the British troops were forced to retreat 100 yards. Julian reported to the
family that 'You will see it is quite impossible to get the body back, but . . . I
never felt so strong in my faith that the dear lad is not dead but lives.' Julian
was grateful that his brother died instantly, which he verified by talking to a
soldier who was by Morris's side. The sights and sounds of the last few days
on the Somme would live with Julian all his life, 'and fill me with an agony
of sympathy for those suffering indescribable things'. He had identified over
seventy bodies, some scarcely recognizable, and been surrounded by blood for
three days.[89]

The Bickersteth family knew that Morris was spiritually prepared for his
fate, with a strong, simple faith in God. Morris had written a letter for his
parents in the event of his death, assuring them that death had no terror for
him and little sorrow, 'because in thirty or forty years the whole family will
be together for ever in eternal life'.[90] But even the most devout Christian faith
left room for anxiety after such a death as Morris's, as the parents and
brothers continued their enquiries to locate his body. Many years later, Revd
Samuel Bickersteth's written memorial to his son included details of these
exhaustive searches. No man's land at Serre, where Morris was killed, was not
captured by the Allies until February 1917, but twice in 1918 was again lost to
the Germans, and so was continually swept by opposing armies. Burying-
parties were unable to reach the bodies in July 1916, and so much high
explosive was used there for days afterwards that recovery became for ever
impossible.[91] On 23 July 1916 Ella Bickersteth reported in her journal that
Morris's body still lay unburied, and her suffering was acute: 'We sit in the
garden and think of Morris our soldier saint . . . I can't bear to think of our
darling's body lying in the open, and we should love the things he carried in
his pockets.' On 24 August the mother noted sadly, 'As I write our Morris'
body has never been found, nor will it be.' Any normal process of mourning
was impossible when uncertainty and anxiety about the location and condition of the body persisted.[92]

During the years that followed, the search for Morris's remains continued, while memory seemed to offer the primary consolation, even for such devout parents. Late in August 1916 Ella Bickersteth noted how good it was to talk to a friend about Morris's life and death. By September 1916 she reported that she and Sam were slightly better, 'but not strong'. A parcel of Morris's winter clothes had been returned, but it was 'hard work unpacking them'. Their youngest son, Ralph, took some of these clothes as a remembrance, having inherited them in Morris's will. One of the few consolations in 1916 came when Ralph presented his parents with a 'most beautiful crayon portrait of Morris done by Eric Jameson' as a surprise memorial present. The parents were delighted with the lifelike portrait: 'you might think Morris would step out of the frame and speak . . . [It] is such a joy to us.' Ella's journal recorded in April 1917 that after eight months Julian was still finding the bodies of his own officers lying unburied at Gommecourt, nor had he abandoned hope in his search for Morris at Serre.

The Bickersteth archives demonstrate the importance of war memorials in local churches, and of memorial services and honour rolls, for those parents whose sons' bodies were never found, identified, and buried. Just after the first anniversary of Morris's death his parents erected a memorial tablet on a pillar in Leeds parish church. They had to obtain special permission for this when they left Leeds for Canterbury, late in 1916, since it was generally felt such memorials should usually not be placed in churches until after the war. The mother's grief was unabated in January 1918: 'I yearn for Morris with my whole being sometimes.' In June 1918 the parents attended the quarterly memorial services at Rugby School for the boys killed in the war. 'Our Morris' seemed very close at the early service in the chapel, which Ella found very moving. Afterwards she 'communed with my darling', sitting near Morris's former school house. From Rugby the parents proceeded to Leeds parish church to commemorate the second anniversary of their son's death, placing a flowering rose under his memorial in the side-chapel. They also left a wreath beneath the roll of honour in memory of all the brave soldiers who fell on the first day of the Somme.[93]

On 1 July 1919 and again two years later Morris's parents made the pilgrimage with Julian and Burgon to the desolate scene of their son's death at Serre. The closest a motor-car could approach to the front line was within an hour's difficult walk across 'a sea of shell-holes', testimony to the destruction of modern warfare, with no house standing. Closest to the place where they thought Morris had fallen, they found two or three hundred wooden crosses erected by the War Graves Department to mark, as far as possible, the place where the bodies were buried. They found Morris's cross, which was later replaced by a more permanent headstone, when the wooden cross was sent to the family home at Canterbury.[94] The Bickersteth parents continued to grieve deeply through the 1920s. Just as Lady Wemyss produced a written memorial to her soldier sons in 1932, so did Revd Samuel Bickersteth for Morris in 1931, also for private circulation only. His 146-page volume was dedicated to his grandchildren on his Golden Wedding day, to secure for Morris 'a place in our home on that day, a place which he always fills in our hearts'.[95]

In both these families it took over a decade before the parents felt able to produce their written memorials, which maintained some continuity with the Victorian past. Perhaps it became even more important to commemorate their lost sons in a written recollection of their lives when the actual memorial to their deaths had been so woefully inadequate. Lavinia Talbot, daughter of Mary Lyttelton and wife of the Bishop of Winchester, wrote a similar memorial for her son Gilbert, killed in 1915. His brother Neville had crawled out to Gilbert's body in no man's land under shelling, checked that he was killed outright, and retrieved his body later, when the shelling subsided, noting 'how strong is the sense of outrage at non-burial'.[96]

The Charteris and Bickersteth families' experiences of death in the Great War help to explain why a new form of national memorial to the dead was needed at the end of the Great War. The Bickersteths did all they could to memorialize Morris, in the absence of a corpse and the normal funeral and burial obsequies. But the memorial tablet at Leeds parish church and the memorial services at Leeds and Rugby had their limitations, while the visits to Serre seem to have been less than consoling. More was needed to commemorate their soldier son, who died so violently for his country and whose body was never properly buried.

Commemoration by the state seemed necessary when nineteenth-century forms of burial and ritual were unavailable, when individual ceremonies were impossible, and when Christian ritual seemed inappropriate for so many. New civic forms of remembrance of the dead and new forms of ritual were needed—the prominent communal war memorials in churches, towns, and villages, the ritual of Armistice Day, and the immense popular appeal of London's Cenotaph and the tomb of the Unknown Soldier. Ken Inglis and David Cannadine have shown how the initial urge to salute the war dead with a temporary shrine in July 1919 was translated by popular demand into the erection of the Cenotaph—the empty tomb—as a permanent 'site for continuing acts of commemoration'.[97] C. F. G. Masterman said of the Unknown Soldier in Westminster Abbey, 'we were burying every boy's father, and every woman's lover, and every mother's child'. That soldier represented Morris

Bickersteth, Hugo Lord Elcho, and the hundreds of thousands like them, for whom no ordinary burial and ritual had been possible.[98] As Ken Inglis observes, 'The Unknown was understood to represent all his dead comrades, but especially the Missing, the huge numbers of men blown to pieces or rotted in mud or otherwise unrecognisable . . . Bereaved people gave dead soldiers, as nearly as they could contrive, the funeral they never had.'[99] The Great War produced more monuments than any earlier single historical event and these new memorials were to mourn the dead rather than to celebrate war.

Cannadine argues that this 'cult of the dead' in the inter-war years was 'a display of bereavement' on a mass scale by an entire grieving community. The mass outpouring of sorrow during and after the Great War suggests that many families never recovered from the wartime deaths of their sons, husbands, and fathers.[100] Bereavement became a more widespread and harrowing experience than ever before. The only comparable loss for Victorian parents was the death of an adult child by violence or suicide or far from home—all deaths which were identified as 'bad' deaths. As we have seen, in peacetime there were few such cases in these families, but those few had a marked tendency to promote chronic grief, which was otherwise rare in the nineteenth century. It is hardly surprising that in wartime, when the premature death of an adult son was associated with violence, distance, and the denial of conventional burial and ritual, the result was a mass outbreak of chronic and unresolved grief.

Most families needed customary rituals and spiritual consolation more than ever in wartime, but the Great War accelerated the decline of Victorian mourning customs. Colin Murray Parkes, a psychiatrist, observes that bereaved people in Western culture today can be confused and insecure in the absence of clear social expectations and prescribed ritual for mourning; the increasing 'disregard of formal mourning' deprives them of longer-term support from their family and community.[101] Some bereaved families turned instead in the inter-war years to social memory, to spiritualism, or to new forms of civic commemoration of their dead. But the prolonged 'cult of the dead' after the Great War suggests that such alternative strategies were often inadequate.

The war largely destroyed the remaining Victorian spiritual resources which had enabled individuals and families to perceive positive meanings in the deaths of loved ones. The meaning of life and the meaning of death were both transformed by the Great War. In the years after 1918 repression and denial of death frequently replaced acceptance and affirmation. Death itself came to be perceived as a major taboo of the British people, in opposition to life rather than its culmination. The Great War destroyed the links with hundreds of years of Christian history which had taught the importance of the good death and the hope of life eternal. The cultural consequences for a population in mourning in the inter-war years were devastating.

NOTES

The place of publication is London unless otherwise indicated. The locations of manuscript collections are listed after the notes.

ABBREVIATIONS

BL Add. MS	British Library, Additional Manuscripts
Bodl.	Bodleian Library
NLS	National Library of Scotland
PRO	Public Record Office
priv. pr.	printed for private circulation

Introduction

1. Michel Vovelle, 'On Death', in *Ideologies and Mentalities* (Chicago, 1990), 65.
2. David Cannadine, 'War and Death, Grief and Mourning in Modern Britain', in J. Whaley (ed.), *Mirrors of Mortality* (1981), 241.
3. Ruth Richardson, *Death, Dissection and the Destitute* (1987), 262.
4. Leonore Davidoff, 'The Family in Britain', in *The Cambridge Social History of Britain 1750–1950*, ed. F. M. L. Thompson, 3 vols. (Cambridge, 1990), ii. 80.
5. Cited by Walter E. Houghton, *The Victorian Frame of Mind*, 2nd edn. (1969), 341–7.
6. G. M. Young, *Victorian England: Portrait of an Age*, 2nd edn. (1967), 150.
7. Houghton, *The Victorian Frame of Mind*, 341–7.
8. William Wilberforce's diary, 1813, cited in David Newsome, *The Parting of Friends* (1966), 35.
9. David Newsome, *Godliness and Good Learning* (1961), 75.
10. Elizabeth Haldane, *From One Century to Another* (1937), 43.
11. Lady Frances Balfour, *Ne Obliviscaris: Dinna Forget*, 2 vols. (1930), i. 348.
12. Owen Chadwick, *The Victorian Church*, 2 vols., 3rd edn. (1971), i. 1; ii. 424.
13. Jose Harris, *Private Lives, Public Spirit: A Social History of Britain 1870–1914* (Oxford, 1993), 152–5.
14. Lawrence Stone, *The Family, Sex and Marriage in England 1500–1800*, 2nd edn. (Harmondsworth, 1979), 149 *et passim*.
15. R. I. and S. Wilberforce, *The Life of William Wilberforce*, 5 vols., 2nd edn. (1839), iv. 273.
16. See e.g. Newsome, *Godliness and Good Learning*, 26, 83–9, 219, 225–6.
17. *Courtauld Family Letters 1782–1900*, 8 vols. (priv. pr., 1916), vii: *1842–1850*, 3319.
18. B. Askwith, *The Lytteltons* (1975), 143, 182.
19. Newsome, *Godliness and Good Learning*, 26, 83–9, 219.
20. B. R. Mitchell and Phyllis Deane, *Abstract of British Historical Statistics* (Cambridge, 1962), 36–7; Michael Anderson, 'The Social Implications of

Demographic Change', in *The Cambridge Social History of Britain 1750–1950*, ii. 15–16.

21. Rosalind Mitchison, *British Population Change since 1860* (1977), 39–40; Anderson, 'The Social Implications of Demographic Change', 15–16; A. S. Wohl, *Endangered Lives: Public Health in Victorian Britain* (1983), 11.

22. Mitchison, *British Population Change since 1860*, 39–57; Anderson, 'The Social Implications of Demographic Change', 15–16.

23. William Munk, *Euthanasia: or Medical Treatment in Aid of an Easy Death* (1887), 65–105.

24. Cannadine, 'War and Death, Grief and Mourning', 241.

25. Richardson, *Death, Dissection and the Destitute*.

26. Michael Wheeler, *Death and the Future Life in Victorian Literature and Theology* (Cambridge, 1990).

27. Geoffrey Rowell, *Hell and the Victorians: A Study of the Nineteenth-Century Theological Controversies concerning Eternal Punishment and the Future Life* (Oxford, 1974).

28. Ralph Houlbrooke (ed.), *Death, Ritual and Bereavement* (1989).

29. Elisabeth Jay, *The Religion of the Heart: Anglican Evangelicalism and the Nineteenth Century Novel* (Oxford, 1979); John Reed, *Victorian Conventions* (Athens, Ohio, 1975), esp. 156–71; see also e.g. Garrett Stewart, *Death Sentences: Styles of Dying in British Fiction* (1984); Karl S. Guthke, *Last Words: Variations on a Theme in Cultural History* (Princeton, 1992).

30. See Emmanuel Le Roy Ladurie, 'Chaunu, Lebrun, Vovelle: La nouvelle histoire de la mort', in *Le Territoire de l'historien* (Paris, 1973), 393–403.

31. Vovelle, 'On Death', 64–5.

32. Pierre Chaunu, *La Mort à Paris, XVIe, XVIIe et XVIIIe siècles* (Paris, 1978); Michel Vovelle, *Mourir autrefois: Attitudes collectives devant la mort aux XVIIe et XVIIIe siècles* (Paris, 1974); Michel Vovelle, *La Mort et l'Occident: De 1300 à nos jours* (Paris, 1983); Philippe Ariès, *The Hour of our Death*, 2nd edn. (Harmondsworth, 1981); John McManners, *Death and the Enlightenment: Changing Attitudes to Death among Christians and Unbelievers in Eighteenth-Century France* (Oxford, 1981); Thomas A. Kselman, *Death and the Afterlife in Modern France* (Princeton, 1993).

33. See e.g. Jane Littlewood, *Aspects of Grief: Bereavement in Adult Life* (1992), 1–3, 4–5, 18–19, which includes a table presenting a simple form of Ariès's model; Zygmunt Bauman, *Mortality, Immortality and Other Life Strategies* (Cambridge, 1992), 94–5, 136–7; Elisabeth Bronfen, *Over her Dead Body: Death, Femininity and the Aesthetic* (New York, 1992), ch. 5.

34. See e.g. Clare Gittings, *Death, Burial and the Individual in Early Modern England* (1984), 15–17, for a critical view which is indebted to Ariès; B. Hüppauf, 'Prologue', in B. Hüppauf and M. Crouch (eds.), *Essays on Mortality* (Sydney, 1985), 2.

35. Cannadine, 'War and Death, Grief and Mourning', 241–2.

36. The Royal Commission on Historical Manuscripts, HMSO, *Guides to Sources for British History*, 1: *Papers of British Cabinet Ministers 1782–1900*

(1982); 2: *The Manuscript Papers of British Scientists 1600–1940* (1982); 4: *Private Papers of British Diplomats 1782–1900* (1985); 6: *Papers of British Churchmen 1780–1940* (1987); 7: *Papers of British Politicians 1782–1900* (1989).

37. Caroline Fox to nephew, Henry, 4th Lord Holland, 6 Dec. [1840], Holland House Papers, BL Add. MS 52051, fos. 222–3.
38. Eleanor Fazakerley to sister, Jane Goulburn, n.d., [Aug. 1834,] Goulburn Papers, Acc. 319, Box 67.
39. Jeremy Taylor, *The Rule and Exercises of Holy Dying* (Oxford, 1857; 1st edn. 1651), 52–4.
40. P. Fussell, *The Great War and Modern Memory* (1977), 310.
41. E. M. Forster. *Marianne Thornton, 1797–1887: A Domestic Biography* (1956), 67–71.
42. Mary Drew to Henry Gladstone, 8 May 1895, Glynne–Gladstone Papers, MS 43/3.

1. The Evangelical Ideal of the 'Good Death'

1. John McManners, *Death and the Enlightenment* (Oxford, 1981), 125–6, 197–206, 253–4. See also e.g. Michel Vovelle, *La Mort et l'Occident de 1300 à nos jours* (Paris, 1983); Thomas Kselman, *Death and the Afterlife in Modern France* (Princeton, 1993).
2. McManners, *Death and the Enlightenment*, 234–45.
3. R. Houlbrooke (ed.), *Death, Ritual and Bereavement* (1989), 25–42.
4. Jeremy Taylor, *The Rule and Exercises of Holy Dying* (Oxford, 1857; 1st edn. 1651).
5. John Reed, *Victorian Conventions* (Athens, Ohio, 1975), 157.
6. Taylor, *The Rule and Exercises of Holy Dying*, pp. ix–xii.
7. Ibid. 47–55, 95–105, 230–42, 77–8.
8. Christopher Sutton, *Disce Mori: Learn to Die* (1626), ed. J. H. Newman (1839), esp. pp. xiii–xv, i–ii.
9. Charles Drelincourt, *The Christian's Defence against the Fears of Death*, trans. Marius D'Assigny, 27th edn. (Liverpool, 1810), 70–88, 157–213.
10. Michael Wheeler, *Death and the Future Life in Victorian Literature and Theology* (Cambridge, 1990), 29.
11. G. M. Young, *Portrait of an Age* (1967; 1st edn. 1936), 4–5. See also Owen Chadwick, *The Victorian Church*, 2 vols., 3rd edn. (1992), i. 5.
12. David Bebbington, *Evangelicalism in Modern Britain* (1989), 37, 42, 80–1.
13. For a full exposition of these defining features of Evangelicalism, see ibid. 1–17; see also R. J. Helmstadter, 'The Nonconformist Conscience', in G. Parsons (ed.), *Religion in Victorian Britain*, 4 vols. (1988), iv. 61–95.
14. Ibid.
15. Bebbington, *Evangelicalism*, 105–6, 141–2, 146, 149–50.
16. Geoffrey Best, 'Evangelicalism and the Victorians', in Anthony Symondson (ed.), *The Victorian Crisis of Faith* (1970), 54–5. See also Geoffrey Rowell, *Hell and the Victorians* (Oxford, 1974), 7–8.

17. *The Evangelical Magazine* (Jan. 1837), 1.

18. Emily Leakey, *Clear Shining Light: A Memoir of Caroline Leakey* (n.d. [*c.*1883]), 54–61. I am indebted to Sue Rickard for this reference.

19. Best, 'Evangelicalism and the Victorians', 55. See also Elizabeth Jay, *The Religion of the Heart* (Oxford, 1979), 161–3.

20. Leakey, *Clear Shining Light*, 61. See also pp. 54–61, 120–1, 136, for inconsistencies in Emily Leakey's account of Caroline's death in 1880.

21. Robert and Samuel Wilberforce, *The Life of William Wilberforce*, 5 vols., 2nd edn. (1839), v. 110–11.

22. Henry Acland, 8 pp. account of a death, n.d., Acland Papers, MS 1148 M/Box 16/7, Devon Record Office.

23. F. W. Robertson, *Sermons, Preached at Brighton*, 3rd ser. (1874), 224–5.

24. Revd W. Carus, *Memoirs of the Life of Charles Simeon*, 2 vols. (1847), ii. 810.

25. The *Evangelical Magazine and Missionary Chronicle* (Feb. 1837), 'Memoir of the Late Revd Charles Simeon, M.A., of Cambridge', 59–60; cf. Carus, *Life of Simeon*, ii. 825.

26. Walter E. Houghton, *The Victorian Frame of Mind* (New Haven, 1969; first pub. 1957), 277.

27. For analyses of the Victorian death-bed in fiction, see e.g. Wheeler, *Death and the Future Life*; Elisabeth Jay, *The Religion of the Heart: Anglican Evangelicalism and the Nineteenth Century Novel* (Oxford, 1979); Garrett Stewart, *Death Sentences: Styles of Dying in British Fiction* (1984); Karl S. Guthke, *Last Words: Variations on a Theme in Cultural History* (Princeton, 1992); Reed, *Victorian Conventions*, 156–71; Margarete Holubetz, 'Death Bed Scenes in Victorian Fiction', *English Studies: A Journal of English Language and Literature*, 67/1 (Feb. 1986), 14–34.

28. Bebbington, *Evangelicalism*, 96–7; David Newsome, *The Parting of Friends* (1966), 5, 14–15.

29. Newsome, *The Parting of Friends*, 14.

30. Houghton, *The Victorian Frame of Mind*, 231–3.

31. John Warton, *Death-Bed Scenes*, 3 vols. (1827).

32. Mary Ann Wildman to brother, A. C. Tait, [May 1832,] Tait Papers, vol. 76, fos. 60–1.

33. Caroline Parker to Lucy Sharpe, 19 Aug. [1853]; see also e.g. Mary Towgood to Lucy Sharpe, 20 Aug. [1853], Sharpe Papers 127.

34. Angelina Acland to brother, Henry Acland, 26 June [1877], Bodl. MS Acland d. 47, fos. 297–8.

35. J. T. Coleridge, *Memoir of Revd John Keble* (1870), 448.

36. Death of Gib Acland, 1874, Bodl. MS Acland d. 42, fos. 481–2.

37. Death of Sarah Acland, 1878, S. A. Acland, 'Memories in my 81st Year', Acland Papers, MS Eng. Misc. d. 214, fos. 63–7; S. I. Marriott, 'Requested recollections of Sarah Acland's early days, 17 Oct. 1889', Bodl. MS Acland d. 1944, fos. 1–9.

38. 4th Earl of Carnarvon's diary, 18–27 May 1876, Carnarvon Papers, BL Add. MS 60908, fos. 116–21.

39. John Hinton, *Dying*, 2nd edn. (Harmondsworth, 1979), 87–8.

40. Memorandum of May Lyttelton's death, 21 Mar. 1875, Mary Gladstone Drew Papers, BL Add. MS 46269, fos. 110–22.
41. 4th Earl of Carnarvon's diary, 23 May 1876, Carnarvon Papers, BL Add. MS 60908, fo. 119.
42. Lady Carrington's diary, 26 July 1879, Carrington MS Film 1097.
43. Agnes Anson to Fred Anson, 14 May 1892, Acland–Anson Papers, MS 2862 M/ F265a, b, Devon Record Office.
44. Beatrice Webb diary, 6 Apr. 1882, Passfield Papers.
45. Lord Grosvenor to Revd W. V. Harcourt, 3 Feb. 1839, in *The Harcourt Papers*, ed. E. W. Harcourt, 14 vols. (priv. pr., Oxford, 1880–1905), xiv. 70–1.
46. Jane Goulburn to daughter, Jane Goulburn, n.d., Goulburn Papers, Acc. 319, Box 78.
47. *Earl Cowper, K.G.: A Memoir*, by his wife (Katrine Cecilia) (priv. pr., 1913), 283.
48. Margaret King to fiancé, Dr J. H. Gladstone, 29 May 1869, MacDonald Papers, PRO 30/69/861.
49. See e.g. Hinton, *Dying*, ch. 8; E. Kübler-Ross, *On Death and Dying* (1978), chs. 3–7.
50. W. Jackman to Frederick Goulburn, 18 Jan. 1856, Goulburn Papers, Acc. 319, Box 23.
51. Victoria Dawnay to Mary Countess Minto, 28 July, 16 Aug. 1910, Minto MS 12431, fos. 106, 126.
52. Henry Venn, *The Complete Duty of Man: or A System of Doctrinal and Practical Christianity* (1841), 240.
53. Ibid. 235.
54. *The Correspondence of William Wilberforce*, eds. R. I. and Samuel Wilberforce (1840), ii. 20–8.
55. R. and S. Wilberforce, *The Life of William Wilberforce*, iv. 272–3.
56. Robin Furneaux, *William Wilberforce* (1974), 347.
57. Ibid. 168.
58. Jane Goulburn's diary, 21 June 1843, Goulburn Papers, Acc. 319, Box 64.
59. Emily Palmer's account of Dorothea's death, n.d. [Jan.–Feb. 1852), William Palmer's abstract, Selborne Papers, MS 1903, fos. 12–13.
60. Richard Cavendish to Edward Goulburn, 9 June 1843, Goulburn Papers, Acc. 319, Box 31.
61. Elizabeth Herbert to W. E. Gladstone, 30 Aug. 1857, W. E. Gladstone Papers, BL Add. MS 44212, fos. 48–50.
62. *The Harcourt Papers*, xiv. 205–7.
63. [Samuel Beckett,] *My First Grief: Recollections of a Beloved Sister, by a Provincial Surgeon*, 2nd edn. (Bath [, 1854]), 129–31.
64. Ibid.
65. Lady Anne Blunt's diary, Apr. to Aug. 1872, Wentworth Bequest, BL Add. MSS 53840–1.
66. *Catharine and Crauford Tait, wife and son of Archbishop A. C. Tait: A Memoir*, ed. Revd William Benham (1879), 194.

67. Archbishop A. C. Tait's journal, 8 Dec. 1878, Tait Papers, vol. 63, fos. 98, 100–3.

68. G. E. Buckle, *Life of Benjamin Disraeli* (1920), vi. 616.

69. M. H., *Death-Bed Thoughts* (1838), 97.

70. *Final Triumph; or, Dying Sayings of Saints, Martyrs and Men and Women of Note*, compiled by M.E.T. (1893), 29; I. A. Taylor, *The Art of Dying* (1894).

71. Leakey, *Clear Shining Light*, 131–5.

72. [Brief Memoir of the Revd John Humphreys, LL D, unsigned,] *Evangelical Magazine* (Nov. 1837), 509–11.

73. 'Memoir of the Revd Samuel Knight', *Christian Guardian and Church of England Magazine* (Sept. 1837), 326–9.

74. 'Memoir of the Revd J. W. Peers', *Christian Guardian and Church of England Magazine* (Feb. 1837), 47–8.

75. *In Memoriam: An Account of the Last Illness and Death of Mrs W——'* (priv. pr., Edinburgh, 1862), 1–28.

76. Account of Revd Dr Thomas Somerville's death written by his son, William, n.d. [1830], Somerville Papers, dep. c. 360, folder MSFP-45.

77. William Roundell to son-in-law, Revd William Jocelyn Palmer, n.d. [1850–2?], Selborne Papers, MS Eng. misc. c. 690, fo. 106. Throughout the book I have avoided using '(*sic*)' to confirm spelling eccentricities.

78. Notes, 8 June 1843, Goulburn Papers, Acc. 319, Box 30.

79. W. E. Gladstone, 'The Last Days of my Father, Sir John Gladstone. 1851', Dec. 1851, W. E. Gladstone Papers, BL Add. MS 44739, fos. 104–20.

80. Louisa Cane to friend, Miss Jane Goulburn (daughter of deceased), 23 Feb. 1857, Goulburn Papers, Acc. 319, Box 30.

81. *Courtauld Family Letters 1782–1900*, 8 vols. (priv. pr., Cambridge, 1916), viii: *1850–1900*, 3605–6.

82. James C. Tait to brother, A. C. Tait, 4 May [1877], Tait Papers, vol. 97, fos. 302–3.

83. Adelaide Drummond, *Retrospect and Memoir* (1915), 291–2.

84. See e.g. Dr William Munk, *Euthanasia: or Medical Treatment in Aid of an Easy Death* (1887), 91, 34–5.

85. Lady Carrington's diary, 29 Jan. 1911, Carrington MS Film 1112. See also e.g. the death of the 4th Earl of Onslow in 1911, 'History of the Onslow Family', by 5th Earl [*c*.1924], Onslow Papers, 173/1/5, ch. XXXIV, pp. 1353–5.

86. Elizabeth Lady Harcourt to Sir William Harcourt, 20 Dec. 1891, MS Harcourt dep. 634, fos. 1–2.

87. W. S. Savory, FRS, *On Life and Death* (1863), 175.

88. Beckett, *My First Grief*, 116–19, 125–6, 128.

89. Emily Harcourt to Sir William Harcourt, Feb. 1884, MS Harcourt dep. 603, fos. 176–80.

90. See Wheeler, *Death and the Future Life*, 30.

91. W. Roberts, *Memoirs of the Life of Mrs Hannah More*, 2 vols. (1836), ii. 192–3.

92. Caroline Fox to Henry, 4th Lord Holland, 23 Oct. 1840, Holland House Papers, BL Add. MS 52051, fos. 200–1.

93. Lady Anne Blunt's diary, 21 Apr. 1872, Wentworth Bequest, BL Add. MS 53840.

94. The death of Charles John Vaughan, Dean of Llandaff, 1897, reported in correspondence to Sir Charles Dalrymple, 9 Oct. 1897, Newhailes (Dalrymple) Papers, NLS Acc. 7228/230.

95. E. M. Forster, *Marianne Thornton* (1956), 70.

2. *The Revival and Decline of the Good Christian Death*

1. John Hinton, *Dying*, 2nd edn. (Harmondsworth, 1979), 84.

2. See e.g. B. Raphael, *The Anatomy of Bereavement* (1984), 280, 310; Jane Littlewood, *Aspects of Grief* (1992), 140–4.

3. F. B. Smith, *The Retreat of Tuberculosis 1850–1950* (1988), 1–2.

4. Quoted in ibid. 225.

5. *Lancet*, 30 Sept. 1882.

6. Margot Peters, *Unquiet Soul: A Biography of Charlotte Brontë* (1977), 228 ff.; Elizabeth Gaskell, *Life of Charlotte Brontë* (Harmondsworth, 1979), 353–6.

7. Kenneth Rose, *Superior Person: A Portrait of Curzon and his Circle in Late Victorian England* (1969), 162–3.

8. Smith, *The Retreat of Tuberculosis*, 224–5.

9. Quoted in *Lancet*, 30 Sept. 1882.

10. Philippe Ariès, *The Hour of our Death*, 2nd edn. (1981), 432–46.

11. Daniel C. Eddy, DD, *The Angel's Whispers . . . [Sermons] Designed to Console the Mourning Husband and Wife* (1885), 121–2.

12. Samuel Beckett, *My First Grief: Recollections of a Beloved Sister, by a Provincial Surgeon*, 2nd edn. (Bath [, 1854]), 125–6, 128.

13. Harry Goulburn's diary, 1843, Goulburn Papers, Acc. 319, Box 63.

14. Ibid.

15. Ibid.

16. Jane Goulburn's diary, 7–8 June 1843, Goulburn Papers, Acc. 319, Box 64; notes on Harry Goulburn's death, 7 June 1843, ibid., Box 65.

17. Dorothea Palmer to William Palmer, 9 July 1851; George Horsley Palmer to William Palmer, 15 July [1851], enclosing copy of Dorothea's letter to father, Revd W. J. Palmer, 6 July 1851, Selborne Papers, MS Eng. misc. c. 691, fos. 5–8, 3–4.

18. Revd Edwin Palmer to Revd William Palmer, 15 Feb. 1852, Palmer Papers, MS 2836, fo. 78.

19. William Palmer's abstract, 'Sister Emily's Account of Dear Dorothea's Last Days', [Jan.–Feb. 1852,] Selborne Papers, MS 1903, fos. 12–13; Mary Richardson Palmer to William Palmer, 6 Feb. [1852], Selborne Papers, MS Eng. misc. c. 691, fos. 25–6.

20. Roundell Palmer to wife, Laura, [29 Jan. 1852,] Selborne Papers, MS 1880, fos. 5–7.

21. Ibid., 29–30 Jan. 1852, fos. 5–7, 11–12.

22. Mary Richardson Palmer to William Palmer, 6 Feb. [1852], Selborne Papers, MS Eng. misc. c. 691, fos. 25–6; Earl of Selborne, *Memorials* (1896–8), ii. 108.

23. John Callcott Horsley's diary, 1852, Horsley Papers, MS Eng. e. 2186, fos. 18 ff.
24. Ibid.
25. Ibid.
26. Ibid., fos. 53–4.
27. Ibid., fos. 47–8, 52–3.
28. Ibid., 1 Dec. 1852, fos. 45–6, 56.
29. Ibid.
30. Ibid.
31. Beckett, *My First Grief,* 113–14, 116–22, 126–7.
32. William Farr, *Vital Statistics* (Metuchen, NJ, 1975; first pub. 1885), 270, 278; J. M. Munro Kerr, R. W. Johnstone, and M. H. Phillips, *Historical Review of British Obstetrics and Gynaecology 1800–1950* (1954), 259, table 1.
33. Kate Potter to fiancé, Leonard Courtney, 6 Sept. 1882, Courtney Collection, vol. III, fos. 153–4.
34. Margaret Gladstone's journal, 31 Dec. 1869, MacDonald Papers, PRO 30/69/852, fo. 143.
35. Elizabeth King's journal of the death of her daughter, Margaret Gladstone, 1870, MacDonald Papers, PRO 30/69/852.
36. Elizabeth King to husband, David King, 10, 11 Aug. 1870, ibid.; E. King to sister-in-law, Margaret Henderson, 15 Aug. 1870, ibid.
37. Elizabeth King's journal of her daughter's death, 1870, MacDonald Papers, PRO 30/69/852.
38. Ibid.
39. Ibid.
40. John H. Gladstone to David King, 30 Aug. 1870, ibid.
41. Samuel Sharpe's journal, 3 June 1851, Sharpe Papers 74/1; see also 21 Feb. 1843 for a similar account of his brother, Sutton's last days, ibid.
42. Mary Reid to daughter, Lucy Sharpe, 11, 24 Dec. 1851; 4, 28 Jan. 1852, Sharpe Papers 118.
43. Samuel Reid to sister, Lucy Sharpe, 4 Feb. [1852], ibid.
44. Anne Rowley to Lucy Sharpe, 1 Sept. 1853, ibid.
45. Lucy Sharpe to husband, William Sharpe, 23, 25 Oct. 1844, ibid. 98, fos. 115–16, 118–19.
46. Dr James Reid to mother, Mary Reid, 26 Oct. 1844, ibid. 169/5.
47. Lucy Sharpe to William Sharpe, [26] Oct. 1844, ibid. 98, fos. 123–4.
48. Mary Reid to daughter, Lucy Sharpe, 16 Aug. 1853, ibid. 118; Dr James Reid to sister, Lucy Sharpe, 3 June 1856, ibid. 122/3.
49. Revd John Kenrick to niece, Lucy Sharpe, 21 Dec. 1874, ibid. 120.
50. Agnes Acland to Fred Anson, 5 May 1884, Acland–Anson Papers, MS 2862 M/F204, Devon Record Office.
51. H. J. Coleridge to John Keble, 25 Apr. 1843, Keble Correspondence 135.
52. Caroline Kerison to Lady Evelyn Mahon, 26 Dec. 1875, Stanhope MS U 1590, C 590/8.
53. Edward W. Harcourt to brother, Sir William Harcourt, 18 Nov. 1876, MS Harcourt dep. 610, fo. 45.

54. Condolence letters to William, 3rd Earl Minto, 23–4 Apr. 1882, Minto MS 12255, fos. 137, 225.

55. Constance Connolly to Margaret MacDonald, 29 Dec. 1908, MacDonald Papers, PRO 30/69/901.

56. B. Askwith, *Lady Dilke: A Biography* (1969), 107–11.

57. 'Annals of our Family', [1886,] uncat. papers of Thorold Rogers family, Box 10, R3.

58. Sarah Bailey to Lady Trevelyan, 9 Dec. 1900, Trevelyan Papers, GOT 123.

59. Alethea Grenfell to Lord Aldenham, 19 Sept. 1902, Gibbs Family Letters, MS 11021/30, fos. 504–5.

60. Dorothy Ward to Sally Norton, 12 Mar. 1901, Ward Papers, Pusey House.

61. Ethel Lady Gainford to daughter, Miriam Pease, 3 Apr. 1917, MS Gainford 18B.

62. Lady Stepney to Mary Drew, [spring 1902,] Mary Gladstone Drew Papers, BL Add. MS 46250, fo. 8.

63. *Earl Cowper, KG: A Memoir*, by his wife (Katrine Cecilia) (priv. pr., 1913), 456.

64. Betty Balfour to husband, Gerald Balfour, 27 May 1900, Balfour Papers (Whittingehame).

65. Molly Trevelyan's diary, 15 May 1911, Trevelyan Papers.

66. Owen Chadwick, *The Victorian Church*, 3rd edn. (1992), ii. 128; B. Caine, *Destined to be Wives: The Sisters of Beatrice Webb* (1988), 194–7.

67. Kate Courtney's diary, Courtney Collection, vol. XXI, fo. 83.

68. Beatrice Potter's diary, Apr. 1882, Passfield Papers; Kate Courtney's diary, Easter 1882, Courtney Collection, vol. XXI, fos. 83–95.

69. Beatrice Potter's diary, Apr. 1882, Passfield Papers.

70. Kate Courtney's diary, Easter 1882, Courtney Collection, vol. XXI, fos. 83–95.

71. Beatrice Potter's diary, Apr. 1882, Passfield Papers; Kate Courtney's diary, Easter 1882, Courtney Collection, vol. XXI, fos. 83–95.

72. Ibid.

73. Beatrice Potter's diary, 27 Aug. 1882, Passfield Papers.

74. Three letters from Frances Balfour to A. J. Balfour, 10 Apr. 1900 and n.d., Balfour Papers (Whittingehame) MS 164.

75. Ibid.

76. Ibid.

3. Bad Deaths, Sudden Deaths, and Suicides

1. W. S. Blunt, 'Autobiography', dictated to his wife, Anne, 1873, Wentworth Bequest, BL Add. MS 54069.

2. *The Journal of Lady Holland*, ed. Earl of Ilchester, 2 vols. (1908), i. 156.

3. Keith Norman MacDonald, MD, *On Death and How to Divest it of its Terrors* (Edinburgh, 1875), *passim*.

4. Elizabeth Palmer to brother, Revd W. J. Palmer, 2 May 1841, Selborne Papers, MS 1890, fo. 111.

5. See Geoffrey Rowell, *Hell and the Victorians* (Oxford, 1974).

6. Ibid., 24–5, 28; Michael Wheeler, *Death and the Future Life in Victorian Literature and Theology* (Cambridge, 1990), 70–9, 175–96.

7. Ada Lovelace to mother, Lady Byron, 16 Aug., 15 Oct. 1851, MS dep. Lovelace Byron 43, fos. 216–18.

8. Ibid., n.d. [end Feb. 1852], MS 44, fo. 30.

9. Mary Somerville to Janet Elliot, 11 Dec. 1852, Somerville Papers, dep. c. 357, folder MSFP-8.

10. Lady Byron's journal, 24 July [1852], MS dep. Lovelace Byron 69, fos. 154–7.

11. Dorothy Stein, *Ada: A Life and a Legacy* (1985), 246.

12. Lady Byron's journal, as written to Emily Fitzhugh, 14 July [1852], MS dep. Lovelace Byron 69, fos. 148–9.

13. Ibid., 14 Aug. [1852], MS 69, fo. 165.

14. Stein, *Ada: A Life and a Legacy, passim.*

15. Ada Lovelace to Lady Byron, n.d. [*c.*Apr. 1851?], MS dep. Lovelace Byron 43, fos. 186–7.

16. Ibid., n.d. [28 Feb. 1852], MS 44, fo. 28.

17. Ibid., n.d. [1852], fos. 60–1, 174–6.

18. Certified copy of Lord Lovelace's journal, 15, 21 Aug. 1852, Wentworth Bequest, BL Add. MS 54089, fos. 2, 5.

19. Lady Byron's journal, 14 Aug. 1852, MS dep. Lovelace Byron 69, fo. 164.

20. Ibid., 22–30 Aug. 1852, fos. 180–6.

21. Ibid., 31 Aug. 1852, fo. 189.

22. Ibid., fo. 188.

23. Ibid., 1, 4 Sept. 1852, fo. 190.

24. Ibid., 7 Sept. [1852], fo. 195.

25. Lady Byron's journal and '"Thoughts of Ada" this last week' in Lady Byron's hand, 27 Aug., 8 Sept. 1852, MS dep. Lovelace Byron 175, fos. 26–7; MS 69, fo. 197.

26. Lady Byron's journal, 27–8 Nov. 1852, ibid., MS 69, fos. 254–8.

27. Stein, *Ada: A Life and a Legacy,* 181.

28. Lady Byron's journal, 11 Aug. 1852, MS dep. Lovelace Byron 69, fo. 161.

29. Lady Byron to Lady Therese Villiers, 13 Nov. 1852, ibid., MS 115, fos. 185–6.

30. Mary Somerville to Agnes Greig, 10 June 1852, Somerville Papers, dep. c. 363, folder MSIF-14.

31. Mary Somerville to son, Woronzow Greig, 14 June 1860, ibid., dep. c. 361, folder MSIF-5.

32. B. Raphael, *The Anatomy of Bereavement* (1984), 28–31.

33. John Hinton, *Dying,* 2nd edn. (Harmondsworth, 1979), 66.

34. Agnes Greig to Martha and Mary Somerville, 20 Oct. 1865, Somerville Papers, dep. c. 364, folder MSIF-25.

35. *The Diary of Lady Frederick Cavendish,* ed. John Bailey, 2 vols. (1927), ii. 218–20.

36. Jeremy Taylor, *The Rule and Exercises of Holy Dying* (Oxford, 1857; 1st edn. 1651), 30.

37. See e.g. Rowell, *Hell and the Victorians*, 164, for F. W. Faber's refusal to endorse Taylor's view.

38. Roundell Palmer to father, Revd W. J. Palmer, 3 Feb. 1835, Selborne Papers, MS 1878, fos. 11–12.

39. Revd W. J. Palmer to son, Roundell Palmer, 4 Feb., 4 July, 3 Aug. 1835, ibid., fos. 13–14, 24–6.

40. Raphael, *Anatomy of Bereavement*, 29.

41. *Autobiography of A. B. Granville, M.D., F.R.S.*, ed. P. B. Granville, 2 vols. (1874), ii. 340–1.

42. Caroline Colville to sister, Eliza, 2nd Lady Phillipps, 7 Jan. 1861, MS Phillipps–Robinson e. 429, fos. 1–4.

43. S. A. Acland, 'Memories in my 81st Year', Acland Papers, Bodl. MS Eng. Misc. d. 214, fos. 63–7.

44. Sarah Acland to son, Willie Acland, 29 July [1877], Bodl. MS Acland d. 43, fos. 244–5.

45. Sarah Acland to son, Henry, n.d. [1877], 18 July 1877, Bodl. MS Acland d. 46, fos. 176, 182.

46. Sophia Marriott, 'Requested Recollections of Sarah Acland's Early Days, 17 Oct. 1889', Bodl. MS Acland, d. 194, fos. 1–9.

47. Selina M. Causton (Lady Southwark), *Social and Political Reminiscences* (1913), 68–73.

48. W. H. Smith to Emily Giberne, 15 Jan. 1887, Hambleden MSS, E/12.

49. Louisa Lady Antrim to Mary Countess Minto, Nov. 1892, Minto MS 12435, fo. 261.

50. Michael MacDonald and Terence Murphy, *Sleepless Souls: Suicide in Early Modern England* (Oxford, 1990).

51. Ibid., 2.

52. Ibid., 42.

53. Ibid., 351.

54. Olive Anderson, *Suicide in Victorian and Edwardian England* (Oxford, 1987).

55. See e.g. *Lancet*, 20 Sept. 1884, 25 Oct. 1884, 27 Feb. 1886, 5 Oct. 1901.

56. *Lancet*, 20 Sept. 1884.

57. W. W. Westcott, *Suicide: Its History, Literature, Jurisprudence, Causation and Prevention* (1885). See also e.g. G. W. Foote, *Atheism and Suicide* (1881); S. A. K. Strahan, *Suicide and Insanity* (1893); H. H. Henson, *Suicide*, Oxford House Papers (1897); F. H. Perry-Coste, *The Ethics of Suicide* (1898).

58. *Lancet*, 25 Oct. 1884.

59. Henson, *Suicide*, 70.

60. Quoted in *Lancet*, 5 Jan. 1901.

61. É. Durkheim, *Suicide: A Study in Sociology* (1897); see also Enrico Morselli, *Suicide: An Essay on Comparative Moral Statistics* (1881); A. Alvarez, *The Savage God: A Study of Suicide* (1974).

62. Morselli, *Suicide*, 5.

63. Bertram M. H. Rogers's notes on family history, uncat. papers of Thorold Rogers family, Box 11, R 5, fos. 134–5; inquest report on Henry R. K. Rogers in *The Times*, 16 Sept. 1876.

64. *The Times,* 16 Sept. 1876.
65. Bertram M. H. Rogers, 'Annals of our Family', No. 5; 'Black Sheep and Tragedies', Aug. 1928, uncat. papers of Thorold Rogers family, Box 10, R 9; inquest report in *The Times,* 16 Sept. 1876.
66. Rogers, 'Annals of our Family', uncat. papers of Thorold Rogers family, Box 10, R 9.
67. James E. Thorold Rogers, open letter, 20 Sept. 1876, uncat. Thorold Rogers MSS, Box 4.
68. Ibid., Box 6, fo. 26.
69. Papers of J. E. Thorold Rogers and family, MS Eng. misc. c. 585, fo. 8; MS Top Oxon, c. 881, Aug. 1987.
70. MacDonald and Murphy, *Sleepless Souls,* 346–9, 42, 15; Westcott, *Suicide,* 45.
71. MacDonald and Murphy, *Sleepless Souls,* 352.
72. Ann Susannah Charlotte Rogers's diary, 1876, Thorold Rogers Papers, MS Eng. misc. g. 101/9.
73. Ibid. 1877, MS Eng. misc. g. 101/10.
74. Rogers, 'Annals of our Family', Aug. 1928, uncat. Thorold Rogers MSS, Box 10, R 9.
75. Ann Rogers's diary, 1879–82, Thorold Rogers Papers, MS Eng. misc. g. 101/12–15.
76. Raphael, *Anatomy of Bereavement,* 29.
77. W. L. de Rosset to Capt. Hamilton, 28 July 1876, forwarded to Lord Selborne, MS Selborne 228(6), fos. 13–18; W. L. de Rosset to Lord Selborne, 12 Aug. 1876, ibid., fo. 47.
78. Lord Selborne to brother, Revd Edwin Palmer, 24 Aug. 1876, ibid., fo. 40.
79. Ibid., 27 July, 10 Aug. 1876, fos. 10–11.
80. W. L. de Rosset to Capt. Hamilton, 28 July 1876, ibid., fos. 13–18.
81. Laura Roundell to cousin, Revd Edwin Palmer, 21 Aug. 1876, ibid., fo. 36; Lord Selborne to brother, Revd Edwin Palmer, 29 July 1876, ibid., fos. 21–3.
82. G. Horsley Palmer to Edwin Palmer, 14, 30 Sept., 5 Oct., 1876, ibid., fos. 50–1, 74–6, 93–4; Lord Selborne to Edwin Palmer, 29, 30 Sept., ibid., fos. 70–1, 87–8.
83. Raphael, *Anatomy of Bereavement,* 30.

4. *Death and the Victorian Doctors*

1. Roy Porter, *Disease, Medicine and Society in England 1550–1860* (1987), 54, 61–5; F. B. Smith, *The People's Health 1830–1910* (1979), *passim.*
2. *Lancet,* 5 Apr. 1862.
3. Ibid., 24 Apr. 1869.
4. 4th Lord Holland to mother, 3rd Lady Holland, 25 Dec. 1841, Holland House Papers, BL Add. MS 51776, fo. 106.
5. Lucy Sharpe to parents, Mr and Mrs Thomas W. Reid, 28 July 1844, Sharpe Papers 169/5.
6. Edward Shorter, 'The History of the Doctor–Patient Relationship', in W. F. Bynum and Roy Porter (eds.), *Companion Encyclopedia of the History of Medicine* (1993), ii. 791–4.

7. Ibid., 788–9.

8. *Cassell's Household Guide* (1869–71), 292.

9. *The Times*, 27 Feb., 26 July, 11 Oct. 1845.

10. Roundell Palmer to father, Revd William J. Palmer, 27 June 1839, Selborne Papers, MS 1878, fo. 52.

11. Dorothea Palmer to brother, Revd William Palmer, 13 Sept. 1851, Selborne Papers, MS Eng. misc. c. 690, fo. 105.

12. 'Copy of William Jocelyn Palmer's Will', 8 May 1852, MS Selborne Adds. 223(5).

13. George Cornish to John Keble, n.d. [1840s], Keble Correspondence 149.

14. Mary Somerville to son, Woronzow Greig, 5 Mar. 1838, Somerville Papers, dep. c. 361, folder MSIF-2.

15. Mary Somerville to brother, Sir Henry Fairfax, 5 July [1844], ibid., dep. c. 357, folder MSFP-6.

16. Letters from Sir Warwick Morshead and Selina Lady Morshead to Sir William Harcourt, n.d. [1883], MS Harcourt dep. 609, fos. 18–38.

17. *Lancet*, 5 Apr. 1862.

18. Sir Benjamin C. Brodie, *Psychological Inquiries* (1854), 127–9.

19. W. S. Savory, *On Life and Death* (1863), 173–82.

20. *Lancet*, 10 Dec. 1887, 7 Jan. 1888.

21. William Munk, *Euthanasia: or Medical Treatment in Aid of an Easy Death* (1887), 4–5.

22. Ibid., 7–8, 18–26.

23. Ibid., 65–105.

24. Ibid.

25. Regulations for Sarah Acland's last illness, 1878, Bodl. MS Acland d. 87, fos. 19–22.

26. *Lancet*, 7 Jan. 1888.

27. William Munk, *The Life of Sir Henry Halford* (1895), 35, 75, 21–7.

28. W. E. Gladstone's memorial on 'The Last Days of my Father, Sir John Gladstone 1851', W. E. Gladstone Papers, BL Add. MS 44739, fos. 104–20.

29. Ibid.

30. Oswald Browne, MA, MB, MRCP, *On the Care of the Dying* (1894), 1–32.

31. Brodie, *Psychological Inquiries*, 130–1.

32. Charles J. B. Williams, MD, FRS, *Memoirs of Life and Work* (1884), 53.

33. *Lancet*, 7 Jan. 1888.

34. Munk, *Euthanasia*, 22–6.

35. Ibid., 26–30, 90.

36. Charles Buttar, MD, *Medicine and Religion* (1910), 38–9, 48.

37. Virginia Berridge and Griffith Edwards, *Opium and the People: Opiate Use in Nineteenth-Century England* (1981), *passim*.

38. Roy Porter, 'Death and the Doctors in Georgian England', in Ralph Houlbrooke (ed.), *Death, Ritual and Bereavement* (1989), 91–4.

39. Dr Colin Murray Parkes, 'The Dying Patient's Grief', conference paper, Perth, Western Australia, 1981.

40. John Hinton, *Dying*, 2nd edn. (Harmondsworth, 1979), 72. But see Sherwin B. Nuland, *How we Die* (1994), 140–4, for a more pessimistic assessment of the proportion of dying people who suffer physical and mental distress until the end.
41. Ibid., 113.
42. C. W. Hufeland, *The Three Cardinal Means of the Art of Healing*, 46, quoted in Munk, *Euthanasia*, 77–8.
43. C. W. Hufeland, *On the Relations of the Physician to the Sick*, 2nd edn. (1846), 18–19.
44. Munk, *Euthanasia*, 73–83.
45. *Lancet*, 7 Jan. 1888. See also 18, 25 Feb. 1899.
46. R. Saundby, *Medical Ethics: A Guide to Professional Conduct* (1902), 11.
47. Dr Locock to Lady Lovelace, n.d., prescribed medical treatment, MS dep. Lovelace Byron 173, fo. 12.
48. Ada Lovelace to mother, Lady Byron, 6 Jan. 1852, ibid., MS 44, fos. 1–3.
49. Ibid., [Mar.?] 1852, MS 44, fo. 44.
50. Ibid., 29 Apr. 1852, MS 44, fo. 81.
51. Lady Byron's journal, 24 July [1852], MS dep. Lovelace Byron 69, fo. 154.
52. Ada Lovelace to Lord Lovelace, c. 10 Aug. 1852, ibid., MS 166, fos. 192–3.
53. Lady Byron's journal, 16–17 Aug. 1852, ibid., MS 69, fos. 169–70.
54. Ada Lovelace to Lady Byron, n.d., ibid., MS 44, fo. 90.
55. Eliza Lady Phillips to mother, Harriet Manse, 28 Nov. 1857, MS Phillips–Robinson e. 431, fo. 55.
56. Munk, *Euthanasia*, 68–71, 84–5.
57. W. S. Blunt to wife, Lady Anne Blunt, 14 Dec. 1871, 14 Mar. 1872, Wentworth Bequest, BL Add. MS 51400.
58. Ibid., 21 Apr. 1872.
59. Elizabeth Pearson to Lady Hambleden, 8 Oct. 1896, Hambleden MSS E58.
60. Helen Gladstone to Ishbel Lady Aberdeen, 28 Mar. 1898, Glynne–Gladstone Papers, MS 52/30.
61. Molly Trevelyan's diary, 15 May 1911, Trevelyan Papers.
62. Parkes, 'The Dying Patient's Grief'.
63. Hinton, *Dying*, 140–3.
64. Munk, *Life of Sir Henry Halford*, 263.
65. Henry Holland, *Medical Notes and Reflections* (1839), 81.
66. Munk, *Euthanasia*, 85–7.
67. R. W. Mackenna, MA, MD, *The Adventure of Death* (1916), 108.
68. Lord Carnarvon's diary, 25 May 1876, Carnarvon Papers, BL Add. MS 60908, fo. 120.
69. Account of Sir Charles Mordaunt's death, 30 May 1823, by his wife, Mary Mordaunt, Acland Papers, MS 1148 M/Box 16/7, Devon Record Office.
70. J. T. Coleridge, *Memoir of John Keble* (1870), 546.
71. Russell Noyes, Jr., 'The Art of Dying', *Perspectives in Biology and Medicine*, 14 (Spring 1971), 432.

72. Hufeland, *The Three Cardinal Means*, 46, quoted in Munk, *Euthanasia*, 77–8.
73. Hufeland, *On the Relations of the Physician to the Sick*, 12–13.
74. Lionel A. Tollemache, 'The New Cure for Incurables', *Fortnightly Review*, NS 13 (Feb. 1873), 222.
75. *Lancet*, 10 Dec. 1887; see also 18, 25 Feb. 1899.
76. Saundby, *Medical Ethics*, 12; Dr S. Russel Wells, cited in *Lancet*, 10 Nov. 1906.
77. Maurice Maeterlinck, *Life after Death* (1911), esp. 10–25.
78. Mackenna, *The Adventure of Death*, 84, 101–8.
79. Lord Lovelace's journal account of his wife's death, 16 Aug. 1852, Wentworth Bequest, BL Add. MS 54089, fo. 2.
80. Dorothy Stein, *Ada: A Life and a Legacy* (1985), 248.
81. Note by Arthur Rogers, 1886, uncat. papers of Thorold Rogers family, Box 11, R3, Box 1, fo. 38.
82. *Lancet*, 20 Feb. 1965, 424–5.
83. Noyes, 'The Art of Dying', 432–47.
84. F. W. Hafferty, *Into the Valley: Death and the Socialisation of Medical Students* (New Haven, 1991).

5. *Nurses, Consultants, and Terminal Prognoses*

1. Dr Oswald Browne, *On the Care of the Dying* (1894), 29–30.
2. *Lancet*, 26 Oct. 1861.
3. Charlotte Maddon, 'Nursing as a Profession for Ladies', *St Paul's Monthly Magazine* (Aug. 1871), 458, cited by B. Abel-Smith, *A History of the Nursing Profession* (1982), 18.
4. Account by Mary Ann Rogers of death of son, George Vining Rogers, 1856, uncat. papers of Thorold Rogers family, Box 14, R2, fo. 25.
5. Elizabeth Parker to Barbara Gandy, 22 Sept. 1865, in 'Letters of Mary Ann Rogers to son, R. N. Gandy', ed. B. M. H. Rogers, uncat. papers of Thorold Rogers family, Box 10, R7, fo. 16.
6. *The Harcourt Papers*, ed. E. W. Harcourt, 14 vols. (priv. pr, Oxford, 1880–1905), xiv. 72–3.
7. Sir Henry Layard to Marchioness of Huntley, 1851–2, Layard Papers, BL Add. MS 57941, fos. 4, 8–10, 13–14.
8. Elizabeth Horsley to Mary Brunel, 18 June 1858, Horsley Papers, MS Eng. c. 2200, fo. 33.
9. Caroline Cane to Jane Goulburn, 18 Feb. 1853; Louisa Cane to Jane Goulburn, 30 Oct. [n.d.], Goulburn Papers, Acc. 319, Box 30.
10. Sir William Harcourt to sister, Emily Harcourt, 22 Apr. 1880, MS Harcourt dep. 606.
11. Abel-Smith, *A History of the Nursing Profession*, 4.
12. Eleanor Fazakerley to sister, Jane Goulburn, n.d. [Sept.? 1843], Goulburn Papers, Acc. 319, Box 67, bundle 'letters to Mrs G. 1843'.
13. Mary Ann Rogers to son, Richard N. Gandy, 27 Oct. 1865, 10 Nov. 1865, uncat. papers of Thorold Rogers family, Box 10, R7, fo. 23.

14. W. E. Gladstone, 'The Last Days of my Father, Sir John Gladstone, Dec. 1851', W. E. Gladstone Papers, BL Add. MS 44739, fos. 104–20.

15. W. E. Gladstone, 'The Last Days of my Father', Dec. 1851, W. E. Gladstone Papers, BL Add. MS 44739, fos. 104–20.

16. Ada Lovelace to Lord Lovelace, c. 10 Aug. 1852, MS dep. Lovelace Byron 166, fos. 192–3.

17. Lord Lovelace's journal, 25–6 Aug. 1852, Wentworth Bequest, BL Add. MS 54089, fos. 9–10, 11–12.

18. Lady Byron's journal, 28 Aug. 1852, MS dep. Lovelace Byron 69, fos. 184–5.

19. Bequest note by Ada Lovelace, 24 Aug. 1852, ibid., MS 175, fo. 124.

20. Charles R. Fox to brother, Henry, 4th Lord Holland, 21 June 1844, Holland House Papers, BL Add. MS 52058, fos. 251–2.

21. Frederick Goulburn to brother, Edward Goulburn, 3 Jan. 1856, Goulburn Papers, Acc. 426, 16/6d.

22. Herbert Luckock to Caroline Lady Trevelyan, 1 Nov. 1890, Trevelyan Papers, GOT 125.

23. Lucy Sharpe to mother, Mary Reid, 22, 25 Oct. 1844, Sharpe Papers, 169/5, 98, fos. 121–2.

24. Sarah Acland to son, William Acland, 13 Apr. [1866], Bodl. MS Acland d. 42, fo. 148.

25. Elizabeth Horsley to daughter, Mary Brunel, 12 Aug. 1854, Horsley Papers, MS Eng. c. 2199, fos. 74–5.

26. Lady Clarendon to Lady Lewis, 27 Feb. 1862, MS Harcourt dep. 632, fos. 102–3.

27. James Tait to A. C. Tait, 13 May [1877], Tait Papers, vol. 97, fos. 304–5.

28. Maddon, 'Nursing as a Profession for Ladies', 460, quoted in Abel-Smith, *A History of the Nursing Profession*, 2 n. 1.

29. W. Munk, *Euthanasia* (1887), 93–6.

30. Quoted in Abel-Smith, *Nursing Profession*, 5.

31. Ibid., 52.

32. Ibid., ch. 4.

33. Lady Ann Blunt's diary, 31 May 1872, Wentworth Bequest, BL Add. MS 53841; Betty Askwith, *Lady Dilke: A Biography* (1969), 107–11.

34. Beatrice Potter diary, Apr. 1882, Passfield Papers.

35. Agnes Mills to cousin, Henrietta, Lady Carnarvon, 25 Aug. 1871, Carnarvon Papers, BL Add. MS 61044.

36. Sarah Acland to son, William Acland, 14 Mar. [1874], Bodl. MS Acland d. 42, fos. 317–18.

37. Sarah Angelina Acland, 'Memories in my 81st Year', MS Eng. Misc d. 214, fos. 63–7; Sarah Acland to son, William Acland, 5 Jan. 1874, Bodl. MS Acland d. 42, fos. 399–400.

38. Edith Bell to J. R. MacDonald, 23 Aug. 1911, MacDonald Papers, PRO 30/69/803.

39. Ellen Webster to J. R. MacDonald, 11 Sept. 1918, ibid., PRO 30/69/740, fos. 8–9.

40. 'In Memoriam, 24 April 1911, Mary Middleton', MacDonald Papers, PRO 30/69/90.

41. Irvine Loudon, *Medical Care and the General Practitioner 1750–1850* (Oxford, 1986), *passim.*

42. F. Parkes Weber, *Death and Doctors: Epigrams and Art in regard to the Relation of Death to the Medical Sciences* (1893), 3–4.

43. C. W. Hufeland, MD, *On the Relations of the Physician to the Sick* (1846), 30–3.

44. Charles J. B. Williams, MD, FRS, *Memoirs of Life and Work* (1884), 190, 213–14.

45. *Lancet*, 16 Jan. 1858, cited in F. B. Smith, *The People's Health 1830–1910* (1979), 369.

46. *My Doctors*, by a Patient (1891), 33–4.

47. Catharine Sharpe to half-brother, William Sharpe, 27 Jan. 1843, Sharpe Papers 97/1, fos. 46–7.

48. Lady Carnarvon to son, Lord Porchester, 27 Feb. 1849, Carnarvon Papers, BL Add. MS 61017.

49. Ibid., 7 May 1849.

50. Ibid., 8 May 1849.

51. W. E. Gladstone, 'The Last Days of my Father, Sir John Gladstone 1851', W. E. Gladstone Papers, BL Add. MS 44739, fos. 104–20.

52. Ibid.

53. A. C. Tait's journal, 14 Mar.–11 July 1856, Tait Papers, vol. 39, fos. 1–14.

54. Roy Porter, 'Death and the Doctors in Georgian England', in R. Houlbrooke (ed.), *Death, Ritual and Bereavement* (1989), 89.

55. Sir Henry Halford, 'On the Influence of Some Diseases of the Body on the Mind', read to the Royal College of Physicians, Feb. 1831, quoted in William Munk, *Life of Sir Henry Halford, Bart* (1895), 178–80.

56. Ibid.

57. Ibid., 261–2, 264–5.

58. Hufeland, *On the Relations of the Physician to the Sick.*

59. Ibid., 11–15.

60. *Lancet*, 13 Mar. 1869. See also 11 Jan. 1890.

61. Munk, *Euthanasia*, 26–30.

62. Sir Henry Holland, *Medical Notes and Reflections*, 3rd edn. (1885), 362.

63. Williams, *Memoirs of Life and Work*, 60–1.

64. Dr Matthews Duncan, 'Concerning Medical Education', cited in Oswald Browne, *On the Care of the Dying* (1894), 22–5.

65. Dr Robert Saundby, *Medical Ethics* (1902), 104–5, 117–18.

66. W. E. Gladstone's memorandum on the death of Jessy, his daughter, 9 Apr. 1850, W. E. Gladstone Papers, BL Add. MS 44738, fos. 122–46.

67. Dr C. Locock to Lord Lovelace, 15 June 1851, MS dep. Lovelace Byron 173, fo. 3.

68. See Dorothy Stein, *Ada: A Life and a Legacy* (1985), 217.

69. Dr West to Woronzow Greig, 20 Aug. 1852, Somerville Papers, dep. c. 368, folder MSBY-13.

70. Ada Lovelace to Lady Byron, n.d. [Nov? 1851], MS dep. Lovelace Byron 43, fos. 253–5.

71. Ibid., [28 Jan?] 1852, MS 44, fo. 21.

72. Dr Locock to Lady Lovelace, 25 Mar. 1852, ibid., MS 173, fo. 9.

73. Ada Lovelace to Lady Byron, [late July?] 1852, MS 44, fos. 128–9.

74. Ada Lovelace to Lady Byron, 25 July 1852, MS 44, fo. 120; Lady Byron's journal, 24 July [1852], ibid., MS 69, fo. 154.

75. Lady Byron's journal, 13 Aug. 1852, MS 69, fo. 164.

76. *Jane May Gladstone and her Children: In Memoriam* (priv. pr., 1864).

77. J. T. Coleridge, *Memoir of Rev. John Keble* (1870), 546, 551–2.

78. Lady Anne Blunt's diary, 1871–2, Wentworth Bequest, BL Add. MS 51400.

79. Lucy Sharpe to Sarah Kenrick, 28 Apr. 1878, Sharpe Papers 185.

80. Adelaide Anson to Agnes Anson, n.d. [1885], Acland–Anson Papers, MS 2862 M/F 154, Devon Record Office.

81. E. B. Turner, FRCS to Elsie Lady Carnarvon, 30 July 1921, Carnarvon Papers, BL Add. MS 61060.

82. Lady Dorothea's account of the death of her mother, Louisa Duchess of Atholl, July 1902, Atholl MS 494.

83. Dr T. Watson to Frederick Goulburn, 26, 31 Dec. 1855, Goulburn Papers, Acc. 426, 16/6c.

84. Frederick Goulburn to Edward Goulburn, 30 Dec. [1855], ibid., 16/6d.

85. Frederick Goulburn, 'FG's Memoranda during my Dear Father's Illness, Jany. 56', ibid., 16/6c.

86. Eleanor Wood to brother, Roundell Palmer, 25 Nov. [1869], Selborne Papers, MS 1879, fos. 113–14.

87. Emma Palmer to brother, Roundell Palmer, n.d. [1869], ibid., fos. 125–8.

88. Eleanor Wood to Roundell Palmer, 25 Nov. [1869], ibid., fos. 113–14.

89. Emma Palmer to Roundell Palmer, n.d. [late 1869], ibid., fos. 125–8.

90. Eleanor Wood to Roundell Palmer, 3 Feb. 1870, ibid., fos. 117–18.

91. William Benham, *Memoir: Death of Crauford Tait* (1879), 167–72.

92. Dr Alfred Carpenter to Catherine Tait, 23 Apr. 1878, Tait Papers, vol. 103, fos. 314–15.

93. Dr Meryon to Lady Carnarvon, 11 Dec. 1849, Carnarvon Papers, BL Add. MS 61019.

94. Katherine Maxse to sister-in-law, Violet Cecil, June [1900], Cecil–Maxse MSS, U 1599, C 65/30.

6. 'That Little Company of Angels': The Tragedies of Children's Deaths

1. Ettie Lady Desborough to [unknown recipient], 2 Jan. 1893, Grenfell Papers, 1627 Box 4.

2. Mary Fairfax to Mary Somerville, [1830,] Somerville Papers, dep. c. 358, MSFP-22.

3. Charlotte Bickersteth, *Doing and Suffering* (1860), 204–8.

4. B. R. Mitchell and Phyllis Deane, *Abstract of British Historical Statistics* (Cambridge, 1962), 36–7.

5. Anthony S. Wohl, *Endangered Lives: Public Health in Victorian Britain* (1983), 10–11. See also F. B. Smith, *The People's Health 1830–1910* (1979), 122–3; Rosalind Mitchison, *British Population Change since 1860* (1977), 49–52; William Farr, *Vital Statistics* (Metuchen, NJ, 1975; repr. of 1885 edn.), 190.

6. Farr, *Vital Statistics*, 203.

7. Ibid., 202–3.

8. R. C. Ansell, *On the Rate of Mortality* (1874), 69, 71; Mitchison, *British Population Change since 1860*, 50.

9. L. Stone, *The Family, Sex and Marriage in England 1500–1800* (1977), 651–2.

10. Colin Murray Parkes, *Bereavement: Studies of Grief in Adult Life* (Harmondsworth, 1978), 148.

11. Linda A. Pollock, *Forgotten Children: Parent–Child Relations from 1500 to 1900* (Cambridge, 1983), *passim*.

12. M. Asquith, *Myself when Young* (1938), 20.

13. 4th Lord Holland to Dowager Lady Holland, 5 Dec. 1842, Holland House Papers, BL Add. MS 51777, fo. 30.

14. B. Askwith, *The Lytteltons* (1975), 125.

15. Stephen Hobhouse, *Margaret Hobhouse and her Family* (priv. pr., Rochester, 1934), 25–6.

16. M. A. Chitty to Margaret MacDonald, 12 Jan. 1910 [1911?], MacDonald Papers, PRO 30/69/904.

17. *Our Children's Rest; or Comfort for Bereaved Mothers* (1863); *To a Christian Parent, on the Death of an Infant*, Religious Tract Society, no. 351 ([*c*.1852]); *Early Death: Thoughts for a Week of Mourning*, Society for Promoting Christian Knowledge ([1861]).

18. *To a Christian Parent, on the Death of an Infant*, 1, 4, 6.

19. Canon W. V. Harcourt to Lord Grosvenor, 6 Feb. 1839, *The Harcourt Papers*, 14 vols. (priv. pr., Oxford, 1880–1905), xiv. 72–3.

20. T. D. Acland to sister, Lydia D. Acland, n.d. [1851], Acland Papers, MS 1148 M/16/2, Devon Record Office.

21. W. H. Smith to 'Aunt Emily' Giberne, 7, 10 Feb. 1866, Hambleden MS, E/1; Charlotte H. Danvers to W. H. Smith, 6 Feb. 1866, Hambleden MS, G41.

22. *Early Death: Thoughts for a Week of Mourning*, 7, 10–12, 17, 19, 21.

23. *To a Christian Parent, on the Death of an Infant*, 4.

24. W. H. Smith to Emily Giberne, 7, 10 Feb. 1866, Hambleden MS E/1.

25. *To a Christian Parent, on the Death of an Infant*, 3, 5.

26. *Early Death: Thoughts for a Week of Mourning*, 13–16.

27. *Our Children's Rest*, 63, 78–9.

28. W. H. Smith to Emily Giberne, 7, 10 Feb. 1866, Hambleden MS E/1.

29. Lord Grosvenor to Canon W. V. Harcourt, 3 Feb. 1839, *The Harcourt Papers*, xiv. 71.

30. Lord Skelmersdale to William Harcourt, 21 Nov. 1864, MS Harcourt dep. 633, fos. 27–8.

31. Maud Lady Selborne to son, Robert Palmer, 18 Nov. [1914], Selborne Papers, MS Eng. lett. c. 454, fo. 173.

32. Jose Harris, *Private Lives Public Spirit: A Social History of Britain 1870–1914* (Oxford, 1993), 54.
33. Smith, *The People's Health 1830–1910*, 136–42.
34. John C. Horsley to Rose Haden, n.d. [7–8 Mar. 1854], Horsley Papers, MS Eng. c. 2206, fos. 24, 28–30.
35. Ibid., 8–11 Mar. 1854, fos. 33–4.
36. Ibid., 9 Mar. 1854, fos. 33–4.
37. Ibid., 12 Mar. 1854, fo. 47.
38. Ibid., 12–15 Mar. 1854, fos. 48, 61, 64.
39. Ibid., 16–17 Mar. 1854, fos. 66, 69–70, 72.
40. Ibid., 18 Mar. 1854, fos. 78–9.
41. Ibid., n.d., 20–4 Mar. 1854, fos. 85, 88, 91, 105.
42. Ibid., 19, 20 [,25] Mar. 1854, fos. 81–3, 85, 114.
43. Ibid., 21–2 Mar. 1854, fos. 88–9, 99–100.
44. Elizabeth Horsley to daughter-in-law, Rose Horsley, [1857,] Horsley Papers, MS Eng. c. 2204, fo. 131.
45. John Horsley to Rose Horsley, 15 Nov. 1866, Horsley Papers, MS Eng. c. 2209, fo. 10; see also Rose Horsley's diary, Feb.–Mar. 1857, ibid., MS Eng. e. 2204, fos. 24–5.
46. Marie B. to Rose Haden, 7 July [1869], Horsley Papers, MS Eng. c. 2235, fos. 1201–2.
47. Peter T. Marsh, *The Victorian Church in Decline: Archbishop Tait and the Church of England 1868–1882* (1969), 13–15.
48. A. C. Tait's journal on the deaths of his children, 1856, Tait Papers, vol. 39, fos. 1–128.
49. Catharine Tait's account of her five children's deaths, in *Catharine and Crauford Tait, Wife and Son of Archbishop A. C. Tait: A Memoir*, ed. Revd William Benham (1879), 403, 408–9, 251–3.
50. Catharine Tait's account, ibid., 284, 289, 305; A. C. Tait's journal on the deaths of his children, 1856, Tait Papers, vol. 39, fos. 29, 41–3.
51. A. C. Tait's journal, 1856, Tait Papers, vol. 39, fo. 88.
52. Catharine Tait's account, in *Catharine and Crauford Tait*, 304–12.
53. Catharine Tait's account, ibid., 336–66; A. C. Tait's journal, 1856, Tait Papers, vol. 39, fos. 64–87.
54. Ibid.
55. Ibid.
56. Ibid.
57. Ibid.
58. Catharine Tait's account, in *Catharine and Crauford Tait*, 257–89.
59. James Walvin, *A Child's World: A Social History of English Childhood 1800–1914* (1982), 29–44.
60. Catharine Tait's account, in *Catharine and Crauford Tait*, 276, 293, 297–8, 302–3; A. C. Tait's journal, 1856, Tait Papers, vol. 39, fos. 31, 37.
61. Catharine Tait's account, in *Catharine and Crauford Tait*, 308, 320, 329, 343, 371–2; A. C. Tait's journal, vol. 39, fos. 53, 107–8, 123–4.

62. Catharine Tait's account, in *Catharine and Crauford Tait*, 286.

63. Ibid., 290–1, 299, 315, 384.

64. A. C. Tait's journal, 1856, Tait Papers, vol. 39, fos. 7, 14, 116–17, 122.

65. Catharine Tait's account, in *Catharine and Crauford Tait*, 287–9, 299, 304, 311–12.

66. Ibid., 327.

67. Ibid., 331–3.

68. Ibid., 333–5, 339–65.

69. Ibid., 391–2.

70. A. C. Tait's journal, 9 May 1856, Tait Papers, vol. 40, fos. 7–9.

71. Ibid., 1, 20 June 1856, vol. 40, fos. 28, 32–3.

72. Ibid., fos. 3, 8, 17.

73. Ibid., 'Whitsunday, 1856', [mid-May,] 8–9 May 1856, vol. 40, fos. 15, 17, 3, 8.

74. Ibid., 8 May, 10 May 1856, vol. 40, fos. 3, 10–13.

75. Ibid., 20 July 1856, vol. 40, fo. 44.

76. Ibid., 26 Oct. 1856, vol. 42, fos. 7–8.

77. David Newsome, *Godliness and Good Learning: Four Studies on a Victorian Ideal* (1961), 148–93.

78. Randall I. Davidson, *Archibald Campbell Tait, Archbishop of Canterbury*, 2 vols. (1891), i. 190.

79. A. C. Tait's journal, 26–30 May 1878, Tait Papers, vol. 62, fos. 84–90; Catharine Tait's account, in *Catharine and Crauford Tait*, 160–72.

80. A. C. Tait's journal, [1878,] Tait Papers, vol. 62, fo. 131.

81. Davidson, *Archibald Campbell Tait*, ii. 334–5.

82. *Catharine and Crauford Tait*, 37, 251.

83. 'In Memoriam: Mrs Tait', 3 Dec. 1878, Tait Papers, vol. 103, fo. 336.

84. Ibid.

85. A. C. Tait's journal, [May,] 21 May, 19 Jan. 1879, Tait Papers, vol. 64, fos. 61, 63–4, 6–8.

86. F. Max Muller to A. C. Tait, n.d. [1878], ibid., vol. 98, fos. 227–8.

87. Sarah W. Jones to A. C. Tait, [1879/80,] ibid., vol. 99, fos. 346–7.

88. W. H. Jellie to A. C. Tait, 27 Sept. 1881, ibid., vol. 100, fos. 17–18.

89. Robert Spence to A. C. Tait, 7 Oct. 1879, ibid., vol. 99, fos. 304–7.

7. Death in Old Age

1. R. Mitchison, *British Population Change since 1860* (1977), 76; David Cannadine, 'War and Death, Grief and Mourning in Modern Britain', in J. Whaley (ed.), *Mirrors of Mortality* (1981), 193; M. Anderson, 'The Social Implications of Demographic Change', in F. M. L. Thompson (ed.), *The Cambridge Social History of Britain 1750–1950*, 2 vols. (1990), ii. 15–16.

2. Anderson, 'The Social Implications of Demographic Change', 46–7.

3. See table in Mitchison, *British Population Change*, 44.

4. Ibid., 55.

5. Cited in *Lancet*, 30 July 1881.

6. Hugh Percy Dunn, 'What London People Die Of', *Nineteenth Century*, 34 (Dec. 1893), 893.

7. Edwin Chadwick, *Report on the Sanitary Condition of the Labouring Population of Great Britain: Special Inquiry into the Practice of Interment in Towns* (1843), 42–3.

8. F. B. Smith, *The People's Health 1830–1910* (1990), 316–17, 320.

9. See e.g. T. H. Hollingsworth's 1964 study of life expectancy in the peerage, 'The Demography of the British Peerage', suppl. to *Population Studies*, 18 (1964).

10. *Earl Cowper, K.G.: A Memoir*, by his wife (Katrine Cecilia) (priv. pr., 1913), 135–6.

11. J. Wilson, *A Life of Sir Henry Campbell-Bannerman* (1973), 515–21.

12. Beverley Raphael, *The Anatomy of Bereavement* (1984), 307.

13. Henry R. Reynolds to granddaughter, Annie S. C. Reynolds, 26 Oct. 1846, uncat. papers of Thorold Rogers family, Box 4.

14. Caroline Fox to nephew, Henry, 4th Lord Holland, 23 May 1843, Holland House Papers, BL Add. MS 52055, fo. 108.

15. Mary Somerville to son, Woronzow Greig, 25 Dec. 1859, Somerville Papers, dep. c. 361, folder MSIF-4.

16. 3rd Lord Holland to son, Henry E. Fox, 31 July 1840, Holland House Papers, BL Add. MS 51757, fos. 240–1.

17. Lady Stepney to Mary Drew, 31 Mar. 1911, Mary Gladstone Drew Papers, BL Add. MS 46250, fo. 123.

18. Kate Courtney's diary, 12 May 1910, Courtney Collection, vol. xxxiv, fo. 115.

19. Elizabeth Haldane to mother, Mary Haldane, 19 Mar. 1909, Haldane Papers, NLS, MS 6050, fo. 92.

20. Mary Haldane to son, R. B. Haldane, 17 Apr. 1903, ibid., MS 6008, fos. 143–4.

21. Edith to Alfred Lyttelton, Oct. 1911, Chandos Papers, II, 3/11.

22. Caroline Fox to nephew, Henry Lord Holland, 23 May 1843, Holland House Papers, BL Add. MS 52055, fo. 108.

23. Anna Merivale to Lord Aldenham, 22 Apr. 1902, Gibbs Family Letters, MS 11021/29, fos. 423–4.

24. Anderson, 'The Social Implications of Demographic Change', 30.

25. Mary Ann Rogers to daughter-in-law, Mrs Alfred Rogers, 14 Sept. 1851, uncat. papers of Thorold Rogers family, Box 4.

26. Mary Ann Rogers to son, James E. Thorold Rogers, 21 Dec. 1864, ibid.

27. Mary Ann Rogers to son, Richard N. Gandy, 26 Dec. 1864, in 'Letters of Mary Ann Rogers to son Richard N. Gandy', ed. B. M. H. Rogers, ibid., Box 10, no. 7, R7, fos. 7–8.

28. Ibid., 12 Oct. 1865, fo. 17.

29. Ibid., 23 Feb. 1867, fo. 38.

30. Ibid., 1 May 1867, fo. 44.

31. Ibid., 6 Jan. 1870, 2 Dec. 1871.

32. Ibid., 15 May, 7 Nov. 1872, fos. 82–5.

33. Ibid., Box 4, no. 23.

34. Roundell Palmer to wife, Laura, 27 Dec. 1867, Selborne Papers, MS 1880, fos. 33–4.

35. A. C. Tait's journal, 19 Jan. 1879, Tait Papers, vol. 64, fos. 3–8.

36. Frances Lupton to Marion Bryce, 26 Dec. 1891, MS Bryce Adds. 41.

37. Charlotte Portal to nephew, Bertie, 4th Earl Minto, 18 Mar. 1891, Minto MS 12376, fo. 148.

38. Maud Lady Wolmer (later Selborne) to husband, William Lord Wolmer, May 1891, MS Selborne Adds. 1, fo. 101.

39. Marion Bryce to husband, James Bryce, 27 Aug. 1901, MS Bryce Adds. 24.

40. See e.g. Avery D. Weisman and Robert Kastenbaum, *The Psychological Autopsy* (New York, 1968), 27; Sir W. Savory, *On Life and Death* (1863), 178–9.

41. Sir Benjamin Brodie, *Psychological Inquiries* (1854), 127–8.

42. Ann Reynolds to granddaughter, Annie S. C. Reynolds, 21 July 1841, uncat. papers of Thorold Rogers family, Box 4.

43. Charles R. Fox to brother, Henry E. Fox, 2 Feb. 1835, Holland House Papers, BL Add. MS 52058, fos. 180–1.

44. Martha Somerville, *Personal Recollections from Early Life to Old Age of Mary Somerville* (1873), 373–4; Frances Power Cobbe's obituary of Mary Somerville, offprint from the *Echo*, 3 Dec. 1872, Somerville Papers, dep. c. 360, folder MSFP-56.

45. Caroline Fox to Augusta Lady Holland, 12 Apr., 19, 21 June 1842, Holland House Papers, BL Add. MS 52149, fos. 113, 124–6.

46. Ibid., 5, 12 July 1842, fos. 129–32.

47. Ibid., 12 July 1842, fo. 132.

48. Agnes Anson to husband, Fred Anson, 8 Jan. 1887, Acland–Anson Papers, MS 2862 M/F265, Devon Record Office.

49. Ibid., n.d. [1887], F270.

50. Ibid., 12–14 May 1892, F310–12.

51. Elizabeth King to sister, Agnes King, 12 Nov. 1894, Ramsay MacDonald Papers, PRO 30/69/969.

52. Margaret Gladstone to fiancé, Ramsay MacDonald, 20 July 1896, ibid., PRO 30/69/778.

53. M. Gladstone to Annie Ramsay, 15 July 1896, ibid., PRO 30/69/775.

54. M. Gladstone to R. MacDonald, 15 July 1896, ibid., PRO 30/69/778.

55. Mary Drew to Catherine Gladstone, 7 Sept. [1897], Mary Gladstone Drew Papers, BL Add. MS 46225, fos. 299–300.

56. Alice Balfour's diary, 14–15 Feb. 1898, Balfour Papers (Whittingehame) MS 224.

57. Frances to Arthur Balfour, [n.d.,] ibid., MS 165.

58. James Cecil to Violet Cecil, 1 Dec. 1899, Cecil–Maxse MSS, U 1599, C 101/12.

59. Alice Cecil to Violet Cecil, 24 Nov. 1899, ibid., C 77/7.

60. Beatrice Potter (Webb) diary, Feb. 1883, Passfield Papers.

61. Ibid., 7 Mar., [Sept.] 1889.

62. Ibid., 29 Mar. 1890.

63. Ibid., 22 Apr. 1890.

64. Ibid., 1 Jan. 1892.

65. Kate Courtney's diary, 1 Jan. 1892, Courtney Collection, vol. xxvi, fos. 85–7.

66. Agnes to Elizabeth King, 21 Apr. 1911, MacDonald Papers, PRO 30/69/970.

67. Elizabeth to Agnes King, 10 Feb. 1912, ibid.

68. Agnes King's 'Prayers during the Long Struggle AGK', 9 Sept. 1911, ibid.

69. Ibid., 29 Sept. 1911.

70. Ibid., 30 Nov. 1911.

71. Ibid., 29 Feb. 1912.

72. Dr Edmund Lambert to George Henry Dashwood, 5, 11 Jan.; [*c.*6–17] Jan.; 8, 18 Mar. 1848, MS D. D. Dashwood (Bucks), G 5/6/1–5.

73. Ibid., 11, 16 Nov. 1848, 24, 26 Jan. 1849, G 5/6/8–9, 11–12.

74. Ibid., 6 Mar. 1849, G 5/6/14.

75. Mrs Mary Berkeley to brother, George Henry Dashwood, 28, 30 May 1849, ibid., G 3/21/3–4.

76. Ibid., 11 June, 26 July 1849, G 3/21/6, 10.

77. G. H. Dashwood to wife, Elizabeth, [*c.*26 July 1849]; John Lechmere to Elizabeth Dashwood, 24 Oct. [1849], ibid., G 3/11/5, G 3/24/4.

78. *Earl Cowper, K.G.*, 392–3.

79. Margot Asquith to Mary Drew, 15 Feb. 1895, Mary Gladstone Drew Papers, BL Add. MS 46238, fos. 228–9.

80. J. D. Hooker to Charles Darwin, 19 Oct. 1872, Darwin Papers, DAR 103, fo. 125.

81. Violet Cecil to husband, Edward Cecil, 26 Jan. 1909, Cecil–Maxse Papers, U 1599, C 705/43.

82. Lady Abercromby to Mary Haldane, 6 Feb. 1898, 3 Apr. 1912, Haldane Papers, NLS, MS 6093, fo. 235, MS 6094, fos. 118–19.

83. Sarah A. Acland to brother, William A. D. Acland, 22 Oct., 22 Nov. 1900, Bodl. MS Acland d. 108, fos. 64–5, 74–5.

84. Cited in C. M. Parkes, *Bereavement: Studies of Grief in Adult Life* (Harmondsworth, 1978), 29–31, 227–8.

85. Raphael, *The Anatomy of Bereavement*, 313–14. See also Parkes, *Bereavement*, 41.

86. Dr J. H. Gladstone, *In Memoriam: Jane May Gladstone and her Children* (priv. pr., 1864), 17–19.

87. Evelyn Stanhope to Arthur Lord Stanhope, 12 Dec. 1875, Stanhope MS U 1590, C 513/3; Aubrey N. Newman, *The Stanhopes of Chevening* (1969), 314.

88. *Emma Lady Ribblesdale: Letters and Diaries*, ed. Beatrix Lister (priv. pr., 1930), 62.

89. Anna Merivale to Lord Aldenham, 22 Apr. 1902, Gibbs Family Letters, MS 11021/29, fos. 423–4.

90. Kate Courtney's diary, May 1905, Courtney Collection, vol. xxxii, fo. 47.

91. See e.g. M. Pelling and R. M. Smith, *Life, Death and the Elderly* (1991), 6–7.

8. *In Search of the Good Death: Death in the Gladstone and Lyttelton Families 1835–1915*

1. S. G. Checkland, *The Gladstones: A Family Biography 1764–1851* (1971), 78, 85.
2. H. C. G. Matthew, *Gladstone 1809–1874* (1986), 27, 52–5.
3. G. Battiscombe, *Mrs Gladstone* (1956), 31.
4. Memorandum on the death of Mary Lady Lyttelton, 1857 ('the Hagley Record'), Mary Gladstone Drew Papers, BL Add. MS 46269, fo. 65.
5. Mary Gladstone to Lord Rosebery, 21 Jan. 1885, Rosebery MS 10015, fo. 93.
6. Mary Drew to mother, Catherine Gladstone, 12 Mar. 1888, Mary Gladstone Drew Papers, BL Add. MS 46224, fo. 122.
7. Note by Mary Drew in March 1888 with her copy of W. E. Gladstone's account of Jessy's death, Mary Gladstone Drew Papers, BL Add. MS 46269, fos. 130, 131.
8. Richard Shannon, *Gladstone*, i: *1809–1865* (1982), 4.
9. This section on the death of Anne Gladstone is entirely based on the memorandum by W. E. Gladstone, 'Recollections of the Last Hours of my Mother. Fasque Sept 23 1835', Gladstone Papers, BL Add. MS 44724, fos. 164–75.
10. Ibid.
11. Ibid.
12. Ibid.
13. *The Gladstone Diaries*, ii, ed. M. R. D. Foot and H. C. G. Matthew (Oxford, 1974), 196–7 (21–5 Sept. 1835).
14. *The Gladstone Diaries*, iv, ed. H. C. G. Matthew (Oxford, 1974), 196 ff., Mar.–Apr. 1850; memorial by W. E. Gladstone on the death of his daughter, Jessy, 9 Apr. 1850, marked 'Most Private', W. E. Gladstone Papers, BL Add. MS 44738, fos. 122–46 (copy in Mary Gladstone Drew Papers, BL Add. MS 46269, fos. 130–43).
15. Ibid.
16. Ibid.
17. Virginia Berridge and Griffith Edwards, *Opium and the People* (1981), pp. xix, 24. See p. 103 for the medical debate on the use of opium in treatment of young children.
18. *The Gladstone Diaries*, iv. 196 ff., Mar.–Apr. 1850; memorial by W. E. Gladstone on the death of his daughter, Jessy, W. E. Gladstone Papers, BL Add. MS 44738, fos. 122–46 (copy in Mary Gladstone Drew Papers, BL Add. MS 46269, fos. 130–43).
19. Ibid.
20. W. E. Gladstone's memorial on Jessy's death, Mary Gladstone Drew Papers, BL Add. MS 46269, fos. 130–43.
21. Ibid.
22. Ibid.
23. W. E. Gladstone, 'The Last Days of my Father, Sir John Gladstone. 1851', Dec. 1851, W. E. Gladstone Papers, BL Add. MS 44739, fos. 104–20.

24. Matthew, *Gladstone 1809–1874*, 100–1.
25. W. E. Gladstone, 'The Last Days of my Father, Sir John Gladstone. 1851', Dec. 1851, W. E. Gladstone Papers, BL Add. MS 44739, fos. 104–20.
26. *The Gladstone Diaries*, ed. Matthew, iv. 372, 29 Nov. 1851; W. E. Gladstone, 'Last Days of my Father', W. E. Gladstone Papers, BL Add. MS 44739, fos. 104–20.
27. W. E. Gladstone, 'Last Days of my Father', Gladstone Papers, BL Add. MS 44739, fos. 104–20.
28. Ibid.
29. Ibid.
30. Ibid.
31. Memorial on the death of Mary Lady Lyttelton, 1857 ('the Hagley Record'), Mary Gladstone Drew Papers, BL Add. MS 46269, fos. 65–109.
32. Betty Askwith, *The Lytteltons* (1975), 137.
33. Memorial on the death of Lady Lyttelton, 1857, Mary Gladstone Drew Papers, BL Add. MS 46269, fos. 65–109; Askwith, *The Lytteltons*, 129–41.
34. Memorial on the death of Lady Lyttelton, 1857, Mary Gladstone Drew Papers, BL Add. MS 46269, fos. 65–109.
35. Ibid.
36. Ibid.
37. Ibid.
38. Ibid.
39. See Askwith, *The Lytteltons*, 135.
40. Memorial on the death of Lady Lyttelton, 1857, Mary Gladstone Drew Papers, BL Add. MS 46269, fos. 65–109.
41. Ibid.
42. Ibid.
43. Ibid.
44. Ibid.
45. Matthew, *Gladstone 1809–1874*, 155.
46. Mary Gladstone's memorial of May Lyttelton's death, 21 Mar. 1875, Mary Gladstone Drew Papers, BL Add. MS 46269, fos. 110–22.
47. Askwith, *The Lytteltons*, 175–7.
48. Lavinia Talbot to sister, Meriel Talbot, Easter Tuesday 1875, Talbot Papers U 1612.
49. Mary Gladstone's memorial of May Lyttelton's death, 21 Mar. 1875, Mary Gladstone Drew Papers, BL Add. MS 46269, fos. 110–22.
50. Ibid.
51. Ibid.
52. Meriel Talbot's diary, 20–1 Mar. 1875, Talbot Papers, U 1612 F 123.
53. Ibid.
54. Lavinia Talbot to Mary Gladstone, n.d., copied into Mary Gladstone Drew Papers, BL Add. MS 46269, fos. 110–22.
55. Mary Dorothea Waldegrave to father, Roundell Palmer, 26 Mar. 1875, Selborne MS 1879, fos. 195–6.

56. Mary Gladstone to mother, Catherine Gladstone, 21 Mar. 1875, Mary Gladstone Drew Papers, BL Add. MS 46222, fos. 237–8.

57. W. E. Gladstone to Lord Lyttelton, n.d., extract in Mary Gladstone Drew Papers, BL Add. MS 46269, fo. 117.

58. W. E. Gladstone to Catherine Gladstone, n.d., ibid.

59. Revd Edward Talbot to mother, Mrs Talbot, extract in Mary Gladstone Drew Papers, ibid., fo. 117; W. E. Gladstone to Lord Lyttelton, ibid., fo. 117.

60. Laura Lyttelton to Edward Lyttelton, n.d. [16 Dec. 1885], in 'Memoir of Laura Tennant by Mary Drew', Mary Gladstone Drew Papers, BL Add. MS 46270, fo. 76.

61. Laura Lyttelton's informal will in 'Memoir of Laura Tennant by Mary Drew', ibid., fos. 76–7.

62. Margot Asquith's [née Tennant] memorandum on the death of Laura Lyttelton, 7 Nov. 1913, in Edith Lyttelton, unpub. typescript, 1938, Chandos Papers, 'Interwoven', 6/1/F.

63. Helen to Henry Gladstone, 22 Apr. 1886, Glynne–Gladstone Papers, MS 44/4; Lucy Cavendish to 'dearest old fellow' [her brother, Spencer Lyttelton?], Good Friday, 1886, Chandos Papers, 1, 2/20, fo. 44.

64. Helen to Henry Gladstone, 22 Apr. 1886, Glynne–Gladstone Papers, MS 44/4.

65. Margot Asquith's memorandum on Laura Lyttelton's death, in Edith Lyttelton, Chandos Papers, 'Interwoven', 6/1/F.

66. Ibid.

67. Margot Tennant's contribution to Mary Drew's 'Memoir of Laura Lyttelton', 1887, Mary Gladstone Drew Papers, BL Add. MS 46270, fos. 80–1.

68. Margot Asquith's memorandum, Chandos Papers, 'Interwoven', 6/1/F.

69. Mary Drew's diary, 24 Apr. 1886, Mary Gladstone Drew Papers, BL Add. MS 46262, fo. 18.

70. Mary Drew to Henry Gladstone, 20 May 1886, Glynne–Gladstone Papers, MS 43/2.

71. Mary Drew to Catherine Gladstone, n.d. [28 Apr. 1886], Mary Gladstone Drew Papers, BL Add. MS 46223, fo. 295; Mary Drew's diary, 27–8 Apr. 1886, ibid., MS 46262, fo. 19.

72. Gertrude Gladstone to Henry Gladstone, 25 July 1889, 21 Jan., 1 Feb. 1891, Glynne–Gladstone Papers, MS 38/4; Catherine Gladstone to Lord Rosebery, 16 June 1891, Rosebery MS 10021, fo. 169.

73. Gertrude Gladstone to Henry Gladstone, 12 June 1891, Glynne–Gladstone Papers, MS 38/4.

74. Catherine Gladstone to Lord Rosebery, 2 July 1891, Rosebery MS 10021, fo. 171.

75. Mary Drew to Lady Stepney, n.d. [July 1891], Mary Gladstone Drew Papers, BL Add. MS 46249, vol. II, fos. 348–9.

76. Catherine Gladstone to Lord Rosebery, 10 July 1891, Rosebery MS 10021, fo. 173.

77. W. E. Gladstone's account of the death of his son, W. H. Gladstone, 4 July 1891, Mary Gladstone Drew Papers, BL Add. MS 46269, fos. 144–52.

78. Mary Drew's account of W. E. Gladstone's last illness, 1898, Mary Gladstone Drew Papers, BL Add. MS 46269, fos. 15–44.
79. Ibid., 4 Apr. 1898, fo. 24.
80. Ibid., 14 Apr. 1898, fos. 25–6.
81. Ibid., 24 Apr. 1898, fos. 27–8.
82. Ibid., 17 May 1898, fo. 33.
83. Ibid., 18 May 1898, fos. 33–4.
84. Ibid., 19 May 1898, fos. 34–5.
85. Lady Stepney to Mary Drew [, c.Apr. 1898], copied in ibid., fo. 26.
86. Helen Gladstone to Mary Drew, 2 Sept. 1903, Mary Gladstone Drew Papers, BL Add. MS 46231, fos. 172–3.
87. John Morley, *Gladstone*, 3 vols. (1903), iii. 528.
88. Mary Drew to Herbert Gladstone, 12, 18 May 1900, Glynne–Gladstone Papers, MS 51/3.
89. Mary Drew to Lord Rosebery, n.d. [May 1900], Rosebery MS 10015, fo. 146.
90. Lady Gwendolen Cecil to Mary Drew, 18 June 1900, Mary Gladstone Drew Papers, BL Add. MS 46238, fo. 148.
91. See Herbert, Viscount Gladstone, *William G. C. Gladstone: A Memoir* (1918), 107.
92. Charles Masterman, 'W. G. C. Gladstone', *Nineteenth Century*, 77 (May 1915), 1196–1202.
93. *Mary Gladstone: Her Diaries and Letters*, ed. Lucy Masterman (1930), 481–2.
94. Mary Drew to sister, Helen Gladstone, 15 Apr. 1915, Mary Gladstone Drew Papers, BL Add. MS 46231, fos. 197–8.
95. *Margaret Cowell Stepney: Her Letters*, ed. B. E. Lockhart (priv. pr., 1926), 340–2.
96. Gladstone, *William G. C. Gladstone*, 121–4.
97. See e.g. Lord Lincolnshire's diary, 18–19 May 1915, Carrington MS Film 1129, fos. 8–13, 16.
98. Gladstone, *William G. C. Gladstone*.
99. Agnes Wickham to Catherine Gladstone, 29 Sept. 1891, Glynne–Gladstone Papers, MS 30/10.
100. Mary Drew to Catherine Gladstone, 17 Mar. 1898, Mary Gladstone Drew Papers, BL Add. MS 46225, fos. 326–7.
101. Mary Drew to Helen Gladstone, 11 Dec. 1913, ibid., BL Add. MS 46231, fo. 189.

9. Funeral Reform and the Cremation Debate

1. Bertram Puckle, *Funeral Customs* (1926), 87, 253–4.
2. John Morley, *Death, Heaven and the Victorians* (1971); J. S. Curl, *The Victorian Celebration of Death* (1972), 7, 20; Julian Litten, *The English Way of Death: The Common Funeral since 1450* (1991), 170.
3. Clare Gittings, *Death, Burial and the Individual* (1984), 25–6.
4. Lawrence Stone, *The Crisis of the Aristocracy* (Oxford, 1965), 576, 784–6.
5. John McManners, *Death and the Enlightenment* (Oxford, 1981), 285.

6. Lou Taylor, *Mourning Dress: A Costume and Social History* (1983), ch. 1.
7. Phyllis Cunnington and Catherine Lucas, *Costume for Births, Marriages and Deaths* (1972), 196.
8. Puckle, *Funeral Customs*, app. 273–5.
9. E. Chadwick, *Report on the Practice of Interment in Towns* (1843), 50–1, the evidence of the undertaker, Mr Wild of London.
10. Chadwick, *Interment in Towns*, 48–9.
11. 'Snells Bill for Funeral' of Henry Goulburn, 1843, Goulburn Papers, Acc. 319, Box 27.
12. Leonard Huxley, *The Life and Letters of Thomas Henry Huxley*, 2 vols. (1900), i. 102 (T. H. Huxley to fiancée, Fanny Heathorn, 28 Nov. 1852).
13. Holland House Papers, BL Add. MS 51472, fos. 8–46.
14. *The Times*, 27 Feb. 1865.
15. G. E. Buckle, *The Life of Benjamin Disraeli* (1920), vi. 620.
16. Mary Anne Disraeli to Benjamin Disraeli, 6 June 1856, Hughenden Papers, Box 24, A, IX, B/2.
17. William M. Sinclair to Revd Randall T. Davidson, A. C. Tait's son-in-law, 3 Dec. 1882, Tait Papers, vol. 104, fos. 3–6.
18. Memorial to A. C. Tait by J. H. J. Ellison, 3 Dec. 1882, ibid., fos. 214–16.
19. Press cutting, *Clerical World*, 3 May 1882, Darwin Papers, DAR 215.
20. Sir John Lubbock to William E. Darwin, 25 Apr. 1882, ibid.
21. Morley, *Death, Heaven and the Victorians*, chs. 2–3; Litten, *The English Way of Death: The Common Funeral since 1450*, 225.
22. *The Times*, 27 Feb. 1865.
23. *Cassell's Household Guide* (1869–71), iii. 292.
24. *Lancet*, 20 Jan. 1894.
25. Lady Colin Campbell, *Etiquette of Good Society* (1893), 211.
26. Chadwick, *Interment in Towns*, 107.
27. Memorandum by Margaret Lady Fairfax, 5 Aug. 1823, Somerville Papers, dep. b. 205, MSFP-60.
28. Caroline Fox to nephew, Henry, 4th Lord Holland, 12 July 1842, Holland House Papers, BL Add. MS 52054, fo. 7.
29. Gen. Charles Fox to brother, Henry, 4th Lord Holland, 27 Oct. 1840, ibid., MS 52051, fo. 209.
30. Sir John Dashwood King, 'Instructions for Codicil', n.d., MS D.D. Dashwood (Bucks), F 6/1/2.
31. *The Times*, 27 Feb. 1845.
32. Ibid., 4 Mar. 1845.
33. Ibid., 9, 11 Oct. 1845.
34. S. G. Checkland, *The Gladstones: A Family Biography 1764–1851* (1971), 373.
35. 'FG's Memoranda during my Dear Father's Illness, Jany. 56', Goulburn Papers, Acc. 426, 16/6c.
36. Copy of Revd William Wood's will, 22 Feb. 1832 (proven 12 July 1841), MS Selborne 230 (11).
37. Copy of William Jocelyn Palmer's will, 1 Jan. 1852, MS Selborne 223 (5).

38. Accounts various, MS Selborne 223 (13), 224 (6) item 5, 227 (9), 230 (4).
39. Mattie A. Vivian to cousin, Rose Horsley, 7 Dec. 1875, Horsley Papers, MS Eng. c. 2235, fos. 126–8.
40. Anon. press cutting, Dec. 1875, Childers MS 9/11.
41. *North Kent Spectator*, n.d. [*c*.30 Mar. 1876], Conway Papers, Add. 7676/V(2).
42. Egerton Harcourt's will, 15 May 1880, MS Harcourt dep. 670, fo. 2.
43. Agnes Anson to husband, Fred Anson, 16 May 1892, Acland–Anson Papers, MS 2862 M/F 313, Devon Record Office.
44. Francis Seymour Haden, 'The Ethics of Cremation', *Quarterly Review*, 192 (July 1900), 45–67.
45. 'Copy of William Jocelyn Palmer's Will', 1 Jan. 1852 [he died 20 Sept. 1853], MS Selborne 223(5); see also Earl of Selborne, *Memorials* (1853), i. 160–1.
46. Press cutting, *c*.4 June 1878, Tait Papers, vol. 62, fo. 131.
47. 2nd Countess Morley's diary, 19, 24 Jan. 1877, Morley Papers, BL Add. MS 48263, fo. 5.
48. Mary Drew's will, 1 Jan. 1890, Mary Gladstone Drew Papers, BL Add. MS 46268, fo. 1.
49. *Lancet*, 27 Aug. 1892.
50. John Morley, *The Life of William Ewart Gladstone*, 3 vols. (1903), iii. 533.
51. Cunnington and Lucas, *Costume for Births, Marriages and Deaths*, 240.
52. Lucy Cohen, *Lady de Rothschild and her Daughters 1821–1931* (1935), 261.
53. William G. Wickham to Herbert Gladstone, [29 May 1898,] Viscount Gladstone Papers, BL Add. MS 46046, fos. 72–3.
54. *Lancet*, 6 Dec. 1873, 2 June 1877.
55. Sir Henry Thompson, 'The Treatment of the Body after Death', *Contemporary Review*, 23 (Jan. 1874), 319–28. See Jennifer Leaney, 'Ashes to Ashes: Cremation and the Celebration of Death in Nineteenth-Century Britain', in R. Houlbrooke (ed.), *Death, Ritual and Bereavement* (1989), 118–35, for a more detailed survey of the history of Victorian cremation.
56. See Haden's arguments in e.g. *The Times*, 12 Jan., 17 June 1875, 11 Apr. 1898; *Lancet*, 18 Aug. 1894, 20 May 1893, 14 May 1898, 27 May 1899; Haden, 'The Ethics of Cremation', 45–67.
57. Ibid.
58. Henry Thompson, 'Cremation: A Reply to Critics', *Contemporary Review*, 23 (Mar. 1874), 553–71; *Modern Cremation: Its History and Practice* (1889).
59. Morley, *Death, Heaven and the Victorians*, ch. 8, pp. 91–101; Adolphe Wahltuch, MD, *The Dead and the Living: Earth Burial One of the Causes of High Mortality* (1891), 6. See Morley's ch. 8 for a more detailed study of the history of cremation in Britain; also Leaney, 'Ashes to Ashes'.
60. See e.g. *Lancet*, 3 Jan., 7 Mar., 9 May, 6 June 1874, 18 Mar. 1876.
61. Ibid., 3 Jan. 1874.
62. Ibid., 16 May 1874, letter by W. F. Sheard.
63. Ibid., 11 July 1874.
64. Ibid., 14 Nov. 1874.
65. Ibid., 11, 18 Jan., 8 Feb., 29 Mar. 1879.

66. Ibid., 20 Feb. 1885.
67. Ibid., 27 Aug. 1892.
68. Ibid., 6 Sept. 1902, 9 May 1903.
69. Puckle, *Funeral Customs*, 222.
70. Certificate of embalming, 24 Sept. 1874, Dilke Papers, BL Add. MS 43902, fo. 206.
71. *Lancet*, 17, 24 Oct. 1874.
72. Arthur Galton, 'An Elegy in Memory of my Grandmother, Isabella Galton, Christmas 1885', Galton Papers 24.
73. Kate Courtney's diary, 'Easter Sunday' 1896, Courtney Collection, vol. xxviii, fos. 120–1.
74. Letter from John W. Martin, MD, *Lancet*, 12 Dec. 1896.
75. Eleanor Rathbone, *William Rathbone: A Memoir* (1905), 490.
76. Kate Courtney to Margaret Courtney, 16 Dec. 1903, Courtney Collection, vol. IX, fos. 37–8.
77. Leaney, 'Ashes to Ashes', 125.
78. Ibid., 118–35.

10. The Funeral Week

1. John Hinton, *Dying* (1979), 186–7. See also John Bowlby, *Attachment and Loss* (1980), 93.
2. B. Raphael, *The Anatomy of Bereavement* (1984), 37.
3. Hinton, *Dying*, 174; see also Colin Murray Parkes, *Bereavement: Studies of Grief in Adult Life* (1978), 85.
4. Parkes, *Bereavement*, 56.
5. Lucy Sharpe (née Reid) to husband, William Sharpe, 28 Oct. 1844, Sharpe Papers 98, fos. 127–9.
6. T. W. Reid to daughter, Lucy Sharpe, 29 Oct. 1844, Sharpe Papers 118.
7. Ellen Stark to future mother-in-law, Mary Reid, 6 Nov. 1844, Sharpe Papers 169/5.
8. Lucy Sharpe to husband, William Sharpe, 1 Apr., 21 May 1845, Sharpe Papers 98, fos. 148, 165.
9. 3rd Lord Holland to son, Henry E. Fox, 5 May 1840, Holland House Papers, BL Add. MS 51757, fo. 306.
10. Mary Somerville to Agnes Greig, 22 Nov. 1867, Somerville Papers, dep. c. 363, folder MSIF-17.
11. A. C. Tait's journal, Dec. 1878, Tait Papers, vol. 63, fo. 105.
12. Miss Cameron's diary, May 1897, Atholl MS 650.
13. W. J. Butler, Canon of Worcester (ed.), *A Short Manual for Nurses* (1881), pp. vi–vii.
14. *Simple Instructions for the Laying Out of the Dead*, by Two Queen's Nurses, L. C. and A. E. H. (Richmond, 1910), 1–8. The pamphlet could only be obtained on application, but the authors were gratified by the 'demand for a fresh supply' which took production up to 3,000 copies.

15. Lady Anne Blunt's diary, 11–13 Aug. 1872, Wentworth Bequest, BL Add. MS 53841.

16. Agnes Greig to Martha Somerville, Nov. 1865, Somerville Papers, dep. c. 364, folder MSIF-25.

17. Elizabeth Horsley to daughter-in-law, Elvira Horsley, [1849,] Horsley Papers, MS Eng. c. 2204, fos. 26–7.

18. Elizabeth Horsley to daughter, Mrs Mary Brunel, 15 June 1858, ibid., MS c. 2200, fo. 20.

19. Mattie A. Vivian to Rose Horsley, 7 Dec. 1875, ibid., MS Eng. c. 2235, fo. 126.

20. Edwin Chadwick, *Report on the Practice of Interment in Towns* (1843), 45.

21. Emily Harcourt to brother, Sir William Harcourt, n.d. [Feb.–Mar. 1863], MS Harcourt dep. 603, fos. 19–22.

22. Lord Carnarvon's diary, 28 May 1876, Carnarvon Papers, BL Add. MS 60908, fos. 121–2.

23. 2nd Countess Morley's diary, 25 Jan., 9 Feb., 2, 22 Mar. 1877, Morley Papers, BL Add. MS 48263, fos. 5–6.

24. John Callcott Horsley's diary, 2–7 Dec. 1852, Horsley Papers, MS Eng. e. 2186, fos. 57–62.

25. Lord Lovelace's journal, 15, 21, 24, 31 Aug. 1852, Wentworth Bequest, BL Add. MS 54089, fos. 1, 5–6, 8, 13; Ada Lovelace's notes, n.d., 30 Sept. 1852, MS dep. Lovelace Byron 175, fos. 142, 144; Lady Byron's journal, 18 Aug. 1852, ibid., MS 69, fo. 173.

26. Agnes Wills to Henrietta, Dowager Lady Carnarvon, 24 July 1871, Carnarvon Papers, BL Add. MS 61044.

27. Frank S. Rogers to brother, Richard Gandy, 21 Nov. 1878, uncat. papers of Thorold Rogers family, Box 11 R3, Box 1, fos. 31–2.

28. Kate Courtney's diary, 1905, Courtney Collection, vol. xxxii, fos. 47–51.

29. Sophy Horsley to friend, Rose Haden, [July 1849,] Horsley Papers, MS Eng. c. 2212, fos. 102–3.

30. Sir William Harcourt to sister, Emily Harcourt, 'Sunday Morning', [1 Mar. 1862?,] MS Harcourt dep. 606, fo. 130.

31. Emily Harcourt to Sir William Harcourt, 'Sunday', [Mar. 1862,] ibid., dep. 603, fos. 14, 16.

32. Revd W. V. Harcourt to son, Sir William Harcourt, 2 Mar. 1862, ibid., dep. 602, fos. 30–1.

33. John Callcott Horsley's diary, 8 Dec. 1852, Horsley Papers, MS Eng. e. 2186, fos. 62–5.

34. For a useful brief survey of the history of undertakers, see Clare Gittings, *Death, Burial and the Individual in Early Modern England* (1984), 94–100.

35. *The Funeral*, Pamphlet no. 295, Society for Promoting Christian Knowledge (c.1858).

36. Agnes Greig to Martha Somerville, 1 Nov. 1865, Somerville Papers, dep. c. 364, folder MSIF-25.

37. *Mary Gladstone: Her Diaries and Letters*, ed. Lucy Masterman (1930), 448–9.

38. *Earl Cowper K.G.: A Memoir*, by his wife (Katrine Cecilia) (priv. pr., 1913), 565.

39. John Callcott Horsley's diary, 8 Dec. 1852, Horsley Papers, MS Eng. e. 2186, fos. 62–5.

40. Ibid.

41. Emily Frances Palmer to brother, William Palmer, 6 Feb. [1852], Selborne Papers, MS Eng. misc. c. 691, fo. 17.

42. Meriel Lyttelton's diary, 3–17 Aug. 1857, Talbot Papers, U 1612, F 105.

43. Sarah Acland to son, William A. D. Acland, 9 Dec. [1866], Bodl. MS Acland d. 42, fos. 386–8.

44. Laura Harcourt to Sir William Harcourt, 24 Oct. [1883], MS Harcourt dep. 610, fo. 210.

45. George H. Dashwood, MP to wife, Elizabeth, 25 Feb. 1846, MS D. D. Dashwood (Bucks), G 3/9/18.

46. Sophy Horsley to sister, Mary Brunel, 16 June 1858, Horsley Papers, MS Eng c. 2200, fo. 25.

47. Augusta Touzel to sister, Eliza Lady Phillipps, 22 Mar. 1856, MS Phillipps–Robinson e. 425, fos. 100–1.

48. 4th Earl of Carnarvon's diary, 31 May 1876, Carnarvon Papers, BL Add. MS 60908, fo. 123.

49. E. Longford, *A Pilgrimage of Passion: The Life of Wilfrid Scawen Blunt* (1979), 19.

50. Lady Anne Blunt's diary, 22–4 Apr. 1872, Wentworth Bequest, BL Add. MS 53840.

51. Ibid.

52. Gwendolen Cecil to sister-in-law, Violet Cecil, [17 Nov. 1899,] Cecil–Maxse MSS, U 1599, C 101/11.

53. Evan Thompson to Caroline Lady Trevelyan, 12 Nov. 1890, Trevelyan Papers, GOT 125.

54. Basil Montagu, *The Funerals of the Quakers* (1840), 23–4, 47–50, 55–6.

55. Unidentified press cutting, possibly from the *Northern Echo, c.*10 Aug. 1892, MS Gainford 48, fo. 83.

56. Charles Darwin to friend, Sir Joseph D. Hooker, 25 Feb. 1875, Darwin Papers, DAR 95, fos. 380–1.

57. *Emma Darwin: A Century of Family Letters*, ed. H. E. Litchfield, 2 vols. (priv. pr., Cambridge, 1904), ii. 177–8.

58. *Court Etiquette, by a Man of the World* (Charles Mitchell) (1849), 82.

59. 3rd Lord Holland to son, Henry E. Fox, 5 May 1840, Holland House Papers, BL Add. MS 51757, fo. 306.

60. Marie-Thérèse Harcourt to mother, Lady Lewis, 10 Mar. 1862, MS Harcourt dep. 618, fo. 306.

61. Roundell Palmer to wife, Laura, [29 Jan. 1852,] Selborne Papers, MS 1880, fo. 7.

62. Sophy Horsley to Mary Brunel, 16 June 1858; Elizabeth Horsley to Mary Brunel, 18 June 1858, Horsley Papers, MS Eng. c. 2200, fos. 24–5, 33.

63. *Cassell's Household Guide*, iii (1869–71), 344.

64. Emily Harcourt to brother, Sir William Harcourt, [late 1883,] MS Harcourt dep. 603, fo. 163; see also Anna Pitman to uncle, A. C. Tait, 19 Jan. 1879, Tait Papers, vol. 99, fos. 32–5, for funeral of J. C. Tait.

65. Lady Colin Campbell, *Etiquette of Good Society* (1893), 213.

66. Jeremy Taylor, *Holy Dying*, cited in Chadwick, *Interment in Towns*, 157–8.

67. Frederick Goulburn to Edward Goulburn, 21 [Jan. 1856], Goulburn Papers, Acc. 426, 16/6 d.

68. Revd Edwin Palmer to brother, Roundell Palmer, 25 May 1870, Selborne Papers, MS 1879, fos. 54–5.

69. H. M. Stanley to Elsie Pease, 31 Jan. 1898, Gainford MS 518.

70. Mary to Beatrice Chamberlain, 23 Nov. 1897, Chamberlain Papers, BC 1/3/3 [fo. 2].

71. Evan Thompson to Caroline Lady Trevelyan, 12 Nov. 1890, Trevelyan Papers, GOT 125.

72. Richard Davey, *A History of Mourning* (1889), 96, 111.

73. Mrs Humphry Ward to Dorothy Ward, 13 Apr. 1888, Ward Papers, Pusey House.

74. Victoria Dawnay to Mary Countess Minto, 4 Aug. 1910, Minto MS 12431, fo. 110.

75. Gittings, *Death, Burial and the Individual in Early Modern England*, 97–8.

76. J. S. Curl, *The Victorian Celebration of Death* (1972), 13.

77. Ruth Richardson, *Death, Dissection and the Destitute* (1987), 8–9, 22–3.

78. *Court Etiquette, by a Man of the World*, 81.

79. John Callcott Horsley's diary, 8 Dec. 1852, Horsley Papers, MS Eng. e. 2186, fos. 62–5.

80. Sophy Horsley to sister, Mary Brunel, 16 June 1858, ibid., c. 2200, fos. 24–5.

81. Mattie A. Vivian to Rose Horsley, 7 Dec. 1875, ibid., c. 2235, fos. 126–8.

82. Lady Anne Blunt's diary, 16 Aug. 1872, Wentworth Bequest, BL Add. MS 53841.

83. 'Copy of William Jocelyn Palmer's Will', 1 Jan. 1852, MS Selborne 223 (5).

84. Funeral expenses, 6 Apr. 1866, Keble Correspondence 168.

85. A. C. Tait's journal, Dec. 1878, Tait Papers, vol. 63, fos. 105–6.

86. R. Houlbrooke (ed.), *Death, Ritual and Bereavement* (1989), 29–32.

87. Copy of William Horsley's will, 5 Feb. 1843, Horsley Papers, MS Eng. d. 2059/1; see also e.g. Revd William Wood's will, 22 Feb. 1832, MS Selborne 230 (11); copy of William Jocelyn Palmer's will, 1 Jan. 1852, MS Selborne 223 (5).

88. Evelyn Lady Stanhope to husband, Arthur, 6th Earl Stanhope, 28 Dec. 1893, 1 Feb. 1894, Stanhope MS U 1590, C 513/10.

89. Lady Stanhope to son, Jem, 7th Earl Stanhope, 27 June 1905, Stanhope MS U 1590, C 642.

90. Documents concerning the disposition of Lord Carnarvon's property, 1884–9, Carnarvon Papers, BL Add. MS 61054.

91. Ibid.

92. 4th Earl of Carnarvon's diary, 28–9 May 1876, Carnarvon Papers, BL Add. MS 60908, fos. 121–2.

93. Kate Courtney's diary, 1 Jan. 1892, Courtney Collection, vol. xxvi, fos. 85–7; will of Richard Potter, 1 Jan. 1892.

94. Mary Somerville to James Graham, [12] Nov. 1865, Somerville Papers, dep. c. 357, folder MSFP-11.

95. James Graham to Mary Somerville, 18 Dec. 1865, ibid.

96. Ibid., 4 Dec. 1865.

97. Henry E. Fox to wife, Mary Augusta Fox, 5 May 1837, Holland House Papers, BL Add. MS 52026, fos. 8–9, 12; see also Earl of Ilchester, *Chronicles of Holland House 1820–1900* (1937), 222, 286.

98. Henry Fox to Augusta Fox, 8–9 May 1837, Holland House Papers, BL Add. MS 52026, fos. 20–2, 27–30.

99. Ibid., 14, 23 May 1837, fos. 44–6, 67–9.

100. Henry, 4th Lord Holland to mother, Dowager Lady Holland, 10 May [1842], ibid., MS 51776, fos. 241–4.

101. *Dictionary of National Biography*, 116.

11. *Widows: Gendered Experiences of Widowhood*

1. Michael Anderson, 'The Social Implications of Demographic Change', in F. M. L. Thompson (ed.), *The Cambridge Social History of Britain 1750–1950* (Cambridge, 1990), ii. 30–1.

2. Colin Murray Parkes, *Bereavement: Studies of Grief in Adult Life* (Harmondsworth, 1978); John Bowlby, *Attachment and Loss*, iii: *Loss* (Harmondsworth, 1985). For details of the various studies, see Parkes, *Bereavement*, 227–49; Bowlby, *Attachment and Loss*, 106–11. Their results cannot be quantitatively precise, since 'no very systematic comparative data are available' (Parkes, *Bereavement*, 131). See also Beverley Raphael, *The Anatomy of Bereavement* (1984), 177–228.

3. Parkes, *Bereavement*, chs. 3–7; Bowlby, *Attachment and Loss*, iii. 85–100.

4. Harriet, Baroness de Clifford to Nina, Countess Minto, Aug. 1877, Minto MS 12257, fo. 149.

5. Lady Stepney to Mary Drew, 1 Apr. 1910, Mary Gladstone Drew Papers, BL Add. MS 46250, fos. 92–3.

6. Kenneth Young, *Arthur James Balfour* (1963), 5.

7. Agnes Greig to Mary and Martha Somerville, 1 Nov., 12, 29 Dec. 1865, Somerville Papers, dep. c. 364, folder MS 1F-25.

8. Alice Latham to Lily Harcourt, 25 Oct. 1884, MS Harcourt dep. 633, fos. 22–3.

9. Journal of Mary, Countess Minto, June 1914, Minto MS 12463.

10. Edith Lyttelton to A. J. Balfour, 23 Aug. 1913, Balfour Papers (Whittingehame), MS 166.

11. Lavinia Talbot to Meriel Talbot, 21 July 1913, Talbot Papers, U 1612.

12. Victoria Dawnay to sister, Mary, Countess Minto, 11 Aug. 1910, Minto MS, 12431, fos. 116, 138.

13. Emily Yates to Sir Ernest Satow, 20 Oct. 1919, Satow Papers, PRO 30/33/13/8, items 41–2.

14. Catherine Gladstone to Mary Drew, 1 Aug. 1891, Mary Gladstone Drew Papers, BL Add. MS 46224, fo. 292.

15. Ibid., 28 Aug. 1891, fos. 311–12.

16. Gertrude Gladstone to W. E. Gladstone, 12 Nov. 1891, Glynne–Gladstone Papers, Box 22/8.

17. Ibid.

18. Ibid., 27 Dec. 1891.

19. Gertrude Gladstone to Catherine Gladstone, 24 Nov. 1892, ibid., Box 30/4.

20. Alice Lubbock, Countess Avebury, to Kate Courtney, 1 Aug. 1913, Courtney Collection, vol. x, fos. 229–30.

21. Lady Wantage to Evelyn, Lady Stanhope, 22 Apr, 1905, Stanhope MSS, U 1590, C 573/3.

22. *The Times*, 19 May 1845. Leonore Davidoff notes that the widow's right to one-third of her husband's property was slowly superseded in the period after 1750 by individual arrangements in marriage settlements; 'The Family in Britain', in *The Cambridge Social History of Britain 1750–1950*, ii. 74.

23. 3rd Lady Holland to son, Henry, 4th Lord Holland, 11 Oct. 1842, Holland House Papers, BL Add. MS 51776, fos. 309–10.

24. Henrietta E. M. Phillipps to J. O. Halliwell, 27 June 1842, MS Phillipps–Robinson d. 247, fos. 73–4.

25. Agnes Greig to Mary Somerville, 12 Dec. 1865, Somerville Papers, dep. c. 364, folder MS 1F-25; Annabella King to [?], 16 Nov. 1865, Wentworth Bequest, BL Add. MS 54094.

26. Ada Burlingham to Lord Aldenham, 17 Dec. 1901; Fanny Remmett to Lord Aldenham, 3 Jan. 1902, Gibbs Family Letters, MS 11021/29, fos. 376–8.

27. Cecilia, Lady Rice to brother, Sir William Harcourt, Dec. 1891, MS Harcourt dep. 609, fos. 94–5.

28. May Harcourt to Elizabeth, Lady Harcourt, 23 Aug. 1909, ibid., dep. 648, fos. 28–9.

29. Marion Montagu to Margaret MacDonald, 5 Feb. 1911, MacDonald Papers, PRO 30/69/905.

30. Lady Wantage to Evelyn Lady Stanhope, 22 Apr. 1905, Stanhope MSS, U 1590, C 573/3.

31. Mathilda M. Harcourt to Sir William Harcourt, 13 Apr. 1871, n.d. [1872], MS Harcourt dep. 602, fos. 84, 98–9.

32. Elizabeth Horsley to daughter, Mary Brunel, 29 July 1858, Horsley Papers, MS Eng. c. 2200, fo. 113.

33. Bowlby, *Attachment and Loss*, iii. 86, 90–2.

34. Ibid.; Parkes, *Bereavement*, 100–3. See also Raphael, *The Anatomy of Bereavement*, 185–6.

35. Lucy Masterman (ed.), *Mary Gladstone: Her Diaries and Letters* (1930), 459–61.

36. Mary Drew to Lord Rosebery, 20 Apr. 1910, Rosebery Papers, MS 10015, fo. 205.

37. Mary Drew to Lady Stepney, 20 May 1910, Mary Gladstone Drew Papers, BL Add. MS 46250, fo. 98.

38. Mary Drew to Lavinia Talbot, 15 June 1910, in Masterman, *Mary Gladstone Diaries*, 462–3.

39. Parkes, *Bereavement*, 100–8, esp. 106.

40. Kate Courtney's diary, Easter Sunday 1896, Courtney Collection, vol. xxviii, fos. 120–1.

41. Journal of Mary Countess Minto, June 1914, Minto MS 12463.

42. Mary Somerville to Agnes Greig, 16 July 1860, Somerville Papers, dep. c. 363, folder MS 1F-15.

43. Duchess of St Albans to Evelyn, Lady Stanhope, 'Easter Monday' 1905, Stanhope MSS, U 1590, C 573/3.

44. Journal of Mary Countess Minto, June 1914, Minto MS 12463, fo. 40.

45. J. D. Coleridge to John Keble, 1 Feb. 1843, Keble Correspondence 136.

46. Sarah Cotton to son, William Cotton, 21 Dec. 1866, Bodl. MS Acland d. 184, fos. 165–6.

47. Winifred Byng to father, Lord Carnarvon, 29 Dec. 1887, Carnarvon Papers, BL Add. MS 61060.

48. Agnes Greig to sister-in-law, Martha Somerville, 1 Nov. 1865, Somerville Papers, dep. c. 364, folder MS IF-25.

49. Agnes Greig to Capt. Henry Fairfax, 2 Jan. 1866, ibid., dep. b. 205, folder MS FP-64.

50. Agnes Greig to Mary Somerville, 12 Dec. 1865, ibid., dep. c. 364, folder MS IF-25.

51. Harriet Agnes, Baroness de Clifford, to Nina, Countess Minto, Aug. 1877, Minto MS 12257, fo. 149.

52. Lady Musgrave to Miss Wood, n.d., Rous Papers, Hall A/14/2.

53. Lady Stepney to Mary Drew, 1 Apr. 1910, Mary Gladstone Drew Papers, BL Add. MS 46250, fos. 92–3.

54. Emily Harcourt to brother, Sir William Harcourt, [20 Oct. 1883,] MS Harcourt, dep. 603, fos. 154–5.

55. Elizabeth Rathbone to daughter-in-law, Emily Rathbone, n.d. [c.1861], Rathbone MS, X.1.147.

56. Constance Shaw-Stewart to Lord Aldenham, 21 June 1900, Gibbs Family Letters, MS 11021/29, fos. 203–4.

57. Alice Lubbock, Countess Avebury, to Kate Courtney, 1 Aug. 1913, Courtney Collection, vol. x, fos. 229–30.

58. Emily Yates to Sir Ernest Satow, 20 Oct. 1919, Satow Papers, PRO 30/33/13/8, items 41–2.

59. *Earl Cowper K.G.: A Memoir*, by his wife (Katrine Cecilia) (priv. pr., 1913), 72.

60. Woronzow Greig to mother, Mary Somerville, 2 July 1860, Somerville Papers, dep. c. 364, folder MS 1F-20.

61. Mary Somerville to Agnes Greig, 16 July 1860, ibid., dep. c. 363, folder MS 1F-15.

62. Emily, 4th Lady Lansdowne to Augusta, 4th Lady Holland, 10 July 1866, Holland House Papers, BL Add. MS 52156, fos. 77–8.

63. Harriet Agnes, Baroness de Clifford, to Nina, Countess Minto, Aug. 1877, Minto MS 12257, fo. 149.

64. Victoria Dawnay to Mary, Countess Minto, 18 Aug. 1910, ibid., MS 12431, fo. 118.

65. *Emma Lady Ribblesdale: Letters and Diaries*, ed. Beatrix Lister (priv. pr., 1930) 35 (9 Oct. 1878).

66. Lavinia Talbot to Mary Drew, 7 Mar. 1914, Mary Gladstone Drew Papers, BL Add. MS 46236, fo. 352.

67. Lady Stepney to Mary Drew, [15 July] 1910, Mary Gladstone Drew Papers, BL Add. MS 46250, fos. 101–2.

68. Elizabeth S. Haldane, *From One Century to Another* (1937), 69–70.

69. Lucy Cohen, *Lady de Rothschild and Daughters 1821–1931* (1935), 285.

70. See e.g. Gertrude Gladstone to Herbert Gladstone, 17 Nov. 1891, Glynne–Gladstone Papers, Box 47/10; Gertrude to Henry Gladstone, 29 Sept., 17 Oct. 1891, ibid., 38/4.

71. Victoria Dawnay to Mary, Countess Minto, 11, 18 Aug., [?]Sept. 1910, Minto MS 12431, fos. 116, 118, 144.

72. Victoria Dawnay to Mary Countess Minto, 23 Aug., [?]Sept. 1910, ibid., fos. 132, 144.

73. See Earl of Ilchester, *Chronicles of Holland House 1820–1900* (1937), 348–9.

74. Ethel Peel (ed.), *Recollections of Lady Georgiana Peel* (1920), 70–1. (Lady Holland's illegitimate son, Charles, was excluded entirely from this reference.)

75. Caroline Fox to nephew, Henry, 4th Lord Holland, 23 Oct. 1840, Holland House Papers, BL Add. MS 52051, fos. 202–3.

76. Ibid., 27 Oct. 1840, fos. 208–9.

77. 3rd Lady Holland to son, Henry, Lord Holland, [4 Dec. 1840,] Holland House Papers, BL Add. MS 51775, fos. 206–7.

78. Caroline Fox to Lord Holland, 6 Dec. [1840], ibid., BL Add. MS 52051, fos. 222–3.

79. Lord Holland to mother, Lady Holland, [c.2 Nov. 1840,] ibid., BL Add. MS 51775, fo. 199.

80. See e.g. Ilchester, *Chronicles of Holland House*, 330.

81. Charles Greville, *Journals*, i. 367, cited in Ilchester, *Chronicles of Holland House*, 285.

82. Charles R. Fox to mother, Lady Holland, 24 May 1841, Holland House Papers, BL Add. MS 51790, fos. 92–5.

83. Lord Holland to Lady Holland, [c.23 Mar. 1842,] ibid., BL Add. MS 51776, fo. 197.

84. Ibid., 24 Mar., 10 May [1842], ibid., fo. 199, 241.

85. Lady Holland to Henry Lord Holland, [25 Mar. 1841,] ibid., BL Add. MS 51775, fos. 210–11.

86. Ibid., [21 May 1841], fos. 228–9.

87. Caroline Fox to Lord Holland, [11 Dec. 1840,] ibid., BL Add. MS 52051, fos. 230–1.

88. Lady Holland to son, Lord Holland, 12 May [1843], 30 May [1843], 18 July [1843], ibid., BL Add. MS 51777, fos. 114, 127, 186.

89. Lord Holland to aunt, Caroline Fox, 13 Apr. 1843, ibid., BL Add. MS 52055, fos. 49–50.

90. Ibid., 20, 22 Apr. 1843, fos. 55, 62–3.

91. Lord Holland to wife, Augusta, 27, 29, 30 Nov. 1845, ibid., BL Add. MS 52034, fos. 178, 181–2, 185.

92. Greville, *Journals*, ii. 306, quoted in Ilchester, *Chronicles*, 355.

93. Lord Holland to wife, Augusta, 25, 26, 29 Nov., 2 Dec. 1845, Holland House Papers, BL Add. MS 52034, fos. 169, 171–2, 183, 188–9.

12. *Widowers: Gendered Experiences of Widowhood*

1. Colin Murray Parkes, *Bereavement: Studies of Grief in Adult Life* (Harmondsworth, 1978), 147–9, 244.

2. John Bowlby, *Attachment and Loss*, iii: *Loss* (Harmondsworth, 1985), 103–5.

3. Roundell Palmer to father, Revd W. J. Palmer, 27 June 1839, Selborne Papers, MS 1878, fo. 53.

4. Sarah Disraeli to sister-in-law, Mary Anne Disraeli, 23 June [1857], Hughenden Papers, Box 186, D/III/A/429.

5. Eveline Lady Portsmouth to brother, 4th Earl of Carnarvon, 20 Feb. 1875, Carnarvon Papers, BL Add. MS 61048.

6. Katharine Bruce Glasier to Margaret MacDonald, n.d. [Apr.–May] 1911, MacDonald Papers, PRO 30/69/902.

7. Caroline Fox to brother, 3rd Lord Holland, 13 Nov [1838], Holland House Papers, BL Add. MS 51743, fo. 83.

8. Letters from Mary Ann Rogers to son, Richard Norris Gandy, 29 Nov. 1865, uncat. papers of Thorold Rogers family, Box 10, R7, fo. 19.

9. Sir Warwick Morshead to brother-in-law, Sir William Harcourt, n.d. [1883], MS Harcourt dep. 609, fos. 41–2.

10. A. W. Roffen to A. C. Tait, 14 Dec. 1878, Tait Papers, vol. 98, fos. 192–4.

11. L. J. L. Dundas, Marquess of Zetland, *Life of Evelyn Baring, First Earl of Cromer* (1932), 286–7.

12. Margaret Pelling, 'Old Age, Poverty and Disability in Early Modern Norwich', in M. Pelling and R. M. Smith (eds.), *Life, Death and the Elderly* (1991), 87–90.

13. S. J. Wright, 'Elderly and Bereaved in Eighteenth Century Ludlow', in Pelling and Smith (eds.), *Life, Death and the Elderly*, 102–33, esp. 106–9. See also B. Todd, 'The Remarrying Widow: A Stereotype Reconsidered', in M. Prior (ed.), *Women in English Society 1500–1800* (1985).

14. William Farr, *Vital Statistics* (Metuchen, NJ, 1975; repr. of 1885 edn.), 79–80.

15. Michael Anderson, 'The Social Implications of Demographic Change', in F. M. L. Thompson (ed.), *The Cambridge Social History of Britain 1750–1950* (1990), ii. 31.

16. 3rd Lady Holland to son, Henry E. Fox, 24 Mar. [1835], Holland House Papers, BL Add. MS 51772, fos. 6–7.

17. Lady Holland to Caroline Fox, [7 Dec. 1841,] ibid., MS 51747, fos. 228–9.

18. Evelyn Lady Stanhope to Lord Derby, 11 Nov. 1887, Stanhope MS U 1590, C 717/5.

19. Lady Holland to son, Lord Holland, 15 June [1841], Holland House Papers, BL Add. MS 51775, fos. 266–7.

20. Mary Somerville to Agnes Greig, 5 Jan. 1853, Somerville Papers, dep. c. 363, folder MS IF-14.

21. Earl of Ilchester, *Chronicles of Holland House* (1937), 426.

22. Betty Askwith, *The Lytteltons* (1975), 148–51, 169.

23. An account by her husband of Deborah Reynolds's death, 11 July 1803, Rathbone MS IV.1.110A.

24. John C. Horsley's diary, [c.Nov. 1852,] Horsley Papers, MS Eng. e. 2186, fos. 37–8.

25. Katharine Bruce Glasier to J. R. MacDonald, 9 Dec. 1912, MacDonald Papers, PRO 30/69/734, fos. 21–4.

26. Count de Franqueville to Lord Selborne, 29 Oct. 1916, MS Selborne 113, fos. 114–15.

27. Dr Seth Thompson to brother-in-law, John C. Horsley, [1849,] Horsley Papers, MS Eng. c. 2205, fo. 32.

28. Ibid., n.d., fo. 38.

29. Ibid., fo. 34.

30. Ibid., fo. 52.

31. Ibid., fos. 32–4, 43.

32. Elizabeth Horsley to anon., n.d. [1849], Horsley Papers, MS Eng. c. 2204, fo. 36.

33. Dr Seth Thompson to John C. Horsley, n.d. [1849], ibid., MS Eng. c. 2205, fo. 38.

34. Sophy Horsley to Rose Haden, n.d. [July 1849], ibid., MS Eng. c. 2212, fos. 102–3.

35. Mathilda M. Harcourt to William Harcourt, [Mar. 1863,] MS Harcourt dep. 602, fos. 78–9.

36. William Harcourt to Mathilda Harcourt, [1863,] ibid., dep. 601, fos. 195–6.

37. William Harcourt to sister, Emily Harcourt, [1863,] ibid., dep. 606, fos. 138–9.

38. William Harcourt to Mathilda Harcourt, [1863,] ibid., dep. 601, fo. 199.

39. Theresa Lady Lewis to Mathilda Harcourt, 23, 27 Feb. [1863], ibid., dep. 632, fos. 59–60, 63–4.

40. Ibid.

41. Ibid., fos. 64–5.

42. Thomas Villiers Lister to William Harcourt, 19 Feb. 1863, ibid., dep. 633, fos. 94–5.

43. William Harcourt to Mathilda Harcourt, [1863], ibid., dep. 601, fos. 199, 203.

44. Edward W. Harcourt to William Harcourt, 8 Feb. 1863, ibid., dep. 610, fos. 8–9.

45. Egerton Harcourt to William Harcourt, 5 Feb. 1863, ibid., fos. 191–2.

46. Lady Lewis to Mathilda Harcourt, 27 Feb. [1863], ibid., dep. 632, fo. 65.

47. Lady Lewis to William Harcourt, 14 Mar. 1863, ibid., dep. 631, fos. 45–7.

48. Lady Lewis to Mathilda Harcourt, 31 Mar. 1863, ibid., dep. 632, fo. 74.

49. A. G. Gardiner, *The Life of Sir William Vernon Harcourt* (1923), 118, 242, 280.

50. Ibid., 386, 241–2, 268.

51. Diary of 4th Earl of Carnarvon, 25 Feb. 1875, Carnarvon Papers, BL Add. MS 60908, fo. 24.

52. Eveline Lady Portsmouth to brother, Lord Carnarvon, 20 Feb. 1875, ibid., BL Add. MS 61048.

53. Lord Carnarvon's diary, 23 Mar. 1875, ibid., BL Add. MS 60908, fo. 35.

54. Ibid., 13 May 1875, fo. 57.

55. Ibid., 17 July 1875, fo. 85.

56. Lady Portsmouth to Lord Carnarvon, 6 Nov. 1875, Carnarvon Papers, BL Add. MS 61049.

57. Mary Drew to A. J. Balfour, n.d. [before 6 May 1886], Balfour Papers, BL Add. MS 49794, fos. 179–80.

58. Alfred Lyttelton to Mary Gladstone Drew, 14 May 1886, in Edith Lyttelton, *Alfred Lyttelton: An Account of his Life* (1917), 149–50.

59. Alfred Lyttelton to Lavinia Talbot, 8 Nov. 1886, ibid., 156.

60. Alfred Lyttelton to Edward Talbot, 30 July 1886, ibid., 151–2.

61. Edward Talbot to Alfred Lyttelton, n.d., ibid., 152–3.

62. Alfred Lyttelton to anon., ibid., 155.

63. Alfred Lyttelton to Lavinia Talbot, 8 Nov. 1886, ibid., 156.

64. Alfred Lyttelton to anon., 14 Nov. 1885, ibid., 160.

65. Alfred Lyttelton to Lavinia Talbot, [*c*.21 May 1888,] ibid., 161.

66. Mary Drew to Alfred Lyttelton, 21 May 1888, Mary Gladstone Drew Papers, BL Add. MS 46234, fos. 114–15.

67. Edith Lyttelton, Chandos Papers, 'Interwoven', 6/1/J.

13. *Christian Consolations and Heavenly Reunions*

1. Revd William Benham to A. C. Tait, Archbishop of Canterbury, 11 Mar. 1878, Tait Papers, vol. 98, fos. 54–7.

2. Ibid., 7 May 1878, fos. 78–9.

3. Michael Wheeler, *Death and the Future Life in Victorian Literature and Theology* (1990), 69–118, 175–218; Geoffrey Rowell, *Hell and the Victorians* (Oxford, 1974).

4. Colleen McDannell and Bernhard Lang, *Heaven: A History* (New Haven, 1988), 277, 287; see ch. 8: 'Love in Heaven'; ch. 9: 'Eternal Motion: Progress in the Other World'.

5. Ibid.

6. 'The Soul and Future Life', *Nineteenth Century*, 2 (Sept. 1877), 329–34.

7. Ibid., 2 (Oct. 1877), 517–21.

8. Ibid., 511–17.

9. Edwin Arnold, 'Death and Afterwards', *Fortnightly Review*, NS 38 (Aug. 1885), 218–27.

10. Revd Richard Baxter, *Saints' Everlasting Rest and Other Selected Works* (1817; 1st edn. 1650).

11. Wheeler, *Death and the Future Life*, 120.

12. Ibid., p. xii.

13. Lucy Sharpe to aunt, Lucy Smith, 22 Feb. 1862, Sharpe Papers 183/1.

14. Lord Lovelace's journal, 17 Aug. 1852, Wentworth Bequest, BL Add. MS 54089, fo. 3.

15. Bishop of Madras to A. C. Tait, 15 Feb. 1879, Tait Papers, vol. 99, fos. 48–9.

16. *Death and the Hereafter: Sermons Preached by Harry Drew, Rector of Hawarden, 1904–1910* (Oxford, 1911), 12–30, 43–50.

17. Mary Flounders to Henrietta E. M. Phillipps, 18 July 1838, MS Phillipps–Robinson d. 247, fos. 62–3.

18. Mary Palmer to nephew, George Horsley Palmer, 4 May 1843, Selborne Papers, MS 1903, fos. 73–4.

19. *In Memoriam: Jane May Gladstone and her Children* (priv. pr., 1864), 44.

20. Mary Waldegrave to brother, Lord Selborne, 13 Apr. 1885, Selborne Papers, MS 1880, fos. 174–5.

21. Priscilla Maurice, *Prayers for the Sick and Dying* (1853), 191–2.

22. Lord Carnarvon's diary, May 1876, Carnarvon Papers, BL Add. MS 60908, fo. 119.

23. Mrs Benson to Laura Ridding, 31 Aug. 1904, Selborne Papers, MS 9M 68/3, Hampshire Record Office, Winchester.

24. Hugh Cecil to William Lord Selborne, [Oct.–Nov. 1915,] MS Selborne 113, fos. 148–9.

25. Wheeler, *Death and the Future Life*, 126.

26. H. E. Litchfield (ed.), *Emma Darwin: A Century of Family Letters*, 2 vols. (1904), i. 347–8.

27. William Sidgwick to fiancée, Mary Crofts, 3 Apr. 1833, Benson Papers, dep. Benson 3/1.

28. Lady Anne Harcourt to son, Henry Harcourt, 25 Dec. 1831, *The Harcourt Papers*, ed. E. W. Harcourt, 14 vols. (priv. pr., Oxford, 1880–1905), xii. 324–5.

29. Mary Palmer to nephew, George Horsley Palmer, 4 May 1843, Selborne Papers, MS 1903, fos. 73–4.

30. Sarah Acland to son, W. A. D. Acland, 8 May [1855–7?], Bodl. MS Acland d. 53, fos. 145–6.

31. Rowell, *Hell and the Victorians*, 9–10; Robert Bickersteth *et al.*, *The Recognition of Friends in Heaven* (1866).

32. Archbishop Harcourt of York to nephew, Lord Vernon, 28 Nov. 1832, *The Harcourt Papers*, xii. 223–5.

33. Mary Morice to John Keble, 14 Aug. 1860, Keble Correspondence 108.

34. Lady Lovelace to mother, Lady Byron, n.d. [1852], MS dep. Lovelace Byron 44, fos. 174–6.

35. William Branks, *Heaven our Home* (Edinburgh, 1861), pp. iii–iv, vii.

36. McDannell and Lang, *Heaven: A History*, 264–8.

37. Boyd Hilton, *The Age of Atonement: The Influence of Evangelicalism on Social and Economic Thought 1795–1865* (Oxford, 1988), 335–6.

38. Revd John Stoughton of Kensington, 'Heaven', *In Heaven: Glimpses of the Life and Happiness of the Glorified*, by various authors (1865), 21–34.

39. Emma Lee to Maria Sharpe, 13 June 1870, Sharpe Papers 139/6.

40. Elizabeth King to Dr J. H. Gladstone, 20 Dec. 1874, MacDonald Papers, PRO 30/69/861.

41. A. C. Tait's journal, 15 Dec. 1878, 18 Jan. 1879, Tait Papers, vol. 63, fo. 108; vol. 64, fo. 12.

42. Bishop of Gloucester to A. C. Tait, Ash Wednesday 1879, Tait Papers, vol. 99, fos. 52–3.

43. James Tait to A. C. Tait, 29 Dec. 1878, Tait Papers, vol. 98, fos. 222–3.

44. Lord Selborne to Archdeacon Palmer, 11 Apr. 1885, in Earl of Selborne, *Memorials* (1896–8), ii. 166.

45. Lady Cairns to Lord Selborne, [Apr. 1885,] Selborne Papers, MS 1880, fos. 148–9.

46. Lucy Stanhope to Evelyn Lady Stanhope, [25 June 1886,] Stanhope MSS, U 1590, C 590/19.

47. Louisa Antrim to sister, Lady Minto, 1 Dec. 1890, Minto MS 12435, fo. 129.

48. *Death and the Hereafter: Sermons Preached by Harry Drew*, 48–50.

49. See e.g. B. Raphael, *The Anatomy of Bereavement* (1984), 280, 310; Jane Littlewood, *Aspects of Grief: Bereavement in Adult Life* (1992), 140–4.

50. Raphael, *Anatomy of Bereavement*, 31–2. See also Edgar N. Jackson, 'Grief and Religion', in H. Feifel (ed.), *The Meaning of Death* (1959), 219, 221.

51. Colin Murray Parkes, *Bereavement: Studies of Grief in Adult Life* (Harmondsworth, 1978), 177–8.

52. Littlewood, *Aspects of Grief*, 37–8.

53. See e.g. condolence letters to Jane and Henry Goulburn, from John Thornton (9 June 1843); Gurney Hoare (9 June); H. P. Bayley (13 June); Charles Wordsworth (9 June); Richard Cavendish (11 June), Goulburn Papers, Acc. 319, Box 67.

54. Jane Goulburn's diary, 21 June 1843, ibid.

55. Ibid., 27–30 June, 1–2 July 1843.

56. Ibid., 15 Aug., 5 Sept. 1843.

57. Eleanor Fazakerley to sister, Jane Goulburn, n.d. [July–Aug. 1843], 15 Oct. 1843, Goulburn Papers, Acc. 319, Box 67.

58. Jane Goulburn's diary, 9, 16 July, 18 Aug. 1843; Goulburn Papers, Acc. 319, Box 64.

59. Ibid., 8 Oct. 1843.

60. Ibid., 12, 26 Nov. 1843.

61. Ibid., 31 Dec. 1843, 1 Jan. 1844.

62. Col. Edward Goulburn to Jane Goulburn, 20 Feb. 1858, Goulburn Papers, Acc. 319, Box 78.

63. Maurice, *Prayers for the Sick and Dying*, 185; *Sacred Poems for Mourners* (1846).

64. Archdeacon Samuel Wilberforce to Jane Goulburn, 17 Oct. 1843, Goulburn Papers, Acc. 319, Box 67.

65. Louisa Cane to friend, Jane Goulburn, 16 June 1843, Goulburn Papers, Acc. 319, Box 30, bundle II/7.

66. Caroline Cane to Jane Goulburn, 30 [June 1843], ibid.

67. Emma Haden's 'Book of Meditations on Bereavement, 1858–61', Horsley Papers, MS Eng. e. 2300.

68. Owen Chadwick, *The Victorian Church*, 2 vols., 3rd edn. (1992), i. 68.

69. David Newsome, *The Parting of Friends* (1966), 74–5.

70. George Cornish to John Keble, n.d. [1837–40], Keble Correspondence 148.

71. John Keble, *The Christian Year: Thoughts in Verse for the Sundays and Holydays throughout the Year* (Oxford, 1827), 192–5. Stanzas were included with many condolence letters, e.g. Emily Palmer to brother, William Palmer, 14 Apr. [1852], Selborne Papers, MS Eng. misc. e. 691., fo. 22.

72. Revd W. V. Harcourt to sister, Georgiana Malcolm, [1853,] in *The Harcourt Papers*, xiv. 206.

73. See A. O. J. Cockshut, *The Unbelievers: English Agnostic Thought 1840–1890* (1964), 168–71.

74. Chadwick, *The Victorian Church*, i. 566–7. For an excellent detailed analysis of *In Memoriam*, see Wheeler, *Death and the Future Life*, ch. 5, pp. 221–64.

75. Mary Gladstone Drew's will, Sept. 1886, and amendments Jan. 1890, Mary Gladstone Drew Papers, BL Add. MS 46268, fos. 1–61.

76. Countess Avebury to Kate Courtney, 7 Feb. 1914, Courtney Collection, vol. XI, fos. 7–9.

14. The Consolations of Memory

1. Beverley Raphael, *The Anatomy of Bereavement* (1984), 186–9.

2. William Somerville to sister, Janet Elliot, Dec. 1841, Somerville Papers, dep. c. 357, folder MSFP-8.

3. Rebecca Kenrick to cousin, Lucy Sharpe, Mar. [1845], Sharpe Papers 122/13.

4. Lucy Sharpe to husband, William Sharpe, 19 May 1845, Sharpe Papers 98, fos. 160–1.

5. Basil Montagu, *The Funerals of the Quakers* (1840), 56–7, 59, 69.

6. A. C. Tait's journal, 11, 13 Apr. 1879, Tait Papers, vol. 64, fos. 42, 44–6.

7. Charles Darwin to J. D. Hooker, 11 Apr. 1861, Darwin Papers, DAR 115 (ii), fo. 96. In fact this letter was premature, for Henslow did not die until May.

8. Henry, 4th Lord Holland to mother, 3rd Lady Holland, 12 July 1843, Holland House Papers, BL Add. MS 51777, fo. 181.

9. Annabella King to grandmother, Lady Byron, 8 Dec. [1852], Wentworth Bequest, BL Add. MS 54090, fo. 47.

10. *Emma Darwin: A Century of Family Letters*, ed. H. E. Litchfield, 2 vols. (Cambridge, 1904), ii. 381.

11. John Callcott Horsley's diary, 8 Dec. 1852, Horsley Papers, MS Eng. e. 2186, fo. 65.

12. Katharine Anne Elliot to Nina, Countess Minto, 16 Aug. 1865, Minto MS 12259, fo. 1.

13. *Emma, Lady Ribblesdale: Letters and Diaries*, ed. Beatrix Lister (priv. pr., 1930), 130–1.

14. Lavinia Talbot to sister, Meriel Talbot, 6 Feb. 1910, Talbot Papers, U 1612.

15. Alec Macmillan to A. C. Tait, 25 Aug. 1880, Tait Papers, vol. 100, fos. 21–2.

16. A. G. Butler to A. C. Tait, 4 Oct. [1880?], ibid., vol. 99, fos. 300–2.

17. Agnes Moore to A. C. Tait, [1880,] ibid., fo. 237.

18. Joseph Parker to A. C. Tait, 30 Oct. 1880, ibid., vol. 100, fos. 15–16.

19. S. Beckett, *My First Grief: Recollections of a Beloved Sister*, 2nd edn. (Bath [, 1854]), 138–9.

20. Emily Leakey, *Clear Shining Light: A Memoir of Caroline W. Leakey* (n.d. [*c.* 1883]), 49.

21. Lord Lovelace to son, Ralph King, 13 Aug. 1852, MS dep. Lovelace Byron 167, fo. 80; Annabella King to brother, Ralph King, 3 Aug. 1852, Wentworth Bequest, BL Add. MS 54098. The artist in question might have been John Phillip.

22. John Callcott Horsley's diary, 24 Apr. 1852, Horsley Papers, MS Eng. e. 2186, fo. 25.

23. Sophy Horsley to sister, Mary Brunel (wife of Isambard Kingdom Brunel), 4 June 1858; Elizabeth Horsley to daughter, Mary Brunel, 2 July 1858, Horsley Papers, MS Eng. c. 2200, fos. 18–19, 58.

24. E. Finch, *Wilfrid Scawen Blunt 1840–1922* (1938), 58–9; Elizabeth Longford, *A Pilgrimage of Passion: The Life of Wilfrid Scawen Blunt* (1979), 59; Lady Anne Blunt's diary, 21 Apr. 1872, Wentworth Bequest, BL Add. MS 53840.

25. Lady Anne Blunt's diary, 21 July, 4 Aug. 1872, Wentworth Bequest, BL Add. MS 53841.

26. Lady Angela Forbes, *Memories and Base Details* (1922), 11.

27. Mary Somerville to James Graham, 24 July 1860, Somerville Papers, dep. c. 357, folder MSFP-11.

28. A. C. Tait's journal, 12 Jan. 1879, Tait Papers, vol. 63, fo. 136.

29. Robert Wilkins, *The Fireside Book of Death: A Macabre Guide to the Ultimate Experience* (1990), 184–5.

30. See Plate 7, Cast of Harry Horsley, 1854.

31. Elizabeth Horsley to daughter-in-law, Rose Horsley, 8 July [1854], Horsley Papers, MS Eng. c. 2204, fo. 87.

32. Agnes Greig to sister-in-law, Martha Somerville, 1 Nov. 1865, Somerville Papers, dep. c. 364, folder MSIF-25.

33. Lady Charlotte Phillimore to W. E. Gladstone, 10 Feb. 18[85], W. E. Gladstone Papers, BL Add. MS 44279, fos. 62–3.

34. Egerton Harcourt's will, copy 18 May 1880, MS Harcourt dep. 670, fos. 3–4.

35. Annabella King to brother, Ralph King, 3 Aug. 1852, Wentworth Bequest, BL Add. MS 54098.

36. Mary Drew to Lord Rosebery, 19 Oct. 1901, Rosebery MS 10015, fo. 153.

37. Thomas Keble to John Keble, 6 Nov. [1860?], Keble Correspondence 22.

38. Martha Somerville to half-brother, Woronzow Greig, 6 July 1861, Somerville Papers, dep. c. 365, folder MSIF-33.

39. Letters of Mary Ann Rogers to Richard Norris Gandy, 30 May; 10, 13 Aug.; 12 Oct. 1865; 19 Apr. 1869, uncatalogued papers of Thorold Rogers family, Box 10, R7, fos. 13–15, 17, 58.

40. William Somerville to Janet Elliot, Dec. 1841, Somerville Papers, dep. c. 357, folder MSFP-8.

41. Thomas Lister to Sir William Harcourt, 31 July 1866, MS Harcourt dep. 633, fos, 98–9, 101–2.

42. J. II. Gladstone to sister-in-law, Elizabeth King, 22 May 1871, MacDonald Papers, PRO 30/69/852.

43. See John Morley, *Death, Heaven and the Victorians* (1971), 32–51.

44. Catherine Ellen Taylor to uncle, George Courtauld II, 29 Mar. 1850, *The Courtauld Family Letters 1782–1900*, 8 vols. (priv. pr., Cambridge, 1916), vii: *1842–1850*.

45. Catherine Taylor to sister, Sophia Courtauld II, 11 Feb. 1851, ibid., viii. 3510–11.

46. Lady Anne Blunt's diary, 14 June 1872, Wentworth Bequest, BL Add. MS 53841.

47. Rose Horsley's diary, 28 July 1858–60, Horsley Papers, MS Eng. e. 2205, e. 2206, fo. 54; e. 2207, fo. 40.

48. Lucy Sharpe to mother, Mary Reid, 6 Mar. 1846, Sharpe Papers 169/7.

49. J. E. Thorold Rogers diary, 3 Feb. 1854, papers of Thorold Rogers family, MS Eng. misc. fo. 476.

50. Lord Carnarvon's diary, 26 May 1877, Carnarvon Papers, BL Add. MS 60909, fo. 61.

51. Elizabeth Horsley to Elvira Horsley, [1849,] Horsley Papers, MS Eng. c. 2204, fos. 35–6, on the death of her daughter, Fanny Thompson, née Horsley.

52. John Callcott Horsley's diary, 9–10 Dec. 1852; Elizabeth Horsley to Rose Horsley, 8 July [1854], Horsley Papers, MS Eng. e. 2186, fo. 58; c. 2204, fo. 82.

53. Gertrude Gladstone to Herbert Gladstone, 7 Oct. 1891, Glynne–Gladstone Papers, MS 47/10.

54. Victoria Dawnay to Mary Countess Minto, 26 Aug. 1892, Minto MS 12428, fo. 135.

55. Mary to Austen Chamberlain, 3 Sept. 1911, Chamberlain Papers, AC 1/8/7/16.

56. Hilda to Austen Chamberlain, 8 Sept. 1911, ibid., AC 1/8/8/26.

57. Mary to Austen Chamberlain, 16 Sept. 1911, ibid., AC 1/8/7/18.

58. Lady Stepney to Mary Drew, 28 Apr. 1910, Mary Gladstone Drew Papers, BL Add. MS 46250, fo. 94.

59. Raphael, *The Anatomy of Bereavement*, 194. See also e.g. Colin Murray Parkes, *Bereavement: Studies of Grief in Adult Life* (Harmondsworth, 1978), ch. 4: 'Searching', 57–76; John Bowlby, *Attachment and Loss*, iii: *Loss* (Harmondsworth, 1985), 86–90.

60. Mary Ann Rogers's notebook of bequests, 10 May 1865 (with later additions and amendments), uncat. papers of Thorold Rogers family, Box 12. See also Ada Lovelace's detailed bequest instructions, n.d. [1852], MS dep. Lovelace Byron 175, fos. 161–2.

61. Margot Asquith's 'Autobiography', Mary Gladstone Drew Papers, BL Add. MS 46270, fos. 76–7.

62. Copy of extract from Laura Lyttelton's informal will, Feb. 1886, Balfour Papers (Whittingehame) MS 166.

63. Mary Drew's Will, Sept. 1886, with alterations and additions Jan. 1890, Mary Gladstone Drew Papers, BL Add. MS 46268, fos. 1–61. By the time she altered the will in 1890 she had a daughter, so the list was much reduced. The

information here and in succeeding paragraphs is drawn from the more comprehensive 1886 will.

64. Ibid.

65. Ibid.

66. Ibid.

67. Theresa Villiers to granddaughter, Marie-Thérèse Lister, 25 Dec. 1848, MS Harcourt dep. 620, fos. 98–9.

68. Dr Seth Thompson to brother-in-law, John C. Horsley, and wife, Elvira, 25 Apr. 1849, Horsley Papers, MS Eng. c. 2205, fo. 46.

69. Ada Lovelace's bequest instructions, n.d. [1852], MS dep. Lovelace Byron 175, fos. 161–2.

70. Lady Lewis to son-in-law, Sir William Harcourt, 16 July 1863, MS Harcourt dep. 631, fo. 68.

71. J. Cooper to Capt. Edward Goulburn, 10 June 1843, Goulburn Papers, Acc. 319, Box 31.

72. Constance Villiers to Sir William Harcourt, n.d. [1863], MS Harcourt dep. 633, fos. 140, 144.

73. P. Cunnington and C. Lucas, *Costume for Births, Marriages and Deaths* (1972), 253.

74. Ada Lovelace's notes, Sept. 1852, MS dep. Lovelace Byron 175, fos. 152, 154–5.

75. Isaac Disraeli's will, 31 May 1847, Hughenden Papers, Box 271, G/v/2.

76. Emily Frances Palmer to brother, William Palmer, 14 Apr. [1852], Selborne Papers, MS Eng. misc. c. 691, fo. 22.

77. Captain G. H. Gildeas to Mrs Sneyd, 8 May 1864, Sherbrooke Papers, J.

78. Ada Lovelace's bequest instructions, n.d. [1852], MS dep. Lovelace Byron 175, fos. 137–8.

79. Lady Cardwell to Lord Selborne, 12 Apr. 1885, Selborne Papers, MS 1880, fos. 146–7.

80. Lavinia Talbot to Mary Gladstone, Ascension Day 1882, Mary Gladstone Papers, BL Add. MS 46236, fo. 136.

81. Morley, *Death, Heaven and the Victorians*, 14, 17. See also Philippe Ariès, *Western Attitudes towards Death: From the Middle Ages to the Present* (1976), 67–74, on the cult of cemeteries in France.

15. Rituals of Sorrow: Mourning-Dress and Condolence Letters

1. Lou Taylor, *Mourning Dress: A Costume and Social History* (1983), ch. 2: 'The Social Status of Widows'.

2. John Hinton, *Dying*, 2nd edn. (Harmondsworth, 1979), 186.

3. Colin Murray Parkes, *Bereavement: Studies of Grief in Adult Life* (Harmondsworth, 1978), 188.

4. David Cannadine, 'War and Death, Grief and Mourning in Modern Britain', in Joachim Whaley (ed.), *Mirrors of Mortality* (1981), 190.

5. Keith Norman MacDonald, MD, *On Death and How to Divest it of its Terrors* (Edinburgh, 1875).

6. Basil Montagu, *The Funerals of the Quakers* (1840), 39–40.

7. Mrs Fanny Douglas, *The Gentlewoman's Book of Dress* (1890), 109–15; Mrs John Sherwood, *Manners and Social Usages* (New York, 1884), 126–7, 132–3.

8. See Lou Taylor, *Mourning Dress*; Phyllis Cunnington and Catherine Lucas, *Costume for Births, Marriages and Deaths* (1972); John Morley, *Death, Heaven and the Victorians* (1971), 63–79.

9. Elizabeth Horsley to daughter-in-law, Rose Horsley, n.d. 'Sunday', 'Tuesday' [1857], Horsley Papers, MS Eng. c. 2204, fos. 129–30, 132–4.

10. Sophy Horsley to sister, Mary Brunel, 17, 21, 30 June 1858, Horsley Papers, MS Eng. c. 2200, fos. 30–1, 43, 57.

11. Mary Reid to daughter, Lucy Sharpe, 14 Dec. 1848, 19 Aug. 1853, Sharpe Papers 118.

12. Based on Cunnington and Lucas, *Costume for Births, Marriages and Deaths*, esp. 241–69; Taylor, *Mourning Dress*; Morley, *Death, Heaven and the Victorians*, 63–79.

13. Quoted in Morley, *Death, Heaven and the Victorians*, 76.

14. Sherwood, *Manners and Social Usages*, 126–7, 132–3.

15. Ibid., 67.

16. Agnes Greig to Martha Somerville, 6 Dec. 1865, Somerville Papers, dep. c. 364, folder MSIF-25.

17. Agnes Anson to husband, Fred Anson, 18 June 1888, Acland–Anson Papers, MS 2862 M/F 283, Devon Record Office.

18. Victoria Dawnay to Mary Countess Minto, 12 Nov. 1887, Minto MS 12427, fo. 203.

19. Elizabeth Haldane to mother, Mary Haldane, 19 Jan. 1889, Haldane MS NLS 6046, fo. 197.

20. Elizabeth King to niece, Margaret Gladstone, 13 Oct. 1896, MacDonald Papers, PRO 30/69/887.

21. Mary Anne Rogers to son, James E. Thorold Rogers, 21 Dec. 1864, uncat. Papers of Thorold Rogers family, Box 4.

22. Marianne Malcolm's diary, 10 Jan. 1884, Milner Papers, Bodl. MS Eng. hist. e. 305, fo. 18.

23. Mrs Rogers to future son-in-law, Harry Acland, 27 Oct. 1878, Bodl. MS Acland d. 103, fos. 194–6.

24. Sarah Acland to son, 'Willie' A. D. Acland, 30 Dec, 1866, Bodl. MS Acland d. 42, fo. 175.

25. *Earl Cowper, K.G.: A Memoir*, by his wife (Katrine Cecilia) (priv. pr., 1913), 226, 223–4.

26. Augusta Touzel to sister, Eliza, 2nd Lady Phillipps, 3 May 1857, MS Phillipps–Robinson e. 425, fos. 129–30.

27. Lady Lincolnshire's diary, 14 Jan. 1892, Carrington MS Film 1099; Mary Chamberlain's diary, 4 Jan. 1892, Chamberlain Papers, c. 5/1.

28. Audrey to Graham Wallas, 6 May 1910, Graham Wallas Papers, Box 46.

29. Lady Lincolnshire's diary, 4 June 1880, Carrington MS Film 1098.

30. Lady Stepney to Mary Drew, 16 Aug. 1913, Mary Gladstone Drew Papers, BL Add. MS 46250, fo. 193.

31. William, 4th Earl of Ilchester, to Augusta, 4th Lady Holland, 2 Nov. 1842, Holland House Papers, BL Add. MS 52152, fos. 106–7.

32. Lady Cardwell to Lord Selborne, 12 Apr. 1885, Selborne Papers, MS 1880, fos. 146–7.

33. Amelia Mary Villiers to Sir William Harcourt, 11 Feb. 1863, MS Harcourt dep. 633, fos. 166–7.

34. See e.g. George W. E. Russell to A. J. Balfour, 1882, BL Add. MS 49838, fos. 168–9.

35. Louisa Cane to friend, Jane Goulburn, 16, 22, 27 June 1843, Goulburn Papers, Acc. 319, Box 30.

36. Henrietta Martin to Dr Henry Acland, 30 Oct. 1878, Bodl. MS Acland d. 84, fos. 50–5.

37. Constance Leconfield to Evelyn Stanhope, 2 July 1886, Stanhope MSS, U 1590, C 590/19.

38. William Somerville to Martha Somerville, 3 Nov. [1837], Somerville Papers, dep. c. 363, folder MSIF-18.

39. Emily Harcourt to Sir William Harcourt, [2 Feb. 1863,] MS Harcourt dep. 603, fos. 17–18.

40. Richard Cane to Frederick Goulburn, 19 Jan. [1856], Goulburn Papers, Acc. 319, Box 23.

41. Condolence letters to Frederick Goulburn, 1856, from J. Braybrooke, 24 Jan.; W. Dalby, 18 Jan.; Thomas Freemantle, 21 Jan.; Lady Ripon, 14 Jan.; Goulburn Papers, Acc. 319, Box 23.

42. Cecilia Lady Rice to brother, Sir William Harcourt, [Feb. 1863,] MS Harcourt dep. 609, fos. 56–7.

43. Lady Susan Harcourt to Sir William Harcourt, [1863,] MS Harcourt dep. 610, fos. 4–6.

44. Lord Lansdowne to 3rd Lady Holland, 23 Oct. 1840, Holland House Papers, BL Add. MS 51690, fos. 114–15.

45. Mary Gladstone to Lavinia Talbot, [1875,] Mary Gladstone Drew Papers, BL Add. MS 46269, fo. 117.

46. See e.g. Mabel[?] to 'darling Elsie', Lady Carnarvon, 28 June 1890, Carnarvon Papers, BL Add. MS 61054.

47. Auberon Herbert to Lady Carnarvon, [1890,] Carnarvon Papers, BL Add. MS 61054.

48. Sherwood, *Manners and Social Usages*, 140.

49. Beverley Raphael, *The Anatomy of Bereavement* (1984), 44, 60, 179, 188, 207, 222; see also Hinton, *Dying*, 187.

50. Mary Somerville to Sir Henry Fairfax, 14 July [1844], Somerville Papers, dep. c. 357, folder MSFP-6.

51. Constance Villiers to Sir William Harcourt, [Feb. 1863,] MS Harcourt dep. 633, fos. 138–9.

52. Agnes Greig to sister-in-law, Martha Somerville, 9 Dec. 1872, Somerville Papers, dep. c. 364, folder MSIF-25.

53. Cecilia Lady Iddesleigh to Evelyn Lady Stanhope, 22 Apr. [1905], Stanhope MS U 1590, C 573/4.

54. See e.g. Raphael, *The Anatomy of Bereavement*, 188, 222.

55. Kate Courtney's diary, 10 Dec. 1908, Courtney Collection, vol. XXXIII, fo. 102.

56. Dr F. T. Watson to Frederick Goulburn, 14 Jan. 1856, Goulburn Papers, Acc. 319, Box 23.

57. Arnold Wheeler to Edward Goulburn, 13 Feb. 1856, ibid.

58. Thomas Pemberton Leigh to Edward Goulburn, 17 Jan. 1856, ibid.

59. Lady Ripon to Henry Goulburn, 10 June 1843, Goulburn Papers, Acc. 319, Box 67.

60. John Thornton to Henry Goulburn, 9 June 1843, ibid.

61. H. V. Elliott to Henry Goulburn, 9 June 1843, ibid.

62. Lord Bathurst to Henry Goulburn, [June 1843,] ibid.

63. Serjeant Edward Goulburn to brother, Henry Goulburn, 9 June 1843, ibid.

64. Revd Edward Meyrick Goulburn to cousin, Capt. Edward Goulburn, 12 June [1843], ibid.

65. Charles Edward Horsley to brother, John C. Horsley, 14 Mar. 1854, Horsley Papers, MS Eng. c. 2213, fos. 27–8.

66. Mary Haden to brother-in-law, John C. Horsley, 2 Mar. 1857, Horsley Papers, MS Eng. c. 2213, fos. 92–3.

67. J. W. Buckley to Elizabeth Horsley, 13 Mar. 1854, Horsley Papers, MS Eng. c. 2198, fos. 281–2.

68. Marquess of Donegall to Evelyn Lady Stanhope, 25 Dec. 1875, Stanhope MS U 1590, C 590/8.

69. K. Bruce Glasier to Margaret MacDonald, 15 Feb. 1910; Mrs B. Wayles to M. MacDonald, 6 Feb. 1910, MacDonald Papers, PRO 30/69/802.

70. Condolence letters to Rose Horsley on her husband's death, Oct. 1903, Horsley Papers, MS Eng. c. 2236, fos. 16–62.

71. Letters to Edith Lyttelton, 17 July, 14 Aug., 23 Sept. 1913, Chandos Papers, II, 3/12.

72. Mary Barham to Maria Sharpe, 10 June 1870, Sharpe Papers 139/1.

73. Mary Dorothea Waldegrave to father, Roundell Palmer, 14 Jan. 1892, Selborne Papers, MS 1871, fos. 87–8.

74. Gen. Charles Fox to Henry, 4th Lord Holland, 27 Oct. 1840, Holland House Papers, BL Add. MS 52051, fo. 209.

75. Caroline Cane to Jane Goulburn, 18 Feb. 1853, Goulburn Papers, Acc. 319, Box 30.

76. Aubrey Harcourt to Sir William Harcourt, n.d. [1876], MS Harcourt dep. 610, fos. 200–1.

77. A. C. Tait's journal, Dec. 1878, Tait Papers, vol. 63, fos. 104, 108–9.

78. Louisa A. Lane to Archbishop A. C. Tait, 27 Mar. 1879, ibid., vol. 99, fos. 83–4.

79. Lavinia Talbot to Meriel Talbot, 21 July 1913, Talbot MS U 1612, Kent Archives Office.

80. Constance Flower to Marion Bryce, n.d. [1894], MS Bryce Adds. 42.

81. Mary Herbert to Marion Bryce, 15 July [1902], ibid.

82. Mary Bryce to James Bryce, n.d. [Sept. 1903], ibid., Adds. 15.

83. Lady Mary Fox to sister-in-law, Augusta Lady Holland, 19 Dec. 1859, Holland House Papers, BL Add. MS 52151, fos. 69–70.

84. A. C. Tait's journal, Dec. 1878, Tait Papers, vol. 63, fos. 108–9.

16. Chronic and Abnormal Grief: Queen Victoria, Lady Frederick Cavendish, and Emma Haden

1. Lou Taylor, *Mourning Dress: A Costume and Social History* (1983), 61, 122, 154–5. See also Clare Gittings, *Death, Burial and the Individual in Early Modern England* (1984), 16, for the assumption that the Queen epitomized 'the Victorian attitude towards death and bereavement'.

2. Philippe Ariès, *Western Attitudes towards Death: From the Middle Ages to the Present* (1976; first pub. 1974), 66–8; Philippe Ariès, *The Hour of our Death* (Harmondsworth, 1981; first pub. 1977), ch. 10: 'The Age of the Beautiful Death'.

3. David Cannadine, 'War and Death, Grief and Mourning in Modern Britain', in Joachim Whaley (ed.), *Mirrors of Mortality* (1981), 190–1.

4. This section on Queen Victoria's experience is based on evidence in *The Letters of Queen Victoria*, ed. A. C. Benson and Viscount Esher (1908), iii; Christopher Hibbert (ed.), *Queen Victoria in her Letters and Journals* (Harmondsworth, 1985); Elizabeth Longford, *Victoria R.I.* (1964).

5. Longford, *Victoria R.I.*, 364–6, 378; M. Ponsonby, *A Memoir* (1927), 47.

6. *Letters of Queen Victoria*, iii. 473, 476.

7. Ibid., 477–8.

8. Longford, *Victoria R.I.*, 486, 489.

9. C. M. Parkes, *Bereavement: Studies of Grief in Adult Life* (Harmondsworth, 1978), 130–42; J. Bowlby, *Attachment and Loss, iii: Loss* (Harmondsworth, 1985), 141–51; Geoffrey Gorer, *Death, Grief and Mourning in Contemporary Britain* (1965), 79–83. See Bowlby, 106–11, for details of the various studies. Results cannot be quantitatively precise, since 'no very systematic comparative data are available' (Parkes, 131).

10. Parkes, *Bereavement*, 143–75.

11. Ibid., 133.

12. Lucille Iremonger, *Lord Aberdeen* (1978), 26–40, 43, 97–107.

13. See e.g. Beatrice Chamberlain to Mrs Endicott, 26 Feb. 1905, Chamberlain Papers, AC 1/8/8/14.

14. Lord Elton, *Life of James Ramsay MacDonald* (1939), 196.

15. D. Marquand, *Ramsay MacDonald* (1977), 132–5.

16. Memorandum on death of Mary Lady Lyttelton, 1857, Mary Gladstone Drew Papers, BL Add. MS 46269, fos. 65–109.

17. Ibid.

18. Mary Gladstone to Alfred Lyttelton, 7 Dec. 1881, in ibid., BL Add. MS 46233, fos. 239–40.

19. *The Diary of Lady Frederick Cavendish*, ed. John Bailey, 2 vols. (1927), ii. 287 (4 June 1881). See also e.g. pp. 11, 192, 228, 240, 300.

20. Memorandum on death of May Lyttelton, 1857, Mary Gladstone Drew Papers, BL Add. MS 46269, fos. 110–22.

21. *The Diary of Lady Frederick Cavendish*, ii. 191, 194 (10 July, 15–21 Nov. 1875).

22. Mary Gladstone to Catherine Gladstone, n.d. [*c*.18–20 Nov. 1875], Mary Gladstone Drew Papers, BL Add. MS 46222, fos. 258–9.

23. *The Diary of Lady Frederick Cavendish*, ii. 195–6 (17–23 Apr. 1876).

24. Mary Gladstone to Catherine Gladstone, 19 Apr. 1876, Mary Gladstone Drew Papers, BL Add. MS 46222, fos. 272–5.

25. Certified copy of an entry of death for George William Lyttelton, General Register Office, London.

26. Sarah Acland to daughter, S. Angelina Acland, 20 Apr. 1876, Bodl. MS Acland d. 140, fo. 112.

27. *The Diary of Lady Frederick Cavendish*, ii. 183.

28. Mary Gladstone to Catherine Gladstone, 19 Apr. 1876, Mary Gladstone Drew Papers, BL Add. MS 46222, fos. 272–5.

29. *The Diary of Lady Frederick Cavendish*, ii. 197.

30. Revd Stephen Gladstone, 'A Life Given for Ireland', memorial sermon, 1882.

31. W. E. Gladstone's poem on the death of Lord Frederick Cavendish, 7 May 1882, Mary Gladstone Drew Papers, BL Add. MS 46269, fos. 127–8.

32. *The Diary of Lady Frederick Cavendish*, ii. 318.

33. Ibid., ii. 320.

34. Ibid., 319–21.

35. Mary Gladstone's diary, 6–7 May 1882, Mary Gladstone Drew Papers, BL Add. MS 46259, fo. 133.

36. Mary Gladstone to Lord Rosebery, 7 May 1882, Rosebery MS 10015, fo. 66.

37. Lavinia Talbot to Mary Gladstone, 12 May 1882, Mary Gladstone Drew Papers, BL Add. MS 46236, fos. 127–8; Lavinia Talbot to Herbert Gladstone, Herbert Gladstone Papers, BL Add. MS 46047, fos. 180–1.

38. Agnes Wickham to Mary Gladstone, 9 May 1882, Mary Gladstone Drew Papers, BL Add. MS 46230, fo. 100.

39. *Mary Gladstone: Her Diaries and Letters*, ed. Lucy Masterman (1930), 250–1.

40. Lavinia Talbot to sister, Meriel Talbot, 15 May 1882, Talbot Papers, U 1612.

41. Ibid.

42. Lavinia Talbot to Mary Gladstone, 18 May 1882, Mary Gladstone Drew Papers, BL Add. MS 46236, fo. 135.

43. Mary Gladstone to Lavinia Talbot, 18 May 1882, ibid., fos. 129–30.

44. Lavinia Talbot to Mary Gladstone, 18 May 1882, ibid., fo. 137.

45. Helen to Henry Gladstone, 12 May 1882, Glynne–Gladstone Papers, MS 44/3.

46. Mary Gladstone to Lavinia Talbot, June 1882, Mary Gladstone Drew Papers, BL Add. MS 46236, fos. 137–8.

47. Ibid., 18 May 1882, fos. 129–30.

48. Helen Gladstone to Henry Gladstone, 16 June, 28 July 1882, Glynne–Gladstone Papers, MS 44/3.

49. Mary Gladstone to Henry Gladstone, 13 July 1882, Glynne–Gladstone Papers, MS 43/2.

50. Lavinia Talbot to Mary Gladstone, 19 Aug. 1882, Mary Gladstone Drew Papers, BL Add. MS 46236, fo. 156.

51. *The Diary of Lady Frederick Cavendish*, ii. 327.

52. Lucy Cavendish to Mary Gladstone, 7 Feb. 1883, Mary Gladstone Drew Papers, BL Add. MS 46235, fos. 223–4.

53. Lucy Cavendish to Catherine Gladstone, 23 Sept. 1884, Glynne–Gladstone Papers, MS 32/9.

54. Frances Balfour to Mary Gladstone, 19 May 1914, Mary Gladstone Drew Papers, BL Add. MS 46238, fos. 74–5.

55. Lavinia Talbot to Meriel Talbot, 15 May 1882, Talbot Papers, U 1612.

56. Mary Gladstone to Lavinia Talbot, June 1882, Mary Gladstone Drew Papers, BL Add. MS 46236, fos. 137–8.

57. Lavinia Talbot to Mary Gladstone, 7 July 1884, ibid., fo. 223.

58. Lucy Cavendish to Mary Gladstone, 9 July 1884, ibid., MS 46235, fo. 228.

59. Lucy Cavendish to Mary Gladstone, 6 Mar. 1883, ibid., fo. 226.

60. *The Diary of Lady Frederick Cavendish*, i, pp. xxviii, xxx.

61. Mary Drew to Lavinia Talbot, 21 Nov. 1892, Mary Gladstone Drew Papers, BL Add. MS 46236, fos. 315–16.

62. Lucy Cavendish to Lady Stanhope, 19 May 1905, Stanhope Papers, MS U 1590, C 573/3.

63. Lucy Cavendish to Edith Lyttelton, 16 July 1913, Chandos Papers, II 3/12.

64. *The Diary of Lady Frederick Cavendish*, ii. 320.

65. See Beverley Raphael, *The Anatomy of Bereavement* (1984), 187, on the normal process of mourning.

66. Margaret to Ramsay MacDonald, 10 Oct. 1896, MacDonald Papers, PRO 30/69/778.

67. Parkes, *Bereavement*, 159–60.

68. Raphael, *The Anatomy of Bereavement*, 280, 310.

69. Jane Littlewood, *Aspects of Grief: Bereavement in Adult Life* (1992), 140–4.

70. Elizabeth Horsley to daughter, Mary Brunel, 18 June 1858, Horsley Papers, MS Eng. c. 2200, fo. 33.

71. Mabel A. Allan to M. E. MacDonald, 9 June 1911, MacDonald Papers, PRO 30/69/905.

72. Rose Horsley to John C. Horsley, 30 July [1858], Horsley Papers, MS Eng. c. 2201, fos. 64–5.

73. Sophy Horsley to sister, Mary Brunel, 1 Aug. 1858, ibid., fo. 1.

74. Rose Horsley to John C. Horsley, 30 July [1858], ibid., fos. 64–5.

75. Elizabeth Horsley to Mary Brunel, 31 July 1858; Sophy Horsley to Mary Brunel, 1 Aug. 1858, Horsley Papers, MS Eng. c. 2200, fos. 119–20; c. 2201, fo. 1.

76. Emma Haden's Book of Meditations on Bereavement, 1858–61, Commonplace Book, 10 July 1861, Horsley Papers, MS Eng. e. 2300, fos. 59–60.

77. Emma Haden's Commonplace Book, 1858, Horsley Papers, MS Eng. e. 2300, fos. 17–18, 25.

78. Ibid., [1859–60,] fos. 31–2.

79. Emma Haden's 2nd Commonplace Book, 1 June 1862, Horsley Papers, MS Eng. d. 2095, fos. 15–16.

80. Ibid., 28 July 1862, fo. 21.
81. Ibid., 28 July 1865, 13 Oct. 1865, 2 Nov. 1865, fos. 44, 46–8.
82. Emma Haden's Commonplace Book, 1858, Horsley Papers, MS Eng. e. 2300, fos. 24, 26, 30.
83. Emma Haden's 2nd Commonplace Book, 28 July 1863, Horsley Papers, MS Eng. d. 2095, fos. 32, 39.
84. Emma Haden's 2nd Commonplace Book, 1861–78, 17 Nov. 1861, 28 July 1862, Horsley Papers, MS Eng. d. 2095, fos. 4, 20.
85. Ibid., 13 Oct. 1865, MS Eng. d. 2095, fos. 46–7.
86. Ibid., 2 Nov. 1866, MS Eng. d. 2095, fo. 51.

17. 'A Solitude beyond the Reach of God or Man':
Victorian Agnostics and Death

1. G. M. Young, *Portrait of an Age*, 3rd edn. (1967; first edn. 1936), 109.
2. Harriet Martineau, *Autobiography* (1983; first edn. 1877), ii. 286.
3. Leonard Huxley, *The Life and Letters of Thomas Henry Huxley*, 2 vols. (1900), i. 239.
4. Mary Drew to Henry Gladstone, 8 May 1895, Glynne–Gladstone Papers, MS 43/3.
5. Mary Booth to Beatrice Potter, [Sept. 1886,] Passfield Papers, II, 1 (ii), fos. 394–7.
6. W. S. Blunt's Autobiography dictated to his wife, Anne, in 1873, Wentworth Bequest, BL Add. MS 54069.
7. Wilfrid Blunt's diary, Apr. 1872, quoted in Elizabeth Longford, *A Pilgrimage of Passion: The Life of Wilfrid Scawen Blunt* (1979), 86.
8. Lady Anne Blunt's diary, 21, 24 Apr. 1872, Wentworth Bequest, BL Add. MS 53840.
9. Martineau, *Autobiography*, ii. 435–8.
10. Ibid., ii. 442, 147–9, 152.
11. See G. W. Foote, *Infidel Death Beds* (1886), 43–4.
12. Revd Charles Maurice Davies, *Heterodox London: or Phases of Free Thought in the Metropolis*, 2 vols. (1874), ii. 398–403, which provides extensive quotations from Austin Holyoake's 'Sick-Room Thoughts'.
13. Ibid., ii. 404–6.
14. Maurice Maeterlinck, *Life after Death* (1911), 51–3, 56, 94–5.
15. See James R. Moore, 'Freethought, Secularism, Agnosticism: The Case of Charles Darwin', in Gerald Parsons (ed.) *Religion in Victorian Britain*, i: *Traditions* (Manchester, 1988), 289, 296–7; John Bowlby, *Charles Darwin: A New Biography* (1991), *passim*.
16. See e.g. Bowlby, *Darwin; Autobiography of Charles Darwin*, ed. Sir Francis Darwin (1929), 139–54, app. ii: 'The Religion of Charles Darwin'; *The Autobiography of Charles Darwin, 1809–1882*, ed. Nora Barlow (1958), 85–95; Moore, 'Freethought, Secularism, Agnosticism', 289, 296–7; Owen Chadwick, *The Victorian Church* (1987), ii. 15–20; Adrian Desmond and James Moore, *Darwin* (1992), *passim*.

17. *Autobiography of Charles Darwin*, ed. Barlow, 85–95; Bowlby, *Darwin*, 90–1, 227–8.
18. *Autobiography of Charles Darwin*, ed. Darwin, app. II, pp. 139–54.
19. Charles Darwin to sister, Caroline Wedgwood, 20 Sept. 1881, Darwin Papers, DAR 153.
20. Bowlby, *Darwin*, 34, 56–60, 67, 76–9.
21. Ibid. 282–3, 286–7.
22. *The Correspondence of Charles Darwin*, ed. F. Buckhardt and S. Smith, 8 vols. (Cambridge, 1985–), ii. 315–16, 352; see also Martha McMackin Garland, 'Victorian Unbelief and Bereavement', in R. Houlbrooke (ed.), *Death, Ritual and Bereavement* (1989), 154–6, on condolence letters by unbelievers.
23. *Correspondence of Charles Darwin*, vii. 138.
24. Charles Darwin to J. D. Hooker, 25 Sept. [1866], Darwin Papers, DAR 115 (iv), fo. 300.
25. *More Letters of Charles Darwin*, ed. Francis Darwin and A. C. Seward, 2 vols. (1903), i. 477.
26. Charles Darwin to J. D. Hooker, 9 Feb. 1865, Darwin Papers, DAR 115 (iv), fo. 260.
27. *Emma Darwin: A Century of Family Letters 1792–1896*, ed. H. E. Litchfield, 2 vols. (priv. pr., Cambridge, 1904), ii. 50.
28. *Correspondence of Charles Darwin*, vol. vii. app. v.
29. Ibid. vii. 116–21.
30. Bowlby, *Darwin*, 292–8; Desmond and Moore, *Darwin*, 381–4.
31. *Correspondence of Charles Darwin*, v. 13–24. Darwin Papers, DAR 210.13.
32. Ibid.
33. Fanny E. Wedgwood to Emma Darwin, [23 Apr. 1851,] Darwin Papers, DAR 210.13.
34. *Correspondence of Charles Darwin*, vol. v. app. II, pp. 540–2. Darwin Papers, DAR 210.13.
35. Ibid. v. 28.
36. *Emma Darwin*, ii. 147.
37. Charles Darwin to cousin, W. D. Fox, 3 Oct. [1856], *Correspondence of Charles Darwin*, vi. 238.
38. *Correspondence of Charles Darwin*, viii. 365–6.
39. *Emma Darwin*, ii. 187–8.
40. Cited in Desmond and Moore, *Darwin*, 281.
41. Emma to Charles Darwin, June 1861, *Emma Darwin*, ii. 189.
42. Ibid. ii. 190.
43. *Correspondence of Charles Darwin*, v. 13–25.
44. Ibid. v. 27.
45. *Emma Darwin*, ii. 142, 147.
46. J. D. Hooker to T. H. Huxley, 'Monday' [1863], Hooker Papers, letters from Hooker to Huxley, 1851–94, fo. 91.
47. J. D. Hooker to C. Darwin, [28 Sept. 1863,] Darwin Papers, DAR 101, fo. 159.
48. Ibid., 1 Oct. 1863, DAR 101, fos. 160–2.

49. Ibid.

50. Huxley, *Life and Letters of T. H. Huxley*, i. 220. See also Garland, 'Victorian Unbelief and Bereavement', 156–8, for the problems of funeral services for unbelievers.

51. J. D. Hooker to C. Darwin, 2[3?] Oct. 1863, Darwin Papers, DAR 101, fo. 170.

52. J. D. Hooker to C. Darwin, 16 Sept. 1864, ibid., fo. 245.

53. Ibid., 1 Oct. 1863, fo. 162.

54. Ibid., 16 Sept. 1864, fo. 245.

55. Hooker to Darwin, 25 Nov. 1874; Darwin to Hooker, 22, 25 Nov. 1874, Darwin Papers, DAR 103, fos. 228–9; DAR 95, fos. 342, 396.

56. Ibid., Hooker to Darwin, 8 Dec. 1874, DAR 103, fos. 232–3; see also Hooker to Huxley, 7 Dec. 1874, Hooker Papers, letters from Hooker to Huxley, 1851–94, fo. 142.

57. Hooker to Darwin, [*c.*mid Sept. 1876,] Darwin Papers, DAR 104, fos. 62–5.

58. Leonard Huxley, *Life and Letters of Sir Joseph Dalton Hooker*, 2 vols. (1918), ii. 66.

59. Hooker to Darwin, 30 Feb. 1865, Darwin Papers, DAR 102, fo. 9.

60. Ibid.

61. Ibid., [1875,] DAR 104, fo. 16.

62. Adrian Desmond, *Huxley: The Devil's Disciple* (1994), 3–49.

63. Ibid. 3–17.

64. 'The Soul and Future Life', *Nineteenth Century* (Sept. 1877), ii. 340.

65. Desmond, *Huxley: The Devil's Disciple*, 75, 80–1, 132.

66. Huxley, *Life and Letters of T. H. Huxley*, i. 99.

67. Ibid. i. 81–3; Desmond, *Huxley: The Devil's Disciple*, 178.

68. Huxley, *Life and Letters of T. H. Huxley*, i. 118–19.

69. Ibid. i. 150–2.

70. T. H. Huxley to Revd Charles Kingsley, 23 Sept. 1860, 5 May 1863, ibid., i. 217–21, 240–1.

71. Ibid.

72. Huxley, *Life and Letters of T. H. Huxley*, ii. 128.

73. Ibid., i. 213, 216.

74. Desmond, *Huxley: The Devil's Disciple*, 286–98.

75. Huxley, *Life and Letters of T. H. Huxley*, ii. 179.

76. T. H. Huxley to J. D. Hooker, 21 Nov. 1887, Hooker Papers, letters from Huxley to Hooker 1854–95, fos. 186–7.

77. Huxley, *Life and Letters of T. H. Huxley*, ii. 179.

78. A. O. J. Cockshut, *The Unbelievers: English Agnostic Thought 1840–1890* (1964), 150.

18. Epilogue. After the Victorians: Social Memory, Spiritualism, and the Great War

1. Jose Harris, *Private Lives, Public Spirit: A Social History of Britain 1870–1914* (Oxford, 1993), 253, 171–2, 179.

2. David Cannadine, 'War and Death, Grief and Mourning in Modern Britain', in Joachim Whaley (ed.), *Mirrors of Mortality* (1981), 230.

3. John McManners, *Death and the Enlightenment* (Oxford, 1981), 167–72.

4. See e.g. Thomas A. Kselman, *Death and the Afterlife in Modern France* (Princeton, 1993), 132–43.

5. Frederic Harrison, 'The Soul and Future Life', *Nineteenth Century*, 1 (July 1877), 836–7.

6. Ibid., 2 (Oct. 1877), 523.

7. Ibid., 1 (July 1877), 836–9.

8. Ibid., 2 (Sept. 1877), 338–40.

9. Dorothy Stanley to Kate Courtney, 13 May 1918, Courtney Collection, vol. xiii, fos. 102–3.

10. Janet Ward to Molly Bell, 16 Apr. 1903, C. P. Trevelyan Papers.

11. Janet Trevelyan, *Two Stories* (1954), 128–9.

12. George Trevelyan to parents, Sir George and Lady Trevelyan, 19 Apr. 1911, Trevelyan Papers, GOT 189.

13. Janet Trevelyan to Molly Trevelyan, 21 Apr. 1911, C. P. Trevelyan Papers.

14. Ibid.

15. Janet Trevelyan to Lady Trevelyan, 23 Apr. 1911, Trevelyan Papers, GOT 189.

16. Mary Humphry Ward to Sir George Trevelyan, 4 May 1911, ibid.

17. Sir Hugh Bell to Molly Trevelyan, 19, 22 Apr. 1911, C. P. Trevelyan Papers.

18. Molly Trevelyan to Lady Trevelyan, 20 Apr. 1911, Trevelyan Papers, GOT 189.

19. Janet Trevelyan to Lady Trevelyan, 23 Apr. 1911, ibid.

20. George Trevelyan to Lady Trevelyan, ibid.

21. Trevelyan, *Two Stories*.

22. Charles Trevelyan to G. O. Trevelyan, 20 Apr. 1911, Trevelyan Papers, GOT 189.

23. G. M. Trevelyan to parents, 21 Apr. 1911, ibid.

24. Charles Trevelyan to Lady Trevelyan, 19 Apr. 1911, ibid.

25. George Trevelyan to Molly Trevelyan, 29 Apr. 1911, and to his mother, 23 Apr. 1911, ibid.

26. Mary Humphry Ward to Sir George Trevelyan, 4 May 1911, ibid.

27. Molly Trevelyan's diary, 19 Apr. 1911, Trevelyan Papers.

28. Molly to Charles Trevelyan, 7 Jan. 1914, C. P. Trevelyan Papers.

29. Katherine Trevelyan, *A Fool in Love* (1962), 39–40.

30. Molly Trevelyan's diary, 23 May 1916, Trevelyan Papers.

31. Ibid., 3 Aug. 1917.

32. Lady Byron to Lady Theresa Villiers, 11 May [1853], MS dep. Lovelace Byron 115, fo. 214.

33. Charles Darwin to J. D. Hooker, 18 Jan. 1874, Darwin Papers, DAR 95, fos. 311–12.

34. G. K. Nelson, *Spiritualism and Society* (1969), 124.

35. Renée Haynes, *The Society for Psychical Research 1882–1982: A History* (1982), p. xiii.

36. Nelson, *Spiritualism and Society*, 134.

37. Ruth Brandon, *The Spiritualists: The Passion for the Occult in the Nineteenth and Twentieth Centuries* (1983), 87–8, 145.

38. Leonard Huxley, *The Life and Letters of Thomas Henry Huxley*, 2 vols. (1900), i. 420.

39. Haynes, *The Society for Psychical Research*, 63, 70, 72.

40. Edith to Alfred Lyttelton, 1906, Chandos Papers, I, 5/14.

41. Edith Lyttelton's account of the death of her son, Antony, 1902, Chandos Papers, II, 3/2.

42. Edith Lyttelton, Chandos Papers, 'Interwoven', 6/1/L.

43. Edith to Alfred Lyttelton, 10 May 1902, Chandos Papers, II, 3/11.

44. Ibid., 1906, Chandos Papers, I, 5/14.

45. Ibid., 19 Oct. 1910, 14 Sept. 1911, Chandos Papers, II, 3/11.

46. Edith Lyttelton, *Alfred Lyttelton: An Account of his Life* (1917), 402–9.

47. Ibid.

48. Ibid.

49. Lavinia Talbot to sister, Meriel Talbot, 21 July 1913, Talbot MS U 1612.

50. Edith Lyttelton to A. J. Balfour, 23 Aug. 1913, Balfour Papers (Whittingehame) MS 166.

51. Edith Lyttelton's account of Alfred's 'appearances', 1913–43, Chandos Papers, I, 6/11.

52. Ibid.; Edith Lyttelton, Chandos Papers, 'Interwoven', 6/I/L.

53. Haynes, *The Society for Psychical Research*, 68, 206–7.

54. Stephen Koss, *Nonconformity in British Politics* (1975), cited in John Stevenson, *British Society 1914–1945* (Harmondsworth, 1984), 357.

55. Stevenson, *British Society 1914–1945*, 356–7.

56. Alan Wilkinson, *The Church of England and the First World War* (1978), 174–84.

57. Revd Cyril E. Hudson, 'A Current Tendency in Popular Religion', *Nineteenth Century*, vol. 84 (Nov. 1918), 880–1.

58. Ella Bickersteth's journal, XIII, 15 June, 11 Apr. 1919, Bickersteth Family Papers, Box 25.

59. James Obelkevich, 'Religion', in F. M. L. Thompson (ed.), *The Cambridge Social History of Britain 1750–1950* (Cambridge, 1993), iii. 349.

60. Nelson, *Spiritualism and Society*, 155–64; Cannadine, 'War and Death, Grief and Mourning', 228–9; Brandon, *The Spiritualists*, 215–17.

61. John Morley, *Death, Heaven and the Victorians* (1971), 76–7.

62. D. C. Coleman, *Courtaulds: An Economic and Social History*, 3 vols. (Oxford, 1969), i. 165–6, 194.

63. See e.g. Geoffrey Gorer, *Death, Grief and Mourning in Contemporary Britain* (1965), 6–8.

64. Ethel Lady Gainford to daughter, Miriam Pease, 15 July 1916, MS Gainford 18A.

65. Ella Bickersteth's journal, XII, July 1916, Bickersteth Family Papers, Box 25.

66. Julian Litten, *The English Way of Death: The Common Funeral since 1450* (1991), 171.

67. Dr R. W. McKenna, *The Adventure of Death* (1916), 2, 28.
68. C. E. Lawrence, 'The Abolition of Death', *Fortnightly Review*, 101 (Feb. 1917), 326–31.
69. Edward Mercer, DD, *Why do we Die?* (1919), 23–5.
70. K. Rose, *The Later Cecils* (1975), 119–20.
71. H. H. Asquith, *Letters of the Earl of Oxford and Asquith to a Friend*, 2 vols. (1933–4), i. 10.
72. J. M. Winter, *The Great War and the British People* (1987), 71–2, 92, 99, 281, and 65–99 on 'The Lost Generation'; see also R. Wohl, *The Generation of 1914* (1980), 85–121.
73. Winter, *The Great War*, 305.
74. Wohl, *The Generation of 1914*, 92, 94–7, 104.
75. Wilkinson, *The Church of England and the First World War*, 302.
76. *The Autobiography of Margot Asquith*, ed. Mark Bonham Carter (Bath, 1972), 315.
77. B. Raphael, *Anatomy of Bereavement* (1984), 28–9.
78. Jane Littlewood, *Aspects of Grief: Bereavement in Adult Life* (1992), 33–4, 142–3.
79. Bernd Hüppauf 'War and Death: The Experience of the First World War', in B. Hüppauf and Mira Crouch (eds.), *Essays on Mortality* (Sydney, 1985), 68–9.
80. See e.g. Trevor Wilson, *The Myriad Faces of War: Britain and the Great War, 1914–1918* (Cambridge, 1986); Winter, *The Great War and the British People*; Wohl, *The Generation of 1914*; Cannadine, 'War and Death'; Paul Fussell, *The Great War and Modern Memory* (Oxford, 1977).
81. Mary Wemyss, *A Family Record* (priv. pr., 1932), 274.
82. Ibid. 330–4.
83. Ibid. 337.
84. Ibid. 351.
85. Ibid. 372–6, 402.
86. Ibid. 399–403.
87. Ibid., preface and pp. 408–10.
88. Wilkinson, *The Church of England and the First World War*, 169.
89. Revd Samuel Bickersteth, *Morris Bickersteth, 1891–1916* (Cambridge, 1931), 122–33.
90. Ibid. 137, 130.
91. Ibid. 139–41.
92. Ella Bickersteth's journal, XI–XII, 1916–17, July 1916, [23] July 1916, 24 Aug. 1916, Bickersteth Family Papers, Box 25.
93. Ella Bickersteth's journal, XII–XIII, Aug. 1916–June 1918, ibid.
94. Bickersteth, *Morris Bickersteth, 1891–1916*, 139–40, 145–6.
95. Ibid., 'dedication'.
96. Lavinia Talbot, *Gilbert Walter Lyttelton Talbot: A Memoir* (1916).
97. Cannadine, 'War and Death, Grief and Mourning', 217–26; Ken Inglis, 'War Memorials: Ten Questions for Historians', *Guerres mondiales*, 167 (1992), 13.

98. Wilkinson, *The Church of England and the First World War*, 298–9.
99. Inglis, 'War Memorials', 12.
100. Cannadine, 'War and Death, Grief and Mourning', 217–32.
101. Colin Murray Parkes, *Bereavement: Studies of Grief in Adult Life* (Harmondsworth, 1978), 24, 189.

LOCATION OF MANUSCRIPT COLLECTIONS

ACLAND MSS, Bodleian Library, Oxford.

ACLAND MSS, Devon Record Office, Exeter, including the Acland–Anson correspondence.

ATHOLL MSS, Blair Castle, Scotland, seen by kind permission of the Duchess of Atholl.

BALFOUR MSS, British Library, London.

——Whittingehame Tower, East Lothian, consulted in the National Register of Archives (Scotland) by kind permission of Lord Balfour.

BENSON MSS, Bodleian Library, Oxford.

BICKERSTETH MSS, Bodleian Library, Oxford.

BRYCE MSS, Bodleian Library, Oxford.

CARNARVON MSS, British Library.

CARRINGTON MSS, Bodleian Library, Oxford (on microfilm).

CECIL–MAXSE MSS, Kent Archives Office, Maidstone, by courtesy of the Hardinge family.

CHAMBERLAIN MSS, Birmingham University Library.

CHANDOS MSS, Churchill College, Cambridge. (The Lyttelton family archive.)

CHILDERS MSS, Royal Commonwealth Library, London.

CONWAY MSS, University Library, Cambridge. (The papers of the family of Lord Conway of Allington.)

COURTNEY MSS, British Library of Political and Economic Science, London.

DARWIN MSS, University Library, Cambridge.

DASHWOOD MSS, Bodleian Library, Oxford. (The papers of the family of Sir John Dashwood King.)

DILKE MSS, British Library.

DREW MSS, British Library. (The diaries and correspondence of Mary Drew (née Gladstone).)

GAINFORD MSS, Nuffield College, Oxford.

GALTON MSS, University College London Library.

GIBBS MSS (Vicary Gibbs), in the archives of Anthony Gibbs and Sons Ltd., deposited in the Guildhall Library, London.

GLADSTONE MSS, British Library.

GLYNNE–GLADSTONE MSS, St Deiniol's Library, Hawarden, consulted in the Clwyd Record Office.

GOULBURN PAPERS, Surrey Record Office, Kingston. (The papers of Henry Goulburn and family.)

GRENFELL MSS, Hertfordshire Record Office, Hertford.

HALDANE MSS, National Library of Scotland, Edinburgh.

HAMBLEDEN MSS (W. H. Smith), seen by kind permission of the Viscount Hambleden at Strand House, London.

HARCOURT MSS, Bodleian Library, Oxford.

HOLLAND HOUSE MSS, British Library, London. (The papers of the Fox family, Barons Holland and Earls of Ilchester.)

HOOKER MSS (Sir Joseph Dalton Hooker), Library of the Royal Botanic Gardens, Kew.

HORSLEY MSS, Bodleian Library, Oxford.

HUGHENDEN MSS (Benjamin Disraeli), Bodleian Library, Oxford.

HUXLEY MSS, Imperial College, London.

KEBLE MSS, Keble College, Oxford.

LAYARD MSS (Sir Austen Henry Layard), British Library, London.

LOVELACE BYRON MSS, Bodleian Library, Oxford. (The papers of Anne Isabella King, Lady Byron and Ada, Lady Lovelace.)

MACDONALD MSS, Public Record Office, London. These include the family papers of Ramsay MacDonald's wife, Margaret (i.e. the King and Gladstone families).

MILNER MSS, Bodleian Library, Oxford.

MINTO MSS, National Library of Scotland, Edinburgh. (Elliott–Murray–Kynymoud family.)

MORLEY MSS, British Library, London. (The papers of the Parker family, Barons Boringdon and Earls of Morley.)

NEWHAILES (DALRYMPLE) MSS, National Library of Scotland, Edinburgh.

ONSLOW MSS, Surrey Record Office, Guildford.

PALMER MSS, Lambeth Palace Library. (The papers of William Jocelyn Palmer, rector of Mixbury, and his sons.)

PASSFIELD PAPERS, consulted in the British Library of Political and Economic Science by kind permission of the Passfield Trust and the London School of Economics and Political Science. References to the Beatrice Webb diary relate to the typescript volumes which I consulted in the LSE Library.

PHILLIPPS–ROBINSON MSS, Bodleian Library, Oxford. (The papers of Sir Thomas Phillipps and family.)

RATHBONE MSS, University Library, Liverpool.

ROGERS MSS, Bodleian Library, Oxford. (The papers of Prof. James E. Thorold Rogers and family.)

ROSEBERY MSS, National Library of Scotland, Edinburgh.

ROUS MSS, Ipswich and East Suffolk Record Office, Ipswich. (The papers of the Earls of Stradbroke.)

SATOW MSS (Sir Ernest), Public Record Office, London.

SELBORNE MSS, Lambeth Palace Library. (Papers of the first Earl of Selborne.) (Ref.: MSS 1861–1906.)

——Bodleian Library, Oxford. (Papers of the second and third Earls of Selborne.) (Ref.: MSS Selborne; MSS Selborne Adds.; MSS Eng. hist; MSS Eng. lett; MSS Eng. misc.)

SHARPE MSS, University College, London. (The papers of the Rogers, Sharpe, Reid, and Kenrick families.)

SHERBROOKE (LOWE) MSS, seen by kind permission of Mrs R. T. Sneyd at her home in Hinton Charterhouse.

SOMERVILLE MSS, Bodleian Library, Oxford.

STANHOPE MSS, Kent Archives Office, Maidstone.

TAIT MSS, Lambeth Palace Library. (The papers of Archibald Campbell Tait, Archbishop of Canterbury.)

TALBOT MSS, Kent Archives Office, Maidstone.

TREVELYAN MSS, consulted at the Robinson Library, University of Newcastle upon Tyne, by kind permission of the Trevelyan family.

WALLAS MSS (Graham Wallas), British Library of Political and Economic Science, London.

WARD MSS, University College Library, London.

——Pusey House, Oxford.

WENTWORTH MSS, British Library, London. (The family papers of Wilfrid Scawen Blunt and Lady Anne Blunt.)

INDEX

Compiled by John Hooper

Abel-Smith, Brian 100, 103
Abercromby, Lady 159
Aberdeen, Catherine Lady 321
Aberdeen, Lord 321–2
abnormal grief, *see* chronic and abnormal
  grief
Acland family 52, 83, 103, 151, 314, 326
Acland, Agnes (m. Fred Anson) 27, 51–2,
  104, 151, 202, 305
Acland, Lieut. Gilbert (Gib) 27, 104
Acland, Harry 306
Acland, Dr Henry Wentworth (later 1st
  Bt.) 23, 68, 104, 107, 115–16, 159, 309
Acland, Herbert (Herbie) 26, 68–9, 278
Acland, Mary Lady 27, 104, 151, 202
Acland, Sarah (*née* Cotton, wife of Sir
  Henry Acland) 27, 68–9, 83, 102, 104,
  218, 272, 278, 306
Acland, Sarah Angelina (Angie) 26, 104, 159
Acland, Sir Thomas Dyke, 10th Bt. 103,
  122, 215
Acland, Willie 69
Acton, Lord 316
addiction, fear of 91
Adventure of Death, The 94
'affective revolution' (Lawrence Stone) 276
Affleck, Mary Lady 149
afterlife, *see* heaven
Age of Atonement, The 274
agnostics 9, 11, 12, 54, 55, 58, 59, 60, 61–2,
  86, 95, 179, 183, 186, 193, 198, 208, 220,
  266, 269, 273, 276, 284, 286, 314, 315,
  339–57, 358, 360, 366, 367
Aids epidemic 97
Albert, Prince (Prince Consort) 27, 318–21
alcohol 6, 83, 84, 86, 89, 90, 92, 102, 166;
  see also brandy; champagne
alcoholism 102, 147, 251
Aldenham, Lady 243
Aldenham, Lord 53, 236
Allan, Mabel A. 335
Allen, Dr John 246, 248
Ampthill, Emily Lady 232, 331
anaesthesia 78
Anatomy Act 7
Anderson, Dr 114

Anderson, Michael 143, 230, 253
Anderson, Olive 70
angels 48, 123, 126, 128, 131, 173, 175, 243,
  289, 311
Anglican(s)/Anglicanism 9, 18, 19–20, 23,
  25, 30, 31, 32, 34, 39, 42, 43, 53, 55, 65, 67,
  70, 71, 75, 119, 124, 128, 161, 178, 198,
  207, 216, 219, 222, 237, 241, 257, 263,
  267, 268, 269, 273, 274–5, 277, 303, 323,
  360, 365, 367, 370, 375
Ann, a servant 102
Annan, Noel 3
anniversaries 138, 141, 145, 219, 263, 293–4,
  322, 337, 345, 351, 366
Ansell, Charles 144
Ansell, R. C. 121
Anson, Adelaide 113
Anson, Agnes, *see* Acland, Agnes
Anson, Fred (m. Agnes Acland) 51
antibiotics 47, 78
antisepsis 78
Antrim, Dowager Lady 69
Antrim, Louisa Lady 69, 276
appendicitis 360
Argyll, Duchess of 66
Argyll, 8th Duke of 57–8, 66
Ariès, Philippe 7–8, 41, 318–19
Armistice Day 379
Arnold, Edwin 267–8
ars moriendi 17, 18, 19, 33
Art of Dying, The 33
Ashley, Lady Constance 306
aspirin 86, 87
Asquith, H. H. 372
Asquith, Margot 158
Asquith, Raymond 372, 374
assassination 178, 239, 316, 318, 323, 326,
  328, 329, 330, 332, 334, 338
atheist/atheism 86, 339, 340, 341, 342, 343,
  353, 360
Atholl, Louisa Duchess of 114, 211
Atkinson, Henry 340
Austen, Jane 306
autobiography 341
autopsy 64
Avebury, Countess, *see* Lubbock, Alice

447

Babbage, Charles 63
'bad deaths' 46, 59–76, 182–3, 325–6, 358, 373–8, 380; *see also* sudden death; suicide; World War I
Bailey, Sarah 53
Balfour family 367
Balfour, Arthur J. 5, 57, 179, 233, 296–7, 308, 366, 369
Balfour, Betty 54
Balfour, Blanche 232
Balfour, Frances 3, 57–8, 153, 331, 366
Balfour, Gerald 296
Baptists 19
Barham, Mary 315
Barnes, Dr 108
Barwell, Dr 101, 215
Bathurst, Lord 313
Battersea, Lady 203, 244
Battersea, Lord 244
Battiscombe, Georgina 163
Battley's Sedative Solution (Battly) 89
Baugh, Mr 254
Baxter, Revd Richard 44, 268
Beaconsfield, Lord, *see* Disraeli, Benjamin
Beagle 343
Bebbington, David 20
Beckett, Dr Samuel (surgeon) 31, 36, 41, 46, 288
Bede, Adam 18
Bedford, Duke of 207
Belgium, King of 319
Bell, Edith 104
Bell, Sir Hugh 362
Benenden Letters 195
Benham, Revd (later Canon) William 140, 265
Benson, Edward White, Archbishop of Canterbury 139
Benson, Martin 139
Benson, Mary 139, 271
Bentinck, George 236
bequests, *see* commemorative bequests; wills
Bergeron family 293
Bergeron, Emma (*née* Haden) 293, 335–8
Berkeley, Mary (*née* Dashwood) 157–8
Berridge, Virginia 86
Best, Geoffrey 20, 23
Bickersteth family 119, 370, 375, 376, 377, 379
Bickersteth, Burgon 370, 378

Bickersteth, Ella 370–1, 377–8
Bickersteth, Julian 377–8
Bickersteth, Morris 371, 376–9
Bickersteth, Ralph 371, 378
Bickersteth, Revd Samuel (Sam) 377–9
Birks, Elizabeth 119
Blackstone, Sir William 295
Blake, Dr 115
blister 92
Blunt family 9, 224, 343
Blunt, Alice, 31–2, 103, 212, 224, 289–90
Blunt, Lady Anne (*née* Annabella King, dau. of Ada Lovelace) 38, 65, 212, 219, 236, 286, 289–90, 293, 341
Blunt, Elsie 305
Blunt, Francis 31–2, 38, 90–1, 113, 219, 289–90, 340–1
Blunt, Mary 219
Blunt, Wilfrid Scawen 9, 31, 60, 65, 90–1, 219, 266, 289–90, 340–1, 357
Booth, Mary 340
Boswell 296
Bowlby, John 231–2, 237, 251, 320, 344
Bowles, a servant 100
Bradlaugh, Charles 341, 342
Brandon, Ruth 366
brandy 47, 83–5
Branks, Revd William 273–4
Bright, Dr 106
British Cremation Society 203, 204–7
Brodie, Sir Benjamin 82, 85, 111, 149
bronchitis 120, 367
Brontë family 8, 41
Brontë, Charlotte 40
Brontë, Emily 40
Brown, Revd James Baldwin 267–8
Browne, Dr Oswald 85, 88, 98
Brunel, Isambard Kingdom 237
Brunel, Mary (*née* Horsley) 214, 237, 289
Brunton, Dr 58
Bryce, James 316
Bryce, Marion 149, 316
Bryce, Mary 316
Buckland, Minnie 104
Bunny, Dr 106
Burdett-Coutts, William 290
burial 7, 70, 73–4, 75, 126, 129, 170, 198, 199, 204, 207, 213, 214, 215, 216, 219, 220, 221, 223, 225, 335, 357, 374, 379, 380
burial-service, *see* funeral service
Burlingham, Ada 236

Burne-Jones, Sir Edward 40, 297
Butler, Revd A. G. 288
Butler, Josephine 331
Butler, Samuel 3
Butler, W. J., Canon of Worcester 211
Buttar, Dr Charles 86
Byng, Winifred 241, 254
Byron, Lady 62-5, 89-90, 101, 298, 341, 365
Byron, Lord 61, 215

Cairns, Lady 276
Cameron, Miss, a servant 211
Campbell family 66
Campbell, Lady Colin 200, 221
Campbell-Bannerman, Sir Henry 144
cancer 12, 37, 41, 53, 61-2, 80, 86, 87, 89,
    91, 93, 95, 103, 104, 112, 113, 143, 144, 183,
    184, 233, 252, 255, 288, 298
Cane, Caroline 100, 281, 316
Cane, Louisa 35, 100, 281, 308-9
Cane, Richard 309
cannabis 89
Cannadine, David 1, 7, 8, 302, 319, 358,
    379-80
Canning, Lady 255
Canning, Lord 319
Canterbury, Lord 80
Cape, Dr 112
Cardwell, Lady 299, 307-8
Carlisle family 211
Carlisle, Bishop of 198
Carlisle, Lady 221
Carlisle, Lord 54
Carnarvon, 3rd Earl of (1800-49) 106-7,
    117
Carnarvon, 4th Earl of (1831-90) 92,
    113-14, 214, 219, 226, 252, 254, 256,
    260-2, 264, 271, 294
Carnarvon, Elizabeth (Elsie) Lady (*née*
    Howard, 2nd wife of 4th Earl) 226, 262
Carnarvon, Evelyn Lady (1st wife of 4th
    Earl) 28, 260-1
Carnarvon, Henrietta Lady (wife of 3rd Earl
    and dowager Countess 1849-76) 27, 92,
    106-7, 117, 214
Carpenter, Dr Alfred 32, 111, 116
Carrington, Charles Lord 27
Carrington, Lady 35
Carrington, 'Minim' (Lord Carrington's
    sister) 27
Carus, Revd William 24

Casciolini 219
Cassell's Household Guide 79, 199, 201, 202,
    221, 223
catacombs 68
Catholic(s)/Catholicism 7-8, 9, 17-18, 21,
    31-2, 43, 59, 60, 85, 110, 208, 219-20,
    266, 267, 268, 340, 341, 359
Cavendish family 66, 330
Cavendish, Edward 149
Cavendish, Lady Frederick (Lucy Caroline,
    'Locket', *née* Lyttelton) 66, 75, 164, 176,
    177, 178, 193, 238, 239, 263, 299, 316,
    318-19, 321, 322-34, 338
Cavendish, Lord Frederick (Fred/Freddy)
    178, 291, 297, 324, 326, 329-30, 332-3
Cavendish, Richard 30
Cecil family 153
Cecil, Alice 153
Cecil, Gwendolen 219
Cecil, Hugh 271
Cecil, James 153
Cecil, Violet 159
Cecil, William, Bishop of Exeter 372
cemetery 199, 208, 214, 291, 292-3, 294,
    335, 337, 342
Cenotaph (London) 379
Chadwick, Edwin 144, 195, 199, 200, 213
Chadwick, Owen 3-4, 282-3
Chamberlain family 222
Chamberlain, Agnes 222
Chamberlain, Austen 294-5
Chamberlain, Ethel 295
Chamberlain, Joseph 222, 294, 322
Chamberlain, Mary (*née* Endicott, 3rd wife
    of Joseph Chamberlain) 222, 294-5, 306,
    322
Chamberlain, Walter 222
Chambers, Dr 106
champagne 47, 83
charity 236
Charlotte, a servant 100
Charteris family 370, 375, 376, 379; *see also*
    Elcho; Wemyss
Charteris, Mary (dau. of Lady Wemyss)
    375
Charteris, Yvo 375-6
Chaunu, Pierre 1, 7
Chief Secretary for Ireland 326
child deaths 5, 12, 119-42, 151, 160, 168-70,
    237, 265, 277-80, 293, 313, 338, 339, 343,
    345, 348, 350, 356, 360, 367

children's views of death 132–5
Childers, Mrs Hugh 202
Childers, Katharine 52
chloroform 89, 92, 183
cholera 40, 78
Christ, *see* Jesus Christ
Christian consolations 265–83; *see also* heavenly reunion
Christian Defence against the Fears of Death, The 19
Christian Guardian and Church of England Magazine 22, 33, 34
Christian Remembrancer 40
Christian Year, The 43, 48, 281–2
chronic and abnormal grief 7, 66, 68, 69, 74, 318–38
Church of England, *see* Anglican
Church of Scotland 3
Churchill, Lady Randolph 256
Clarendon, Lady 102
Clark, Dr Andrew (later Sir) 113, 182
Clark, Sir James 112
Clear Shining Light 22, 23, 165
Clemens, Louisa 35
Clifford, Harriet Agnes, Baroness de 232, 241, 243
Cobbe, Frances Power 149, 207
Cockshut, A. O. J. 357
coffin 196, 199, 202, 203, 207, 212, 213, 214, 217, 218, 219, 220, 222, 289, 297, 350
Coleman, D. C. 371
Coleridge family 52
Coleridge, Fred 52
Coleridge, Henry J. 52, 240
Coleridge, J. D. 240–1
College of Physicians 109
Collier, Marion (*née* Huxley) 356
Colville family 68
Colville, Caroline 68
Colville, George 68
Colville, Henry 68
commemorative bequests/keepsakes 295–9
commemorative jewellery 298–9
Communion of Saints 275
Complete Duty of Man, The 29
Comte, Auguste 359
condolence letters 9, 187, 193, 210, 215–16, 244, 246, 262, 275, 277, 281–2, 286, 300, 303, 307–17, 326, 330, 333, 344–5, 372
Congregationalists 19, 141, 267
Connolly, Constance 52

consolation literature 122–3, 141–2, 336
consolations of widowhood 240–4, 262, 265
consultant physicians 47, 77, 79, 87, 98, 105–8, 112, 175, 179
consumption, *see* tuberculosis
Contemporary Review 203
contraception 207
Conway, Canon William 202
Cooper, Beth, nurse 139
Cornish, George 76, 80, 282
Cornwallis-West, George 256
coroner 71
coroners' juries 70, 72
Cotton, Sarah 241
Cotton, William 102, 218
Courtauld, Ruth 35
Courtauld, Sarah 5
Courtauld, Sarah 5
Courtaulds 300–1, 302, 304
Courtney, Kate (*née* Potter) 47, 55–6, 145, 154, 160, 208, 227, 283, 311
Cowell-Stepney, Margaret 'Maggie', *see* Stepney, Lady
Cowper, Anne Lady 54, 158, 243, 306
Cowper, Lord 144, 217, 243, 306
cremation/-ists 12, 193, 202, 203–9, 357, 372
Cremation Act (1902) 205, 206, 208
Cripps, Blanche 215
Cripps, Theresa 47
Crofts, Mary 271
Cromer, Lord 253
Crosse, John 63, 297
Cumberbatch, Dr 258
Curl, James Stevens 194, 223

Dante 374
Danvers, Charlotte 122
Darwin family 9, 339, 343, 351, 353
Darwin, Annie 220, 346–8, 349, 350, 356
Darwin, Charles 9, 198, 208, 220–1, 271, 282, 286, 339, 343–52, 353, 355, 356, 357, 363, 365
Darwin, Charles Waring (son of Charles Darwin) 345
Darwin, Emma (*née* Wedgwood) 198, 271, 286, 343, 345–50, 356, 357
Darwin, Erasmus 86
Darwin, Henrietta 346, 348, 349
Darwin, Mary 345
Darwin, Dr Robert 343–4
Darwin, Susan 345

Darwinism 276, 339, 353
Dashwood, George Henry, MP 156–8, 218
Dashwood, Revd Henry 218
Dashwood King, Sir John 156–8, 200, 219
Davidoff, Leonore 2
Davidson, Randall 140
Davies, Revd Charles Maurice 342
Dawnay, Guy 245
Dawnay, Lewis 29, 243, 244–5
Dawnay, Victoria 223, 233, 243, 244–5, 294, 305
Death and the Enlightenment 17
death-bed attendants 27, 84–5, 130, 132, 152, 166–7; *see also* servants at the death-bed
death-bed farewells 7, 44, 117–18, 131, 169–70, 340
death-bed memorials 10–11, 25, 128–39, 151, 164–89
death-bed portrait 257, 288, 289–90, 291, 378
Death-Bed Scenes 25
Death-Bed Thoughts 33
death certificate 155, 182, 204, 213
death denial 209, 380
death duties 245, 303
Death, Heaven and the Victorians 194
death in childbirth 181–2, 260, 296, 309, 331, 334, 335, 367
death in surgery 183
death-mask/bust 288, 290–1
death of children, *see* child deaths
death-rate, *see* mortality rates
death, sudden, *see* sudden death
dementia (senile) 57–8, 155–8, 186, 219
demography 5–6, 46–7, 143–4, 230
depression 71, 72, 74, 153, 183, 186, 231, 241, 251, 256, 261, 305, 320–1, 324–5, 343, 344, 351, 352, 369–70; *see also* manic depression
Desborough, Ettie Lady 119
Desmond, Adrian 353
devil 21, 22, 23, 342, 354–5
Devonshire, Duke of 328
diabetes 41
diarrhoea 120
Dickens, Charles 7, 24, 36, 37, 102, 301
Diderot 359
digitalis 92
Dilke family 207
Dilke, Sir Charles 207, 260
Dilke, 1st Lady 207

diphtheria 113
Disce Mori: Learn to Die 19
diseases 40, 46, 55, 59, 77, 78, 100, 335; *see also* cancer; fever; puerperal fever; scarlet fever; tuberculosis; etc.
Disraeli, Benjamin (Lord Beaconsfield) 32, 144, 197–8, 261, 320
Disraeli, Isaac 298
Disraeli, Mary Anne 198
Disraeli, Sarah 252
Dissenters, *see* nonconformists
doctor(s) 6, 24, 26, 27, 28, 31, 32, 36, 41, 55–6, 57–8, 60, 66, 70, 72, 77–97, 98, 101–2, 105–18, 131, 132, 153, 155, 157–8, 166, 169, 171–2, 179, 183, 184–5, 203, 206, 207, 223, 224, 237, 249, 312, 320, 343–4, 355, 369
Doddridge, Philip 281
Donegall, Marquess of 314
Douglas, Fanny 302
Dover's Powder 86, 169
Doyle, Sir Arthur Conan 371
Drelincourt, Charles 19
Drew, Berthe 283
Drew, Revd Harry 185, 187, 225, 238, 239, 242, 269, 276, 295, 296
Drew, Mary (*née* Gladstone) 152–3, 164, 179, 180, 181, 182, 183, 184–9, 203, 232, 237–8, 239, 242, 243, 262, 263–4, 283, 291, 296–7, 310, 324–5, 326, 327–8, 329–30, 331, 332–3, 369
dropsy 92
Drummond, Adelaide 35
Dugdale, Alice 53–4
Duncan, Dr Matthews 110, 182
Durkheim, Emile 71
Dyson, Rosie 239

Early Death 123
Earth to Earth Society 204
Eddy, Daniel C., DD 41
Edward VII, King 145, 306–7
Edwards, Griffith 86
Egerton, Lady Louisa 331
Elam, Dr Charles 78
Elcho, Hugo (Ego) Lord 375–6, 380
Elcho, Letty Lady 376
Eliot, George 18
Elliot, Janet (*née* Somerville) 284, 292
Elliot, Katharine Anne 287
Elliott, H. V. 313

Ellison, Lt.-Col. Robert 278
embalming 207
Empress of Russia 307
enema 84
Enlightenment 70, 71, 109, 359
epidemics 78
epitaph 215, 220, 269
erysipelas 166
ether 90
ethics 91, 93–5, 109–10
Etiquette of Good Society 200
euthanasia 81, 82–6, 92–5
Euthanasia : or Medical Treatment in Aid of an Easy Death 82–6, 88, 93
Evangelical Magazine (1793–1892) 21–2, 24, 33
Evangelicalism 2–5, 11, 17–38, 39, 47, 49, 50, 51–2, 59, 77, 82, 84, 118, 128, 130, 132, 133, 136, 161–89 *passim*, 246, 314, 339, 358
Evans, Dr, consultant physician 175
evolution, theory of 268, 339
executors of wills 76, 195, 249
Exercises of Holy Dying, see *The Rule and Exercises of Holy Dying*

Fading Away 40
Fair Rosamund 40
Fairfax, Captain Henry 241
Fairfax, Margaret Lady 200
Fairfax, Mary 119
Fairfax, Montgomerie 311
Falconer, Prof. Hugh 345, 352
family reunions, *see* heavenly reunion
Farr, William 46, 120, 253–4
Fazakerley, Eleanor 10, 100, 278–9
Fazakerley, Ellen 278–9
feather-man 195, 196, 199, 203
Ferguson, Dr 102
Ferriar, Dr 92
fever 36, 41, 78, 92, 117, 147, 166, 168, 171, 179, 199, 335, 345, 346, 347, 360
Final Triumph 33
Fitzhugh, Emily 63
Flounders, Mary 270
Flower, Constance 316
Forbes, Edward 354
Forster, E. M. 11
Fortnightly Review 93, 267–8, 372
Fox family (at Holland House) 227–8, 246–8, 286
Fox, Caroline 9, 37, 101, 145, 146, 149–50, 246–7, 248, 252

Fox, General Charles 228, 246, 247, 249, 255, 316
Fox, Charles James 101, 149, 197, 200, 246
Fox, Elizabeth 149–50, 200
Fox, Henry E. (4th Baron Holland), *see* Holland
Fox, Lady Mary 246, 316
Fox, William (Charles Darwin's cousin) 344–5
Franciscan 219, 290
Franqueville, Count de 255–6
free thinkers, *see* agnostics
Freeborn, Dr W. D. 83
French Revolution 57
funeral(s) 12, 80, 120, 126, 127, 130, 132, 136, 138, 170, 173, 183, 184, 188, 193, 194–203, 210, 216–29, 244, 262, 263, 294, 295, 303–4, 307, 316, 328, 337, 340, 341, 342, 344, 348, 350, 351, 363, 371–2, 375, 379; *see also* state funeral
Funeral and Mourning Reform Association, *see* National Funeral and Mourning Reform Association
funeral attendants 195, 220, 221; *see also* mutes
funeral costs 195–7, 199–202, 223, 224, 235; *see also* funeral extravagance
Funeral Customs 194, 372
funeral extravagance 194–200, 216, 223, 225, 304, 306
funeral feast 223–4
funeral haberdashery/millinery 196, 199, 202, 203, 216
funeral reform/reformer 194, 196, 199–200, 216, 305, 371
funeral sermon 198
funeral service 29, 75, 130, 132, 138, 170, 183, 188, 196, 198, 216, 218, 219, 221, 263, 342, 350, 357, 361
funeral week, 210–29, 316
Funerals of the Quakers, The 220
Furneaux, Robin 30
Fussell, Paul 10

Gainford, Ethel Lady 53, 371
Galton, Arthur 208
Galton, Francis 208, 365
Gamp, Mrs 102
Gandy, Richard Norris (son of Mary Ann Rogers) 147, 252, 291
Garibaldi 363
Gates Ajar, The 274

gendered experiences 12, 98–104, 136–41, 147, 212, 219, 221, 230–64, 286–7

Gentlewoman 301

George, Dr 101

germ theory 78

ghost 321

Giberne, Emily 91

Gildeas, Capt. G. H. 299

Giles, Dr 175, 177, 178, 179

Gipp, Mr 129, 132

Gittings, Clare 223

Gladstone (W. E. Gladstone family of Hawarden Castle) 11, 32, 66, 71, 111, 161, 167, 179, 181, 183, 184, 186–9, 314, 322, 332, 347, 349, 365

Gladstone (and Lyttelton) family tree 162

Gladstone, Agnes, *see* Wickham

Gladstone, Anne (mother of W. E. Gladstone) 161–3, 165–8, 181

Gladstone, Anne (sister of W. E. Gladstone) 166

Gladstone, Annie (m. Stephen Gladstone) 296

Gladstone, Catherine (m. W. E. Gladstone, *née* Glynne) 27, 66, 163–4, 168–70, 174, 176, 177, 179–80, 183, 185, 186–7, 233–4, 323, 324, 328, 329, 349

Gladstone, Gertrude (m. William H. Gladstone) 233–4, 244, 294

Gladstone, Helen 91, 100, 107, 185, 188, 296, 330

Gladstone, Henry 244

Gladstone, Herbert 185, 186, 203, 238, 244, 294

Gladstone, Jessy 111, 164–5, 168–71, 173, 181, 184, 287, 347, 348, 354, 355

Gladstone, Sir John (father of W. E. Gladstone) 33, 35, 84, 100, 101, 107, 161, 171–3, 188, 201

Gladstone, John (brother of W. E. Gladstone) 166

Gladstone, Lord, *see* Gladstone, Herbert

Gladstone, Mary, *see* Drew, Mary

Gladstone, Revd Stephen 32, 185, 326

Gladstone, Tom (brother of W. E. Gladstone) 166, 167

Gladstone, William Ewart (W. E.) 10, 27, 30, 32, 61, 84, 91, 99, 107, 111, 144, 161, 162–74, 177, 178, 179, 181, 183–9, 197, 203, 225, 234, 244, 269, 280, 283, 287, 296, 323, 326–7, 328, 329, 332, 347, 348, 354, 355, 361, 366, 368

Gladstone, Lieut. William G. C. (Will, grandson of W. E. Gladstone) 187–8, 244

Gladstone, William Henry (Willy, son of W. E. Gladstone) 165, 170, 183–4, 233–4, 244

Gladstone (King/Gladstone/Ramsay MacDonald family):

Gladstone, Dr John Hall (m. Margaret King) 46–9, 270, 292

Gladstone, Jane May (1st wife of Dr J. H. Gladstone) 113, 160, 270

Gladstone, Margaret (*née* King, 2nd wife of Dr J. H. Gladstone; died 1870) 28, 46–9, 79, 103, 292

Gladstone, Margaret (m. Ramsay MacDonald, daughter of Margaret Gladstone *née* King, died 1911), *see* MacDonald, Margaret

Glasier, Katharine Bruce 252, 255

Gloucester, Bishop of 275

Gloucester, Duchess of 306

Glynne family 163, 175

Glynne, Revd Henry 32, 177

Godding, Miss, governess 129, 131, 132

Godfrey's Cordial 86

Good Shepherd, The 296

Girton College, Cambridge 332

'good death', 20th-century perception 117–18

'good death', Victorian ideal of 2–3, 8, 11, 17–38, 39–58, 59, 76, 77, 81, 161, 165, 168, 171, 173, 175–6, 178, 179–80, 183, 185, 186, 189, 381

Goodfellow, Dr 108, 129, 131

Gordon, Sir William 211

Gorer, Geoffrey 301, 320–1

Gosse, Edmund 3

Goulburn family 50, 277, 280, 313, 314

Goulburn, Edward 30, 114, 313

Goulburn, Revd Edward Meyrick 313

Goulburn, Frederick 101, 114, 201, 222

Goulburn, Henry, MP (Chancellor of the Exchequer in Peel's Cabinet) 29, 42, 114–15, 196, 201, 277, 280, 309–10, 312–13, 315

Goulburn, Henry ('Harry', son of Henry Goulburn MP) 30, 35, 42, 43, 180, 196, 199, 201, 277–80, 281, 298, 308, 312–13

Goulburn, Jane (wife of Henry Goulburn, MP) 28, 30, 35, 222, 277–80, 281, 338

Goulburn, Jane (daughter of Henry Goulburn MP) 28, 222, 281, 308

Graham, Dr 137
Graham, James 227
Granville, Dr A. B. 68
Granville, Charles 68
grave 69, 73–4, 125, 139, 198, 200, 202, 204, 208, 220, 222, 223, 258, 259, 275, 291–5, 322, 328, 335, 337, 342, 348, 361
grave visiting 74, 125, 139, 258–9, 291–5, 318, 337, 348
gravestone 215, 291–2
graveyard, *see* cemetery
Great War, *see* World War I
Greens, Miss, three nurses 104
Greig, Agnes 65, 66, 211, 212, 227, 232, 236, 241, 290, 305, 311
Greig, Woronzow 66, 212, 227, 232, 241, 243, 290, 291
Grenfell, Alethea 53
Grenfell, Sir Francis 253
Grenfell, Henry 53
Grenfell, Julian 375
Grenfell, Lady 253
Greville, Charles 247, 249
grief/grieving 1, 2, 4, 5, 7, 9, 11, 12, 137, 193, 210, 222, 230–50, 252, 265, 276, 284, 311, 344, 346, 349, 351, 352, 354, 355, 370, 374, 375, 380
grief, stages of 193, 210, 217, 231–5, 237, 252, 259, 278–81, 284, 288, 307, 318, 328, 333, 336–7, 339–40
Grosvenor, Lord 28, 123
Grosvenor, Sibell 283
Guest, Lady Charlotte 99
Guest, Sir John 99
Guides to Sources for British History 9
Gully, Dr James 346–7
Gurnhill, Revd J. 71
Guthrie, Dr 107, 167, 172
Guy, Dr William 144

Haden family 255
Haden, Charles, surgeon 125, 335
Haden, Emma 193, 281, 318–19, 321, 335–8
Haden, Sir Francis Seymour 202, 204, 205, 206, 335
Haden, Mary 314
Haden, Rose, *see* Horsley, Rose
Hafferty, F. W. 97
Hagley Record 164–5, 174–89, 297
Haldane, Elizabeth 3, 146, 244, 305
Haldane, Mary 146, 244

Halford, Sir Henry 6, 82, 84, 85, 86, 91, 108–9, 110, 111
Hallam, Arthur 282
Halliday, nurse 179
Hamilton, Edward 297
hanging 72
Hankey, General 276
Harcourt family 100, 259–60, 314
Harcourt, Lady Anne 272
Harcourt, Aubrey 316
Harcourt, Edward (Archbishop of York, Sir William's grandfather) 273
Harcourt, Edward (Sir William's brother) 52, 259
Harcourt, Egerton 202, 259, 291
Harcourt, Lady Elizabeth Cabot Ives (2nd wife of Sir William) 36, 260
Harcourt, Emily 37, 100, 213, 215, 309
Harcourt, Col. Henry 30, 272
Harcourt, Julian 102, 215, 257, 258
Harcourt, Laura 218, 221, 242
Harcourt, Lewis (Sir William's son) 213, 257, 260
Harcourt, Louisa 99, 122
Harcourt, Marie-Thérèse (Thérèse, *née* Lister, 1st wife of Sir William Harcourt) 213–14, 221, 257–9, 308–11
Harcourt, Mathilda M. (Sir William's mother) 237, 257–8
Harcourt, May (Mary, m. Lewis Harcourt 1899) 236
Harcourt, Lady Susan (*née* Holroyd) 310
Harcourt, Sir William (1827–1904, barrister and Liberal politician, k. 1873) 36, 80, 100, 213, 215, 237, 256, 257–60, 261, 264, 292, 298, 308, 309, 310
Harcourt, Revd (later Canon) William Vernon (1789–1871, father of Sir William) 28, 30, 99, 122, 216, 236, 282
Harkness, Maggie (*née* Potter) 56
Harris, Jose 4, 124, 358
Harrison, Frederic 359–60, 362
Havelock, Sir Henry 33
hearse 196, 197, 199, 201, 220
hearse-pages 195, 196, 197
heart disease/attack 41, 66, 68, 69, 92, 115, 143, 160, 174, 323, 341, 354
heaven 7, 12, 17, 18, 22, 34, 37, 43, 44–5, 48, 59, 64, 85, 120, 123, 124, 125, 126, 128, 131, 133, 134, 135, 136, 137, 138, 139, 140, 146, 149, 156, 160, 170, 172, 173, 176, 177, 180,

193, 218, 240, 241, 242, 258, 266–83, 310,
    311, 328, 335, 337, 338, 339–40, 342, 349,
    352, 353, 359, 360, 370, 381
Heaven: A History 266
Heaven our Home 273
heavenly reunion 45, 48, 49, 123, 125–7, 132,
    135, 137, 139, 140, 152, 156, 160, 171, 173,
    183, 187, 193, 218, 240, 241, 242, 250, 256,
    257, 265, 266–83, 310, 315, 332, 347, 349,
    352, 355, 356, 360, 362, 377
hell 7, 12, 17, 18, 21, 59–61, 64, 266, 268,
    273, 274, 276, 302, 339, 340, 342, 343,
    350, 374
Henderson, Mr, consultant physician 112
Henry VII 194
Henslow, Prof. John S. 220, 286, 351
Henson, Revd H. H. 71
Herbert, Auberon 310
Herbert, Dolly, *see* Herbert, Florence
Herbert, Elizabeth 30
Herbert, Florence ('Dolly') 54, 158, 217
Herbert, Mary 316
Herbert, Reginald (Reggie) 297
Herbert, Rolf 217
heroin 86
Hervey, Captain F. F. 242
Heterodox London 342
Hewitt, Dr, consultant 47
Hilton, Boyd 274
Hinton, John 27, 66, 77, 82, 87, 91, 97,
    210, 301
Hobhouse, Lady 160
Hodge, Mrs 289
Holland, Augusta Lady (wife of 4th
    Baron) 228
Holland, Elizabeth Lady (wife of 3rd
    Baron) 60, 228–9, 245–9, 253–4, 286
Holland, Henry Fox, 3rd Baron
    (1773–1840) 37, 145, 200, 211, 228–9, 245,
    246–7, 248, 310
Holland, Henry E. Fox, 4th Baron
    (1802–1859) 78, 121, 228–9, 246, 247,
    248, 249, 286
Holland, Sir Henry 88, 92, 110
Holt, Robert 311
Holyoake, Austin 341–2, 343
Home Secretary 205
honour rolls (World War I) 378
Hood, Thomas 235
Hooker family 9, 339
Hooker, Fanny (*née* Henslow) 351

Hooker, Joseph Dalton 9, 159, 286, 339,
    343, 345, 350–2, 355, 356, 357, 361, 363,
    365
Hooker, Minnie 350–1
Horne, Bishop 30
Horsley family 50, 124, 142, 255, 256, 289,
    294, 302–3, 314, 347, 349
Horsley, Charles 314
Horsley, Edward 45, 124, 125–6, 314
Horsley, Elizabeth 99, 102, 213, 221, 237,
    257, 294, 303, 335
Horsley, Elvira 43–6, 47, 124–7, 214,
    217–18, 223–4, 255, 294
Horsley, Emma 127
Horsley, Frank 124, 127, 290, 303, 314
Horsley, Harry 126–7, 290
Horsley, Hugh 127, 303
Horsley, John Callcott 44–6, 124–7, 129,
    138, 213, 214, 216, 217–18, 255, 256–7, 278,
    280, 287, 289, 290, 294, 297, 303, 314–15,
    338, 347, 352
Horsley, Rose (*née* Haden, 2nd wife of J. C.
    Horsley) 125–7, 202, 213, 214, 255, 293,
    294, 303, 335
Horsley, Sophy 214, 217, 219, 237, 303–4,
    335
Horsley, Walter 303
Horsley, William 213, 221, 224–5, 303
hospice 87, 97, 104
hospitals 78, 96, 103, 183
Houghton, Walter 2, 24
Houlbrooke, Ralph 7, 18, 224
Hour of our Death, The 8
Howard, Geoffrey 54, 91
Hudson, Revd Cyril 370
Hufeland, Prof. C. W. 82, 87–8, 93, 105,
    108, 109, 110, 117
Humphreys, Revd John 33
Hunt, William Holman 40
Hunter, Charlie 53
Hunter, Dr 166
Hüppauf, Bernd 374
Hutton, R. H. 267, 360
Huxley family 9, 339
Huxley, Dr 113
Huxley, Henrietta ('Nettie') 353–6
Huxley, Leonard 354, 356
Huxley, Noel 350, 354–5, 356
Huxley, Thomas Henry 9, 196, 339, 340,
    343, 348, 350, 352–7, 360, 361, 365, 366
hydrophobia 82

hymn 48, 133, 134–5, 151, 180, 185, 220, 223, 266, 267, 270, 281, 309, 323, 360
hypodermic injection 86, 87, 89

Iddesleigh, Cecilia Lady 311
Iddesleigh, Lord 69
Ilchester, William, 4th Earl 307
Illustrations of Political Economy 341
Imitation of Christ, The 297
immortality 3, 12, 124, 265, 266, 267, 272, 273, 276, 283, 315, 340, 341, 342, 352, 353, 355, 356, 359–60, 366, 370; *see also* heaven
In Memoriam 48, 282–3
Infant Pilgrim's Progress 133
Inglis, Ken 379–80
inquest 72, 326
insanity 40, 41, 70, 72, 320, 375
insurance policy 237
intercession 137
Irvine, Mr, clergyman 107

Jameson, Eric 378
jaundice 92, 99
Jay, Elisabeth 7
Jellie, W. H. 141
Jenner, Sir William 320, 321
Jersey, Lady 254
Jesus Christ 3, 4, 18, 22, 29, 31, 34, 37, 42, 45–6, 47, 61, 64, 123, 124, 126, 133, 134, 138, 139, 141, 170, 172, 177, 225, 243, 265, 270, 272, 274, 275, 276, 280, 282, 309, 310, 328, 337–8, 340, 364
Johnstone, Dr 92
Jolly, Mr, consultant physician 106–7
Jones, Sarah 141

Kaye, Dr 254
Keble family 273
Keble, Charlotte 92, 113
Keble, Elizabeth 273
Keble, John 25, 27, 43, 48, 80, 92, 113, 123, 132, 180, 224, 273, 281–2, 291
Keble, 'Kenie' 27
Keble, Thomas 291
Kelvin, Margaret 28
Kelvin, Uncle William 28
Kempis, Thomas à 297
Kenrick family 49, 50
Kenrick, Revd George 51
Kenrick, Revd John 51
Kerison, Lady Caroline 52

kidney disease 47, 55
King, Agnes 152, 155–6, 305
King, Annabella, *see* Blunt, Lady Anne
King, Revd David 46, 49
King, Elizabeth (mother of Margaret Gladstone, *née* King) 47–9, 151–2, 275
King, Elizabeth (sister of Margaret Gladstone, *née* King) 151–2, 155–6, 305
King, Margaret, *see* Gladstone, Margaret
Kingsley, Revd Charles 273, 354–6
Knight, Revd Samuel 33
Knutsford, Lady 53
Koch, Robert 40
Koss, Stephen 370
Kselman, Thomas A. 7
Kübler-Ross, Elisabeth 77, 82, 97

La Traviata 40
Lambert, Dr Edmund 157–8
Lancet 40, 70, 71, 78, 82, 84, 85, 88, 93, 96, 98, 110, 111, 143, 199, 204, 205–8
Lane, Louisa A. 316
Lang, Bernhard 266–7, 268–70, 276
Langton, Catherine (*née* Darwin) 345
Lansdowne, Lady 243
Lansdowne, Lord 310
Last Judgement 266
last words 33–7, 48, 170, 172, 175, 180, 182, 185, 186
Latham, Alice 232
Latham, Dr Peter 80
laudanum (tincture of opium) 86, 89, 90
Lawrence, C. E. 372
Lawrence, Sir William 105
Layard, Sir Henry 99
laying out the body 66, 100, 130, 132, 211–12, 217
Lazarus 48, 133
Leakey family 288
Leakey, Caroline 22, 23, 33
Leakey, Emily 22, 23
Leakey, Sophia 22–3, 288
Leaney, Jennifer 209
Leconfield, Constance 309
Lee, Emma 274–5
Lee, Dr Robert 112
leeches 108, 132
Lewis, Theresa Lady (mother of Marie-Thérèse Harcourt) 102, 258–60, 298
life expectancy, *see* mortality rates
Life of Gladstone 186

Life of Samuel Johnson 296
Lilford, Mary Lady 246
Lincolnshire, Lady 306, 307
Lister family 259–60, 292
Lister, Thomas Villiers 258–9, 292
Litchfield, Henrietta (*née* Darwin) 348
Litten, Julian 194, 371–2
Little Nell 24, 36, 37
Littlewood, Jane 277, 334, 374
Lloyd, Mrs Ann 21
Locock, Dr Charles, consultant 61, 89, 111–13, 168–9, 174–5
Lodge, Sir Oliver 371
Lodge, Raymond 371
Lothian, Concy 299
Loudon, Irvine 105
Lovelace, Ada Lady (daughter of Lord Byron) 9, 61–5, 89–90, 95, 101, 111–13, 215, 254, 266, 269, 273, 286, 288–9, 291, 297, 298, 299, 340, 341
Lovelace, Lord 62–5, 95, 111, 112, 215, 254–5, 298
Lubbock, Alice, Countess Avebury 234–5, 242, 283
Lubbock, Sir John 198
Luckock, Herbert 102, 220, 222
Luckock, Margaret (Maggie) 220
Lumleian Lecture 78, 81
Lupton, Frances 148
Lyell, Sir Charles 220, 352
Lyttelton family 11, 32, 71, 161, 179, 181, 183, 184, 187, 189, 263, 314, 322, 365, 367, 369
Lyttelton (and Gladstone) family tree 162
Lyttelton, Alfred 181–3, 187, 189, 233, 243, 256, 262–4, 296, 315, 331, 334, 352, 363, 366, 367, 368–70
Lyttelton, Antony 367–8
Lyttelton, Arthur 32, 177
Lyttelton, Charles 326
Lyttelton, Christopher 263, 331
Lyttelton, Edith ('D. D.', *née* Balfour, 2nd wife of Alfred Lyttelton) 146, 187, 233, 243, 264, 315, 333, 365, 366–70
Lyttelton, Edward 182
Lyttelton, Aunt Emy (Emily, m. Revd William) 180
Lyttelton, George 4th Baron 5, 71, 92, 163–5, 174–8, 179, 181, 187, 189, 225, 255, 323, 325–6
Lyttelton, Kathleen 297
Lyttelton, Laura (*née* Tennant, 1st wife of

Alfred Lyttelton) 181–3, 262–4, 296, 297, 366, 367, 369
Lyttelton, Lavinia, *see* Talbot
Lyttelton, Lucy, *see* Cavendish, Lady Frederick
Lyttelton, Mary Lady (*née* Glynne, wife of George Lord Lyttelton) 30, 121, 162, 163, 164, 165, 172, 173–8, 179, 181, 188, 189, 218, 255, 297, 323, 366, 379
Lyttelton, Mary (daughter of Alfred Lyttelton) 243, 368
Lyttelton, May 5, 27, 164, 179–81, 187, 189, 297, 310, 323, 324–5, 366
Lyttelton, Meriel, *see* Talbot, Meriel
Lyttelton, Neville 324
Lyttelton, Oliver 243
Lyttelton, Spencer 179, 180, 189, 297
Lyttelton, Sybella Lady 255, 329
Lyttelton, Revd William (Billy) 163, 177, 180, 323

Macaulay, Lord 247
McDannell, Colleen 266–7, 268–70, 276
MacDonald, Keith Norman, MD 302
MacDonald, Michael 70
MacDonald, Ramsay, family 104
MacDonald, David 122, 314
MacDonald, Malcolm 322
MacDonald, Margaret (daughter of Margaret Gladstone *née* King) 52, 104, 122, 151–2, 155, 255, 322, 334
MacDonald, Ramsay 151, 155, 255, 314, 322
Macgregor, Miss 211
Mackenna, Dr Robert W. 92, 94–5, 372
Macleod, Dr 81
McManners, John 7, 17, 194–5, 359
Macmillan, Alec 287
Maddon, Charlotte 98, 102
Madonna of St Sixtus 219
Madras, Bishop of 269
Maeterlinck, Maurice 94, 95, 342–3
Malcolm, Georgiana (*née* Harcourt) 30
manic depression 62, 174
Manners and Social Usages 302
Marquand, David 322
marriage rates (table) 253–4
marriage settlement 235, 236
Married Women's Property Acts (1870, 1882) 295
Marriott, Elizabeth 69
Marriott, Sophia 69

Marsh, Peter 128
Marston, Miss 150
Martin, Dr 102, 114, 208
Martin, Henrietta, governess 309
Martin, upholsterer/undertaker 214, 216
Martineau, Harriet 148, 340, 341, 342, 343
Masterman, Charles F. G. 187, 379
Matthew, Colin 163, 171, 178
Maurice, Priscilla 270, 281
Maxse, Katherine 117
Maxse, Leo 117
measles 120
Medecine and Religion 86
Medical Ethics 88, 93
medical fees 102, 106
Medico-Legal Society 94
medium(s) 365, 366, 371; *see also*
  spiritualism
melancholia, *see* depression
Melbourne, Lord 247, 319
memorial likenesses 288–291
memorials, war, *see* war memorials
memory, as consolation 10, 12, 193, 240,
  242, 256–8, 262, 284–99, 307–15, 331,
  335–7, 347–8, 356, 358, 359–64, 378
memory, social 12, 333, 358, 359–60, 361–4,
  372, 378, 380
meningitis 165, 168, 173, 263, 364
mental illness/disorders 71, 76
Mercer, Edward, DD 372
mercy killing, *see* euthanasia
Merivale, Anna 146, 160
Meryon, Dr 107, 117
mesmerism 62, 90
Methodism 19, 342
Middleton, Agnes 104
Middleton, Jim 252
Middleton, Mary 104
Mildmay, Sybella, *see* Lyttelton, Sybella
  Lady
Millais, John Everett 40, 207
Miller, Prof. 107
Mills, Agnes (*née* Acland) 104
Minto, 4th Earl of 240
Minto, Mary 4th Countess of 232–3,
  239–40, 294
Minto, Nina 3rd Countess of 52, 287
miscarriage 121, 296, 364
Moloney, Mr 290
Montagu, Basil 220, 302
Montagu, Marion 236

Montgomery, Mary Millicent 299
Moore, Agnes 288
Morals of Suicide, The 71
Mordaunt, Lady 51
Mordaunt, Sir Charles 92
More, Hannah 25, 30, 37
Morice, Mary 273
Morley, Countess 202–3, 214
Morley, John (W. E. Gladstone's
  biographer) 185–6, 203, 361
Morley, John (1970s author) 194, 299
Mornington, Earl of 200
Morpeth, Lord 247
morphine/morphia 45, 55, 84, 86, 87, 89,
  90, 94, 176
Morris, Dr, consultant 47
Morselli, Enrico 72
Morshead, Selina Lady 37, 80–1, 100, 260
Morshead, Sir Warwick 80, 252
mortality rates 78, 120–1, 124, 143–4, 160,
  230, 253, 358
mourning-coach 196, 197, 199, 200, 201,
  202, 218, 223
mourning-dress 183, 193, 220, 285, 298, 299,
  300–7, 317, 371, 372; *see also* widows'
  weeds
mourning ritual 1, 7, 12, 183, 193–203,
  210–29, 248, 284, 300–7, 318–22, 371–2,
  380–1
Muller, F. Max 141
Munk, Dr William 6, 77, 81, 82–6, 88, 91,
  92, 93, 95, 96, 97, 102, 109, 110, 111
Mure, Jemima 160
Mure, Kate 160
Murphy, Terence 70
Musgrave, Lady 241
mustard plasters 101
mutes 195, 196, 197, 199, 203
Myers, F. W. H. 366
Myers, Frederic 297

National Funeral and Mourning Reform
  Association 199, 304, 371
National Reformer 342
natural selection, theory of 198, 282, 343
New Testament 268, 271, 274
Newcome, Colonel 24
Newman, John Henry 7, 25
Newman, Mrs, nurse 179
Newsome, David 25, 281–2
Newton 281, 359

Nightingale, Florence 103
Nineteenth Century 267-8, 353, 359
nonconformists 31, 75, 198, 268-9, 270
Norfolk, 2nd Duke of 194
Northumberland, Duke of 197, 199
novels/novelists 11, 18, 24-5, 36, 40, 102,
    181, 301
Noyes, Russell, Jr. 96-7
nurse/nursing 12, 26, 27, 28, 31, 40, 45-6,
    48, 50, 55, 66, 77, 83, 97, 98-104, 107,
    125-6, 131, 139, 147, 159, 166, 168, 171,
    176, 177, 179, 185, 210, 211-12, 346
nursing-home 187, 368-9

Obelkevich, James 371
Observer 196
obsessive grief, *see* chronic and abnormal
    grief
old people's deaths 27, 35, 57-8, 107-8, 119,
    143-60, 165-7, 171-3, 184-7
On the Care of the Dying 85
On Death and How to Divest it of its Terrors
    302
On Life and Death 82
On the Relations of the Physician to the Sick
    109
opium/opiates 6, 47, 61, 62, 83, 86-91, 101,
    113, 166, 169
Origin of Species 282, 343, 353
Othello 95
Ottley, Revd Edward 297
Our Children's Rest 122, 123
Owen, Robert 342
Owen, Wilfrid 374
Oxford movement, *see* Tractarians
oxygen 58, 117

Page, Mr, consultant physician 108
Paget, Sir James 116, 144
Paget, Lady 54
Paget, Revd 276
Paget, Victor 54
palliative care 6, 47, 77, 79, 81, 86-91,
    98-118, 129
Palmer family 48, 50, 68, 69, 71, 75-6, 201,
    221
Palmer, Dorothea (Do) 30, 43-4, 80, 180,
    201, 202, 218, 221, 298
Palmer, Revd Edwin 75, 222
Palmer, Eleanor, *see* Wood, Eleanor
Palmer, Elizabeth 60

Palmer, Emily Frances 43, 218, 298-9
Palmer, Emma 44, 115, 201
Palmer, Revd George Horsley 43, 75-6
Palmer, Henry 67-8
Palmer, John Horsley 80, 252
Palmer, Mary 44, 201, 270, 272
Palmer, Roundell, 1st Earl of Selborne, *see*
    Selborne, Roundell Palmer
Palmer, Thomas 202
Palmer, William (son of Revd William
    Jocelyn Palmer) 43
Palmer, Revd William Jocelyn 43, 44,
    67-8, 80, 201, 202, 224
Palmer, William Waldegrave, 2nd Earl of
    Selborne, *see* Selborne, William
Palmerston, Lord 144
Parker, Caroline 26
Parker, Joseph 288
Parker, Marianne (*née* Darwin) 345
Parker, Robert 100
Parkes, Dr Colin Murray 87, 91, 121, 231-2,
    237, 239, 251, 277, 302, 320-1, 334, 380
Pattison, Frances 53
Pattison, Mark 53, 103
Peach, Mrs, housekeeper 130, 132
Pease, Elsie 222
Pease, Mary Lady 220
Peers, Revd John Witherington 34
Pelling, Margaret 253
Pembroke, Lord 297
pension 235
Percy, Henry 194
Percy, Henry (Harry) 271
Phelps, Elizabeth Stuart 274
philanthropy 159, 331
Philip, Dr 47
Philips, Mr 289
Phillimore, Lady Charlotte 290
Phillipps, Henrietta E. M. 235
Phillips, Mr, physician 113
photographs 288, 289-90, 294, 295, 329, 347
Pilgrim's Progress 133, 270
Plato 296
Playne, Mary (*née* Potter) 56
pleurisy 55
pneumonia 53, 55, 120, 186
Poe, Edgar Allan 41
poetry/poets 28, 33, 40, 43, 48, 60, 123, 132,
    134, 140, 148, 178, 215, 235, 263, 268, 270,
    274, 281, 282-3, 289, 297, 299, 336, 337,
    340, 361, 362, 363, 369

Pollard, Mrs, nurse 126
Pollock, Linda 121
Ponsonby, Mary 319
Poor Law 236
Portal, Charlotte 148–9
Porter, Roy 78, 86–7, 108
Portsmouth, Eveline Lady 252, 261
positivists/positivism 359, 360
Potter family 226
Potter, Beatrice (m. Sidney Webb) 27,
    55–7, 153–4, 155, 208
Potter, Kate, *see* Courtney, Kate
Potter, Lawrencina 27, 54–7, 103, 121, 287
Potter, Richard 54, 153–4, 225, 226
Potter, Rosie 55
prayer 69, 133, 136, 137, 138, 140, 149, 167,
    172, 177, 180, 185, 211, 212, 217, 218, 241,
    256, 281
Prayers for the Sick and Dying 270
Presbyterian, English 9, 19, 39, 48, 270,
    274–5
Presbyterian, Scottish 34, 46, 128, 151, 155
Priestly, Dr 80–1
probate duty 214, 244
Protestant Christianity 59, 61, 193, 230,
    266, 285
psychiatrists, *see* psychologists and
    psychiatrists
psychologists and psychiatrists 8, 27, 28, 39,
    65–6, 68, 75, 87, 96, 97, 121, 145, 149,
    160, 193, 210, 231, 239, 251, 277, 284, 301,
    302, 311, 319, 320–1, 334, 373, 380
Puckle, Bertram 194, 372
puerperal fever 12, 28, 41, 46–9, 79, 103, 255
purgatives 101, 169
purgatory 17–18, 59, 61, 266
Pusey, Edward 25, 60

Quaker 9, 20, 220, 285, 288
quarantine 126, 129, 134, 136
Queen 301, 304

Raphael, Beverley 65–6, 75, 76, 145, 160,
    210, 231, 277, 284, 295, 311, 334, 374
Rashdall, Revd J. 23
Rathbone, Elizabeth 242
Rathbone, William 208
reading the will 226
Recognition of Friends in Heaven, The 272
Reed, John 7
Reformation 8, 18, 59, 70, 266

Reid family 49, 50
Reid, Dr James 50
Reid, Kenrick 50
Reid, Laetitia (Letty) 50, 78, 102, 210–11
Reid, Mary 50, 51, 102, 211, 304
Reid, Thomas 211, 285
Religion of Humanity 359
*Report on the Practice of Interment in
    Towns* 195, 199, 200, 213
Report on the Sanitary Condition . . . 144
resurrection 24, 29, 34, 48, 133, 135, 205–6,
    216, 220, 265, 266, 269, 270, 271, 282,
    339, 342, 350
retirement 144
Retreat of Tuberculosis, The 40
Revelation, Book of 268, 270, 271
Reynolds, Ann 149
Reynolds, Deborah 255
Reynolds, Henry R. 145
Ribblesdale, Charty 40, 181, 182, 263
Ribblesdale, Emma Lady 160, 243, 253
Rice, Cecilia Lady (*née* Harcourt) 236, 291,
    310
Richardson, Ruth 1, 7, 223
Ridding, Laura 271
Ripon, Lady 309, 312
Rise and Progress of Religion in the Soul 281
Roberts, Caroline 123
Robertson, Revd F. W. 23–4
Robinson, H. P. 40
Roffen, A. W. 252–3
Rogers family 71, 72–5
Rogers, Ann (m. James Thorold Rogers)
    72–5, 318–19, 321, 337, 338
Rogers, Arthur 53, 74
Rogers, Bertram 72–4
Rogers, Clement (Clem) 53, 74
Rogers, Edmund 147
Rogers, Elizabeth (Mrs Parker) 99, 100, 147
Rogers, Francis (Frank) 53, 95, 215
Rogers, George Vining 99
Rogers, Henry 71, 72–4, 76, 325
Rogers, Prof. James E. Thorold 71, 72–3,
    99, 147, 293–4, 295
Rogers, Louisa 99, 147, 291–2, 305
Rogers, Maggie 306
Rogers, Mary Ann (mother of James
    Thorold Rogers) 99, 100, 147–8, 252,
    291–2, 295–6, 305
Rogers, Murray 296
Rogers, William 296

Roman Catholicism, *see* Catholic
Romantic/Romanticism 4–5, 8, 20, 40–1,
  128, 130, 182, 215, 282, 299, 361
Rosebery, Lord 164, 291
Rosset, W. L. de 75
Rossetti, D. G. 40
Rothschild family 244
Roundell, Currer 71, 75–6
Roundell, Laura 75–6
Roundell, William 34
Rowell, Geoffrey 7, 266
Rowley, Anne 50
Rowse, Mr, consultant physician 115
Royal College of Physicians 78, 81, 84
Royal Institute of Great Britain 36
Royal School of Mines 353
Royal Society 350, 353
Rugby School 128
Rule and Exercises of Holy Dying, The
  18–19, 20, 25, 140, 221–2, 281, 313
Ruskin, John 2, 297, 366
Russell, George W. E. 308
Russell, Lord John 35, 245, 252, 253
Russell, Mr 252
Ryle, Revd H. E., Dean of Westminster
  368

Sacred Poems for Mourners 270, 281
St Albans, Duchess of 240
St Matthew's Gospel 135
Saints' Everlasting Rest 44, 268
Salisbury, Lady 152–3, 158
Salisbury, Lord 153, 373
Sarah, a servant 100
Saundby, Dr Robert 85, 88, 93–4, 110–11
Saunders, Cicely 82, 97
Savory, Sir William S., FRS 36, 82, 149
scarlet fever 41, 65, 100, 108, 119, 120, 122,
  124–37, 141, 143, 282, 290, 303, 345, 354
Scott, a male nurse 102
secularism 183, 314, 358
Selborne, Laura Lady (*née* Waldegrave, m.
  1st Earl) 270, 299, 308
Selborne, Maud Lady (m. 2nd Earl) 124,
  149
Selborne, Roundell Palmer, 1st Earl of
  43–4, 67, 75–6, 115, 148, 201, 221, 299,
  308
Selborne, William Waldegrave Palmer, 2nd
  Earl of 255, 271, 275–6
sermon 269, 274, 276, 279, 281, 326

servant-mourners 196
servants at the death-bed 98, 100, 125, 129,
  132, 150, 178, 211
servants' wages 195
Sesame and Lilies 2
Shaftesbury, Lord 306
Shakespeare, William 133, 215
Shannon, Richard 166
Sharpe family 49, 50, 304
Sharpe, Catharine 26, 50, 106
Sharpe, Daniel 51
Sharpe, Lucy (*née* Reid) 50, 78–9, 113,
  210–11, 269, 285, 293, 304
Sharpe, Maria 274, 315
Sharpe, Mary 113
Sharpe, Samuel 50, 113
Sharpe, Sarah 50
Sharpe, Sutton 106
Shaw-Stewart, Constance 242
Sherbrooke, Lord 203
Sheridan, Thomas 108
Sherwood, Mrs John 302, 304, 311
shooting 75
Shorter, Edward 79
Sidgwick, Eleanor (*née* Balfour) 366
Sidgwick, Henry 366
Sidgwick, William 271–2
Simeon, Revd Charles 24, 25
Simpson, Prof. James Young 84–5, 107–8,
  171
Sinclair, Archdeacon William M. 45, 126,
  198
Skelmersdale, Lord 124
smallpox 40
Smith, Barry (F. B.) 40–1, 78, 124
Smith, Lucy 287
Smith, Miss, governess 177
Smith, Dr Protheroe 112
Smith, W. H. 69, 122, 123
Sneyd, Clement 299
Sneyd, Mrs 299
social workers 97
socialist/socialism 154, 273, 274, 354
Society for Promoting Christian
  Knowledge 216
Society for Psychical Research 365–8
Some Cases of Prediction 370
Somerville, Martha 243, 291, 305
Somerville, Mary (*née* Fairfax), scientist 61,
  65, 80, 145, 149, 211, 212, 227, 240, 243,
  254–5, 290, 311

Somerville, Mary (dau. of Mary Somerville)
243
Somerville, Revd Dr Thomas 34, 35
Somerville, William 240, 284–5, 292, 309
Southwark, Lady (Selina Mary Causton)
69
Spectator 144, 267
Spence, Robert 142
Spencer, Earl 80, 200, 329
Spencer, Herbert 207, 208, 356
spinsters 99, 147, 151, 155, 159, 230–1, 237,
253, 303
spiritualism/spiritualist 12, 62, 187, 315, 358,
365–70, 371, 374, 380
Springer, Miss, dressmaker 303–4
Stanhope family 225
Stanhope, 5th Earl of 52
Stanhope, Arthur, 6th Earl of 225, 240, 311
Stanhope, Evelyn Lady, 6th Countess 225,
235, 240, 254, 309, 314, 333
Stanhope, Harry 225
Stanhope, James Richard (Jem), 7th Earl of
225
Stanhope, Lucy 276
Stanhope, Philip 225
Stanley, Lady Augusta 320
Stanley, Dorothy 360
Stanley, H. M. 222
state funeral 194, 196–9, 203
Stein, Dorothy 62
Stephen, Sir James 205, 206, 208
Stephen, Sir Leslie 3, 207, 366
Stephenson, Lady 332
Stepney, Lady (Margaret 'Maggie' Cowell
Stepney) 145, 185, 188, 232, 238, 242,
243–4, 295, 307
Stevenson, John 370
Stone, Lawrence 4, 121, 194, 276
Stoughton, Revd John 274
strychnine 58, 92
sudden death 6–7, 11, 41, 59, 65–9, 76, 117,
239, 318, 321, 334, 367, 374
suicide 59, 69–76, 156, 178, 207, 215, 255,
318, 323, 325–6, 334, 338, 380
Suicide: A Study in Sociology 71
Sumner, J. B., Archbishop of Canterbury
20
Sunday at Home 22
Sunday School 49
Sutton, Christopher 19
syphilis 208

Tait family 102, 116, 124, 129, 132–3, 135,
140, 142, 280, 314, 347, 348, 349, 350, 354,
361
Tait, Archibald Campbell, Archbishop of
Canterbury, Dean of Carlisle 10, 26, 32,
35, 100, 108, 116, 127–39, 140–2, 148, 198,
202, 211, 224, 252, 265, 269, 275, 278, 281,
285–6, 287–8, 290, 316–17, 338, 347
Tait, Catharine (*née* Spooner) 10, 32, 100,
116, 128–39, 140–2, 349
Tait, Cattie 128, 129, 130–2, 133, 134, 137,
138, 347, 348
Tait, Chattie 127, 129, 130, 132, 133, 134, 135,
136, 142
Tait, Revd Crauford 114, 116, 133, 134,
140–1, 148, 202, 265, 281, 285
Tait, Frances 128, 130–1, 133, 136–7
Tait, James 35, 148
Tait, John 35, 102
Tait, May 108, 128, 129, 131, 132, 133, 134–5,
137, 138
Tait, Susan (Susie) 128, 129, 130, 134, 136
Talbot, Revd Edward (m. Lavinia Lyttelton,
Bishop of Winchester) 32, 181, 262–3,
287, 325, 369, 379
Talbot, Gilbert Walter Lyttelton 379
Talbot, Mrs John (mother of John and
Edward) 174, 176, 177, 178
Talbot, John Gilbert (Johnny, m. Meriel
Lyttelton) 287
Talbot, Lavinia (*née* Lyttelton, m. Edward
Talbot 1870) 189, 233, 238, 243, 287, 299,
324, 328–9, 330, 331, 332, 366, 369, 379
Talbot, Meriel (*née* Lyttelton, m. John
Talbot 1860) 174, 176, 177, 179, 180, 218,
287, 323, 324, 326, 329, 331, 332
Talbot, Neville 379
Talbot, Peggy 219
Taylor, Catherine Ellen 293
Taylor, Jeremy, Bishop of Down 10, 18–19,
20, 25, 28, 67, 69, 140, 165, 216, 221, 281,
313
Taylor, Lou 195, 301, 318
Tennant family 183, 263
Tennant, Lady 287
Tennant, Margot 121, 181, 182
Tennant, Pauline 40, 181
Tennyson, Alfred Lord 7, 48, 282–3, 366
Tennyson, Hallam 283, 297
terminal care, *see* palliative care
tetanus 82

Thackeray 24
Thompson, Evan 220
Thompson, Fanny (*née* Horsley) 213, 215, 256, 294, 297
Thompson, Sir Henry 203, 204, 205, 207
Thompson, Mrs, servant 226
Thompson, Dr Seth 45, 213, 214, 215, 256–7, 261, 264, 297
Thornton family 11
Thornton, Henry 11
Thornton, Mrs Henry 4, 29
Thornton, John 312
Thornton, Marianne 11, 38
Times, The 197, 199, 200, 204, 235
To a Christian Parent, on the Death of an Infant 122, 123
Todd, Alice 104
Tollemache, Lionel 93
Touzel, Augusta 219, 306
Tractarians 21, 25, 30, 39, 49, 161, 163, 167, 171–2, 246, 268
Trench, Revd Richard Chenevix 281
Trevelyan family 9, 355, 359, 360, 361
Trevelyan, Charles, MP 360, 363–4
Trevelyan, George Macaulay 360–4
Trevelyan, Hugh 364
Trevelyan, Humphry 363
Trevelyan, Janet (*née* Ward) 360–4
Trevelyan, Katherine 364
Trevelyan, Mary 363
Trevelyan, Molly 54, 360–4
Trevelyan, Theodore (Theo) 360–3
Trollope, Anthony 24, 207
truth for the dying 108–18
tuberculosis 11, 22, 29, 30, 31–2, 35, 38, 39–46, 50, 79, 80, 90, 102, 103, 111, 113, 114, 139, 143, 166, 181, 255, 277, 288, 289, 324, 340, 356
Tucker, Mrs, servant 150
tumour, *see* cancer
Turner, E. B., FRCS 113–14
turning points in the history of death 6, 96, 120, 199, 358
Tutankhamun 194
typhoid 100, 102, 117, 143, 220, 319, 335, 346
typhus 27, 41, 78, 123, 143, 179, 180, 324, 366

unbelievers, *see* agnostics
undertakers 195–6, 199–200, 202, 214, 216

Unitarian 9, 49–51, 54, 56, 161, 210, 222, 223, 269, 274–5, 285, 341, 343
Unknown Soldier's tomb 379–80
utilitarian 352, 356

Vaughan, Charles, Dean of Llandaff 38
venereal diseases 40, 239; *see also* syphilis
Venn, Henry 10, 29, 30
Vernon, Colonel Francis 100
Victoria, Queen 195, 198, 201, 306, 316, 318–22, 334, 338, 371
Victorian Celebration of Death, The 194, 223
viewing the body 37–8, 46, 132, 170, 212–13, 214, 335
Villiers, Amelia Mary 308
Villiers, Constance 298, 311
Villiers, Henry, Bishop of Durham 308
Villiers, Theresa 297
Vivian, Mary 202, 224
Vivian, Mattie A. 213
Vovelle, Michel 1, 7

Wade, Dr, consultant physician 179, 180
Walcot, Mary 90
Waldegrave, Lady 29
Waldegrave, Mary 270
Waldegrave, Mary Dorothea (*née* Palmer, dau. of 1st Lord Selborne) 181
Wallas, Audrey 307
Walton, William 27
Walvin, James 133
Wantage, Lady 235, 236
war, *see* World War I; World War II
war memorials 376, 378, 379
Ward family 223
Ward, Dorothy 53
Ward, Mrs Humphry (Mary) 52, 223, 360, 362
Ward, Dr W. G. 267
Warton, John 25
water cure 346
Waterford, Lady 255
Watson, Dr T. 79, 80, 102, 114
Watt, Sir Aloitius 146
Webb, Beatrice, *see* Potter, Beatrice
Webb, Sidney 154
Weber, Dr F. Parkes 105
Webster, Ellen 104
Wedgwood, Caroline 286
Wedgwood, Fanny 271, 346, 347, 348, 349
Wedgwood, George 365

Wedgwood, Hensleigh 365
Wedgwood, Sarah 221
weepers 203
Wellesley, Lady 235
Wellington, Duke of 194, 196–7, 199, 203
Wells, Dr S. Russel 94
Wemyss, Hugo Charteris, 11th Earl of 375
Wemyss, Mary Charteris Lady 375, 376, 379
Wenham, Canon 32
Wenneslaus, Father 32
Wesley, John 10, 20
West, Dr 90, 101, 112, 113
Westcott, Wynn 71
Westminster, Dean of 198
Westminster, Duke of 207
Westminster, Marquis of 80, 200
Wheeler, Michael 7, 19, 266, 268, 271
White, Mrs (*née* Greig) 227
whooping cough 120
Wickham, Agnes (*née* Gladstone) 177, 188, 324, 328
Wickham, Katie 296
Wickham, Margaret 296
Wickham, William 203
widower 12, 160, 220, 230, 251–64, 293, 301, 331, 334, 352
widowhood 12–13, 145, 230–64, 318, 329, 331, 332
widows 12–13, 146, 147, 156, 187, 230–50, 251–64, 300–7, 315, 317, 318, 321, 322, 330, 331, 332, 334, 371
widows' weeds 231, 249, 300–7, 329; *see also* mourning-dress
Wilberforce, Barbara (dau. of William Wilberforce) 23
Wilberforce, Barbara (wife of William Wilberforce) 30
Wilberforce, Archdeacon (later Bishop) Samuel 281, 353

Wilberforce, William 3, 4, 10, 23, 25, 29–30, 51, 281
Wildman, Mary Ann 26
Wilkinson, Alan 370
Wilkinson, Sir Gardner 89
Williams, Dr/Prof. Charles J. B., FRS 78, 81, 85, 105–6, 110, 111, 175
Williams, Dyson 208
wills 18, 80, 101, 164, 182, 195, 200, 201, 202, 203, 214–15, 223, 224–9, 236, 244, 246, 249, 283, 291, 295–9, 329; *see also* commemorative bequests; executors of wills; reading the will
Winks, Mrs, nurse 102
Winter, Jay 373
Wiseman, Cardinal 199
Wohl, Anthony 120
Wohl, R. 374
Wood family 201
Wood, Revd Cyril 114, 115, 116
Wood, Eleanor (*née* Palmer) 115, 201, 222
Wood, Revd William 201
Wordsworth, Dr, Bishop of Lincoln 205–6
Wordsworth, Mrs 128
Wordsworth, William 361
workhouse 144, 331
working class 1, 7, 40, 86, 103, 124, 144, 209, 213, 221, 223, 224, 330
World War I 2–3, 6–7, 68, 76, 187–8, 318, 338, 358, 365, 370–81
World War II 79
wreath 222
Wright, S. J. 253

Yates, Emily 233, 242
York, Archbishop of 272
Young, G. M. 2, 19, 339
Young, Michael 160